Professing
THE·FAITH

ALSO BY DOUGLAS JOHN HALL

Confessing the Faith:
Christian Theology in a North American Context (1996)

God and the Nations
(with Rosemary Radford Ruether, 1995)

Thinking the Faith:
Christian Theology in a North American Context (1989)

God and Human Suffering:
An Exercise in the Theology of the Cross (1986)

Professing
THE·FAITH

Christian Theology in a North American Context

DOUGLAS JOHN HALL

FORTRESS PRESS

Minneapolis

PROFESSING THE FAITH
Christian Theology in a North American Context

First Fortress Press paperback edition 1996

Scripture quotations from the New Revised Standard Version Bible are copyright © 1989 by the Division of Christian Education of the National Council of Churches of Christ in the U.S.A. and are used
by permission.

Cover design: Judy Swanson/David Lott
Text design: David Lott

The Library of Congress has catalogued the hardcover edition as follows:

Library of Congress Cataloging-in-Publication Data

Hall, Douglas John, 1928–
        Professing the faith : Christian theology in a North American
context / Douglas John Hall.
            p.   cm.
        Includes bibliographical references and index.
        ISBN 0-8006-2546-3 :
            1. Theology, Doctrinal—North America.   2. Christianity and
culture.   I. Title.
BT75.2.H34   1993
230'.097—dc20   93-27772
                                                                                CIP

        ISBN 0-8006-2548-X (paperback)

The paper used in this publication meets the minimum requirements of American National Standard
for Information Sciences—Permanence of Paper for Printed Library Materials, ANSI Z329.48-1984.

Manufactured in the U.S.A.   AF 1-2548

00   99   98   97   96   1   2   3   4   5   6   7   8   9   10

To my Colleagues,
Students,
and Staff Associates
at the Faculty of Religious Studies,
McGill University

CONTENTS

CONTENTS

PREFACE

This is the second volume in a projected trilogy. The question to which it is addressed is, What would it mean to profess the faith as North American Christians living at the close of the second millennium C.E.?

I have felt it necessary to raise that question, because I think that we have become very confused about the core of our belief. We have lost touch with the tradition, and even the Bible is (almost) an unknown book in the churches. Because we do not remember and struggle with that past, we are also uncertain what it is that we ought to profess today. If we have no coherent basis of faith's profession, how shall we *confess* the faith?*

The "we" of the preceding paragraph refers especially to those of us who remain in and around the churches that used to be called "mainline Protestantism." What we can be called now that our old, classical denominations have been edged out of the center, when the political powers-that-be are more interested in having the blessing of a quite different segment of American and Canadian Protestantism I am not sure. Somebody used the term "sideline churches," and that is an instructive turn of phrase. Perhaps from the sidelines of the dominant culture of this continent there can be a more prophetic sort of Christian witness than there ever was when "mainline Protestantism" was the stained-glass dimension of "mainline culture."

But this will only happen, I believe, if we stop being demoralized by our reduced status vis-à-vis power and learn enough about what the Christian faith really means to enable us to disengage ourselves from the dominant culture also at the level of what we believe and profess. Without that, our disestablishment will be merely a pathetic occurrence, benefiting no one. If, having been edged out physically, we can discover intellectual and spiritual foundations that are also different from the values of the majority culture, we may in the

---

*The title of the projected third volume will be *Confessing the Faith*.

end have something worthwhile to profess in this society, and even to the forces and classes that dominate it.

Dying to Christendom, we could become the church.

■   ■   ■

This large tome has not come to be without a great deal of encouragement and help from others. For the project as a whole—the trilogy—I have received grants from the Social Sciences and Humanities Council of Canada, the Association of Theological Schools, and the Graduate Faculty of my university. I also acknowledge, with gratitude, the opportunity to begin work on the present volume in the quiet precincts of the School of Theology of Doshisha University in the ancient city of Kyoto, Japan, where I was Visiting Scholar in the Spring of 1989.

The book is dedicated to my colleagues, students, and staff associates of the Faculty of Religious Studies of McGill University, where I have held the chair of Christian Theology for the past seventeen years. Dean Donna R. Runnalls and my other colleagues, as well as my graduate students, have been extremely generous and understanding of my preoccupation with this project and my other writing and lecturing activities. Apart from the atmosphere of support, mutual respect, and desire for excellence that obtains in my academic setting, such an undertaking as this would not be possible.

Finally, it is customary for authors to thank their wives or husbands, "who typed the manuscript," or performed other necessary functions. When it comes to that, I hardly know what to say. I typed the manuscript myself, every word of it. I composed every word of it, too, with the exception of a line here and there. But there is not an idea herein expressed that has not been hammered out on the anvil of our ongoing dialogue, Rhoda's and mine. Behind some of the ideas and the words are hours of discussion, some of which would have to be qualified by the adjective "heated." A very great deal of the research necessary to documentation has been hers, and she has not only read but read, marked, learned, and inwardly digested (and in some instances refused inwardly to digest) the six or seven preliminary manuscripts that were required to come up with this one. To thank her, therefore, would be an act of sheer condescension on my part. Where she is concerned, I can only thank divine providence.

Douglas John Hall

Notre-Dame-de-Grâce,
Montréal, Québec

INTRODUCTION TO VOLUME TWO

Professing the Faith

1. The Profession of Faith in North America Today

The first volume of this trilogy is entitled *Thinking the Faith,* but Christianity is not only a thinking faith; it involves thinking *about* a particular tradition of belief. Christians bring to the contemplation of existence a perspective that they gain primarily from their ongoing dialogue with an explicit theological heritage. They look at their world through the window of that received tradition. It is the "lens" (George Lindbeck) that enables them to see what they see. It is the "great code" (Northrop Frye) on whose basis they seek to decipher their *hic et nunc.* It is the meditative core of their life together, the focal point of their thought and their discourse, the inspiration for their worldly work and witness.

When in Christian settings we employ the term "profession" (for instance, when it is said that persons join the church "on profession of faith"), we refer to this meditative core of the faith. One *professes* the faith as and when one submits, not necessarily to some prescribed set of dogmas but to the discipline of regarding one's life and all of life from the vantage point of that "story"[1] that is the ground of all quests for purity of dogma and the judge of them all.

---

1. See *Thinking the Faith; Christian Theology in a North American Context* (Minneapolis: Fortress Press, 1991), 89ff. The best background known to me for an understanding of the concept *story* as I am using it here is found in one of Isak Dinesen's last published stories, "The Cardinal's First Tale." Here the great Danish writer contrasts contemporary literature, with its concentration upon 'the individual,' with classical stories, in which the story has its own inner logic and momentum, and in which the characters—the heroes and heroines—are evoked by the inherent needs of the story itself. The classical story thus understood implies the dialectic of freedom and destiny that characterizes the biblical story of divine-human encounter (*The Last Tales* [New York: Vintage Books, 1975], 3ff.).

As such, this submission is by no means the end of the matter, as if to be a Christian meant, simply, to adopt this "professional" stance. Submission to this particular heritage of belief is in fact nothing more than a means to the end. The goal in relation to which the profession of faith is way and means is faith's *confession.* [2] We confess the faith when, through this process of contemplating our world in the light of that whole heritage of meditation, we are thrust into an active engagement with that which threatens the life of our world.

Profession of the faith is therefore always a penultimate stage in the life of the disciple community. It must not be elevated to the status of ultimacy. Others, who have not heard this story or who have heard it and reject its import, may be as diligent as Christians in confronting evil and seeking to "change the world" (Marx). This is surely the point of Jesus' enigmatic statement about the children of "this age" and "the children of light" (Luke 16:8), as of many other biblical references. But so far as Christians are concerned the "insight" (Lonergan) and the motivating power of their engagement with the world emanates from a spiritual and intellectual contemplation of this tradition, this account of reality, this "message" (Tillich). For that reason, the profession of faith, while penultimate, is never merely incidental. It is indispensable to the life of discipleship; indeed, without it, what *is* ultimate with respect to that life, namely, obedient *con*fession of the Christ, is unthinkable.

Two basic assumptions are already present in what we have said so far. The first is that profession of the faith implies knowledge of the tradition. The second is that it entails, beyond mere knowing, a high degree of commitment to what is known. We shall see that in both of these assumptions Christianity in a North American context is obliged today to struggle with certain characteristic problems.

Knowing the Tradition.   Knowledge (in Greek, *gnosis*) is of the essence of Christian faith. If anyone seriously professes this faith it must be assumed that he or she does so on the basis of some genuine acquaintance with the primary data of this religious heritage—especially, though not exclusively, the Scriptures of the two testaments.[3] It was just this prominence of *gnosis* in the early church that lent power to the greatest temptation of primitive Christianity, the temptation known as Gnosticism. Gnosticism,[4] at base, is a religion of knowing; that is, its premise is that salvation comes through the sort of illumination that accompanies the extraordinary impartation and reception of truths otherwise hidden from human view. Historic Christianity resisted this temptation,

---

2. Hence the projected third and final volume of this work will be entitled *Confessing the Faith.*

3. See *Thinking the Faith,* 257ff.

4. See Hans Jonas, *The Gnostic Religion: The Message of the Alien God and the Beginnings of Christianity* (Boston: Beacon Press, 1963).

though only just barely and never quite permanently; overtly or covertly, Gnosticism has entered the history of the church again and again. Yet after the initial struggle with this temptation, the marks of its character and the nature of its misappropriation of the gospel have at least been recognized, if not always or consistently acted upon. Without attempting to enter into a full discussion of the subject at this juncture, we may say that Gnosticism errs precisely at the point of failing to incorporate the distinction that we have just made—that between profession and confession of the faith. There were enough vigilant minds at work in the first centuries of the church's history (Irenaeus being chief among them) to realize that people may know or claim to know a great deal and yet fail to deploy their knowledge in the service of Christ in the world. They may indeed use their *gnosis* as a bulwark against worldly involvement—a heresy that is as modern as it was ancient, and as applicable to secular as to religious communities.[5] For authentic Christian belief, salvation is "by grace alone," not by knowledge; and it entails love, not merely comprehension. Knowing, which is certainly the sine qua non of Christian profession of the faith, belongs, with profession as a whole, to the level of penultimacy and of means. We are not redeemed by what we know but by the One by whom we are known. And our being known by that One is tested, not by our "correct" answers to doctrinal questions, but only by our readiness to know as we are known—that is, to love as we are loved (1 John 3:13f.).

The danger of falsely elevating knowledge, however, should not in reaction encourage denigration of the role of knowing in the life of faith. Wherever such a denigration occurs (and it has occurred very often in the history of the church) the demons that enter the community of belief that has been swept clean of the dangers of Gnosticism may be seven times as deadly. Overemphasizing faith's transcendence of *gnosis,* the disciple community easily drifts into spiritualistic, moralistic, activistic, and other forms of religious behavior from which precisely the "professional" dimension is lacking. Knowledge of "the things of faith" is often subordinated to reputedly better ends—piety, morality, work (and also less admirable qualities than these!)—which are then raised up to a prominence that biblical testimony hardly affords them. In such communities some people may even take a certain pride in downplaying the significance of "theology," and those who pursue theological work profession- Mennos ally are then regarded with suspicion by the "real Christians," the "front-line

---

5. C. F. von Weizsäcker attributes much of the contemporary predicament of Western civilization precisely to the pursuit of knowledge devoid of responsibility for that which is known. At the end of his important early work, *The History of Nature* (trans. Fred D. Wieck [Chicago: Univ. of Chicago Press (Phoenix Books), 1949], 190), he writes: "The scientific and technical world of modern man is the result of his daring enterprise, *knowledge without love"* (emphasis added). For a discussion of Gnosticism "modern and secular," see Eric Vogelin, *Science, Politics, and Gnosticism* (Chicago: Henry Regnery Co. [A Gateway Edition], 1968).

Christians," whose days are so taken up (they say) with "*being* Christian" that they have no time for studying the tradition or meditating upon its noetic core.

Anyone familiar with the ethos of Christianity in the North American context, and more particularly with most so-called mainline Protestantism, will recognize how uncomfortably close this comes to denoting our ecclesiastical situation. Not only did the churches here inherit the general Constantinian character of European Christendom, with its assumption that one is Christian as a matter of course and not through an unrelenting struggle to *understand;* but beyond that the very practicality of religious observance on this continent has rendered the study of the faith at best secondary, if not merely expedient— for example, as a necessary (and, to many, tedious) preliminary to ordained ministry. Distinctions may certainly be drawn between various ecclesial communions and denominations, with some being more and some less serious in the impartation of "sound teaching." The Reformed tradition, for instance, has (whether justifiably or not) prided itself on being a teaching faith, with clergy whose office is understood to be that of the "teaching elder," while in the Anglo- and Roman Catholic communions the emphasis has been more sacramental and in the "free" churches piety has had precedence over learning— partly, one must admit, as a consequence of class distinctions. Moreover, in most Protestant expressions of Christian faith in North America, as elsewhere, study of the Scriptures has to some extent qualified the generalization that I am making here.

Despite these nuances, however, Christianity in our historical setting has not created the impression of being a faith that emphasizes the importance of knowing. Gnosticism has never, I think, been our great temptation. The practice of catechetical instruction, which is still a relatively serious (if largely cultural) undertaking in many "Old World" as well as some younger church settings, has been even more perfunctory with us than in Europe. Sermons, once the main cultic medium of edification in the faith, degenerated in the late nineteenth century into moral pep talks or discourses on broadly religious and ethical topics. As for Bible study, while in name it has suggested a resolute grappling with the scriptural texts, as practiced in and around congregations it has normally connoted a sort of vague Protestant spirituality: The Bible was revered as an object around which a group of particularly earnest Christians might gather in order to "share." These groupings have in fact frequently been designated "Bible fellowship"—an instructive nomenclature. For in truth fellowship and not disciplined study was normally the object of the exercise—to the extent that a rigorous intellectual dimension, when introduced into such circles, was regularly regarded with mistrust and sometimes hostility.

We have spoken here in the past tense, though a case could be made for the accuracy of these observations as descriptive also of the present. Certainly in

4

some parts of the continent, and in particular ecclesiastical settings, variations on the above themes persist unabated.[6] But I believe that the present context—the situation obtaining during the second half of the current century—has seen the introduction of new factors that are germane to this discussion.

The negative aspects of these factors (we shall later notice some positive aspects as well) are in part related to dimensions of our context discussed in the first volume of this work, such as "the end of the Constantinian era," religious pluralism, the new apocalypticism, and others.[7] In a way that was not formerly so decisive, the inherent challenge of faith to "seek understanding" (Anselm) is dampened in our time by subtle forces at work in our society. Two of these can be identified fairly straightforwardly, one emanating from a fear that learning will dispel belief, and one from a kind of activistic impatience with all "theory."

The first stems from preoccupation, open or subconscious, with the prospect that the claims of the Christian faith may be insupportable. Can the Christian religion bear the scrutiny of a serious intellectual investigation? This question predates the contemporary period, but as a question affecting large numbers of Christians, and not only the Christian intelligentsia, it is new. In the nineteenth and early twentieth centuries, the great bulk of churchgoers were not personally threatened by the agnosticism or radical disbelief of the few outspoken doubters. Robert Ingersoll's antireligious antics,[8] one senses, were more interesting as entertainment than they were challenging as an alternative to nominal faith. A business-as-usual mentality persisted in the churches well into the 1950s. One might have one's doubts, but one's predisposition was to go along with the majority (or what could still appear the majority) and abide in "the faith of the fathers." Today, the non- or antireligious alternatives to belief are not only more numerous, they are also more ubiquitous and compelling. The question whether religious faith can survive the inquiries of a lively mind, even when that mind is basically friendly to faith, is a question that affects everyone

---

6. The tendency to accentuate immediacy and "fellowship" is exacerbated by the television conditioning of the so-called baby-boomers. Ironically, some of the more "conservative" denominations are more affected by this phenomenon than are the liberal churches. "'Churches have to get into the entertainment business,' said Rev. David Brandon, the 41-year-old senior pastor at the Alliance Church. . . . 'We're dealing with a television generation that has a short attention span and doesn't like to waste time.'" Wasting time seems to include exposure to the profundities of the tradition in favor of, for example, "Bible-based discussions of women's issues with aerobics classes and craft demonstrations." ("Saving the Boomers: Churches Shun Tradition to Attract Young Adults," *Macleans* [June 3, 1991], 50f.)

7. *Thinking the Faith,* 197ff.

8. Robert Green Ingersoll (1833–99) was the son of a Congregational minister in New York State, a colonel during the Civil War, and a lawyer. He was known as "the great agnostic." He lectured widely throughout the United States and Canada, publishing his lectures under such titles as "The Gods" (1872), "Some Mistakes of Moses" (1879), and "Why I Am an Agnostic" (1896). Editions of his works in twelve volumes are still available.

to some extent. We do not laugh at atheists any more; we are too worried that the truth may be on their side.

Thus the habit of wanting to *know,* which the medieval schoolmen insisted is inherent in faith, is for many of our contemporaries countered by a strong suspicion that any kind of knowing could be fatal for believing. If one attempted quite deliberately to acquire an informed grasp of the tradition, would one not run the risk of seeing at first hand its improbabilities and flaws, its biases, its relativity, its incompatibility with present-day scientific data, and so on? One of the reasons for the growing popularity of thought-*less* forms of Christianity in our context—by which I mean Christianity based on sheer authority, Christianity that subsists by squelching doubt and refusing discourse with worldly reason—lies just here. If a faith that desires to know must entertain profound challenges to itself, then the natural tendency of the human spirit might well be to avoid knowing and simply . . . *believe!* "True belief" thus becomes an alternative to the quest for knowledge and all that is associated with serious reflection. One side of the anti-intellectualism that pervades North American Christianity today is surely related to this type of religious repression.

While that may explain in part what in the earlier volume I called "the rise of religious simplism,"[9] it does not explain the paucity of a sustained search for understanding within the so-called mainline denominations, for whom these pages are chiefly intended. Here, I think, the question is not so much whether Christianity could bear honest intellectual scrutiny as whether such scrutiny is necessary—whether, indeed, it does not function detrimentally in the Christian community, for instance, by putting between theory and practice a permanent no-man's-land where one can dally with ideas without the inconvenience of having to act upon any of them.

For our purposes, this is the more serious question, because what is really being asked here is whether what I am calling faith's *profession* is necessary to genuine *confession* of Christ in the world; whether the former may not in fact deter and deflect the latter.

There are very good reasons why this question should be asked, and is asked. It can hardly escape the attention of anyone who has followed the course of church history, and especially of recent church history, that those most diligent in the pursuit of a professional grasp of Christian teaching have all too consistently failed to rise to the occasion when the disciple community was being called to radical obedience. With every crisis in human affairs in the West, the most dominant professional groupings within the churches have habitually cautioned against hasty decisions and one-sided acts. The period in our own century that saw the birth of new and courageous forms of resistance to evil, namely, the 1930s and 40s, also bore strong witness to the propensity of

---

9. *Thinking the Faith,* 228f.

the Christian intelligentsia to find in their doctrinal preoccupations both grounds for confirming the status quo and reasons for maintaining a safe detachment from all parties. In our immediate period, it is often this same professionalism that warns liberationists, feminists, and others with urgent messages for the churches that there is always an "on the other hand," that one must maintain a professional distance, that "ideologies" cannot be endorsed, and so on.[10] In short, the actual record of professional Christianity testifies rather shockingly to the truth of the suspicion that the profession of faith may function more consistently to *prevent* than to facilitate confession. Reading modern and contemporary church history, one might well conclude that a faith which is not too nuanced (spoiled?) by the exercise of professional dialectics is more apt to "do the right thing" than is a sophisticated faith—and even perhaps to do it "for the *right* reason" (T. S. Eliot). The paradigms of Christian life whom we honor today are, like the St. Francises of yesteryear, women and men of deed rather than, in the primary sense, of thought and word: Martin Luther King, Jr., Archbishop Romero, Mother Teresa, Jean Vanier, Dorothy Day. . . .

Yet this line of reasoning can also lead to a simplistic and romantic promotion of immediacy and intuition. That many Christian professionals have used their knowledge of the complexities and ambiguities of reality to avoid involvement or passively to approve questionable systems does not add up to the conclusion that the profession of faith actually breeds disobedience; it only indicates that human beings, being sinful, are able to discover subtle ways of hiding from the One who walks in the garden in the cool of the day. Truly, theology may be one of the best ways of avoiding God. But it is not the subject matter of Christian theology as such that provides this escape hatch; it is the human spirit, which flees the "Hound of Heaven" along many and devious routes. If Christian professionals have failed during this century to give decisive leadership in concrete obedience, they only reflect a hesitancy that can be observed throughout the churches. The way of the cross is not easily followed.

Besides, on the other side of the coin, it must be recognized that the leadership that has been and is present in the modern and contemporary church has often if not always been inspired by professional theologians who did *not* seek refuge in thought. Not only Barmen—perhaps the most dramatic episode in this recent confessional history—but also the renewal of the church through lay academies, through base communities, through the work of individual theologians concerned for the accessibility of their work to the laity—all this and much more could be cited in this connection. The very exemplars of Christian

---

10. See Frederick Herzog's discussion of the implications of this attitude for theological education in *God-Walk: Liberation Shaping Dogmatics* (Maryknoll, N.Y.: Orbis Books, 1988), 253–54, nn. 31, 32.

living named above are not only in some sense theologians in their own right, but they have been inspired by theological schools and movements, some of which were certainly very professional. The only antidote to the kind of theological professionalism that takes refuge in "knowledge" is a professional theology that deliberately pursues its task as a catalyst to fresh encounter between doctrine and life.

But the defense of knowing must be carried beyond mere defense. The truth is that the quest for knowledge of the tradition cannot be *neglected* without very serious consequences. That this is so is not a matter of theory but of plain observation. All around us in the churches of this continent today we are seeing what happens when neither the fundamental sources (the Scriptures) nor the supporting traditions of the faith are pursued with any passion or seriousness. Precisely at a point in history when knowledge of the faith is most indispensable (for no one is any longer a Christian by birth), we in the North American context who think ourselves inheritors of the classical traditions of the Reformation are becoming—have become—functionally illiterate. Even milder critics of the ecclesiastical status quo speak openly now of the loss of contact with the Christian past. "There is no more conversation with the tradition," says Mac Watts of Winnipeg. "The connection has been snapped. We cut knots—we're not willing to take the time to untie them."[11] In some quarters, biblical and theological illiteracy are almost celebrated!

Conspicuous in this regard is biblical illiteracy. For more than a century, professional biblical scholarship has pored over the texts of the two testaments and, using methods that are at least in some real sense comprehensible to ordinary twentieth-century intelligence and sensibilities, produced all kinds of data that could render biblical authority for faith both more effective and more intelligible. Yet in our churches (and I mean the churches of once-mainline Protestantism, where these data are both readily available and potentially meaningful) there is hardly any awareness on the part of average churchfolk of such established facts as the multiple authorship of the Pentateuch, the oral traditions preceding the written Gospels, the existence of a Pauline "school" and of a Johannine "school" that took a somewhat different approach, and hundreds of insights resulting from the application of historical-critical method to the ancient texts. It is as if all this scholarship had occurred on some other planet! The appalling ignorance of the Bible in so-called Protestant circles— not only of the nuances of scholarly interpretation but of the most basic teachings of the texts themselves—makes any further discussion of the principle of *sola scriptura* as the authenticating, "formal" mark of Protestantism ironic from the start. It is no wonder that most alleged Protestants, if and when they

---

11. Janet Somerville, "Different Paths, One Mission," *The United Church Observer* 53/12 (June, 1990), 44.

are actually called upon to refer to biblical precedence in matters of faith and morality, turn out to be either as literalistic as their sectarian counterparts or as vague as the average secularist.[12]

If most Christians are abysmally uninformed in relation to biblical scholarship, the situation is even more unfortunate when it comes to knowledge of the postbiblical Christian tradition, including both the evolution of doctrine and the concerns of contemporary professional theology.

This aspect of our context has immediate and explicit consequences for what we will undertake in this book. Instead of beginning immediately a contextual critique and restatement of the three main doctrinal areas that constitute the core of this study, I shall provide in each case a brief summary chapter of historical background in order to give the reader some awareness of the emergence, over many centuries, of the central beliefs that mainline Protestants still claim to profess. To begin otherwise would be contextually irresponsible, for one cannot assume this necessary background. For example, in regard to "the trinitarian history of God" (Moltmann), most Christians on this continent, if they think about it at all, are simply confused. In their churches they sing trinitarian hymns and pray "in the name of the Father, the Son, and the Holy Spirit" (or contemporary equivalents of the same); but if their children ask them what this language really means, they end up citing views that were long ago declared to be rank heresies. *And they do not know the difference.*[13]

Is there a difference? Does the dogmatic core of our belief matter? Does our profession of the faith condition in any material way the manner in which we *live* the faith? Does knowledge of what has been handed over (*tradere*) lead to changed perception, changed behavior? Or, conversely, does ignorance of what the fathers and mothers have professed end in aesthetic, axiological, and ethical

---

12. To illustrate: In the many discussions surrounding the knotty question of the ordination of self-declared homosexual persons, discussions that have shaken the foundations of most of the older Protestant bodies on this continent, the most notorious sort of biblicism has generally prevailed. Without so much as a suspicion of the significance of its historical setting (its context), with its pervasive sense of the subtle ties between sexuality and idolatry, the bald statement of Leviticus that sexual relations between two men constitute an "abomination" punishable by death (20:13) has again and again been cited as the biblical teaching on the subject, supported at times by equally uninformed, single-line quotations from St. Paul. In a similar vein, the biblicism emanating from the studios of the "televangelists," instead of being countered with something approaching knowledgeable exposition of the Scriptures, is either summarily dismissed as fanaticism or (far too often) imbibed and accepted without question by avowed mainstream Protestants. The state of confusion and plain ignorance about the Bible that is rife in our churches, together with the often pathetic and even tragic ethical consequences of this state, ought by itself to persuade concerned North American Christians today that new and serious efforts really to know the faith must be embarked upon.

13. Recently Gabriel Fackre conducted a survey on "The State of Theology in Churches." He reports: "The vast majority of respondents judged the state of theology in the churches to be 'abysmal,' 'dismal,' 'confused,' 'mushy,' 'sparse,' 'inarticulate,' 'deplorable.' . . ." (*Theology and Culture Newsletter* No. 30 [Advent, 1991], 1.)

behavior that from a more informed posture might have been prevented? Are heresies only errors of the mind, or do they lead to errors of the heart and the hand? Is "sound teaching" (in that sense, "orthodoxy") in any way mandatory for those who desire to engage in "sound practice" ("orthopraxy")?

Both of the foundational traditions of our civilization as well as our own theological past affirm the indispensability of sound teaching. Both Jerusalem and Athens assume that there is a decisive and inevitable link between knowing, being, and doing. While cognizant of the fact that the quest for *gnosis* may constitute an effective retreat from real life, these traditions insist that fullness of human being entails a never-ending search for depth of understanding—not only for knowledge (*scientia*) but for that possibility to which the earnest and prayerful quest for knowledge may lead, the possibility namely of acquiring *wisdom* (*sapientia*).

Wisdom is not the greatest gift of God, at least as far as the tradition of Jerusalem is concerned. *Sophia* is not mentioned by St. Paul when, in the famous hymn to love (1 Corinthians 13), he undertakes to speak of the greatest gifts of the Spirit. Yet the same Paul can call Jesus Christ "the wisdom of God" (1 Cor. 1:24); and does he not assume, this dialectician of wisdom and folly, that wisdom *en Christo* is in fact the *conditio* sine qua non of all three virtues that he names? Faith without wisdom might be fervent enough—but indistinguishable from credulity, true belief. Hope apart from wisdom might be abundant—and naive. Above all, love without wisdom, as ordinary human experience regularly and painfully confirms, is a love that is "all heart and no head."

Add to this the fact that for Jerusalem, in particular, the acquisition of such wisdom is bound up with the remembrance of things of which none of us has immediate, firsthand experience, namely, the contemplation of historical occurrences and of verbal testimony to these occurrences that belong to the past. A disciple community that fails to rehearse, struggle with, and reformulate for itself these collective memories that constitute its very foundation is a contradiction in terms; for it begs the question, disciples of what? of whom?

The general intellectual nonchalance of North American liberal Protestantism with respect to Christian theological tradition—a nonchalance that is partly explicable on the basis of modernity's rudimentary assumption of its superiority over all that preceded it—is today complicated by an attitude of deep suspicion on the part of certain groupings and movements that feel betrayed by the Christian past. Many women, native people, African Americans, and other marginalized groups whose identity seems to them jeopardized by dominant aspects of received "Christianity" now outrightly protest: "But this is not *my* tradition!" Such outcries within our own geographic context find much in common with new Christians in non-Western societies, who ask why they must submit to almost two millennia of Euro-American religious and dogmatic history. In order

10

to be Christians, must they also become pseudo-Westerners? Is not such an implied requirement the contemporary equivalent of the insistence on the part of the Jerusalem disciples that converts to the Christ must be circumcised—an insistence passionately contended by the apostle to the Gentiles, Paul?[14]

The present work assumes a sympathetic but not uncritical response to this kind of protest. It shares with the protesting movements a strong suspicion of traditionalism, and an equally strong intention to engage the real world of the present. This ought already to be obvious from the first volume, which interprets contextuality in theology as being the quest for a theology appropriate to the specifics of the here and now and is therefore inherently critical of any exposition of Christian belief as a deposit of truth to be accepted everywhere and anywhere in the same manner.

To deny primacy to the past, however, is not to exclude the past. A faith that presupposes the high significance of historical experience, as the Judeo-Christian tradition does, cannot endorse the sort of ahistorical approach that simply disowns the tradition. For one thing, such a disavowal too easily confirms the general anti-intellectualism and individualism of so much North American Christianity, thus supporting the belief that all that matters is "my" or "our" spirituality, stimulated by whatever remnants of Scripture and tradition appeal to me or to us.

Beyond that, there is in reality no such thing as a Christianity that is unrelated to the actual history of the Christian churches and their historical traditions. Even in the remotest parts of the so-called developing world (remote in relation to intercourse with Western civilization), any faith identifiable as Christian bears the earmarks of this or that strand of the long and diverse tradition of Christendom. Even the protest against the weight of regnant traditions is, after all, part of this tradition, and (especially for historic Protestantism) a very important part.

The principle of faith's innate quest for knowledge of what has been passed on is in fact upheld more effectively than elsewhere today precisely by those movements that protest against the oppressiveness of dominant forms of Christian dogma, whose dominance is often palpably inseparable from their questionable service to powerful conventions and elites within Christendom. Informed expressions of feminist, African-American, or aboriginal Amer-Canadian religious concern have indeed led the way for the rest of us when it comes to what I have been calling here struggle with the tradition. Such Christians often know—better than do those of us who can still in some ways seem to benefit from the perpetuation of certain presuppositions, biases, and distortions—that they must acquire an enlightened grasp of the history of Christian dogma and practice. It is not possible to challenge anything of which we are

---

14. See, e.g., 1 Cor. 7:18; Gal. 2:3ff., 5:6f.; Eph. 2:11.

insufficiently cognizant. While we may indeed rail against the unknown oppressor, we shall do so effectively only if we become better acquainted with the sources of the oppression that we sense. Even to disown the tradition, one has first—in some genuine sense of the word—to own it. If, however, one sets out seriously to investigate the tradition one has owned, one soon discovers that it is so broad, diverse, and even diffuse, that a quick, preliminary response of disavowal ("It's not *my* tradition") is quite out of place. For "it" is not an "it." It is a multiplicity, an ongoing dialogue with recurrent yet nuanced themes and variations, in which, as Peter Abelard discovered centuries ago, there is always a yes and a no (*Sic et Non*) to every proposition proffered. This multiplicity is already present in the biblical foundations of the tradition, and it is there for the good reason that the truth, toward which both the Bible and the faithful of all the ages desired to point, *lives.*

In particular, the serious student of the Christian tradition will always discover alternatives within that tradition which will inevitably qualify, if not altogether silence, his or her too hasty disavowal. This is in fact what the most engaged and disciplined protesting movements in our own time have discovered—as did the Reformers and all previous movements of protest. For the rich tradition that faith professes contains at every point neglected, hidden, minority, or submerged traditions that, when they are unearthed under new contextual circumstances, can become foundational not only for forceful Christian protests against the continued power of dogmatic conventions that are oppressive, exclusive, or dehumanizing, but for the constructive restatement of the faith.[15]

This again reinforces the importance of genuine knowledge of the tradition. None of the foundational insights out of which contemporary feminist, liberationist, nature, and ecological theologies have based themselves would exist, and exist as decisive challenges to conventional Christianity, had not theologians like Ruether, Sittler, Cobb, Cone, Sölle, Sobrino, Song, and many others understood from the outset that a major aspect of their work as theologians was the historical work of acquiring an informed awareness of the evolution of Christian thought. In the process of pursuing that necessity, they found within the tradition not only some of the doctrinal sources of the oppressiveness they darkly sensed, but also alternative theologies, Christologies, eschatologies, and so forth on whose foundations they might rebuild their own houses of faith and understanding.

There is no doubt always some sense in which "the tradition" is apprehended as enemy, that is, as the enemy of present faith, and more especially of a faith whose present and future orientation stems from a high degree of

---

15. See Letty M. Russell on "The Search for a Usable Past," in *Human Liberation in a Feminist Perspective—A Theology* (Philadelphia: Westminster Press, 1974), chap. 3, especially 88–89.

religious commitment. Tradition represents, after all, the ponderous weight of the past. As such, it constrains us. It limits our bid for unfettered freedom. Between our personal sensitivity and "the gospel" it sets this testimony of the ages, and there are few who can bear this without some twinge of deep resentment. For it constitutes in truth an existential denial of autonomy, an affront to self-sufficiency.Moreover, because tradition always has its present-day, usually self-appointed guardians, and because these guardians are almost always wholly unaware of the one-sidedness of their grasp of what has been handed over, tradition can seem all the more opposed to vital faith and spirituality in the here and now. But this apparent enmity of the tradition, like most enmity, is in large measure the consequence of its unknownness, including the abysmal inadequacy of its representation by "the guardians." Those who devote themselves to searching the Scriptures and traditions of the faith, while they will almost certainly encounter some aspects that are more alien to their own preferences than they had imagined, will also discover that the tradition can be user friendly. Indeed, they will probably find out that, without the usable past that the great tradition can provide, their own gropings for truth for the here and now would be quite insubstantial.

Profession as Commitment.   Profession in the sense in which we are using it here not only presupposes knowledge of the tradition, and wisdom that may come with the prayerful habit of seeking to know; it also presupposes commitment to that which is known or sought. This is already implicit in what we have said about knowledge, but it needs to be made explicit; for knowledge or the act of seeking to know does not necessarily imply commitment to what one knows or hopes to comprehend. Both in theory and (today especially) in practice, it seems possible to know a good deal about many subjects without in any way intending to *profess* them. This is evidently true also where religion in general, as well as the Christian religion in particular, are concerned. The "science of religion" (*Religionswissenschaft*) is premised on the assumption that knowledge and commitment are wholly separable. Indeed, in academic circles where the "phenomenon" of religion is studied, it is often thought that commitment is positively detrimental to the pursuit of reliable knowledge. Even seminary educators ask today whether the teaching of Christian theology should involve "advocacy."[16]

It is my opinion (I am, fortunately, not alone in this) that Christian theology as distinct from the "religiological" study of Christianity rejects and *must* reject this divorce of knowing and commitment. The object of the theologian's search for understanding is not a matter of the intellect alone but of the will

16. Cf. *Theological Education,* Supplement 1, 1988, vol. 24 ("Theological Education as the Formation of Character").

and even of the body—in short, of the whole person. Who can read any of the most excellent exemplars of this theological tradition (Augustine, Luther, Kierkegaard, Barth, Suzanne de Dietrich, Tillich, the Niebuhrs, Ruether, et al.) and imagine that he or she is encountering a detached and dispassionate inquiry? Professing the faith means submitting in a holistic, existentially engaged way to the exploration of what has been handed over. It is (to use Tillich's well-known term) a matter of ultimate concern. Doubt is by no means excluded from this concern;[17] it is indeed a prominent dimension of the concern in question, and it is for that reason precisely more than mere intellectual doubt. As "existential doubt" (Tillich), it adds its own high degree of *necessitas* to the quest for knowledge. The idea of detachment, however, or of a value-free examination of the scriptural and historical-theological data, has only a very limited place in this undertaking. It is part of that "technical reason" (Tillich) which *of course* binds the knower to what is actually there in the texts of Scripture and in the documents of the councils and the theologians. But this limited application of the research honored by Academe so uncritically in our historical moment, in theology does not permit of becoming the habitual stance of the knower. For the presupposition of the whole theological undertaking is after all that what is being explored is a treasury of wisdom that is *saving* knowledge, namely, a type of *gnosis* which, when it is sanctified by grace and suffering, saves one not only from the state of ignorance but from the state of profound and many-sided estrangement, that is, of sin.

It is just here, of course, that liberal forms of Christianity experience particular difficulties. These difficulties are naturally related to the fact that much of this same Christianity has bought into the whole ideology of value-free inquiry and a detached openness to truth that must find nowhere to lay its head; and therefore it fears above all and precisely . . . *commitment.* This ideology is augmented for sensitive Christians today, moreover, by the recent and growing awareness of the plurality of religious commitments, and of the fanaticism that often accompanies the most vociferously "committed" believers in all of the world's major religions. The intelligent modern Christian, hearing such a term as *commitment*—or even less emotionally charged language such as discipleship, obedience, or theological seriousness—is prone to suspect that no good will result from such earnestness. Will not the commitment that is called for end in the kind of exclusivism that is already the cause of so much suffering in our world? Can anyone submit so totally to one religious tradition without courting the specter of dogmatism? In North America we are well aware of what happens to Christians who give themselves unrestrainedly to "Bible faith" and to certain traditions of dogma. Liberal Christianity stands for tolerance, and tolerance is not a virtue lightly to be dismissed. In the Anglo-Saxon tradition of this heritage

---

17. *Thinking the Faith,* 248ff.

of tolerance (what a difference was made by the Act of Toleration of 1689!), we rightly feel reluctant to sacrifice such hard-won openness to "the other" for any kind of religious loyalty that may end in bigotry and the humiliation of all beyond the pale of this or that little orthodoxy.

This right concern for tolerance and inclusivity compels us to expatiate more precisely on the connotation of the term *commitment* as we intend it here. It is true that its usage, particularly in religious circles, inclines one to think in terms of a stance admitting neither doubt nor the capacity to entertain alternatives. "Committed" Christians, in the popular imagination that has been fueled by the pyrotechnics of American television religion,[18] are persons virtually incapable of receiving new thoughts even about their own religion, let alone listening to advocates of other religious faiths. They have committed themselves—"made up their minds": they are determined to stick by the "truths" they have accepted.

Is there any way of conceiving of Christian commitment that avoids this caricature but avoids at the same time the pitfalls of a liberality that is so afraid of explicit commitments of any sort that it functions, regardless of its intentions, to deny the very possibility of professing the faith?

The present work is premised on the belief that such a way does exist. The rectitude of the claim can only be tested, finally, by what is actually said in this book. Perhaps I shall not always be able to avoid both the Scylla of conservative exclusivity and the Charybdis of liberal generalities. The proof is in the pudding. But at the outset certain intentions of the author can at least be set out.

1. I reiterate what has already been said in passing (and may, for that reason, have been overlooked), namely, that the commitment about which I am writing here should not imply adherence, rigid or otherwise, to specific systems of doctrine or dogmatic tradition. The profession of the faith does not mean: "I accept all the creeds" (the ironic statement of Hitler's *Reichsbischof,* Ludwig Müller). It does not even mean that I accept this creed or that one—the Apostles', the Nicene, the Westminster Confession of Faith, the Barmen Declaration, the Augsburg Confession, the Heidelberg Confession, the Formula of Chalcedon, and so on. Nor is it implied that I dismiss or sit lightly to any of these historic statements. Certainly not! But they are not what I *profess.* What I profess is Christian faith, and I think there is no better way of stating it, nebulous as this may sound to persons whose "commitment" is bound up with more explicit doctrinal conventions.

Christian faith has found expression in a great many ways, some more and some less explicitly doctrinal. These ways share, to be sure, recurring motifs and

---

18. On the subject of televised Christianity, see Neil Postman, *Amusing Ourselves to Death: Public Discourse in the Age of Show Business* (New York: Penguin Books, 1985), 114–24; William F. Fore, *Television and Religion* (Minneapolis: Augsburg, 1987); and Jerry Mander, *Four Arguments for the Elimination of Television* (New York: Quill, 1978).

claims—a "common heritage" (Robert McAfee Brown). Some of these, obviously enough, I shall find more compelling than others. But what I *profess* when I profess the faith is not my commitment to a set of dogmas or religious ideas; rather, it is the act of acknowledging my intention to give to this whole account of reality called Christian, in all of its biblical and doctrinal variety and riches, a certain priority. It is my determination (though not on my own initiative) to listen with special attentiveness to the witnesses to this tradition, commencing with the biblical witness; to wrestle with the meaning of this diverse testimony to the living Word; to live my life and think my thoughts in dialogue with this testimony; to risk seeing "everything"[19] *sub specie Christi.* Commitment is here a matter, not of the possession of truth (the language of possession, as I have previously insisted, is simply not appropriate to this tradition), but of memory and expectation: *I profess the faith as I remember its foundations and hope for its continuing illumination of the present and the emergent future.*

Such an explication of commitment will not satisfy some of those in all of our denominations who like to style themselves conservatives. They can be satisfied only with affirmations of the absolute truth of the propositions they themselves advocate (which are many, and often contradictory). But my purpose here is not, in any case, to appease religious conservatism. I mean rather to speak to those who inherit the broad categories of Christian liberalism (for want of a better term), for it is that tradition which, in my view, must be liberated. It must be liberated from its fear, precisely, of commitment. It rightly spurns dogmatism and exclusivity; but in its commitment to noncommitment it is in danger of dissipating the witness of the church by denying faith a *professional foundation.*[20]

Especially in its socially conscious expressions, particularly the Social Gospel movement, liberalism called the churches to a greater moral and political responsibility in the world, and for this all North American Christians ought to be grateful. But a strong imperative requires an equally strong indicative. The ethic must have a basis in theology. Liberalism begs the question, Why? Without the kind of commitment to doctrinal clarity that is required of those who profess the faith, any alleged Christian ethic, regardless of its appeal, lacks an ontic foundation. As the history of theological liberalism shows, moreover, it will not suffice to substitute for a nuanced and ongoing struggle for adequate theological underpinnings the sort of "simple gospel" that, throughout its history, the church has frequently tried to have. Already in the earlier part of this century, the churches had to learn that—the hard way! The

---

19. See *Thinking the Faith,* 323.
20. See Joseph C. Hough, Jr., "The Loss of Optimism as a Problem for Liberal Christian Faith," in *Liberal Protestantism: Realities and Possibilities,* ed. Robert S. Michaelsen and Wade Clark Roof (New York: Pilgrim Press, 1986), 145ff.

complexity of existence cannot be answered by easy declarations of "the fatherhood of God and the brotherhood of man." In the situation of today, with ever-deepening human questions posed to all classical systems of meaning (for example, in the area of medical ethics),[21] Christians who wish to shed light on our darkness must commit themselves to a search for theological depth that is at least as demanding as anything undertaken by the medieval scholastics or the Protestant reformers. While it is our ethic that is being most conspicuously tested for its adequacy in the "postmodern" world, it is in reality our theology—as the foundation of that ethic—that is being weighed in the balance.

2. I intend in these pages to elaborate a profession of Christian commitment that does *not* end in or lead to religious exclusivity. I am in full agreement with those who decry religious commitment of the sort that *must* end in the exclusion of other faiths and other interpretations of Christian faith. But does commitment to the Christian faith—to this particular religious tradition—necessarily result in exclusivity? Why should the decision to pay serious attention to Christian foundations produce an attitude of Christian superiority and a posture of rejection where all other claims to truth are concerned? That many of the most "committed" Christians and Christian endeavors *have* engendered and *do* engender such an attitude and posture cannot be denied. But is this a matter of theological or rational necessity? Is it not better accounted for on the basis of psychological rather than logical causation?

Logically, the determination to orient oneself toward a particular tradition does imply an initial and in some sense an arbitrary choice, in that other religious alternatives are in the process denied that kind of initial prioritizing. Similarly, the choice of a mate involves commitment to a particular human being—"forsaking all others," as the traditional marriage ceremony stated it. But does this logic then extend to the end-product of the marriage relationship? Having committed myself to this *one* as the necessary condition for depth of relatedness, have I also entered into a covenant that will prevent proximity to and dialogue with "all others"?

Surely the answer will depend upon the nature of that one, and of my relationship with her or him. We know from experience that some marital relationships do indeed exclude others—that sometimes exclusivity is their most visible trait. Former friends, acquaintances, parents, even occasionally the very children of the union are shut out. But are not such alliances unhealthy from the start? If the person to whom I am married demands of me that I devote my attention exclusively to him or her, to the point, say, of manifesting extreme jealousy with respect to all other human contacts, then most marriage

---

21. See Jacques Ellul, *The Technological Bluff,* trans. Geoffrey W. Bromiley (Grand Rapids: Wm. B. Eerdmans Pub. Co., 1990), 402–5. See also Margaret A. Somerville, "The Song of Death: The Lyrics of Euthanasia" (McGill University, Faculty of Medicine, unpublished paper, 1993).

17

counselors will want to examine that partner carefully. Ironically, when *religious* allegiances function in the same way there is a tendency on the part of many to admire the tenacity of such "devotion." But could it not be that the same psychic insecurity that produces suspicion and jealousy in marriage is at work in religious circles where closed loyalty to the one system is demanded?

Let us state the matter positively: Should not particulars of every type function to open us to the wide world—to the universal? Is it not in fact the authenticating mark of any particular when it does, without negating itself, point beyond itself? We are dependent upon particulars for our experience of the universality that they can and do reveal; for we do not meet universals except through these particulars. I have never met Childhood nor The Coming Generations. But through the lives of particular children to whom providence has committed me, I have been led beyond the confines of my own generational cohort to the world of the young, so that sometimes I am even permitted to glimpse the world through their eyes. Through them, the future is no longer simply my future—which is certainly limited in scope. Through them the more distant future has been given faces—and so I have learned to care about the consequences of our present acts and failures to act, and not just for the next decade or so but for the world of my children's children.

Nor have I ever met Tree, or Tree-ness. But I have known and nurtured and loved particular trees, and they have taught me something about forests—and more. They have wholly conditioned my science. From them I know that the whole realm of nature vastly transcends our no doubt partially correct theories about nonhuman forms of life. From them, and from certain dogs and cats and cows and grasses and bodies of water (all intensely particular) I have contemplated the interrelatedness of all that is with sufficient seriousness to recognize, if not always to emulate, the truth of what Albert Schweitzer meant by "awe before life" (*Ehrfurcht vor das Leben*).

In all such instances, the intensity of commitment to the particular is sustained; yet, along with it, through its instrumentality, there is an equally intensive commitment to that which particulars *disclose,* which always exceeds their own particularity while at the same time binding us all the more to themselves as embodiments of a mystery that they cannot in themselves contain. Why then should it not also happen that one's attachments to the particular religious alternative called Christian faith—if indeed it is a worthy particular—serves to give one a new understanding of and appreciation for the greater whole, including other religious traditions? And if it does not do so, then is it not possible that one's alleged Christianity is functioning for one in the same manner as a jealous husband or a spoiled child functions in familial relations, that is, destructively?

Commitment, whether in ordinary human relationships, in vocational choices, in political allegiances, or in religion, always involves particularity.

We acknowledge this, in recent theology, when we speak about "the scandal of particularity." But what must be learned by conservative and liberal Christians alike is that the role of the particular ultimately is not to exclude but precisely to include. For the sake of depth, mystery, transcendence; for the sake of getting beyond the It to the Thou; for the sake of encountering life itself, and not just theories about life, our commitments—all of them—must pass through the narrow door of the particular. But it is a door. It is not a barrier, a dividing wall of hostility, or a restrictive place from which there is "No Exit" (Sartre).

Christian exclusivism has always made much of John 10: "'I am the door . . .'" (RSV). If, instead of concentrating so narrowly on the "I" of this sentence the people who employ the passage to rule out all but those who can "name the Name" had explored the informing metaphor of the sentence (the door) more imaginatively, they might have helped the church avoid much unwholesome bigotry and proneness to violence. For Christians, Jesus Christ is indeed "the door": without this Christocentrism the Christian faith dissolves into a general theism indistinguishable in essence from any other abstract discourse about God. But doors are not chiefly for keeping people out. Why bother with doors at all if what is wanted is exclusion of the outsider and protection of those inside? Walls are much better adapted to that purpose. Both in general usage and in this metaphoric utterance of Jesus, doors are intended primarily for *access* to something. The purpose of the door that Jesus "is" (or, to refer to another dimension of the parable, through which as "Shepherd" he leads "the sheep") is to provide access to "pasture" (v. 9), that is, to more abundant life (v. 10). Far from accentuating the uniqueness and exclusivity of this one entree to "salvation," the whole passage moves toward the *inclusiveness* of Jesus' redemptive work. As in that other well-known reference to the door metaphor ("Listen! I am standing at the door, knocking. . . ," Rev. 3:20), the symbol of the door in this passage is one of invitation and openness. And, as if to warn against exclusivism, the author uses the same context to have the "Good Shepherd" declare that he has "other sheep" which are "not of this fold." This open-endedness is finally carried to its logical and theological conclusion with the expression of "the Father's" intention of there being but "one fold"—that through the "one shepherd" there should come to be an ecumenical unity and harmony, the same idea that John expresses in many places, especially in the high-priestly prayer "that they may all be one" (chap. 17). In other words, the goal of this particular Gospel is its provision of access to universal wholeness. Commitment to Jesus as the Christ is only legitimate commitment if it reflects this same concern for and orientation toward the whole.

3. I intend here to demonstrate (what I have attempted from the outset with the centrality of the language of Christian discipleship)[22] that the commitment

---

22. See especially *Thinking the Faith,* "Introduction to Volume I," 57ff.

which belongs to the church's profession of faith is a matter of discipleship, not merely or even primarily of scholarship.

It is characteristic of most forms of historic Christianity that they have understood their primary loyalty, where the exposition and inculcation of doctrine is concerned, to be the faithful perpetuation of theological teachings inspired by founding individuals or movements. To be a committed Lutheran meant and means to sustain faithfulness to the basic insights of Martin Luther and the doctrinal symbols of historic Lutheranism. Those committed to the Reformed tradition have been and are oriented rather to the works of Calvin, Knox, and others; and so on. In other words, doctrinal commitment has for most of us a connotation decisively associated with the past. One professes the faith as one maintains this orientation toward the particular theological heritage in which one stands, with a view to keeping it alive in the present life of the church.

Such a preconception is not wholly misleading, for, as we have already acknowledged, commitment in the sense in which we must use it here does involve the willingness to hear and receive and interpret what has been handed over. But the notion of faithfulness to a doctrinal past is certainly inadequate as a total conception of what is meant by profession of the faith. It is especially inadequate to a theology that consciously seeks to be contextual. The mentality that desires above all to be faithful to some past expression of the Christian faith is in no position to take with seriousness what is indispensable to contextuality in theology, namely, the formative influence of the here and now. The past is not dismissed in this mode of theological reflection. If anything, it is taken more seriously than by traditionalism, because it is needed for the illumination of the present. But contextual theology respects the doctrinal traditions within which it works, not out of faithfulness to them but rather out of faithfulness to the Spirit who spoke through them and who continues to speak to the church today.

Our conception of the kind of commitment that belongs to faith's profession must be conformed to this existential, pneumatic dimension of theology. Doctrine is created by the coming together, in the disciple community, of the memory of what has been vouchsafed to past generations and the ongoing experience of being grasped by the divine Spirit here and now. It is not only a question of sensitivity to confessional traditions, therefore, but faith's profession (not only its confession but already its *pro*fession) involves a special receptivity to what is occurring within the disciple community right now and right here. What *is* (present tense) the Spirit saying *to the churches* (see Revelation 2–3)? How does discipleship under the conditions of this quite specific historical moment affect our articulation of that meditative core that, at their best, church doctrines and dogmas are intended to characterize?

A number of contemporary theologians have made this same point. *"Discipleship,"* writes José Míguez Bonino, "is the only epistemological location for understanding Jesus Christ. In traditional Protestant theology discipleship, when discussed at all in systematic theology, was seen as an ethical consequence or, at best, as part of a sanctification conceived as a 'second moment' after justification." [23] Similarly, Frederick Herzog insists that "doctrine arises from discipleship—God-walk rather than God-talk." He continues:

> Just as the civil rights struggle, born in the God-walk of the black church, helped shape Christian doctrine (as became clear in the work of James Cone and Gayraud S. Wilmore, among others) so today the battle against apartheid in South Africa is affecting doctrine, as is the women's movement and other similar struggles.[24]

Contextual theology is a theology in which doctrine is shaped, not only by positive responses of prophetic movements within the disciple community but also by negative factors in church and society. For example, in a context conditioned by what I have dubbed "official optimism," what the church must learn to profess is a Christology and ecclesiology that permit people to be honest about their real pessimism. In a context which reflects an anthropology that makes a clear-cut distinction between humankind and all other creatures, the Christian doctrine of humanity should accentuate the ways in which, according to our profession of the faith, human beings participate in the whole creaturely condition. In other words, our doctrine will be significantly affected by our call to present discipleship as well as by responses to this call on the part of faithful minorities.

To summarize: The commitment that is implied in the profession of faith is characterized by three qualities. (1) It is faithfulness to remembered tradition that is always more comprehensive than any of its explicit credal or systematic formulations; therefore it is a matter of memory and expectation, rather than the possession of inherited truth. (2) While it entails orientation to an intensely particularized tradition, this commitment does not end in exclusivity, since at least *this* particularity, whose center is Jesus as Christ, leads to an inclusivity that transcends itself while not negating itself. (3) The commitment required of those who profess the faith is part and parcel of their total discipleship, and this discipleship is not only the condition for their comprehension of doctrine

---

23. "On Discipleship, Justice and Power," in *Freedom and Discipleship: Liberation Theology in an Anabaptist Perspective,* ed. Daniel S. Schipini (Maryknoll, N.Y.: Orbis Books, 1989), 132.

24. "A New Spirituality: Shaping Doctrine at the Grass Roots," *The Christian Century* 103, no. 23 (July 30–Aug. 6, 1986): 680–81.

but an ongoing source of their apprehension of what it is that they are called to profess.

2. The Contextual Appropriateness of the Profession of Faith

To this point, we have been concerned chiefly with two aspects of our subject: first and foremost, we have wanted to inquire about what is actually involved in the profession of faith, and this has led us to discuss the place of knowing and commitment in the disciple community. Secondly, in keeping with the concern for contextuality by which this whole work is informed, we have had to acknowledge and address the difficulties that are encountered in such an attempt at faith's profession within the socioreligious setting of the two northern nations of our continent. Along the way, however, we recognized[25] that the same North American context contains factors that render sustained endeavors to articulate what Christians profess both positive and contextually appropriate. To these we shall now turn. They can be treated more succinctly, not only because their details will form part of the larger content of this volume, but also because they are, in fact, the other side of the story that has already been introduced in our discussion of negative factors affecting faith's profession in this context.

A New Demand for Knowledge. The same sociohistorical forces that have deprived Christianity of its cultural and political supports and thus generated a reaction that substitutes credulity for knowledge have fashioned, as well, a quite different response in some quarters. In and around all of the ecclesial communities of our continent today, one finds people who are newly awakened to the need to *know* the faith they profess, desire to profess, or at least cannot fully renounce. The very deprivation that has been brought about by the demise of "Christendom," the bewildering plurality of religions in our midst, and other dimensions of our historical experience that have had the effect of challenging an automatic or merely cultural Christianity have caused such persons to demand of Christian institutions a more rigorous and informed attention to the core of belief. They cannot be satisfied with "Sunday school religion," and they are not prepared to sacrifice their minds on the altar of "true belief." Neither are they predisposed to adapting themselves to the general apathy of the secular, hedonistic society by which they are surrounded. For one reason or another, they find they cannot entirely dispense with theism; yet they are characteristically critical (and sometimes contemptuous) of the "sweet nothingness" and "bourgeois

---

25. See above, p. 5.

transcendence" (Käsemann) that they are offered in the middle-class sanctuaries with which, in most cases, family and class conventions have associated them.[26] Neither the dogmatism of much convervatism nor the laissez-faire of much liberal Christianity appeals to such persons. They want to know the fundamental basis of Christian belief, not merely some of the useful consequences of believing, but they do not intend to imbibe these fundamentals after the manner of fundamentalism. The only faith that can speak to them is one that allows them the freedom to explore its claims without restrictions, and one that is profound enough to engage their deepest anxieties and give substance to whatever remains of their highest ideals.

We may safely assume, I think, that the segment in question represents a minority in our society. We should certainly not immediately jump to the conclusion (a favorite conclusion with all promoters) that here is a vast market that the churches could tap if only they would recognize the demand for their "product" and learn how to "package" it more attractively.[27] The great portion of our contemporaries appear all too ready to squelch whatever questions the discomforts of the intellect arouse, so long as their bodies and emotions are enveloped in the comforts offered by a relatively affluent society. All the same, as the affluence of our society is increasingly taxed by economic recession and violence, it can be reasonably expected that the numbers of those seeking greater depth will increase.

In any case, biblical faith is keenly interested in minorities—more directly, indeed, than in majorities. For its most basic soteriological assumption is that the salvation of the many is bound up with the spiritual ventures of a few, through whose subjection to the hard quest for truth and justice the world may be preserved from its preference for "easeful death," falsehood, and the maintenance of the status quo. The dissatisfied, the disenchanted, the restless searchers after meaning have always been those in whom the Spirit of this faith has been especially interested—not because it would redeem them alone (that is elitism), but because it regards them as the salt and yeast and light through whom the food may be prevented from insipidity, the loaf from flatness, and the soul of humanity from its captivation by mediocrity (Matt. 5:13-16; 13:31-33). That is what this tradition means by *election*.

It would be salutary if Christianity in North America today were to regard as the sign of divine election precisely such dissatisfaction and disenchantment,

---

26. Margaret Atwood characterizes the sentimentalized remnants of classical Protestantism on this continent cunningly in her novel *Cat's Eye* (Toronto: Seal Books, McClelland-Bantam, 1988), 332. "Theology," she writes, "has changed, over the years: *just deserts* used to be what everyone could expect to get, in the end. Now it's a restaurant specializing in cakes."

27. Such a conclusion seems to have been reached by Reginald W. Bibby and his researchers in *Fragmented Gods: The Poverty and Potential of Religion in Canada* (Toronto: Irwin Publishing, 1987).

such determination to demand of life something better than comfort. So long as the churches make their appeal to those who desire security, calm, and consolation, they will have little room for the kind of intellectual, ethical, and spiritual rigor that is required of any resolute attempt at professing the faith. We have seen that one of the chief reasons why the North American Protestant churches have been so inconstant in their theological work is that their dominant "clientele" has consisted of persons who are seeking peace of mind, and a thinking faith disturbs the mind! There will no doubt always be a market for peace-of-mind religion, but it will be inimical to a faith that demands extraordinary exertions of both mind and heart if it is to be *professed* by anyone.

Those, however, who are driven by the "spirit of the times" to search in old places for new meaning, regardless of the risk—they are the ones from whom the churches may expect a hearing whenever Christian communities are sufficiently faithful not to be threatened by unfaith or by that keen scrutiny of faith that emanates from the necessary doubt that is part of genuine human need. It is particularly provocative for Christian apologetics in our time and place that such persons, while certainly in the minority, constitute a significant minority, and that, despite the general failure of the churches to present a gospel that addresses their need, representatives of such a posture are still to be found within and around Christian congregations.

Often, in fact, they are at the very center of congregational life, cheerfully camouflaging their disappointment through exceptional patience with what is there, yet hoping always for something better to emerge. The truth is, all extraneous reasons for remaining in the church having been dispersed by the winds of time, it is now necessary to assume that a great many of those who continue to have some association with organized Christianity are looking for something more than what, on the whole, they are receiving. Many of them are prepared to be entirely serious about the faith. If they are half inspired by any presentation of Scripture or doctrine, they will go to considerable lengths to obtain more of the same. Often they will be capable of feats of intellectual discipline far in excess of anything that the professional clergy has been conditioned to expect of the laity. It is almost a rule of contemporary ecclesiastical experience that wherever truly dedicated, sustained, and imaginative efforts at lay education have been mounted, the response is beyond all expectations. The German *Kirchentag,* an intellectually demanding annual event in a society numerically far more advanced than ours along the path of post-Christian existence, is a splendid example of what I mean.

It is this quest for depth on the part of searching and disaffected minorities in and around all of our churches that makes the serious profession of the faith a contextually appropriate undertaking. If half the energies expended on church growth, modern techniques of communication (communication of *what?*), and the usual maintenance of the ecclesiastical machine were devoted instead to truly responsible work in the area of Christian adult education, the failing mainline churches of this continent might discover a new vitality. I do not suggest that they would experience numerical and material success. That was never promised, in any case, to the followers of the crucified one. It is just *that*, in fact, that must be overcome; for it is a continuing temptation. The vitality—the *life*—that is appropriate to the disciple community is a vitality that depends upon quality, not quantity; and part of that quality is determined by the earnestness with which the community seeks to know the truth that makes it free. I have suggested that there is, in our social and ecclesiastical context, a certain readiness—even a certain demand—for such quality. Insofar as this is so, the first step of a Christian leadership that wishes to contextualize the faith is to return to the basics of the faith—not as a refuge from the complexities of contemporary life but as a source of wisdom, courage, and direction.

Commitment in a "Free" Society. We have seen that the profession of the faith involves not only a willingness to subject oneself to the discipline of seeking knowledge but also to risk commitment to what is known. This is undoubtedly a more complex aspect of our subject than is the search for knowledge in itself. Commitment is not easily espoused in a society that celebrates self-determination and the individual's inalienable rights. The power of individualism in North America militates against the prospect that a person might suspend his or her autonomy long enough to permit the claims of a faith-tradition to make their impact. In short, commitment goes against the grain of a social milieu that has apotheosized freedom, glorified the free-ranging individual whose only "commitment" is to his or her own unrelenting pursuit of personal happiness, and reduced Truth to objectifiable data.

Here again, however, the student of contemporary North American civilization will have noted an interesting development. There is an almost palpable discontent among us, and it is often most conspicuous in circles that, on account of material security, have promoted the greatest and least inhibited exploits of personal freedom. The restlessness that unimpeded freedom breeds is of course not always admitted. But those who can admit it, or who recognize its distinguishing features, are able to detect its presence on a large scale in our social context.

The explanation of this phenomenon is not terribly obscure. When freedom virtually means license to pursue whatever—with or without the help of advertisers—occurs to one; when it connotes freedom *from* forces external to the self without a corresponding freedom *for* anything more expansive than the self; when, in short, freedom is no longer held in correlational tension with responsibility, it can come to be felt as the greatest tyranny.

Recently a young woman gave spontaneous expression to this ancient wisdom when she wrote to me that the baby she was expecting, though not willed by her, would perhaps be a welcome deliverance from the "bondage of Self." She was recognizing that personal liberty, apart from commitment to something transcending one's own person, could in fact prove the most wretched and subtle form of human oppression.

This recognition, at varying levels of consciousness, informs the daily life of more than a few of our contemporaries. Nor is it unreasonable that this should be the case; for many in our society have gone far enough toward realization of the dream of personal security and individual autonomy to know that its reality is by no means so desirable as its promoters promised. A surfeit of freedom has as a reaction bred something like a demand for more worthy forms of dedication and duty. In many persons this demand, under duress, is too quickly assuaged. People all around us today appear ready to give themselves to schemes, programs, and belief systems that are calculated precisely to relieve them of their burdensome freedom. Religious and quasi-religious agencies offer them total belief systems, complete with techniques for dispelling any lingering misgivings. Not only the notorious "Moonies" but many socially more acceptable forms of religion, including a good deal of what advertises itself as Christian, capitalize precisely on this need to escape from the spiritual oppression that is an unwanted by-product of idealized individual freedom. Their success, however deplorable, is eloquent documentation of the discontent to which I am referring.

Christians who are faithful to the sources of their own discipleship know that they are not at liberty to offer the gospel as an antidote to oppressive freedom. There can be no commitment, no discipleship, where freedom has simply been forfeited. Even a distorted freedom, even a freedom that has been conditioned to hear only the demands of self, retains some semblance of an orientation to "the other." It is still able now and then to recognize the inappropriateness of mere *self*-service.

The existence, even in the midst of a consumer society that finds ever new ways of indulging the self, of persons and whole movements that reach out for more profound forms of human and worldly service can be understood by Christians as being indicative of vestiges of that freedom which seeks its counterpart in greater responsibility. Observing the rather impressive numbers of individuals and organizations whose commitments to such causes as the preservation of species, of peace, and of justice carry them toward forms of self-sacrifice for which they may not have bargained, anyone familiar with biblical faith is liable to conclude that the juxtaposition of freedom and responsibility present in that tradition may after all have had its foundations in the deepest realities of the human spirit. According to biblical faith, human beings were created for service—the enjoyment and service of God, which is the service of one to "the other" and the mending of creation. Our freedom, along with our rationality and other related gifts (speech, for instance), is a thing to be cherished not for itself but only as it equips us for our stewardly role within the whole created order. Freedom, in other words, is precisely for the sake of commitment; and a freedom that has not found that to which it can commit itself profoundly is a restless sort of thing. It belongs to that same *cor inqui- etum* ("restless heart") that, according to the most famous sentence of Augustine of Hippo, is the very thing that marks us created by God and for God.[28]

The question that is put to North American theology and faith both by our cultural "restlessness"[29] and by the apparent readiness of minorities to take up new and exceptionally demanding forms of worldly responsibility is this: Can we learn to profess the Christian message and the life of discipleship as a commitment worthy of the best efforts of those who are ready for great responsibility and a challenge to those who are languishing in their oppressive "freedom"? The onus is upon the Christian community to test whether what it professes is capable of eliciting explicit commitment within a social context redolent of an implicit, if cloaked and imprecise, readiness for commitment. Until the present, it seems to me, the most established forms of Christianity on this continent have been so hesitant to make any demands, so fearful of any sort of rigor, that they have been in no position to appeal either to the idealism or to the anxiety that is present in "restlessness" North American style. If the disciple community is to alter that, it shall have to begin with an exploration of the basis of our belief that makes real demands upon both the intellect and the will. The new preparedness for commitment that seems present in many within our society should not be interpreted as a desire for more volunteer work, more weekly discussion groups, more congregational participation in worship, and so on. Churches are being invited to offer profound and timely presentations of the very foundations of Christian belief. Can Christianity today learn to profess a faith that is able to engage the rekindled aspiration to *know* and the latent will to responsible commitment that informs many of our contemporaries, especially those who have allowed themselves consciously to undergo the failure of modernity?

In a recent, perceptive essay entitled "The Year 2000: Is It the End—or Just the Beginning?" Henry Grunwald notes that "we are witnessing the end, or at least the decline, of an age of unbelief and beginning what may be a new age of faith," and he comments:

> The mainstream churches have tried various ways to adapt themselves to a secular age. The Roman Catholic Church made its liturgy accessible in the vernacular and turned increasingly from saving souls to saving society. The major Protestant

---

28. *Confessions,* Book 1, para. 1.

29. "A perennial restlessness and yearning dogs our steps." Wendy Farley, *Tragic Vision and Divine Compassion: A Contemporary Theodicy* (Louisville: Westminster/John Knox Press, 1990), 35.

denominations also increasingly emphasized social activism and tried to dilute dogma to accommodate 20th century rationality and diversity. . . .

But none of these reforms are arresting the sharp decline of the mainstream churches. Why not? The answer seems to be that while orthodox religion can be stifling, liberal religion can be empty. Many people seem to want a faith that is rigorous and demanding.[30]

The hypothesis that a serious attempt at faith's profession is contextually appropriate today is confirmed by one of the most impressive contemporary sociological studies of the religious situation in the United States. In concluding their work on *American Mainline Religion: Its Changing Shape and Future,* Wade Clark Roof and William McKinney accentuate the potentially vital role of "the liberal churches" in providing "a vocabulary of symbols, beliefs, moral values, and feeling-responses for articulating a socially responsible individualism."[31] The condition apart from which such a public role could not be achieved, according to these authors, is that liberal Protestantism must acquire a more informed, inspired, and committed sense of what it is called to profess.

A crucial challenge for liberal Protestantism is to recapture some sense of particularity as a community of memory and not merely as a custodian of generalized cultural values. This will require among other things a countering of the secular drift that has had a disproportionate impact on its traditional constituency. The liberal churches need their own particular language of faith to communicate with the "cultured despisers" of the modern world, in a manner that lays claims upon the self and the community.[32]

Theology, far from being peripheral in this project, must be brought to the center: "If a revived public church is indeed on the horizon . . . [it] will require forms and qualities of leadership that have seldom been forthcoming from the Protestant middle; a revitalized ecumenicity and *new, bold theological affirmations are critical as well, especially a theology that resonates with and gives meaning to the experience of middle Americans.* "[33]

Such a theology cannot be a mere repetition of any of the orthodoxies of the past. But unless the Christian past is wrestled with, we shall once more end up with little more than a stained-glass version of our own cultural values and aspirations.

---

30. *Time* (March 30, 1992), 61f.

31. (New Brunswick, N.J.: Rutgers Univ. Press, 1987), 241. (The choice of the term "individualism" is unfortunate. "Individuality" would have been better. Following Robert Bellah and Martin E. Marty, the authors insist upon the importance of Christian community as a public witness ["public church"—Marty]; they are critical precisely of an "individualism" that lacks any sense of worldly responsibility.)

32. Ibid.

33. Ibid., 243 (emphasis added).

3. The Organization of the Subject

The Major Divisions.   Professing the faith, we have said, does not mean giving consent to specific creeds, dogmas, or theological systems. Even though such doctrinal materials are essential to the process of recall that faith's profession entails if the church is to become such a "community of memory" as Roof and McKinney envisage, they are not in any direct sense what faith professes. At base, we affirmed, professing Christian faith means submitting to the discipline of regarding one's life and all of life from the vantage point of that "story" that is the ground of all quest for purity of dogma and the judge of them all.

Implicit in this concise definition of Christian profession of faith is a question that becomes explicit as we approach the task of ordering our thought for this study: How should theology organize its subject matter so as to do justice to the breadth and depth of that "story"? Within the question, moreover, is a warning that every attempt at formal theology needs to recognize. It is a warning that is issued, in a way, to all who dare to comment on stories—any stories—and it is made necessary by two ineluctable facts of human experience: first, that great stories always transcend the commentaries upon them; second, that (unfortunately) commentators on stories seem perennially prone to overlooking just that transcendence, and so tend to attribute more finality to their commentaries than the latter warrant.

This warning is issued a fortiori to the commentators on the story that is told in the continuity of the two biblical testaments—or rather, the story upon which the testaments themselves comment. For the Bible does recognize in a quite remarkable way the limitations of its capacity to do justice to the story that it wants to tell. In this respect as in many others it should be regarded as paradigmatic for all theological commentary. If we affirm the principle *sola scriptura,* it is in part precisely this that we should mean—namely, that we are beholden to Holy Scripture because, while it tells us in a unique and indispensable manner of basic things, it never does so as though it were itself the basic thing. The story that it relates, interprets, exposes, ponders, explains, puzzles over—the *original* story, so to speak—vastly transcends its most authoritative version (an observation that is upheld in a concrete way by the recognition of oral traditions that preceded so much of the written word of Scripture). The Bible knows this about itself—that it is itself only commentary, midrash.

Theological commentary can, however, if it is willing to assume a modest role, illuminate the story. I mean that it is the task of theology to draw attention to certain themes, nuances, patterns, and the like which, when they are pointed up, help one to hear and understand the gospel story better than one might have done without the help of this running commentary. Like the critic who has made a profession of knowing Shakespeare's plays, professional theology is intent upon comprehending as much of the story testified to in Scripture and tradition as will assist the listening community of faith to recognize depths and heights, shadings and turnings that otherwise might have been passed over unnoticed.

The analogy with literary criticism is useful also for our present task, the organization of our subject matter. Like every good story, the story that is the subject of Christian Scripture and tradition contains certain primary motifs. Thus, even though the profession of Christian faith cannot be easily circumscribed as to its basic subject matter—for it incorporates literally "everything"[34]—it is able to encompass most of what it has to contemplate within the parameters of three or four major subject areas.

These areas, as one might anticipate given the narrative and historical character of Christian foundations, reflect the main personages of the Christian drama—as it were, the dramatis personae. Here, of course, as is true also in connection with great secular literature such as the plays of Shakespeare, there is room for difference of opinion. Who precisely *are* the main figures of the Christian drama? Medieval spirituality, as the Everyman plays illustrate graphically, would certainly include Satan, in one guise or another, among these. It could be insisted, too, that "the Church" belongs to this list, for "she" not only appears prominently in the doctrine of the faith but is conspicuous in art and symbol, where "she" is frequently depicted as a queen, sometimes in juxtaposition with the deposed queen conventionally called "Synagogue."[35] One may, as well, want to consider supernatural beings, the "whole host of heaven"—Karl Barth, hardly a medieval thinker, devotes a large section of his famous *Church Dogmatics* to angels.[36] And today many, like Jürgen Moltmann, would like to see nature and the cosmos, the extrahuman creation, raised to high prominence in this narrative.

Certainly the meditative core to which we refer when we ask about the content of the Christian profession of faith is very rich in subject matter. None of the figures (themes, dimensions, motifs) mentioned above can be wholly ignored by anyone wishing to do justice to the foundational story—and many more such could be included. Yet for both theoretical and practical reasons I shall base the subsequent organization of this book on the assumption that we have to do here with three major points of focus.

The latter correspond to the three central figures of the drama of creation, fall, and redemption: God, creaturely being (with emphasis upon the human creature), and the Christ. Faith's profession, I shall argue, revolves around the three basic doctrinal areas conventionally called Theology (God), Christian

---

34. *Thinking the Faith,* 323ff.
35. See my essay "Rethinking Christ," in *Anti-Semitism and the Foundations of Christianity,* ed. Alan T. Davies (New York: Paulist Press, 1979), 167ff.
36. *Church Dogmatics,* vol. 3/3; 426–623.

Anthropology (formerly, "the Doctrine of Man"), and Christology. These, accordingly, are the divisions that will determine the organization of this volume.

I admit at once that there is in this selection a certain degree of arbitrariness. I myself would not want any of these three areas of concentration to be conceived of narrowly, that is, in such a way as effectively to exclude most of the dimensions that are inherent in them. What I mean is most easily illustrated by the second area, anthropology.

Creaturehood could be thought of as referring exclusively to the human creature only if one were to take as one's basis for such reflection some other sources than the story to which Christian theology is bound. For the human creature in that story is a creature among creatures, inconceivable apart from its reciprocity vis-à-vis all the others. Thus nature does belong to this area of doctrinal concentration, and the second part of this present study, in which we shall treat the Christian doctrine of humanity, will have to devote a good deal of space to the question of the relation between human and extrahuman being. In fact I shall depart from convention here and name this second major division of the work, "Creaturely Being." It would be literally impossible to understand faith's profession on the subject of human nature and destiny without serious reflection on the larger whole of which the human species is part; moreover, at a time when precisely the biblical view of the relation between human and extrahuman is accused of promoting the false elevation of humanity above the rest of nature and thus of begetting a society prone to destroy the natural processes without which life cannot continue, it would be irresponsible to speak only of *anthropos*.

At the same time, we must recognize that the human creature is central to the action and dialogue of this drama; and not only faithfulness to our classical sources but also responsibility to our planetary future depend upon achieving a better understanding of this central actor in creation, especially of the role that this creature is called to play—and *being healed may play*—in relation to all the others.

A final, and finally insoluble, limitation must be acknowledged. Like every great story, the story with which Christian theology has to concern itself is characterized by one overarching feature: integrity. However nuanced and unpredictable the interaction of the "characters" at its center, this is a single drama, whose essential unity and integrity has grasped every mind that has contemplated it profoundly. Thus the entire practice of separating the parts, of ordering them according to a certain schema, of giving them a particular nomenclature (Theology, Creaturely Being, Christology) is at some basic level artificial and potentially misleading. Where does Theology leave off and anthropology begin? How does anyone discuss Christology apart from a simultaneous consideration of divinity and creatureliness?

31

In saying this, we are only reiterating the demand for modesty—modesty, not as a virtue but as a necessity. Theology is, and can only be, commentary. It necessarily divides the indivisible. It shares this dissecting (one could almost say vivisecting) activity with all human science. Recognizing this, we are thrown back on the reality that our discipline is penultimate at best. To substitute for what is ultimate any theological commentary on the ultimate is comparable to substituting for the rose a botanist's description of the rose. Yet, it may be given to the botanist to know that her work could help others to be in the presence of the rose more knowingly, that is, with greater awe. And that is all that Christian theology, too, could ask with respect to its subject matter.

The Ordering of Thought within the Three Divisions. Conscious of the breadth of our subject, we must determine in advance how best to do justice to each of these three vast and complex areas of Christian doctrine within the confines of a single volume. We are to bear in mind, not only the extensive history of each area but also the specific aim of our own presentation of this material as it was described in the first volume. Our basic purpose is to offer a statement of the Christian faith that is *contextually* sensitive, that is, one which is crafted within and for the North American situation and therefore maintains throughout a consciousness of the ways in which that situation impacts what we have received as the core of the Christian profession of faith.

There is, I suspect, no single formula by means of which such an undertaking can be achieved. The success of any method that might be followed would depend upon the actual content of the presentation. A schema that suggests itself to me on account of its relative simplicity and adaptability, however, is to order the discussion in each of the three main divisions according to three dimensions of the whole discipline of systematic theological thought: namely, historical theology, critical theology, and constructive theology.[37] In following this schema I hope to sustain my own and the reader's attention to three requirements of a study adopting the approach for which I have opted here: (1) to recall the tradition of Christian thought in the light of its reception—including its neglect—within our ecclesiastical context (historical theology); (2) to point up flaws and problematic elements within the received tradition, as well as alternatives overlooked by evolving Christendom (critical theology); and (3) to propose ways in which the faith might be professed responsibly under the present sociohistorical conditions in our North American context (constructive

---

37. Here I am in fundamental agreement with Rosemary Radford Ruether, who explains that she has "made use of the basic paradigm of Christian systematics" because she feels that it "continues to be a powerful and formative structure . . . [providing] an interpretive framework for human situations of conflict and struggle for justice" (*Sexism and God-Talk* [Boston: Beacon Press, 1983], 38).

theology). It will be expedient at this juncture to comment briefly on each of these dimensions of the work of "professional" theology.

a. Historical Theology.   Historical theology has as its object the articulation of the belief of the Christian community as it has developed over the centuries. It is not, however, synonymous with the history of doctrine. The history of doctrine may be pursued without any sense of responsibility toward an existing Christian community. Historical theology, on the other hand, as an aspect of systematic theological reflection, has in view definite service to a living *koinonia.* That is, it exists to keep before a body of believers the nature of the doctrinal past that they have inherited, to interpret it to that body in ways accessible to its understanding, and to raise questions concerning their appropriation and misappropriation of that past.

Thus conceived, historical theology is a necessary dimension of systematic theology. From the previous discussion in this as well as the first volume, it will be clear that the author of this work—a work whose object is to address the present and the impending future—would reject any conception of the discipline of theology that eliminates or minimizes dialogue with the church's past. Christian theology is never (legitimately) simply a religious stream-of-consciousness on the part of present-day Christians. We who profess the faith *here* and *now* are persons who have been brought into a long tradition, one that existed for centuries before we arrived on the scene. A conversation has been in progress and we, who have entered the room late in time, are obliged to listen carefully if our own contribution is to be pertinent. We may want to be very critical of some things, but we have first to find our proper place in the established dialogue: "One cannot wield the lever of criticism without a place to stand."[38]

Theology is not made up out of one's own head, or from the collective entelechy of the contemporary church or of especially vociferous elements within it. It is a matter of receiving, not only of giving. It is what happens when what has been received is appropriated, made our own. For that to happen, the received tradition must of course pass through the sieve of our own individual and contemporary-collective experience; we cannot give it, profess it as ours, unless such a process occurs. And it never occurs easily.

Part of the struggle entailed in this process is simply *finding out* about the Christian theological past. That is why, earlier in this discussion, we insisted that *knowing* belongs to the act of professing the faith.[39]

---

38. Ibid., 18.

39. To speak of the Christian theological past is to speak in particular of a European past. I have been criticized by Susan Thistlethwaite for paying too much attention to European theologians and theological movements (see *Theology Today* 46 [Oct. 1989]: 312–13). She appears to

In addition to this inherent reason for the inclusion of historical theology in this study, three pragmatic reasons may be mentioned. First, it can never be assumed that the historical tradition being rethought by constructive theology *is* known by those who would and should participate in the theological work of the disciple community. We have seen that there is in fact reason to believe that sheer ignorance of the Christian tradition is one of the most conspicuous aspects of our ecclesiastical and social context in North America today. Second, it is always important to ascertain what, out of the great variety of the doctrinal past of our faith, has been picked up and accentuated by the churches, and what on the contrary has been intentionally or unintentionally ignored. We have indeed claimed[40] that the point of view that will inform this entire study—the *theologia crucis*—has been consistently neglected by evolving

---

think that a work purporting to articulate Christian theology "in a North American Context" should sit lightly to European theological traditions and consciously evolve out of an internal North American dialogue. She complains that I do not quote enough North Americans (though perhaps she does not recognize that many of those whom I have quoted in the first volume are North Americans, namely Canadians).

In any case, I am not able to endorse the point of view implied in this criticism. It seems to me to verge on a type of American isolationism and self-sufficiency that is, in the end, detrimental to genuine contextuality. It overlooks the plain historical fact that what we call the Christian tradition is largely a European tradition. For good or ill, we are all inheritors of this tradition. It is both over against and alongside this past that we must conduct our specifically North American reconstruction of the faith. Moreover, we may count on the support of many European Christians as we do so. Sensitive, globally conscious European theologians themselves understand the need to distinguish Christian theology from its past European domination (see, e.g., Jürgen Moltmann, *The Way of Jesus Christ: Christology in Messianic Dimensions,* trans. Margaret Kohl [Minneapolis: Fortress Press, 1993], 64), and therefore we need not fear that in turning to them we are necessarily perpetuating our old dependency syndrome.

My entire project is premised on the assumption that the future of Christianity in the North American context hinges upon the theological "coming of age" of Christian scholarship on this continent. I have made no secret of the fact that I think such a prospect requires the termination of North American dependency in relation to European theological scholarship and trends. That will not be achieved, however, by an indigenous scholarship that circles about itself and its own internal debates and discussions. Not only could such a scholarship easily slip into that sort of parochialism which, in Volume I, I identified as one of the salient dangers of contextuality in theological thought; it could never come to grips with the subtle nature of our dependency. To gain a mature and healthy independence from the parental cultures, churches, and theological guilds, we must continue to acquaint ourselves with them and with the weight of the traditions of which they are representatives and guardians. Only an adolescent bid for autonomy wants to break off the dialogue with the parental home. Besides, there is not a doctrine in the annals of our historic faith that can be pursued without a great deal of discourse with European thought, past and present.

In short, in this matter, I am entirely in agreement with Leonardo Boff when he writes: "A Christology thought out and vitally tested in Latin America must have characteristics of its own. The attentive reader will perceive them throughout this book. The predominantly foreign literature that we cite ought not to delude anyone. It is with preoccupations that are ours alone, taken from our Latin American context, that we will reread not only the old texts of the New Testament but also the most recent commentaries written in Europe." (*Jesus Christ Liberator: A Critical Christology for Our Time* [Maryknoll, N.Y.: Orbis Books, 1984], 43.)

40. *Thinking the Faith,* 22.

Christendom. It is the task of theology to explore such neglected or submerged motifs within the tradition, and, as was stated earlier, today the most engaging theological movements, especially feminist theology, involve a drastic rereading of Christian theological history for this very purpose.[41] Third, an author can never take for granted that readers will be able to divine where he or she stands with respect to the interpretation of the tradition. For instance, the early church's important decisions about the "two natures" of the Christ can be viewed in many ways. It will facilitate understanding if the author not only alludes to major alternatives present in the actual historical discussion of this subject but also provides the reader with evidence of his or her own position— for example, whether he or she is more attracted to the school of Alexandria or to that of Antioch. Faithfulness to the continuity of the theological dialogue of the disciple community requires such historiographic work on the part of systematic theologians.

For these auxiliary reasons, as well as to honor the fundamental link between the past and present witness of the church, each of the three divisions of our study will begin with a brief exercise in historical theology (chapters 1, 4, and 7).

b. Critical Theology.   Critical theology is that aspect of the total theological discipline which cultivates a special awareness of the human situation and of the manner in which, in a given context, religious ideas and practices function. Unlike historical theology, it is not a separable branch of Christian theology, though it is sometimes treated as such. It belongs to the discipline inherently and is more a dimension of the theological task as a whole than a stage or step in the process of theological reflection. It would not be incorrect to say that Christian theology is a critical reflection upon existence.

While this stance affects the whole, however, it can become a particular emphasis in certain phases of theological work—and especially where the issue turns upon the analysis of the apologetic situation. This is how I am using the term at present. The second part of each of the three doctrinal areas dealt with will be a concentration of critical thought, in that it will ask specifically about the historical-sociological context in which the doctrine is to be interpreted. An illustration will help to establish my meaning:

Let us say that the discussion concerns the subject of belief in God. It would be possible for the Christian community to take any number of approaches to this subject, basing itself on this or that facet of biblical or traditional theology. It could emphasize the rationality of belief in the style of high scholastic Christianity, or of Deism; it could, in contrast, stress a fideist position, depicting belief as response to specific revelation; or it could devise

---

41. See in this connection Pamela Dickey-Young, *Feminist Theology/Christian Theology* (Minneapolis: Fortress Press, 1989), especially chap. 4, "The Place of Christian Tradition."

some combination of the two poles, apologetic and kerygmatic, after the manner of most mediating theologies. What should determine the approach?

Surely the answer must be: the situation in which this discussion is occurring. All of the various approaches to belief in God have in fact come into existence in response to different historical circumstances. The perpetuation of any tradition (let us say the apologetic tradition associated with the Thomistic synthesis) out of loyalty to the tradition as such is at best a naive dependency. St. Thomas himself devised his arguments for God's existence within the context of what he (with justification) perceived as a new social environment—a "paradigm shift"—in which the Platonic-Augustinian presuppositions of the old approach to belief had been silently but decisively supplanted. So the church must always engage in the critical theological task, analyzing the nature of the human *krisis* as it manifests itself here and now, in order to engage in its ongoing task of constructing or reconstructing its articulation of gospel.

It would be accurate to say that the critical theological task refers in a special sense, then, to *contextual* analysis. But at the same time, the contextual dimension is involved at every step of the way. It was because of the contextual concern that we could not be satisfied with historical theology as an end in itself but had to go on to ask how the tradition has been received by the church within which the theological community is at work. So also in the constructive stage we are concerned, not with stating a theology that would be pertinent under all circumstances, but with a contextually responsible articulation of Christian belief. Yet it is true that the context is the decisive concern of critical theology, and therefore the second part of each division will concentrate upon that within the social and ecclesiastical context which has particular relevance for that doctrinal area. Chapters 2, 5, and 8 will thus constitute the sort of "clearing" process necessary to the "building" that is the object of the third stage, constructive theology.

c. Constructive Theology. Constructive theology, as has just been intimated, is the ongoing attempt of the disciple community to shape its theological understanding—and hence the church's kerygma—to meet and engage the realities of its situation. Two factors are in tension here: the Christian message, as that to which the biblical and historical traditions point, and the worldly context for which the gospel has now to be reformulated. The object of constructive theology is to attempt this reformulation. Constructive theology, in other words, is theology formulated in such a way that it can be professed *today*, in this quite specific place and time. It is the church ordering its thought so as to address the world, namely the world within itself and the world beyond itself—to rediscover the meaning of gospel.

We are not yet thinking of *con*fession but only of the *pro*fession of the faith. Already in the professional mode, it is the disciple community's quest for gospel—its evangelical impulse—that exercises greatest influence upon the character and content of its profession of the faith. The distinction between the confessional and the professional modes is that in the former it is the disciple community's hope to engage that within its world which is (as we put it earlier) threatening the life of creation. In *pro*fessing the faith, the worldly context of the church is already that which must be engaged, but *what* the witnessing community hopes to sort out at this stage is the intellectual and spiritual foundation of its faith and life. With faith's profession, the church's question is: How shall we articulate the rudiments of our belief in such a way that the world within us and around us will be existentially grasped by this account of reality? What do we ourselves believe? How may we formulate here and now this "meditative core" of faith that is and must become the basis and presupposition of our confession of Jesus as the Christ?

Addressing the world does not mean speaking to the dominant classes and value-setters of a society in a way that they would approve (which is too often what people mean when, in this connection, they speak about the "relevance" of the gospel or of Christian doctrine). If we may trust the biblical precedent, the genuineness of faith's articulation and address is probably more aptly attested by the world's disapproval—including the disapproval of "the world" that is present in the community of discipleship itself. Neither approval nor disapproval, however, should be made the aim of faith's profession. Sometimes Jesus' teaching was rejected, but sometimes it was accepted. There will always be an element of *skandalon* in the gospel, but there will also, usually, be an element of curiosity and attention where the quality of genuine address is sustained. Indeed, the "scandal" presupposes interest, and of an existential nature. People are not scandalized by what fails to arouse any animus within them.

The point to be emphasized here is that the object of constructive theology is neither to accommodate nor to repulse but to achieve a real meeting between the foundational claims of the faith and the world with its working assumptions, ideologies, worldviews, and values. It would not be profession (that is, witness *for* or *before* [*pro*] anything or anyone) unless it bore about it this aura of encounter and dialogue. Already in its professional stance the church should know itself to be meeting its world and, conversely, its world should be able to recognize in the church's profession of faith that it is being taken very seriously.

This has to be said, because too often "professional" theology has been unconscious, or only superficially conscious, of its world. Thus it may think that the world is rejecting it, when in reality the world is only bored. Or it may imagine, vainly enough, that it is terribly *au courant* because the world seems to accept its statement of faith, when in fact the world is simply exercising its famous capacity for tolerance—that is, nonchalance in relation to that which doesn't affect it one way or another. Genuine profession of the faith is a very *worldly* matter. Constructive theology succeeds or fails in direct proportion to its awareness of the actual context for and within which the faith is professed.

Thus any constructive theology relies heavily on the two previous exercises, whether it engages in them explicitly or implicitly, formally or informally. Without historical theology there is a tendency for the church's faith not only to lose touch with its roots but to become an indistinct and vaguely spiritualistic version of current and popular trends.[42] This is a present danger in North America, where, like every other activity that is conscious of and in some sense dependent upon public response, Christian theology too is tempted to confuse trendiness with truth. But without critical theology, which questions what is "handed over," there is an equally dangerous tendency for the dominant strands of the received tradition to be put forward as if they were the professional foundations of faith, unchanged and unchanging. In relation to constructive theology, historical theology is an ongoing recollection of what the church has professed, and critical theology is a continuous reminder of the fact that what has been professed cannot simply be repeated. Constructive theology fashions the Christian profession of faith as it deconstructs the church's past profession and reconstructs it in the light of the world's present and future reality.

The construction of theology is therefore an unending task. What is today constructed may tomorrow constitute the entrenched, hardened, and even debilitating convention that critical theology must once more break down. The point is not that yesterday's theology is always wrong, but that it may well be wrong *for today*. In saying so, it is necessary to recognize that we are using the language of today and yesterday metaphorically, not literally. There are yesterdays that are more appropriately honored today, and yesterdays that should not be prolonged any more than is absolutely necessary. Certainly we should not give way to the kind of situationalism that is sometimes mistaken for contextuality and adopt a dull chronology capable of thinking in decades at most, and devoid of any real kairotic intuition. Obviously it would be a false sort of faith—a bizarre iconoclasm—that literally destroyed each day's or each decade's theological work because tomorrow God would (quite predictably) be "making all things new." Yet at the symbolic level at least, the churches must be prepared to regard their work as "sufficient for the day" and not fall into the habit of thinking it a monument to eternal truth. Theology will most honor truth if it is willing to live in tents and move along, craving neither towers nor temples made with hands.

---

42. "Perhaps now even liberation theology language, not just religious language in general, is being used to keep the real conflicts of society concealed" (Herzog, *God-Walk*, 204).

Chapters 3, 6, and 9, as the constructive statements regarding Theology, Creaturely Being, and Jesus Christ (respectively), will at least aim to honor Truth in that fashion.

Alternative Approaches to the Reading of This Volume.   While the book is designed to be read chapter by chapter, it may also be read by combining the chapters in which the reader is particularly interested. For example, readers who have already acquired a significant background of historical and critical theology may wish to concentrate on the three chapters of constructive theology (3, 6, and 9), reading them consecutively. Similarly, the first (historical) chapters of each part (1, 4, and 7) may be read one after another, as may the second (critical) chapters (2, 5, and 8) of each part.

PART I

THEOLOGY: THE CHRISTIAN DOCTRINE OF GOD

CHAPTER ▪ ONE
"Credo in Deum"

Introduction

While many approaches are open to us as we attempt to review the most significant aspects of the Christian tradition concerning the Deity, for the sake of convenience we shall divide the material into three considerations: the knowledge of God, the being of God, and the works of God. This should enable us to touch upon the most important elements in the tradition, and at the same time provide some of the necessary background for the interpretive thesis that will be developed in the course of these three chapters on the doctrine of God.

1. The Knowledge of God

Since the question of the knowledge of God is the basic subject matter of theological epistemology and was treated as such in the first volume,[1] I do not intend to dwell upon it here extensively. Nevertheless it must come into the discussion of God because it is part of Theology, in the restrictive sense of the term.[2] The whole question of knowing in Christian faith and theology is of course focused in a particular sense on the knowledge of God, but it is more inclusive than that. When we ask about the knowledge of God under the aegis of the doctrine of God as such, we are asking about God and not only about human knowing. The manner in which anything is known already assumes

---

1. *Thinking the Faith,* 369ff.
2. N.B.: I shall capitalize the term Theology and its derivatives when it refers to the doctrine of God; the lowercase spelling will be reserved for the discipline of theology.

something about the thing itself. The question we are addressing here as distinct from the epistemological considerations of Volume I is what sort of "picture of God" is presupposed by the Christian tradition when it speaks of our way of knowing God.

The answer is not a simple one, because different traditions of theological epistemology assume differing conceptions of the One who is known. We cannot do justice here to all the nuances of this broad tradition; three themes, however, dominate the Christian Theological tradition in this respect: God is presented (1) as Revealer, (2) as counterpart of creaturely (specifically of human) being, and (3) as the reasonable consequence of human reflection upon the world. These three themes are not necessarily mutually exclusive, though certain thinkers and schools are to be distinguished by their adherence to one theme more emphatically than to the others.

1.1. God as Revealer.

The first and undoubtedly the most decisive thing that the tradition has said about the God Christians profess to know is that the Judeo-Christian God is a *revealing* God. If God is known by us, according to this claim, it is because God is Self-communicating. Only where the biblical witness has been set aside or given a purely poetic function, as in eighteenth-century English Deism or certain expressions of nineteenth- and early twentieth-century Modernism, have Christians found it possible to dispense with this central affirmation. Even those traditions that stress the other two alternatives to be treated below normally combine them in some manner with this fundamental theme.

Behind this conception of God as Self-revealing deity we may detect both a negative and a positive presupposition. The negative presupposition is that we human beings do not, will not, or cannot know God immediately or naturally, apart from God's Self-manifestation. Older Theologies, which could still assume the temporal reality of a pre-fallen state, presented the human pair in the Garden of Eden as having immediate fellowship with their Creator. Revelation as God's mode of Self-communication in that case might be understood as belonging to the order of fallen creation—God's recourse to human consciousness, so to speak, in the postlapsarian situation. The permanent insight contained in this premodern account of the history of salvation is that faith recognizes, in the experience of revelation, the dullness, imperfection, and even absurdity of "unaided" human apprehension of the divine. The revealing God, when experienced as such, throws all previous pretensions to knowledge of the divine into question. "Surely the Lord is in this place, *and I knew it not*" (Gen. 28:16, KJV).

Again discounting extreme positions, it must be said that this negative assumption informs most of the diverse expressions of our wider tradition. To be sure, the assumption is given varying emphases, all the way from the absolute denial of any kind of natural awareness of God (or Natural Theology), as in Tertullian or Karl Barth, to the milder recognition of the limitations of humanity's capacity for personal knowledge of God in Thomas Aquinas, Schleiermacher, Reinhold Niebuhr, and many others. No one, however, within the mainstream of Christian thought broadly conceived would altogether deny this negative assumption. If God is Self-revealing it is at least in part because God cannot be known by us otherwise—not, at any rate, in a manner sufficient to our own inherent need for the knowledge of God.

There is, as well, a positive assumption in the picture of God as Revealer. It is that God both *must* and *can* reveal God's person. The "must" of the divine Self-manifestation does not, of course, refer to a law binding upon the Deity; it expresses, rather, something integral to God's person as professed by Christian faith. It affirms that God wills to communicate with us ("I will be your God"), and it also affirms that God can only communicate with us *as God* if God assumes and retains the initiative in this communication. Like every other subject, the mystery and otherness of the divine Subject are posited on God's personal transcendence of those by whom God is known. The "thou-ness" of the "Eternal Thou" (Buber) could not be sustained apart from this insistence upon Self-revelation. God could not be Thou for us if we suspected that we were ourselves responsible for God's being known by us. Revelation is a positively conceived activity of God, then, and not merely an emergency measure, as it were, taken by the Deity in view of our postlapsarian dullness of soul. Even if a historical pre-fallen state could be imagined, the pair in the Garden could only encounter God as a revealing Presence, however open (by comparison with fallen humanity) they might themselves be vis-à-vis that Presence.

But God not only must, God also *can* (according to this profession of faith) reveal God's Self. Unlike the far-off, expiring deity of Franz Kafka's unforgettable parable, "The Imperial Message,"[3] who, even though he desires to communicate with his subjects, cannot traverse the infinite distance between himself and them, the God of Christian profession can and does bridge the gap. The distance is great, as Kafka's parabolic story insists; it may even be said to be infinite.[4] In this Kafka has correctly appropriated his Judaic heritage. But the distance is not untraversable, for either Judaic or Christian faith.

Here, of course, our tradition wavers between those who locate the possibility of revelation more or less exclusively in God, those who find humanity open to receiving the divine Self-impartation, and those who combine the two

---

3. "Eine Keiserliche Botschaft," in Franz Kafka, *Gesammelte Werke,* ed. Max Brod (Berlin: S. Fischer Verlag, 1967), 169–70.

4. One remembers the early Barth's answer to some of his critics: "If I have a system, it is limited to a recognition of what Kierkegaard called the 'infinite qualitative distinction' between time and eternity, and to my regarding this as possessing negative as well as positive significance: 'God is in heaven, and thou art on earth.'" Karl Barth, *The Epistle to the Romans,* trans. Edwyn C. Hoskyns (London: Oxford Univ. Press, 1950), 10 (from "The Preface to the Second Edition," written in 1921).

emphases. As might be anticipated, theologians who accentuate the negative presupposition of revelation (discussed above) invariably stress that revelation is strictly God's possibility. Karl Barth is the primary exemplar of this insistence in twentieth-century theology. Others, without denying the divine initiative in revelation, hold out for the positive anthropological presupposition in the whole concept of a revealing God: namely, that if God *can* reveal Godself to us it is because there is within us, fallen though we be, a continuing capacity for divine revelation (*capax Dei*). For some theologians, this capacity is very prominent; for others, like Emil Brunner, who named it our "addressibility" (*Offenbarungsmächtigkeit*),[5] human beings contribute nothing substantive to the revelatory experience, but at least they constitute in themselves as such an unquenchable potentiality for the hearing of the divine Word.

There is, then, a variety of ways in which the tradition articulates the profession of belief in God as a revealing God. The Christian past is no more monolithic here than at most other points of doctrine, and perhaps it is even more diversified; for the whole process of *knowing* is always a complex one in human discourse. Yet there is a certain conformity (not uniformity) of thought behind the many variations and shadings that color the picture of God at this juncture. All but the most doubtful expressions of belief affirm that the God in whom Christians profess to believe is a revealing God; that is, that the-will-to-reveal is integral to this God.

This affirmative generalization about the Christian tradition, when it is pondered with some care, incites a question that must become part of the critical theological reflection brought to bear upon our attempt to reconstruct Theology. The affirmation that God is by definition a revealing God suggests to the mind a negative or opposing proposition: If God is Self-revealing, why do so few apprehend God? And why is it that even those who do profess the experience of divine revelation must at the same time honestly acknowledge their misgivings, the inconstancy of their faith, the sense of God's absence?

This is, of course, the interrogation of the doubting spirit, and because there have always been doubting spirits within the disciple community, the Theological tradition has gone a little way toward response to this interrogation—but only, I think, a little way. Some few voices out of the Christian past have addressed themselves to the reality of doubt within the community of belief. But prior to the modern and contemporary period, the doubt that certainly always existed existentially in the face of the affirmation under discussion was rarely voiced openly.[6] Now, on the contrary, this doubt is prominent—and perhaps

---

5. Literally the term means "capacity for revelation," and as such it formed the central point of contention between Barth and Brunner in their historic exchange on the subject of Natural Theology. See *Natural Theology,* trans. Peter Fraenkel (London: Geoffrey Bles: Centenary Press, 1946).

6. For many North American students of theology in the decades following 1934, one of the most liberating aspects of the theology of Paul Tillich was his recognition of the positive role of

more prominent within the community that professes faith in this revealing God than it is in the secular world by which this community is surrounded, which hardly gets so far as "existential doubt." Yet *as we have received it,* the tradition seems ill equipped to take into itself the critical question that this profound doubt represents.

In the North American context particularly, this is a highly problematic aspect of the tradition. The "true belief" alluded to in the Introduction is a direct consequence of the failure of the most persistent expressions of Christianity in our context to absorb the ongoing existential doubt of those who profess belief. Not only in the ecclesiastical groupings that treasure "true belief" explicitly but also among more "liberal" expressions of the church in our setting, it is exceptionally hard for people to be straightforward about the disbelief that accompanies their belief. We appear to be laboring under a conception of divine revelation that leaves little room for the acknowledgment of God's hiddenness.

Our mandate therefore for the entire discussion of God, but especially for our attempt at reconstructing Theology in the third chapter, would seem to be to discover whether it is possible to profess belief in a revealing God without suppressing the reality of the divine concealment as it is felt in our present context. To state the question explicitly: Can Christians bear witness to the revealing God in such a way as to sustain a meaningful dialogue with the contemporary experience of God's hiddenness, absence, eclipse, or "death"? We shall carry this question over into the critical and constructive statements made in the two chapters following.[7]

---

doubt in the life of faith. He insisted that the doctrine of justification applies not only to the anxiety of guilt but also to the anxiety of doubt, and that faith itself must be understood as involving an ongoing dialogue with "unfaith." For North Americans this was—and for many still is—an unusual exposition of the nature of the human relationship with God; and among other things it demonstrates the relative failure of the theology of the cross to penetrate Anglo-Saxon Christianity generally. For Tillich's juxtaposition of faith and doubt is certainly a contemporary application of the theology of the cross to the nature of the divine/human relationship. See Paul Tillich, *Dynamics of Faith* (New York: Harper & Brothers Publishers, 1957), 16ff.; see also James Luther Adams, "Tillich's Concept of the Protestant Era," in Paul Tillich, *The Protestant Era* (Chicago: Univ. of Chicago Press, 1948), 292f.

7. In his insightful study, *Luther's Theology of the Cross* (Oxford: Basil Blackwell, 1985), Alister McGrath draws attention to the fact that Luther's theology of the cross, with its "proclamation of the hidden presence of God in the dereliction of Calvary," came into its own once more after the devastations of World War II. It "struck a deep chord of sympathy in those who felt themselves abandoned by God, and unable to discern his presence anywhere." McGrath (pp. 179–80) cites the diary of Karl Goerdeler, who was executed as a conspirator against Hitler: "'In sleepless nights I have often asked myself whether a God exists who shares in the personal fate of men. It is becoming hard to believe this. For this God must for years have allowed rivers of blood and suffering, and mountains of horror and despair for mankind to take place. . . . Like the Psalmist, I am angry with God, because I cannot understand him. . . . And yet through Christ I am still looking for the merciful God. I have not yet found him. O Christ, where is truth? Where is there any consolation?'"

1.2. God as Counterpart. While the Christian tradition concerning the knowledge of God necessarily emphasizes revelation as God's mode of being known by human beings, revelation (as we have noted in the first volume)[8] has hardly ever stood alone. It is even doubtful that it could, for unless the revelation is received it is no revelation; and its reception has seemed to most expositors of the faith to assume a capacity for the knowledge of God inherent, to one degree or another, in human beings. It may be the achievement of the Barthian school that it has come closer than any other exposition of Christian faith to offering an interpretation of revelation that rejects this assumption.[9]

Broadly speaking, two types of explanation have been offered concerning the human capacity for the knowledge of God, with variations on the two themes. Classically, their chief exponents have been Augustine and Thomas Aquinas. The first, which we shall consider under the present subheading, is given what may be its most beautiful as well as most influential expression in Augustine's *Confessions,* though it is even more consistently articulated in the less well-known work, *Soliloquies.* [10]

This approach posits that it belongs to human nature as such to seek its divine origination. That is, of course, stating the matter from the anthropological side. It may also be stated from the Theological side, and then it would mean something like this: God, while unique as the Creator of all that is, has nevertheless implanted some reminiscence of their divine source in human creatures. God is present to us, then, not only as the Revealer who comes upon the scene of our life unknown, unanticipated, and "a Stranger" (Tillich), but as one who is never wholly absent from us.[11] There is, thus, an ontic connectedness between God and human being, analogous to the physical connection between a human parent and his or her offspring. It cannot be broken. The son may leave

---

8. *Thinking the Faith,* 369ff.

9. It is true that in the Reformation teachings of both Luther and Calvin it is God who makes possible in us the reception of divine revelation. That is, God the Spirit prepares us internally for the reception of God the Son or Word. Only by grace can grace be received. This led Luther to make almost violent judgments about the presumptions of human rationality, and Calvin to take up the path that led him, reluctantly, to the concept of double predestination. But neither Luther nor Calvin is quite so clear about the total incapacity for God on the part of human beings as was the early Barth—despite the fact that in his earlier works Barth consistently claimed these two reformers as his mentors in what Bonhoeffer later called Barth's "positivism of revelation." See in this connection Karl Barth, *The Holy Ghost and the Christian Life,* trans. R. Birch Hoyle (London: Frederick Muller Ltd., 1938).

10. Indeed, a text for this approach to the knowledge of God might well be the famous sentence found in the first paragraph of the first book of the *Confessions:* "Tu fecisti nos ad te, Domine, et inquietum est cor nostrum donec requiescat in te." ("You have created us for yourself, Lord, and our heart is restless til it reposes in you.") Well-known exemplars of the God-as-counterpart tradition include Anselm of Canterbury, Bonaventura, Schleiermacher, Tillich, and many others.

11. See Paul Tillich, "The Two Types of Philosophy of Religion," in *Theology of Culture* (New York: Oxford Univ. Press, 1959), 10ff.

his father's house, but he may not shed the indelible ties that forever bind him to his father (Luke 15:11-32).

Again from the anthropological side, the classical dogma in which this sense of ontic relatedness has again and again been articulated is the *imago Dei* concept. As we shall see in the chapters on Creaturely Being, it is necessary to question precisely the substantialistic versions of this dogma today, and from the side of biblical ontology. Yet there can be no doubt whatever that the dominant expressions of the *imago Dei* within the total Christian tradition have been those that assumed precisely an ineradicable continuity between the divine and the human at the level of being as such. The obverse, Theological side of this teaching is that God is not only external to us ("out there, up there," as Bishop Robinson put it[12]) but is also imparted to us *within* ("in there"). God transcends us as our Source, but God is also immanent to us, inseparable from our own being.

Christians who have pursued this line of thought about the Deity have sometimes found themselves accused of pantheism. (The charge was frequently made against such theologians as Meister Eckhart, Nicholas of Cusa, Catherine of Sienna, and, in the present epoch, Paul Tillich, Matthew Fox, Sallie McFague, and most of the process school.) It is not usually a true pantheism that such theologians represent, however, for they do not deny the divine transcendence (for example, for Tillich God is always the "*Ground* of Being"), nor do they overlook the discontinuity between God and the human being that is present by reason both of creaturely finitude and creaturely disobedience. Yet the position we are describing, which is sometimes called panentheism,[13] does share with classical pantheism a feeling for the immanence of the divine within the sphere of the creaturely. A strictly secular view of the world is incompatible with this position. It is simply not possible to get away from Augustine's God!

Here again we must take note of a negating sentiment in our present context that is almost inevitably inspired by this affirmation of the inescapable God. When God is so conceived, the idea of our being "alone" is virtually inadmissible. Camus's solitary, abandoned Stranger, alone in an indifferent universe, has

---

12. J. A. T. Robinson, *Honest to God* (London: S.C.M. Press, 1963), chap. 1, 11ff.

13. Literally, "God-in-everything," as distinct from "God-as-everything" (suggested by pantheism). See Jürgen Moltmann, *God in Creation: An Ecological Doctrine of Creation* (The Gifford Lectures of 1984–1985), trans. Margaret Kohl (Minneapolis: Fortress Press, 1993), 103. Sallie McFague writes: "Paul Tillich was right to say that God is 'Being-Itself,' for even though, once again, the only kind of 'being' we know is creaturely existence and hence 'Being-Itself' is a metaphor, still, the phrase points to God as the source and depth of our being. We have no words for this sense of radical and absolute dependence on Another for life itself. We know it is not of our making or doing, that all that is derives from 'not itself,' that we are something but come from nothing." (*Metaphorical Theology: Models of God in Religious Language* [Philadelphia: Fortress Press, 1982], 192.)

little in common with the protagonist of the *Confessions*.[14] The same could be said of Marie Claire Blais's Emmanuel, a figure who, despite his name, bespeaks the contemporary sense of the divine absence.[15] In short, insofar as we are faithful to the attitudinal realities of our own epoch, we are compelled to recognize that a sense of aloneness and radical alienation has come over the soul of twentieth-century Western humanity with great power. Acknowledging this, we must raise the critical question: How can a Theological tradition that assumes imperishable ties of being between Creator and (human) creature engage a society that experiences great difficulty in locating a transcendent respondent to its (perhaps at times nostalgic) longing for the divine counterpart?

1.3. God as Reasonable Consequence of Thought. With the questioning of Augustinian epistemological assumptions in the High Middle Ages, the knowledge of God became, under the tutelage of Albertus Magnus and Thomas Aquinas, a matter of inductive reasoning—so far, that is, as its philosophic, nonrevelational aspect was concerned. This "logical" approach to deity,[16] combining the evidence of the senses with cause-and-effect argumentation, did not intend to do so but in fact it substituted a new type of rationality for the old, intuitive type. On the one hand, it could seem more modest than Augustinian reason in that it only aimed at knowledge *about* God, not knowledge *of* God; on the other hand, it could appear to the age more intriguing, because it began with observable data and proceeded step by step to its supramundane conclusions. To be sure, a later period of history would judge that the step from secondary to primary causation was not a step but a leap!

Despite the debunking both of the theological and philosophical critics of Natural Theology, however, the power of this tradition has been felt even into our own era. For the most part it is no longer considered a positive force supportive of theism; rather, it is present as an entrenched tradition that, because of its impressive associations with an outstanding period of the Christian past, can be treated by some of our contemporaries as if it represented *the* Christian approach to the knowledge of God. University sophomores are still subjected to "brilliant" refutations of St. Thomas's five arguments for God's existence by witty professors, and the sophomores are still temporarily impressed by these cheaply won victories. Why? Because the rationality honored by our own age is still, largely, the empirical thought of the natural sciences and technologies, whose rudiments St. Thomas well understood. So long as "God" is not *reasonable* according to the rubrics of this rationality, "he" can be effectively banished.

---

14. Albert Camus, *L'Etranger* (Paris: Editions Gallimard, 1957).

15. *A Season in the Life of Emmanuel,* trans. Derek Coltman (New York: Universal Library, Grosset & Dunlap, 1966).

16. See Jürgen Moltmann, *God in Creation,* 76.

It is no doubt futile to demand that those who visit this past should try, like good historians, to judge it first by its own standards and assumptions. What Christians have rather to ask themselves is whether they have not cheapened their own better traditions by allowing them to seem applicable and current beyond the point of their effective demise. If God is presented as a wholly reasonable conclusion to our rational observations of the universe, then what happens when the unreasonable and irrational and random side of the universe overwhelms us? A reasonable world may suggest a reasonable—perhaps even a benevolent—Cause, Mover, Orderer, Authority. But it is impossible to move from the irrational and absurd, which is what has impressed itself upon the deeper spirit of many twentieth-century people, to a God who is all reason, order, and purpose. The question here becomes: Given a tradition that associates God with the highest rationality, how can Christianity incorporate into its Theology a dialogue with the absurd?

To recapitulate: Each of the three motifs in the traditional exposition of the knowledge of God accentuates the positive dimension of divine knowability: (1) God reveals God's person (does not God also conceal?). (2) God is indelibly imprinted upon the human soul (how is it that we feel we are alone?). (3) God is the reasonable conclusion of our observation and experience of an ordered world (why is the world so fragmented, vulnerable, and directionless?). The questions are the more powerful because on the whole the tradition, at least as it has been received by us, does not anticipate or articulate them. Are there, perhaps, minority or neglected traditions that can help us move beyond the impasse represented by the unacknowledged questions? We shall elaborate on this critique in chapter 2, and attempt to speak to it constructively in chapter 3.

2. The Being of God

The two primary areas of Theological teaching where the tradition has permitted itself to describe God's being are the so-called attributes of God and the doctrine of the Trinity. Of these, the latter is no doubt the more important for Christians; it is certainly the more complex. At the same time, the questions addressed in the discussion of the divine attributes are highly significant questions, and in some ways they anticipate the great Theological issues that came to a head in the trinitarian debates of the early centuries.[17]

---

17. It is also unfortunately true that the attributes have been treated too often without sufficient reference to the issues at the core of trinitarian doctrine. Thus, as Karl Barth has forcibly demonstrated, even Calvin was given to the habit of considering the divine "perfections" (attributes) without sufficient reference to God's Self-manifestation in the Christ, through the Spirit. (Karl Barth, *Church Dogmatics,* vol. 2/1, *The Doctrine of God,* trans. T. H. L. Parker et al. [New York: Charles Scribner's Sons, 1957], 322ff.)

51

2.1. The Divine Attributes.   There are perhaps as many ways of designating the divine attributes or "perfections" (also called predicates, properties, and virtues) as there are theologians. This is partly because different qualities of divinity have appealed to different ages and branches of Christendom. It is also of course attributable to the fact that one cannot easily curtail the predicates of a being (who to begin with is not "a" being), one of whose attributes is infinity![18]

This diversity of attributes within the Theological conventions of Christendom is not without its problems. Among the many attributes that have accumulated over the centuries there are sufficient conflicts, not to say outright contradictions, so that anyone who considers them studiously may well conclude that for all their insistence upon the divine unity, Christians may in fact be worshiping quite different gods. A notorious example of the conflict in question is that between the attribute generally named the divine immutability (the idea that God is not subject to change, since divinity cannot be moved by what is external to itself) and the attribute of love. What kind of love would it be, by any known standard of discernment, that remained unmoved by the condition and the response of the beloved? The whole concept of immutability, which must certainly be traced to the Greek side of our heritage, was introduced to guard the triune God from the kinds of passionate involvements that reduced the popular gods of the ancient world to personifications and caricatures of human follies. But this no doubt understandable concern to avoid ludicrous anthropomorphisms ended (in the Patripassian controversy) with the strange spectacle of a transcendent Deity who had no vital, personal stake in the suffering of "his only begotten Son"—a God who is not only "behind it all" but (in the colloquial sense) "above it all."[19]

---

18. Not only are various qualities attributed to God by the many schools of the tradition, but there are as well many different ways of classifying them. John Macquarrie, for example, groups the traditional attributes under four headings: Mystery (incomprehensibility, incomparability); Overwhelmingness (immensity, infinity, eternality, omnipotence, omniscience, omnipresence); Dynamism (immutability, perfection); and Holiness (loving, merciful, just). (*Principles of Christian Theology* [London: S.C.M. Press, 1966], 186ff.)

The Canadian theologian of Queen's University, the late J. M. Shaw, made an interesting distinction between "relative" and "absolute" attributes, the former (omnipotence, omniscience, and omnipresence) being those whose character and manifestations are determined by the latter (holiness and love). This is a device that makes it possible to exclude interpretations of power (perforce attached to all the omni-attributes) that contradict the character of the revealing God as "holy love." (*Christian Doctrine* [Toronto: Ryerson Press, 1966], 36ff.)

Hendrikus Berkhof (*Christian Faith: An Introduction to the Study of the Faith,* trans. Sierd Woudstra [Grand Rapids: Wm. B. Eerdmans Pub. Co., 1979]) makes an important distinction between attributes of transcendence and attributes of condescension, which I shall quote in the course of the text below.

19. "Attributes are ascribed to the divine nature of Christ which the God of Abraham, Isaac and Jacob, 'the Father of Jesus Christ' never knew. His faithfulness is transformed into a substantial immutability, his zeal, his love, his compassion—in short his pathos, his capacity for feeling—are supplanted by the essential apathy of the divine. . . . The God of History, 'the coming God,' disappears in favor of the eternal presence of the heavenly Lord." (Jürgen Moltmann, *The*

While this represents perhaps the most notorious difficulty that historical Christianity experienced when it attempted to combine an emphasis upon the divine otherness with the declaration of God's unrestrained participation in the life of the world, it is not unique. How is it possible to insist upon God's infinity, eternality, omnipotence, omniscience, omnipresence, and so on, and at the same time affirm that our God is compassionate, long-suffering, merciful, just, faithful, patient, and kind? In other words, how was Theology able to retain the high picture of God presented in classical philosophies as well as most monotheistic faiths and at the same time remain loyal to the fundamental Christian belief that God is revealed supremely in the ignoble, sacrificial death of the man of Nazareth?

It would seem that historical Christianity resolved this knotty problem for the most part by accentuating the attributes that depict the divine power and transcendence, and causing its Christology to fit that Theological mold. The full significance of this tendency cannot be pursued here; it will become a recurring theme, and will be prominent especially in Part III of this volume. For the present, we confine ourselves to the Theological implications of this working "resolution."

God, not only for classical and medieval forms of Christianity but also for much Reformation and post-Reformation doctrine,[20] is presented as a figure of almost unapproachable majesty. God's perfections must perforce include ("weak," "feminine") traits such as mercy, long-suffering, and patient, unrequited love; but the shapers of the tradition are wonderfully careful to keep these qualities as noble, dispassionate, and steeped in an unearthly holiness as possible.[21] As we shall argue at greater length in chapter 2, God emerges first and foremost "the Father Almighty" in this tradition, and there is no mistaking the fact that both the "fatherhood" and the "might" which inform the *Gottesbild* (God-picture) of Christian orthodoxies are based on models from which

---

Way of Jesus Christ: Christology in Messianic Dimensions, trans. Margaret Kohl [Minneapolis: Fortress Press, 1993], 53.)

20. Moltmann draws our attention to a "new picture of God offered by the Renaissance and by nominalism," in which "God is almighty, and *potentia absoluta* is the pre-eminent attribute of his divinity" (*God in Creation,* 26).

21. In the preface of her passionate work on the nature of radical evil and suffering, Wendy Farley writes: "I have found the history I live in intolerable and the solutions of classical Christian theodicy unhelpful. Augustine watched as the barbarians of the north spread destruction like a virus through what was to him the entire known world and the apex of civilization. But his theory of predestination seems as morally bankrupt as the violence that surrounded him. Thomas Aquinas lived in more placid times, but surely even he should have known something about the harshness of medieval life. Was Calvin too innocent or too cruel to imagine the possibility of unjust and destructive suffering? Why do these men, so brilliant in other ways, have so little wisdom to offer those who suffer?" The answer, surely, is that they felt called upon, not only to "justify the ways of God to men" but to preserve God from personal involvement in creaturely suffering. (*Tragic Vision and Divine Compassion: A Contemporary Theodicy* [Louisville: Westminster/John Knox Press, 1990], 12.)

most traces of tenderness have been expunged. "The typical picture of divine *omnipotence*," writes W. Norman Pittenger, "is a case of 'giving to God that which belongs exclusively to Caesar.'"[22] Even the *love* of God, as for instance it is handled by Anselm in *Cur Deus Homo?*[23] is a highly "masculine" affair— or rather a caricature of masculinity, though one that has been extremely potent right into our own epoch. This "love" can identify with the beloved in a mathematical sort of way, but there are no tears in it; it is finally more concerned for its own "honor" than for the redemption of the beloved (which is why Peter Abelard, the lover, found it so hateful).

The message conveyed by the Father Almighty image of the various orthodoxies is the same message that human "fathers almighty" always convey to their progeny—namely, that it would be better to stay close to one's mother. The cult of the Virgin in Catholicism and the feminization of the Son in sentimental Protestantism were surely direct consequences of the orthodox insistence upon professing God as omnipotent Father, a being almost exclusively depicted in terms of sacred remoteness, absolute power, and unearthly glory and exaltation. As Berkhof rightly observes of this tradition,

> Due to the one-sided emphasis on God's transcendence in the traditional doctrine of God, in the history of theology especially the attributes that denote God's supernatural exaltation have been studied and developed, such as his infinity, incomprehensibility, immutability, omnipresence, omniscience, omnipotence, simplicity, eternity, spirituality, holiness. The attributes of God's condescension remained much more obscure, the most significant of which were wisdom, goodness, love, and righteousness. *God's essence was not derived from his condescension to Israel and in Christ.* In that way there was constructed the image of a God who is far away, aloof, and cold.[24]

It would be misleading, however, for North American comment upon the tradition concerning the divine attributes merely to echo this assessment of the matter. Insofar as various orthodoxies persist also on this continent, whether in the older Catholic, Protestant, or Eastern Orthodox forms or in sectarian and fundamentalist circles, the critique voiced by Berkhof applies to our context as well as to his. But the North American situation is in this respect more complex than that of the Netherlands. Reformed Protestantism in Europe was not radically affected at the grass-roots by theological liberalism. Among the major Protestant denominations in North America, on the contrary, liberalism was at many points very successful—and nowhere more successful than in connection with our reimaging

---

22. *Goodness Distorted* (London: Pitman Press, 1970), 54.
23. Eugene R. Fairweather, ed., *A Scholastic Miscellany,* Library of Christian Classics, vol. 10 (Philadelphia: Westminster Press, 1956).
24. *Christian Faith,* 113 (emphasis added).

of God. Liberalism reacted more strongly than does Berkhof to the one-sidedness of the God depicted by the classical traditions. Indeed, liberalism exchanged the orthodox picture of God for its antithesis.

Love—and precisely love of the most unjudgmental variety—became the norm by which every other quality attributed to the Deity was tested, altered, or discarded. The Father Almighty became the Grandfather All-merciful. What the Japanese theologian Kazoh Kitamori has insightfully identified as a "monism of love"[25] replaced, in the liberal milieu, the monism of might. Whole generations of North American liberal Protestants have by now grown used to a "Christian" God who is incapable of anger—and they have treated "him" accordingly: with condescension and often secret contempt.

At the same time, conservative forms of Christianity, spurred to even greater feats of one-sidedness by the liberal critique and alternative, have continued to bear stringent testimony to the God who rules in majesty and will punish all offenders. Thus North American Christians are victims of both unhappy traditions, sometimes displayed simultaneously in curious admixtures of doctrinaire transcendence verging on Deism and undialectical immanence verging on sentimental pantheism. It is no wonder that many sincere Christians in our context resolve this contradiction by associating the images of supernatural majesty and might with "the Father" (and the older Testament) and those of an all-embracing and forgiving love with "the Son" (and the newer Testament).[26]

The question posed by this contextual confusion of divine attributes is: How is it possible to think of God within the parameters of Christian faith without either projecting upon the divine person our entrenched models of power or, in reaction, making a romantic caricature of divine love?

This question begs precisely the question to which the doctrine of the Trinity was addressed early in the history of the Christian movement. We shall continue the discussion of God's being under the aegis of that doctrine.

2.2. The Triunity of God. To try to grasp the being of God according to the Christian profession of faith is to encounter from the start the strange yet overfamiliar and frustratingly unbiblical term, "Trinity." From time to time Christians have attempted to have it otherwise and, as the existence of a Christian Unitarianism testifies, they have occasionally succeeded—or seemed to. The

---

25. See Kazoh Kitamori, *Theology of the Pain of God* (Richmond: John Knox Press, 1965), 117ff. See also Carl Michaelson, *Japanese Contributions to Christian Theology* (Philadelphia: Westminster Press, 1960), 73ff. In conversation with me in Tokyo in 1989, Professor Kitamori again emphasized his conviction that Western Christian liberalism failed to understand the biblical God on account of its too undialectical pre-understanding of the nature of love.

26. Rosemary Radford Ruether draws attention to the role that Christian sculpture and painting have played in representing God "as a powerful old man with a white beard," as contrasted with the proscription against idolatry honored by Israel. (*Sexism and God-Talk* [Boston: Beacon Press, 1983], 66.)

historical course of Unitarianism, itself an important aspect of our continental history, also indicates that such successes not only regularly entail separation from the mainstream of the Christian movement but raise a fundamental question of identity. Is Unitarianism Christian? Certainly there are Unitarians who want to retain that nomenclature. Yet other Unitarians, as well as staunchly "trinitarian" Christians, insist with some justification that if the being of God is not related in a quite basic way to the being of Jesus Christ, then it is artificial to apply the designation "Christian" to Unitarianism.

A less dramatic but perhaps more cogent form of the same question was brought to the fore within the churches as a result of nineteenth-century liberal theology, some of whose representatives asserted that while trinitarianism may be a legitimate way of conceiving of God in terms of God's relation to us, it is presumptuous to make triunity descriptive of God's own being. Technically, the former conceptualization was designated the "economic Trinity" or the "Trinity of experience," and distinguished from the latter, the "immanent Trinity." The critical principle implied in this distinction cannot be taken lightly, for it has its origins in the same theological modesty that gave us the Third Commandment and was strongly at work in the Reformation as "the Protestant Principle."[27] Certainly the doctrine of the Trinity must never be accorded the kind of devotion that can only legitimately be given to the mystery of the godhead whom it seeks to describe. Yet the question of the neo-orthodox thinkers who criticized liberalism's "trinity of experience" remains: Can one take seriously the belief in a Self-revealing God if one begins by supposing that, inherently and immanently, God is perhaps fundamentally different from God's Self-manifestation to us?[28] The power of this question obliges us to consider the Trinity under the heading of the being of God rather than that of the divine works.

It is a truism to say that trinitarian teaching is complex, but we should distinguish between its inherent or necessary complexity and the complexity associated with its historical evolution. The Trinity is necessarily complex because it represents an attempt to describe the indescribable. *Deus non est genera*—God is not one of a species. While trinitarian thought has always had to use analogies, similitudes, and metaphors, it has been humbled by the fact that its subject is utterly unique.

Yet a good deal of the complexity associated with trinitarian thought is an acquired complexity, bound up with the history of its development as doctrine.

---

27. Tillich's term, by which he referred to Protestantism's *protest* against regarding finite, historically conditioned realities such as the church, church authorities, codifications of belief, and even the Scriptures as though they were ultimate. See *Systematic Theology,* vol. 1 (Chicago: Univ. of Chicago Press, 1951), 37, 227.

28. See Karl Barth, *Church Dogmatics,* vol. 1/1, chap. 2, Part 1, "The Triune God," trans. G. T. Thomson (New York: Charles Scribner's Sons, 1936), 339ff.

It is part of an almost impossibly tangled story, interwoven with the vacillations and inconstancies of a faith that was (after all) being equipped for imperial service,[29] and with often sordid and devious motives on the parts of persons whose political futures depended upon the success of their ideas in the courts of power.

One cannot escape that history entirely, even in such a brief account of the formation of the doctrine as we shall offer here. But since—unless it is treated with great depth and thoroughness—its history can only obscure the meaning of what actually came to be, I shall approach the doctrine rather more thematically than chronologically. After orienting ourselves to the problem through a brief reflection on the biblical background, we shall think of the genesis of the doctrine mainly from the standpoint of what it tried to *avoid*.

a. Why Did the Church Develop a Doctrine of the Divine Trinity?

I began by applying the word "unbiblical" to the doctrine of the Trinity. This does not infer that the doctrine is inconsistent with the biblical testimony to the being of God. It does mean, however, that the Trinity as such is not a biblical idea. The term never appears in the newer Testament, even though the so-called trinitarian formula (itself a later designation) is employed or suggested in certain places.[30] Not only is there no specifically trinitarian teaching in the newer Testament, but the characteristic language associated with the evolving doctrine is conspicuously unbiblical. Terms like "substance," "essence," "hypostasis," "perichoresis," and even "person" (as the latter word is employed classically and technically) all derive from the Greek and Roman background of the postbiblical era. The disciples of Jesus would have been baffled by these terms, and indeed by the whole debate that gave rise to them.

This constitutes a barrier for many, especially for Protestants who have been taught to take seriously the *sola scriptura* principle. Emil Brunner, for example, in his *Dogmatics* refused to discuss the Trinity at all until he had treated the biblical qualities of God, particularly holiness and love. He upheld trinitarian Theology, but not as kerygma.[31]

---

29. *Thinking the Faith,* "The End of the Constantinian Era," 200ff.

30. Explicitly, in Matt. 28:19 and 2 Cor. 13:13. For a discussion of the biblical background of the doctrine of the Trinity, see William G. Rusch, *The Trinitarian Controversy* (Philadelphia: Fortress Press, 1980), 2–3; also, Edmund J. Fortman, *The Triune God: A Historical Study of the Doctrine of the Trinity* (Philadelphia: Westminster Press and London: Hutchinson, 1972), 3–33.

31. "The ecclesiastical doctrine of the Trinity established by the dogma of the ancient Church, is not a Biblical kerygma, therefore it is not the kerygma of the Church, but it is a theological doctrine which defends the central faith of the Bible and of the Church. Hence it does not belong to the sphere of the Church's message, but it belongs to the sphere of theology; in this sphere it is the work of the Church to test and examine its message, in the light of the Word of God given to the Church. Certainly in this process of theological reflection the doctrine of the Trinity is central." (*The Christian Doctrine of God: Dogmatics,* vol. 1, trans. Olive Wyon [London: Lutterworth Press, 1949], 206.)

One can readily sympathize with this hesitancy. The translation of Hebraic-Christian faith into the Hellenistic and Romanic world was a complex operation indeed, and it is necessary for the survival of the faith to ask whether what emerged as the Christian profession of faith is really faithful to the original oral and written testimony of the early Christian community. Linguistically, much of the theology of the patristic or classical period is certainly very different from the writings of the newer Testament; and nowhere is the difference more conspicuous than with these trinitarian developments. Moreover, historical sensitivity has taught us to suspect that fundamental shifts of meaning as well as of language occurred in this movement of the early church beyond the context of the tradition of Jerusalem.

Yet, given the testimony of the Gospels and epistles, must one not conclude that it was almost inevitable that something like the Trinity concept would have come to be, regardless of subsequent historical circumstances? For while the newer Testamental writers do not employ the term or anticipate any of the ontological and epistemological nuances to which the formulators of the doctrine had recourse, they do leave us with what may be called *the problem* of the Trinity.

The nucleus of that problem can be stated fairly straightforwardly: As soon as the Christian community makes Jesus as the Messiah (Christ) the center and foundation of its profession of faith, but without intending that Jesus should simply displace the God of Abraham and Sarah, the first and great stage of the trinitarian enigma has been effectively introduced. For then one must immediately ask: What is the relation between this Jesus and the "one God" of the *Shema* ("Hear, O Israel: The LORD our God is one LORD"—Deut. 6:4)?

Historically, that is where trinitarian reflection began; existentially, it is where it always begins: with Christology.[32] If Jesus had been regarded by the postresurrection disciple community as (say) a teacher, a prophet, or even a high, heavenly being (as the heretic Arius more or less considered him), there would have been no such problem. But Jesus was not so regarded. The newer Testament's "community of the Way" would not have come into being if he had been regarded in that manner. The Christian movement was formed, not around the memory of a great rabbi, a heavenly messenger, or a prophet and judge (Israel already had many such); it was founded upon the insistent belief that in *this* person, and in a manner both unique and ultimate, humanity had been visited by the Eternal. Time had been invaded by the Creator of time. Not merely a *kairos* among *kairoi;* not merely a manifestation of the divine, which might be superseded by subsequent manifestations (such as certain sects later made of "the Paraclete"); not merely a Son of David bearing

---

32. See Moltmann, *The Way of Jesus Christ,* 140.

extraordinary authority, but rather (declared the community of Pentecost) in this one we have experienced Emmanuel, God-with-us.[33]

And yet (to repeat) the Christians did not say this in such a way as to suggest that Yahweh, the Father, the One God, had been superseded by God's Messiah, the "only-begotten Son." Jesus is not presented by this literature as he is presented by so much North American conservatism—simply as Deity. Nowhere in the canonical writings does one encounter flat declarations of the kind that one can hear hourly on "the electronic church," that "Jesus is God." On the contrary, the sacred literature is at pains to sustain Hebraic monotheism, and therefore it shows Jesus teaching his followers adherence to the Father,[34] and himself living to the full the obedience that he asks of them (Philippians 2).

Without the latter emphasis there would be no trinitarian problem in the newer Testament, any more than would be the case had Jesus been treated there as teacher or prophet alone. There is a trinitarian problem in this biblical literature because the earliest witnesses will neither present Jesus as strictly different from the Father nor strictly the same. If he were wholly distinguishable from the One God, it would raise the question why he should be offered such unconditional loyalty. These first Christians were after all Jewish. On the other hand, had the earliest disciple communities thought him simply God—all the God they needed—this would beg the question both of his real humanity and of their continued worship of the transcendent God, both of which are amply testified to in the literature concerned.

This christological problem does not by itself constitute the matrix for trinitarian Theological reflection. What we have so far is not a trinitarian problem but a "binitarian" one. Does the newer Testament go beyond this?

Although some interpreters have suggested that it may not,[35] most believe that it does. Certainly the relation of God and Jesus is the catalyst of the whole discussion. There is another dimension of the problem, however—one moreover of which the biblical authors seem entirely aware, and its presence makes the Bible already the matrix of what could be called proto-trinitarian contemplation of deity. I refer to the discussion of the Holy Spirit, particularly in Luke-Acts but also in the letters of the Pauline and Johannine schools.

We may express this aspect of the trinitarian problem in the following way: Newer Testamental faith is conscious not only of *having met* the Eternal in, or through, Jesus; it is also (and ecstatically) conscious of *continuing to meet* its

---

33. See below, chap. 9.
34. See Jon Sobrino, *Christology at the Crossroads: A Latin American Approach,* trans. John Drury (Maryknoll, N.Y.: Orbis, 1978), 384ff. See also in this connection Moltmann's discussion of the trinitarian God as "Father," especially his timely insight that "patriarchal religion is quite obviously not trinitarian" and that the doctrine of the Trinity in fact "makes a first approach towards overcoming sexist language in the concept of God" (*The Trinity and the Kingdom,* 162–65).
35. See Cyril Richardson, *The Doctrine of the Trinity* (New York: Abingdon Press, 1958).

Lord beyond the point of his historical sojourn. The writers are obviously unprepared to attribute this continuing experience of the Lord's presence to the disciple community's power of recall. In any case, recall would scarcely apply once the immediate contemporaries of Jesus had died. But even with his contemporaries, and in a sense especially with them, the newer Testament is clear that little can be attributed to the power of recall understood in strictly human terms.

Indeed, one of the most remarkable features of the Gospel records is their candor in depicting the incapacity of the original disciples even for ordinary human comprehension, let alone anything that could be called spiritual receptivity. Not only are they shown to be poor in imagination and understanding, they are in fact depicted as failing to comprehend the most elementary points of Jesus' teaching and mission. And finally, on the slim basis of what they do comprehend, they are presented as being adamantly opposed to Jesus' own understanding of his vocation, to the point of desertion and denial. Peter, "the Rock," represents an "agenda" that is in fact the very antithesis of Jesus' "way of the cross" and constitutes, in reality, a betrayal of his Lord far more subtle than is the tactical betrayal arranged by the pathetic figure Judas Iscariot (Matt. 16:18-28).

The Gospel writers know all of this perfectly well. Subsequent ecclesiology and legend made far too much of Judas's betrayal and far too little of Peter's (perhaps, given the symbolic power of Peter for the evolving Ecclesia, for reasons that are all too transparent). At every step of the way, the future vicar and symbol of the church not only demonstrates his fisherman's stubbornness but represents an alternative vision. To the way of the cross his back is turned (according to the beautiful and insightful *Quo Vadis?* legend, not even Pentecost fully transformed him). His proposal, voiced at several points but most unguardedly on the Mount of the Transfiguration (Matt. 17:4), could be called "the way of friendship." To the suffering-love (*agape*) of Jesus' interrogation at the end of John's Gospel (21:15), Peter insistently opposes his "philanthropic" devotion (*philia*)—and promptly demonstrates his inability to live that way. (One may be permitted to observe that in this respect Peter really has been the most fitting symbol and representative of historic Christianity, which has seldom grasped the way of the cross better than he did.)

The point is that this realism of the newer Testament's portrayal of the very persons who are, after all, both the sources of its basic information and the heroes of its drama, is not simply a victory of modesty over the human tendency to exaggerate the role of reputed founders and champions. It is integrally bound up with the message that these writings intend to communicate. Through the literary device of self-disparagement (a device that is prominent in the older Testament as well), the authors reinforce their positive message, namely, that their subsequent comprehension, faithfulness, and sense of mission are matters of sheer grace. We cannot read their honest testimony to their own actions, including not only their pathetic lack of comprehension but their actual disloyalty and cowardice, and come away thinking that the Christian movement was inaugurated *by them.* Thus they buttress, *via negativa,* the positive affirmation by which they hope to explain Christian beginnings—that is, that a transforming spiritual power has come to be among them, enlightening their mental dullness and making bold their weak wills: the promised Paraclete, the sacred wind and fire, the Spirit.

It is true that the Holy Spirit was not prominent in the discussions that came to a head at the Council of Nicaea in 325 C.E. It is often remarked that the doctrine of the Spirit is the most neglected area of the Christian profession of faith, and this neglect can be noticed already in the earliest phases of the trinitarian debate. In another sense, however, the Spirit could be regarded as the foundational Theology of Christianity, because without the *metanoia* that from the outset the church has attributed to the *testimonium Spiritus sancti internum* (internal testimony of the Holy Spirit), there would have been no enlightened remembrance of the Christ in the biblical sense of the term.[36]

We may therefore conclude (to state the matter as concretely as possible) that there is a *binitarian* problem in the Theology of the newer Testament only because there is a prior trinitarian problem.[37] It is only the pentecostal experience that causes the disciple community to look upon Jesus in such a way as to cast the question of his identity in the Theological mode. Flesh and blood have not revealed this to us (Matt. 16:17). The Holy Spirit must therefore be understood as present from the beginning, at least as the presupposition of the whole discussion, in this biblical and ecclesiastical reflection on the being of God.

It is understandable, however, that the christological aspect of the problem should have engendered the most controversy; for, unlike the Spirit, the second person of the Trinity represents the concrete, the historical, the particular—in short, flesh and blood. And if one says that in this historically conditioned, vulnerable human being, "crucified, dead and buried," one encounters the Eternal, then one poses in the most conspicuous way the problem to which the church of the early centuries had to address itself, and to which its doctrinal response was the declaration of God as triune being.

---

36. As Christianity emerges from its long Constantinian phase, the role of the Holy Spirit in all aspects of the life and faith of the church necessarily increases; for the reality of the church is then seen to be dependent upon charismatic rather than institutionalized foundations. It is symptomatic of this transition that, increasingly, pneumatology is brought into the center of the theological discussion. See, e.g., the prominent role assigned to the Spirit in creation in Moltmann's Gifford Lectures (*God in Creation,* 95–98, 263, and elsewhere).

37. In this respect, Henry Pitney Van Dusen's thesis in *Spirit, Son and Father: Christian Faith in the Light of the Holy Spirit* (New York: Charles Scribner's Sons, 1958), is more important than subsequent theological discussion has recognized, though it may be true that Van Dusen made too much of his important insight concerning the priority of the Spirit.

In turning now to the thematic discussion of this doctrine, it is important for us to assume, in this chapter on the historical background of the doctrine, a sympathetic posture. As in the previous subsections, my interpretation here too will lead to certain questions which, in my view, need to be put to this material. We may only acquire the right to articulate such questions, however, by first demonstrating a willingness to open ourselves to the best intentions of the tradition. The Trinity is bound to fail as doctrine. Its subject matter condemns it to failure before it begins. We should nevertheless try to appreciate the intellectual imagination and courage of the attempt. The church, as I have endeavored to show, did not have the alternative of silence on the matter. Its own Scriptures left it with a fundamental Theological problem, and the militantly pluralistic context of its early years accentuated that problem. Perhaps the greatest failure of the attempt to answer it was the sense, on the part of some, of having succeeded! But that failure is as much the responsibility of the subsequent ages of Christendom as of those who "resolved" the mystery classically.

b. The Genesis of the Doctrine.   What emerged from the long and tortuous discussions about the nature of godhead is perhaps best appreciated, not as a positive identification of the being of God but rather as a negation of certain alternatives that the church found to be misleading and dangerous (heretical). Through the gradual elimination of these heterodox opinions, an area of accord was finally reached—a kind of clearing at the center where, in the opinion of the councils, the mystery of the divine could be safely contemplated.

Given the fact that the biblical testimony bequeathed to the early church a problem of overcoming the seeming contradictions involved in three manifestations of an indivisible divinity, it can readily be seen that the positions that emerged as heterodox in the debate came from two sides of the problem. The one, which I shall call the danger of polytheism, accentuates the side of distinct or different manifestations of God; the other, for which I shall use the term undialectical monotheism, overstresses the divine indivisibility.[38]

The polytheistic danger.   From the perspective of monotheism, which was certainly the background of the first Christians, polytheism must be seen as dangerous because it implies the fragmentation of life and a lingering uncertainty about the character of the ultimate. To whom is obedience due? Before what sort of "transcendence" is one finally accountable? Polytheism is a vastly

---

38. It should not be thought that monotheism is of one type only, or that all actual and possible forms of monotheism are compatible with biblical faith. The monotheism of Neoplatonism, for example, with its fixation upon the unity principle, is quite different from that of Israel, which not only requires creaturely differentiation from the Creator but recognizes the supernatural influence of "principalities and powers" that are not of God. See the discussion of this subject in Tillich, *Systematic Theology,* vol. 1, 225ff.

unsatisfactory religious framework for all who look to religious faith to provide some sense of the integrity of existence.

The form that the polytheistic impulse characteristically assumed within Christian circles was tritheism. Tritheism is the natural heresy of those who for one reason or another are especially conscious of distinctions in the godhead. Even today when church members and adherents attempt to define the Trinity, they frequently offer explanations that are patently tritheistic: there is God, and there is Jesus, and (as a kind of ultimate vagueness) there is the Holy Ghost. For the casual Christian, the language of liturgy and hymnody largely confirms this heretical position—a language that is particularly misleading on account of the quite different connotation the word "person" has acquired in modern as contrasted with classical speech. It is difficult for the modern mind to sustain the overarching sense of the divine *unity* while singing,

> Holy, holy, holy. . .
> God in three persons,
> Blessed Trinity!

Although contemporary American and Canadian congregations are not likely to be cognizant of the dangers they are courting on such occasions, the church in its initial struggles with the nature of the being of God certainly was aware of these pitfalls. Moreover, it knew that the dangers were by no means only theoretical ones. Doctrine incarnates itself in ethics and in life. The Christian community that permits the polytheistic impulse to go unchecked runs the risk of destructive fragmentation of its always fragile unity. The history of the church amply testifies to this tendency, and our own religious situation in North America today may be more illustrative of it than is any previous period. All about us on this continent parties, sects, and "churches" exist, some of which identify themselves decisively with the Spirit, others of which have adopted working forms of Christomonism, and still others of which continue along lines that are vaguely theistic (and often virtually indistinguishable from non-Christian expressions of theism). The disunity of the church in a context boasting fifteen hundred to four thousand or more denominations is explicable at least in part on the basis of a de facto polytheism whose existence begs the question of the fundamental Theology of the Christian movement.

Tritheism, however, is only the beginning, even in Christian contexts. The polytheistic impulse cannot easily be limited, once indulged. In the Middle Ages it gave way to exponentially increasing cults of saints, whose prominence in daily life (though rarely in high theological theory) effectively expanded the pantheon of Christendom.

The ancient church fought against polytheism in the name of biblical monotheism. It recognized that certain natural inclinations of the human spirit toward polytheism were encouraged by elements of the biblical narrative over-laid by subsequent legend and myth. The foreign-sounding, technical language that the theologians came to employ was, much of it, brought in to ensure that the triune nature of the Christian profession of faith would not unwittingly support a tritheistically inclined religious praxis.

Despite my earlier observation that polytheism is unsatisfactory for all who look to religion for the integration of life, the power of the polytheistic impulse should not be underestimated. By positing a plurality of divine beings, whether hierarchically conceived or in mutual tension with one another, the human spirit may account for existential ambiguities and contradictions while retain-ing both belief in the supernatural and ritual means of influencing earthly events. It is surely always an act of spiritual audacity when a person affirms, in spite of everything in the world that speaks of chaos, conflict, contradiction, and caprice, that reality is ultimately fashioned from a single fabric; that it is only our human confusion and duplicity that hide from us the many-splendored integrity of all that is. The more immediate implication of raw human experi-ence of the world is that life is full of an almost infinite variety of occurrences, some pleasurable, some painful, which do not lend themselves to a holistic con-ception of reality. The modern mind faces the consequences of such an impres-sion by affirming that human beings are capable of creating the order that they need to achieve a sense of purpose. The tendency of premodern societies has been to achieve the sense of purpose by attributing the seeming randomness of things to a plurality of supramundane influences. To know these influences was not only to understand something of the *why?* of events but also to acquire a certain power in relation to the supernatural causation of events.

The plethora of gods in the ancient world testifies to the fact that this poly-theistic solution was appealing to many. Perhaps because of the meeting of di-verse cultures and cults, the sense of ambiguity and contradiction seems to have achieved a certain intensity, particularly in the Hellenistic world. The struggle for meaning in the midst of this cacophony formed itself around the war between spirit and matter. The terrible conflict of body and spirit could be explained—and therefore in part accepted—by projecting it into the supernat-ural sphere: the battle within us is a microcosmic manifestation of a macro-cosmic struggle. What saved the discerning from total victimization by the plurality of warring deities and heavenly influences was a modification of polytheism, through which the supernatural powers were assigned a hierarchic order, with ultimacy of power given to the god or gods most clearly identifiable with spiritual virtues.

It is against this Hellenistic background that we must view the man Arius (d. 336), who in some sense is responsible for inaugurating the trinitarian de-bate *as debate*. What this tall, lean, ascetic presbyter of the Alexandrian church feared was that the transcendent, utterly spiritual Deity who alone could claim his ultimate fidelity would be rendered ineffectual through a too close proximity to the material world. Perhaps as one whose polytheistic temptations had been resisted through a hierarchic ordering of the supernatural and natural universe, Arius would not have the floodgates of an undifferentiated polytheism opened again by a religion that wanted, apparently, to secure an intense connection between ultimate divinity and the world of matter. Consequently, and in a manner altogether predictable given such a background, he insisted that the omnipotent God of the Christian profession did not *personally* create the material world; that this was the work of "the Logos" (by which Arius meant the Demi-Urgos, a vastly inferior worker-god); and that it was just this "Logos" that in Jesus of Nazareth assumed flesh. Far from being "of the same substance" (*homoousios*) with the high and holy God, therefore, the one professed by Christians as the Son is of an altogether different *ousia* (*esse*), one that is neither fully divine nor yet fully human, but a being in between, like a demigod or a superman.

Thus—and this is not without irony—it happened that in the name of preserving a sort of monotheism, or perhaps henotheism (that is, the supremacy of the one transcendent Deity), Arius provided the rationale for a working Christian polytheism in which, below the Almighty though nevertheless in some affiliation with that high God, first the Christ and then other divine or semidivine beings could be posited.

The great champion against the Arian heresy, Athanasius (d. 373), was moved by a very different fundamental concern. If Arius feared that God would end by being less powerful and transcendent through a too great proximity to matter, Athanasius feared that *unless* God achieved full solidarity with the flesh, God would in fact have no power at all over the forces that prevent human redemption. Again and again, therefore, he insisted upon his special word, *homoousios* (of the same substance), despite the fact that this term was already associated with another heretical position, that of Sabellius.

Athanasius never truly succeeded in convincing Eastern Christians of the importance of what lay behind this word, and his long career was full of sorrow on account of his single-minded devotion to the belief that Jesus Christ participates in the very being (*ousia*) of God. His concern was entirely soteriological—we might say existential. The Son must be "of the same substance" as the Father, for otherwise we cannot expect ultimate salvation through him. If the Christ of our profession is other than or different from the God by whom he is sent and whom he represents, then one can in no way trust that in the encounter with Jesus Christ faith meets the Ultimate. And if it is not the Ultimate (God-with-us) whom faith meets in Jesus Christ, Athanasius insisted, then the grace of that meeting by no means suffices for our ultimate redemption.

The danger of undialectical monotheism. The name of Sabellius has been invoked. The course chosen by Athanasius was one that many thought too close to what the church had already declared to be the monarchian heresy, a position on the godhead put forward by Sabellius, a third-century Roman theologian, and his followers and, in another version, by the school of Paul of Samosata (Bishop of Antioch from ca. 260 C.E.). The monarchian heresy was a capitulation to what I am calling the danger of undialectical monotheism.

By an undialectical monotheism I mean the type of belief in "one God" that amounts to an a priori commitment to the unity principle as principle, an abstract devotion to theistic oneness. Trinitarian monotheism insists that there is dialogue (dynamism, relatedness, yes-and-no, give-and-take) *within* the one God. Undialectical monotheism is by contrast static and unbending. It fixes upon oneness as an implacable given. It is as far as possible removed from the picture of God presented in the Scriptures of ancient Israel, in which the Deity is in continual conversation with himself, struggling with different dimensions of his own response to creation, changing his mind ("repenting of the evil"), letting justice be qualified by mercy—in short, *responding*. In a real sense the unity of the God of Israel is a unity that is not given but constantly being achieved. It must be so, because the God of this tradition allows and even encourages dialogue with that which is not God, and such dialogue could not be taken seriously by exponents of belief in a God whose homogeneity is fixed and untouchable.

It would of course be misleading to say that the Christian view of God is nothing more than an extension of the Hebraic understanding of Yahweh because, as Christians and Jews recognized from the outset, the Christian identification of Jesus with the divine Word and essence constitutes a special problem for the "exclusive monotheism" (Tillich) of Israel. Still, the monotheism of Israel is not (at least in its primary biblical expression) the undialectical monotheism that became dangerous for early Christianity and has continued to exist in the Christian world. For in the monotheism of the Hebrew Bible the affirmation of the oneness of God does not entail commitment to a metaphysical principle of unity that excludes the very possibility of relationship *within* the godhead as well as relations of a genuinely covenantal nature *with* the godhead. This is even shown linguistically by the fact that Israel never excludes plurality from its concept of God—as is evidenced by the plural form of the divine name, *Elohim.*

If the danger of polytheism is the fragmentation not only of deity but of life under the conditions of such a religion, the danger of undialectical monotheism is a forced, theoretical integration of reality at the expense of life's real diversity. There *are* incongruities in our experience of God and the world. Religious faith in a God whose purposes are not contradictory helps us to live through the worst of these incongruities, and the particular genius of biblical faith lies precisely in the fact that the courage to live with the ambiguities of historical existence comes from the faith that God graciously participates in these ambiguities, and that through God's participation the "broken" character of existence is challenged and continually transformed ("mended"—Fackenheim). The monotheism of the Bible is dialectical monotheism in just that sense.

Of course Judeo-Christian faith knows that God is not internally ambiguous, that incongruous and warring elements are not present in God: this is the meaning of the attribute traditionally called the divine simplicity. But biblical faith also knows that God *loves*.[39] It professes, moreover, that love is not only a divine attribute but is of the very essence of God: "God *is* love" (1 John 4:8). When therefore that which God loves, the creation, exists under conditions of radical disjunction and alienation, the loving God "must"[40] participate in these incongruities of creaturely existence; for only from within can the destructive, annihilating power of creaturely ambiguity and estrangement be overcome without destroying creation as such. This is why biblical monotheism, in its Hebraic as well as its Christian expression, should be called dialectical: it takes into itself the negating dimension that does not belong to itself but is the immediate and necessary consequence of the love that does belong to itself. Just here we are at the heart of the theology of the cross, which as we have argued in the first volume has its roots in the Theological traditions of Israel.[41]

Undialectical or static monotheism must be regarded as a danger from the perspective of biblical faith because in place of this Hebraic readiness to find in God a personal acquaintance with the contradictions to which human life under the conditions of existence is heir, it presents us with a deity from whom all traces of suffering, or even of *movement,* have been expelled. With this deity there is no on-the-one-hand/on-the-other-hand. Everything is clear-cut, straightforward. The same theistic mind-set is at work here as we shall see presently in connection with the *creatio ex nihilo* dogma. It is a mind-set that dislikes very much the ongoingness, the livingness, and above all the struggle-character of biblical faith. It desires to have everything settled. But the trouble is, "everything" is only settled—ever!—theoretically. And the danger of all theory that emanates from the spirit of this Theology—especially when it is expounded within the context of religious establishment—is that life, which is always unsettled and organic, must then be forced to conform to theory.

It is important to note at this juncture a point on which we shall dwell more fully in the succeeding chapter. The danger of undialectical monotheism is the one that Western Christendom habitually courted. One may well ponder

---

39. See Moltmann, *God in Creation,* 85.
40. I shall frequently place the word "must," used in such constructions as this, in quotation marks, because I wish the reader to recall the theme of *necessitas* or destiny that runs throughout the length and breadth of the biblical story and is explicitly present in the predictions of the passion ("The son of man must suffer many things and be rejected . . ." Mark 8:31; 9:12).
41. *Thinking the Faith,* 26ff.

(1) whether the kinds of doctrinal orthodoxies of both Protestant and Roman Catholic traditions and (2) the type of political imperialism of the successive "Christian" empires of the West could have come to be without the underlying theoretical aid of such a conception of the deity.[42]

In the trinitarian debates of the early centuries, this predilection toward a static form of monotheism, combined with the desire (also a strong one in the West) to preserve the absoluteness of the revelation in Christ, gave the church the other great heresy that classical Theology had to try to avoid. This was the aforementioned Monarchianism, so named because of the fundamental desire informing it, the desire to sustain the undivided monarchy of the one God. Dynamic Monarchianism maintained this indivisible sovereignty by claiming that at a certain point in his life the man Jesus had been taken up into (adopted by) the divine Monarch; that is, it sustained the unity principle through an adoptionist Christology. The more popular form of Monarchianism has been termed Modalistic Monarchianism; its chief exponent was Sabellius. Sabellianism offered a rather simple and direct explanation of deity to Christians who were simultaneously committed to a rigorous theistic unity and to the finality of the Christ event: God, it contended, appears in three modes, successively: Father, Son, and Spirit. The three are masks of the same inseparable sovereignty.

The fight against this solution was led by followers of Tertullian and Origen. They argued that Monarchianism maintains the unity of the godhead at the expense of ignoring real distinctions.[43] In particular, Sabellianism raises grave christological questions: If Jesus is fully and exclusively divine, what are we to make of his humanity? Surely the newer Testament is quite decisive in its witness to the fact that, whatever his origin and destiny, Jesus as he appeared among his contemporaries was a thoroughly human being. To make of him God in God's second mode of appearance is not only to call his humanity into question, but it is to alter substantially the newer testamental witness. If Jesus were simply God come among us, to whom did he himself pray? To whom did he refer in his teaching when he spoke of "the Father"? Of whom did he have to "learn obedience" (Heb. 5:8)? To whose "will" did he submit, finally, in the garden of sorrows (Matt. 26:36ff.)?

The "clearing in the middle." Having over a period of approximately two centuries identified these theological dangers and their ethical and practical consequences; having in effect declared that these are *not* the ways in which Christians ought to think about the being of God, the church found itself, as we may say, with a small space, an intellectual "clearing" defined by the process

42. See J. Moltmann, *The Trinity and the Kingdom,* trans. Margaret Kohl (Minneapolis: Fortress Press, 1993), 136.

43. See William G. Rusch, ed., *The Trinitarian Controversy* (Philadelphia: Fortress Press, 1980), 8ff.; also Moltmann, *The Trinity and the Kingdom,* 130–32.

of elimination, within which reflection on the essence of the godhead might profitably take place. If we ask for some nomenclature or sign designating this elusive space, there could be no doubt about the answer that should be given. It would be the phrase, *una substantia et tres personae.*

This phrase, which was first thrown into the debate—almost at random—by the impulsive Tertullian, became the doctrinal motto or symbol which (in terms of the metaphor we are using) gave a nomenclature to the little clearing where the mystery lay. It served as such two functions. It reminded Christians of the routes to be avoided: God is one substance (*una substantia*), therefore everything that may promote polytheism is to be rejected; but God is three "persons" (*tres personae*), therefore everything that denies any distinctions within the godhead is to be shunned. This negative or critical function of the formula was certainly its most important contribution. On the positive (constructive) side, however, the formula and its accompanying commentary invite subsequent discipleship to conduct its Theology along lines that maintain continuity with biblical monotheism while at the same time providing a solid foundation for the centrality of Jesus Christ in the Christian profession of faith.

The trouble was (and is) that as a positive statement of the identity of God in Christian belief, the trinitarian formula never functioned well. The weakest part of it is the second key term—in Latin, *personae;* in Greek, *hypostaseis.* Ironically, these terms permitted a kind of linguistic agreement between Eastern and Western branches of Christendom, while allowing each branch to pursue its own peculiar temptation. For Eastern Christianity that meant the polytheistic temptation that was already, if unintentionally, present in the theistic thought of Arius of Alexandria. For Western Christianity, as has been noted, it meant the temptation toward Sabellianism.

Like so many of the "agreements" within Christendom, this linguistic agreement was attributable only to different nuances of the two primary languages used, Greek and Latin. The Cappadocian theologians, through whom the long debate was resolved, took up the Latin phrase of Tertullian and rendered it in Greek as *mia ousia kata treis hypostaseis.* The term *hypostaseis* had for the Eastern mind a strong flavoring of "distinctions." Thus it was able to placate those who feared that the first part of the formula, which depicts Jesus as sharing the same essence [*ousia*] as God the Father, would compromise the transcendence of the high and holy One. When, however, the Cappadocian formula was rendered again into the Latin and the old, Tertullian language reinstated, the supposed equivalent of *hypostaseis,* namely *persona,* far from affirming the side of divine distinctions, tended to duplicate the sentiment already expressed in the first part of the formula, that is, the affirmation of the indivisible unity of the Deity. For, unlike its contemporary equivalent in English ("person"), *persona* was not for that fourth-century Western setting a term denoting individuality but stressed rather the common humanity, the humanity in which all human beings participate and out

69

of which they "stand" [*ex sistere*].[44] The image conjured up by the formula in Latin, then, is that the God who is "one substance" speaks through three different media (modes), but it is always the same God. In other words, the West got what it really wanted from the outset—a strong declaration of the divine unity and indivisibility. It is no wonder that Athanasius, the Easterner, found his niche finally in the Latin West.

The same logic that was irrevocably at work in the christological phase of the trinitarian discussions manifested itself some century and a half later when the Western church clarified its pneumatology (doctrine of the Spirit). There are good reasons why an "ungrounded" Paraclete must be clearly identified. The newer Testament already knows of these (see especially 1 John 4). One cannot therefore be wholly out of sympathy with the decisions of the Third Council of Toledo (C.E. 589) concerning the question of the divine Spirit's "procession." Yet it confirms the general direction of this interpretation (and of the questions that I shall presently formulate) that Western Christianity should sooner or later have had to insist upon something approximating the *Filioque* clause that Toledo added to the Nicene Creed: "And I believe in the Holy Ghost, the Lord and Giver of Life, who proceedeth from the Father *and the Son*. . . ." For the whole direction of Western Theology was (and to some extent still is) to accentuate the divine unity and indivisibility; or—to put the matter from the side of what the West historically fears—to avoid any hint of plurality in the godhead. Toledo therefore attempted to ensure that the Spirit would not be able, in orthodox circles, to introduce into the "settled" Theology, ecclesiology, and political theory of the church any new and unpredictable elements.[45]

Numerous questions emerge for us out of this long and complex history, but one question dominates them all (though I speak here only for Western Christianity; so far as the Christian East is concerned, a different question would have to be asked). Because it is a profound and many-sided question, we shall have to put it in a variety of ways, though it is finally the same question: How is it that the tradition as we have received it accentuates so strongly the divine unity? What is lost when this happens? Are there broadly political as well as psychological and religious reasons why the Western church opted for this emphasis?

---

44. *Persona* originates with ancient theater. In classical drama, one actor often played several parts, using masks to mark the visible distinctions between characters. It was always, however, the same sound (*sona*), i.e., the same voice, that came through (*per*) the different masks. In the evolution of the word "person" in modern languages, especially English, we have passed from a highly realist (in the Platonic sense) usage of the term to an extreme nominalism that accentuates individual uniqueness; nowhere in the world is this individualism so blatantly present as in the contemporary North American employment of the word "person."

45. Rosemary Radford Ruether's earlier works, *Liberation Theology* (New York: Paulist Press, 1972), chap. 5, and *Faith and Fratricide: The Theological Roots of Anti-Semitism* (New York: Seabury Press, 1974) are both important background reading for this formative period in the development of Christian Theology.

What sort of rethinking of the trinitarian Theology of the West is required of us if we are to correct this one-sided emphasis?

The foregoing discussion of the tradition will, I trust, assure the reader that I am not here suggesting that we should opt for the polytheistic side of the problem. That this is tempting for many Christians today is clear. Our pluralistic religious situation, our incapacity for the philosophic realism that informs classical Western Theology (we are nominalists all), and many other general and concrete factors incline us toward tritheism in church theology and a working polytheism in interfaith apologetics. But to follow that path consistently would mean the demise of the Christian movement. The future of the ecumenical church depends above all upon some agreement about the identity of the God whom we serve.

Agreement, however, does not necessarily mean unanimity. Historically we have been extraordinarily committed to the unity principle in our Theology, our ecclesiology, and in most other aspects of our doctrine and practice. As intimated in the foregoing, I suspect that this commitment has from the outset been bound up with the political role played by the dominant forms of Christendom in the Western world. There are strong sociological impulses driving an imperial religion away from a too consistent emphasis upon the elements of diversity and mystery in its own Theological traditions.

The price that we have paid for this commitment to the unity principle is on the one hand theological and on the other cultural and political. Theologically, it has meant the creation, generation after generation, of systems of doctrine whose guiding mandate has been the affirmation of unity: God's unity, of course, but God is never merely God. It has meant the affirmation of a unity symbolically expressed in Theology but inclusive of all reality. This can be justified by insisting that Truth is one, that God works in all things for a unitary good, and so on. But the accentuation of unity can also become a cloak for covering the real disjointedness of the world—and therefore a useful ideological tool in the suppression and repression of diversity.[46] That is the cultural and political side of the price we have paid. A one-sided, single-minded theism in the service of a dominant culture and an imperial state is almost invincible. Who can withstand the pressures of conformity under such conditions?

Are we to settle, then, for diversity and fragmentation? Are we to abandon the quest for the integrity of all that is, the unity of Truth, the interrelatedness of all reality? Certainly not. Yet, hearing the voice of the One who declares, "I *am* the Truth," we must be more consistently inclined than we have been toward modesty with respect to our own apprehension and comprehension of the Truth of God. We cannot possess truth—least of all truth concerning God. The

---

46. See Ruether's documentation of this repression as experienced by Jews and followers of Mithraism, etc., in the fourth and fifth centuries C.E. (*Liberation Theology*, 74ff.).

most impeccable trinitarianism cannot comprehend the triune God. God lives! Is there not something altogether too apposite about an established religion which first determines that the Father is Almighty, then establishes that the Son has once-for-all achieved the victory of the divine sovereignty over all its enemies, and finally insists that the Spirit exists to bring us into this already-realized state of harmony?

The question thus articulated anticipates other claims of this discussion; but already with the trinitarian dimension we have the elements of what follows. What it comes to is the sacrifice of the dynamic side of trinitarian Theology (which is maintained, at least in theory, in Eastern Christianity especially by the second phrase of the formula—*kata treis hypostaseis*) for the sake of the apparently more stable side (*mia ousia/una substantia*). To state it in another way, one that will become central to our continuing discussion here, it means the sacrifice of the *relational* dimension of the divine being to the *substantial* dimension.[47]

What has to be asked of Western Theology, to summarize this discussion, is: How can we explicate what was important in this trinitarian Theology respecting the unity and faithfulness of God without in the process losing touch with the *living* God who participates in the real, unfinished, unsettled, and threatened life of the creation? Trinitarian Theology may be the most monumental contribution of the Christian intellect in all of our inherited tradition. Tom Driver doubts whether Christianity would have survived without it.[48] But like most monuments, it easily becomes a memorial without meaning, having no existential basis in contemporary consciousness. The trinitarian monument will have to be recast if the Truth to which it was supposed to point is going to become newly visible and viable within the disciple community today. Trinitarian theology is not served well in North America today by those who simply repeat that God is "Father, Son, and Holy Spirit."

3. The Works of God

There is no simple way of classifying God's works;[49] they are both manifold and mysterious. It has been customary in systematic treatments of the doctrine

---

47. In this I am in complete agreement with Jürgen Moltmann when he states that his intention is "to free the Christian doctrine of God from the confines of the ancient metaphysics of substance, and from the framework of the modern metaphysics of transcendental subjectivity, in order to develop a social doctrine of the Trinity in the different context of a metaphysics of community, process and relation." (*The Way of Jesus Christ*, xv.)

48. *Christ in a Changing World: Towards an Ethical Christology* (New York: Crossroads, 1981), 97.

49. Moltmann observes, insightfully, that the entire concept of God's "works" reflects a masculine and patriarchal point of view, and that this has questionable implications today especially

of God, however, to subsume the divine works under three cat
preservation, and redemption.

Two general observations must be made before we consic
separately. The first is that the tradition recognizes the imp
arating the being and the works of God. God's being is ex~~pressed in God's~~
works, and God's works are consequent upon God's being. If, for example, it is
asked *why* God created the world (a question that may be asked frivolously, but
also out of existential concern), the answer given by the tradition is normally
some version of that stated by Paul Tillich when he writes, "God is creative
because he is God."[50]

The second introductory point is that the three categories of God's work are
not to be conceived as though they referred to three separable works. It follows
both from the discussion of the divine attributes and the doctrine of the Trinity
that faith professes God's works to be integrated, each work already implying
the others. For instance, creation as it is treated in the tradition presupposes
redemption noetically. That is, the community of faith (Israel/the church) professes belief in God's creation of the world as a community that is itself being
created—and indeed, as both testaments would insist, created *ex nihilo*. Similarly, preservation can be referred to in the tradition as *creatio continuo* (continuing creation), and preservation and redemption follow an obvious line of
continuity. Redemption in turn implies both creation, as God's "good" first
work, and is itself a work of ultimate preservation.

3.1. Creation

God *Creates*—God Creates! Although the chronological beginnings of
our Scriptures are different from the order in which the writings actually appear, the ordering of the biblical writings is by no means lacking in theological
significance itself. The fact that the opening verses of the Bible describe God
in the act of creation reinforces the point that we have just made, namely, that
the Bible does not manifest any fundamental interest in God's *being* as distinct
from God's works. God's being is already God's being-*with*.[51] The myths of

---

for the "work" of creation: "A child is conceived and grows in the mother's womb, and the mother
bears it. But the man works on something external, creating a world which exists outside himself."
(*God in Creation*, 312f.) While I agree with this insight, I shall retain the conventional nomenclature of divine "works" in this chapter treating historical theology.

50. Tillich continues: "Therefore it is meaningless to ask whether creation is a necessary or a
contingent act of God. Nothing is necessary for God in the sense that he is dependent upon a necessity above him. Nor is creation contingent. It does not 'happen' to God, for it is identical with
his life. Creation is not only God's freedom but also his destiny. But it is not a fate; it is neither a
necessity nor an accident which determines him." (*Systematic Theology*, vol. 1, 252.)

51. See my *Imaging God: Dominion as Stewardship* (Grand Rapids: Wm. B. Eerdmans Pub.
Co., 1986).

_eation in Genesis chapters 2 and 1 may be said to presuppose certain ideas that are important for the biblical view of reality (for instance, the whole concept of "the void," to which we shall speak presently); but they do not manifest the curiosity about pre-creational reality—including in particular God's own internal reality—found in many other ancient myths, legends, and sagas. Already from the outset, the tradition of Jerusalem pictures God as oriented toward the world: "In the beginning God created the heavens and the earth." This orientation never changes. It is one of the great constants of the whole scriptural record.

Whether the Christian church has been faithful to this orientation is another question, and it will become an aspect of the larger critical question that shall emerge from this brief consideration of the work of creation. The pull toward an otherworldly and indeed an antiworldly posture has been strong in Christendom, especially since the "natural" psychic impulse toward world-ambiguity received its first great formative influence in the meeting of early Christianity with Hellenistic world views.

Ostensibly, the most blatant form of otherworldliness was put aside in the early Christians' struggle against Gnosticism. The Gnostics were adamant in their rejection of matter as being neither good nor real. Like Arius, they could not accept the notion that the material order had been created by the same God who, through Christ, redeemed it. The power of the gnostic interpretation of the faith was very strong in the second century of the Christian era particularly. In resisting it, the theologians insisted on the unity of God as creator and redeemer (the second general point made above). According to Bernhard Lohse, their rejection of the gnostic way was decisive: "The theologians of the time did this circumspectly and thoroughly, so that ever since that day the danger that the doctrines of creation and redemption would be separated has hardly ever become as acute as it was then."[52] While the final phrase of the quotation safeguards Lohse's generalization somewhat, it seems to me a rather too optimistic assessment of this aspect of the history of Christian thought.[53] It would be accurate enough to say that the Christians have never been tempted actually to name two deities, a greater who redeems and a lesser who creates; but this technical adherence to the decisions of the early church in relation to the Trinity and other, related dogmas has hardly prevented a certain "depreciation of creation"[54] from dogging the steps of

---

52. *A Short History of Christian Doctrine: From the First Century to the Present*, trans. F. Ernest Stoeffler (Philadelphia: Fortress Press, 1966), 103.
53. Rosemary Radford Ruether would, I think, agree. See her discussion of the "extreme ascetical spirituality" and "withdrawal from the world" in *Liberation Theology*, 69f., 81, and elsewhere.
54. Ibid., 29.

Christian spirituality. And the test of Gnosticism lies precisely in one's "working" attitude toward creation.[55]

The depreciation of creation can be expressed in more ways than one. For the Gnostics it was a rather clear-cut rejection of materiality: the material world is not and could not be "good," for it is material. A more subtle but just as effective form of the denigration of creation deploys the theology of redemption to secure for the elect a certain vital transcendence of creaturehood. This has been so constant a temptation in historical Christianity that one must wonder whether the gnostic heresy, in its supposed defeat, did not channel its power into transcendental theories of redemption. The question is not only whether the God who creates is also the God who redeems, but whether what God redeems is the world that God created.

This question is entirely pertinent in the North American context today, for new expressions of theological dispensationalism are strongly present in popular versions of the faith that capitalize on "future shock" within our society. No serious work of Christian theology should be allowed to neglect the fact that the best-selling book in any category of literature during the decade of the 1970s was Hal Lindsey's *The Late Great Planet Earth*—a book that "demonstrated" that the redemption of the few ("the raptured") entails the destruction, not only of the many, but of creation itself.[56]

Despite both modern and ancient temptations of this sort, what Christians have claimed historically to profess is that God *created* the world and that the world is the creation of none other than *God.*

***God Creates* ex Nihilo.**   If the first insistence of our tradition is that it is God who has created and is creating the world, the second is that God creates "out of nothing." *Creatio ex nihilo* is not, as is sometimes thought, a concept demonstrating the divine omnipotence, as if God were a great magician who could cause worlds to appear out of thin air. Like the two Christian teachings with which it shares a common background in the theology of grace—namely, justification by grace through faith, and the resurrection of the dead—*creatio ex nihilo* points to a profound existential depth. It expresses the fundamental and recurring experience of faith, that the impossible becomes possible

---

55. See my *The Steward: A Biblical Symbol Come of Age,* rev. ed. (Grand Rapids: Wm. B. Eerdmans Pub. Co., 1990).

56. Hal Lindsey with C. C. Carlson, *The Late Great Planet Earth* (Grand Rapids: Zondervan, 1970). To such a scenario, the only appropriate response from the perspective of biblical faith is that voiced by Moltmann in his Gifford Lectures: "The expectation of 'the end of the world' is a vulgar error. Like the expectation of the *annihilatio mundi,* it is gnostic in origin, not biblical." (*God in Creation,* 93.)

through the love, faithfulness, and life-commitment of God: where there was only sin, there is forgiveness and a new beginning (justification); where there was only death, there is life (resurrection); where there was nothing, there is something (creation). All of these are expressions of the rudimentary theology of grace that informs the biblical story from beginning to end.

What *creatio ex nihilo* explicates within this larger category of divine grace is the concept that, like the "new creaturehood" (2 Cor. 5:17) that is being given us through God's justifying grace and shall be given us finally in what the Apostles' Creed designates as "the resurrection of the body," the being of creation as a whole is a matter of pure gift. It is God's possibility. There was no preexistent potentiality for it apart from God's creating love. Just as Israel was conscious of being transformed from a state of slavery and wandering into peoplehood; just as the early Christians were conscious of being shaped into a body, where before there had been only disparate groups and alienated persons incapable of sustained mutuality, so (reasons faith) the world itself came to be.[57] This is what was meant earlier when we spoke of redemption as the noetic presupposition of creation.[58]

This, at its best, is what the Christian profession of faith has intended in its affirmation of the dogma *creatio ex nihilo*. There is, however, a nuance in the concept that has not so often been acknowledged and has perhaps been consciously avoided by many. This is the suggestion, implicit in the phrase itself but explicit in the account of creation from which the technical term sprung, that the *nihil* out of which creation comes is not merely the absence of being but the *negation* of being. In other words, while the accent must fall upon the first word of the Latin phrase (*creatio*), it should also be noted as a kind of subtheme that that out of which (*ex*) the world is fashioned is a something-or-other that is not merely neutral but actually resists the creating fiat (word-command) of the Creator.

Not only does the biblical text that is the *locus classicus* of the *ex nihilo* dogma suggest such a rendering, but it belongs to the same existential or experiential framework of grace to which we have already referred.[59] Sin is not neutral

---

57. Bruce C. Birch accentuates this point in *Let Justice Roll Down: The Old Testament, Ethics, and Christian Life* (Louisville: Westminster/John Knox Press, 1991): "Israel first came to know God as Creator in its own story as a people, and not in abstract reflection on the beginning of all things. The earliest references to God as Creator come in relation to God as the Creator of Israel" (p. 76).

58. See in this connection Romans 4.

59. Although the second (and older) saga of creation provides a better (because more graphic) pictorial basis for the point being made here, the *creatio ex nihilo* concept must be traced in particular to Genesis 1:2 (RSV): "The earth was without form and void [*tohu wabohu*], and darkness was upon the face of the deep. . . ." Hendrikus Berkhof notes that many interpreters have recognized the certain incongruity of this verse in relation to the rest of the Priestly account of creation. "This verse is a 'foundling from a distant time' (W. H. Schmidt), 'an erratic block' (Kuitert), and therefore a '*crux interpretum*' (Barth). The explanations for it are legion. In my

with respect to forgiveness; it positively resists the preferred transformation. "The body" is not passive; "death" is not dormant—not in the tradition of Jerusalem. There is a persistent opposition to the grace that "gives life to the dead and calls into existence the things that do not exist" (Rom. 4:17). So with creation: not only is the "nothingness" (whether that *tohu wabohu* of Genesis 1 or the "clay" and "dust" of Genesis 2–3) as such incapable of producing anything, it seeks to withstand the creative act. Preservation is in fact just the

---

judgment we look here deep into the heart of Israel, which cannot break herself free from the fear of the dark powers which cross Yahweh's plans, and which nevertheless, rising above her own fear, confesses that there are no gods before the face of Yahweh, who created the world." (*Christian Faith,* 158–59.)

At the same time, Berkhof admits that "most of the creation traditions in the OT do not know of a creation out of nothing and . . . it is not explicitly mentioned until 2 Macc. 7:28" (ibid., 155); and later he affirms that "most" of the older Testamental passages to which he is referring as offering "important statements about creation" (to wit: Gen. 1–2:4a; 2:4b–7[J]; Job 26:12f.; 38:8–11; Ps. 74:13f.; 89:10ff.; 104:5–9; Prov. 8:28; Isa. 27:1; 51:9–11) "give the impression that the world originated out of a struggle between Yahweh and a primeval sea monster which he overcame." This notion, he affirms, "is also found in the Babylonian creation account *Enuma elish*" and other ancient myths. He concludes that "There must . . . have been an earlier period in which Israel still thought in terms of this dualistic pattern and had to wrestle with it." But with the Priestly account "dualism has been overcome," "Yahweh creates solely through his word"— excepting that the verse in question (Gen. 1:2) "does not appear to fit"; and this leads Prof. Berkhof to the aforementioned conclusion.

Although it is not without persuasive power, Berkhof's solution seems to me somewhat artificial and doctrinally determined rather than exegetically sound. Not only does it fail to answer why, when it contained such a potential contradiction, the verse in question was retained by the Priestly writer, but it gives the victory to the remainder of the Priestly account without any mention of the Yahwist tradition and other references that Berkhof himself has faithfully noted. Surely the more reasonable explanation for the continuation of this theme in the "mature" reflections of Israel is that Hebraic faith does acknowledge a kind of provisional dualism. It is not a full-fledged dualism, as in Zoroastrianism, for that would contradict the confession of the one God. But it is the recognition that that which negates is real; that creation as such is already a struggle of grace and love; that evil, while certainly not a transcendent force on a par with the One God, constitutes a negating potential against the creation of God—and that before the "fall of Adam." This would also account for the presence of the Tempter in the Garden.

John Macquarrie's analysis appears to me more trustworthy than Berkhof's: "The importance of a doctrine of *creatio ex nihilo* would seem to be that it draws attention to the fact that any particular being stands, so to speak, between nothing and Being . . . or that the nullity (nothingness) is an essential constituent of creaturehood . . . something of the dualistic view is found in all religion, and certainly in Christianity. Dualism genuinely reflects the twofold possibility of all creaturely being—to advance into fuller being, or to slip back into the nothing from which it has come." (*Principles of Christian Theology,* 198.)

Tillich makes essentially the same point: "The term *ex nihilo* says something fundamentally important about the creature, namely, that it must take over what might be called 'the heritage of nonbeing.' . . . Being a creature includes both the heritage of nonbeing (anxiety) and the heritage of being (courage).

"The doctrine of creation out of nothing expresses two fundamental truths. The first is that the tragic character of existence is not rooted in the creative ground of being; consequently it does not belong to the essential nature of things. In itself, finitude is not tragic. . . . The second truth expressed in this doctrine is that there is an element of nonbeing in creatureliness; this gives insight into the natural necessity of death and into the potentiality but not necessity of the tragic." (*Systematic Theology,* vol. 1, 253–54.)

logical and existential consequence of this assumption: since, contrary to Deism, creation is not *sui generis* or self-sustaining once set in motion; since on the contrary there is a sort of natural slide toward oblivion, creation must be continually affirmed, upheld, sustained, nourished.

It is obvious enough why throughout its history Christian doctrine avoided this nuance, and not only avoided it but used the *creatio ex nihilo* dogma to proscribe the idea. The reason is that it can appear straightforwardly dualistic—as if, alongside the Eternal One there were another, opposing force. Furthermore, it can seem to support the very antimaterial bias that we have seen at work in Gnosticism and Arianism. Certainly the church has been called to walk a precarious tightrope between two equally dangerous positions: on the one hand the courting of dualism, on the other the embracing of a monism so unrelenting that it could only regard evil, sin, death, the demonic, and the whole spectrum of nonbeing as deprivation and the absence of being.

The fact is, surely, that historic Christendom errs on the latter side. In order to avoid any hint of dualism (partly, one supposes, because the dualistic temptation was so great, especially in the early church), Christian profession has courted the kind of monism that has great difficulty giving the devil his due. The whole horrendous range of that which negates—the cosmic *Todestrieb* (death-wish), so to speak—has lacked substance for the most classical expressions of our faith from Augustine to Karl Barth. And when (as in fact it characteristically happens) this monism is combined with a triumphalistic resurrectionism and a strongly "realized" eschatology, it is even less possible within the parameters of the received tradition to take evil seriously.

This is by no means a purely doctrinal matter. It has the most immediate ethical consequences. If one believes that the raw stuff of creation is wholly malleable to the divine creative will; and if one further believes that the sin which entered through the human will has been overcome in the Christ event; and if one adds to all this the sense that the divine victory has been realized already, then what can (for example) Auschwitz be but the *appearance* of evil? That which radically negates has no ontic standing in such a system. And certainly there may be contexts where precisely such a message can and should be experienced as gospel—moments of failure, defeat, and hopelessness when the human spirit has to be encouraged to think that the demonic and life-denying dimension of our experience is nothing more than an appearance, is fundamentally unreal. But such a message, while contextually appropriate from time to time, should not be put forward as *the* Christian profession of faith. In the hands of the self-confident and powerful of the earth, it is an exceedingly dangerous point of view, for it carries with it the psychic machinery that individuals and societies need in order to justify their failure to combat existing evil. Christian triumphalism, which derives its greatest ideational power from a one-sided theology of redemption, already begins with a creation theology that accentuates the positive and eliminates any hint of an abiding negative.

The antidote to this triumphalism, which must become part of our deliberations in the third chapter, is not to leap over the opposite edge of the precipice into dualism. Dualism ends in an ethic that provides equal justification for Auschwitz, Hiroshima, poverty and injustice on a global scale, and so on and on. It allows for an eternal negative that, for all our efforts at banishing it, will remain; and it offers as salvation the acceptance of this state. Christianity fails to express its most important basic belief either when it embraces a theory in which the Nothing has no substance at all or one in which it is all too substantial. Whatever emphasis may be called for in the context where faith is *con*fessed, the *pro*fession of the faith always must entail the courage to affirm the reality of that which negates while at the same time insisting upon the gracious possibility of negating the negation. The profession of the faith must do this because precisely the core of that upon which the disciple community meditates is a gospel which declares that the great negation by which creaturely life is continuously threatened has been entered into and is being overcome by a God who, by personally submitting to the aboriginal Nothingness, nullifies its power over us.[60]

Is being overcome . . . "The darkness is still there and the chaos still returns!" These words of a Third World theologian must become part of the story that is told also in our First World. For it is our very self-confidence as children of light and order and *seeming* good that has perpetuated the appalling condition called the Third World. This necessity will again enter our deliberations in chapter 3.

God's Creation Is Good.　God created the world; God created the world "out of nothing"; the world as God's creation is good. This unmistakable theme of creation's goodness not only dominates the first (Priestly) account of creation in Genesis, but it is a supposition permeating the faith of Israel. Whether the newer Testament follows this all-important assumption of its Judaic progenitor is one of the most agonizing questions of the Christian profession of faith. The ambiguity about this world, to which I have already drawn attention, is undoubtedly present in some of the sentiments expressed by the

---

60. In his long and illuminating discussion of *creatio ex nihilo,* Moltmann draws what is to my mind the appropriate soteriological conclusion from this teaching of the church when he writes: "The eternal God enters the Nothingness out of which he created the world. God enters that 'primordial space' which he himself conceded through his initial self-limitation. He pervades the space of God-forsakenness with his presence. It is the presence of his self-humiliating, suffering love for his creation, in which he experiences death itself. That is why God's presence in the crucified Christ gives creation eternal life, and does not annihilate it." (*God in Creation,* 91.) This accurately identifies the connection between the *creatio ex nihilo* concept and the *theologia crucis.*

newer Testament—for example, James's blatant, "know ye not that friendship of the world is enmity with God?" (4:4, KJV).[61] The question is, is it basic?

Provisionally (because this is not yet the time to give ourselves unreservedly to that knotty question) I answer that it is not basic. While an anti-world attitude hovers on the fringes of newer Testamental faith, it cannot touch the core—that is, the theology of the incarnation and humiliation of the Word. Over against its own hesitancy about world-affirmation, the central declaration of the newer Testament's *koinonia* is the message of Calvary—that "God so loved the world . . . " (John 3:16). So fundamental is this divine orientation *toward* the world that even that Gospel account most influenced by Hellenizing tendencies is driven to express it, and in language that is both unambiguous and memorable. For God, at least, the world in its essence is so very good that it cannot and must not be abandoned; it must be redeemed. This is the "must" that rings throughout the newer Testament's so-called predictions of the passion. "The Son of Man *must* suffer. . . ." And why? Because the Father—the Creator—will not withdraw from the world, will not forsake it, will not give it up to the annihilating processes that are at work within it; will, on the contrary, personally assume the anguish that must be borne by anyone seeking to mend the world. And why? Because the world is very good.

This essential goodness of the creation certainly does not mean that the tradition of Jerusalem is naive about evil and suffering. We have just been at some pains to accentuate that tradition's sensitivity toward that which negates. The declaration of creation's goodness is made by the God of this tradition in full view, as it were, of the darkness and chaos that "is still there and still returns." What the declaration of creation's goodness rules out is that finitude as such constitutes the locus of the negating element. On the contrary, while the Hebrew-Christian tradition affirms that the peculiar temptations of earth and its creatures are bound up with their being material and finite (how could it be otherwise?), materiality and finitude as such do not constitute humanity's "bondage to decay" (Rom. 8:21). When Paul employs that provocative phrase, he is not thinking of the aging and disintegration that belongs to our *sarx* (flesh) as such; rather, he is thinking of the temptations and anxieties that play upon these physical realities—spiritual temptations and anxieties of the *psyche* (soul).

Since we are finite, limited in power, in need of food and warmth and shelter, craving sexual expression and procreation, conscious of existing as "being-towards-death" (Heidegger), the temptations and anxieties to which our creaturely consciousness opens us will as a matter of course be connected with

---

61. It must be said at once that such passages frequently (and this is a case in point) have reference to the world (*kosmos*) as it is defiled by human sin, not the creation as such. Christian pietism, however, has consistently found in such declarations a sufficient basis for its other-worldliness.

these physical realities. Presumably the temptations and anxieties of angels are something else! We are not angels but creatures of flesh and blood and gland; therefore the choices within which the love of God sets us are related to our actual, physical-psychological life. To what else could they be related? But this does not mean that the choice of the forbidden, the demonic, the death-prone—in short, sin—is determined by our enfleshment. Finitude is the condition for human sin because it is our human condition, but sin and finitude are by no means synonymous or inevitably correlated.[62] Something else has to enter the picture for the creation that is "very good" in all of its finitude to actualize the potential for evil. And that something else, as we shall see more fully when we discuss human being, is a thing of the spirit.

Again, however, it must be asked whether this biblical affirmation of creation's essential goodness as God's own work has been faithfully professed within the dominant traditions of the church; and I think that it must be said in all honesty that it has not. At very least, popular Christianity has failed grievously in this respect. Generations of Christians—and not only the illiterate, premodern masses—have simply assumed that everything connected with matter is tainted. Archbishop William Temple was quite right when he pronounced that Christianity is the world's most materialistic religion.[63] It is that, for it finds the material world to be God's own good work. More than that, it declares in its doctrine of incarnation that God, even God, who "is spirit" (John 4:24), does not despise materialization when the good destiny of the world is at stake.

While this may be true of the biblical rudiments of our faith, however, and of those exponents of the faith who have been moved, as Temple was, by the Bible's primal affirmation of the world, it has been far from dominant in the broad stream of the Christian profession. Attachment to this world; the love of nature; the satisfactions of the body; joie de vivre—the sheer exuberance of living; an appreciation for "the infinitely various, lovely fecundity of concrete existence":[64] all this has had to find expression outside or alongside that broad stream. And, as might be expected, it has frequently found expression in melancholy and sometimes tragic ways; for when the flesh has discovered its way barred to the sanctuary, it has often made unholy alliances with other reputedly supernatural forces, all the way from witches' sabbaths to contemporary "hard rock" and the drug culture.

In all of this we discern a strong propensity to equate sin and finitude. Perhaps such an equation is understandable: It is simpler to say that sin resides in the flesh and righteousness in the spirit that resists the flesh than to embrace

---

62. See Farley, *Tragic Vision and Divine Compassion*, 124.
63. *Nature, Man and God* (London: Macmillan and Co., 1951), 478.
64. Farley, *Tragic Vision and Divine Compassion*, 59.

a biblical faith that thinks in more psychosomatic terms about both sin and righteousness. But when the simpler path is followed it results in the undoing of the whole biblical tradition, beginning with its Theology. It represents a move from Jerusalem to Athens—or rather to that stream of Greco-Roman thought that distrusts materiality, while being fascinated by it.

This raises one of the most salient questions the Christian movement has to face in our time. Today as never before in Western history, as I have maintained in the first volume,[65] the question put to all human beings is, What is your attitude toward *this world?* The urgency of this question derives from the multifaceted prospect that, in the absence of positive, responsible, and enthusiastic affirmation of the world on the part of human cults and cultures, it is likely that civilization will perish; for the means are at hand to dispense with a world for which no operative raison d'être can be discovered. In this discussion of creation we have seen that the tradition of Jerusalem demands of those who profess the faith an unambiguous affirmation of creation and creaturehood. Against the whole antiworld impulse of so much religion, including prominent neoapocalyptic and other movements in North America today; against the nihilistic tendencies in so much of human society generally, biblical faith compels us to profess creation's fundamental goodness, both in word and deed. To profess that fundamental goodness, however, does not mean to ignore or minimize the actual evil and radical suffering present in the world; and therefore the celebration of existence currently popular in liberal middle-class contexts can be a very shallow affair.

In view of this, the question we are to carry with us as we move from God's work of creation to that of preservation, to state it in the most direct way, is: How under the conditions of our present context can we learn how to say "Amen" to the Creator's "very good," recognizing that this is not to be equated with the smug bourgeois approval of our own favored life-style? Or, to put the question more technically: How can Christians in North America today express a theology of creation which, without simply celebrating the status quo and without obscuring our complicity in the forces that are destroying the planet, affirms the reality, order, beauty, and goodness of the world as God's own work?

3.2. Preservation

A Matter of Faith. Christians profess that God not only created the world but that the world is sustained by God. God's preservation of the creation is a profession of faith; therefore where it has been profound it has not involved the disciple community in a rush for evidence of divine preservation. Where faith

---

65. *Thinking the Faith,* chap. 3, 197ff.

did not satisfy, the evidence that has been proffered has usually consisted of variations on the theme of the steadfast and purposeful order of nature. This in turn has encouraged the thought that those who are able to discern nature's order will be enabled thereby to benefit personally: they will not only be preserved but they will prosper.

This deuteronomic conception of the workings of providence was, however, rejected by the prophetic and wisdom traditions of Israel, which recognized how frequently the evil prosper and the good are given up to failure, defeat, and torments of soul. The so-called pessimistic wisdom literature, especially Job, made this its particular theme, and in the Beatitudes Jesus recapitulates the whole prophetic distrust of such a conception of the *providentia Dei* when he declares, "Blessed are you when people revile you and persecute you and utter all kinds of evil against you falsely on my account. Rejoice and be glad, for your reward is great in heaven" (Matt. 5:11-12). In other words, the divine preservation of creation follows a pattern and a logic very different from what is assumed by human self-seeking. Like the profession of creation, faith's profession of the divine preserving of life is truly a matter of faith, not of sight (2 Cor. 5:7).

Providentia Dei *and the Religion of Progress.* The Christian teaching concerning God's preservative work can be appreciated fully only if it is viewed over against the alternative that it negates, namely that the world is a product of chance and is self-sustaining. The concept of divine providence does not deny that there are laws of nature and that these laws are oriented toward the preservation of life. Biblical faith gives full assent to the future-thrust that is present in all of nature. Long before Darwin, the tradition of Jerusalem knew something of this rudimentary quest for survival inherent in the plant and animal world: they multiply; they have their seeds within them (Genesis 1). This too belongs to the goodness of creation that is celebrated by our tradition.

However, contrary to Deism and to every view that assumes that the preservational dimension is simply inherent in the process as such, biblical faith insists upon the active agency of God in the preservation of creation. Laws there certainly are, but the laws are *means* of God's preserving work, not in themselves the final cause. The existence of natural laws does not warrant the conclusion that the life process is *sui generis*. When faith considers the world it does not see day and night, seedtime and harvest, birth, maturation, and death, the succession of generations, and so on, as though it were all a matter of course. Behind the conformity and continuity of nature, faith professes the faithfulness of God.

Historical theology has often been at pains to secure this priority. Thus Calvin, who in his discussion of divine providence in the *Institutes* no doubt carries his point too far, while giving due respect to the sun as the most "wonderful" and "illustrious" of all the creatures, notes that "the Lord, to reserve the praise of all these things entirely to himself, was pleased that the light should exist, and the earth abound in every kind of herbs and fruits, before he created the sun."[66] Luther makes essentially the same point in a more down-to-earth way when, in his commentary on Psalm 111, he writes:

> Here the Psalmist indicates how few are the righteous who consider or see these works of the Lord. They neither praise nor give thanks, not even when they say, "Great are the works of the Lord." They are used to them and saturated with them, like an old house with smoke. They use them and root around in them like a hog in a bag of feed. They say, "Oh, is that such a great thing that the sun shines, or fire warms, or water gives fish, or the earth yields grain, or a cow calves, or a woman bears children, or a hen lays eggs? That happens every day." My dear Mr. Simpleton, is it a small thing just because it happens every day? If the sun did not shine for ten days, then it would be a great thing.[67]

Above all, the Christian profession of divine preservation resists the conclusion to which, under the impact of modernity, many were led, namely, that the process as such is oriented not only toward survival but toward enhancement and perfection. That the Christian doctrine of divine providence could be transmuted into the "Religion of Progress" (George P. Grant) only indicates that the dominant forms of Protestantism in North America had ceased to have any vital awareness of the Reformation's radical theology of grace.[68] Providence, as the word itself indicates, means that the continuance of life in the face of death, of order in the face of chaos, of plenty in the face of want is a matter of sheer grace. Nothing at all, not even the most steadfast-seeming phenomena of the natural order (that the sun will rise, or that spring will follow winter) can be taken for granted. Nature is sustained by grace. While nature's steadfastness can be relied upon for practical purposes, there is no cause for human presumption in this. The habit of such reliance, unless it is accompanied by gratitude and care, is misguided and dangerous. For if nature is reliable it is because God, its Preserver, is not capricious but faithful. Apart from gratitude to God, human beings are prone to presumption in their attitude toward creation; and between presumption and arrogance there is a very fine line—a truth whose evidence is all too plain in our ecologically threatened context.

---

66. Book 1, chap. 16, trans. John Allen (Philadelphia: Presbyterian Board of Christian Education, n.d.), 220.

67. Jaroslav Pelikan, ed., *Luther's Works,* vol. 13 (St. Louis: Concordia, 1956), 366–67.

68. Moltmann asks: "Isn't history, pictured as progress, always at the same time an instrument of domination—the domination of one society, one class and the one, present generation, as instrument used to suppress all the others and take possession of them? And isn't history, pictured as progress, also an instrument for subjecting nature to the will and intentions of human beings?" (*God in Creation,* 125.) The question is particularly apt in the North American setting.

It was on the basis of such reflection that the reformers and others were liable to exclaim that if God for an instant neglected the care and nurture of creation it would simply disintegrate. Modernity smiled at such a thought. The whole of modern scientific and technological literature is filled with references to the former naiveté of the race, which in its innocence imagined that "the gods" were necessary to the ordinary workings of the life of the world.

Intentionally, I speak in the past tense. There are of course many in our midst who still profess that modern credo, and who smile at the Christian profession as at other "primitive" explanations of the cosmos. But some of our contemporaries, including many who have been at the cutting edge of the natural sciences,[69] are less prone to condescension now. They know that the modern credo takes at least as much psychic energy to sustain as does the most primitive providentialism. What can be taken for granted about the continuation of a world like ours? What laws of nature are so eternal that they can defy the rapaciousness of the developers or the revenge of societies caught up in nuclear madness and in consumerism? Moreover, are there not, besides those laws upon which modernity depended so one-sidedly, other forces that are less favorably disposed to its optimistic outlook?—processes that point up the inevitable consequences of the rape and defilement of nature by a civilization that has forgotten the rudiments of gratitude and care? It may indeed be childlike at the end of the twentieth century to insist that it is only the divine love that keeps our world from falling apart; but many of earth's most thoughtful children have had to conclude that, in the face of human destructiveness and arrogance, such naiveté may not be far from the truth. At a time when it is possible to sense the proximity of the disintegrative thrust at every turn, it requires more than confidence in nature's laws and human technical know-how to hope for the continuing future of the planet, and particularly the future of its human inhabitants.

Divine Providence and Human "Dominion." That the world is being preserved from beyond its own internal processes is a profession of faith, then, and it is made over against the presumption that the future is simply guaranteed. To this we now add a third aspect of the Christian teaching concerning God's preservative work, one that has to do with the role of the human creature in the divine preservation of creation. As such it is one of the many places where Theology cannot avoid the fact that the Christian profession of faith is "theoanthropological" (Barth) throughout.

---

69. See, e.g., J. C. Polkinghorne, *Science and Providence: God's Interaction with the World* (London: SPCK, 1989); *The Particle Play: An Account of the Ultimate Constituents of Matter* (Oxford: W. H. Freeman, 1979); and Arthur Peacocke, *Religion Can Help the World: A Symposium* (London: World Congress of Faiths, n.d.).

Clearly, it is unthinkable that the biblical tradition could ever have envisaged a scenario in which God would not be necessary to the everyday life of the world. Even if the human creature had become the kind of responsible steward of earth that the Creator obviously intended, the Theological as well as the anthropological assumptions of the tradition would require us to think of God's sovereignty in terms of a constant, overseeing care: the Monarch as Shepherd (Psalm 23). The human role, even if it had been taken up as it was evidently intended by the Creator, is after all strictly limited. The great movements of the planets and stars, the astonishing and scarcely known forces and interactions of nature, the underlying cosmic "laws": these are not the prerogative of humanity, even in its "pre-fallen" conception (Job 38–41). We can speak here only of a covenant-partnership, and it is evident from the outset that the tradition regards the human creature as the junior partner.

Yet it is equally plain that such a partnership is intended, and that therefore the preservation of the world as conceived by biblical faith is a work shared by the Creator and that creature who is the articulate center of the creation. The ill-fated word "dominion" (Genesis 1; Psalm 8) should be heard in this connection. Human dominion means in the first instance humanity's participation in God's preserving work. It is humanity's stewardship of that part of creation to which the human creature has access.

This is the Creator's intention. But whether we rely upon the third chapter of Genesis (as Christianity has done rather too exclusively) or take a more inclusive view of Scripture and tradition, it will be evident that the Christian past is exceptionally unanimous in its belief that the divine intention for humanity has been and is thwarted. Over against the possibility of participating in God's preservation of the whole creation, the human creature chooses narrow self-preservation. This not only means that the biblical God can no longer rely upon the human partner in the sustaining of life; it means that God must, as it were, take the destructive consequences of this creature's choices into account in God's providential work. Having desired a creature who could freely share the divine love for the good creation, God had to risk the prospect of the creature's antithetical choice. Since the latter is the choice out of which historical humanity habitually lives, according to biblical faith, God in the present dispensation has not only to sustain the ordinary workings of nature but also to engage in an *extra*ordinary work: the transforming of the negations brought about by human mismanagement, exploitation, and hostility in relation to extrahuman and human creation.

The preservation of a fallen creation already anticipates the divine work of redemption; for with the anticreational activity of the human species, annihilating powers are unleashed that are over and above the merely limiting aspects of creation's finite vulnerability. With the refusal of the steward's role and the assumption, on the contrary, of a false mastery over the earth, and/or an equally false withdrawal from earthly responsibility, the human creature has activated the negating potentiality within finitude ("the fall of creation"). Hence God's preserving work in a creation fallen from the divine intention is virtually indistinguishable from God's redemptive work. It is now no longer a matter simply of sustaining the life of the creation; it is rather one of transforming the annihilating impulses set in motion by the human will—of causing even "the wrath of man to praise thee" (Ps. 76:10, KJV).[70]

Just here we may introduce the question that contemporary Christians inherit from the church's historical appropriation of this aspect of the profession of faith. The tendency of all conservative forms of Christianity has been to place such a strong emphasis upon the sinful, fallen nature of the human creature that any thought of a continuing vocation to preserve the creation as God's covenant-partner has had little chance to flourish. Particularly where "the fall" could be regarded as an actual event in time, the preservation of the world in its post-fallen condition has depended almost exclusively upon the sovereign God in these expressions of the tradition. Even where such renditions of Christian doctrine have stressed the responsibility of "the saved" among the human race (as in Calvinism), the stress has usually fallen so exclusively upon the divine initiative that our human responsibility for the earth has not been adequately explored.

In reaction against this and other aspects of conservative traditions, liberal Christianity tried to discover the human potentiality for earthly responsibility. The theology of stewardship is, not accidentally, coincidental with the liberal movement, and it is almost wholly a North American emphasis. But this commendable enough attempt to explore human powers for preserving the life of the world was and is rendered rather ineffectual by two notorious weaknesses: it fails to take seriously enough the residual selfishness of the community of the redeemed, and it identifies itself too uncritically with the anthropological and societal values of modernity. As conservative Christianity *under*estimates the human capacity for entering into the preserving work of God, so Christian liberalism *over*estimates it. Unlike Judaism, which on the whole seems to have found a way both of confessing the indispensability of divine grace and working as though everything depended upon human vigilance and care, Christianity has wavered between an orthodoxy that turns everything over to the sovereign Deity and a humanistic religiousness that turns everything over to supposedly good and inspired human beings.

The question as it confronts us in connection with this aspect of the Christian profession is, therefore: How can we articulate a doctrine of divine providence without either rendering the activity of human beings superfluous on

---

70. Therefore, the theological concept of divine preservation cannot be conceived adequately as the sustaining of the original creation; and Moltmann is quite right in insisting that preservation is not just *creatio continua* but *creatio nova* (*God in Creation*, 209).

the one hand, or making it too readily and naively continuous with the divine preservation of the world on the other?

3.3. Redemption.   The work of redemption is the basic subject matter of the third part of this volume. It will not be so fully treated in the present chapter, therefore, as were the works of creation and preservation.

At the same time, it is a mistake (and one that frequently finds expression in Christian literature) to subsume the whole discussion of redemption in the Christian tradition under Christology. Obviously for Christians the supreme statement of God's redeeming work is and must be a christological statement—a position that we have adopted here in our presentation of the triune nature of God's being. But apart from the most christomonistic renderings of the Christian profession of faith, the tradition has always acknowledged that redemption is, after all, the work of God; and while it has concentrated upon the second person of the Trinity in this connection, it has hardly been able, given the trinitarian unity, to separate the work of the Son and the work of the Father. As the dogma of perichoresis (or coinherence) has insisted, the unity theme within the trinitarian doctrine implies that in the working of each "person" the other "persons" are also at work.

A particular reason for wariness against a monopolistic soteriology of the Christ is the fact that from earliest times the story forming the basis of the Christian profession of belief was understood to begin, not with Jesus but with Abraham—or, in a manner of speaking, not with the second Adam but the first. The guardians of our tradition have never been wholly able to forget the consequences for the faith stemming from the Marcionitic attempt to dispense with Israel. Not only Jesus himself but also Paul and the other epistle writers assume the whole long story of God's dealings with Israel as a messianic people, a "priestly nation." To dispense with this is not only to relinquish the sacred texts of the foundational faith but, as the early church discovered to its chagrin, it is to alter the Gospel accounts so significantly that the result is the presentation of a Jesus quite different from the one remembered by the first disciple community. Apart from sporadic attempts to rid Christianity of its Judaic connections, the church has therefore been obliged to recount the story of redemption as an extended narrative, a "holy history" (*Heilsgeschichte*) beginning with the patriarchs and matriarchs of Israel and finding its denouement in the "second Adam," the "son of David," who fulfills God's promises to Abraham, Sarah, and their progeny.

The work of redemption as God's work already begins, then, with that preserving activity of God which, given the divine agape, "must" commence immediately within the fallen creation. In the earlier accounts and doctrines, where one could still assume a historical moment when the fall occurred, this could be associated with the Creator's gracious behavior toward the sinning pair in the Garden. While God might justly have punished them mortally, or left them to the destructive consequences of their own deed, God took pity upon them, clothed them against their own sense of shame, gave them children, allowed their labor to prosper in some real measure (though with pain). Even in later expressions, the tradition has looked upon the adamic beginnings as mythic or symbolic presentations of the redemptive work of God. Nor has that ancient tradition ever quite succumbed which believed that, since God, being omniscient, must have known beforehand that the creature would fall, the fall must somehow have been preordained: the position named supralapsarianism. In other words, the redemptive activity of God commences, perhaps, already prior to history. Or, to state the matter in less provocative terms: redemption is already in the mind of the Creator, for it belongs to the divine essence, which is love. God does not *will* the fall of the creature; yet God graciously anticipates it as one who is able to make of this tragic turn of events a new beginning that is even, perhaps, more glorious than the first.[71]

In Christian supralapsarianism supremely, but to a lesser extent in most other interpretations of the divine work of redemption, the ultimate redemption wrought by and through the Christ is the goal of all God's work in and with Israel. From the outset, the church read the Scriptures of Israel as a process leading to the final enactment of the redemptive plan (*boule*) in the "fullness of time" (Gal. 4:4).

The sermon attributed to Stephen in the seventh chapter of Acts is perhaps the best newer Testamental statement of this perspective. Beginning with God's appearance to Abraham "in Mesopotamia," the writer of Acts has the first Christian martyr recount the whole history of salvation—through Isaac, Jacob, Joseph, Moses, David, and Solomon. His conclusion is that Israel has always rejected the emissaries of God; that the redemption offered by God has not been accepted by Israel; and that once again, with Jesus, Israel has behaved in relation to God's offer of redemption as it always behaved: "'Which of the prophets did not your fathers persecute? And they killed those who announced beforehand the coming of the Righteous One, whom you have now betrayed and murdered, you who received the law as delivered by angels and did not keep it'" (7:52-53, RSV). Nevertheless, far from being a straight denunciation of Stephen's own people, the author understands all of this to have been part of God's redemptive work:

"Men of Israel, hear these words: Jesus of Nazareth, a man attested to you by God with mighty works and wonders and signs which God did through him in

---

71. The supralapsarian position, which developed among the stricter exponents of Calvinism, was bitterly opposed by infralapsarians, who insisted that the divine omniscience must not be interpreted in such a way as to lead to a kind of puppetry on the human scene.

your midst, as you yourselves know—this Jesus, delivered up *according to the definite plan and foreknowledge of God,* you crucified and killed by the hands of lawless men. But God raised him up. . . ."

(Acts 2:22-24, RSV, emphasis added).

It is this handling of the redemptive history as it relates to Israel that evokes for us the question contained in this dimension of our tradition. It is a question that must become one of the most urgent issues of all Christian theology "after Auschwitz."[72] Introducing Rosemary Ruether's seminal study tracing the roots of anti-Judaic bias to Christian theology,[73] Gregory Baum has stated our question in the following way: "Is it possible to purify the Christian message of its anti-Jewish ideology without invalidating the Christian claims altogether?" For the purposes of our present discussion we may refine that question in more explicitly Theological terms: Is it possible to discuss the divine work of redemption in such a way that Jesus remains central in it without superseding God's redemptive activity in and through both ancient and modern Judaism? May it not be, in fact, that the way toward such a discussion can be found by concentrating upon redemption as *God's* work, rather than permitting the whole question of salvation to be subsumed under the aegis of Christology, as has so characteristically occurred?

Within this rather specific question is a more inclusive one. For if Christianity is capable of including Israel in the whole work of divine redemption, it may also find a way of relating to other religions and movements with which, in our pluralistic society, it must certainly be prepared to converse on this subject.

Conclusion

The Christian profession concerning God cannot be limited to the subject matter touched upon in this brief historical interpretation; for God is for this tradition "above all and through all and in all" (Eph. 4:6). Yet the major aspects of the doctrine of God have at least been considered. It is assumed that the serious student of theology would, in the process of reading this chapter, supplement this material with literature from primary and secondary sources. My intention in this chapter has been to provide a brief, overall interpretation of the received tradition on whose basis it would then be possible to engage in meaningful dialogue with the tradition. Chapter 2 will concentrate upon that which, in the author's opinion, contemporary theology in a North American context must view with critical concern in the church's profession of God; and chapter

---

72. See *Thinking the Faith,* 210ff.
73. Ruether, *Faith and Fratricide,* 8.

3 will attempt to build on both the received tradition and the critique of it presented in chapter 2.

One recognizes, of course, some of the hazards of such an approach. It would be all too tempting to find in the received tradition precisely the problems that one intended, from the outset, to correct in the subsequent stages of the argument! This is a problem that must be faced by every theological enterprise, however, no matter how the material is organized. The historical review is never a recitation of sheer fact; it is always a matter of fact-plus-interpretation. I do not doubt that the interpretational dimension is prominent in the foregoing; but, as with all historical and theological thought, the test of its authenticity will depend upon its essential faithfulness to what is known of the past and upon its own internal coherence and integrity.

What we are left with after this summarization of the Christian profession of faith concerning God is a question. It is a many-sided question, of course, but it may be stated in this way: How, given such a doctrinal heritage, can Christians in our present time and place embrace belief in God that stands in continuity with this tradition? That is to say, *essential* continuity. Clearly enough, we do not live in an era that finds belief in God natural. Even though sheer secularity is less attractive to us now than it was mid-century; even though we may indeed be entering a new "age of faith" (Grunwald), an explicitly Christian belief in God cannot be presumed upon. The ages out of which the Christian profession concerning God was shaped were, in comparison with our age, not only ages of belief but predominantly "Christian" ages. Most North Americans are not ready to rush headlong into the disbelief that produced so much of the nihilism of our own epoch. We "mourn the loss of God" (as Samuel Beckett did). But the positivism—or let us say the lack of tentativeness and modesty—that informs the traditional Christian profession of God makes it difficult for most of our contemporaries to join the ages of Christendom in declaring, *"Credo in Deum"* ("I believe in God"). It may be that the need to believe in God has seldom been so keenly experienced among human beings as it is in our own context. But between this human demand and the traditional Christian supply, no conspicuous correlation exists; the laws of supply and demand do not seem to apply here.

To be sure, the truth of the church's profession of God is not to be determined by public opinion. Yet the gospel is intended for humanity, and in all the specificity of its "here and now." How much of our conventional belief in God is of the essence, and how much of it is the accretion of the ages, false scandal, dispensable and dated dogma? What would have to be changed to make this theistic profession accessible to North Americans at the end of their Age of Progress and already more than familiar with the Age of Anxiety? Accessible—not acceptable merely: that is, a spiritual and intellectual statement commanding enough to engage our gnawing quest for mystery and for meaning.

CHAPTER ▪ TWO

Questioning the Father Almighty

4. A Critique of Pure Power

After nearly two thousand years, Christian profession concerning God is sufficiently varied to render generalization hazardous. For every generalization, exceptions can be found that may qualify or disprove the rule. I shall myself presently evince from the long history of Christian God-talk alternative traditions that constitute exceptions to the norm. At the same time, I am prepared to risk assuming that there has been a dominant Theology within the Christian tradition broadly considered. It is certainly not uniform, but it is nonetheless sufficiently widespread as a general approach to deity within Christendom that it may be analyzed, reflected upon, and challenged.

Summarizing the discussion of the previous chapter, and bearing in mind particularly the questions that were registered at the end of each section, I would ask the reader to consider the following critical hypothesis: The Christian doctrine of God has tended to accentuate the aspects of transcendence and power, as befits a patriarchally conceived deity in the service of empire; but in doing so it has severely jeopardized the essence of God testified to in Holy Scripture, and has risked confining belief in God to contexts amenable to "positive religion."

The intention of this chapter will be to demonstrate the plausibility of this thesis. It will do so, first (sections 4 and 5), by engaging in a general critique of power as the primary concept informing the Theological tradition that we have considered in Chapter 1; second (section 6), by reflecting upon the peculiar appropriation of that tradition within the North American context; and finally (section 7), by relating this analysis to other critical Theologies present in theological discourse today. *God vs. Evil*

4.1. The Triumph of Certitude.

Reviewing the preceding discussion of the three basic components of Theological thought (the knowledge, being, and works of God), we are made conscious of the tendency within each component for Christians to enucleate what may be termed an ideological triumph of the positive over the negative elements of the subject under consideration.

In the realm of the knowledge of God, the negative element is of course ignorance. This could mean the simple ignorance of not-knowing, but it could also refer to lack of certitude—to the point of actual doubt. It would be reasonable to suppose that the Christian tradition concerning knowledge of God would oppose to this negative dimension a stronger positive. If the negative dimension alone were present; if doubt were insufficiently countered by its antithesis; if, in short, there were no reliable knowledge of God, or no possibility of confidence in what one believed concerning God, then that would be the end of the matter. We should have had, in that case, no Christian doctrine of God at all. But in relation to what there *has* been by way of a Theology, we must ask: Was it necessary to banish the negative so thoroughly?

As we have seen, all three conventional paths to the knowledge of God have stressed the positive element to the virtual exclusion of the negative: (1) God is Self-revealing, but few have explored the depths of the *concealment* that is entailed in every profound self-revelation. (2) God is the counterpart of our human being and quest, but few of those who formulated for the church the normative outlines of its Theology have pondered how such knowledge of God is affected by our real alienation, our sense of being-alone and being-against. (3) God is the conclusion our minds must reach if they observe the cosmos rationally, but few have struggled with the irrational, the absurd, the contradictory and chaotic dimensions of our human experience of the cosmos, which, at least today, can hardly be ignored.

In short, there has been little space for not-knowing *(agnosis)* and for "existential doubt" (Tillich) in the dominant traditions of the faith concerning the knowledge of God. Or, to speak more accurately, these traditions have too categorically celebrated the victory of knowledge and certitude over ignorance and unbelief. They have not been content to engage in an ongoing dialogue with the antithesis, but have presented the knowledge of God as a finished accomplishment for those who could profess the faith. At best, they have left the impression that agnosticism and doubt (to say nothing of atheism) are pre-Christian or sub-Christian states of mind, which in the community of faith itself should never be conspicuous. The practical consequence of this mode of faith's profession is that the doubt which is actually (and inevitably) present within the church has usually

93

had to suppress itself, thus making for an exaggeration of the rhetoric of belief and opening the door to hypocrisy.

Stating the matter in other terms, the knowledge of God in dominant Christian conventions has received the connotation of *knowing* rather than *believing*. The Greek *pistis* (trust, faith, belief) contains within itself the prospect of disbelief and distrust; for faith involves decision, a decision taken not only once but continuously reconsidered and renewed. Unlike the state of knowledge, faith admits the real and continuing presence of its opposite—if not plain ignorance, at least of never-quite-knowing. Stated more directly, faith is a continuous and unfinished dialogue with doubt.

This is because faith is a category of relationship—as we affirmed in the first volume.[1] The "knowing" that is appropriate to faith is determined by its fundamentally relational character: one knows God in a manner analogous to the way in which one may be said to know another human being. Of such knowledge one may legitimately posit confidence (*con + fide* = "with faith") but not certitude. Where there is certitude the relationship has been violated; the other has been objectified. Where there is certitude faith is unnecessary; it has been replaced by "sight," to use the Pauline distinction. But "sight" is not a possibility this side of the consummation of the Reign of God: "we walk by faith, not by sight" (2 Cor. 5:7).

Because of the association of the knowledge of God with certitude and noetic conclusiveness, it has in fact been singularly difficult and rare in the Christian church to think of God in terms of faith. For precisely as a category of relationship faith is also an eschatological concept: that is, it describes a state of hope that anticipates consummation but is perennially denied it as an accomplished reality. Because the relationship with God, like all relationships, is an ongoing one, and one that has always to be reaffirmed and reconstituted by the Spirit in the face of the remnants of mistrust and autonomy in the souls of the faithful, faith contains a future orientation: it may be experienced as sufficient (Hebrews 11), yet like love—including the love of God by which it is evoked—faith longs for a consummation that, itself, it can neither compel nor ensure.

It is perhaps no wonder, therefore, that the Christian religion has regularly substituted knowing for believing, credulity for faith. One could say that religion as distinct from discipleship is primarily characterized precisely by this substitution. Yet this religious ineptitude for faith, this need to embrace a knowledge of God from which the negative components have been eliminated in favor of an unassailable positive, has profoundly affected not only the Christian understanding of faith itself but also the Christian profession of belief concerning the One in whom faith is placed. If the mode of knowing

---

1. *Thinking the Faith*, 248f.

God is one that discourages the contemplation of God's actual hiddenness and inaccessibility, this already contains a decisive statement about the nature of the Deity. What it precludes is the ineffable otherness of God. Only faith—that is, faith understood as trust within the context of relationship—enables the disciple community to preserve a Theology that takes seriously the mystery and livingness of God. And faith does this just because it does not attempt to overcome the negating dimensions inherent in the knowledge of God (doubt, distance, lack of certitude), but rather takes these dimensions up into itself. "Lord, I believe *[pisteuo]*; help thou mine unbelief *[apistia]*" (Mark 9:24, KJV).

The phenomenon of "true belief" that is so prevalent in North American popular Protestantism is an ironic testimony to the failure of classical Protestantism on this continent to inculcate the profoundest meaning of the Reformation's guiding principle, *sola fide* (by faith alone). As such, however, it is only one of the many consequences of the subtle transformation of the reformers' theology of the cross into ever new yet ever old and predictable renditions of the theology of glory. The same process that is at work here is also at work in the other two components of conventional Theology.[2]

4.2. Triumph over Nonbeing. That process is particularly visible in connection with the traditional presentations of the being of God. The negative that corresponds to the category of being is nonbeing; it can also be identified as anything that detracts from the fullness of being or threatens or negates being: death, obviously, but also finitude, weakness, suffering, vulnerability, inconclusiveness or lack of centeredness, and so on. As with the category of knowledge, it was obviously necessary for Christians to present their God as one in whose being the threat of nonbeing is at every point being overcome. Without this, no Christian Theology as such would have come to be—or at best it should have emerged as a dualistic Theology. But again one must ask: Was it necessary to achieve, in God's behalf, so overwhelming a victory of being over nonbeing?

The most conspicuous expression of this victory is the doctrine of the resurrection of the Christ. God in Christ encounters, supremely at Golgotha, the ultimate nonbeing—traditionally, not only death but also the dominion of death: hell. The resurrection of the Christ is decisive in this Theology because it affirms that precisely in the encounter with ultimate nothingness God is ultimately victorious: Death cannot hold the source of life (1 Cor. 15:55).

---

2. This is part of what Dietrich Bonhoeffer had in mind when, upon his return to Germany from the United States in 1939, he wrote about Protestantism on this continent under the title, "Protestantism Without Reformation." The text of Bonhoeffer's essay is reproduced in John de Gruchy, *Dietrich Bonhoeffer: Witness to Jesus Christ* (London: Collins, 1987).

There can be no question that the resurrection of the crucified one is therefore foundational for the Christian conception of God. Where questioning must be engaged in, however, is where the resurrection of the Christ constitutes in God's behalf a triumph so complete, immediate, and unparadoxical that it effectively displaces the cross and supercedes the whole story of the crucified one, upon whose passion the newer Testamental witness clearly and (we must believe) purposely concentrates. And that propensity within the received traditions of Christendom is both intense and almost unrelieved.

The price that is paid for this Theological victory is virtual removal of the Christian God from the sphere of the continuing struggle of being and nonbeing that is the actual substance of historical existence. God emerges from the tussle with death and hell as one who is above it. But we are not above it, obviously enough; and the "divine pathos" (Heschel) that led the loving God toward solidarity with us is exchanged in this Theology for the kind of transcendence that simply displaces everything intended by the incarnation and humiliation of the divine Word. The resurrectionism[3] that colors most forms of Christianity on the North American continent is a late adaptation of this long-standing tendency of Christian Theology to remove the cross from the heart of God. It makes for a religion that is attractive to those within our society who are still moved by success stories, or are neurotically incapable of contemplating failure; but it is inaccessible to all who are (perhaps newly)[4] conscious of the incredibility of most unalloyed success stories.

While the triumph of being over nonbeing is expressed most graphically and centrally in a resurrectionism that is shaped by the theology of glory, it is already present in the usual description of the Deity according to the divine attributes or perfections. God is depicted as one who, unlike us, does not exist under the threat of nonbeing in any of its manifestations. Thus, the divine power (omnipotence) is not challenged by any lack or weakness; the divine knowledge (omniscience) is not circumscribed by ignorance, uncertainty, or inherent limitation; the divine presence (omnipresence) is not subject to the constraints of

---

3. I use the term "resurrectionism" intentionally to distinguish this phenomenon, which is a blend of cultic-folkloric heroism, New World optimism, and religious triumphalism, from the Christian theology of the resurrection of Jesus Christ.

4. While the theme of success still bedevils North American society, rendering the "downs" of personal and corporate life all the more shocking and unacceptable, imaginative literature in both Canada and the United States has throughout this century mirrored the sense of failure that is never far from the surface of human consciousness and becomes a prominent sociological factor in times of economic recession like the present. In his recent best-seller, *Hocus Pocus,* Kurt Vonnegut draws attention to this dichotomy of contemporary America: "This library is full of stories of supposed triumphs, which makes me very suspicious of it. It's misleading for people to read about great successes, since even for middle-class and upper-class white people, in my experience, failure is the norm. It is unfair to youngsters particularly to leave them wholly unprepared for the monster screwups and starring roles in Keystone Kop comedies and much, much worse." (New York: Berkley Books, 1990, p. 33.)

time and space; and God is not vulnerable to change or prey to passions that may be aroused by any external eventuality (immutability). Indeed, so consistently have such attributes been associated with the Deity that it has been extremely difficult for Christians to reflect upon God, "the Father Almighty," according to the primary categories of biblical Theology, which, as many have pointed out, are not categories of pure power; or, to be more exact, they are categories that in themselves entail a subordination of power as it is normally conceived to its apparent opposite, weakness.[5]

The reference here, as was intimated in chapter 1, is primarily to holiness and love. Both of these biblical categories represent an enormous critical challenge to the whole power orientation of historical Christian Theology. This is most obvious in the case of divine love, that is, agape or "*suffering* love" (Aúlen). As soon as God loves—loves, namely, a world and creatures whose condition is that of being-threatened-by-nonbeing—then God too must be seen to participate vicariously in nonbeing. For love, if it is genuine, assumes as its own the condition of the beloved. The loving God of the Bible is evidently not interested in a personal triumph of being over nonbeing, but only in a triumph that incorporates the salvation of the beloved; and that is no facile matter.

As for the divine holiness, it is not to be conceived of as awe-inspiring grandeur, as of great worldly potentates, but as the mysterious otherness of one who, without having to, dwells with the humble and meek.

> For thus says the high and lofty one
>> who inhabits eternity,
>> whose name is Holy;
> I dwell in the high and holy place,
>> and also with those who are contrite
>> and humble in spirit,
> to revive the spirit of the humble,
>> and to revive the heart of the contrite.
>
> (Isa. 57:15)

---

5. "One of Luther's most profound insights was that God made Himself small for us in Christ. In so doing, He left us our freedom and our humanity. He showed us His Heart, so that our hearts could be won.

"When we look at the misery of our world, its evil and its sin, especially in these days which seem to mark the end of a world period, we long for divine interference, so that the world and its daemonic rulers might be overcome. We long for a king of peace within history, or for a king of glory above history. We long for a Christ of power. Yet if *He* were to come and transform us and our world, we should have to pay the *one* price which we could not pay: we would have to lose our freedom, our humanity, and our spiritual dignity. Perhaps we should be happier; but we should also be lower beings, our present misery, struggle, and despair notwithstanding. . . . Those who dream of a better life and try to avoid the Cross as a way, and those who hope for a Christ and attempt to exclude the Crucified, have no knowledge of the mystery of God and of man." Paul Tillich, *The Shaking of the Foundations* (New York: Charles Scribner's Sons, 1953), 148.

In short, God's holiness is inseparable from God's love—*is* God's love, apprehended in awe by love's always unworthy recipients.

Both holiness and love thus enter a profound biblical judgment against the "religious" propensity to depict deity in terms of sheer power. Every one of the "attributes of transcendence" (Berkhof) is assessed by the criterion of the love enacted upon the cross, and, in their characteristic presentation in the annals of Christendom, they are found wanting.

What shall we say of the Trinity in this respect? We have considered the doctrine of the Trinity Christianity's supreme statement of God's being; but, looked upon from the vantage point of critical theology, the Trinity too may require further reflection. In fact, it raises one of the most perplexing questions of our subject: Was the doctrine of the Trinity as it emerged in some sense an attempt to acknowledge the divine participation in the negation of being, but without in the end necessitating a Theology centrally and fundamentally colored by this participation? As we have seen earlier, resurrection theology has frequently been used to extricate God from any continuing struggle with that which negates or detracts from fullness of being. Is the Trinity as a whole susceptible to this same "religious" impulse?

There is, I think, some cause for suspecting that classical Eastern Theology was conditioned in part by such an impulse. Even the danger of tritheism could be courted, if only the transcendent God could be kept transcendent. Western Christendom chose another route. It knew that the unity of God must be maintained—that diversity is also a potential threat to being, for the line between diversity and diffusion is difficult to sustain. So the West settled for a highly integrated deity, even though this meant that its God (in God's second "mode") must be brought very near to earth and all that is earthy.

Yet the almightiness of the Western heavenly Father did not suffer ultimately from this proximity to creaturely ambiguity, finitude, suffering, and death; for what the West risked in its exegesis of the *being* of God it regained in its discussion of God's *work*. It was necessary for the triumph of God's redemptive work (Athanasius had insisted upon it) that the Son, *homoousios* with the Father, should also be *homoousios* with respect to human being. For the sake of a soteriological triumph over the negative in humanity's behalf, a (temporary) christo-ontic identity with the finite is required. This is perhaps a gain over a purely transcendental (and usually docetic) rendering of the Christ-event. But it does not mean that in the West there was a greater willingness than in the East to let the positive and negative within the heart of God struggle together still. On the contrary, it was for the sake of an end to the struggle that the unity of the divine being was emphasized over against its hypostatic diversity, and the Christ's triumph over nonbeing thus rendered a triumph of the full godhead.

Western Christian liberalism may be thought, on the surface of it, to constitute an exception to this analysis. After all, did not liberalism make precisely *love* the core of its Theology?

While it is common to think of the liberal accentuation of divine love as an explicit, or at least implicit, critique of power, what such an assessment obscures is the triumphalism precisely of "love" in liberal Theology. The prominence of the language of love in religion is never self-explanatory. It is always necessary to ask what love implies concretely, how it manifests itself, what it exacts both of its giver and its receiver. The truth is, nothing in the liberal exposition of divine love is so conspicuous as its *power*. Love conquers all. What Kitamori has called the "monism of love" in liberal Christianity may indeed represent the final triumph over nonbeing in Christian Theology. Traditional orthodoxy in Theology, however fixated on the power principle, could never quite avoid the unsettling paradox of love and justice (not to mention judgment and even wrath) in its reflections on the being of God. When the liberals opted for a nonjudgmental love as the guiding principle of their Theology, they abandoned that ancient paradox and, with it, the vestiges of a continuing struggle within the divine person. We shall return to this consideration in subsequent discussion.

4.3. The Triumph of Finality. The same tendency to overwhelm the negative is present in every phase of the traditional discussion of God's work. The Creator God, contrary to the ambiguity of the pentateuchal antecedents, does not wrestle with a negating something-or-other in the act of creation, but creates out of a "nothing" that is either neutral or simply nonexistent. The Preserving God of the dominant tradition is not involved in a limiting partnership with the human element but causes the movements of history to display God's will and serve God's purposes, as befits an absolute sovereign. Above all, as was said earlier in connection with the resurrection, the Redeemer God effects a triumph over all that negates (sin, death, devil).

Moreover, while the tradition regularly makes room for a future-oriented eschatology in terms either of a heavenly or an earthly consummation and manifestation of the triumph, or both, all the dominant conventions of Christian theology clearly favor a realized eschatology, in which the divine work is truly finished already and remains only to be displayed to full view and acknowledged universally. The "not yet" of the modern "already/not yet" exposition of eschatology has seldom achieved the attention paid to the "already."

Again, one must certainly admit that nothing could have come of a religion that made too much of the negation of God's work, or offered the "negation of the negation" only in vaguely proleptic terms, as a matter of promise ungrounded in remembrance. One must nevertheless once more ask: Was it necessary to negate the negation so unstintingly as has occurred in our doctrines of creation, preservation, and (especially) redemption? Was it imperative that the negating realities of existence should be so thoroughly put to flight as they are (for example) in most theories of atonement, especially the two so-called classical/objective theories? Or, to state the matter more explicitly, was it mandatory so consistently to replace the category of *promise* (the primary eschatological category of Israel's faith) with that of *fulfillment?* Could the gospel not have been announced more faithfully from the outset as a Theology of hope?—that is, with hope as a fundamental earmark of the doctrine of God, and not just an aspect of theology in general.

The danger of a Theology in which the divine work is already triumphant over all obstacles is that it requires of believers that they dismiss from their consciousness everything that could constitute a contradiction of such a creed. We shall acknowledge in a moment that there is something within the human psyche that is positively attracted to this type of religion, and even demands it. Beyond that, we must recognize its particular appeal within our own social context. Our argument, however, in keeping with the discussion of repression in the first volume,[6] will be that the conscious or subconscious elimination of contradictory evidence not only involves a falsification process within the life of belief but constitutes a possibility only where the external and internal circumstances of human existence are amenable to the repressive impulse. Under relatively stable social and personal conditions, people may give themselves to a doctrine of God in which every trace of tentativeness and incompleteness is denied: God is clearly in charge, God's will is being done, God's plan is visibly efficacious, and so on. But in the first place such a determination always entails a highly selective approach to experienced reality, and in the second place it is a viable approach only under favorable contextual conditions. In the First World generally, and in North America particularly, the extent to which this kind of Theology has been dependent upon economic stability alone is very great; and even in the First World— finally even in North America—a spiritual and intellectual climate has come to be that is increasingly inhospitable to a God who is unambiguously "Lord of the Dance."

Obviously enough, the Christian testimony to God must be based upon the confidence that God is at work in the world and that God's work is decisive for the fate of the world. But the Christian profession will only acquire depth and credibility if and when it is able to undertake this testimony in the full knowledge and acknowledgment of that which calls the whole witness into question. Both within and beyond the disciple community, the profession of faith in God will be tested for its authenticity, not so much by its ability to squelch every

---

6. *Thinking the Faith,* chap. 2, especially 174f., 182f.

contradictory piece of evidence as by its readiness to open itself to the contradictions and, in the face of them, to utter its "Nevertheless."

5. Reasons for the Ideological Triumph of the Positive

Summarizing the discussion thus far, we may suggest that: (1) in its zeal to present the knowledge of God as a triumph over ignorance and doubt, historic Christendom forfeited the language of *faith;* (2) in its zeal to present the being of God as a triumph over nonbeing, historic Christendom forfeited the language of *suffering love;* (3) in its zeal to present the work of God as a triumph over evil, death, and sin, historic Christendom forfeited the language of *hope.* Or, to speak less absolutely, if in each case the language or mode of reflection was not altogether forfeited, neither was it adequately explored and exploited. And, given the centrality of these three categories in biblical thought (and not only in 1 Corinthians 13), one must certainly ask why they were not exploited.

Three types of reasons may be given in response—one from the standpoint of psychic and "religious" considerations; one on the basis of philosophic influences in the life of the early church; and one relating to the political functioning of the Christian profession concerning deity. The first reason belongs to the human condition existentially and can be discerned under all historical conditions. The second reason, like the third, is more expressly historical.

5.1. Human Need for Symbolic Fulfillment. We are asking why Christianity in its Theology developed a picture of God in which, at every point, the positive decisively triumphs. To begin with we do not have to go farther than our own conscious and unconscious human experience for an answer. There is that within us which wants and even needs the positive to triumph and which, precisely because the positive does not obviously triumph in the realities of our daily experience, creates images of triumph that bolster within us the will to affirm life despite its negations and ambiguities—the courage to "go on." Such images may be secular, this-worldly ones, and in recent Western history this has indeed been their characteristic form (for example, the belief that medical and other sciences will overcome all illnesses and threats to life). But historically they have usually been otherworldly, supranatural, and in the usual sense "religious" conceptions of reality. The divine reality is held over against the realities of earthly experience, and the resolution and victory that are absent from mundane experience are affirmed by belief as nonetheless real—as ultimate reality.

"God" thus becomes the symbol of a wholeness, unity, power, majesty, simplicity, righteousness, and wisdom that we lack and for which we long. No god is ever exempt from this human longing for fulfillment, and even human figures or historical events that become the vehicles of this overpowering psychic need for completion tend to lose their creaturely qualities or are frankly apotheosized. Later we may speak of the fate of Jesus in Christendom in just these terms. Every hero from Moses to Lenin has suffered the loss of purely human qualities because humanity demands of its gods and of its substitutes for gods that only the positive should triumph. It would be remarkable indeed if the Christian God had not been subjected to this same psychic-religious need, especially after Christianity had become the religion of a whole civilization; then—at least then—its God had to stand for all that the gods usually stand for.

But the need of which we are speaking predates the Establishment and is present in every historical situation. That the godhead should function as a fulfillment symbol is already well known to biblical literature. Indeed one could say that such a deity is the great option with which biblical Theology struggles from beginning to end. This deity is present not only in the alternative "pagan" religions with which Israel and the new church do battle. The deity who conquers every negating reality is the ever-present alternative god of Israel and of the church. This is the god for whom Israel longs in its wandering in the wilderness; the god whose promptings, despite the prophetic protest, lead to the establishment of the kingship as the earthly model and mirror of heavenly power; the god for whom the heroic warrior, David, comes to stand; the magnificent god whose house Solomon builds; the god whom Satan quotes before Jesus in the wilderness, whom Peter represents on the Mount of the Transfiguration, whom the disciples serve when they vie for prestige in "your kingdom" (Matt. 20:20f.), and so on.

And precisely this is the god by whom Jesus is deserted on Calvary. For prophetic religion, whether of the Hebrew Scriptures or of the faithful church, resists this god steadfastly. Why? Because this god can only produce a people that settles down, secure in the knowledge of the power of its deity, basking in the wake of divine triumph; a people, therefore, that shuts its eyes to the reality of evil, injustice, death, bondage, and sin—especially its own sin; a people that no longer struggles with evil, no longer searches for truth and justice, no longer hungers and thirsts for righteousness, no longer feels an evangelical responsibility for the world.

The God of the prophets and of the crucified one will not have such a people. The God of Pentecost does not aim to achieve a ready-made triumph for the disciple community. That is not the meaning of prevenient grace. God's aim is rather to achieve a victory with the covenant partner—that is, to instill in human beings the courage to be in the face of that which negates being. For, unlike the "Almighty Father" of Christendom tradition (and of so many of this world's religions and quasi-religions), the holy and loving God of biblical tradition does not function to protect "his children" from life, giving them the

[handwritten margin note: God does not cause evil, but is present during suffering.]

consequences of a victory in which they have not participated as combatants; rather, God aims to bring the "children" to maturity, to lead them through suffering and trial to the glad acceptance of their creaturehood and the responsible use of their freedom. Certainly, this is a matter of grace, not of works—of permission, not only of command: without God's own gracious participation in the structures of negation, human beings do not find the will or the courage to enter that struggle. For it is truly not a struggle with flesh and blood but with powers and principalities (Eph. 6:12; Col. 1:16), and with human beings this is impossible (Luke 18:27). Responding faith enters the darkness because it believes the darkness to be inhabited. It believes that even at the darkest hour it will be given light enough. But this is very different from a religion whose God is said to have banished the darkness.

The trouble with "the Father Almighty" is that "he" necessarily belittles those to whose need "he" stoops. The child remains the child; he or she does not become the "friend" of whom Jesus spoke (John 15:15). The Father God does it all for the child and, precisely like the children of overprotective human parents, Christian "children" have too often remained at the level of the child, waiting for the Father's power to effect its miracles and victories, down to the last little need. Meanwhile, the God of the tradition of Jerusalem calls for friends, for covenant partners, for laborers in the vineyard, for stewards.

There can be no doubt that the fulfillment symbol of a deity who has triumphed for us over every negating element is psychically appealing from one standpoint, that of our dependency syndrome. As Feuerbach and, following him, Freud, Marx, and Nietzsche have variously shown, such a theism is deeply rooted in the psychological and social needs of the human creature. But far from condoning these needs and simply supplying what they demand, biblical faith in its prophetic expressions calls for a trust that will enter more consciously and deeply into the negations that are there—into "the rupture of creation";[7] a trust that will find its courage, not by embracing a theological ideology in which all the negations have been negated already, but through believing that the struggle with them is an integral part of their overcoming.

5.2. Transcendence: Athens and Jerusalem. The triumphant deity of Christendom is thus not to be traced solely to historical factors but also to that deep religious longing for fulfillment that will always use whatever is at hand to satisfy its demands. Yet, without the historical influences to which we now move, this longing would surely not have been sufficient to turn the *koinonia* from the wilderness God, the "Abba" of that One who had no place to lay his head, to the settled, opulent monarch of the evolving Christian religion. After

---

7. Wendy Farley, *Tragic Vision and Divine Compassion: A Contemporary Theodicy* (Louisville: Westminster/John Knox Press, 1990), chap. 2.

all, Israel resisted (though with difficulty) capitulation to that deity for centuries, and in spite of the fact that Israel did manage, at times, to become a settled people. Something had to be added to the religious needs of the human psyche to give us the "Father Almighty" of Christendom.

Observing the proper chronology, we may say that the first dimension of this external historical influence comes from the traditions of Greek and Hellenistic religion and philosophy. There can be no doubt that the intellectual and spiritual climate into which early Christianity moved brought the faith ever closer toward a Theology that embraced a "high" account of the divine transcendence. We may mark negative as well as positive reasons for this. On the negative side, serious Christianity did not want to—and as the offspring of Hebraic monotheism, could not—identify itself with popular religions of the polytheistic variety. Positively speaking, it did want—and could in some sense legitimately attempt—to enter into dialogue with the higher philosophic traditions of the Hellenic world: Stoicism, and the Platonic and Aristotelian remnants that, later on, became even more important in their Islamic, Judaic, and Christian revivals.

In these philosophic traditions, the deity is characterized above all by transcendence—partly as a result of the philosophic struggle against popular Hellenistic religions and superstitions of the ancient world. As the career of Arius and most of the Alexandrian school illustrates, the most difficult aspect of Judaic-Christianity for this mentality was its habit of associating the deity too familiarly with creaturehood.

Israel too, of course, believed in God's transcendence: "My thoughts are not your thoughts, nor my ways your ways" (Isa. 55:8). But Israel articulated God's otherness, not in spatial, antimaterial terms, but temporally and ethically. God is the Eternal—the creator of time, not time's captive. God brings to pass what God will bring to pass and makes human wrath the vehicle of divine purposes (Ps. 76:10). God breaks the strict cause-and-effect sequence of historical events, causing *chronos* to bear kairotic meaning, meaning that time has not itself begotten. God is the "high and lofty one who inhabits eternity" and as such communes with the humble and meek (Isa. 57:15). Therefore God's transcendence is to be seen in dialectical tension with God's critical involvement in time. God's love qualifies God's unapproachable majesty: qualifies it, but also serves it. For the wonder of God in Hebraic and biblically Christian profession is precisely that in being *totaliter alliter* (wholly other), God *is* love. In accepting what is not acceptable, in justifying what is not justifiable, in loving what is not lovable, God is . . . different, wholly different.

The philosophic forms in which the tradition of Jerusalem had to be articulated as, with the Christian mission to the Gentiles, it entered into the sphere of Greco-Roman culture, could not endure the vulnerability of such a God. The open-endedness of the working out of God's love and justice; the inevitable proximity of divine and human being (a proximity as much Judaic as Christian); above all, the agapaic suffering that could not be avoided by such a divine orientation and presence: all this was foreign to the spirit of high philosophic thought about deity. The tradition of Athens is very great, but it cannot bear the idea of a suffering God.[8] In the meeting of Athens and Jerusalem, nothing was more at issue than this. And despite the relative victory of soteriology in Western Christendom, the Greek traditions of philosophic Theology have exercised a lasting influence upon empirical Christianity's conception of deity. In most of its historic manifestations, Christianity has never overcome the transcendentalization of its Theology through the encounter with the tradition of Athens. Even in the 1960s, a Christian bishop could startle Christendom by announcing that God is not "up there and out there."[9] Apparently even liberal Protestantism, which seemed to stress the divine immanence to the exclusion, sometimes, of God's transcendence, did not prepare us for this kind of critique.

In fact, while theological liberalism, especially in the North American context, modified classical Theology by sentimentalizing "the Fatherhood of God," it can hardly be said to have entered a serious critique of the power/transcendence principle. The "Father Almighty" may indeed, under the aegis of liberalism, have become (as I put it earlier) "the Grandfather All- Merciful," but there was at least as much power behind the ubiquitous and unquestioning love of this benevolent deity as there was in the more traditional Theologies of the Classical and Reformation periods. Liberalism was no fight against the entrenched triumphalism of Christendom's Theology. Indeed, it would be more accurate to see the liberal revisions of conventional theism as a strategic updating of Theological triumphalism; for neither the Thomistic Final Cause nor the Calvinistic Sovereign God could claim any longer the respect of enlightened modernity. A God of inspiring and uncritical love could command more influence in the world of progressive ideals than could the exacting and distant judge of human perversity known to our Puritan forebears. Ironically, the liberal insistence upon the divine immanence functioned—for a time—to reinstate a waning emphasis upon the transcendent power of God. It was a

---

8. "Greek epistemology was based on the principle of analogy: We come to know something through its resemblance to something already known. If the deity is pictured in terms of power or intelligence or wisdom, then one can hardly recognize God on the cross of Jesus because it displays no trace of power or wisdom. The principle of dialectical knowledge, of coming to know things through their seeming contrary, was not developed by Greek philosophy. That is in marked contrast to the gospel scene of the last judgment, where it turns out that the Son of Man was concealed in the oppressed and needy and persecuted. Greek epistemology could not take account of the surprise needed to recognize God on the cross. . . . It did not envision suffering as a source of knowledge." (Jon Sobrino, *Christology at the Crossroads: A Latin American Approach,* trans. John Drury [Maryknoll, N.Y.: Orbis Books, 1978], 373.)

9. J. A. T. Robinson, *Honest to God* (London: S.C.M. Press, 1963).

variation on a very old theme. For all its sentimentality, it was at base a novel and temporarily effective application of the *theologia gloriae*. [10]

5.3. The Political Co-optation of the Christian Doctrine of God. The all-powerful Father God of Christendom was not created, however, by psychic needs and philosophic associations only. There was a third influence and it seems to me to have been the decisive one. Without it, the prophetic protest against the God of transcendent power could have endured throughout the history of the church as it endured (and endures) throughout the history of Israel. Psychic needs and philosophic conceptions, strong as they may be in molding our views of reality, do not altogether preclude criticism coming from alternative visions and traditions. When, however, these more nebulous spiritual and intellectual influences are accompanied by sociopolitical structures that sustain similar or compatible aims, the prospect of consistent protest is more difficult to mount.

This is precisely what the Establishment of Christianity meant and means. [11] A religion designed to serve the purposes of empire cannot present the spectacle of a God whose kenotic long-suffering detracts from "his" majesty. A less-than-absolute deity; a deity torn between impartial judgment and unwarranted mercy; a deity who "stoops to our weakness" and actually becomes weak for our sake: such is not the blueprint for a god designed for empire, any empire. If the aims of those who, like Arius, were deeply influenced by Greek philosophic Theology were to preserve the Christian God from a compromising participation in mundane materiality, the struggle of Constantine and his theological servants was to exploit the power potential of the Christian God and minimize everything reminiscent of divine vulnerability and self-emptying. An empire founded on military might, carefully layered structures of authority, the subordination of inferiors, and the unity of political intention and order—such an empire simply could not take as its primary religious cultus a faith whose deity struggles

---

10. This ironic aspect of liberalism's Theology is more conspicuous in the art to which it gave rise than in its doctrine. For example, Lloyd C. Douglas's *Magnificent Obsession,* first published in 1932 (Toronto: Thomas Allen Publisher), presents the Christian God, supremely exemplified in Jesus, as the "Great Personality" whose resources may be tapped for the enhancement of our own personalities. It is in fact a very entrepreneurial concept of the deity, and it is not accidental that the protagonist and all the major characters of the novel belong to upper-middle-class American society and would hardly be attracted to presentations of the divine power along the lines of earlier forms of Christian triumphalism. They are not, after all, feudal lords and ladies but New World business and professional people. Their conception of "victorious living" requires, accordingly, a deity who reflects their own brand of ambition, success, and happiness and can help them to acquire and maintain the same. Divine transcendence, conceived in the mode of the *theologia gloriae,* only "works" if it accommodates itself to the existing values of its clientele, elevating those values to the level of the eternal.

11. See Jürgen Moltmann, *The Way of Jesus Christ: Christology in Messianic Dimensions,* trans. Margaret Kohl (Minneapolis: Fortress Press, 1993), 31, 104, 135, 313.

with the paradoxes of love and justice, forgives the gravest of offenders, punishes inordinate human pride and ambition, questions every authority structure, and listens to the pleas of the lowest citizens while putting down the mighty from their seats.

So much of what happened in the early decisions of the church is attributable to the religio-political needs of empire—particularly in the areas of trinitarian and christological thought—that one is tempted to wonder whether Christianity is not permanently and irrevocably shaped by this influence. The struggle to maintain the divine transcendence in Eastern Christianity served not only the philosophic and psychic needs discussed above but also this sheer political need; for under the conditions of establishment heavenly governance mirrors and is mirrored by earthly governance. The insistence upon the unity of the divine being that dominated Western Theological preferences even at the risk of courting forbidden Sabellian Monarchianism also clearly serves an imperium requiring allegiance to a single emperor/monarch. In the christological discussions, as we shall see later, the most difficult thing for the church to preserve was the real humanity of Jesus, and in fact it did so only in a formulary sort of way. What prevailed, for all intents and purposes, was a docetism that either through straightforward divinization or by making Christ's "humanity" the *perfection* of humanity removed the Christ effectively from the actualities of "finitude in anxious self-awareness" (Tillich).

Let us not forget: What Constantine heard, according to the legend, was that "in this sign" he would "conquer" *(In hoc signo vinces)*. It was a conquering, heroic God that his counselors in the church gave him; and those who objected in the name of the crucified one (particularly the school of Antioch) were rejected.

The political co-optation of Christian Theology did not end with the Roman Empire. It has been present in all the empires with which, in subsequent history, Christianity has commingled. As we shall see presently, it is an unmistakable motif in the religious history of the American empire. The young airmen who bombed Vietnamese and Iraqi towns and cities after training sessions that were closed with prayer were invoking the same God that Constantine's soldiers were ordered to invoke prior to the battle of the Milvian Bridge.

Power—and precisely power understood in the usual sense—is of the essence of divinity shaped by empire. The purposes of the imperial god are sure and this god's power is absolute. It does not matter greatly what specific mores he upholds or what language he uses, whether it is the language of unrepentant fascism or of liberal, militarily maintained democracy. The chief thing is that this god is unambiguously supportive of the established earthly powers that honor him, fully in accord with the aims of the imperium, and unassailed by self-criticism. He is always "the Father Almighty," even when he is grandfatherly, and he triumphs over every enemy, no matter who, in that historical moment, the enemy happens to be.

But the great enemy of this god is the God of prophetic faith, who is always conceived critically precisely over against this deification of the power principle.

6. God in the North American Context

6.1. The Weakness of Power. There is a tragic flaw in the religion of the Almighty Father. A god who consistently negates the negation satisfies, to be sure, many perennial human needs: the need of the psyche for a fulfillment mythos; the need of the mind for a transcendent guarantor of its ambition to possess controlling knowledge; the need of a society for order and of a nation for coherence and might. But such a god is credible only under certain well-defined sociological conditions. When the desire for fulfillment can still conquer the lived experience of incompleteness; when the need for transcendence is able to keep at bay the gnawing sense of universal indifference to the human project; when the pride of empire is able to brush aside the always uninvited suspicion of transience: then such a god may be believed and worshiped vigorously.

When these conditions are altered by internal and external circumstances, however, the vision of a conquering God fails to inspire the souls of people and the spirits of nations. Powerful peoples demand powerful deities—and get them! But the deities created by empires seldom survive the empires that fashioned them; for supernatural power has nothing to say in the face of our finally unavoidable, natural weakness. The powerful gods of yesterday's empires are all silent today, although—perhaps for that reason—their adherents are often still noisy enough. The whole continent of Europe is a museum of Theology, a pantheon to failed gods whose failure is directly attributable, not to their lack of power but to their incapacity to come to terms with historical human weakness.

In North America too the Father Almighty is failing fast. For a society whose fulfillment impulse ("the American Dream") has become clouded, whose sense of transcendent purpose has given way to narcissistic individualism, and whose empire is being eaten away from without and within—for such a society, that God could indeed be . . . "dead."

6.2. A Necessary Distinction: Canadian Skepticism. "American Christianity," states the revised edition of Williston Walker's influential work, *A History of the Christian Church,* "is primarily an importation from the Old World." We may say, accordingly, that the God professed in New World experience is an adaptation of the "Father Almighty" of the dominant tradition about which we have been thinking. This Theology is, however, an adaptation, involving (as Walker would claim with respect to our Christianity in general) "modification

[of] European forms."[12] In order to grasp something of the peculiarity of this application of Christendom's historically dominant Theology, we shall need now to ask more precisely how God has functioned in North American experience, and what the present status of this Theology appears to be.

A preliminary concern must be expressed, however, before we undertake this aspect of our critical reflections. A certain differentiation needs to be made between the two northern nations of this continent in the matter precisely of their Theology.

As even a passing acquaintance with the history of the United States suggests, God has been singularly important in the life of that nation: "the North American Enlightenment heritage, conflated with the Constantinian mood of Christianity in the West, makes God a peculiarly American God."[13] The Canadian experience, on the other hand, is not conspicuously a God-centered one. While there have of course been explicitly religious movements and experiments throughout Canadian history, and while Canada's vast land space and relative toleration of "otherness" have continued to provide havens for countless religious minorities to pursue their beliefs in relative peace and quiet,[14] Canadian history provides nothing quite like the national sense of being God-directed that is of the essence of the American pattern.[15] On the whole, Canadians are conscious of a past that is much less intentional—almost to the point

---

12. New York: Charles Scribner's Sons, 1959, 430.

13. Frederick Herzog, *God-Walk: Liberation Shaping Dogmatics* (Maryknoll, N.Y.: Orbis Books, 1988), 61.

14. Numerous examples of this phenomenon can be cited, but perhaps none is more dramatic than the 1898–99 mass exodus from Russia to Canada of the sect known as Doukhobors (in Russian, "spirit wrestlers"), an exodus financed in large measure by Count Leo Tolstoy. It is highly doubtful whether the United States, with its strong quest for unity and its melting-pot philosophy of society, could have tolerated this band of communalistic, state-resisting, antimilitary, and sometimes (especially with the radical wing, the "Sons of Freedom") anarchistic Christians. A similar observation could be made about the Finnish settlers in northern Ontario and other parts of Canada who fled, not Russia but the midwestern American states, in order to pursue their communistic approach to religion and life.

15. New France, it is true, came to think itself a kind of holy, Catholic nation, an island of pure Catholicism in the sea of Protestant and secular modernity—"Moloch," as Lionel Groulx designated Protestant America. (See Norman F. Cornett, *The Incarnational Thought of Lionel Groulx* [Ph.D. diss., McGill University, n.d.]. Cornett discusses this aspect of Groulx's thought in a chapter entitled "New France, New Israel.") This sense of being a sacred remnant was strengthened, moreover, when in the aftermath of the French Revolution, pre-Enlightenment Catholic doctrine and morality were furthered by conservative priests who fled to Quebec and other parts of French Canada from the ungodly state of modern France. There may be some reminiscences here of attitudes that shaped the development of the Protestant empire *south* of the 49th parallel, but it is certainly in another mode, and the French Canadian sense of religious vocation has never played a significant role in the religious self-understanding of the Canadian nation as a whole. It is even questionable that it has played a lasting role in the history of Quebec, which in the wake of *"La revolution tranquille"* of the 1960s is today one of the more secular provinces of the Canadian federation. See in this connection Gregory Baum, *The Church in Quebec* (Outremont, Quebec: Novalis, 1991).

of being haphazard. Canada has hardly been able to think itself a viable human experiment, let alone imagine Almighty God as its designer.

The obvious consequence of this distinction for our present purposes is that we shall have to concern ourselves primarily with American God-consciousness. This does not mean, however, that such an exercise is less than immediately pertinent to Canadians. For one thing, nothing so vital as God has been for Canada's powerful southern neighbor can be safely ignored by Canadians. Indeed, part of the current Canadian crisis has directly to do with that nation's proximity to an overwhelmingly influential neighboring state whose identity has been shaped by its sense of possessing a peculiar relation to God. Of all the world's peoples, Canadians should have some feeling for the practical, worldly significance of empire when it is imbued with the convictions of supernatural purposing.[16]

---

16. Beyond this, the study of God in the American experience is a necessary exercise for Canadians because, particularly since the end of World War II, American-style Christianity of the "televangelical" type has made significant inroads in Canada. In view of the fact that fully 88 percent of the television that Canadians watch emanates directly from the United States, it is inevitable that "God," along with other aspects of life, should be defined increasingly by American Theological presuppositions. While it is true, then, that Canadians on the whole do not derive from their own past the kinds of Theological conventions permeating the history of the United States, it is equally true that many Canadians show themselves more than willing to borrow these conventions from their U.S. neighbors. At the political level, this willingness manifests itself in the advent of movements like the so-called Reform Party, which links religion with capitalism and with Anglophone social, moral, and racial assumptions.

Television has immensely facilitated this process, but the process itself is the fruit of many factors working together: the fact that the natural lines of communication and public commerce in North America have been north/south rather than east/west; that much Christianity in Canada (not only recently but—with Methodism and Congregationalism—in the nineteenth century) is the result not of European but of explicitly American missions; and that the Americans have been far more vociferous, single-minded, and mythically inclined than have Canadians in the telling of their story. It is neither unusual nor surprising, given such factors, that many Canadians feel closer to the Pilgrim fathers, George Washington, Abe Lincoln, and Paul Bunyan than they do to the mostly unsung and often more prosaic heroes, sages, and mythic figures of Canada's own history. That "God" should also have become an American is, accordingly, not astonishing.

Yet traditionally, and among a significant portion of the population (including many artists, intellectuals, and free-thinkers) still today, a critical, even skeptical and sometimes cynical strain can readily be detected in the Canadian temperament. It may belong to our northernness, for a similar phenomenon can be observed among other northern peoples—the Scandinavians, the highland Scots, northern Germans, Russians. In a strange and not merely metaphoric way, the great problem of Canadian identity is bound up with this "feeling of North" (Glenn Gould) and with the growing temptation to disown it in favor of the powerful fantasies that draw Canadians southward. As novelist Rudi Wiebe writes: "Canadians have so little comprehension of our own *nordicity*, that we are a northern nation and that, until we grasp imaginatively and realize imaginatively in word, song, image and consciousness that North is both the true nature of our world and also our graspable destiny we will always go whoring after the mocking palm trees and beaches of the Caribbean and Florida and Hawaii; will always be wishing ourselves something we aren't, always stand staring south across that mockingly invisible border longing for the leeks and onions of our ancient Egyptian nemesis, the United States." (*Playing Dead: A Contemplation Concerning the Arctic* [Edmonton: NeWest Publishers Ltd., 1989], 111.)

Whether Canadian skepticism can be attributed to geography or to history—and undoubtedly both are involved—I regard it as perhaps the single most significant theological factor in the

6.3. "In God We Trust." The Christian God, variously arrayed and interpreted, has been bound up with numerous empires ever since Constantine first discerned the potential for imperial service in the Christian movement. It may well be, however, that no empire in history has achieved so intimate a link between the Christian God and nation as has the United States of America. This in itself may be the greatest irony in all of the "ironies of American history" (Reinhold Niebuhr); for after a brief flirtation with Christian establishment in certain of its earlier, colonial manifestations, the determination strictly to separate religion and state entered fixedly into the minds of the founders of that nation, and has ever since been given off as one of the most basic tenets of American society and government.

As a matter of fact, however, while the United States is a society without official religious connections, it is nevertheless a thoroughly religious society. The de facto, cultural establishment of Christianity in the American states has long and successfully outlived the old de jure establishments of the European parental nations—the very cultic patterns that the patriarchs of America were determined not to emulate.[17] There are, to be sure, qualifying statements to be made about the status of God in America today; we shall do so in the subsequent subsection. But so far as the past is concerned—the formative and still rhetorically normative past—it is necessary to state that when we reflect on the American pilgrimage we are reflecting upon a self-consciously Christian society, whose primary religious symbol is the Christian God. Few could doubt, even today, that the God in whom America "trusts" is that God.

The indelible link between God and America is, like all such relationships, complex; indeed, it is one that wholly mystifies non-Americans. But it may be rendered a little less esoteric, if not exactly lucid, if we recognize four factors contributing to its early formation.

The Mythology of Providential Beginnings. The beginnings of European society in the United States were conceived of in explicitly religious terms,

---

Canadian context. "True belief"—whether in God, nation, political system, the future, or whatever—is not compatible with this "nordic" condition. And of this I feel certain: The displacement of such skepticism by the less cantankerous, more benign and accepting mentality of middle-class America would signal the virtual demise of Canada as a distinctive culture.

It may be that this has already occurred.

17. "Americans succeeded in creating a legal non-establishment whose security lay in the ethos, customs, habits, and practices of popular government. . . .

"A *de facto* establishment grew where the old legal one had fallen. Later Americans of many persuasions from anti-religious to fanatically pro-religious have lived with and claimed the [Christian] charter. . . . Daniel Webster said that 'Christianity—general, tolerant Christianity—Christianity independent of sects and parties—that Christianity to which the sword and the fagot are unknown . . . is the law of the land,' even though the authors of that law had studiously avoided Christian reference." (Martin E. Marty, *Righteous Empire: The Protestant Experience in America* [New York: Harper Torchbooks, 1970], 37–44.)

and this has continued to exercise a powerful symbolic influence upon successive generations. From the outset, a parallel was seen between the beginnings of European America and those of ancient Israel.[18] As with the Abrahamic covenant (Gen. 12:2-3), the creation of America was interpreted in terms that were both providential and messianic—with, one must however add, little of the prophetic vigilance against presumption informing Israel's own "holy history." Thus the nineteenth-century church historian, Leonard Woolsey Bacon, presents what Sydney Ahlstrom aptly calls "yet another version of the Protestant American's *theologia gloriae*" when he writes:

> By a prodigy of divine providence . . . the secret of the ages [i.e., that a new world lay beyond the Western Sea] had been kept from premature disclosure. . . . If the discovery of America had been achieved even a single century earlier, the Christianity to be transplanted to the western world would have been that of the church of Europe in its lowest stage of decadence [i.e., the pre-Reformation church].[19]

With the War of Independence and the departure of the United Empire Loyalists, the association of America with God's own purposes was strengthened by the recognition that America alone had been singled out for decisive leadership. "In many minds the American was conceived as a new Adam in a new Eden, and the American nation as mankind's great second chance."[20] Abraham Lincoln, though by no means conventional in his faith, "could speak of the United States as 'the last, best hope of the earth' and of its citizens as 'the almost chosen people.'"[21]

This mythic interpretation of the genesis of America has informed the whole history of the United States. It has provided the spiritual energy for America's great accomplishments as well as much of what, from the perspective of many of the other nations in the hemisphere, would have to be regarded as U.S. imperialism. What is not always noticed about this mythos, however, is that in subtle ways it makes "God" dependent upon the success of the American experiment. The reputation of "the Almighty" is inextricably bound up

---

18. In April, 1609, when the Reverend William Symonds preached at White Chappel "In the Presence of . . . the Adventurers and Planters of Virginia," the text for his impressive sermon was Genesis 12:1-31 (God's calling of Abram to leave his ancestral home, with the promise that a new and "great" nation would come of these uncertain beginnings). Martin Marty notes that Christians were "so successful . . . at making the identification with Israel" that this became a recurrent theme of American imaginative literature even where—as in the case of Herman Melville—the authors themselves were far from Christian orthodoxy (cf. *Righteous Empire*, 46).

19. From Bacon's *History of American Christianity*, pp. 2, 419, as quoted by Ahlstrom in *A Religious History of the American People*, vol. 1 (Garden City, N.Y.: Doubleday & Co. [Image Books], 1975), 36–37.

20. Ahlstrom, *A Religious History of the American People*, vol. 1, 34.

21. Howard Clark Kee et al., *Christianity: A Social and Cultural History* (New York: Macmillan Pub. Co., 1991), 693.

with the might (world leadership, economic prowess, military invincibility, and general sense of public well-being) of the Republic. We shall notice subsequently what this implies for contemporary religious life in the United States.

Protestant Internalization of Doctrine and "This-Worldliness." The sincere and intense conviction with which, historically, Americans have embraced the myth of divine origins and destiny can be traced in particular to the impact of Protestantism on American God-consciousness. More specifically, it is a by-product of Reformed Christianity, the most influential form of Protestantism in American history.[22]

The internalization of doctrine is of the essence of the Reformed tradition. Earlier forms of Christianity were able, it is true, to compel allegiance to the Christian religion more lastingly than democratic government could expect to do. But as the continuing undercurrent of paganism in European societies has demonstrated down to our own century,[23] neither Constantine nor Charlemagne nor any other European prince was able to bring about such an internalization of Christian faith as was achieved in American history. This has largely to do with the Protestant conception of conversion and of the relation between faith and doctrine. Neither the old Roman form of Christianity nor those of the Middle Ages required of believers that they personally decide upon, endorse, and seek to comprehend the faith. It was indeed assumed that few among those who belonged to the church (that is, nearly everyone) would be capable of or interested in professing their faith at the level of understanding and articulating it. The practice of religion prior to the Reformation meant chiefly observance of the rights, rituals, and sacraments of the church. Theology was for scholars.

Not only the internalization process as such, however, but also *what* was internalized bespeak the singular importance of the Reformed tradition in America. Here the concept of God is of specific significance, for the Reformed tradition is in an explicit sense a God-centered interpretation of Christianity, and in a way that neither Roman Catholicism nor other forms of Protestantism, whose Theology is more soteriologically informed, can be said to be.

---

22. Of the two principal classical Protestant streams originating in continental Europe, the one that clearly dominates American history is the Reformed or Calvinist stream. Not only was most Lutheranism later in making its appearance in the United States, but it was so consistently identified with ethnic enclaves and, in its doctrine, so incommensurate with "New World" expectancy that it did not deeply influence the evolving culture. Ahlstrom estimates that "if one were to compute [the percentage of Calvinist heritage in the United States] on the basis of all the German, Swiss, French, Dutch, and Scottish people whose forebears bore the 'stamp of Geneva' in some broader sense, 85 or 90 percent would not be an extravagant estimate" (*A Religious History of the American People,* vol. 1, 169).

23. It was not very difficult for Nazi propagandists to rekindle interest in the old gods of the Teutonic forests, despite the fact that Germany was perhaps the most secular of all European societies in the 1920s and '30s.

The Calvinists' insistence upon God's absolute sovereignty results not only in God-orientation but also in a species of world-orientation; for this world is, for that tradition, the concrete locus of God's monarchy. What many have resented as Calvinist or puritan moralism, "workaholism," and lack of humor has its roots in this conviction: God is at work in the world, and Christian obedience means faithful and unstinting involvement in God's worldly work.

Combined with another prominent Reformed teaching, the doctrine of election, this gave rise to what many regard as a distortion of Calvinism—the deuteronomic sense of the worldly success of the elect. For the most part, original Reformed teaching maintains a high degree of modesty with respect to the identity of the elect. In the first place they are denied certitude concerning their salvific status, and in the second place they are perhaps as likely to experience suffering as satisfaction in their earthly sojourn.[24] In the practical working out of the dogma of election in American and other experience, however, the element of uncertainty was often greatly reduced. The success of human ventures could be regarded as a sign of divine approval. Thus Reformed Theology, pragmatically purged of nuance, could contribute to the supposition that America's success demonstrated America's special election by the Sovereign of history.

Again, the question that is begged by this logic is what, in that case, the failure of America could mean for its God-consciousness, or whether failure could even be entertained as a possibility by a people grasped by such a Theology.

A Theological **Carte Blanche.** A third factor in the composition of the affiliation between God and America has to do with the relative monopoly of the Christian God in the European settlement of the whole North American continent. If one regards the implantation of Christianity in North America from the perspective of Christian missions elsewhere—including the Pauline, Gregorian, and other missions in early Christian Europe itself—what stands out starkly is that Christianity in North America encountered no effective rival claims. Even in medieval Europe there were always, besides the concealed paganism of the various christianized tribes, Jews and Moslems. In North

---

24. Some teachings of Calvin and others, however, seem to authenticate the idea of reward for faithful obedience. Reinhold Niebuhr notes: "In Calvinist thought prosperity as a mark of divine favor is closely related to the idea that it must be sought as part of a godly discipline of life. 'There is no question,' declared Calvin, 'that riches should be the portion of the godly rather than the wicked, for godliness hath the promise in this life as well as the life to come'" (*The Irony of American History* [New York: Charles Scribner's Sons, 1952], 51). See also in this connection M. Douglas Meeks's comments on "the preeminent American 'theologian,' Andrew Carnegie," in *God the Economist: The Doctrine of God and Political Economy* (Minneapolis: Fortress Press, 1989), 20f.

America, on the contrary, the Christian God could flourish unchallenged well into the late nineteenth century.[25]

The questionable—indeed, the damning—reality that is hidden by this fact of the progress of Christendom cannot be bypassed in any responsible introduction to Christian Theology in North America today, particularly in the wake of the five hundredth anniversary of Columbus's historic voyage. I refer to the absolute disregard for the spirituality of the native peoples of this continent on the part of the European missioners.

The fact is, the North American landspace was not an empty stage, a *carte blanche*. There were people here to meet the boats.[26] These people held distinctive views, including views about God. Yet it was universally assumed by the Christian newcomers that the natives' conceptions of deity were worthless. The question was not whether Christians should hold dialogue with these "lesser tribes without the law," but whether the native peoples were worthy of conversion to the Christian God. While there were both Protestant and Catholic efforts at conversion or assimilation through marriage, the question never quite disappeared from view whether these "inferior races" should not simply be eliminated, leaving the stage entirely unpeopled.

In this connection it is worth contemplating whether the superficial hold on the life of this continent that, in the last analysis, Christianity has been able to achieve, is in some mysterious way related to its missionary refusal to enter humbly into the life of the land's own peoples and to respect the gods of the land. Autochthonous religion should never be lightly brushed aside, for it is the deepest expression of the relationship between humanity and the world of nature and spirit that has been acquired by centuries of love and suffering in that place. As such it contains wisdom that cannot be imported from elsewhere. Perhaps we are just now seeing the terrible consequences of the noncontextual, European conquest of a continent whose gods have been deeply offended by the emissaries of a foreign deity.

---

25. "While through their Bible studies many Protestants came to hold views that may be classified as theologically anti-Semitic, the Jews were too small a presence (about 3000 people in 1815) to represent any threat to the spread of Christian empire. They had been in America since colonial days, and by 1848 numbered only about fifty congregations. Anti-Judaism became a social reality in the 1880's only. It was a feature of the early post-Civil War Ku Klux Klan. But prior to World War I American Judaism attracted little attention." (Marty, *Righteous Empire,* 124.)

26. "While it is difficult to estimate populations or death tolls of five centuries ago, historians agree that most of the tens of millions who were overrun in just a couple of decades met death. No words in our time can make up for the terror and the tears of those years, or evoke the pain that produced rivers of blood.

"Yes, among the explorers and expropriators there were humane people; many of these were missionaries who began to speak up for the rights of Native Americans [and Canadians—DJH]. But almost no record shows that any of the Spanish or Portuguese intruders looked positively on Indian religion and culture. Nor have we any such record from Dutch or English colonizers, traders or missionaries, and only a few traces from the French." Martin E. Marty, "Discovering Columbus: A Quincentennial Reading," *The Christian Century* (Nov. 20–27, 1991), 1105.

However that may be, what must be noted seriously in connection with the American appropriation of European Christianity's doctrine of God is that, in contradistinction to every previous Christian expansion, the God testified to by Christians entering the new sphere of the Americas went unchallenged and unchanged by any external Theology. Surely the peculiar brand of Theological triumphalism that came to be in American Christianity should not be dissociated from this fact.

A Grateful, "Believing" People.   A fourth and deceptively significant factor in the American adaptation of European Theological tradition is bound up with the identity of the Europeans who actually cleared and settled this continent from the seventeenth until the nineteenth centuries. Not discounting the fact that some of their leaders (including the many clergy) were persons of learning, nor overlooking the sterling accomplishments of many of their own numbers, still it must be recognized that the majority of the settlers were uneducated men and women—peasants, soldiers, adventurers, and refugees from an Old World that was full of revenge, class conflict, religious persecution, and economic chaos created by industrialization, famine, war, and greed.

These ordinary settlers had not read the philosophic treatises of the Renaissance and the Enlightenment. They were not imbued with the spirit of agnosticism that had already permeated the European intellectual community. Moreover, though they experienced many and terrible hardships, they did not find their life in the New World productive of the kind of despondency that might have been experienced by their "betters" in old Europe, for they were Europe's victims. Their expectations were not the exaggerated dreams of the affluent. They could endure abysmal physical deprivation because they had already, most of them, experienced the numbing despair of the poor and oppressed. Their life in the new situation, even when it was full of practical anxieties, seldom led to cynicism. Hardly any of the literature that we have from them (their poetry, letters, stories, hymns, and reminiscences) reflects anything verging on pessimism. This is remarkable because, from the standpoint of contemporary expectations in North American and other "developed" world societies, they had much to be pessimistic about.

It is in this sense that I use the phrase, "a believing people." I do not mean "true belief" in the present-day idiom, but rather the kind of human serenity and expectancy that is frequently displayed by those "extraordinary ordinary people" who, having known great deprivation, are capable of entertaining modest visions if they are given the slightest opportunity to do so. Something akin to this phenomenon can be observed in the attitudes of contemporary immigrants coming to these shores from Asia, Africa, the Caribbean, and elsewhere.

In time, this humble contentment of the pioneers would be taken up into the grand utopian (and essentially secular or deistic) ideology that we name the

American Dream. But the original, I think, was purer than what came to be under the tutelage of Enlightenment bravado. Certainly it is more significant religiously. For in ways that perhaps parallel Christian liberationist movements in Third World settings today, the kind of hope that was manifested by the early European pioneers in North America—as distinct from the historical optimism that later emerged from, or was superimposed upon, that hope—was an essentially spiritual phenomenon and therefore, not unnaturally, associated with God, open to God, grateful to God.

6.4. God and the Transition from Republic to Empire. While the potentiality for a deeply felt linkage between the purposes of Almighty God and the American "experiment" was already present, then, in the pioneering and republican phases of European America, the hardening of the logic of this association must be traced to a later period. Until that point in U.S. history when the promise of a distinctive destiny "under God" could seem to be confirmed by actual experience, a certain tentativeness attends the belief that God had destined America for greatness: America was still the "*almost* chosen people" (Lincoln). Greatness having been achieved—at least in the eyes of the influential—in the period following the Civil War, the association of America with God's own design became, for many, more a law of history than a historical hope. With a hindsight born of the liberal doctrine of historical progress, Horace Bushnell (1802–1876) could write:

> We associate God and religion with all that we are fighting for. . . . Our cause, we love to think, is especially God's and so we are connecting all the most sacred impressions with our government itself, weaving it in a woof of holy feeling among all the fibres of our constitutional polity and government. . . . The whole shaping of the fabric is Providential. God, God is in it, everywhere . . . every drum-beat is a hymn, the cannon thunder God, the electric silence, darting victory along the wires, is the inaudible greeting of God's favoring work and purpose.[27]

According to Henry Steele Commager, it was the Civil War that gave rise to modern America:

> That conflict gave an immense stimulus to industry, speeded up the exploitation of natural resources, the development of large-scale manufacturing, the rise of investment banking, the extension of foreign commerce, and brought to the fore a new generation of "captains of industry" and "masters of capital." . . . It put a premium upon inventions and labor-saving devices and witnessed the large-scale application of these to agriculture as well as to industry. . . . It created conditions

---

27. Quoted by Sydney E. Mead, *The Lively Experiment: The Shaping of Christianity in America* (New York: Harper & Row Publishers, 1963), 142–43.

favorable to the growth of cities and offered work to hundreds of thousands of immigrants who soon crowded into the New World. . . .

. . . The small republic became a world power. . . . No other generation in American history witnessed changes as swift or as revolutionary as those which transformed the rural republic of Lincoln and Lee into the urban industrial empire of McKinley and Roosevelt.[28]

Summarizing this period, Sydney E. Mead writes that the belief in inevitable progress gripped the United States as though it were standing on "a teleological escalator."[29] Protestantism, which as we have seen played so important a role in the initial fashioning of America, now became the chief cultic vehicle for the expression of an Americanism that went considerably beyond the tentative God-association referred to above. "During the second half of the nineteenth century there occurred an ideological amalgamation of Protestantism with 'Americanism,'" wrote Mead, "and we are still living with some of the results."[30]

Gore Vidal's 1987 historical novel, *Empire,* is an imaginative reconstruction of the period in question. From the perspective of the troublesome imperialism of late twentieth-century U.S. history, Vidal looks back upon the historical moment almost a hundred years earlier when the republicanism of Lincoln passed almost unnoticed through the hands of McKinley to become, under Theodore Roosevelt and the reinterpretation of the Monroe Doctrine, a "world-class" imperial power. In an imagined conversation between Henry Adams and John Hay that is no doubt intentionally reminiscent of more recent talks in high places, Vidal has Hay announce:

> "Surely we have a *moral*—yes, I hate the word too—duty to help less fortunate nations in this hemisphere. . . ."
>
> [Adams] "And in sunny Hawaii, and poor Samoa, and the tragic Philippines. John, it is empire you all want, and it is empire that you have got, and at such a small price, when you come to think of it."
>
> "What price is that?"
>
> "The American republic. You've finally got rid of it. . . . The republic is dead; long live the empire."[31]

At the novel's end, Vidal depicts a portrait of Abraham Lincoln hanging in Theodore Roosevelt's presidential office, his "eyes fixed on some far distance

---

28. Allan Nevins and Henry Steele Commager, *A Pocket History of the United States,* 7th ed. (New York: Washington Square Press Publication, Simon and Schuster, 1981), 236–37.

29. *The Lively Experiment,* 145.

30. Ibid., 134.

31. New York: Random House, 1987, 399.

beyond the viewer's range, a prospect unknown and unknowable to the mere observer, at sea in present time."[32]

With the birth of empire, the logic of the God-connection is consummated. America has been vindicated in putting its trust in God, for it has achieved the preeminence that such trust promised from the outset. The God who is "great"[33] has made America great.

But, as we have suggested in the foregoing, this logic contains a hidden connotation that is unsettling: If a God conceived of in terms of power and primacy only becomes wholly credible when "he" has given birth to a people that reflects "his" own preeminence, will not the credibility of that God depend upon the continued ascendancy of that people? What will be the fate of the "great" God if, instead of sustaining and enhancing its might, the nation that so conceives of deity finds its powers waning, its problems increasing, its ebullience assailed by "future shock"? The very intimacy of the association of God and America makes this question more critical for both the religious and the postreligious in the United States today than it has been for previous empires, which deployed God-talk in more objective and perfunctory ways. When the coalescence of God and nation is a matter, not only of official policy, but of the consent and belief of the majority, the state of the nation will quite naturally affect popular belief in God, and vice versa. It is not surprising, therefore, that all recent administrations in Washington have incorporated a great deal of "positive religion" into their policies, regardless of the personal religious leanings of presidents, senators, and representatives.

6.5. The Inadequacy of the "Old Theology." "America," announced President Dwight D. Eisenhower, "is the mightiest power which God has yet seen fit to put upon his footstool." He added: "America is great because she is good."[34] By the 1950s, however, this "generalized religion [which] adapted the Protestant doctrine of God and marketed him as a convenient and benign fixture, a 'man upstairs,'"[35] simply did not ring true. For already the secret melancholy that has visited the American spirit frequently in the second half of the twentieth century had begun to disturb the illusions of progress and superiority that prevailed, publicly, until the end of World War II.[36] While the

---

32. Ibid., 486.
33. "Great," as in the popular modern hymn "How Great Thou Art!" is the highest tribute North American Volk-Christianity knows how to pay to the Deity. It is the ultimate "attribute of transcendence," the everyday equivalent of "almighty" and "omnipotent," and as such far more descriptive of Deity as conceived by American Christians of all hues than terms like "compassionate," "forgiving," or even "loving."
34. Quoted by Marty in *Righteous Empire*, 259.
35. Ibid.
36. According to Mark A. Noll, this more somber spirit has been part of the U.S. landscape from early times: "The mood of common Americans was . . . closer to the melancholy of

"newly converted Presbyterian," Eisenhower, was praising America's greatness and goodness, Reinhold Niebuhr was documenting the "refutations" of America's "original pretensions of virtue, wisdom, and power":[37]

The prosperity of America is legendary. Our standards of living are beyond the dreams of avarice of most of the world. We are a kind of paradise of domestic security and wealth. But we face the ironic situation that the same technical efficiency which provided our comforts has also placed us at the center of the tragic developments in world events. There are evidently limits to the achievements of science; and there are irresolvable contradictions both between prosperity and virtue, and between happiness and the "good life" which had not been anticipated in our philosophy. The discovery of these contradictions threatens our culture with despair.[38]

Words like "despair" and "tragic" were not part of the pre-twentieth-century American vocabulary, even though Calvinism knew well the language of original sin. They appear rather frequently in twentieth-century American literature, especially (as noted earlier) imaginative literature, and they spell not only a new social-cultural ethos but also a new dissatisfaction with the old Theology. This disenchantment entails, among other things, an open or covert rebuttal of the assumptions contained in all four of the historical factors referred to above as having been productive of America's peculiar God-consciousness.

Refuting the Myth of Holy Origins. Five hundred years after Columbus's discovery of America, the entire providentiality of the well-rehearsed tale of American beginnings is questioned by many and frankly renounced by vocal minorities. To the secular mentality that has been in the making for a century, the narrative of New World origins appears biased, promotional, and naive. A more critical approach among intellectuals of the left insists upon recounting, along with the anecdotes of heroism and inventiveness, the conditions of class conflict, oppression, and violence that accompanied these events. "God," they say, has (predictably enough) functioned as a convenient camouflage for human rapacity.

African-American activists, many of them Christians, question whether the five-hundredth anniversary of Columbus's voyage is to be celebrated or lamented. A new word has entered our vocabulary in consequence: decelebration.

Abraham Lincoln than to the cosmic optimism of Ralph Waldo Emerson" (*Christianity: A Social and Cultural History,* 683). This seems plausible, since there is a kind of folk wisdom that usually resists, at some deep level, the rhetoric of the image-makers. At the same time, such folk wisdom is remarkably flexible, and during periods of general political and economic stability it seems entirely capable of suspending disbelief.

37. *The Irony of American History,* viii.
38. Ibid., 45.

How can Christians celebrate a civilization that was built upon the foundations of slavery? They are joined by indigenous peoples in Canada and the United States, from the perspective of whose newly gained sense of racial pride the advent of the white race in North and South America must be perceived with sorrow and anger.[39] Moreover, the power of this criticism, far from being limited to nonwhites, has captured the sympathy and imagination of many Caucasians as well, particularly among the young. Genocide, slavery, and gross dehumanization do not harmonize nicely with the high religious or secular idealism of traditional American mythology.

Perhaps one must even ask today whether the repetition of the myth of holy origins and destiny does not confirm more North Americans in their agnosticism and disbelief than it undergirds theism. For many it can only seem hypocrisy to associate a God of reputedly holy love with the inhumane behavior of the white "developers" of this continent.[40]

The Displacement of Mainstream Protestantism. The Protestant hold on the soul of America had begun to diminish even before the end of the nineteenth century. Mark A. Noll locates the beginnings of the end of Protestant "hegemony" in the same period that marks, according to Mead, the "ideological amalgamation" of Protestantism and Americanism. Noll associates the displacement of mainstream Protestant influence with a number of rather swift social and cultural changes: the population shift away from "the small towns and rural settlements in which that Protestantism had dominated" toward the cities;[41] the loss of Protestant control of higher education;[42] the growing influence of modern natural science;[43] the emergence, with Julius Wellhausen, of higher criticism of the Scriptures, and so on.

---

39. In this connection, see Joyce Carlson, ed., *The Journey: Stories and Prayers for the Christian Year from People of the First Nations* (Toronto: Anglican Book Centre, 1991).

40. The film *Dances with Wolves,* which presented both the European newcomers and the native peoples in terms very different from the "cowboys and Indians" films of the first half of this century, may mark a perceptual watershed in the dominant understanding of North American beginnings. And the historical restraint of *Dances with Wolves* is thrown to the winds in the (Canadian and Australian) film version of Brian Moore's historical novel, *Blackrobe.* Quite apart from its general public reception, however, this new consciousness of white, Western injustice raises for serious Christians the question whether there is not something abysmally wrong with our conception of God.

41. "A simple statistic highlights the great changes underway in American society after the Civil War. In 1870, 9.9 million Americans (or 26 percent) lived in towns and cities with 2,500 people or more. By 1930, the absolute number had risen to 69 million Americans and the national proportion to 56 percent." (Kee et al., *Christianity: A Social and Cultural History,* 704.)

42. "In 1839 fifty-one of the fifty-four presidents of America's largest colleges were clergymen. . . . By 1900 that number was greatly reduced" (ibid.).

43. Darwin's *Origin of Species* (1859) not only shook the faith of those who believed that the world had been created in six days, but more importantly it "seemed to call into question a treasured proof for God's existence, the Argument from Design . . . a mainstay of American higher education" (ibid., 706).

While modernists sought to adjust Christian faith to these new, secular winds, and were to a certain extent successful, the changing profile of the American population made it unlikely that Protestantism would any longer sway the future. Not only was mainline Protestantism challenged from within, with fundamentalists and, at times, dispensationalists[44] claiming large numbers of adherents, and African-American Christians founding their own denominations, but for the first time Protestantism found itself confronted by significant representations of both Eastern Orthodox and Roman Catholic Christianity.[45] Thus, by 1926 "Church life in America had become pluralistic in the extreme" and the largest denomination "by far" was the Roman Catholic Church.[46]

"Other Gods." Not only has Christian Theology become diversified on account of the late nineteenth- and twentieth-century influx of ecclesiastical bodies previously far less influential in the New World, but the increasing multiculturalism of the entire continent means that non-Christian faiths—faiths whose deities were formerly, for most North Americans, mere rumors and legends—are now present in an increasing and almost fantastic array. We have already cited religious pluralism as one of the important components of the North American context,[47] and we have noted that this diversity introduces qualitative and not only quantitative considerations. Theistic multiplicity inevitably poses the question whether God, if God exists at all, may not entirely transcend all historic accounts of deity.

In the new atmosphere created by the combination of religious pluralism, secularity, and (what we shall address in chapter 3) an indistinct though insistent quest for transcendence, it is increasingly difficult for people to give themselves wholeheartedly to one religious tradition; and in the American context this poses cultural and political as well as religious questions, for the American commitment to societal unity seems to many to require the foundation of a common religion, a single deity in whom "we trust."[48]

---

44. The interesting thing about dispensationalism in this connection is that it signals a significant relocation of Christian hope. While classical (especially Reformed) Protestantism as well as liberalism considers this world the scene of divine "mending," dispensationalism locates its hope in a supramundane kingdom and frequently (as in the case of Hal Lindsey) regards worldly destruction as a condition for the salvation of the chosen ("raptured"). The popularity of this response is naturally, therefore, associated with periods of historic pessimism.

45. "A great surge in immigration in the last third of the nineteenth century brought millions of Catholics to the United States from Italy, Poland, and other places in southern and central Europe" (Kee et al., *Christianity: A Social and Cultural History,* 718).

46. Ibid., 721.

47. *Thinking the Faith,* 207ff.

48. See Martin Marty's discussion of this in John McManners, ed., *The Oxford Illustrated History of Christianity* (Oxford & New York: Oxford Univ. Press, 1990), 384ff.

The Loss of Spontaneous Theism. Despite the fact that many surveys indicate a high incidence of theistic belief among Americans (nine out of ten Americans still claim to believe in God, according to some pollsters); despite the popularity of neoconservative, fundamentalist, and pietistic forms of Christianity in the United States; despite the power of religious rhetoric in all public discourse, it seems to me very dubious to posit continuity between the relative "belief-fullness" of the pioneering and republican past and the religious situation in America today. Not only have all the once-mainline denominations suffered loss of numbers and influence, but the militant Christianity of the more vociferous "sects" (as they would formerly have been designated) lacks conspicuously the spontaneity of the earlier forms of the church. It is militant because it is fashioned over against the obvious secularity and religious apathy of the society at large and of "liberal" Christianity's capitulation to ever-changing social trends.

While it may in one sense be true, as Martin Marty has recently argued, that Christianity will "remain somehow the dominant force" in the United States and that Justice William O. Douglas's 1952 summary statement that "We are a religious people" still remains accurate,[49] taken by itself such an assessment seems to me misleading. What Reinhold Niebuhr wrote in 1958 appears closer to reality: "Here we are in the twentieth century, at once the most religious and the most secular of Western nations. How shall we explain this paradox? Could it be that we are most religious partly in consequence of being the most secular culture?"[50] The earlier "openness to God," specifically the Christian God, has for large numbers of Americans (as for even larger numbers of Canadians and Europeans) given way to doubt, confusion, and indifference. In response—and in the United States particularly in a response born of shock over the consequences of God's "death" for humanity's and the nation's life—there has come to be a hardened, dogmatic backlash of "true belief." But the backlash as well as the overt secularity that has evoked it demonstrate that "the old American theology no longer works very well."[51]

One conclusion that cannot, I think, be avoided by serious Christians is that the "old theology" does not "work" because it was posited on the mythology of power: a powerful God, whether presented in fatherly or grandfatherly mien, would ensure the empowerment of the nation. This Theology "worked" while America could seem—at least to a large number of its citizens—unambiguously great. But from the 1960s onward, and from a bewildering variety of perspectives, dashed hopes, and contrary experiences,

---

49. Ibid., 384, 419.
50. *Pious and Secular America* (New York: Charles Scribner's Sons, 1958), 1.
51. Lance Morrow, *Time* (March 31, 1980), 41. (See *Thinking the Faith,* 171.)

vast numbers of American people have had to confront negations undreamt by the architects of the Dream: the ambiguities, limits, and real dangers of power; the emptiness of material prosperity; the falsification of reality necessitated by the ideology of success; the "Catch-22" of the bid for mastery over nature (that we ourselves, being part of nature, must be mastered!); the many tokens of our actual failure—to achieve happiness, to eradicate poverty and pain, to befriend and liberate oppressed peoples, and so on.

The attitudinal change brought about by all such experiences and realizations was perhaps most poignantly expressed at the symbolic level by the Death-of-God movement—or rather, by the public response to it. While at the intellectual core of that movement something far more profound was taking place, what it symbolized for many people in and on the edges of ecclesiastical life was precisely the demise of the "old Theology": God, in whom we trusted, has turned out to be ineffectual.[52]

But what is even more telling than the emergence of a Death-of-God Theology in the midst of a "religious" people was the early death of the Death-of-God movement. Unlike most Europeans, Americans on the whole cannot endure the thought of a world without God, indeed without a powerful, winning God. Such a prospect raises the bleak question about America's own status. Therefore the refusal of God's "death" (William Hamilton's chair of theology was actually removed, and he received death threats),[53] the return in the 1980s to "old-time religion," and the concomitant drive to overcome the image of a weakened and perhaps failing America are all part of the same logic, the same "old Theology."

Periodic successes can of course be expected. The exaggerated celebrations of U.S. victory in the Persian Gulf War—perhaps the war itself—are to be explained precisely in terms of the attempt to revive the "old Theology."[54] But the deeper challenge to that Theology will not disappear. That challenge comes in many forms—from process theology, from all theologies employing the metaphor of liberation, and above all from feminist theology.[55] What Christians faithful to the biblical and best traditions of the faith are required to do

---

52. See Lloyd Steffen, "The Dangerous God: A Profile of William Hamilton," *The Christian Century* (Sept. 27, 1989), 844ff.; see also Isabel Carter Heyward, *The Redemption of God: A Theology of Mutual Relation* (Lanham, New York, London: Univ. Press of America, 1982), 8.

53. Steffen, "The Dangerous God," 844.

54. Significantly, polls indicated that American confidence in "the churches" increased by about 2 percent in the wake of the U.S. triumph over Iraq.

55. "Feminism may well be the most radical challenge ever to arise within the church," writes Harold H. Oliver ("Beyond the Feminist Critique: A Shaking of the Foundations," *The Christian Century* [May 1, 1985], 446f.). He continues: "However, by facing feminism's challenge to the tradition, the church, I believe, stands to gain much more than it conceivably could lose. . . . If there is one truth at the heart of both Judaism and Christianity, it is that no representation of the divine—either visual or verbal—is finally adequate, and that failure to accept this judgment leads to idolatry."

today is *not* to join the ranks of those who are trying to resuscitate the Theology of power and glory, but to bear witness in thought, word, and deed to the God who enters into the depths of human distress, failure, and despair, particularly, in our case, the despair of those who do not know how to admit despair.

7. Summary: Power and the Powers

The thesis of this chapter of critical theology has been that the dominant Theology of Christendom has suffered from a too consistent application of the power principle to the godhead; that this Theology not only fails to represent the biblical testimony to God, but also contains inherent contradictions and inadequacies; and that these latter become conspicuous and intolerable when the historical conditions that gave rise to such an image of God are replaced by conditions incompatible with the conclusion that the world is governed by a God of power and glory.

It will be evident that this critique has a good deal in common with other theological movements and schools present in our continental context. It shares with process theology the assumption that a purely transcendental conception of deity falls short of Christian Theology, because if God "is" love then God's necessary involvement with the beloved creation entails divine participation in the unfinished, dynamic, suffering world and precludes the sort of Theology that "gives God the glory" at the expense of extricating God from any real, incarnational engagement with the livingness of the whole creaturely condition. Perhaps more conspicuously, it shares with the various expressions of liberation theology a basic suspicion of the uncritical association of God with existing powers.

For all theologies employing the metaphor of liberation, power represents the central problematic component of the inherited traditions of Theology. Despite their different emphases, liberationists are united in the belief that God must be distinguished (liberated) from hermeneutical captivation by specific manifestations of human dominance. Thus for black theology the problem is that the Christian God has been distorted through association with the power-quest of the white race, which (perhaps in consequence of its exaggerated anxiety over finite powerlessness) developed techniques of mastery and read its own explicit and implicit assumptions of superiority into its conceptions of deity.[56] Similarly, for representatives of Christian and other religious thought among indigenous peoples of this continent, the problem with conventional Christian conceptions of God is that they habitually apotheosize human qualities treasured by

---

56. See James Cone, *Speaking the Truth: Ecumenism, Liberation and Black Theology* (Grand Rapids, Mich.: Wm. B. Eerdmans, 1986).

European civilization, such as the primacy of rationality, the extrication of Homo sapiens from—and that species' domination over—the rest of nature, and so on. For ethnic Christians—for example, the growing numbers of Korean, Japanese, Vietnamese, Philippine, Indian, and Pakistani Christians in Canada and the United States—Theology in the modern West is problematic on account of its preoccupation with triumphant individualism; its lack of communal consciousness encourages the promotion of a deity who empowers private lives but leaves the tribe to its own devices, or to the devices of the powerful. Among gay and lesbian Christians, the God of the received tradition is so inextricably bound up with heterosexual stereotypes of "true humanity" that the acceptance and celebration of their own humanity must entail either the straightforward rejection of that deity or a drastic rethinking of God—and in particular of Jesus Christ—along lines less homophobic.

Most conspicuously, feminist theologies struggle against the domination of male assumptions that have been transferred to the knowledge, being, and work of God throughout the centuries of Judeo-Christian history. Characteristically masculine forms of rationality, pride, ambition, and sheer physical dominance have been projected onto the deity. Not only is the conventional God of Christendom indisputably masculine "himself"; not only is the Christ depicted as the bearer of virtues treasured by Western males; but the deity acts in ways calculated to inspire the ideals of masculinity that have held sway in Christendom— differing ideals, of course; for, like all fashions, fashions in male behavior change; yet always *male* behavior, and therefore behavior that implicitly excludes women.

All of these protesting movements (especially feminism, since it incorporates persons in all of the other groups as well) have made and are making highly significant contributions to the critique of power that, in my opinion, must inform centrally Christian reflection on deity in our time. Because power is never merely abstract; because the models of power that human beings employ in their depiction of God are always concrete and historical, the critique of power absolutely requires criticism of "the powers that be." Inevitably, we give to God what belongs to Caesar: that is, we project upon the deity or deities of our choice what most impresses us in our experience of earthly power and glory. In popular religion, moreover, such projection usually lacks the self-critical recognition that historical models of any quality which human beings transfer to deity are at best analogies and quite possibly inappropriate.

Therefore when black theology opposes the white God, and indigenous theology the European God, and ethnic theology the modern Western God, and gay theology the "straight" God, and feminist theologies the masculine God, they are all performing an invaluable service for all Christian theology; for they introduce into theological reflection the self-critical dimension that, almost always, is underdeveloped by those who "do theology." Myopia and self-interest cannot be underestimated in the execution of this discipline—perhaps especially this discipline. Particularly our portraits of God regularly turn out to be self-portraits, idealized and never quite honest representations of the perfections that we personally strive for or have been socially conditioned to covet. Even the critical insight called (by Tillich) "the Protestant principle," where it is present, does not guarantee that such a thing will not be done. Even under the aegis of the theology of the cross, which knows that power is a dangerous and misleading entree to the understanding of God, it can happen that God is portrayed along the lines of, for example, masculine preconceptions of the heroic. Therefore it belongs essentially to the discipline of theology as a corporate undertaking of the disciple community that there should be voices from the ranks of the victims of power, who will bear witness to the obvious or hidden power assumptions in all of our discussions of God.

Power, however, is a restless thing. It seeks ever new auspices. The various revolutions that have taken place in our own historical period almost all illustrate the manner in which the once-powerless, having achieved their victory over corrupt power, are themselves quite capable of manifesting the very tyranny that they overthrew. This is not to say that revolutions are always wrong; it is only to observe, once more, inherent vagaries within power itself.

Not all of the concrete forms and representations that power can assume have been assumed. It is entirely within the realm of possibility that some of those who today struggle for liberation could tomorrow become forces against which other human beings would have to struggle for liberation. Therefore, while it is important that there should be an ongoing protest in the church against specific, existing expressions of power and against the theological by-products of those expressions, the Christian community must at the same time continue to wrestle with the idea of power as such. Without this (if you like) more theoretical vigilance—this work of professional as distinct from confessional theology—the practical opposition to concrete expressions of human domination too easily devolves into a struggle of power against power. Then, the principle of power in itself is no longer seriously questioned as to its appropriateness, theologically and anthropologically, doctrinal and ethical rectitude is determined by the dominant camp within the struggle.

In registering this caveat, I am not unconscious of the fact that one of the ways in which the powerful keep the powerless "in their place" is by perpetuating images of God that discourage self-fulfillment, pride, achievement, autonomy, and the quest for power. Under the impact of that knowledge, some feminists today resist the theology of the cross and the presentation of God as "the crucified God" or the "self-emptying God" because they are aware that such conceptions of the deity have been employed, and have the potential to be employed, to deter women from achieving their rightful equality in church and society. In this connection, Catherine Keller writes:

The politics of kenotic humility incarnates itself all too clearly in the willingness of most male ministers. . . to deal with situations of physical, often life-endangering, abuse by counseling the woman to remain and submit. Christianity has been perennially tempted to glorify victimization in its glorification of its central victim. The cross, when rendered normative rather than descriptive, can indeed work to create submissive martyrs rather than revolutionary risk-takers. The root of compulsive self-victimization lies in the underdevelopment of the self.[57]

Keller is in my opinion entirely justified in rejecting a type of Christian witness that conceives of the "word of the cross" in terms of resignation, and applies such an interpretation to all and sundry. The acceptance of "what cannot be changed" (Reinhold Niebuhr) does belong to this tradition; but unlike Stoicism, Christianity does not elevate such acceptance to the status of a universal "ought." The fundamental message of the cross, as I have interpreted it in the first volume,[58] is not the acceptance of the status quo, which would frequently if not habitually mean the acceptance of death, but rather the lived recognition of God's abiding commitment to the world and to life. The manner in which this message will be received and enacted varies with differing contexts. Faith honors God's life-commitment sometimes by accepting, graciously, what may seem far from life-giving, even death. But this will be turned into a "law" only at the expense of replacing the theology of the cross with an ideology of the cross. The theology of the cross is about the courage to enter the darkness so that the light may be seen. An ideology of the cross counsels a priori acceptance of the darkness: "Life in this world is a cross that must be borne."

When life is diminished and denied in the name of the crucified, we may be sure that it is an ideology and not the gospel that is at work. Preventing blacks, native peoples, ethnic minorities, women, or anyone else from achieving their full potentiality as human beings is not what the cross of Jesus Christ is all about. It concerns rather the quest for wholeness ("abundance") of life: that we should become truly human. But the wisdom of the cross entails a judgment against the sinful attempt to seize our life at the expense of the life of "the other." Power is judged by this theology, not as a quality and quest for the realization of human potentiality but as a bid for preeminence—"being first" (*arche*). To this bid, the response of Scripture is: "The first shall be last."[59]

It is an indisputable fact of Christian history that "Patriarchy [has been] the original and most pervasive model of systematic exploitation."[60] In church and

---

57. In *The Emptying God: A Buddhist-Jewish-Christian Conversation,* eds., John B. Cobb, Jr., and Christopher Ives (Maryknoll, N.Y.: Orbis Books, 1990), 106.

58. *Thinking the Faith,* 22ff.

59. For an alternative to feminist rejection of the theology of the cross, see Elisabeth Moltmann-Wendel's essay, "Is There a Feminist Theology of the Cross?" in Elisabeth Moltmann-Wendel and Jürgen Moltmann, eds., *God—His and Hers,* trans. John Bowden (New York: Crossroad, 1991), 77ff.

60. Keller, in *The Emptying God,* 103.

theology, males have been "first." This being so, patriarchy must be named and judged by the Word of God. Yet, the theoretical problematic implicit in patriarchy is not fatherhood (*patros*) but the sinful propensity, which males have been the most successful in exploiting, of seeking primacy (*arche*). Without setting aside the critique of patriarchy and hierarchy, Christian theology must contend simultaneously with the rudimentary (and in that sense theoretical) problematic that these concrete, historical forms of domination and exploitation embody. Apart from such contention, there can be no viable alternative to the continued, idolatrous presentation of doctrines of God that, in one way or another, render the deity first among the first. Power itself must be critically engaged, for not all the forms and representations that power can assume have been assumed. Apart from an ongoing struggle with the bid for power that arises ubiquitously and spontaneously in human souls and communities, we shall never know how to profess faith in a God who declares, "My grace is sufficient for you, my power is made perfect in weakness" (2 Cor. 12:9). "The crux of the cross is its revelation of the fact that the final power of God over man is derived from the self-imposed weakness of his love."[61]

---

61. Reinhold Niebuhr, *The Essential Reinhold Niebuhr: Selected Essays and Addresses,* ed. Robert McAfee Brown (New Haven: Yale Univ. Press, 1986), 22.

CHAPTER ▪ THREE
A Suffering God?

8. After the Death of God, A Quest for Transcendence

8.1. Disenchantment with Secularity.   The nations of the North American continent began as European colonies with high religious intent. Without God we are perhaps inconceivable. Yet belief in God does not come easily to us today. How shall we speak of God after the "death of God"? That, in its starkest expression, is the question to which this chapter of constructive theology is addressed.

What can we say about the context in which we find ourselves—and which is found *within* ourselves—as it relates in particular to God-talk and belief in God?

It is plausible, I think, to observe about the Theological situation that obtains in the North American context today that it is a strange and in some ways contradictory one, though not altogether unintelligible, given the past upon which we have been reflecting. Two impulses seem to inform our collective spirit, and they are not easily compatible. On the one hand, spontaneous acknowledgment of a recognizably Christian God in our vaguely "religious" society is conspicuously diminished in comparison with the past. While television evangelists and some "conservative" expressions of Christianity can still achieve an impressive following, their following does not represent the dominant middle of the society but rather a segment of the population (albeit a large one) made fearful by events and seeking in religion a refuge from the wanton spirit of the age. Because we are a society experiencing manifold crises, the most critical dimension of which is our incapacity to confront forthrightly the deeper crises that we face, the clamor for an "old-time religion" is strong among us; this does not mean that genuine belief in God characterizes our society, it only means that we are afraid.

But while the biblical God certainly bids those who "labor and are heavy-laden" to "come to me" (Matt. 11:28), Christians in North America today are greatly deceived if they think that the periodic rushes upon the divine mercy seat that characterize our public are unambiguous spiritual quests. However humanly understandable they may be, these so-called revivals—and especially these twentieth-century revivals—have more to say about our "future shock" than about our spiritual depth. The God of the Bible comforts the afflicted, certainly. But this God also "afflicts the comfortable" (Reinhold Niebuhr), exchanging their usually rather private anxieties for a new, deep, and caring vigilance for the world that is greatly loved. To picture God as the healer of sick and weary souls without mentioning God's habit of placing a heavy public responsibility upon these same souls, being somewhat healed, is to do grave injustice to the tradition of Jerusalem. "Come unto me"—yes. But. . . "take my yoke upon you" (Matt. 11:29, KJV).[1]

While the conventional deity of Christendom is by no means ignored in our context, serious theology and faith cannot afford to assume an apologetic that accepts the public demand for "God" at face value. The truth is, surely, that North America too, along with the Western world in general, has for a long time now experienced a distinct distancing from "the Father Almighty." The God of Christendom is not only inaccessible to many, perhaps most, but "he" is incredible to many—and obnoxious to some.[2] Vast numbers of us, including many within the churches, are increasingly alienated from this "old Theology." Not only the intelligentsia, which has long been absent from the heart of Christendom, but also most of our young find it quite impossible to relate to the quasi-official theism of church and society. Women, as we have recognized in the preceding chapter, are conspicuously and vociferously at odds with this still highly masculine deity.[3] And those who are least able to protect themselves from the slings and arrows of outrageous fortune twentieth-century style—the growing "underclass"[4] in our midst—for the most part find that a God whose primary virtue is might, success, or winning has little to say to them. That kind of power only makes the powerless more conscious of their

---

1. See Ben Smillie, *Beyond the Social Gospel: Church Protest on the Prairies* (Toronto: United Church Publishing House, and Saskatoon: Fifth House Publishers, 1991), especially chaps. 1 and 2, 23–45.

2. "Both western accounts of Christianity—Protestant and Catholic—have emphasized the arbitrary power of God in a way which seems to me fundamentally wrong and which has produced a picture of God whom one should not worship." George P. Grant, in *George Grant in Process: Essays and Conversations,* ed. Larry Schmidt (Toronto: Anansi, 1978), 103.

3. See in this connection Doris Jean Dyke, *Crucified Woman* (Toronto: United Church Publishing House, 1991), a study of reactions to a sculpture entitled "Crucified Woman" erected in a garden at the University of Toronto.

4. See John Kenneth Galbraith, *The Culture of Contentment* (Boston: Houghton Mifflin Co., 1992).

impotency. The official God of the official culture still functions to insulate certain classes of people against the sharp pains of finitude—especially the pain of self-knowledge. But this Theology "works," as we have seen, only where there are other types of insulation as well, such as economic security, diversions made possible by relative wealth and free time, and a general atmosphere of well-being. God really is, in this sense, rather "dead" among us; and we are apologetically insensitive if we do not know that we are bearing witness to God *post mortem Dei.*

On the other hand, a quite different impulse also governs the mood of our society. We do not experience what might theoretically have been thought would be the case—what indeed was assumed by some earlier studies would be the case—namely, the more or less nonchalant acceptance of a world without God. Some considered that such acceptance would be the natural reaction to that secularity that has been stealing over the Western world for a century or more. Pockets of celebrators of God's "death"—some of them refugees from the Beat Generation or the Age of Aquarius—dot the landscape; and certainly most people in our society are far from being anguished over God's "eclipse" (Buber). At any rate, their anxiety does not normally attach itself directly to that absent Source. Yet, quite in defiance of Friedrich Nietzsche, we are decidedly not happy in the God-forsaken world.

On the contrary, it becomes increasingly clear that we may be quietly lamenting the loss of God. Not only is there very little militant atheism among us today, such as one could discover in the nineteenth century,[5] but the atheism that exists does not find much to be militant about. Few are simply detached, religiously speaking, few indifferent, few content with one-dimensional secularity. Perhaps little overt theological discourse takes place outside the churches, synagogues, mosques, and academic religious circles, but there is much covert searching after . . . something. Mystery? Transcendence? Meaning? Besides the emergence of "New Age" and other alternatives to conventional religion, one is conscious of a vast and even palpable dissatisfaction permeating the status quo, a disenchantment that can be interpreted—and by many non-Christians is interpreted—as inarticulate religious longing, "sighs too deep for words." Many of the most promising young, who on the one hand do not appear in churches but on the other openly resist their generation's alarming proneness to self-destruction, are even open to God-talk.

The brush with the enormous problems that beset humankind in our age, perhaps especially problems relating to the deterioration of the natural environment, has created what may be regarded as a whole new species of North American intellectuals: the this-worldly, scientifically oriented and trained researcher who is driven to metaphysical questions through his or her close

---

5. See the earlier reference to Robert Ingersoll in the Introduction, n. 8.

contact with impossible and unacceptable physical realities.[6] There is perhaps more authentic questing for transcendence in unchurched circles of social justice, peace, and environmental concern than in all of our evangelism put together. We find ourselves, if we roam widely enough in our marketplace, in a new era of ultimate questions—indeed, of ultimate concern. Traditional metaphysics may not suffice, but neither do traditional physics. There is not half the confidence in science and technology that there was in the 1950s, or even a decade ago; on the contrary, more people seem to fear and resent unlimited application of technology than trust it implicitly.

A great skepticism about humanity in general and Western civilization in particular has swept over us[7]—to the point that sensitive Christians have themselves, often, to become defenders of Homo sapiens and of our own civilization as much as apologists for God. Often it is easier for Christians and other theists to bear witness to God today than it is to testify to the inherent meaningfulness of the human project. The failure of modern humanity has obscured the demise of premodern Divinity. The God of conventional Christian theism may be dead, yet the divinity that replaced "him"—Man, the Measure of All Things—may have turned out to be an impotent idol.

8.2. No Simple Apologetic. What are Christians to make of such a situation? I think that we must see it, first, as a rather clear rejection of the Theology that Western Christendom has habitually offered. If it is true, as I have argued in the previous chapter, that "the Father Almighty" functions primarily in our society to insulate people from the reality of their situation; that such a Theology constitutes part of the repressive mechanism of a class that can still camouflage the truth because it is well-padded economically and psychically; and that this Theology, accordingly, is partly responsible for the oppression of others who suffer from First World luxury, aggressiveness, and self-deceit,

---

6. "The contemporary conversation between theology and the sciences is little known by many, even though the picture of reality coming to us from the sciences is not only one that we must take seriously if our planet is to survive and flourish but also probably the most attractive picture for theology since the medieval synthesis. I suspect this conversation is seen by some as erudite and irrelevant, at best material for academic conferences between the elite few theologians who can understand the complexities of quantum physics and the equally few scientists who find religious questions interesting if not necessarily important.

"Nothing, I believe, could be further from the truth. For the first time in several hundred years we have the possibility of thinking holistically about God and the world, and this possibility is being given to us by the 'common creation story' coming from the sciences, from cosmology, astrophysics, and biology." Sallie McFague, "Cosmology and Christianity: Implications of the Common Creation Story for Theology," in *Theology at the End of Modernity,* ed. Sheila Greeve Davaney (Philadelphia: Trinity Press International, 1991), 23.

7. See Jacques Ellul, *The Betrayal of the West,* trans. Matthew J. O'Connel (New York: Seabury Press, 1978); Jerry Mander, *In the Absence of the Sacred: The Failure of Technology and the Survival of the Indian Nations* (San Francisco: Sierra Club Books, 1992).

then as responsible "professors" of Christian faith in our time we must drastically alter our Theology. It is not just a question of correct doctrine, it is a matter of discipleship. A Theology that maintains the image of deity based on a power principle that can only comfort the comfortable is a flagrantly disobedient, not merely a doctrinally distorted, Theology.

While some may consider that to be too strong a statement, I shall not retract it. Ideas are not neutral. Theological ideas are terribly potent, even where they are only implicit and only halfheartedly believed. The idea of God is still the most potent of all theological ideas. A people's God is always in some measure a collective representation of the people, of their self-image, their expectations and fears, their ambitions and values. The imperial God of the "Christian" nations of the West, even in "his" decadent—even in "his" dead—estate, still wields enormous ideological force in the world. Perhaps this God is even more powerful dead than alive. For when this God was alive "he" was still somewhat unpredictable. "The Father Almighty," alive, did indeed sometimes put down the mighty from their seats and exalt the humble and meek—because the mighty actually believed in God's reality and therefore occasionally, in spite of themselves, felt themselves judged. The trouble with a dead or only half-alive Almighty is that "he" seldom interferes with the predilections and plans of the mighty. Since God is for them little more than a convenient memory of the omnipotence they covet for themselves, they can always interpret the other side of God's reputed character (for example, God's "preferential option for the poor") in a manner favorable to their own continued preeminence.

At very least, Christians in North America today who are called to the vocation of thinking the faith must begin to delete from their professing of it everything that functions to confirm the powerful in their unrepentant oppression of the powerless. If we were to do nothing more than that—a work of penitent deletion—we would be contributing a great deal to the *shalom* of the earth.

Can we go farther? Beyond the work of deletion and the renunciation of theistic concepts that have proven to be dangerous as the basis of discipleship, is it possible for us to propose other emphases, stress other aspects (perhaps neglected or submerged dimensions) of the long history of God-talk in Christianity? Beyond the necessary work of distinguishing God from America, or rather from those elements of North American reality that have adapted divinity to their own imperial inclinations, is it possible for the church today to entertain a Theology that positively engages the second impulse described above—the quest for transcendence, for meaning, for purity, for a future that is not simply shocking?

Answers, it seems to me, must not be given too quickly. It is tempting to take up the societal quest for mystery and meaning and cause it to correlate nicely with the God Christians have always professed. The apologist in all

Christians is excited by that prospect, but it is much too easy. Christians in North America today cannot without pain—that is, without a painful rethinking of their own tradition and a painful realignment of their own loyalties—hold up God to those who have begun, despite the rhetoric of light, to suspect that they may be sitting in darkness and the shadow of death.

The one absolutely clear message that we are getting from our world is that it is not necessary for us any longer to be chaplain to the imperium. God and America, for at least a significant minority of our contemporaries, are no longer simply interchangeable or mutually inclusive realities. God may become God again, also in North America, for those who have ears to hear. Disciples of Jesus Christ in the United States and Canada at the end of what was to have been "the Christian Century" are under no obligation to speak and act as though they had to uphold the whole value system of their society, or at least not set God in opposition to the pursuits of the dominant culture. In short, prophetic Theology is possible, and on a scale that may never have been the case in our context heretofore.

Beyond the prophetic critique of the equation of God with our way of life, may we also hope to offer a witness to divine presence that engages the real quest for truth and transcendence that is certainly also part of the fabric of our context?

Not a facile answer, yet something approaching an authentic one may be given to this question: We may do this, on condition that we are able to revise, imaginatively, our profession of the faith, beginning with what we believe concerning God. We may go beyond merely critical Theology and toward a more constructive Theology if and insofar as we demonstrate our readiness to listen to the quest for transcendence and to explore, in the light of it, some of the minority traditions of historic Christianity that were suppressed by the dominant Theological convention I have named "the Father Almighty."

Such minority traditions do exist.[8] Deletion (as distinct from some types of deconstruction) does not simply mean jettisoning the past, as the modernists thought; it also means rediscovering the past. We are not alone in our present. There is another succession, another apostolic tradition, and it is not easily identifiable with the one that was counted so. Even today, God is able to raise up from theological stones that were rejected by the builders of Christendom foundations for a "new" Theology.

If we are faithful in such a work of tearing down and building up (Jer. 1:10), then I suspect that one theme will prevail, namely, the reinstatement of that banished negative, that presentiment of Nothingness at the very core of things,

---

8. See Rosemary Radford Ruether's discussion of tradition as it relates to feminist theology ("usable tradition") in her *Sexism and God-Talk: Toward a Feminist Theology* (Boston: Beacon Press, 1983), chap. 1, 12ff.

that frustrating lack of finality, which had to be expunged from the ideologically triumphant Theology of Christendom.

9. Knowing the Living God

In order to retain a modicum of order in a subject that can easily become confusing, I shall return now to the structure of the discussion followed in both preceding chapters. Using the three basic headings established there (the knowledge of God, the being of God, and the works of God), I shall endeavor to outline the directions in which God-talk today might be more responsibly and faithfully professed in our North American context. I shall also retain the same subdivisions within these three larger divisions, except that in the case of the main headings and the subheadings, I shall use nomenclature different from that of the previous chapters, in order to suggest through the headings themselves something of the content that I should like to develop in each.

9.1. "Lord, I Believe; Help Thou Mine Unbelief." We return first, then, to the question of the knowledge of God. Here, to recapitulate briefly, each of the three major "ways" of knowing pursued within the regnant traditions of the church have accentuated (according to the preceding analysis, unduly) the positive dimension of each type. Thus (1) the revealing God has been presented too consistently as one in whom the (negative) dimension of concealment is lacking; (2) God as counterpart of the human spirit has taken too little account of the human sense of "being alone"; and (3) God as the reasonable consequence of thought about the world has not been sufficiently cognizant, at least for our epoch, of the unreasonable, disjointed, and absurd world, the world that would hardly lead anyone to the splendid conclusion that it is the beloved of a Creator.

As we undertake to explore a Theology that engages our own context, we need to be conscious particularly of the excluded negative. In the first place we should ponder whether it *is* a matter of negation. Is concealment simply the negation of revelation, or does it in some way define the nature of revelation? Is the experience of alienation ("being alone") simply the negation of reconciliation ("being with"), or is it somehow necessary to the latter—perhaps even its *conditio sine qua non?* Is the sense of the absurd simply the negation of reasonability? May not it be the dialogue partner of reason—as it is, for example, in the work of contemporary authors like Elie Wiesel?[9]

These are not merely theoretical questions; they are bound up with concrete reality—the reality of our North American context. In a context where negation is now not easily negated, it is at least in part precisely the undiluted

---

9. See Maurice Friedman, *To Deny Our Nothingness* (New York: Dell Pub. Co., 1967), Part 10, 309–54.

triumph of the positive in the Christian tradition's treatment of Theological knowledge that constitutes the most effective barrier to faith. Where faith too often means sight and knowledge connotes certitude rather than confidence, those who cannot see so much and are far from certain even of themselves, let alone God, are discouraged from the outset from taking seriously the Christian profession of God. It could be that our very positivism of Theological knowing is the false *skandalon* that has to be removed so that the true scandal may be perceived and the world, *our* world, may become a little more disturbed and surprised by the Christian account of ultimate reality.

But let us follow the established pattern and consider, in turn, the three modes of the knowledge of God in the light of such a hypothesis.

9.2. Revealing and Concealing.

The tradition in all of its expressions excepting the most questionable, we have affirmed, insists that God is a revealing God. Revelation is not just an emergency measure, so to speak, adopted by a deity whom human fallenness has deprived of the possibility of immediacy. God is Self-revealing: that is of the essence of the godhead in this tradition. As such it presupposes both necessity and possibility: necessity, in that apart from God's Self-manifestation we should not know God, truly; possibility, in that God may reveal the divine Person to human beings since, as their Creator, God has given them a capacity for receiving the mystery of the divine Presence (a theme taken up in the second mode of the knowledge of God).

But let us consider more extensively the affirmation of God's Self-revelation; particularly let us do so in the light of the (possibly false) offense that is created by a conception of revelation that becomes detached from the Person who is its subject and its agent. In the first volume we have already noted the distinction between revelation as data (propositional revelation) and revelation as encounter.[10] We should pursue this now as it relates to the question of God and our knowledge of God. Two points in particular need to be discussed.

First, consider the distortion that occurs in our Theology when revelation connotes primarily the impartation of information about God. What happens is that God then becomes identifiable with a collection of supposed theistic verities. These "truths" lend themselves to being imbibed and imparted. On their basis one may seem to know a great deal about God. But is that not a false impression, always? Karl Barth, who wrote more about God than, perhaps, any other Christian in recorded history, nevertheless declared that theology has to be "the most modest science"; it is determined to be so, he said, because of its object, who is no object at all but a living Subject.[11]

---

10. *Thinking the Faith*, 402ff.
11. *Evangelical Theology: An Introduction*, trans. Grover Foley (New York: Holt, Rinehart and Winston, 1963), 7.

When revelation is separated from the revealing "Thou" it does permit of being possessed, multiplied, and manipulated. There is no end to the Theological "truth" that can then be amassed and mastered!

But if one is on the outside of this religious enterprise that is so knowledgeable about the Deity, then is it not likely that one will be amazed at the extent of its comprehension? In an age of belief such as the European Middle Ages are said to have been, public amazement over Christian near-omniscience was evidently not common. The scholastics were capable of astonishing feats of speculative Theology, and few people appear to have found these feats presumptuous. But we are not part of an age of belief. On the contrary, despite the lamentation over our unfortunate incapacity for faith, most of us are deeply impressed by the silence of eternity. In such a state, to be met by representatives of a religion that is so very knowledgeable is simply to encounter beings of another order altogether. One is hardly engaged by such a witness, but only made more certain of one's not belonging to that company.

Earlier we introduced the concept of theological reconstruction as deletion, and in this connection nothing seems more in need of being deleted from Christian Theology in North America today than this tendency of almost all expressions of Christianity, even the most liberal, to possess greater knowledge of God than we both do have in fact and can have in theory.

By "theory" I mean the kind of sound teaching that recognizes more exactly what biblical faith and the best testimony of the tradition of Jerusalem understand by revelation as God's mode of Self-communication. This is the second point requiring attention here: What does it mean for our Theology that God is Self-revealing?

The answer that must first be understood in the light of the distortion under discussion is that it does not mean that God, in this tradition, is characterized by a willingness to give out extraordinary information about divinity and all else. That there are data associated with God's revealing is not denied; it is after all a historically grounded concept.[12] But the idea that data are the heart of the revelation is entirely false and misleading. At the heart of revelation is the disclosure of a Presence. It is *Self*-revelation. This is not only a fine sentiment of Christian piety; it is a highly critical first principle of biblical thought about God. For it means that every assertion about God, every doctrine, every dogma, every hymn and prayer, stands under the judgment of a Presence that it cannot possibly define; and that, the more it thinks to define and confine this Presence, the more idolatrous it must be judged.

There is in other words a kind of refusal in God's invitation to communion, a kind of distancing in God's proximity, a kind of hiding in God's making-known.

---

12. See *Thinking the Faith*, 409ff.

A Suffering God?

Is this after all so very strange? Is it not at least analogous to every sort of self-revealing known to human experience? Who is so profoundly known to us as those whom we know we can never fully know? Who is so unconfinable by us as those who give themselves to us freely? Who is so far as those who are close, so other as those who are familiar, so mysterious as those who reveal to us their innermost selves?

Why is it that this sort of knowing is so little in evidence in our conventional presentations of the Christian God? We who know so very much about God—how did it happen that we failed to discern the theme of unknownness and unknowability running throughout the Scriptures and the most gripping traditions of our faith? "I will be who I will be," insists the God of Sinai, the unnameable one. And Jesus, in whom Christians say God has gone all the way and revealed the very mind and heart of Divinity—this Jesus remains a stranger to his closest associates, is constantly misnamed by them, is forever having to distinguish himself from their misapprehensions of him, is recognized for the mystery that he is, apparently, only by lunatics and demons . . . who therefore tremble.

Where has this biblical sense of the divine remoteness ever found a home in the church?—in the "liberal" churches of North America, especially, with their awesome familiarity, their chatty piousness in the presence of God. From what pulpits does one regularly learn anything of the unavoidable biblical theme of divine and human hiddenness: the God who hides from people and the people who hide from God? In what classrooms of theology is close attention paid to the recurring motif of the divine concealment? Where besides in a few books of theology, written mainly by Jews and other persons never quite acceptable to Christendom (Nicholas of Cusa, Kierkegaard, Miskotte[13]) does one read anything at all about the darkness of God, the eclipse of God, or even that "God-above-God" of whom Paul Tillich occasionally spoke and wrote? Yet if concealment is there in the tradition of Jerusalem, at the very heart of the revelatory act; and if it is there, analogously, in our profoundest relationships with our own kind and with the earth itself; and if we know perfectly well that it is there (and we do!), how has it come about that we Christians have found out so very much about God—have indeed convinced ourselves (some of us) that we have exclusive knowledge of this One, who in revealing conceals and in concealing reveals?

Were we even now to rediscover this dialectic, which incidentally has not been without its witnesses (though they represent a thin tradition), what difference might it make to the credibility of our witness?

It could make a great deal of difference. For in a context where at the level of existing, if not always at the level of conscious thinking, people have discovered

---

13. See Kornelius H. Miskotte, *When the Gods Are Silent*, trans. John W. Doberstein (London: St. James Place, 1967).

139

the eternal silence, the "death" of God, no Theology will prove the least engaging unless it makes room for all that emptiness. Of course the disciple community does not confine its witness to the divine concealment. But unless it knows something of that hiddenness, it will not know anything of the condition of most of its worldly contemporaries. Unless it has experienced something of the divine refusal that is present in the divine acceptance, it will have no grounds for discourse with the spirit of our age. And without such solidarity, every other bid for relevance is sheer condescension. Unless Christian profession of God is in some fundamental way conscious of God's inaccessibility, our witness to the living God will engage no quest for transcendence known to late twentieth-century humanity.

Nor should this be thought a brazen innovation, a gesture in the direction of existentialism or some other modern phenomenon. It is rather the recovery of a pitifully neglected theme, a theme present, among other places, at the core of the Reformation. Martin Luther, who understood well this dialectic of revealing and concealing—*Deus revelatus/Deus absconditus*—regarded it as the cornerstone of the *theologia crucis*. [14] Luther learned this dialectic, not only from the Scriptures of Israel and the church, but from the whole submerged tradition of Christian mysticism. What we have inherited by way of the knowledge of God is, by comparison, the product of an almost unrelieved scholastic triumphalism. We "professionals" know so much—about God!

The point of departure for any doctrine of God that is contextually responsible in North America today is a theology of the cross that begins with the humbling of Theology in the presence of *Theos*. If what God reveals is not a "what" but God's own Person, then unknowing and even unknowability must be found at the very core of our knowing such a One.

9.3. (Nevertheless) "We Are Not Alone . . . ". If a reconstruction of God-talk in our context must first involve a reconstruction of the meaning of revelation, one that leaves room for the mystery of divine Presence, it also entails a rethinking of the human sense of being a counterpart of something, of someone. This ancient theme, classically expressed in Augustine's middle works but informing the whole apologetic tradition from Paul's sermon on Mars Hill to Paul Tillich's "method of correlation," has perhaps new coinage in our context, but only, I think, if Christians are willing to resist the temptation to usher in the Deity as the answer to every twinge of cosmic loneliness.

---

14. See Walther von Loewenich, *Luther's Theology of the Cross,* trans. Herbert J. A. Bouman (Belfast: Christian Journals Ltd., 1976), chap. 1, 27ff.; Alister E. McGrath, *Luther's Theology of the Cross* (London: Basil Blackwell, 1985), chap. 5, 148ff.; Alister McGrath, *The Enigma of the Cross* (London: Hodder and Stoughton, 1987), chap. 5, 102ff.

Augustine's God, we have seen, is virtually inescapable. So is Schleiermacher's.[15] The human experience of contingency for the "Father of Liberal Theology" inevitably implies the intuition of that upon which we are ultimately dependent. Perhaps even Tillich, who understood much about the depths of twentieth-century alienation, was too bound to an apologetic tradition that was ready to offer God as answer to the human question, and Jesus Christ as the bringer of a "New Being" that resolves the contradictions of our existence.

Late twentieth-century disenchantment with secularity, which is perhaps the core of postmodernity, does not easily lend itself to Christian apologetics of the traditional variety. North Americans who have ceased giving credence to the salvific possibilities of technology and the "religion of progress" (G. Grant) should not be considered immediate candidates for Christian evangelization. Like Margaret Drabble's nonhero in *The Ice Age,* many of our contemporaries "do not know how man can live without God," but like the same fictional figure they have not received the gift of faith along with this insight.[16] In the age of ecology most people have at least begun to understand their dependence upon other creatures, but the sense of ultimate dependency—dependence upon a Creator—still involves a leap of more than "natural" reason.

In short, it seems clear that any discussion of deity as the presupposition of our humanity will have to occur in proximity to the lived experience that we may really be alone; that there is no sublime correspondent to our anxious quest for transcendence; that our intimation of being counterpart to something, someone, is just an all-too-human longing.

Can the Christian profession of God's reality make room for such an apparently antithetical impulse? Should it even attempt to do so?

There is of course no call for Christians to tailor-make their profession of belief in God to the religious or cryptoreligious sensibilities of their context. The leap and the *skandalon* cannot be removed by apologetics. But neither is there any reason for continuing to profess a Theology whose content further alienates the alienated. The Christian *apologia* is not committed to the dominant forms of

---

15. See Isabel Carter Heyward, *The Redemption of God: A Theology of Mutual Relation* (Lanham, New York, & London: Univ. Press of America, 1982), 63, n. 26.

16. "Anthony Keating found himself thinking, I do not know how man can do without God.

"It was such an interesting concept that he stopped in the roadway, like Paul on the way to Damascus: not exactly felled by the realization, for alas, faith had not accompanied the concept. But it stopped him in his tracks, nevertheless. He stood there for a moment or two, and thought of all those who accept so readily the non-existence of God, who find such persuasive substitutes, such convincing alternative sanctions for their own efforts. Anthony had never been able to accept the humanist argument that man can behave well through his own manhood. Man clearly does not do so: that is that." (New York: Penguin Books, 1977; p. 258.)

its own past, which were elaborated in response to contexts more inclined to specific theistic belief than is our own. It is possible in the post-Christian era that has also invaded North America to live one's entire life in the supposition that one lives and dies alone. One probably does not do so happily, but perhaps one is able to cope. Moreover, this supposition is not entertained only by those who decisively turn away from formal religious belief. Doubt does not know any neat statistical boundary between belief and unbelief, but invades also communities of faith. That we are perhaps quite alone: this is the configuration of the doubt, unbelief, and spiritual anguish that accompany the life of faith today. As in the Middle Ages spiritual anguish took the form of a recurrent suspicion of eternal damnation, so in our age faith lives with the prospect that "out there" (J. A. T. Robinson) there is no objective correlate to its devotion—that it is just faith; that it is neither engendered nor met by grace.

This is certainly a new phenomenon in Western spirituality so far as its particulars are concerned, including the sheer preponderance of the experience, yet it is not without precedent. Indeed, some of the most evocative prototypes of this abiding sense of aloneness are found in the Scriptures themselves. The Psalms— the very hymns of Israel—are virtually teeming with the fearful intimation of our creaturely solitariness: "I am like a vulture of the wilderness, like an owl of the waste places; I lie awake, I am like a lonely bird on the housetop" (Ps. 102:6-7, RSV). Lamentations, that forgotten book, is at least as conscious of the absence of God as are contemporary post-Holocaust commentators like Richard Rubenstein. The book of Job details the career of one utterly estranged, who hears at last the "voice out of the whirlwind" only as a response wholly unexpected and perhaps not permanently comforting. Ecclesiastes is the philosophic counterpart of the poem of Job—a biblical writing, not incidentally, that has been for many twentieth-century Christians an unlikely doorway into the house of God.

And what shall we say of Jesus? Whoever is able to break through the welter of pious, sentimental, and callously doctrinal characterizations of the Christ to the human being upon whom these well-intentioned images have been heaped, will discover a person who probably has more in common with the protagonist of *Jesus Christ Superstar* or the Quebec film *Jesus of Montreal* than with the heroic orthodox divinity or the equally heroic liberal humanity that have dominated in Christendom.[17] Who is more alone than Jesus? Moreover, his being-alone is not only the consequence of his desertion by the former companions of his humanity. The cry of dereliction is there—and is it accidental that this cry, among all the events and words and teachings of the newer Testament, is the

---

17. See below, chap. 9, sec. 38.2.

moment in the biblical story before which the spirit of twentieth-century humanity feels something like reverence?[18]

In sum, we do not have to invent a Theology that incorporates (or at least does not exclude, a priori) the sense of our being pathetic counterparts of an absentee deity. We only have to cease treating our own best sources as if their Theology were ante-Christian! As if, in the postresurrectional situation, so to speak, all that unbelief, betrayal, foresakenness, and *tentatio* (temptation) had been supplanted by a victorious assurance that no longer doubted the answering Presence. Newer Testamental faith, like the faith of Israel before it, is by no means so certain about God as subsequent stages of Christendom have led us to think. That is to say, it is faith, not sight. It is confidence, not certitude. It is therefore in dialogue with its antithesis, not only at the beginning but perpetually (Romans 7). It is trust in a divine Presence which, since God cannot be "had" but only "lived with," must contend also with the divine absence.

It is therefore capable of being surprised at God's sometimes "being there." Since it is denied the assurance of divine reciprocity, the experience of God's presence, when it occurs, is in fact far more deeply moving than can ever be the case where that presence is presumed upon.

The contemporary creed of the United Church of Canada, the opening phrase of which I have used in the subheading above, captures in a remarkable way the existential situation of humankind in North America and elsewhere today. As creeds should always do, it identifies explicitly that in the face of which Christians profess their faith: for us that means the experience of abandonment, the abiding suspicion that there is no divine partner in the covenant that is our ecclesiastical charter. Against this, the creed rightly asks the congregation to profess: "We are not alone, we live in God's world. . . ."

The authenticity of this creed, like that of all historic creedal summations, however, depends upon serious prior contemplation, on the part of the professing community, of that over against which the positive declaration is uttered as "hope against hope." A silent "Nevertheless" has always preceded all profound

---

18. "Jesus' death cry on the cross is 'the open wound' of every Christian theology, for consciously or unconsciously every Christian theology is a reply to the 'Why?' with which Jesus dies, a reply that attempts to give theological meaning to his death. But when Christian theologians do not accept what Jesus suffered from God, they are like Job's friends, not like Job himself. The contradiction between the Sonship of God and forsakenness by God is a contradiction that cannot be resolved, either by reducing the divine Sonship or by failing to take the forsakenness seriously. Even the words of Psalm 22 on Jesus' lips do not solve the conflict, for the psalm ends with a prayer of thanksgiving for rescue from deadly peril. There was no such rescue on Golgotha; and with the psalm Jesus no longer speaks to God as his 'Father'; he addresses him as the God of Israel. Early manuscripts of Mark's Gospel intensify the cry into: 'Why have you exposed me to shame?' and 'Why have you cursed me?'" (Jürgen Moltmann, *The Way of Jesus Christ: Christology in Messianic Dimensions,* trans. Margaret Kohl [Minneapolis: Fortress Press, 1993], 166–67.)

declarations of faith in God. Today this "Nevertheless" must become less silent if our expressions of belief in the "Thou" who responds to our "I" and "We" are to be lifted out of the morass of religious predictability to become genuine professions of faith.[19]

9.4. God and Postmodern Rationality.

It was the achievement of Western modernity to demonstrate that God could not be demonstrated. The postponement of this insight was itself impressive, lasting as it did for five centuries. St. Thomas first sensed the trend and temporarily calmed the misgivings of Christian intellectuals with his new synthesis of faith and reason. The nominalists, Ockham particularly, gave reason its due while reserving a clear space for faith. Kant (according to Nietzsche the "great postponer") still found a "practical reason" that could retain a space for deity in the face of an increasingly earthbound rationality. Schleiermacher located the path to God through suprarational yet thought-filled sensitivity (*Gefühl*). But the trend was strong, and Reason had perhaps already gone over to the side of agnosticism long before Hume and others announced the fact.

Yet nothing is static in human history, least of all humanity's estimation of itself. With its rationality in full bloom, Western humanity invented marvels of technique, conquered ancient diseases, overcame distance and barriers to communication . . . and produced, in the process, the wherewithal necessary to its own and perhaps all nature's annihilation. Fortunately, the object lesson apparently has not been altogether lost on the human race. Though it has apparently effected in large numbers of the affluent peoples of the earth a state of programmed indifference and a flight into irrationality, it has raised for some the question: Could our conception and use of reason itself have been too narrow?[20] Thus, at the end of the century of technological prometheanism there is, among significant numbers of North Americans today, a new uncertainty concerning the possibilities and limits of human rationality.

---

19. A brilliant illustration of the "Nevertheless" as I am using it here is provided by Günter Grass in his 1979 novel, *Das Treffen in Telgte*. Grass stages in the small pilgrimage town of Telgte an imaginary meeting of all the poets of Germany, paralleling the great political gathering in nearby Münster, Westphalia, which brought to an end one of the most terrible conflicts in European history, the Thirty Years' War. The object of the (purely fictional) meeting of the poets is to determine whether something positive can still be said about the human project in the wake of all that chaos, bloodshed, and nihilism. In the process, the poets themselves become profoundly discouraged, for they realize how thoroughly they are themselves implicated in the causes of violence and warfare.

At the height of their debilitation, the famous musician, Heinrich Schütz, rises at last to confront the failure everyone feels. Why have they assembled? "For the sake," says Schütz, "of the written words, which poets alone [have] the power to write in accordance with the dictates of art. And also to wrest from helplessness—he knew it well—a faint 'and yet' [*dennoch* = nevertheless]." English translation by Ralph Manheim, *The Meeting at Telgte* (London: Secker & Warburg, 1981), 69.

20. See the discussion of "Two Types of Reason" in *Thinking the Faith,* 390ff.

A Suffering God?

Does this mean that God may be allowed back into the discussion? It should not, it seems to me, be taken to imply that at this juncture in history Western Christians are at liberty to reach back behind the Enlightenment (as some nineteenth-century Romantics did) and speak and act as though we could again have immediate discourse with premodern metaphysics. The Enlightenment was not only a necessary human rejection of the kind of religious determinism that took everything, the plague included, as being the will of God; it also raised intellectual questions of lasting import to the profession of theistic belief. It is impossible, after the modern critique of religion, to come to God authentically as the conclusion of reasonable discourse. The Christian nominalists were right, in my view, in insisting that revelation is the norm where Christian theology is concerned. And classical Protestantism was also right in accepting that judgment.

There is, however, a tendency in Christianity where it has been most affected by the watershed separating medieval from modern world views to calcify the juxtaposition of reason and revelation, as though nothing could happen to their relationship after the division agreed upon by the Renaissance and Reformation. An internal development in the school of Reason has clearly left many of its best representatives in a humbler frame of mind than when Reason first began to entertain its potentiality for autonomy. Today human rationality thinks itself divine only in those backwaters where it has not yet contemplated with any seriousness the destructive capacities of a bid for mastery on the part of Homo sapiens, which does not revere the world it seeks to understand. Reason after the Enlightenment, it is true, is no longer the compliant Beatrice who leads the soul to the courts of heaven; but neither is Reason—after Auschwitz and Hiroshima—the Mephistopheles whose only office is to lure humanity away from God.

God cannot be for us the logical consequence of thought about the world; but neither is No-God the consequence of thought about the world. Reason does not provide a viable and satisfying alternative to faith, as it once seemed to do. Nothing would be more absurd today than to set up temples to Reason, as did the enthusiastic of the French Revolution. There is in fact some cause for those who care about the fate of the earth to fear that many temples that *are* being erected to reason (alias Research) in our time are in reality monuments to unreason and, perhaps, to oblivion.

What reason's own critique of reason has produced, where our present topic is concerned, is a conspicuous vacuum: reason itself can no longer satisfy its own deepest questions: "I have come to believe that in the world there is nothing to explain the world," wrote the great American scientist Loren Eiseley.[21]

---

21. Richard E. Wentz, "The American Spirituality of Loren Eiseley," *The Christian Century* (April 25, 1984), 430.

145

This does not mean that Christians are at liberty to rush in with their answers. It does mean, however, that Christians have once more to enter seriously into dialogue with the most responsible representatives of nonpartisan human thought.[22]

That is a demanding challenge for Protestants in particular; for, on the basis both of the Renaissance/Enlightenment rejection of theistic reason and the Reformation's accentuation of revelation, Protestants have tended to conduct their discourse in a separate court. For the most part, we are still professing a God who is suprarational, thus avoiding the stringent demands of a rationality that, while it cannot be smug, cannot be expected to accept faith statements at face value, either.

There is, then, a new possibility—which is also a demanding kind of necessity—for dialogue with reason, and it is not being met in North America by either Christian pietism or Christian activism. The point of the dialogue cannot be persuasion, as in earlier versions of Christian apologetics, but engagement and mutual enhancement. The juncture at which this may and must occur is wherever reason recognizes the need for a mode of reflection and decision-making that cannot be attained by pursuing empirical and value-free investigation alone. "Unaided reason" has in many quarters today reached the surprising conclusion that it is gravely in need of aid. As knowledge (*scientia*) it needs, and knows that it needs, wisdom (*sapientia*). Only from some source of human wisdom can principles be derived that can guide, direct, and above all limit the endless pursuits and inventions of functional rationality.

The "God of the gaps" approach has been rightly scorned. But those who profess God must be willing to submit to the intellectual stringency that rationality necessarily brings to any dialogue with faith, in order humbly to point to the resources of wisdom to which the mind is opened through genuine profession of faith in a Creator God.

10. Emmanuel: God-with-Us

10.1. "I Will Be *Your* God."   Logically, of course, the knowledge of God and the being of God are inseparable. In speaking about the knowledge of God we have therefore had to assume some highly significant things about God's being. If, as we have affirmed, we know God as a revealing Presence who meets us in our state of estrangement, then we must recognize in this an implicit first

---

22. See McFague statement in n. 6 above. See also Jürgen Moltmann, *God in Creation: An Ecological Doctrine of Creation* (The Gifford Lectures of 1984–1985), trans. Margaret Kohl (Minneapolis: Fortress Press, 1993), 2–4.

principle in relation to the question of God's being—namely, that there is no interest here in depicting divinity in its solitude, a being among all the others, though higher, greater, more enduring. It must be taken quite literally that when this tradition insists upon God's being a revealing God, whose revelation is not the unveiling of secret truths but the presentation of Truth as the divine Presence as such, it intends us to consider the very being of God in relational terms. That is to say, the first principle of this Theology is that God's being comprises an orientation toward "the other"—is God's being-*with*.

We shall encounter this principle frequently in all phases of the present study, and it is possible that we should pause at this point in our Theological deliberations to explore the ontology that is here assumed. In the present context, however, it seems more advisable to continue along the lines of the structure that has been established in the foregoing and to allow the ontological assumptions of the whole study to penetrate it gradually. Increasingly it has seemed to me that in the tradition of Jerusalem we do not have to do only with a different way of thinking about divinity, humanity, and salvation, but with a different conception of that which is presupposed in all of these and in every other area of religious and philosophic thought, namely being itself. That is to say, Jerusalem presupposes an ontology that is unique and distinguishable both from "classical" (that is, largely Greek) and-modern ontologies.

Both of the latter consider being substantially. "To be" means to be endowed with certain qualities, properties, or substances that sustain existence. Different beings possess different endowments, and in varying degrees of intensity. God, in classical terms, possesses being fully and without any admixture of nonbeing. All the attributes conventionally associated with divinity are like so many variations on this fundamental theme.

In the tradition of Jerusalem, however, the primary interest is not with various distinctive beings and the qualities that constitute them but rather with their interrelatedness. "There is no substance of any kind, not even an ontological substance and certainly not a divine substance, prior to relating."[23] To put it in a formulary way, being itself for this tradition is relational—is "with-being" (*Mitsein*). This applies not only to the creation but also to the Creator, the ground and source of all that is: God is not a being, whose existence faith is called upon to accept, demonstrate, and testify to. God is rather a revealing Presence, a Companion—"*your* God." It is accordingly the object of the church's profession, not to demonstrate that God must *be* but to bear witness to God's being-there, being-with, and being-for the creature. Just as in its anthropological testimony it is the disciple community's vocation to show that we

---

23. Tom F. Driver, *Christ in a Changing World: Towards an Ethical Christology* (New York: Crossroads, 1981), 104.

human beings are creatures whose primary character stems from our being-in-the-presence-of-God (*coram Deo*), so in its Theology this community's calling is to picture God as the Mystery before, alongside, and in relation to whom "we live, move and have our being"—that is, as Emmanuel, God-with-Us.

If this ontological presupposition of the tradition is grasped in a rudimentary way from the outset, it will cast a whole new light on the discussion of the being *of God* as we turn to consider this subject, once more, under the aegis of the so-called attributes of Deity and the doctrine of the divine triunity.[24]

10.2. The Perfections of a Searching God. In our brief review of historical Theology, we noticed that the primary attributes of God as these are maintained within the inherited conventions of doctrine describe qualities that accentuate God's distinction from the creation: Unlike the human creature, who is bound to time, the Creator God is infinite, eternal; unlike the creature, who is weak and vulnerable, the Deity is all-powerful; unlike the creature, who is subject to radical change, God is immutable; unlike the creature, who is limited in knowledge, the divine being is omniscient. Or, to pick up the liberal Christian theme of themes: Unlike the human creature, whose love is always partly selfish and mixed with antithetical proclivities and emotions, the divine being is all-loving, all-merciful, all-forgiving.

What is wrong with this way of thinking about the fundamental character of God is that it regularly bypasses the aforementioned first principle of the biblical tradition concerning God. In distinguishing God so enthusiastically from the creature, it creates a false impression, which then informs every aspect of conventional Theology. Biblically, the essential factor in the being of God is not God's absolute distinction from all else but rather God's determined orientation toward the creation. "I will be *your* God!" God's differentiation from creation is by no means denied. One may even say, with Rudolf Otto and the early Barth, that God is "wholly other" (*totaliter alliter*). But this distinctiveness, including all the perfections of knowledge, presence, and power that constitute or describe it, is not what is primary. It is presupposition and means, not end. Later we shall claim something comparable with respect to human being, namely that it manifests certain qualities (rationality, freedom, dexterity, and so on) that are means to the end of its peculiar relatedness to God and to its fellow creatures. Likewise God may be said to manifest certain distinctive qualities, qualities different from those of any creature; but these qualities or perfections as such do not describe for biblical faith the essence of the divine. It is rather the character of the relationship with

---

24. For a discussion of "relational ontology" from the perspective of Christian anthropology, see my *Imaging God: Dominion as Stewardship* (Grand Rapids: Wm. B. Eerdmans Pub. Co., 1986), chaps. 4, 5, 6.

creation for which these attributes (so to speak) equip God that must occupy our full attention. We shall not even understand such attributes as omnipotence, omniscience, omnipresence, simplicity, and mercy, unless we regard them within the context of the divine determination to seek communion with the creature—to be "your God."

Strangely, for those who approach God-talk with what may indeed be "the usual" expectations, there is in this tradition no interest in providing answers to the question, What is God like internally, within God's own inner Self? It is assumed from the outset that God *is* who God reveals Godself to be; that God's becoming-present-to the creature is not an appendix to more weighty aspects of divinity, but of the first order. Therefore to speculate about (for example) the extent of God's power in isolation from the orientation of God toward creation is to engage in abstraction. Power, majesty, transcendent "overwhelmingness" (Macquarrie) are not absent from biblical testimony, to be sure; but they are there in the service of something very different from the mere show of superior strength on the part of deity. They serve the divine will to be "your God."

For this reason, all of the divine attributes—and especially this must be insisted upon with regard to the attributes associated with divine superiority—are strictly conditioned from the outset. For if it is proximity to the creature that God chiefly desires, then every potentiality that may be attributed to God has to accommodate itself to that end. Not even God can force creaturely reciprocity. Power, even God's power, cannot behave powerfully when its object is loving proximity to that which is weaker. All-knowingness, even God's omniscience, cannot act all-knowingly when its object is fellowship with beings whose knowledge is strictly circumscribed. Ubiquity of being, even when it refers to the divine omnipresence, can only hope to communicate with creatures of time and space if it focuses itself in particularity—in being-*there*. Likewise must eternality subject itself to temporality, immutability to change, simplicity to complexity, incomprehensibility to comprehension, spirituality to materiality, holiness to the ordinary, and infinity to finitude—if, in each case, its object is to be "with us."

Therefore we are confronted from the beginning (it is present already in the narrative of the Yahwist; one does not have to wait for Bethlehem) with a God whose transcendent otherness is radically shaped by the divine insistence upon communion with that in relation to which it is, indeed, "wholly other." At very least, we must think of the whole biblical testimony to this deity as involving something like a kenosis—an emptying of that which prevents or could prevent God's full communion with the covenant partner. This kenosis may be most conspicuously recognizable at the point of the incarnation of the Word; but to confine it to the newer Testamental portion of the whole scriptural story is surely to miss the point: the parental yearning that is present from creation onwards, far from being one divine attribute among others, is the foundational dimension of deity as deity is conceived in this tradition.[25]

"Like as a father pitieth his children, so the Lord pitieth them that fear him" (Ps. 103:13, KJV): When we read such statements as that, we should recognize that we are in the presence of the Bible's rudimentary ontological/theological presupposition. To name this presupposition love or mercy or goodness or compassion, and then to list it as one of the divine perfections is to engage in a reductionist hermeneutic. The truth is, of course, that no one term, not even the term *agape*, captures this most basic assumption of biblical Theology, for it expresses a reality that is hardly graspable even by the saints and wise ones: that God should be concentrated upon . . . *us;* that the Creator should yearn toward the creation; that the Eternal should desire above all else to become companion to creatures of time; that no barrier to such companionship, no distinction of being, no hierarchy of worth, no height nor depth should be allowed to prevent, ultimately, the consummation of this desired communion—this friendship (John 15:15).

Yet it is there, and it is there as the foundational assumption of everything else. Whether it should even be named kenosis is a moot question; for while that concept, derived from Philippians 2, preserves the necessary belief that grace is "costly" (Bonhoeffer)—costly *to God*—it can too easily also suggest that what is essential to God as God is that of which God empties Godself, the seemingly superior reality that must be forfeited, at least temporarily, in order to enable proximity to the beloved inferior. Whereas, with its refusal of abstract speculation about deity, its historical concreteness, and its persistent anthropomorphicity, biblical faith dares almost to suggest that grace is God's nature. To be sure, grace remains grace. It is not simply natural for us. To the contrary. But for God? Biblical faith entertains the prospect that it is God's very nature to be gracious—without, however, leaving the impression that God dispenses grace as a matter of course, like Voltaire's, "Dieu pardonnera, c'est son metier" ("God will forgive; that's his business").

Insofar as gracious orientation toward the creature is the foundational Theology of the tradition of Jerusalem, all of the qualities that we attribute to God must be built on this foundation and no other. It will not be a matter, therefore, of collecting superlatives and attributing them to Deity. It will be a work, rather, of trying to discern how or whether the various perfections

---

25. "God's self-humiliation does not begin merely with creation . . . : it begins beforehand, and is the presupposition that makes creation possible. God's creative love is grounded in his humble, self-humiliating love. This self-restricting love is the beginning of that self-emptying of God which Philippians 2 sees as the divine mystery of the Messiah. Even in order to create heaven and earth, God emptied himself of his all-plenishing omnipotence, and as Creator took upon himself the form of a servant." (Moltmann, *God in Creation*, 88.)

that Scripture and tradition have associated with God serve or can serve to illuminate this most basic Theology, the Theology of grace.

This insight, wherever it is grasped, immediately casts up problems for all who have been schooled in the Theology of divine hierarchic superiority—that is to say, in the *theologia gloriae* as it applies to the doctrine of God. One suspects that, in one degree or another, that means nearly all of us.

The divine superiority in by far the most influential forms of Christian doctrine (so influential that they are perpetuated even among many who have seemed to renounce them) centers in the idea of God's infinite power. As we have seen, no adjective is more consistently applied to God (in prayer, for instance) than "Almighty." Since, as was suggested in chapter 2, the models for divine power have been drawn, quite understandably, from human experience, God's power invariably turns out to be a magnification of the most powerful instances of creaturely being accessible to humans—traditionally, kings and military heroes, but perhaps today more abstract instances like "the power of the atom" or of advanced technology. With such a preconception of power, all-powerfulness can only suggest something basically incongruous with a Theology of grace.

Influenced by such a preconception (and it is normally a *pre*conception— usually a completely unacknowledged one), we habitually subsume the "attributes of condescendence" under the "attributes of transcendence" (Berkhof). Mercy, goodness, compassion, and love are then thought of as the temporary setting aside of power: like a great emperor, God sometimes shows unwarranted magnanimity to his subjects. Such a picture of God may not be wholly reprehensible. As a model for the behavior of superiors to inferiors it has a rather more honorable history than, say, a model of power that never strays from the idea of total subordination. It is nevertheless a conspicuous misrepresentation of biblical Theology, and in the end it may betray the latter more effectively than do models of deity based on unambiguous power. For it leaves the impression that the real nature of God is God's high and holy otherness and not God's "tabernacling" with the creature (Rev. 21:3).

Scripture reverses this. With striking frequency, the One revealed as God is remarkably powerless. This God does not show up with the usual accoutrements of might but quietly, inconspicuously, privately, often incognito, and always in ways that are frustratingly roundabout. Certainly there are sometimes signs and wonders that may be predictable enough, given the history of epiphanies: lightning and thunder, of course, and darkness, voices, miracles. And one is usually given to understand that God could do all such fantastical things to which human gods are regularly prone. Sometimes (Moses before Pharoah!) God *does*. But normally the revealing Presence is "elusive" (Samuel Terrien). It is only afterwards that some among those present realize what was happening in their midst. "'Surely the Lord is in this place—and I did not know it!'" (Gen. 28:16).

This regular practice in the older Testament's depiction of Deity becomes thoroughly normative in the newer. The incognito idea, of which Luther was so fond, is here indeed the informing Theology:

> How silently, how silently
> The wondrous gift is given!
> So God imparts to human hearts
> The blessings of his heaven. . . .
> (Phillips Brooks, "O Little Town of Bethlehem")

The categorical, voluntary refusal of power is here the norm. The post-Event recognition of divine Presence is here almost a principle—the Pentecostal principle, as one might designate it. But these newer Testamental testimonies to God's hidden presence in the Christ are appropriations of a pattern that is already well-established in the faith of Israel. However often it is possible to discover in the older Testament passages and references to the God of power, a sort of Hebraic Thor, these depictions cannot be designated normative for Israel's faith; they represent, rather, reversions to earlier or extra-Judaic material that, in certain specific contexts, may indeed serve to say something important about Yahweh/Elohim. The norm—for Israel, too—is not the God of battles but the "still small voice," the God who waits, the "defenseless" God:

The general and popular idea is that in the biblical witness concerning God the emphasis is on God's omnipotence. But this is a great mistake. On the contrary, the first impression one gets from the biblical account of revelation is that of God's *impotence*, of how man has taken the initiative away from him, of what we shall call here God's "defenselessness." By this we understand that attribute by which he leaves room for his "opposite" and accepts and submits himself to the freedom, initiative, and the reaction of that "opposite." It has to do with the passive and receptive, the *enduring and the suffering of God.* The traditional doctrine of God has had no place for this aspect, not even in the discussion of the patience and long-suffering of God, though it is very prominent in the Bible. . . . What is at stake here is the very special way in which God makes his power felt.[26]

Not only omnipotence but all of the superior attributes of Deity must be put in subjection to the fundamental Theology of grace. As it would be appropriate under the aegis of this Theology to speak of divine power only by emphasizing the power of God to refrain from the use of power or (which is to say the same thing) the power to love, so it would be appropriate to think of the divine omniscience as the wisdom that does not think itself above being

---

26. Hendrikus Berkhof, *Christian Faith: An Introduction to the Study of the Faith*, trans. Sierd Woudstra (Grand Rapids: Wm. B. Eerdmans Pub. Co., 1979), 134.

considered foolishness by the wise (1 Corinthians 1, 2); and of the divine omnipresence as a presence that becomes universal only through particularization; and the divine immutability as a changelessness of intention that therefore adapts itself willingly to every contextual change; and of the divine infinity as an eternality that subjects itself to, and permeates, temporality, thus hallowing time itself. In every case, the transcendent attribute "must pass through the eye of the needle of the properly understood concept of the death of God"[27]—that is, to speak historically and concretely, through the humiliation and crucifixion of the Word. Otherwise we shall end with *Deus* and not *Theos,* with Jehovah and not Yahweh, with Thor and not with the one whom Jesus called Abba.

Yet, far from being a reduction and belittlement of God, this subjection of the divine attributes to the foundational Theology of the Bible constitutes an enhancement and even an exaltation of the divine being. For in the last analysis nothing is more easily managed (or more ludicrous) than an account of deity in which all that human beings wrongly aspire to be and are not is heaped upon the head of some paper god. The really difficult but also moving and even humanly inspiring thing is to contemplate a Deity whose greatness lies in the capacity to go in and sup with sinners and tax collectors and harlots.[28]

The impression should not be created here, however, that it is only the attributes of superior power that must be subjected to the foundational Theology, the Theology of the cross (that is, the picture of God that emerges from that thin tradition). Such an impression would seriously jeopardize our contextual concern. In the first chapter we advanced the opinion that, in our particular context, Christians fluctuate between a wooden orthodoxy that exalts divine power at the expense of the divine mercy and a liberalism that so apotheosizes simplistic love that it is incapable of judgment—and so of justice. This reminds us that the so-called attributes of condescendence must also be submitted to the foundational Theology. Just as might, majesty, dominion, power, and all the superior qualities attributed to God achieve authenticity, biblically, only as they are defined by the grace that is actually described in the continuity of the story told in the two testaments, so mercy, goodness,

---

27. Eberhard Jüngel, *God as the Mystery of the World: On the Foundation of the Theology of the Crucified One in the Dispute between Theism and Atheism,* trans. Darrell L. Guder (Grand Rapids, Mich.: Wm. B. Eerdmans, 1983), 63. See also J. B. Webster, *Eberhard Jüngel: An Introduction to His Theology* (Cambridge: Cambridge Univ. Press, 1986).

28. Again the novelists are able to capture this age-old truth better than theology. There is something inherently, profoundly moving whenever "the Good and the Great" is seen to move among ordinary, fallen creatures—for instance, as John Steinbeck achieves this in his 1945 novel, *Cannery Row.* The reason for this is obvious enough: however we may act, we know at some infallible level of comprehension that we are neither good nor great; therefore the only superiority that can touch us profoundly is a superiority that lives among us and uplifts us through its willing subjection, in our behalf, to all that demeans and corrupts our existence.

compassion, gentleness, and love must acquire their Theological meaning through a strict association with that story.

To put it in a simple phrase: God defines love, not love God.[29] The object of the God who "is love" is after all to communicate that love to a being—the human being—who is for the most part unloving and afraid of love. A love that "lays down its life for its friends" (John 15:13) is not easily brought home to such a being. There is judgment in it, and if it is truly communicated to anyone it will always be mingled with disbelief, rejection, and even hate. For who can believe that he or she is *so* loved? Beyond that, who is ready to become the lover that this same "suffering love" persistently wills to beget in its recipients (1 John 4:19ff.)?

It is vital for a responsible Theology in the North American context to come to terms with this strange side of the gospel of love. For in our context, the sentimentalization of divinity under the impact of cheap religious romanticism has inflicted upon the Christian faith a "monism of love" (Kitamori) that renders such Christianity simplistic and untrue to the experience of the honest. Perhaps one of the most effective deterrents to faith in our situation is that the utterly uncritical equation of God with love that still characterizes mainstream liberal Protestantism is literally incredible and distasteful to any who have had firsthand experience of the ecstasy and turbulence that are part of unfictionalized human love, and are able to be truthful about both sides of the experience. Moreover, in a context where stylized representations of human love no longer inform even the most popular forms of art; where private lives are riddled with grief because our ordinary loves cannot bear the burden of meaning that has been thrust upon them by a disenchanted secularity; and where love is for millions only a polite four-letter word for a three-letter word, sex: in such a context, for Christians to keep on repeating that "God is love" without mentioning the suffering that this divine love entails for both God and its human recipients is to invite scorn—and to deserve it richly.

In short, if love and all the other attributes of divine proximity are really to convey God's "with-being" in such a context, then the dark, negative side of this same love must no longer be neglected. Truly to be Emmanuel, the loving God must suffer and be rejected. Truly to be with us, the people of a continent that is at the heart of a world called "First," the loving God must be a God of judgment—perhaps even of wrath. Even with our limited experience of love at the human level, we know that genuine love can and must sometimes feel like hate. Because it cares, it will not just accept everything. It is a travesty of love,

---

29. "The definition 'God is love' acquires its full weight only if we continually make ourselves aware of the path that leads to the definition: Jesus' forsakenness on the cross, the surrender of the Son, and the love of the Father, which does everything, gives everything and suffers everything for lost men and women. God is love: that means God is self-giving. It means God exists for us: on the cross." (Moltmann, *The Way of Jesus Christ,* 175.)

mercy, forbearance, forgiveness, and all the other qualities of divine condescension when, Sunday after Sunday, North American churchgoers, representatives before God of one of the richest families of earth, are enabled by their worship to sally forth into the violent and hurting world of their towns and cities with peace and joy in their hearts, unburdened even of the cares with which they entered their pretty sanctuaries—cares which, in most cases, were (alas) purely personal. It is fashionable now to think of worship as celebration and to say that talk of the divine wrath belongs to an outmoded neoorthodoxy. But what kind of celebration is it that glosses over truth, and what kind of love is it that is incapable of saying no to greed, smugness, and self-deceit?

The key to the whole discussion of the divine attributes is relationship, that is, the ongoing encounter between God and human beings that is characterized by trust and truth. The will of the biblical God is to achieve communion with the creature who is called to respond to God in behalf of all the creatures—the only creature among them all who is deeply alienated from its Source, and whose alienation is dangerous for all the others as well as for itself. The relationship that God seeks to establish with this creature is therefore not a sign of divine exclusivity but of the inclusiveness of God's grace. The whole fate of the creation is bound up with the righting of this particular relation, with the reorientation of human life and work through the overcoming of human estrangement. This is the core. It is superfluous and misleading therefore to approach the discussion of the nature of God by accumulating high-sounding qualities and characteristics that seem magnificent enough to be thought divine. Any deity derived from such speculation remains a total abstraction, a pure construct. The test of the church's God-talk at any point in time is its contextual authenticity: Does it illuminate God's being-with-*us*? Does it foster and contribute to a profession of faith that flows from a *relationship* with God, one characterized by truth-orientation (*Wahrheitsorientierung*)?

More explicitly, do the attributes that we, who profess this faith, assign to God express themselves ethically in our own lives? For the perfections we profess as belonging to God are at the same time qualities that we, who are called to image God, are commanded and enabled to manifest in our lives. "Be perfect, therefore, as your heavenly father is perfect" (Matt. 5:48). The faithful descriptions of the being of God must illuminate the nature of God's being-with-us; and the genuineness of this Theology will be discerned, as belief always is, by its fruits. In describing God, does our Theology also describe the charter of our discipleship?

10.3. Rethinking the Trinity in the Light of God's Search for Humanity.

The same mandate applies to the doctrine of the Trinity. Here again it is a question of relationship, namely God's quest for proximity to us and our consequent vocation to conform to the new identity we are being given through

God's reaching out—to image God's grace in our relations with our own kind and with "otherkind."

A statement of Hendrikus Berkhof could be our text for this section. At the end of an admirably pithy summary of the history of the doctrine of the Trinity, Berkhof writes, "In its NT form . . . the structure of the Trinity describes precisely the fellowship with man, for which God emerges out of himself. We need to return to that intention. We may not let ourselves be held back from it by a tradition, imposing though it may be, which is artificial and in its abstractness dangerous to faith."[30]

However understandable it may be that the church's resolution of the trinitarian problem posed by the newer Testament became entangled with substantialistic concepts and language, it is evident to all who are able to achieve a modicum of liberation from the weight of that complex doctrinal history that in its depiction of God, of Jesus, and of the divine Spirit, the newer Testament is simply not on the same wavelength as the later tradition. To the traditional theist, the biblical presentation of God may beg such questions as were later posed and answered by the early church's resort to the language of substances, essences, and hypostatic distinctions; but this is not the biblical métier. Moreover, when that later trinitarian language is permitted to become the key to the undoubtedly unresolved problems in the Bible's presentation of God; when, to speak more exactly, it becomes the philosophic "science" under whose guidance the biblical story of God's tabernacling with us is dissected, ordered, and interpreted, then a great spiritual and intellectual boundary has been crossed, whether or not this is recognized.

There is a fundamental shift in orientation between the Gospels and the Council of Nicaea. The formulators of classical trinitarianism were preoccupied by a concern quite different from the overarching concern of biblical faith as a whole. Theirs was an abiding preoccupation with what they felt to be the basic incompatibility of spirit and matter. The question seering the minds not only of Arius and Cyril of Alexandria but even—with at least a prominent aspect of his consciousness—of Athanasius was the question whether and how God, being pure Spirit, could cohabit with the flesh, a substance not only radically different from spirit but intrinsically opposed to it. The question confronting Hebraic and early Christian thought about God is of another order altogether—different, not only in terms of its assumptions about spirit and matter, but also in its whole underlying ontology and soteriology.

We have already identified that question in the foregoing. It is the question of how God will be able to become our God, and how we may become God's people. As such, it is the persistent concern of a community that has identified the human *problematique* as being, at base, that of abrogated relationship, not

---

30. *Christian Faith,* 337.

of lost endowments. The salvation sought by this community, Israel, hangs upon the restoration of the broken relationship. And Israel already knows that such a restoration cannot be brought about by human initiative. It already knows (this is what lies behind its messianic longing) that the restoration cannot even be effected by God so long as God remains outside the process, external to the predicament. So intense is this soteriological question for the tradition of Jerusalem that its prophets and wise ones are ready to regard it as God's own question. They believe that God's own heart is aflame with the dilemma: how to become "your God."

This has little if anything to do with the alleged incompatibility of spirit and matter. Materiality is not a problem for Israel. God's own creation, the world, is material—even God can be depicted materially. The dilemma exercising Israel's profoundest spirituality is a dilemma of conflicting intentions—in that sense, therefore, a spiritual dilemma. To the intention of the One who "will be your God" the human will perennially opposes itself. No amount of exhortation ("law," in the restrictive sense), no sacrificial system, no priestly guidance through times of trial, no liberation from oppression appears to touch this aboriginal conflict of wills. How shall God truly communicate with the alienated creature? How shall the father reach the wayward son? How shall the hen gather her chicks under her wings? How shall the shepherd locate his lost, straying sheep? This is the fundamental question, the ultimate concern underlying the whole biblical discourse on deity, and it becomes, in the newer Testamental witness, the clue to the affirmation that God is "with us" in Jesus, the Christ, through the ongoing, internal testimony of the divine Spirit.

10.4. An Ontological Interlude: The Emmanuel Concept. We may elucidate this approach to trinitarian Theology by exploring the implicit trinitarianism of the Emmanuel concept. The "with" of the expression, "God with us," is by no means only a linguistic device; it captures, so far as any language can, the rudimentary relationality that informs the whole of biblical thought. Of all the possible ways of describing the relation between God and humankind, or indeed of all relations, biblically understood, the preposition "with" is the most satisfactory.

There are other candidates, grammatically speaking, for this office. One of the most common (in view of the preponderance of the Theology of almightiness, one should even say that for the tradition it is the most common) is the preposition "above." Certainly there is an "above" as well as a "below" in the divine/human relationship: "as the heavens are high above the earth" (Ps. 103:11); "Set your minds on things that are above" (Col. 3:2), for example. Another important biblical preposition is "in." It is particularly important for the entire mystical component in the history of the church, following Paul's description of the members of "the body" as being "in Christ" (*en Christo*).

157

"With" is nonetheless normative, for it is the language of love; it describes in the briefest possible form "the ontology of communion."[31] Love in this tradition does not incorporate the beloved, as the language of inclusion ("in") too easily suggests. Love not only honors but in a real sense establishes the independent being of the other: I become who I am as I become "thou" for another. God's purpose as the one who loves supremely should not be confused with that type of theistic mysticism which would simply assume human being in its own greater essence. God loves: that is, God wills to have vis-à-vis God's person another center of consciousness, intelligence, and will who is not an extension of God but can respond to God freely. When we affirm that the question that exercised the spirit of Israel was the question of how God could become "your God," we mean that kind of relationship. To be sure, it is not conceived as a relation between equals, and therefore it contains an "above" and a "below"; nevertheless it is a relationship between centered selves, "persons," both of whom could do otherwise than to affirm this relationship, and in the case of the human partner habitually, tragically, do so.

God is and will be "with" us. But this "with" denotes a complex relation, far more complex than the common preposition itself seems to connote. Yet even our ordinary use of the preposition, if examined carefully, contains the two essential thoughts that are necessary to trinitarian reflection in the biblical mode.

First, "with" implies proximity to: I am with someone when I am near at hand—usually it is assumed to mean very near, the nearer the better. "I wish that you could be with us" does not mean within reach by telephone. The metaphoric use of the term reinforces the idea of proximity: "I'm with you!"— that is, I am in total solidarity with you; there are no qualifications, no ifs and buts. Being "with" you, I am (as it goes without saying) "for" you, "on your side." Coexistence implies proexistence.

At the same time, secondly, this metaphoric use of the term points up the limitation implied in the literal sense of the preposition. Physical proximity—

---

31. Joseph Sittler, to whom (on various occasions) I earlier attributed this term, appears to have himself gleaned it from his colleague Joseph Haroutunian. Sittler quotes Haroutunian's book, *God with Us* (Philadelphia: Westminster Press, 1965), 148: "We have no ontological status prior to and apart from communion. Communion is our being; the being we participate in is communion, and we derive our concrete selves from our communion. The old controversy between the realists and the nominalists about universals and particulars is incongruous with the ontology of communion. We have to do, not with universals, but with our neighbors, not with particulars, but with particular fellow-men. We do not participate individually in Being, and Being is not by our own being individually. There is no individual to participate in Being or to make Being to be. In the beginning, by God's creation, is the *fellowman,* and the fellowman is by loving his neighbor. The apparently universal notion, at least in the Western world, that one man can be and that he can have a nature suggests an alienation that gives us, not a human ontology, but one from which the human manner of being is excluded. In the beginning is communion and not being or Being. For this reason, in Christian philosophy, traditional ontology is a source of misunderstanding and confusion." (Joseph Sittler, *Essays on Nature and Grace* [Philadelphia: Fortress Press, 1972], 106–7.)

being with someone in the sense of being beside or alongside the other—is never wholly satisfying for those who really desire closeness. The lover, the parent present during some critical moment in the life of the child, the old companion at the deathbed of her friend, the father trying to "get through" to his alienated daughter: in all such instances (and life is comprised of them!) physical presence, while infinitely preferable to absence, is frustratingly insufficient. It almost heightens the sense of separation—of *not* being with the other; of being alone in one's own skin; of being incapable of ultimate communion with the other. Even sexual intimacy, which may sometimes approach such ultimacy (though not as often as romantic fictions suggest), participates in the poignancy of this profound frustration; in fact, since sexuality in our time has become the unfortunate bearer of almost religious expectations, it is possible that no human experience so regularly underscores the limitations of our quest for togetherness.

In short, the proximity that is implied in the preposition drives to the desire for consummation. "With-ness" can never be wholly satisfied with that state. "With" presses on toward "within." Everything that gets in the way of complete mutuality must be overcome. The external must give way to internality. The veils that separate must be torn away, even to the seventh.

Here, undoubtedly, lies a great danger in the life of humankind; for between the kind of union that this desire for total proximity connotes and the unrightful invasion of the other—invasion and possession—there is a very fine line. The lover who desires to be "within" too easily becomes the possessive husband or wife, who will grant no independent status to his or her partner. The parent who wants to go all the way with the child in crisis may all too predictably prevent the child from achieving maturity.

Biblical faith is wonderfully nuanced at this point. It does not intend to substitute "in" for "with," union for communion, mystically undifferentiated togetherness for identity-with-distinction. All the same, it knows that the "with" itself, intrinsically, drives to greater and greater realization of itself; and therefore, eschatologically, it opts for a final state in which God is "all in all" (*omnia in omnibus*).[32]

10.5. Analogia Entis?   If now we seek to apply this reflection upon "being with" to trinitarian thought, we naturally run into the knotty question: Do we here imply an *analogia entis,* an "analogy of being"? Is it possible to speak of God on the basis of a general analysis of the nature of being as such? Is not God unique, and have we not already done homage to that uniqueness—*Deus non est genera* (God is not one of a species)?

---

32. See Moltmann, *God in Creation,* 89.

The answer is that we are not adopting an *analogia entis* in the usual, classical sense of the term; for in the first place the picture of God to which we have been pointing here—that is, the biblical portrayal of Deity—informs our ontology at least as much as our ontology informs our Theology; and in the second place, more importantly, we have already strictly qualified our conception of being by defining it relationally. All being is with-being—"All real living is meeting."[33] The analogy in question, then, is not an analogy of creaturely with divine being, but an analogy between the relatedness that applies to all creaturely being (not only that of human beings) and to God as well. If that is something like what Karl Barth meant by *analogia relationis,* then we accept the designation.[34]

The analysis of relationship developed above and drawing upon the language of being-with applies analogously to trinitarian Theology as soon as it is recognized that God's search for humankind involves a twofold movement of God toward the creature. To be "with us," Emmanuel must not only be among us but also within us. We shall consider the two claims in that order.

The Scriptures, we have insisted, do not despise physicality; therefore they do not indulge in that kind of spiritualism which can conceive of presence in purely pneumatic terms. There is a good reason for this. For biblical faith, creatures are physical beings—at least in the case of human beings, creatures whose very spirituality is inextricably linked with their physicality. One cannot be present to another in a purely spiritual way where such creatures are concerned. When Adam longs for the presence of a counterpart, he looks for this—naturally enough—first in existing creatures; and when none is found that is right for him (a "help meet"), another creature of flesh and blood has to be created for the purpose. When David longs for Bathsheba or for Jonathan, he wants these persons to be *there;* he will not be satisfied with the thought of them afar.

Is not this same drive toward physical proximity equally applicable to the God of Abraham and Sarah, Isaac, Rebecca, Jacob? Is there not all the way through the Bible—both from the side of humanity and of God—a longing for that kind of presence? Is not the very spirituality of God therefore a highly physical thing, always necessitating at least material tokens of itself: a burning bush (why not just a mystical experience without the bush?); a cloud and fire; three men under

---

33. Martin Buber, *I and Thou,* trans. Ronald Gregor Smith (Edinburgh: T. & T. Clark, 1937), 11.

34. Certainly Barth's discussion of the *analogia relationis* in vol. 3/2 of the *Church Dogmatics* (G. W. Bromiley and T. F. Torrance, eds. [Edinburgh: T. & T. Clark, 1960], 220f.) suggests something similar to my intention here: "This is not a correspondence and similarity of being, an *analogia entis.* The being of God cannot be compared with that of man. But it is not a question of this twofold being. It is a question of the relationship within the being of God on the one side and between the being of God and that of man on the other. Between these two relationships as such . . . there is correspondence and similarity. There is an *analogia relationis.*"

a tree; a writing finger and the fleeting glimpse of someone's back, and so on. Christian modernism put all such references down to primitive anthropomorphism. But is the anthropomorphism of the Bible so primitive—in the pejorative sense in which modernism intended us to hear that term? Must not God assume some recognizable form (*morphe*) if God is to be "with us"? One may well wonder whether Christians have not grasped the Johannine text, "God is spirit," with such excessive zeal that the only kinds of people who are allowed to traffic with the spiritual Deity of Christian pietism are people who have successfully repressed their own physicality!

For biblical faith (surely this must be recognized, finally) there is a thrust toward incarnation of the Deity all the way through. Sadly, the term "incarnation," on account of its early and decisive co-optation by substantialistic ontologies, is almost unusable in this connection. What it points to, however, stripped of its post-Testamental garb, is nothing more nor less than the consummation of the thrust toward enfleshment that can hardly be avoided by anyone who reads the Hebrew Bible. God will be *with* us. And to be with *us*— creatures who cannot even think of our best friends without, in our mind's eye, seeing faces—God "must" assume some kind of recognizable form. Even God's "voice" (the primary category of high Hebraic prophecy) is already such a form; so that those who reject the incarnation on the grounds of the concretization of the Word must ponder whether God's Word to the prophets and lawgivers and wise ones is not already at least a step in that direction. God will be *with us:* present to us, alongside us, beside us, face-to-face with us. This is by no means only a claim of the newer Testament.

Neither, however, does it translate at once into the dogma that in Jesus we have, purely and simply, God in physical form. That is to leap over the boundary between Athens and Jerusalem. It is to substitute for the relational ontology of Jerusalem the substantialism of classical and modern thought. It is not at all the same thing to say, "In Jesus faith encounters the very presence of God— Emmanuel," as it is to say, "Jesus is God." The first statement has to do with communion, communication, relationship; and it combines a christological with a soteriological approach to the first and initiatory problem of trinitarian thought. That is, it makes the christological claim serve the soteriological claim. The end of the matter is not that "God was in Christ" but rather (as the text itself says) "God was in Christ reconciling . . . " (2 Cor. 5:19, RSV).[35]

This may indeed leave the personal identity of Jesus imperfectly defined—but why not? Should it not in fact remain (what it clearly is for the original disciple community) a mystery? That does not imply that the whole christological side of the discussion is mere mystery, inadmissible of any sort of comprehension. What

---

35. See D. M. Baillie, D.D., *God Was in Christ: An Essay on Incarnation and Atonement* (London: Faber and Faber Ltd., 1948).

is to be comprehended is that through this ineffable presence faith discovers God: God with us, God overcoming the distance between us, God near and always nearer. The statement "Jesus is God," on the contrary, and equivalent pronouncements about the divinity of Jesus, are christological statements that in themselves carry no soteriological weight. They are impressive only to those who seek signs and wonders, not to those who hunger and thirst for authenticity. To such a claim as that "Jesus is God," or "Jesus possesses two natures, the human and the divine," those who truly yearn for God are liable to respond with indifference. For it is an existentially extraneous and gratuitous claim. It does not engage any spiritual anguish. It only presents yet another supranatural phenomenon, whose impact in conventionally Christian contexts is more impressive than reports of other extraterrestrial appearances only on account of its long history, its associations with religious dogma, and its symbolic weight within certain religious communities.

Biblical faith (and I would here accentuate the place of the older Testament in this entire discussion) does comprehend the theological assumption that God wills to be present to us, and that to be present to us must mean to approximate some kind of physicality. I do not intend that this should imply an immediate cessation of the distinction between Christians and Jews. To claim to have experienced the presence of God in and through Jesus, in particular, remains a Christian profession, which is by no means already implicit in Jewish belief or in the testimony of the Hebrew Bible. My point, however, is only this: that the *direction* of a Christology and trinitarianism that speaks from the posture of a fundamental concern for divine proximity is the same *direction* as that found in classical as well as in most contemporary Judaism. What is offensive to Jews (and in my view, rightly so) is that conventional Christology and trinitarian thought assumed and assumes a completely different direction: namely, it has opted for a substantialistic rather than a relational approach to the whole question, and is therefore perceived by biblical faith of both branches as "artificial and in its abstractness dangerous to faith" (Berkhof).

10.6. God Within.   The movement of God toward the estranged creature— "the fellowship with man for which God emerges out of himself" (Berkhof)— necessarily involves a second step. To be-with, we said, implies not only to be-among but also to be-within. Here too, as we have already suggested, the first movement begets the second. In the presence of God that the disciple community experienced as it lived in close proximity to Jesus, it also learned its essential distance from God. In a real way, and in many ways, the very proximity of "the Word made flesh" heightened, for these ordinary men and women who were Jesus' contemporaries, their recognition of their terrible separation from God.

It meant on the one hand the sense of their own profound unworthiness: "Go away from me, Lord, for I am a sinful man!" (Luke 5:8). On the other, it meant their offense and rejection: "Then all the disciples deserted him and fled" (Matt. 26:56). Without the concretization of the absolute, the absolute remains theoretical and objectifiable—even optional, so far as its claims upon personhood are concerned. But with the concretization it becomes too close for comfort, for it makes itself felt in all of its theological and ethical radicality. It will not be ignored.

Jesus makes God present to this community, but the presence itself does not heal. On the contrary, it renders the wound more visible, more intolerable. It aggravates the brokenness that, apart from it, may be overlooked and minimized—through, among other things, the ministrations of "religion."

Yet this appears to be a necessary stage in the movement of God toward the alienated creature: the estrangement must be fully exposed. There can be no truth in a relationship that does not confront the negation—every sort of negation—that proximity engenders. The falseness of that bourgeois romanticization of love to which we referred earlier is precisely that it is built on a more or less deliberate suppression of what negates. Love is supposed to be all yes and no no, all come hither and no go away. We are supposed to "fall in love" without pain and sustain love without stress. But love, if it is real, is always costly to us, for we want to have our life on our own terms. The proximity of "the other" is never unambiguously welcome. It is welcome as relief from our loneliness, but it is a burden to our bid for autonomy. If this is not recognized, the burden grows heavier, and finally love becomes a lie.

Jesus brings the Twelve to the point of this recognition. Claiming to want God present and available, humankind only wants its pain assuaged by the Great Physician. It does not want this companionship, which is far too demanding. It does not want to lose itself, but only to find itself. Yet it cannot have the one without the other, and this has to be made perfectly clear.

Golgotha makes it clear. God has come that close. *With* us, in complete solidarity, so close that we have had to back away, our space invaded. But now a beginning can be made. Now at last something new can happen. The falsehood of our religion has been exposed. If grace is willing to go farther, we may find ourselves in a relationship based on truth.

The pentecostal advent of the Spirit is the church's declaration that grace has gone farther. God who was with us, fully and in truth, has followed God's own gracious impulse to fellowship and is now, already, within us. Externality has given way to a process of internalization—the *testimonium Spiritus sancti internum,* the "baptism" of fire. Our spirits, emptied of pretense by the encounter with the divine Presence whom we crucified, are revived again by the divine Presence within, crucifying our need to crucify. The internal Presence does not overwhelm us or simply obliterate our own reality. Nor is this Presence, binding us together humanly in the *koinonia,* destructive of our individual personhood. We are not involved in a merger of selves from which no "thou" but only "we" will emerge. The Spirit remains God's Spirit, neither ontically amalgamated with our spirits nor the personification of an esprit de corps called "church." The relationship with God, and our relationships with one another, are manifestations of love, not of undifferentiated homogeneity. God's love toward us, and our love toward God and toward one another: this is the process to which we have been introduced.

And it is far from over and done with. The end of the process cannot be foretold, though we believe in its consummation, namely in that future in which there will no longer be yes and no but only yes; when that which still resists the indwelling Spirit will be won over wholly. But the point is this: The process has begun. The *koinonia* is real. The reign of God is anticipated—is already becoming present in the daily overcoming of hostilities, the submission to God and to one another, the struggle for truth and for justice.

10.7. The Gospel Recapitulated. It has been said with insight that the doctrine of the Trinity is the gospel in a nutshell. But this is an accurate way of speaking only if, in some such manner as the above, the doctrine of God that trinitarian thought seeks to elucidate is understood in the light of the whole gracious movement of God toward fellowship with the creature. When on the contrary the doctrine of the Trinity is confined to an attempt to define deity, then, while it may certainly become very interesting and even all-engrossing, it will not escape the narrowness of vain speculation and abstraction.[36] Because we have felt obliged to explicate the divine triunity in relational terms, our Theological reflections have drawn us willy-nilly into anthropology, soteriology, ecclesiology, ethics, eschatology—in short, the entire "story."

In the process we have left behind many questions associated with classical trinitarianism, and this will no doubt be seen as a fault. But many of the questions and considerations associated with trinitarian dogmatics are in my opinion extraneous to the tradition of Jerusalem, and I have wanted to say this openly and concretely. They have served, in some cases, important functions in

---

36. "The trinitarian concept describes the particular unity of the living God, while philosophical monotheism conceived of the dead or static unity of a supreme being as an existing entity indistinguishable within itself. The trinitarian idea of God is congruous with historical process, while the notion of a supreme entity speaks of a 'divine thing' outside man's history. The trinitarian doctrine describes the coming God as the God of love whose future has already arrived and who integrates the past and present world, accepting it to share in his own life forever. The trinitarian doctrine is, therefore, no mere Christian addition to the philosophical idea of God. Rather, the trinitarian doctrine is the ultimate expression for the one reality of the coming God whose Kingdom Jesus proclaimed." (Wolfhart Pannenberg, *Theology and the Kingdom of God,* ed. Richard John Neuhaus [Philadelphia: Westminster Press, 1969], 71.)

the past. In the historical discussion of the Trinity in chapter 1, I have acknowledged this. But if we are going to revive trinitarian theology for the profession of faith of communities of faith in North America and elsewhere today, we shall have to sustain a strict vigilance against substantialistic thought about God, which only confuses the church with abstract problems that do not relate to or enable our confession of faith, and which only foster a separation of profession and confession, with parties standing for various emphases, and damning one another, while in the meantime the hungry world to which the triune God intends to extend unwarranted grace "looks up and is not fed" (Milton).[37]

Does the relational explication of biblical trinitarianism represent a return to the liberal concept of "the trinity of experience"? Yes and no. Yes, insofar as it recognizes that Christians cannot speak of God theoretically. The Christian profession of faith in God, including God's triune nature, does not consist of meditation upon Theological "truths"; it originates rather with the church's experience of God. Trinitarian thought is a commentary on this experience, or else it is sheer speculation. The church clings to the trinitary symbol, even where (as in North American "liberal" Christianity) is has all but lost touch with classical trinitarian discussion, only because the Trinity explicates in some way its experience of God. This liberal insight is not less insightful because it is liberal.

But liberalism gave away too much. Why should not the experience of God illuminate the reality of God? It is not necessary (it is in fact precluded by the Reality in question) to insinuate that our Theology is an accurate, or even a very reliable, description of *Theos*. If, however, the experience of God's revealing incorporates the movements that I have attempted here to depict, then ought we not to suppose that God really is something like that? Perhaps liberalism was reluctant to draw that conclusion because it was—despite its attachment to the historical Jesus—still too welded to an abstract Theology to leap to the conclusion that God, precisely in Jesus, suffers.

11. "God Is at Work in the World . . ."

11.1. The Worldly Orientation of God's Labor. One clear mandate emerges from our reflection on the "works" of God in the two previous chapters.[38] It is that these must be shown to have concrete reference to this world. Because they are works of a God who is "one" both in person and intention, moreover,

---

37. See Barbara Brown Zikmund, "The Trinity and Women's Experience," *The Christian Century* (April 15, 1987), 354ff.

38. "God is at work in the world to make and to keep human life human" (Paul Lehmann, *Ethics in a Christian Context* [New York: Harper & Row, 1963], chap. 3, 74ff.).

they must all three—creation, preservation, and redemption—manifest this orientation. The God whose will is to be Emmanuel is turned toward the world, not only in creating and preserving it, but also in the third work, the work of redemption.

It will help to establish the character of this divine orientation, linguistically speaking, if, remembering Moltmann's critique of the language of divine "works,"[39] we introduce as an alternative usage the phrase "God's labor." "Labor" does not overcome all the questionable connotations of "work," and it introduces some complications of its own. But if it is remembered that from at least the sixteenth century this word was used to describe childbirth, and that it is applied to God and God's "work" in precisely that way in several scriptural passages,[40] it will help at least to offset the masculine objectivization implied in "work" and at the same time suggest something of the involvement and suffering that are necessary to a biblical understanding of what God is bringing to pass in the world.

Redemption is the primary consideration here—the test case, as it were. All too consistently, the Christian explication of redemption has involved, implicitly if not explicitly, an orientation that is not only transworldly but anti-worldly. Even in theological systems and popular forms of piety that make a good deal of the redemption of human life and society, the impression is regularly conveyed that the world as such, as distinct from (a portion of) its human element, is bypassed by the Redeemer. It is, so to speak, soteriologically neutral. Human life, perhaps even collectively considered, may be saved out of it, but precisely *out of* it. A vast silence reigns in Christian doctrine where the destiny of the created order as such is concerned. Yet this silence is highly audible, finally, for it implies that the world, apart from the sentient creature Homo sapiens, appears to the Christian religion a merely temporary thing, a stage upon which, for a time, an important historical drama is played, interesting and no doubt necessary as the setting of the drama, but in the end discardable—like so much theatrical scenery.

The audibility of this theological silence has been amplified for us today on account of the threat to the biosphere brought about by this same historical being who, precisely under the influence of a cultic tradition that maintained such a silence about nature, has acted without reference to or respect for the otherness, rhythms, and integrity of nature. The crisis of the environment thus has the effect (a salutary one) of calling Christianity to account for this age-old neglect. But it is shortsighted to assume that this crisis only requires re-thinking the Christian attitude toward extrahuman creation. It does that, certainly; for if only human beings are ultimately interesting to Christianity as

---

39. See above, chap. 1, n. 49.
40. E.g., Isa. 42:14; Jer. 4:31; Hos. 13:13; Rom. 8:22.

objects of God's work, then what ecological and other critics say is eminently true: that the extrahuman world is for this faith tradition a matter of indifference; that the fate of the earth is not a Christian concern; that nature is significant to this religion only as the raw material for human sustenance and aggrandizement.

Beyond questioning Christian attitudes toward the natural order, however, the crisis of nature registers a deeper question about the Christian conception of God and of God's labor. Concretely, we are being asked today whether this faith professes the redemption of creation. Does the Christian conception of the divine work of redemption in some way apply to the creation in its totality, or is it preoccupied only with the salvation of what can be saved *from* creation? If the latter, then does this not introduce a terrible contradiction at the heart of this faith? Is it not then implied that between the divine labors of creation and preservation, on the one hand, and that of redemption on the other, there is a blatant dichotomy—to the extent, perhaps, that redemption virtually nullifies creation and renders its preservation gratuitous? And if such a dichotomy exists at the level of God's labor, does this not imply a dichotomy also with respect to God's very being? Would it not then be more comprehensible for Christians to assume (with Neoplatonism, for instance) an inferior deity who creates and a superior one who redeems?

As the reference to Christian Neoplatonism suggests, these questions are not new. But we have reached a point in our faith's historic sojourn where such questions are no longer merely theological. They never were, of course. But now the very practical consequences of a Theology that is unwilling to speak openly and positively about the redemption of creation have been brought to light. If, in this age of biospheric crises so enormous as to evoke the prospect of an imminent end to planetary existence, Christians are to be found on the side of *life,* we shall have to demonstrate that the unity of God's person and labor demands of us an outlook upon this world very different from the one that has for the most part colored our past. We shall have to show (and in our doctrine, not only in our actions) that God's labors of creation, preservation, and redemption are not three separate or separable works but a single labor, whose object is precisely the birthing of the world that God intends. God is "in labor" *in* the world, *for* the world, that it might become what, in its *conception,* it is. This has to become the leitmotiv of our Theology of the divine work.

11.2. Identifying False Theologies in Our Context. We are, however, attempting to think about these subjects quite consciously as Christians living within a specific sociohistorical context, North America. The *oikumene*—the whole world church—has begun to express a new concern for the this-worldly orientation of God's labor, and much progress has been made along the lines of a theology of creation that lets itself be shaped by the above-named leitmotiv.

But within our specific context there are peculiar religious and other conditions by which any such reflections must be affected.

In particular, two Theologies of the divine "work," influential in the context of the two northern countries of this continent, must be identified by anyone attempting a constructive statement in this area. The two, which are (not unpredictably) shaped by reaction one to another, represent false alternatives in relation to which a constructive statement concerning God's labor may be articulated.

One of these alternatives follows rather straightforwardly the dichotomous tendencies of conventional Theology alluded to in the previous subsection. Its fundamental assumption is that the object of God's work is supramundane salvation. It does not wholly neglect the works of creation and preservation (that is hardly possible); but its emphasis is upon redemption, and redemption as a work of rescue applicable exclusively to human beings. In this Theology, people are redeemed from their creaturely estate, and, one must add, redeemed not as people but as *souls*. [41] For this position usually goes hand in hand with a conception of human being that assumes the divisibility of body and psyche, with ultimacy attributed only to the latter, and a conception of salvation that has more in common with the classical Greek notion of the immortality of the soul than with the early Christian profession of "the resurrection of the body" (Apostles' Creed).

This is a powerful alternative in the North American context; if anything, it is more powerful today than at any other time in history. That is undoubtedly due to the apocalyptic nature of our period.[42] At such a time, the human quest for salvation, which in calmer periods is less prone to finding its outlet in otherworldly accounts, is driven more and more toward extraordinary religion. Heaven or the afterlife becomes the emergency route beyond the impasse of earthly existence.

Yet nothing is quite simple in Christianity, not even in North America. While on the one hand there exists this strong tradition of world-renouncing soul salvation, there exists on the other an antithetical questioning of the very necessity of radical salvation. This alternative, which emanates from a liberalism that may be just as individualistic as the conservative preoccupation with souls, does intend to be this-worldly in its basic understanding of God's work. While pietistic conservatism embraces a redemption theology that in one degree or another rejects the world, liberalism boldly affirms it. But its world-affirmation suffers from a superficial, myopic, and often chauvinistic perception of the world, so that what

---

41. Moltmann traces "the internalized redemption of the saved soul" to the Christendom distortion of newer testamental redemption theology (*The Way of Jesus Christ,* 31).

42. See *Thinking the Faith,* "Apocalyptic Consciousness and the Rise of Religious Simplism," 228ff.

it ends by affirming is not the real world at all but a construct based on its own limited experience, seen through the perspective of an optimistic ideology.

The first Theology is false because it rejects creation as unfit for or incapable of redemption; the second is false because it confirms the basic rectitude of its own little creation, in effect upholding a creational or naturalistic-humanistic Theology that has no need of a Theology of redemption.

Responsible profession of faith in God undertaken within such a context has to sustain a vigilant consciousness of these two popular alternatives. It must simultaneously fend off the temptation to otherworldliness implicit in the first and the superficial this-worldliness of the second. And it will be no easy matter to fend them off. Both positions are not only powerful, but both contain part of the truth that Christians are called to profess. Conservatism knows that there is a tension between creation/preservation and redemption; that is, it rightly insists that the work of redemption is an extraordinary work, not merely an extension of the common grace (*gratia communis*) of preservation. And liberalism knows that God's work must be directed toward this world, even though it knows far too little about the cost of that directedness.[43]

Since I believe that Christians in North America are mandated to profess a consistently this-worldly interpretation of the gospel under our present circumstances, what follows here will, in some quarters, be construed as liberal. But against that too hasty conclusion I should like to say that I regard the more conservative presentation of the divine work as containing a warning that is permanently true: God's great labor of redemption must certainly be articulated in ways that apply concretely to the beloved world, but this can never be achieved easily, and it cannot be demonstrated conclusively. It can only be professed and confessed—and in the face of much evidence to the contrary. It is, once more, the great "Nevertheless" of faith. Any attempt to transmute the "Nevertheless" into "Therefore" will soon encounter the world's own skepticism about its ultimate redeemability.

11.3. The Key: Our Perception of the Negative. The key question that must be put to any Theology of the divine labor is how it interprets that in relation to which this labor is undertaken. As we have already seen, each phase or aspect of the labor of God presupposes a certain opposition. Creation comes to be in the face of a "nothingness" that is not only not neutral but in some manner resistant of formation by the divine command or fiat. The preservation of creation assumes a tendency within the "fallen" creation toward disintegration, decay, and death. Most of all, redemption presupposes deliverance from a

---

43. Western Christianity, writes George P. Grant, "in its moment of pride" forgot "how powerful is the necessity which love must cross" (*Two Theological Languages*, ed. Wayne Whillier [Lewiston: Edwin Mellen Press, 1990], 102).

negative state so unacceptable to the tradition that, without it, all would be lost. Now the question addressed to every Theology of the divine work (though it is not always appreciated that this is so) is: How shall this Theology consider the negating element that is the presupposition of the whole discussion?

It will help us to arrive at and express our own answer to this question if we first identify the answers given (or assumed) by the two alternatives treated above. It is in fact their different perceptions of the negating element that principally shape the two positions—as would be expected of a key question.

The tendency of most Christian conservatism is to assess the negative in such overwhelming terms that it is prevented from developing an unambiguously world-affirming gospel. Deeply impressed with the radicality of finitude, sin, evil, the demonic, and death, it evolves an ethic aimed at curbing, so far as possible, the full consequences of negation; and it presents a gospel that offers the faithful a status ("new birth") that is not only new, but almost wholly discontinuous with the old. For this position, the fall[44] and not creation is the decisive reality, and divine providence implies God's constant prevention of the total disaster that is the natural consequence of human disobedience. Only the redemption through Christ breaks the power of the negative, and that only for the elect.

We have here, in other words, a conception of the *nihil* that is not only exceptionally strong but so determinative from its inception (the fall) that it is finally more decisive for the world than is God's own salvific work. Through extraordinary grace, God is able to rescue some human beings from the doomed world; but the fate of the world itself is sealed from the outset. American dispensationalism has carried this thinking to its logical conclusion and has not flinched at the suggestion that God—even God!—cannot alter the course of the negating process so far as creation as such is concerned.[45] Less doctrinaire forms of conservative Theology introduce nuances that mitigate such a stark conclusion; but it is a question whether the dispensationalists have not followed the logic of this position more faithfully than most.

On the other side of the spectrum, liberalism in all of its manifestations constitutes a protest precisely against any such analysis of that which negates. While there are many shades and variations within the liberal position, all of them reject the deterministic portrayal of negation that is characteristic of Christian conservatism. In all of them there is a decisive overcoming of that which negates—often a progressive overcoming, since theological liberalism is

---

44. See Wendy Farley, *Tragic Vision and Divine Compassion: A Contemporary Theodicy* (Louisville: Westminster/John Knox Press, 1990), 12–13.

45. See Christopher Levan, *Dialogue with Dispensationalism: Hal Lindsey's Dispensational Eschatology and Its Implications for an Articulation of Christian Hope in a Nuclear Age* (Ph.D. diss., McGill University, 1990).

hardly ever free from the ideology of historical progress. Their assessment of the negative is in the first place always less intensive than that of conservative Christianity, including the classical and Reformation traditions. Far from accentuating the inevitability of negation, Christian liberalism presents us with a view of the history of salvation in which negations are themselves progressively negated. Providence and progress are, as we have just noted, inextricably knit together in this conception of God's work, and, as in other modern accounts of history, redemption is frequently understood to be implicit in the movement of time itself.[46] Here, in other words, the decisive component is not an implacable negative but an absolutely reliable positive. This positive element may be named love or grace; it may be identified as providence or sanctification; it may be called the divine plan or the heavenly kingdom that is to be constituted "on earth as it is in heaven"; but it is always the same insistence— that whatever negating realities are present, whether ignorance or illness, whether sins individual or social, whether cancer or war or economic injustice or death itself, they are necessarily subject to the positive working of the divine will.

Both of these positions must be challenged by a Theology that takes seriously the worldly orientation of God's whole labor and wishes, in doing so, to engage the context in which we find ourselves as North American Christians today. For in both of these interpretations there is a kind of determinism at work that does not do justice to the dynamic (living) character of God and of God's relationship with unpredictable humanity. In the conservative position, this determinism attaches to the negative: it has decided in advance that the world is more or less lost, and therefore it discourages, implicitly, any wholehearted attempt to change the world. If even God is working toward the consummation of a new creation, faith is hardly inspired to expend its energies on the renovation of the old one! Let faith instead do what it can to stave off the worst consequences of worldly sin and evil, while setting its sights on the paradise that is being made ready for it.

This position hardly accords with the American Dream, and it would seem an unlikely candidate for any piety nurtured by the New World milieu. But there is a well-known relationship between apparent opposites. To dream of paradise on earth is to feel, at some level of awareness, the risk involved. What will one do if the promised earthly paradise does not materialize?—if instead the dream becomes, or threatens to become, a nightmare? In that case, one would do well to have an alternative, and the alternative will be all the more accessible if it retains the same basic content and involves only a change of direction and context. Where people dream of a heaven-on-earth it is not exceptional that—

46. See Reinhold Niebuhr, *Faith and History: A Comparison of Christian and Modern Views of History* (New York: Charles Scribner's Sons, 1951), chaps. 1–4.

collectively—they should also keep on hand, in case of need, a dream of heaven-beyond-earth. There is in fact an entirely reciprocal relation between the two dreams, the one secular and the other religious; and it is not at all unusual, as we have seen in the decades from 1960 to 1990, for great exponents of the secular dream, in their disillusionment, to show up one fine day as true believers in the religious version.

The liberal position, which is certainly more directly related to the American Dream, is only a little less deterministic than its conservative opposite—perhaps it is even more deterministic, in the end. Here of course we have the rare phenomenon of a determinism of the positive: it has decided in advance that the world is moving toward the good, toward fulfillment and perfection. It can appear to be less deterministic than the conservative version because it makes so much of freedom. It wants to affirm both that progress is inevitable and that we human beings are decisive in the scheme of things. The general pattern is clear: God is bringing about the divine reign on earth (gospel); join your work to God's for the inauguration of this divine project (law).

Identifying God's labor in either of these ways contains no radical call to discipleship in our particular context. Conservatism encourages the continuation of the status quo, politically and economically, by assuming that nothing can be altered significantly. Even critical conservatism—even the sort of apocalypticism that declaims openly that this world is irretrievably lost, is "the late, great planet earth" (Lindsey)—makes an easy alliance with political powers that sustain the status quo. Liberalism, which at least has the benefit of encouraging human responsibility, on account of its positivistic determinism prevents its advocates from entertaining a sufficiently radical view of negation to transform them from being cheerful "improvers" of what already is to builders of what might be.

What is called for in North American Christianity is a conception of the divine labor that provides the disciple community with enough discontent to be driven to clear resistance against the status quo and enough historical hope to believe that the world does not have to remain as it is.[47] What is called for, in short, is a dynamic discipleship that combines realism about the awful discrepancy between the world as it is and as God intends it to be, with the confidence that God's intention for the world is realizable, and in part through our discipleship.

> Scripture and the church, for all of their ambiguity, still can witness to the non-finality of evil by envisioning (and occasionally embodying) an alternative to the "principalities and powers" that dominate history. Neither history nor the church

---

47. See Frederick Herzog, *God-Walk: Liberation Shaping Dogmatics* (Maryknoll, N.Y.: Orbis Books, 1988), 72, 216–17.

are *characterized* by their ability to resist evil. But in our tragic and broken world, any small token of the nonfinality of evil signifies the power of redemption at work against despair and evil.[48]

We shall end this section by attempting to relate just such an affirmation to the three aspects of the divine work, and in doing so we shall return to the questions that were articulated at the end of the parallel sections of this discussion in the first chapter.

11.4. God's Work as the Basis of Christian Discipleship

Creation. The question with which we closed the discussion of the divine work of creation in the first chapter ran as follows: How can Christians in North America today express a theology of creation that, without simply celebrating the status quo, affirms the reality, order, beauty, and goodness of the world as God's own work?

An answer may now be ventured. Two interrelated points must be made: In the biblical tradition, (1) the world—creation—is of God's own conception, and therefore we must learn to resist "religious" and other influences at work among us that tempt us to abandon this world; (2) the world as it is is not to be identified with God's intention for it, and therefore we must resist the temptation to accept it as we find it.

The first point is directed against that type of conservatism which, along with its political allies, is fundamentally skeptical about the prospect of mending the world and concentrates instead on saving souls out of it. Such a position is a very old one, antedating its Christian expression. It is understandable and human, and therefore always a great temptation; for it is impossible sensitively to contemplate the extent of the evil, suffering, and apparent meaninglessness through which, age after age, humanity must pass, without being persuaded of the "vanity" (Ecclesiastes) of the entire project. The Bible itself does not avoid entertaining such a conclusion.[49] Not only Koheleth, Job, and many of the Psalms and Proverbs, but Jesus and Paul as well give vent to this sense of worldly dereliction. A faith that has not entertained such bleak thoughts about historical existence, a faith that does not in fact do daily battle with such thoughts, is no basis for Christian hope. It belongs to the tradition of Jerusalem in that it provides a foundation of meaning that allows us to take into our consciousness a maximum of negativity, without being debilitated by it: "We are afflicted in every way, but not crushed; perplexed, but not driven to despair; persecuted, but not forsaken; struck down, but not destroyed; always carrying

---

48. Farley, *Tragic Vision and Divine Compassion,* 130.
49. See Ronald Goetz, "Jesus Loves Everybody," *The Christian Century* (March 11, 1992), 276.

in the body the death of Jesus, so that the life of Jesus may also be visible in our bodies" (2 Cor. 4:8).

This splendid summation of apostolic courage testifies not only to the capacity of faith to contemplate the negative but to do so without abandoning the life of this world. For faith trusts that despite—and even in and through—these negations, "God is at work in the world." The reference to Jesus in Paul's declaration, explicitly to Jesus' death, is fundamental to his argument, as it is to our own. For the Christian affirmation of creation is an affirmation made possible by the prior affirmation of God's redeeming work. Without denying the life force that can be discerned in the processes of nature themselves, biblical faith nevertheless begins elsewhere. It is not a religion of creation-mysticism—not a celebration of nature or life *in se*. It takes its cue from the revelation of the divine presence within a creation that has been subjected to "futility" (Rom. 8:20). The life of creation that it affirms is a life that it perceives "hidden beneath its opposite" (Luther), death. God is mending the world, not merely by undergirding, deistically, the processes and laws of nature, some (but not all) of which are life-producing; rather, God goes to the heart of that in the world which is productive of death in all of its meanings. Believing this gospel, it is not necessary for the disciple community to close its eyes to the *nihil* that is always eminently visible in the world in order to profess the *creatio ex nihilo*. Faith is commanded and permitted to affirm creation even when creation contains manifold evidence of destruction and decay; it is permitted to affirm "the integrity of creation"[50] even when creation appears to be subject to a process of disintegration. This is the great difference between biblical faith and the kind of "natural theology" that thinks nature sufficient as evidence of creation.

Thus (and now we address the second temptation), faith professes God's labor of creation only as faith, not as a matter of observation and demonstration—not as "sight." Without overlooking the evidence of God's labor that the cosmos does offer, the disciple community is not reduced to proving at every juncture that the creative dimension is always victorious over that which detracts from and threatens it. Christian hope is not to be equated with such "positive thinking." Such thinking, which is like a great spiritual plague in North American religion and culture, simply rules out honesty from the start. The mindless celebrationism that can be observed in many reputedly Christian services of worship has more in common with Dionysius than with Jesus Christ; and there is now, as well, a new influx of nature-romanticism, which seems incapable of contemplating the idea that nature is not always benign. This kind of thought patently reflects the general affluence of a society that no longer lives daily in close proximity to nature but is insulated both physically

---

50. A reference to the World Council of Churches' "process," adopted at the Sixth General Assembly in Vancouver, 1983, "Justice, Peace and the Integrity of Creation."

and intellectually from its realities. It is rightly despised by those who, having to face the great negations that cannot be avoided by the two-thirds world, resent the primacy that is given to environmental concerns in First World societies because this so often camouflages the realities of injustice. It is easy to celebrate the goodness of creation when the harshness and indifference of nature are cushioned by relative affluence and filtered through the sieve of bourgeois domesticity.[51]

But true gratitude for and affirmation of creation involve greater honesty— the honesty that is permitted to faith. The world as it is (including also its natural dimension) is not—decidedly not—the creation that God intends. The creation that God intends (including also its natural dimension) is "groaning in travail," is "waiting" for redemption (Rom. 8:22-23, RSV). To celebrate it as though it were already fulfilled, or perhaps unfallen to begin with, is to embrace a sub-Christian romanticism that leaves no place at all for the reality of evil and radical suffering, let alone for the divine work of redemption, and little enough even for preservation.

In sum, the profession of the divine work of creation can be regarded as a Christian profession only if and insofar as it is simultaneously a profession of the divine work of redemption. We shall learn how to affirm creation and to express this affirmation in a credible theology of nature only if and when we learn how to affirm the transformation of a disintegrating creation through the costly grace of a preserving and redeeming—that is, a suffering—love.

Preservation. At the end of the discussion of the work of preservation in chapter 1, we asked: How can we articulate the doctrine of divine providence without either rendering the activity of human beings superfluous, on the one hand, or on the other making it too readily and naively continuous with the divine preservation of the world? We may now try to explicate a response.

Again it will be useful to introduce our discussion by stating two dialectically related theses: (1) The providential work of God includes the spiritual transformation of sinful humanity, therefore we may affirm that human stewardship is both possible and necessary. (2) The redemption of humanity is an eschatological process, therefore it is presumptuous to think that our preservative work is the decisive component in the preservation of the world.

---

51. "From morning to night we walk through a world that is totally manufactured, a creation of human invention. We are surrounded by pavement, machinery, gigantic concrete structures. Automobiles, airplanes, computers, appliances, television, electric lights, artificial air have become the physical universe with which our senses interact. They are what we touch, observe, react to. They are . . . what we think about and know" (Jerry Mander, *In the Absence of the Sacred,* 31). See Douglas John Hall, with responses by Carl Ridd and Jacob Waschenfelder, "Symposium: The Environmental Crisis and Christian Culpability," *Dianoia: A Liberal Arts Interdisciplinary Journal,* 2/2 (Spring, 1992), 1–63.

The first of these theses is directed against that heavy strain of self-announced orthodoxy in our social context that is so unfailing in its promulgation of the *providentia Dei* and so untrusting with respect to human possibilities that it is productive, finally, of an atmosphere of passivity in both ecclesiastical and social spheres. While it is true that the rhetoric of the New World still indulges in fantastic claims about human know-how, the underside of this same activism is a lingering passivity, born both of the negative and the positive forms of determinism treated above. The latter, an attitudinal consequence of our official optimism, breeds passivity in that it assumes that everything is in any case already "going our way," so that our only mandate is to be in the right place at the right time. The negative determinism, which is more explicitly associated with religious conservatism, has little if any hope for the world as such and is therefore content to view human and (especially) Christian responsibility chiefly in terms of prevention, not preservation.

Our thesis, however, tries once more to take with great seriousness the unity of the divine labor. If the end to which God's labor is directed is indeed the redemption of creation, and if this redemption includes as its central theme the transformation of the one creature most responsible for creation's despoliation, then we must assume that this creature is in some genuine sense being equipped for participation in the preservative work of the Redeemer. Not only the central biblical theme of the covenant, but a great many auxiliary themes (including the metaphor of the steward, the concept of human priesthood, and the theme of discipleship, which has figured prominently in the present study) demand such a view of human being and vocation.

It is in fact time that Christian theology and piety attempted to redeem the much-misunderstood idea of human "dominion" for contemporary usage. With the death of dreams and visions that is being witnessed in Eastern Europe, North America, and many other locations today; with the growing phenomenon of an individualism that is not only passive in relation to society but militantly self-protective; with the general withdrawal of many of the most intelligent and well-trained human beings from any sense of enduring civic responsibility; above all, with the coming to be of an image of the human that is almost diametrically opposed to the promethean anthropocentrism of the nineteenth and early twentieth centuries,[52] there is a new and pressing need to accentuate human accountability and responsibility. Christians are not doing a service to God or the world when they join the nature-romantics who call for humanity to draw back from its managerial stance vis-à-vis the world. Or rather, if that is *all* they do, then they will have contributed to the passivity and apathy that is already far too rampant in our society.

---

52. See below, Part III.

A Suffering God?

It belongs to gospel today to profess that the preserving God is equipping human beings (not only Christians) to assume an appropriate dominion within the world: that is, a leadership that is engendered, not by the desire to dominate but by the desire to love effectively and well. Love entails active responsibility for the other—that is to say, a dominion that is patterned, not upon the *Dominus* called Caesar but upon the *Dominus* called Jesus: a servant . . . a suffering servant.

But, to speak now to the second thesis above: As the reference to suffering implies, any suggestion that human stewardship within the world is strictly continuous with God's preserving work is to be distrusted from the outset. Liberalism was fond of citing St. Teresa's dictum (though it was not meant by Teresa in that way) that God "has no hands but our hands, no feet but our feet," and so on. Such a naive assertion not only ignores the Reformation's *simul justus et peccator* (at the same time justified and sinner), but it displays a woeful ignorance of biblical priorities. The divine labor of preservation is infinitely more expansive and mysterious than can be enfolded in our human works, even when they are "good" works; moreover, it is prior to them, and, when they are authentic, their only real basis.

To illustrate: In the upheavals and changes that have taken place in Eastern Europe in recent years, the church (which apart from Poland is a minority church) has played a decisive role, particularly in the former German Democratic Republic. When, however, the Propst of Erfurt, Dr. Heino Falcke, was asked in a television interview how the church had devised its program for this role and where it had gained the inspiration for it, Dr. Falcke responded: "God is mixed up in (*gemischt*) the world and is freeing people for responsibility." The interviewer appeared not to comprehend this statement and said that it was of course a fine religious sentiment, but what had the church in the GDR really *done?* What was its plan of action?

Perhaps the world will not and cannot understand this. Perhaps *because* it does not understand this it is driven to awkward attempts to have an ethic ("values") without any foundation in reality. But for Christians the raison d'être of their discipleship is clear: they are made capable of participation in God's liberating and life-enhancing labor knowing that God is already "mixed up in" everything that happens; they only follow.

Their following—their discipleship—is a matter of service, often of suffering service. But all the same it is never entirely satisfactory. They take their cue from Jesus' parable: "We are unprofitable servants. . ." (Luke 17:10, KJV). At the end of the day, even if we have done everything that we could, we shall not have stopped Satan from sowing seeds in human history; we shall not have acquired proximity to a "Kingdom" that is very discernible. God's preserving work is the foundation and necessity upon which our stewardship is based; but our stewardship is always a tentative and ambiguous thing, never quite separable from our lingering desire for mastery or—on the shadow side of that same desire—our wish for perfect ease.

Redemption. The question with which we concluded our historical reflections on God's work of redemption was the following: Is is possible to discuss the divine work of redemption in such a way that Jesus Christ remains central to it without superseding God's redemptive activity in and through both biblical and modern Judaism? This is both a specific question about the relation between the Judaic and Christian branches of biblical faith, and a more general question concerning the Christian conception of salvation, which is necessarily christocentric, in juxtaposition with Judaic and other soteriological claims.

To facilitate our response, we may again posit an introductory, two-sided affirmation: (1) Christianity is certainly bound to the profession of salvation through Jesus Christ—even, to use the Reformation formula, *per Christum solum* (through Christ alone); and therefore it will not suffice, in a false accommodation to religious pluralism, to relativize or minimize this claim. (2) The profession of the saviorhood of Jesus as the Christ does not, however, immediately translate into a profession of this or that christological/soteriological doctrine; and therefore the disciple community in our pluralistic context must develop a particular consciousness of the limited nature of its theology of redemption and be prepared to hear the "voice of the Good Shepherd" in places unfamiliar to Theological and christological conventions.

It is extremely difficult to explicate the first point without seeming to nullify the second, and vice versa. We are not, however, dealing here with a paradox, and certainly not with a contradiction. We are confronted by two aspects of the same theology of redemption, which, when they are grasped within the relational mode applying to all doctrine, mutually inform and strengthen each other.

Redemption for Christians is irrevocably and unambiguously a christocentric (though not a christomonistic) category. There would be no point in continuing to employ the adjective Christian were this not the case. When the first Christians introduced the language of the *logos* and of the Christ's preexistence, they intended not only to link Jesus with God's very being but also with God's work. And when they described the ascension, reign, and return of the crucified one they wanted to affirm that the salvation they themselves had begun to experience was applicable to the whole world. They did not entertain the possibility that this redemptive work could be incomplete. For them Jesus as the Messiah of God was a full, perfect, and sufficient response on God's part to the problems and possibilities of existence. They therefore implicitly rejected the prospect that Jesus might be superseded, a prospect that was entertained, apparently, by the disciples of John the Baptist: "Are you the one who is to come, or are we to wait for another?" ask John's disciples; and in answer Jesus indicates his ministry of healing—a symbolic response implying that there is no need for anything more; this is what has been awaited, not only by these individual sufferers but by the whole "groaning" creation (Luke 7:18ff.).

In short, the first disciple community confessed the messiahship of Jesus. Apart from this, they would have had no reason to form a fellowship that was distinct from their own Judaic community. Apart from this, there would have been no vocation to the gentile world. Apart from this, Jesus would have remained, perhaps, a prophetic figure within the Jewish tradition, remembered at best by a few searchers after truth and meaning. It was only the confession, "Thou art the Christ," which was perhaps uttered by Peter at Caesarea-Philippi but was assumed by all who followed "the Way," that created the Christian movement; and it is only this confession, when it is made in sincerity and not as a rote formula, that can sustain the Christian movement in its continued existence.

Does this mean that the Christian profession of God's redemptive work is strictly limited to its specific witness to Jesus Christ? The answer, I think, must be a negative one, and we must learn how to say this "No" without erasing the "Yes" that has already been given. How can that be?

It can only be done if Christians are prepared to make a radical and critical distinction between the reality indicated by this name and title, Jesus the Christ, and our own mental images, doctrines, formulae, poetic and hymnological expressions, theological traditions, and even scriptural testimonies to that reality. That is, the actual person, Jesus, and the actual work of that person must never be thought synonymous with our doctrine of the Christ's person and work. We may retain the singularity of that name; we may live, and even live comfortably, with the particularity of that name, only if we continuously do battle with our own idolatrous tendency to *equate* that name with the substance of our profession of that name.

I underscore the verb "equate." It goes without saying that Christians must assume that there is some correspondence between what Scripture, tradition, and the present deliberations of the *koinonia* tell us concerning this one and his independent reality. But—let us admit it honestly—the problem has not been that the church has been zealous in upholding the centrality of this person and work; the problem has been that the church has been too keen to preserve its own Christology, soteriology, and Theology, and too little given to critical theology. And we do not refer to a merely historical problem. Daily, hourly, representatives of every variety of Christianity from the most illiterate to the most learned utter the name "Jesus Christ" and mean by it their own certainly limited and quite possibly wrong and misleading ideas about the identity, character, and import of the one bearing this name and title. Most of us have sufficient everyday sense to realize that everything and everyone whom we name eludes and transcends our comprehension and apprehension of them. But where Jesus Christ is concerned, Christians have been immodest indeed. As we said earlier concerning the whole godhead, Christians appear to know so very much about Jesus Christ!

It is this that must be changed. Neither we nor the world itself is redeemed by Christology. If and insofar as Christians are ready to allow the bearer of this name to remain "person" in relation to our own personhood, and therefore never possessable by us, we may be permitted to retain the profession of faith that names him as the one in whom God's redeeming work is "finished." We may even be permitted to retain the exclusivity of this profession of faith: *per Christum solum*—provided we train ourselves to dismiss at once any hint of a suggestion that this *solus* applies to our *Christology*. It is one thing to say, as in prayer we normally do, "through Jesus Christ, our Lord," knowing that because he is "our Lord" we have absolutely no claim to the possession of him; and it is something very different to claim such sole redemptor status for him if what we are doing really, pious language notwithstanding, is insisting upon the absolute truth of our particular profession concerning redemption. We can own the latter. We can never own the former.

And if we cannot own—cannot even understand, but only stand under—this one, then the exclusivity of what he stands for cannot possibly be mistaken for *our* exclusive right to truth. If he forever eludes our dogmatic and liturgical grasp; if he frustrates our appetite for finality; if his exclusiveness is also an exclusion of all that—then it is after all an inclusive exclusiveness. For why should we not assume that a Redeemer whom we cannot domesticate is present, on the same or similar terms, to others "who are not of this fold"?[53]

We ourselves were not of *his* fold. We ourselves, most of us, are among the ones who are "grafted on" (Romans 11). We are only at most second in relation to those who, according to Paul's repeated formula, must still and always be regarded as first—the Jews. The redemptive work of which Jesus, according to Christian faith, is the apex, is a work that was fully under way long before the historical Jesus appeared, and certainly long before our profession of faith in him. It is entirely possible—should it not be regarded in fact as likely?—that this far-reaching and mysterious labor of the creating and redeeming God, of

---

53. I am therefore in complete agreement with H. Richard Niebuhr when he writes: "I do not have the evidence which allows me to say that the miracle of faith in God is worked only by Jesus Christ and that it is never given to men outside the sphere of his working, though I may say that where I note its presence I posit the presence also of something like Jesus Christ." ("Reformation: The Continuing Imperative," *The Christian Century* 77 (1960): 249.

which Jesus is for us the window of recognition, is infinitely more extensive than our small, unsteady apprehension of it.[54]

Conclusion

In our pursuit of an appropriate Theology, we have been drawn inevitably into Christology. How could it be otherwise?—and yet, it has been otherwise for the greater share of the history of Christian thought and the mission of the church. Despite the prominence of Jesus in the Christian story, the propensity of Christendom has been to regard Jesus from the vantage point of an a priori conception of deity—a perspective informed primarily, as we have seen, by triumphalistic assumptions drawn from whatever experiences of "greatness" have been entertained by human beings and cultures. As we shall see in Part III, our Christology itself has been shaped by this same Theological preunderstanding, to the point that Jesus' "divinity" has wholly overshadowed his humanity and effectively removed him from the sphere called by the prologue of John's Gospel "flesh."

The revolution in Theology (God-talk) that has been taking place in many different ways during the present century (and that will one day be perceived as the major motif in the great transition between Christendom and the coming diaspora church) is a consequence of the refusal, on the part of Christians of many and diverse backgrounds, to allow this procedure to continue apace. If Jesus is indeed the Messiah of God, God's anointed representative, then all of our prior assumptions about deity must be submitted to that story. And when this is done faithfully, the predilection of people and empires for "great" gods must be understood as part of the pathology of sin and not as if it were a natural religious inclination to which Christian evangelism might attach itself contentedly.

The God whom Jesus reveals is a suffering God: that is entirely clear, and Christians must simply stop trying to have it otherwise.[55] The glory, triumph, and power that belong to this suffering of God are of an altogether different order from the glory, triumph, and power of the imperial imagination of fallen humanity. Moreover, beyond the hints and rumors of them that are given sometimes to the church in its suffering, Christians themselves cannot describe that

---

54. In this connection see the report of Jeffrey Gros on the World Council of Churches' texts on interreligious dialogue and the Vatican encyclical, *Redemptoris Missio*, entitled "Christian Confession in a Pluralistic World," *The Christian Century* (June 26–July 3, 1991), 644–46; also S. Mark Hein's excellent review of the academic debate on pluralism, entitled "Crisscrossing the Rubicon: Reconsidering Religious Pluralism," *The Christian Century* (July 10–17, 1991), 688–90.

55. It would be much better for theology "if we ceased to make God's apathy our starting point, and started from the axiom of God's passion" (Jürgen Moltmann, *The Trinity and the Kingdom* [Minneapolis: Fortress, 1993], 22).

glory and triumph and power positively—beyond the *via negativa*. That is to say, the *gloria Dei* remains for us an eschatological reality—visible only to faith, and under the guise of its antithesis. That applies a fortiori (as was claimed in the immediately preceding subsection) to our Christologies. "Until Christ's parousia, there can only be a historical christology, not a chiliastic one. This shuts out of christology all forms of ecclesiastical and political triumphalism, for the *christologia viae* is *theologia crucis* and nothing else. The coming One is in the process of his coming and can be grasped only in that light: as on the road, and walking with us."[56]

Perhaps the most significant Theological revolution of our era is the one that was signaled by Dietrich Bonhoeffer when on the way to execution he wrote, "Man's religiosity makes him look in his distress to the power of God in the world: God is the *deus ex machina*. The Bible directs man to God's powerlessness and suffering; only the suffering God can help."[57] Some decry such a transformation in Christian God-consciousness and long for the days of philosophic theism, when the Deity could be considered a subject fit for high academic discourse. But Bonhoeffer and his contemporaries, along with those who in the subsequent decades have become conscious of God's strange associations with the world's anxious and oppressed, have felt themselves excluded from the calm atmosphere of scholarly religion—not, let us note, because of their lack of scholarly credentials, but because the God whom they actually met in the world and in the Scriptures made them uncomfortable in that atmosphere.[58] Whoever has traced the faint but persistent lines of *theologica crucis* throughout Christian history can only be grateful that the newer Testamental witness to the crucified one has at long last led a significant body of Christian scholars to draw Theological conclusions from this christological testimony.

But what is still too seldom realized by those who find, today, the way back to God through "the way of Jesus Christ," is that the God to whom they are led is none other than the God of Abraham and Sarah, of Moses and the prophets, of Deborah and Koheleth. At long last, Christians are being guided by Jesus (often unawares) back to the God to whom Jesus himself prayed. That God was set aside

---

56. Moltmann, *The Way of Jesus Christ,* 33.

57. *Letters and Papers: The Enlarged Edition,* trans. Reginald Fuller, Frank Clarke, et al. (London: S.C.M. Press, 1953), 361.

58. Ronald Goetz, in his review of Richard C. Creel's *Divine Impassibility: An Essay in Philosophical Theology* (Cambridge: Cambridge Univ. Press, 1986), rightly notes that the theologians whom Creel criticizes for having "installed theopaschitism as the new orthodoxy" (including Barth, Brunner, Reinhold Niebuhr, Bonhoeffer, Moltmann, Pannenberg, and Rahner) did not arbitrarily *choose* to affirm God's suffering over against the whole tradition of Patripassianism; rather, they "felt compelled to speak of God's suffering because God has revealed that suffering in his incarnate son. For such revelational theology, the suffering of God is a given. It is not an option to be 'rationally' negotiated; it is a reality to be witnessed to." (*The Christian Century* [Jan. 7–14, 1987].)

by Christendom for centuries—and not only by Marcion and his ilk, but (far more effectively) by all who gladly accepted the Old Testament . . . and forced its "I am who I am" into the mold of triumphant divinity, devoid of pathos.

The God of the whole Bible is a suffering God.[59] God suffers because God loves. And until that which God loves—the creation—is healed, the glory of God can only be glimpsed by those who in some measure are given to participate in God's suffering love.[60]

---

59. See in particular Terence E. Fretheim, *The Suffering of God: An Old Testament Perspective* (Philadelphia: Fortress Press, 1984).

60. See Larry Rasmussen and Renate Bethge, *Dietrich Bonhoeffer: His Significance for North Americans* (Minneapolis: Fortress Press, 1990), 129–30.

PART II
CREATURELY BEING

CHAPTER ▪ FOUR

The World and Humanity as Professed by Faith

12. The Perspective

12.1. A Matter of Faith.   There is a kind of unspoken assumption among many Christians that when we turn from the consideration of deity to humanity and the world, we are moving from matters that presuppose belief to aspects of our tradition that are more or less open to the inspection and verification of any intelligent human being who will take the trouble to reflect on them. One supposes that this predisposition is engendered by the fact that, while God and all that the related nomenclature signifies belong to the realm of "things invisible," the world and what it holds seem eminently visible and subject to ordinary investigation. Western literature is filled with diverse and sometimes desperate attempts to answer the question, Does God exist? but no one apart from recent poets of the Absurd has considered it necessary to ask whether the world and human beings exist. The raw fact of existence in this way deceives people into thinking that now, as we turn our attention from the Creator to the creation, we may rely less upon faith and more upon sight.

This is a great deception, and one of which contemporary *non*religious culture has happily made Christians more aware—insofar, at least, as the latter have absorbed the secular critique of religious belief. For in a real sense the cutting edge of the "scandal" of faith must be understood today as having more to do with what Christians profess concerning the world and humanity than

187

with their belief in God.[1] We shall have to develop this thought more fully in both of the succeeding chapters on creaturely being; for the present we need only mention it, because it highlights the epistemological presuppositions with which we approach the entire discussion of creaturely being as professed by faith.

The key concept in our chapter heading is indicated by the phrase, "as professed by faith." What Christians claim concerning "the world and humanity" *is* a matter of faith. Today perhaps one should say of sheer faith, for none of it is self-evident. Even of existence itself fundamental questions are to be asked, where Christian profession is concerned. Obviously enough, few of our contemporaries would be prepared to deny that beings named by the classifying mind of the West as Homo sapiens really do exist and are surrounded by other forms of life. But when Christians speak of existence, they wish from the start to go much farther than that. Their discussion of creaturely existence in general, and of human existence in particular, contains fundamental claims that are, from a strictly observational point of view, extraordinary.

They intend, for one thing, to generalize; that is, they wish to speak of *human* existence—of humankind, and not only of individuals or classes or groupings based on historical, geographic, racial, sexual, linguistic, or other characteristics. While not overlooking such specific realities as these, Christian doctrine assumes and (insofar as it wants to retain the adjective "Christian") must assume certain realities that cut across all distinctions that pertain to life as it is actually lived in all of its specificity.

For example, about all human life Christian profession assumes a certain distortedness. "Christian theological anthropology recognizes a dual structure in its understanding of humanity. This dual structure differentiates the essence from the existence of humanity. What humanity is potentially and authentically is not the same as what humanity has been historically. Historically, human nature is fallen, distorted, and sinful."[2] Whether old or young, black or white, male or female, North American or Asian, prehistoric or modern, "all have sinned and fall short of the glory of God" (Rom. 3:23). All! This is to say that sin—which we have still to define—is a condition of human existence as such; and so long as we wish to remain within the profession of faith called Christian, we are obliged to take this seriously—to profess it. Distinctions are assumed; they are indeed expected, and in an indeterminate variety. But, it is claimed, the condition called sin applies in one way or another to all human creatures. It is part of what it means to exist—though, as

---

1. "[T]here is no more fundamental debate in the world today than that about human nature." T. E. Pollard, *Fulness of Humanity: Christ's Humanness and Ours* (Sheffield: Almond Press, 1982), 19.

2. Rosemary Radford Ruether, *Sexism and God-Talk: Toward a Feminist Theology* (Boston: Beacon Press, 1983), 93.

we shall affirm presently, the connection between existence and sin is not a necessary one.

Now, if one says that existence (or at any rate human existence) is distorted, this implies yet another assumption of faith that is not at all axiomatic. To say "distorted"—or, to use the older, metaphoric terminology, "fallen"—is to imply a condition in relation to which our actual life can be so regarded. The obvious question that has to be asked in the face of the Christian claim concerning the universality of sin is: distorted in relation to what? fallen from what height?

Many, undoubtedly most, of earth's present-day human citizens are conscious of aspects of worldly experience that they regard with apprehension, disgust, or anxiety. It would be hard to live on planet Earth today and remain unaware of the threats to life and happiness by which all of us are surrounded and which none can finally escape, even through habitual and practiced unawareness. War and violence, gross economic disparities, environmental degradation, the depletion of vital resources, racial hatred, suspicion and resentment between the sexes, an expanding human population that threatens extrahuman and human futures: these and countless other ills, dangers, and causes of suffering are daily recounted by the media. But to name all this "distortion" is to assume both that it could be otherwise and that it should be otherwise; that is to say that, were the world as it ought to be, such things would not exist.

It is true that many people who lament the state of the world cannot, when pressed, provide a rationale for their lament. Since they have no position of vantage from which to believe that it could be other than it is, they have no basis on which to assert that it should be other than it is.

Here we touch upon the great moral dilemma of secular civilization. Apart from a few of the more callous nihilists and cynics, nearly everyone today agrees that we must attempt to inculcate some kind of public morality, some sense of limits. In North America the cult of individual freedom has so far given way to public chaos that even the amoral are ready to petition for the institution of public morality. In cities teeming with dirt and crime, it requires extraordinary psychic (and material) insulation to keep from realizing that urban civilization may be impossible without some commonly held values.

Precisely "values" is the language employed by those who have lately come to this conclusion. Value-education is today part of many curricula, even at the primary school level. Undoubtedly it is imperative that this should be so, but it does not alter the dilemma—in fact, it enshrines it. No amount of conditioning aimed at some "should" can hide the chasm over which it is constructed: namely, the metaphysical emptiness whose reality is the very raison d'être of the exercise in value-engineering. Morality based upon such foundations, which are no foundations at all but only the specter of an immense and fearful need for foundations, is an ephemeral thing at best. Values are the basis of an ethic only so long as they

189

are held; and there is nothing beyond the will of the majority to approve them that can sustain them or arbitrate between them and rival values.[3]

Christian faith bases neither its ethic nor its assessment of the distorted state of worldly life upon value-thinking, even though Christians may often make common cause with those who seek to inculcate values in public life. For the Christian tradition, the discrepancy between what *is* and what *ought to be* derives from a perspective on existence coming from the whole substance of what is professed by faith. According to this perspective, the world certainly should not be the way it is—something is wrong at the heart of its life. But this judgment stems, not from personal distaste for or dissatisfaction with what is, and not merely from the pain, danger, chaos, or unhappiness that is experienced on account of what is, but from the belief that what is is not what is intended, and in fact need not *be*.

This statement necessarily conjures up the whole background of Christian profession as the perspective that Christians bring to the contemplation of the world and humanity. How shall we characterize that theological background for our present purposes?

12.2. Not a Failed Experiment. To begin with, the Christian professes that the world and all life must be regarded as creation. Life is not a random thing, a chance happening resultant upon some capricious Big Bang.[4] Whatever the "How?" of the universe may be, it presupposes a "Whence?" Christians name this source God; but they do not stop there. As we have already seen in the discussion of the Christian account of deity, it is impossible within the parameters of this tradition to speak only of God; for God as Judeo-Christian thought depicts deity is already from the outset God-with-us. God, faith affirms, wills to have vis-à-vis God's own person another. This created other is not as such divine, is not to be worshiped as divine, and is not, therefore, the ultimate test of its own worthwhileness. It is valuable because God values it. "God saw everything that he had made, and indeed, it was very good" (Gen. 1:31).

This is the first (though not necessarily noetically first) aspect of faith's perspective on creaturely being. Or, to put it otherwise, this is the ontology (metaphysic) on which Christian faith founds its ethic. The first thing that must be said about this world is that it is the creation of God and as such is

---

3. "If values have no *fundamentum in re* (cf. Plato's identification of the good with the essential structures, the ideas of being), they float in the air of a transcendent validity, or else they are subjected to pragmatic tests which are arbitrary and accidental unless they introduce an ontology of essences surreptitiously." (Paul Tillich, *Systematic Theology,* vol. 1 [Chicago: Univ. of Chicago Press, 1951], 20.)

4. See Ronald Goetz's challenging comments on the moral implications of the Big Bang theory and the "recklessness of God's love" in "Jesus Loves Everybody," in *The Christian Century* (March 11, 1992), 275.

"very good." The affirmation that the world as it exists is distorted, presupposes this prior affirmation of its essential goodness.

The primary reality where the Christian profession of faith concerning the world and humanity is concerned is *not* the distortedness of creaturely being but the insistence that creaturehood as such is not distortion; that it would be possible to *be* and not to be "fallen"; that fallenness is not, so to speak, built into existence but constitutes a discrepancy between what-is-intended and what-has-come-to-be. Because what-is-intended is intended, not merely by human good will or wishful thinking but by the one who has fashioned the world, it may and must be taken with the utmost seriousness by faith. Intentionality (that is, God's will for creation) is in fact more decisive in faith's perspective on existence than is faith's recognition that, from such a vision of what-is-intended, what-has-come-to-be is unacceptable.

This first pillar in faith's foundational perspective on the world and humanity would not, however, in itself suffice either as a basis of hope or as ground for an ethic of worldly concern and responsibility. It could even be argued (and as we shall see later, such a position has not been far from the mind of historic Christianity) that on the basis of the Christian doctrine of creation and fall, all that one could say about the world and humanity as such is that they were intended for a high purpose from which, unfortunately, they fell. In fact, the doctrine of creation can easily function as a posture from whose heights the world as it is, is pathetic indeed. This kind of thinking accompanies every soteriology that announces a prospect of being saved *from* the world; and we have already noticed that such expressions of the meaning of salvation abound in North American religious consciousness. Nevertheless, despite their abundance they do not represent either biblical faith or those traditions faithful to biblical faith. For these latter, the perspective that faith brings to the contemplation of the world and humanity contains another aspect, one that goes beyond the profession of belief in God's creative intention for the world.

This is the aspect that is implied in the doctrine of divine providence and is consummated, for Christians, in the doctrine of the work of the Christ. This world is not only *created* by one whose intention for it transcends and judges its actuality; it is being *redeemed* from its distorted condition by this same God. Even in the midst of its decadence—its "bondage to decay" (Rom. 8:21)—the world is the scene of God's active work of redemption. Because this is so, we have said, we do not have to close our eyes to the negation that is also present in the world's ongoing history; we do not have to confine our view to that which gives some pale evidence of its being the sphere of divine providence; and we do not have to find within ourselves the necessary moral courage to work for earth's betterment. God, we profess, has made good God's own creational intention: the world, which was "very good" at its foundation, is becoming and shall become very good in its unfolding; its *terminus ad quem* (the end toward which it moves) is not destruction but fulfillment, consummation. Creation is not a failed experiment. It has not been abandoned by the one who brought it into being. It is not given over to the processes of disintegration and death that were introduced into it by forces other than the will of its Creator. It is being "mended" (Emil Fackenheim).

These two aspects of faith's perspective on the world and humanity, taken in their unity and continuity, form the vantage point from which Christians both admit the wrongness of the world and profess its being righted. Together, the doctrines of creation and redemption constitute the ontological possibility ("could be") that gives substance and drive to the ethical necessity ("should be") that informs Christian discipleship from beginning to end. Because God is both creator and redeemer of the world, the world, though distorted, could still be different from what it is. And faith hears in this "could still be" both the permission and the command to participate in God's transforming work.

12.3. What This Perspective Allows.

What we have here as the basic perspective of Christian faith as it regards this world, its creatures, and its destiny, is in other words a point of view informed by the three basic categories of Christian doctrine generally: creation, fall, and redemption. These are the three foci—or rather, because it is misleading to separate the three, this is the threefold focus—from which Christians view all that is included in the designation "the world," including humanity. As such, this focus is productive of several important nuances, which, when compared with other possible and actual outlooks upon the world, deserve close attention:

a. *The Christian perspective on the world permits a high degree of realism (using the term "realism" here in its modern connotation).* Because of its doctrine of the fall, Christian faith, unlike the modern progressive account of the world, does not have to search for evidence of continuous improvement in worldly life and history. As we have said previously, it is free to explore that which negates. It is not committed in advance to positions that must corroborate "progress" and accentuate the positive. It expects to find evil in the world, but, when it is true to its own best interpretations, it neither rejoices in evil nor reduces it to predictability. It does not expect sin and evil always and everywhere to be the same. To do so would be to court a cyclical view of history, and the biblical view of history is linear (a matter to be elaborated in Volume III).

b. *The Christian perspective on the world permits a high degree of hope.* Points (a) and (b) are dialectically linked. We are not usually very realistic about life if we have no reason at all to expect anything better. The doctrines of creation and redemption provide a frame of reference for the exploration of worldly despair because they counter worldly despair through the promise of grace that transforms both the causes of human despair and the despair itself. Thus the realism of the first observation does not lead to historical cynicism. Nor, on the other hand, does the hope of the second observation translate into historical optimism. There is a dialectic at work here that moves back and forth between unvarnished honesty about what is wrong with the world and exceptional hope for its righting.

This dialectic, which can be detected in many of the greatest historical expressions of Christian belief from Paul to Augustine to Calvin and Luther and Reinhold Niebuhr, is terribly puzzling to those who are unaware, or insufficiently aware, of the perspective that we have been considering here. To many such persons, and especially those who are committed to a static positive outlook on the world, a figure like Niebuhr seems a veritable pessimist; for he was constantly detailing what was the matter with his world—"America." To others, the same person seems an incorrigible optimist; for they are all too ready to see what is wrong with their world and therefore they are amazed that anyone would continue to hope for change.[5]

c. The Christian perspective on the world precludes reduction to theory. At any rate, it should do so, and in its better articulations it does. The reason is that it is first not a conception of the world—a *Weltanschauung*—but a profession concerning the nature of the living God and God's relationship with a created order that also lives, moves, and constantly changes. Because the Christian view of creaturely being takes history seriously, it is not permitted to indulge in "world views," even though it must always dialogue with these. "Human temporality in its changing historical context sets the condition for the way we are human; it thus also sets the condition for the way we are or are not religious. Our humanity, our action, our religiousness and thus our theology are essentially intertwined with our historicity."[6]

To be sure, there are certain steady themes. We have already named the most rudimentary of them: creation, fall, redemption. But these do not lend themselves to fixed theories concerning the world. There is no automatic movement through creation to fall to redemption. The threefold focus provides for faith a perspective; it does not provide a prospectus, schema, or blueprint. A good deal is spoken in ecclesiastical circles about the "Plan" of God. This can be a useful nomenclature under certain circumstances (for example, to counter randomness), but it can also come dangerously close to suggesting a fixed program, accessible to the faithful, from which there can be no deviation—perhaps not even on God's part![7]

---

5. In this connection see Niebuhr's essay "Optimism, Pessimism, and Religious Faith," in Robert McAfee Brown, *The Essential Reinhold Niebuhr: Selected Essays and Addresses* (New Haven: Yale Univ. Press, 1986), 3–17.

6. Langdon Gilkey, *Reaping the Whirlwind: A Christian Interpretation of History* (New York: Seabury Press, 1976), 9.

7. See the earlier reference to dispensationalism, p. 170 above.

To indulge in such thinking is to move from the stance of faith to imagined "sight" (Heb. 11:1; 2 Cor. 5:7) and from the sphere of theology to that of ideology. Christians may expect to find in their experience of the world intimations of each of these three interrelated themes, but they may not expect to find definite patterns of their interrelatedness or predictable manifestations of their interplay. We have already affirmed, for instance, that sin (fallenness) applies universally; but what, specifically, sin will mean in any given context, or how it may be countered by redeeming grace, is never known in advance, and only imperfectly after the fact. It has been an ongoing temptation of the Christian church to turn faith's perspective on the world into a prospectus. But if we wish to be faithful to the best articulations of the tradition and not the worst, then we must certainly insist that the received tradition itself includes a polemic against the reduction of this perspective on the world to theories about the world's history and its fate.

   d. *Above all, the Christian perspective on the world and humanity is a matter of faith.* This cannot be overemphasized. No aspect of this perspective is subject to clear demonstration. It has been said that the doctrine of sin comes closest to an empirically verifiable facet of Christian doctrine, but this statement is made (for example, by Reinhold Niebuhr) in jest. Sin is what it is only in relation to what, according to the doctrines of creation and redemption, is intended; and no one can prove that a world was intended, or is even now being fashioned, that is radically different from what the world has been and is. Even St. Thomas, for whom much about the Christian faith was "reasonable," left to "revealed truth" the doctrines of creation and redemption.

   In our own time, the faith basis of the Christian perspective on the world and humanity has been accentuated by the pervasive secularity of the West, and to some extent also by alternative religious and quasi-religious views. Nothing that Christians say about the world as Christians can be considered self-evident or universally acceptable in such a context. While parallel ideas may be found in this or that place; while a certain nostalgia for "the Christian world view" may certainly be discovered in many post-Christian circles; and while Christians are never justified in treating their faith as if it were secret knowledge (*gnosis*) inaccessible to any outside the circles of faith, we know today that we are thrown back upon the faith basis of our belief even where "things visible" are concerned. In some respects the churches have not caught up with this fact, and in North America particularly—where, for example, some Christians can still force young people to study the doctrine of creation as if it were a scientific theory—there is a continuing and often militant refusal to acknowledge that what we say about our world is indeed a matter of profession and confession. It must become part of the mandate of anyone who attempts to discuss Christian theology in North America today to challenge and correct this.

12.4. Differing Emphases in Jewish and Christian Perceptions of the World. We have stressed, in the foregoing, the unity and continuity of the three aspects of Christian profession concerning the world and humanity—creation, fall, redemption. We must now, however, draw attention to the fact that, historically speaking, this unity and continuity have not been consistently maintained within the Judeo-Christian stream. The fact that the three prongs of this single focus provide three somewhat different angles on the nature of this world means that it has been possible, among the branches of this faith tradition, to assume different emphases. There is perhaps a parallel here with the doctrine of the Trinity.

While it is impossible in the present work to trace all the turnings and nuances of this subject, I shall venture the generalization that, on the whole, Jewish faith has taken a more consistently positive attitude toward this world than has historic Christianity.[8] This could, I think, be documented, not only from the writings of Jewish authors, including biblical and theological students, but also—and more concretely—from the actual behavior of the Jewish community throughout its history and still today.[9]

By contrast with such a record of world-commitment, it must be admitted that Christianity, empirically speaking, has manifested a consistent ambiguity with respect to this world. It is possible, fortunately, to find impressive exceptions to this generalization—for example, in some aspects of monasticism, particularly the mendicant orders of the Middle Ages; or in the social

---

8. "The Christian emphasis upon the dualities of body and soul, the secular and the sacred, the Church and the world, and even this world and the next, are foreign to Jewish thinking. The hope for the messianic age remains, but it continues to be held as a future horizon of *history*. . . . The word 'heaven' . . . is not so much a place that one goes to by abandoning the earth as that place of God's presence which one seeks to bring near by hallowing daily life. . . . Thus daily life is not lived in a spirituality that abstracts man from creation, the body and society, but rather seeks to draw God's holy presence into these forms of daily life, so that every aspect of ordinary activities becomes a prayer and God's *Shekhinah* comes near and hallows the earth." (Rosemary Radford Ruether, *Liberation Theology* [New York: Paulist Press, 1972], 72.)

9. What I mean is graphically demonstrated in a city like my own, which contains a significant minority of Jews from all over the world, some of whom are recent immigrants, some of whom can claim generations of Canadian citizenship. The extent of their participation in the public life of the city; their impressive and disproportionate contribution to culture and the arts; their leadership in the fields of the natural sciences, and particularly in medicine: all this and much more impresses the observer again and again, presenting to the Christian observer a disturbing contrast with much of his or her own religious community. Even Jewish people who have long since ceased to have any vital connection with the synagogue have often retained an extraordinary degree of world-commitment. It is impossible to visit a Jewish hospital or home for the elderly without coming to the realization that this unusual care for life at its extremities is only an extension of the general stewardship of life informing this faith community, heightened by the proximity of the threat to life. It is not—as is sometimes superficially concluded—merely the consequence of exceptional obedience to the fifth commandment ("Honor your father and your mother . . . ," Exod. 20:12). On the contrary, the fifth commandment (and most of the others as well) is a consequence of this same world-orientation, which is prior to all the law and is the foundation of the older Testament's historical interest as well as its prophetic and wisdom components.

gospel wing of liberalism; or in numerous current Christian movements such as the World Council of Churches' "Justice, Peace and the Integrity of Creation" process. Indeed, it would not be presumptuous to append to the above generalization the qualification that perhaps the most significant distinction between most classical expressions of Christian belief and contemporary theologies, both Catholic and ("mainline") Protestant, is precisely the fact that the latter represent a quite steady movement of faith *toward this world.* In nineteenth-century liberalism and neo-Protestantism this had a certain obvious priority, but it was unfortunately so prone to break with the Christian tradition—including even the Scriptures—that it did not, so to speak, bring the tradition with it as it turned toward the world.

Neoorthodoxy could be interpreted—and in a figure like that of Dietrich Bonhoeffer *should* be interpreted—as precisely the determination to orient toward the world not only the present-day churches but the whole Christian tradition. Similarly, though along very different lines, the priest-scientist Pierre Teilhard de Chardin,[10] together with some Roman Catholic existentialists and political theologians, have wished to be both in and "for" the world, not only in their own behalf, but as representatives of the Christian faith in its total, incarnational thrust. This same movement toward the world has been carried to ever more explicit lengths by such present-day movements as black theology, liberation theologies, and feminist theologies. Increasingly, the world-orientation of the Christian movement is overcoming the ancient and lamentable distinction between Christian theology and Christian social ethics and, even more dramatically, the questionable division of the world into sacred and secular dimensions.

Assuming some acquaintance with the course of Christian history and thought throughout the centuries, however, it is obvious that this is a late emphasis, on the whole, and that it can only be carried out through a critical struggle with the dominant ecclesiastical conventions of the past. Moreover, it by no means holds the field even in the contemporary life of the churches. In some ways, indeed, Christianity in contemporary North America is still more accurately perceived as a religion of world-denial and withdrawal from the world than of orientation toward the world. It is even possible that this propensity is more conspicuous in North American Christianity than in any other province of Christendom today, including Western Europe, where the politicization of the faith is strongly present among those for whom Christianity is no longer simply the established religion.

The importance of these observations for our present discussion becomes obvious if one asks *why* historic Christianity manifests ambiguous attitudes

---

10. See Jürgen Moltmann's recent discussion and critique of Teilhard in *The Way of Jesus Christ: Christology in Messianic Dimensions,* trans. Margaret Kohl (Minneapolis: Fortress Press, 1993), 292f.

toward this world—attitudes that are on the whole not shared by the parental faith. Such an inquiry naturally introduces a complex web of cause and effect, subject to many different interpretations. Certainly Christian ambiguity about the world has something to do with the Hellenization of the faith, to which we have already drawn attention. Since the Hellenistic mentality engenders suspicion about materiality, Hellenized Christianity always had difficulty with the Judaic-Christian explanations of both creation and redemption; for in the minority traditions in which the latter has persisted, the psychosomatic unity of creaturely life has been assumed (for example, in both the Christ's resurrection and the eschatological resurrection of the dead). Christianity, so far as it was permanently impacted by this early spiritualization of the faith, quite naturally turned away from this world for its understanding of ultimate reality and ultimate salvation.

Some recent commentators refer to spiritualistic processes at work in historic Christianity as its inherent Manichaeanism. Christopher Derrick describes Manichaeanism as the attitude that says we are trapped in an evil world. He believes this may even be a majority "Christian" opinion.[11] Conrad Bonifazi emphasizes how this Manichaean orientation has detracted from any sustained Christian contemplation of the "liberation" of the natural order:

> In practice, the church has not been concerned with the liberation and development of the natural world; and, from the second to the fifth centuries particularly, it radically perverted the spirit of the New Testament in its regard for matter. During that time, despite the war waged by Christianity against Iranian dualism, Manichaeism seeped through the Gnostics into the Christian body, and, instead of remaining an indispensable vehicle of spirit, matter came to be regarded as a drag upon it.[12]

Again, from another perspective that has informed our work throughout, the tendency of Christianity to denigrate or to manifest a continuing uncertainty about this world can be traced in part to the fact of Christian establishment. While on the one hand the establishment of Christianity as the religion of empire meant (and still, where it pertains, means) a certain adaptation of

---

11. "The Manichaeans—strictly so called—flourished chiefly in the fourth century: for a time they held the allegiance of the great St. Augustine, and he never entirely shook off their influence. But there is a great deal in common between their view of life and that held by the second-century Gnostics, the medieval Catharists and Albigensians, and the countless similar groups that emerge at intervals in the light of history. . . .

"Manichaeanism (in our broader sense of the word) has thus been present . . . throughout practically the whole history of the Christian West." (*The Delicate Creation: Towards a Theology of the Environment* [Old Greenwich, Conn.: Devin-Adair Co., 1972], 35f.)

12. "The Biblical Roots of an Ecologic Conscience," in *This Little Planet,* ed. Michael Hamilton (New York: Scribner's, 1970), 223.

the faith to worldly standards and goals, it implied and implies on the other hand a stance of superiority and power with respect to this world. The world becomes interesting and acceptable to Christians, as it were, when they can seem to control it. Thus, reading the history of the church one could derive the impression that, where this world is concerned, Christianity has vacillated between a posture of disdain and withdrawal on the one hand and attempted mastery on the other.

However we may interpret such historic influences, what we may and must say theologically in response to the question under discussion is that for a great number of reasons, both religious and sociopolitical, evolving Christianity came to stress the fallenness of the world in a way that had not happened in the parental religion of Judaism.[13] This emphasis can already be discerned in the newer Testamental writings—though it is countered there by other emphases, some of which have been picked up again by contemporary liberationist and other theologies. Did not Jesus speak of this world in negative terms—as "an evil and adulterous generation," for example (Matt. 12:39; 16:4; Mark 8:38)? Did not this same sinful world reject and put to death the one who came "that it might have life"? Did not the early teachers of the "little flocks" warn their charges against a too close affiliation with this world (for example, James 4:4)? And are we not told by these ancient mentors, therefore, to shun worldly associations?

> Do not love the world or the things in the world. If any one loves the world, love for the Father is not in him. For all that is in the world, the lust of the flesh and the lust of the eyes and the pride of life, is not of the Father but is of the world. And the world passes away, and the lust of it; but he who does the will of God abides forever. (1 John 2:15-17, RSV)

Is it then any wonder that the young church, an ostracized and often severely persecuted minority, conceived of itself as an alien colony of heaven, a separated *koinonia,* an ark plying tempestuous waters?[14] Neither the doctrine of creation nor that of redemption, apparently, could offset the impact of the doctrine of the fall. Creation, in fact, as has been demonstrated many times in recent years, has played a very small role in the church's perception of worldly life. For the most part, it has been assumed rather than explored—taken for granted as a necessary backdrop to the fall from grace and as a means, besides, of exonerating the Creator from any responsibility for the world's wickedness. Redemption could not be so thoroughly neglected, of course; but for the most

---

13. That is not to say that Judaism is not profoundly aware of "the unredeemed character of the world" (Moltmann, *The Way of Jesus Christ,* 29).

14. See Hendrikus Berkhof, *Christian Faith: An Introduction to the Study of the Faith,* trans. Sierd Woudstra (Grand Rapids: Wm. B. Eerdmans Pub. Co., 1979), 411.

part in classical expressions of the faith (and I speak of the dominant, not necessarily the most brilliant theologies), redemption has been conceived as a rescue operation. The statement of the famous American evangelist Dwight L. Moody (1837–1899), for all its unsophistication, unfortunately summarizes rather well the salvation theology of many more sophisticated Christian thinkers: "I look upon this world as a wrecked vessel. God has given me a lifeboat and said to me, 'Moody, save all you can.'"[15]

What has been forgotten in this centuries-old conception of the Christian enterprise, as Berkhof has nicely stated it, is that "the ark was to land as soon as possible so that the earth could be newly populated and cultivated."[16] In other words, Christian preoccupation with worldly sin and evil has tended to blind many to the fact that it is *God's* world and that the "rescue operation" has to do not only with elect persons but with the whole wronged and twisted creation. The angle on the world that comes from the hamartiological focus of the Christian perspective does necessitate an enduring realism about what is the matter with the world, as well as the entertainment of radical conceptions of salvation: the "wounds of my people" (Jer. 6:14) cannot be healed lightly. It would be as questionable for faith to underestimate the radicality of evil in the name of a positive doctrine of creation as to neglect the doctrine of creation in the name of Christian realism. An evil and lost world requires more than exhortation, more than law, for its redemption. And since this assumption is necessarily implied in the gospel of redemption, those who bear witness to the gospel will never easily fit in. They will feel themselves, often, aliens in a strange land. They may need to fashion symbols and metaphors that capture this sense of their otherness: a priestly people, a covenant people, an elect people, a separated people, dwellers in an ark.

But they will have gone terribly wrong—even within the terms of most of these symbols of their distinction from "the world"—if they forget that their mission is a mission *to the world*. Truly they are a priestly people; but the priest is there for the people. Truly they are a covenant people; but the end to which their covenant presses is inclusive in the extreme: "in you all the families of the earth shall be blessed" (Gen. 12:3). Truly they are an elect people; but this does not translate forthwith into the related but finally inimical concept of an elite. Truly they are a separated people—called apart in order to be set down again into the midst of that from which they have been and are being separated; so that not being "of" the world they may be the more unambiguously "in" it. Truly they are occupants of an ark riding out troubled waters; but the object of the voyage is to land, to disembark, to begin again.

---

15. Quoted in Howard Clark Kee et al., eds., *Christianity: A Social and Cultural History* (New York: Macmillan Pub. Co., 1991), 696.
16. *Christian Faith*, 411.

Evidently we are already anticipating what may and must become a theme of our discussion in the constructive chapter (6) of this part. We do so only because it is impossible to appreciate the historical temptation of Christianity with respect to its perspective on this world and humankind without recognizing something of the alternative that it did not sufficiently embrace—an alternative rather astonishingly present in the Scriptures and history of Israel, a people far more consistently ostracized from the world than were the Christians; an alternative present, also, at least with high potentiality, in the Scriptures peculiar to the explicitly Christian side of biblical faith; an alternative, finally, which (not without difficulty and not without its own attendant dangers) is being explored on all sides in our own period.

The hint of danger alluded to in the previous sentence brings to the fore the question that must emerge out of this aspect of our discussion: How is it possible for the Christian community unambiguously to affirm the world without courting the sort of uncritical acceptance of the world that minimizes the doctrine of sin and in the end denies the church the possibility of a prophetic perspective, witness, and ethic?

13. The Human Creature

13.1. Humanity, the Point of Concentration. Contrary to some recent commentary on the subject, the Judeo-Christian tradition at its sources is not silent on the subject of extrahuman creaturehood.[17] At least it must be maintained that the Scriptures contain far more potential for the development of this subject than has been actualized in the history of Christian doctrine. From them we learn, for example, that God delights in creation and its great variety (Gen. 1:31; Job 38–39; Psalm 104); that God establishes covenant with all creatures (Gen. 9:10; Hos. 2:18); that nature throughout manifests an aboriginal harmony (Isa. 11:6-9); that the rights of nonhuman beings are to be respected by the human community—for example, animals too are to be allowed to rest on the sabbath day (Exod. 23:12); birds are not to be taken when they are hatching their eggs, oxen at work are not to be muzzled (Deut. 22:6, 25:4); the land is to be cared for and allowed to lie fallow during certain periods

---

17. A typical example of the simplistic reading of Judeo-Christian tradition that has captured the imagination of many, especially within the ranks of those rightly concerned about our deteriorating environment, is given in the Reith Lecture of Frank Fraser Darling: "Our Greek derivation in western civilization gave us the reason which has guided our science, but the Judaic-Christian background gave us a man-centred world. Our technology is a monument to the belief that Jehovah created us in his image, a belief which of course had to be put that way to express the truth that man created Jehovah in *his* own image. The resources of the planet were for man, without a doubt. They could have no higher end than to serve man at the behest of Jehovah. There could be no doubt of the rightness of technology." (Reith Lecture No. 3, reprinted in *The Listener* [Nov. 17, 1969].)

(Leviticus 25); trees are not to be cut down at random (Deut. 20:19-20), and so on. Generalizing on the basis of the creation sagas, Jürgen Moltmann writes, "Every glance at the creation accounts in the Old Testament makes it clear first of all that the human being is one creature among others. There is a fellowship of creation and the human being is a member of it."[18]

In the newer Testament, which, to be sure, does not expatiate on the theme, we are at least given no cause to suppose that this Hebraic sensitivity to the whole creation has been set aside. We do see there passing illustrations of a concern for nature, even for its small and apparently insignificant components (for example, not one sparrow falls to the ground without God's knowing of it—Matt. 10:29); and in the famous eschatological passage of Romans (8:18–39) it is not only the community of faith which, in its suffering, finds intimations of "the glory that is to be revealed," but the creation itself, which "has been groaning in travail," "waits with eager longing" for the liberation from that "bondage to decay" to which it has been subjected through no fault of its own. For, Paul concludes, "the creation itself will be set free from its bondage to decay and obtain the glorious liberty of the children of God" (RSV)—an astonishing statement! The final liberation for which the suffering *koinonia* waits is not its own private liberation but a cosmic hope in which, almost as a latecomer on the scene of creation's ancient "groaning," the disciple community may also be permitted to participate.[19]

Such biblical themes as these are, moreover, only particular consequences of a much larger conception of reality that, as we have already suggested and will presently develop more fully, provides a basis from which the evolving church might have worked out an extensive theology of nature. That it did not do so—that, instead, it concentrated its attention on Theology and anthropology—in no way nullifies the potentiality for a full-fledged creational theology in the most authoritative documents of the tradition, the Scriptures.

While recognizing this, however, we must at the same time acknowledge the centrality of the human creature in this tradition.[20] In what follows in this second part of our discussion of the faith Christians profess, I intend to demonstrate that this biblical concentration upon humanity cannot and must not be construed as if it were an exclusive interest in the human creature. On the

---

18. *God in Creation: An Ecological Doctrine of Creation* (The Gifford Lectures of 1984–1985), trans. Margaret Kohl (Minneapolis: Fortress Press, 1993), 186–87.

19. The reader is referred to the excellent study of Paul Santmire, *The Travail of Nature: The Ambiguous Ecological Promise of Christian Theology* (Philadelphia: Fortress Press, 1985).

20. "In contrast to the other creatures, man's primary bond is with God and not with the earth." (Phyllis Bird, "Images of Women in the Old Testament," in *Religion and Sexism: Images of Woman in Jewish and Christian Traditions*, ed. Rosemary Radford Ruether [New York: Simon and Schuster, 1974], 73.)

"From beginning to end, the earth creature is the center of attention." (Phyllis Trible, *God and the Rhetoric of Sexuality* [Philadelphia: Fortress Press, 1978], 81.)

contrary, from the vantage point of a context that has simultaneously elevated and denigrated humanity, it must be stressed that the tradition of Jerusalem concentrates on the human creature simply because of its concern for all creatures and for all creation. It not only knows that this creature, among them all, is capable of great misconduct in relation to all other manifestations of creaturely life, but it also dares to believe that this same errant creature bears—and even in its state of imperfection is capable of actually undertaking—a high degree of responsibility for all the others. Therefore isolating the human creature from the total created order, a procedure that unfortunately and in subtle as well as obvious ways has characterized so much of the Christian theological tradition, is already the greatest violation of biblical faith. As we can readily observe from the two ancient creation sagas themselves (Genesis 1, 2), human being "makes sense" to this tradition only as it is perceived as a dimension—to be sure, a unique dimension—of creaturely being in general.

This poses, nonetheless, a difficult question of approach to the Christian profession concerning creaturely being. How shall one do justice to the concentration of the tradition upon the human creature without seeming to isolate and elevate it? In faithfulness to the authoritative sources of the tradition, notably the Scriptures, it is incumbent upon us to devote a good deal of specific attention to this one species. Every discussion of creaturely being that purports to be Christian must do so. It is not easy to achieve this, while at the same time conveying the truth alluded to above—namely, that the reason why such attention must be paid to this particular part of creation is that this tradition manifests a vital concern for the whole. The very fact of singling out this creature and of giving it such prominence seems to betray the assumption that creation in its entirety is the ultimate concern of Christian profession.

This danger can never be wholly overcome; the sheer amount of space devoted to *anthropos* in Christian theology will never be acceptable to all who now blame this tradition for Western neglect and ruination of nature. The danger, however, can at least be somewhat alleviated if from the outset we recognize it as a real danger, and if, particularly in our constructive statement of creaturely being (chapter 6), we refuse to engage in an explicit or implicit valuation of creatures based on a hierarchic conception of creaturehood, which is in turn based on a substantialistic ontology. What we shall have to show, then, in this chapter and chapter 5, is that (with exceptions) evolving Christian doctrine did succumb precisely to such a valuational conceptualization; so that "Man" (*sic*) became increasingly interesting to Christian theology as being not only different from other beings (a thing never doubted by the ancients who shaped this tradition) but higher, better, and of greater worth.

Purposely, I say that this occurred "increasingly" in the history of doctrine because, while from the confluence of Jerusalem and Athens onwards there was a strong temptation to hierarchic conceptualization of this sort within the courts of the theologians,[21] it was notably the modern epoch, with its roots going back to the High Middle Ages and Aristotelian influence, that singled out the creature, Man, the *"rational* animal."[22] In fact, what was unabashedly named "the Doctrine of Man" prior to the long-overdue recognition of sexual exclusivity in such nomenclature is, as a separate doctrine of dogmatic consideration, a latecomer on the scene of systematic or dogmatic theology. If it has indeed come to dominate professional theology (and it has), this is a commentary in itself on Western Christianity's capitulation to modernity, which was caught up with the grandeur—and to a much lesser extent the misery—of "Man."

It is perhaps a truism to say that this kind of Christian anthropocentrism has to be challenged and undone by all responsible profession of the faith today; and I can only hope that the present discussion will contribute to its undoing. Yet, theological work is usually complicated by the necessity of fending off several metaphoric dragons at once. Today, and partly as a direct reaction to the above-mentioned anthropocentrism, there has come to be a (postmodern?) tendency, not only to locate the human species solidly and undialectically within nature but to degrade and belittle the species quite mercilessly. The hoary concept of "total depravity" is not dead. It has found a new and fertile outlet in the growing assembly of those who have suddenly discovered the infinite value of nonhuman species. In the necessary struggle against a highly technologized Prometheanism with which, unfortunately, eighteenth- and nineteenth-century Christianity allowed itself to become too uncritically allied, there is now a propensity to tilt one hundred and eighty degrees toward a position of immense disgust with humanity. It is perhaps the intellectual equivalent of physical suicide, whose high incidence in Western cultures provides a more ghastly but perhaps not more effective symbol of contemporary self-loathing on the part of the "rational animal."[23]

---

21. See in this regard the informative essays in Ruether, ed., *Religion and Sexism,* 150–267.

22. "In the middle ages, Christian anthropology accepted the Ptolemaic world picture, and declared earthly beings to be the centre of the world; and in doing this it lost sight of its roots in the biblical traditions. It became one-sided when, in modern times, it continually drew on the biblical traditions solely in order to legitimate the special position of human beings in the cosmos, not in order to illuminate the fellowship of human beings with creation. It became narrow-minded and ultimately barren when it felt obliged to defend modern anthropocentrism against Galileo, Darwin and Freud, in order to rescue human dignity and morality." (Moltmann, *God in Creation,* 186.)

23. Larry Rasmussen reports on a "poll on whether the arrival of humankind was a good thing for the universe," conducted in 1972 by Cosmos Inquiry of Secaucus, New Jersey. "To the question, 'In your judgment, was the arrival of humankind, on balance, a good thing for the universe?' nearly 82 percent replied No; 12.5 percent said Yes and 2.5 percent were 'undecided' or 'failed to reply.'" ("The Late Great Planet Poll," in *The Christian Century* [Oct. 9, 1991], 900.)

Faithfulness to the tradition (by which, to repeat, I mean the biblical literature and those theological systems and other expressions of faith that have manifested a sustained desire to dialogue with and represent the story upon which
that literature focuses) requires that both of these distortions be identified and
actively countered. Insofar as both are still very much at work in the North
American context, the perennial difficulty to which I have referred above is rendered even more delicate. Thus, I have no doubt that some will hear in what I
shall say in these three chapters a continuation of the old or neoorthodox chastisement of the so-called rational animal. Others on the contrary will sense a re-
furbished *liberal* emphasis upon the glory and potentiality of our species. But
some will know from this statement of intention, at any rate, that what I want to
do is to sustain a real semblance of continuity with a tradition that is well aware
of the sin and misery ("vanity") of the human creature, yet cannot forget its
creaturely and grace-given capacity for responsibility—well, let us say it, for
"dominion." Precisely our context, I believe, has to hear both of these emphases,
and in their dialectical but by no means contradictory juxtaposition.

To state explicitly, then, the question implicit throughout this section, which
must become our focus in the two succeeding chapters: How is it possible
simultaneously to do justice to the tradition's concentration upon the human
species without, perhaps unwittingly, relegating the larger creation to a position of at most secondary interest?

13.2. The Knowledge of Human Being.

The first question that confronts
us in this investigation is an old one, but at the same time always new: How do
we know? Specifically, what are our sources of anthropological truth?

We shall not have done with that question in this brief, introductory statement of its importance, for it is in a way *the* question of all Christian anthropology; moreover, through it not only the doctrine of humanity but all Christian
doctrine is confronted in our time by the skepticism of the worldly-wise. For,
as we already proposed in passing, the affront of faith today is not so much
what Christians have to say about God, creation, redemption, and other quite
explicitly Theological matters, as it is the fact that they dare to say these things
of and to a being who, they seem to suppose, is in some way naturally inclined
toward an interest in them and to some degree capable of understanding them.
To many of our contemporaries this is extremely presumptuous. As Hans Urs
von Balthasar has somewhere observed, while the ancient sages of Athens were
offended at the point where they heard the preacher on Mars Hill ("this bab-
bler") begin to speak about the resurrection of Jesus, citizens of contemporary
New York, Moscow, or Peking would find the sermon of Paul in Acts 17 rash
already in what it assumes about humanity: that it is by nature "religious"; that
it intuitively recognizes the distinction between essence and existence; that it
is open to accounts of itself which simply take it for granted that the species

has a purpose, and so on.[24] We shall have to return to this—and as a central concern. But to begin with, and in keeping with the purpose of the present chapter to reflect upon what has been "handed over," we have primarily to remind ourselves of the sources of the knowledge of humanity as these have been considered within the tradition.

So as to be clear about our mandate here, let me compose several questions that, from different angles, highlight the overall design of this subsection: What are the sources of Christian claims concerning the nature and destiny of human being? Can these claims be tested empirically, or on the basis of general observation and universal experience? To what extent are they dependent upon extraordinary experience—revelation? faith? religious experience? Are there parallels between Christian claims about humanity and the claims of other religious traditions?

What we have inherited from the past by way of response to such inquiries is, as can be imagined, a considerable variety; moreover, the positions contained in this variegated theological history are by no means readily compatible with one another. They move, in fact, between two poles that are incapable of fusion, though elements of each may be found in a single system.

The first of these poles—which, in keeping with the categories already established in the first volume,[25] we may identify with apologetic theology—tends to maximize the continuity between Christian anthropology and the anthropological presuppositions current in a given culture and most systematically articulated, often, in philosophic systems that seem generally acceptable and "reasonable." Since, as we have seen,[26] "reason," far from being a constant, is in reality a historically conditioned category, the specific character of the continuity between Christian and cultural descriptions of the human being varies from age to age. "Reason" does not mean the same thing for the early Middle Ages as it does for the modern postindustrial West. It follows therefore that within this apologetic classification it is possible to discern a considerable spectrum of opinion concerning the character of *anthropos* and of human capacities for religiously significant self-knowledge.

For example, for Augustine, who at least during his early and middle periods worked within a generally Platonic frame of reference, it was reasonable to suppose that the human soul retained an aboriginal if diminished *memoria* of its origins and destiny. But for Aquinas, whose dialogue partner was not Platonic but Aristotelian philosophy, the soul, being "in the form of the body,"[27]

---

24. See Hans Urs von Balthasar, *Karl Barth: Darstellung und Deutung Seiner Theologie* (Köln: Verlag Jakob Hegner, 1951), 175.

25. *Thinking the Faith*, chap. 5, "Theological Method," 325ff.

26. *Thinking the Faith*, 390ff.

27. Thomas Aquinas, *Summa Theologica* I, Questions 75–89, in Anton C. Pegis, ed., *Basic Writings of St. Thomas Aquinas*, vol. 1 (New York: Random House, 1945), 682–863.

could only arrive at such knowledge indirectly and inductively, through logical reflection on sensory data. The point in both of these instances, however, is not the consequences of the dialogue but the principle of dialogue as such. That is to say, both believe that the Christian knowledge of human being, while not simply equatable with the best knowledge accessible to human observation and reflection, is nevertheless fundamentally compatible with the latter.

It is important not to exaggerate this observation. The quest for dialogue and continuity with reason, which is characteristic of apologetic theology in all of its aspects—in its doctrine of humanity just as much as in its Theology— should not be thought to exclude revelation and faith. Augustine, Aquinas, and the vast majority of those who belong to this theo-anthropological tradition certainly believed that the Christian message contains extraordinary insight into the human condition. Again to turn to Augustine: The divine counterpart of human existence, while for Augustine a source sought after by human beings even in their state of radical separation from God, can only be addressed as Thou—that is to say, can only be truly present and known—through God's own revelatory act, received in faith. For Aquinas, humanity's knowledge of itself as creature is actually hidden from reason, as is the whole conception of the world as creation. One could in fact say that for *all* Christian thought, the human being's awareness of itself as loved and redeemed through the Christ is strictly a matter of revelation, even though apologetic theology (as exemplified by Schleiermacher, for instance) normally insists that the longing for such "acceptance" (Tillich) belongs to the creaturely condition as such. Only perhaps with some extreme forms of liberal modernism was there a tendency to carry the principle of continuity to such extremes that nothing explicitly and uniquely "Christian" could be retained in connection with human self-knowledge.

Yet the direction taken by the apologetic stream here, as in other aspects of the Christian profession of the faith, is readily distinguishable from the opposite pole, the kerygmatic. As we have already seen,[28] kerygmatic theology is particularly conscious of the principle of discontinuity. In the case of the doctrine of human being, this means that its representatives are deeply impressed by the gap between rational/experiential conclusions concerning human nature and destiny and, on the other hand, the anthropic claims of the gospel (kerygma).

Just as this theological stream emphasizes the total otherness of the God proclaimed in Scripture in relation to "the gods of the philosophers," so it conceives of the relation between anthropologies deriving from human reason and experience on the one hand and legitimately Christian anthropology on the other hand. It does not trust reason, however reason is defined, to provide truthful descriptions of the human condition, for reason is always human, and thus given to bias, distortion, and rationalization. When it does not overly glorify the human, it

---

28. *Thinking the Faith,* 336ff.

sinks into self-loathing. Not even as an analyst of the negative side of human existence can human rationality be trusted; for while Christian faith knows that side very well, it also knows that the negative is not the last word about the human condition. Reason cannot comprehend even the darker aspect of the human character accurately because the presupposition of this dark side (sin) is dependent upon the sense of the presence of that one over against whom sin is committed; and that one is present only through self-manifestation, and only to faith.

This latter observation pinpoints the fundamental presupposition of the kerygmatic position with respect to humanity: namely, that apart from knowing God, humanity cannot know itself. The knowledge of human being is as much a matter of revelation (understood as encounter[29]) as is the knowledge of divinity. While through rational reflection and ordinary observation we may discover a great many things that are true concerning human being, we cannot on our own find out what is *essential* to this being, namely, that it is the creature and covenant-partner of God; that it is truly itself only when, like the prodigal, it returns to the Parental home; and that, apart from that return, it is in a state of radical disorientation, regardless of whether it is living as though it were divinity itself (pride) or in flight even from its human potentiality and calling (sloth). To state the matter more technically: Theology—and for many advocates of this position that must mean a highly christologized Theology—is the indispensable presupposition of Christian anthropology.[30]

If we take these two positions as tendencies rather than as full-fledged and mutually exclusive alternatives, we may carry the generalization further and say that between them we find in the history of Christian thought a whole spectrum, with some closer to the kerygmatic and others to the apologetic end. Indeed, it is probable that the great majority of those who have contributed to this long tradition adhere more closely to the center than to either of the poles. Usually, however, a tendency can be noticed in the work of a given theologian or school. For instance, most Roman Catholic theology has tended toward the apologetic side. For a variety of reasons, not all of them strictly theological or even broadly spiritual, Catholicism has understood its mission as one entailing the establishment of a common basis with whatever, in the context concerned, could be considered "reasonable"; and this common basis has almost always been an anthropological one, with particular emphasis upon the human capacity for self-knowledge.

Classical Protestantism, in contrast, has rather consistently manifested a kerygmatic orientation. This undoubtedly reflects the general milieu of Protestantism; for in its formative stages it was, after all, a protest movement, and

---

29. See *Thinking the Faith,* "What Is Revelation?" 402ff.
30. See Karl Barth, *Church Dogmatics,* vol. 3/2, trans. Harold Knight, et al. (Edinburgh: T. & T. Clark, 1960), 19ff., "Man as an Object of Theological Knowledge."

protesting minorities are not on the whole given to search for common grounds with that against which they are protesting. Only in its own forms of establishment did Protestantism become friendlier toward the general assumptions of its host culture. Whenever it was forced back upon its classical foundations in the Reformation, the kerygmatic element has reasserted itself; and it has done so, not only in the name of a God who is "wholly other," but also in the name of another and different way of being, and in the first place of understanding, the designation "human."

To state this in more explicitly theological terms, Protestantism in its beginnings and at certain pivotal historical moments reflects a rediscovery of biblical anthropology. It is frequently assumed that the greatest distinctions between biblical and nonbiblical accounts of reality are to be found in the realm of Theology (God). This is questionable, however, not only in its hidden assumption that one can isolate the biblical picture of God from its conception of everything else, but also in its failure to notice that the point of greatest distinction may very well lie in its anthropology. One of the reasons (a salient one) why this was and is easily overlooked is that—to speak only for the Christian side of the matter—the one who must be regarded as the newer Testament's final answer to the ancient question, "What or who is this human creature?" was so consistently deified by Christian dogma and piety that the radicality of that answer as an anthropological one was never sufficiently felt in the church. Jesus as the Christ thus became a decisive and sometimes provocative answer to the question, "Who is *Theos?*" but because his true humanity was constantly being lost sight of, absorbed, or legendized beyond all human recognition, he has seldom presented to faith anything like an equally decisive and provocative answer to the question, "Who is *anthropos?*"

Yet the impact of Christology upon anthropology is potentially even greater than its impact upon Theology. The spiritual shock that produced not only the sixteenth-century Reformation but numerous attempts at reform before and since that historical watershed comes from the recognition, in the presence of the crucified one, not only that God is very different from our preconceptions of deity but that humanity essentially, that is, in God's intention for it, is a far cry from what we have become. There is an existential dimension in the human encounter with Jesus' humanity that exceeds even his revelation of God; for the truly human (*vere homo*) in him meets in us a humanity that is not true. In the presence of *this* human being, we, like that apostle who typifies fallen humanity in all its pathos and lost innocence, know within ourselves the depths of our estrangement from the personhood into which from the outset we have been beckoned. Experiencing this, that apostle, Peter, cried, "Depart from me, for I am a sinful man" (Luke 5:8, RSV). Wherever human beings are moved by the *imago hominis* that is presented to faith in the person of the one to whom Pontius Pilate pointed when he uttered his *"Ecce Homo!"* ("Behold, the Human!");

whenever human stories are held in tension with that story and, behind that story, the whole testimony of the lawgivers and wisdom writers and prophets of Israel in whom that same beckoning to true humanity can be felt; then we sense the great gulf that is fixed between our fondly held self-images and the humanity that was intended for us, the humanity that is offered us as gift.

The question is whether this experience leads to a sense of the utter dissimilarity between the Christ's true humanity and the general human condition or to a desire to find, within the latter, points of convergence. Protestantism, which in the sixteenth-century reformers and in neo-Reformation revivals within our own period tended always to accentuate the former position, nevertheless does not necessarily display an exclusivism of revelation in its anthropology. Reinhold Niebuhr, for example, who was certainly deeply influenced by Reformation thought, especially that of Luther,[31] and who was suspicious of Protestant modernism precisely on account of its propensity to identify modern and Christian images of the human, nevertheless sustained throughout his life a passionate search for continuity with worldly wisdom concerning humanity. He based this on the Augustinian assumption that, despite human self-deception and the refusal of grace, the human spirit is incapable of ridding itself of its sense of "essential homelessness":

> This essential homelessness of the human spirit is the ground of all religion; for the self which stands outside itself and the world cannot find the meaning of life in itself or the world. It cannot identify meaning with causality in nature; for its freedom is obviously different from the necessary causal links of nature. Nor can it identify the principle of meaning with rationality, since it transcends its own rational processes, so that it may, for instance, ask the question whether there is a relevance between its rational forms and the recurrences and forms of nature. It is this capacity of freedom which finally prompts great cultures and philosophies to transcend rationalism and to seek for the meaning of life in an unconditioned ground of existence.[32]

Similar affirmations may be found in the works of Emil Brunner, Rudolf Bultmann, and many other representatives of the so-called neoorthodox or postliberal periods.

More recent theologies, particularly in North America, show a general if less purposive movement toward the apologetic side of the spectrum. This is particularly conspicuous in process theology, narrative theology, and some types of political theology—those especially that employ a Marxist frame of

---

31. See my essay, "The Cross and Contemporary Culture," in *Reinhold Niebuhr: And the Issues of Our Time,* Richard Harries, ed. (London and Oxford: Mowbray; Grand Rapids: Wm. B. Eerdmans Pub. Co., 1986).

32. *The Nature and Destiny of Man,* vol. 1 (New York: Charles Scribner's Sons, 1953), 14.

reference. In African American, Native Amer-Canadian, and some feminist theologies the apologetic thrust, which may be in some sense implicit, is countered by the minority status of the theologies in question, which share with classical Protestantism the fact that they are protesting dominant cultural norms. It is rare, however, apart from continuing efforts on the part of a few to perpetuate neoorthodox and especially Barthian emphases, to discover any intentionally and consistently kerygmatic positions in North American theology, particularly where the doctrine of humanity is concerned.

This may be inevitable, given the fact that, for all its seeming appeal at the popular level still, Christianity on this continent is in a process of being disestablished.[33] Because it can no longer rely on convention and custom for its transmission, the Christian message must discover new ways of commending itself to human experience and reflection. The danger in this situation is that, so far as the anthropological side of the Christian profession is concerned, Christianity will be adapted too uncritically to existing cultural presuppositions, trends, and values. We shall discuss further in the next chapter the observation, which is made both inside and outside the churches today, that in fact the Christian conception of human nature and vocation seems to differ from the dominant cultural assumptions on the subject only by retaining a slight aura of piety; that there is no prophetic "bite" in it; that it presents no real alternative to the status quo.

Thus the question with which we emerge from these reflections on the knowledge of humanity in Christian thought can be stated as follows: How, within the present situation of church and society in North America, is it possible to sustain genuine faithfulness to the traditions of biblical anthropology, while at the same time recognizing the necessity for new forms of an apologetic in connection with the Christian profession of human nature and destiny?

14. Human Nature

14.1. Creatures. We turn, secondly, to the question: What, according to the received traditions, must be said about the character or nature of this being upon whom, among all the creatures, biblical thought concentrates? While our answer to this question will begin with this subsection, it will continue through the next two subsections as well, which we distinguish from the present consideration on account of specific aspects of the subject that must be addressed,

---

33. Christianity is "in the awkwardly intermediate stage of having once been culturally established but . . . not yet clearly disestablished." (George A. Lindbeck, *The Nature of Doctrine: Religion and Theology in a Postliberal Age* [Philadelphia: Westminster Press, 1984], 134.) See also Stanley Hauerwas, *After Christendom* (Nashville: Abingdon Press, 1991), 23.

namely, the question of the human calling or vocation and the question of human destiny. Here we want to think about the *nature* of human being as confessed by faith. In accordance with the previously established criteria, this means that we shall have reference in particular to two of the three foci that constitute faith's point of departure: creation and fall.

The first response given by the Judeo-Christian tradition to the question about human nature is that it is a *created* nature. While this affirmation may seem simple enough—even, through pious or familiar usage, banal—it is in fact a highly significant statement about the human being. To begin with, it immediately denies any supracreaturely status for this being. Thus it constitutes a polemic against the whole concept of human immortality, a notion with which Christianity has unfortunately allowed itself to be confused more often than not. Neither about the collective, humankind, nor about the individual person is the Christian permitted to deploy the language of immortality. We are *creatures*. We had a beginning in time and we shall have an ending. This applies to each of us individually and in the psychosomatic unity of our being; and it applies also to the human species. Like all created life, we are mortal, finite, confined to material embodiment, subject to time and the elements, moving inevitably from beginning to ending.

What may and (for Christians at least) must be said about our destiny as individuals and as a species beyond this mortal condition is said, not as if it were a possibility residing in our creaturehood as such, but only as God's possibility for us. This is one reason why, as we shall see, the Christian does not confess "the immortality of the soul" but rather "the resurrection of the body" (that is, of the whole person). We shall return to this theme under the subheading of creaturely destiny.

The profession of human creaturehood is today a necessary aspect of the Christian message. One could almost say that it *is* the gospel. For not only do we find ourselves confronted by a religious (indeed a "Christian") personalism that perpetuates the mythology of the soul's immortality, but we also inherit from the Enlightenment, including Marxism, a philosophy of the immortality of our species. As it has been sloganized by the latter mentality, "Man is mortal; mankind is immortal." Both of these attitudes, the one ultrareligious, the other covertly so, contribute to the separation of the human species from the rest of creation and perpetuate an image of the human as being above nature. To profess, "We are creatures"—a thing that our received tradition actually demands of us—is already (in our context) to move across the invisible line between profession and confession.

The profession of human creaturehood, however, does not convey only or chiefly a message of limitation. Certainly to be a creature is to be circumscribed. It means that one cannot think oneself creator, for example. We use the language of creation loosely in our society ("He is such a creative person!");

211

and while this may be a meaningful way of speaking under certain circumstances, it is strictly relative. Human beings do not create, only God creates. Everything of which it may be said that it is a human "creation" is dependent upon God's creation, both in terms of the external forms and materials that it uses and in terms of the internal talents and imagination that are brought to bear upon these.

All the same, the critical and polemical dimension of the profession of our creaturehood is only one side of the matter. The other, without which this critical side presents a falsification of doctrine, is that as creatures *of God,* human beings are beings of astonishing promise and beauty, who are by no means forbidden to wonder at and rejoice in their own being and their diverse capacities: ". . . Thou hast made [us] a little lower than the angels, and hast crowned [us] with glory and honor" (Ps. 8:5, KJV). We mistake our tradition if we hear only those who remind us of our bleak finitude, our paltry capabilities, our stringent limitations. There *are* boundaries to our being—a fact that must still be learned in America, the land of "unlimited opportunities." We are to seek our own peculiar glory *within* these boundaries.

And within these boundaries, we may find our glory. We do not have to reach beyond our creaturehood in order to discover the *doxa* for which we are intended. Such overextension, according to this tradition, is the beginning of sorrows for us. To be human, "nothing *more,* nothing *less*" (Bonhoeffer): that is the object of our creaturehood, and it is no mean thing. When a human being finds joy in the music that she makes, in the child whom he fathers, in the words and thoughts that he hears, reads, or speaks, in the strength and grace of the body he or she possesses, in the beauty and usefulness of human art and technology—this should not be put down straightaway to inordinate pride.

The puritanical Protestantism that has left its mark on the history of North America tends to frown too readily upon every human achievement. The greater tradition recognizes that all of life is dreadfully complicated by sin, of which we shall speak presently. But it also insists that, despite our sin, we have within us a vestige of that original spontaneity that the saga of creation touchingly depicts, with Adam glorying in his flesh and (all the more so) in the being that is "flesh of [his] flesh." Unless we relegate this joy of creaturehood to a golden age altogether forfeited by humanity's fall, we shall find it present still wherever human beings are sufficiently self-forgetful to *be* and to *do,* to think, speak, work, and play without spoiling it through boastful or morbid self-consciousness. Under the conditions of existence, this may not be a continuous or even a frequent experience; but its occasional occurrence nonetheless illustrates for us the true joy of creaturehood—that we may find our own peculiar glory in that which belongs to our finitude; that we do not have to become gods. Here, the doctrines of creation and redemption converge.

14.2. *Imago Dei.* That we are creatures is a theme within the Judeo-Christian tradition upon which historic Christianity has until now reflected far too little. On certain aspects of the subject, however, a good deal of thought has been devoted. In particular, one aspect of the entire profession of human creaturehood has dominated Christian theology: the concept, linguistically suggested by the Priestly document of Genesis, of *imago Dei.* [34]

In the P document, notably in three instances (Gen. 1:26-27, 5:1-3, and 9:5-6), the human creature is described as being made in the image and likeness of God. While this theme was not explicitly developed in the literature of the older Testament (though there are cognate ideas),[35] it became a highly prominent anthropological preoccupation of Christians almost from the outset of the movement. Already in the Pauline corpus, the *imago Dei* motif is used, although there it is given a specifically christological and ecclesiological connotation and is not directly applied to the original creaturely condition.[36] Paul's deployment of the *imago* concept concentrates upon his depiction of Jesus as the one who is the genuine "icon of God" (*eikon theou*) (for example, 2 Cor. 4:4), and upon the church as that body whose members are being "conformed to the image of [God's] Son . . . in order that he might be the firstborn within a large family" (Rom. 8:28-30).

Given the rather limited use of the *imago* idea in biblical literature, it is something of a wonder that the concept came to play so important a role in Christian doctrine; but that it did so is beyond question. As Emil Brunner put it, "the whole Christian doctrine of man hangs upon the interpretation of this expression."[37] If one asks why this occurred, one may be led along thorny and interminable paths of Christian and particularly European history. For the present, suffice it to say that, where certain assumptions about the human condition could be shared by both Jews and Christians, in its contact with the non-Judaic world Christianity soon found itself confronted by accounts of human nature very different from those of biblical faith. In relation to these "pagan" accounts, Christian theology had to develop certain anthropological ideas that were only implicit in its message. As it did so it both countered and incorporated aspects of the rival or alternative views. The *imago* idea seems to have

---

34. Because I have discussed this at length in my book, *Imaging God: Dominion as Stewardship* (Grand Rapids: Wm. B. Eerdmans Pub. Co., 1986), I shall not duplicate that material here. Nevertheless, enough must be said about the dogma in this place to prepare for the critical and constructive chapters to follow.

35. The *imago* is thought explicitly to inform Ps. 8:5, Wisd. of Sol. 2:23, and Ecclus. 17:3.

36. It may be said to apply to that condition indirectly, however, insofar as Paul obviously regards Jesus Christ as the *authentic* human being, and therefore the one who alone can fully exemplify God's intention for humanity as a whole.

37. Quoted in James Childs, *Christian Anthropology and Ethics* (Philadelphia: Fortress Press, 1978), 13.

lent itself to this necessity as a convenient biblical and doctrinal symbol upon which to construct, if not a full-fledged anthropology, then at least a conception of the human that was both consistent enough with the scriptural sources of faith and broad enough as a basis for the Christian *apologia* to become, in fact, the core of the Christian understanding of essential human nature.

What did and does the *imago Dei* concept mean? The answer is that it can signify a great many things. It has been part of the genius of the symbol that it could adapt itself to a variety of situations and conjure up a variety of human qualities. The question is whether, in the long process of its adaptation to the changing apologetic situation of evolving Christendom, it managed to retain any genuine connection with biblical anthropology, or whether the connection that seems to be present is based chiefly on the retention of the scriptural nomenclature as such.

As Paul Ramsey[38] and others have argued, the conception of the *imago Dei* that has dominated Christian history is a substantialistic one: the image is conceived of in terms of a substance or quality ("endowment" is perhaps the most frequent designation) possessed by the human creature in distinction from all other creatures. The precise identification of the endowment is not universally agreed upon. Classical theologies, however, invariably name two human qualities in this connection: reason and will. While more elusive characteristics have also been put forward (such as simplicity, spirituality, immortality, and integrity), and while one has the impression that the term has served as a carryall for whatever high ideals inspired people contemporaneous with the making of the doctrine, reason and will are the perennial attributes singled out as defining the quintessence of the divine image in the human. Not surprisingly, Pope John Paul II names these two human qualities as foundational; "Intellect and freedom are the essential, inalienable attributes of the human person and the whole natural foundation of his dignity."[39]

Again we must recognize that reason, being a historically conditioned category, signifies different meanings where the *imago Dei* is informed by it. Some types of reasoning presuppose a more relational conception of human being than do others; therefore it may be judged that the distinction that is drawn between substantialistic and relational conceptions of the image of God is not a hard and fast one. Augustine, who defined the image of God as residing in the intellectual nature of the soul, with its three powers of memory, intellect, and will, in doing so presupposes a lingering relatedness of the soul to its Maker. This explanation no doubt comes closer to the relational conception of the *imago* than does the Thomistic idea, which finds the rational process itself the quality in which the

---

38. *Basic Christian Ethics* (New York: Charles Scribner's Sons, 1950).
39. Quoted in M. Malinski, *Pope John Paul II: The Life of Karl Wojtyla,* trans. P. S. Falla (New York: Seabury Press, 1979), 173.

image of God consists. Yet even with the Augustinian interpretation there is a tendency to think of the image of God "in us" as a quality inherent in our human makeup that, especially when we are compared and contrasted with other creatures, must be seen as constituting our human essence.

The Protestant Reformation brought an incipient challenge to this whole tradition—a challenge that, unfortunately, was never fully understood or carried forward. The challenge lies in the reformers' recognition that, with all our human capacity to think and to choose, we think vain and foolish things and choose "the evil that we would not rather than the good that we would," to paraphrase Romans 7:18-20. Ostensibly, in other words, the challenge to the traditional explanation of the *imago Dei* was a consequence of the subtlety that Reformation thinkers brought to their exegesis of the nature of human sin.

The matter came to a head with the question of whether the image of God had been lost with humanity's fall and expulsion. Luther insisted that it had been, and this insistence could only be received by his opponents as a contradiction of the whole, long tradition that, beginning with Irenaeus and basing itself on an erroneous reading of the distinction between "image" and "likeness" in the Genesis texts, argued that while the *similitudo Dei* ("likeness") had been lost and the *imago* weakened by humanity's fall, a total loss of the image of God would mean the entire ruin of humankind. To have lost the "image" as well as the "likeness" would be tantamount to having lost everything that makes the human being human.

What was not and perhaps could not be seen by those involved in this heated debate was that the two parties were presupposing fundamentally different ontologies. For the early ("ancient") Catholic and medieval scholastic position, being itself was thought of substantially and beings were distinguished one from another by the differing qualities of being vouchsafed to them by God, with some closer to their Maker and others more distant. Of earthly creatures, only the human being possessed qualities of being more nearly resembling those of the Creator (an idea made graphic, for example, in Augustine's conception of "vestiges of the Trinity" in the human combination of memory, intellect, and will).

Intuitively, and because he had been so greatly altered by his fresh encounter with the Scriptures, Luther was already thinking in a different mode altogether—though he himself may not have recognized, at every point, how different it was. For him, the essential thing about the human creature was not its rationality (which is so frequently and easily employed for questionable and wicked ends), nor its will (which he considered to be in a state of bondage) but its capacity for relatedness with God—meaning, in the postlapsarian situation, the capacity for faith, for trust. Thus he once remarked that if the image of God consisted of powers named by the scholastics, then the devil must be thought exemplary, "since he surely has these natural endowments, such as memory and a very superior intellect and a most determined will, to a far higher degree than we have them."[40] Luther never liked to contradict Augustine openly, but in this as in many other matters related to the nature of humanity he was in fact well on the way to exploring an anthropology significantly different from that of his ancient mentor, the foundational figurehead of his monastic order.

Calvin appears to have traveled this same way even more daringly than the Wittenberg reformer—perhaps because, in the generation between the two, humanistic and biblical studies had had the effect of lessening the weight of scholastic authority. For Calvin, the concept of the *imago Dei* has already moved from the status of a noun to that of a verb. At base, what is referred to is not something that we *have* or *had* but something that we *do* or *fail to do*. We image God if and insofar as we are oriented toward God. Rightly turned to God, we reflect the divine image, as mirrors reflect what they are turned toward. The image of God is thus not a permanent endowment, any more than a given reflection in a mirror belongs to the mirror, but a quality that is dependent upon our posture vis-à-vis God. If the relationship with God is distorted, or does not exist, or is cut off; if we are "alienated" (Calvin) from God, then, like the mirror turned away from its original object, we may no longer be said to image God; indeed, we reflect whatever we are turned toward—which, in the mind of the reformers, was no admirable thing, so far as the "natural Man" is concerned.[41]

It was, one surmises, this propensity to reflect whatever captivates our spirits that Emil Brunner had in mind with his rather unorthodox yet nonetheless evocative conception of the addressability (possibility of being addressed) of the human creature. For modern Protestantism, Brunner's 1930s debate with Karl Barth over this dogma is undoubtedly the most significant recent chapter in the unfolding of this aspect of Christian anthropology.[42] At least in that moment, which was a critical period in the history of European Protestantism and European civilization as a whole, Barth refused even to accept the idea that human beings as such, in their fallen state, have an inherent capacity for being addressed by the divine Spirit. Barth modified his position somewhat in the

---

40. *Luther's Works,* vol. 1: *Lectures on Genesis, Chapters 1–5,* ed. Jaroslav Pelikan (St. Louis: Concordia, 1958), 61.

41. John Calvin, *Institutes of the Christian Religion,* Book 1, chap. 15, Art. 4. (See my discussion of this in *Imaging God,* 101ff.)

The fact that human beings do not image God when they are "turned away from God" does not mean that the divine-human relationship is nonexistent; for, as Moltmann rightly points out, "Human sin may certainly pervert human beings' relationship to God, but not God's relationship to human beings. That relationship was resolved upon by God, and was created by him, and can therefore never be abrogated or withdrawn except by God himself." (*God in Creation,* 233.) One may therefore conclude that human beings image God even in their "fallen" state, unintentionally. The point remains, however, that the *imago* is dependent upon our relationship with God.

42. Emil Brunner, *Natural Theology,* trans. Peter Fraenkel (London: Geoffrey Bles, Centenary Press, 1946).

postwar situation, but the whole discussion brought once more to the fore the question, What *do* Christians mean by *imago Dei?* While Brunner's position was by no means a return to substantialistic thought, Barth felt that it could be interpreted in such a way as to betray the primary fact of the divine-human relationship as the basis of the whole dogma; and that meant, for him, a relationship initiated and sustained throughout, not by the human will and intellect but by divine grace. Our response to God—our faith—is not strictly speaking ours, but rather the response of the divine Spirit at work within us.

Such has been the power of the classical conception of the *imago,* however, that even in most Protestant circles it is generally assumed that being "made in the image of God" refers to some human quality that human beings, in contradistinction to other forms of creaturely life, possess. Neo-Protestant or liberal theology reinforced this for many; for while the formulators of that movement were not so keen to accentuate the intellect in this regard, following Schleiermacher, Ritschl, and others, they found points of marked correspondence with the divine in human freedom, feeling, aspiration to goodness, spirituality, and other yet more nebulous human qualities.

It should also be recognized in this discussion that modernity generally has conditioned us to think substantially about reality. While many scientists have emphasized the astonishing interrelatedness of all that is, the effect of the scientific revolution upon the popular mind has been to direct attention to the constituents of various forms of life, rather than to consider the myriad ways in which all life is characterized by interdependence. In short, until the present, whose complex *problematique* invites all thinking persons to consider the whole of reality in its integrity and ecological interrelatedness, this doctrinal symbol has stood for an anthropology that ranks human beings higher on the scale of being because they possess mind, or will, or some more rarefied and ethereal capacity.[43]

The point that we shall have to explore in the subsequent chapters is not only that this assumption about "essential humanity" is today put to the test by events that threaten a civilization based upon such clear creaturely distinctions, but that within the history of this tradition there has already come to be an implicit critique of it, based on an alternative conception of the meaning of the divine image. In order to grasp and incorporate this alternative, however, it is necessary to embrace, not only a different anthropology but an entire ontology that is quite distinct from the one that has been largely assumed both in Christian theology and in the (Western) civilization with which this theology has been most closely linked.

---

43. A typical definition of the meaning of the "image of God": "Man is a creature divinely endowed with gifts which set him above all other creatures: he is made in the image of God." (J. S. Whale, *Christian Doctrine* [Cambridge: At the University Press, 1941], 44.

This different anthropology is part and parcel of the same ontology that has expressed itself in a different Theology in many contemporary schools of Christian and Jewish thought—what (with Sittler and Haroutunian) we called earlier "the ontology of communion." This understanding of being is inherently relational: being-with. The "image of God" concept, when it is understood within such an ontological framework, cannot be defined as an endowment but as a quality of the relationship between creature and Creator. Christian feminism, as well as ecologically conscious theological thought, has much to contribute to such a conception of the divine *imago*. [44] The movement toward such a relational ontology is more widespread and inclusive, however, than these anthropological expressions of it, and it may also draw upon a more expansive background in Christian tradition than is sometimes assumed.[45] We shall return to this discussion in chapter 6.

14.3. Fallen Creatures.   The nature of human being is defined, then, by a creaturehood that images God; but this is only part of the story that the tradition with which we are obliged to wrestle wishes to tell us about ourselves. The other side, which it has been impossible for us to neglect even in speaking about this first aspect of human nature, is the declaration that this creature's actual behavior and history (existence) is a contradiction of what is intended for it as God's creature (essence). Of all the creatures of God, this one has deliberately but also tragically (or pathetically?) controverted its very essence. Its nature is a denial of its nature.

As is well known, the concept of the human fall takes the story of the disobedience of Adam and Eve in the third chapter of Genesis as its biblical basis. Partly because the church read both the creation and fall sagas as if they were chronological history, but also partly because developing Christianity needed a way of accounting for evil without attributing it directly to the Creator, the fall, as we have already noted, has played a part in Christian theology far more prominent than has the conception of human distortedness in the theology of the parental faith.[46] Until the modern period—and for many Christians in

---

44. In this connection see Ruether, *Sexism and God-Talk,* 93–99; also Ruether, ed., *Religion and Sexism,* 234–60, 313–14.

45. For example, Rosemary Radford Ruether's treatment of both Luther's and Calvin's anthropology, which in her view represent only "slight modifications" of Augustine and Aquinas, draws upon none of the relational exposition of the "image of God" to which I have made (albeit limited) reference above. Jane Dempsey Douglas ("Women and the Continental Reformation," in *Religion and Sexism,* 309ff.) is more nuanced in this respect.

46. "Where Christianity . . . degraded sexuality, the body and even the goodness of children, seeing even offspring of legitimate unions as a doubtful blessing best dispensed with by those who would live in the new order of the resurrection from the dead, the blessings of children continued to be seen in Judaism as God's highest gift. Strange indeed in Jewish ears would have been that Christian doctrine that the defiling character of sex so tainted the child with an hereditary sinfulness that it

North America still today—the fall of the human being from its "original righ-teousness" (*justitia originalis*) was and is regarded as a historical occurrence. During the past century or so, however, most mainline Christians have learned to think of myth without assuming the basic untruth of the reality thus desig-nated; and while it is still perhaps impossible entirely to separate the myth of the fall from temporal considerations, we may nevertheless recognize some-thing of the profundity of this ancient saga without thinking it an actual event in history.

Of signal importance in this respect is the recognition that the shapers of our tradition have wanted to affirm two things about human nature that, with-out some plausible explanation, would seem contradictory. On the one hand they wanted to say that the essence of human being is good. As we have already seen in connection with the profession of creaturehood, the tradition refuses to believe that we are flawed simply because we are creatures, flesh and blood, finite, limited in power and knowledge. It would be possible to be human, truly human, and not fallen, sinful, distorted. For Christian faith this affirmation stems not only from its creation theology but also from its Christology; for it understands Jesus, the "second Adam," as a true human being (*vere homo,* in the language of Chalcedon) who, though "in every respect . . . tempted as are we" (Heb. 4:15, RSV), did not succumb to disobedience. In view of what has already been said about the Hellenistic and other forms of distaste for creaturely materi-ality, it will be appreciated how important it was and has continued to be for Christians to insist upon the essential goodness of created being.

On the other hand, the tradition has also included a persistent (if not always consistent) effort to be honest about the actual condition of humanity, individ-ually and corporately. Christians felt that they could do this without despair-ing altogether of human life, because this too, they believed, was not the last word; this too was only part of the story, a penultimate statement. Yet as such it was the presupposition of the ultimate—the gospel of redemption. For to say only that creaturehood was good was neither to do justice to the reality of crea-turely suffering and evil nor to anticipate adequately the necessity of radical redemption. A thrust toward realism—and not in the Platonic but in the prophetic sense of the term—has persisted within this tradition. It could not close its eyes to existing wrong, or with Epicurus regard the apparently wrong as nothing more than "nature." Besides, it did not have to ignore and repress its consciousness of the wrongness of existence because, as the core of its mes-sage, it professed God's righting of the wrong.

---

became the means for the transmission of Original Sin. For Jews, man has indeed good and bad tendencies, but he was free and responsible to choose between them. Adam's fall was not treated as an Original Sin that fundamentally removed man's capacity for good. Indeed, Christians should seriously ask themselves whether this doctrine in St. Paul was not more gnostic than Jewish." (Ruether, *Liberation Theology,* 73.)

Yet the question remained: How is the wrong to be accounted for in the first place? To attribute sin and evil to the Creator was unthinkable—even though a few Christians risked advancing the idea that the lapse could be meaningfully associated with the sovereign God, since apart from it God could not appear in the divine fullness as Redeemer. This supralapsarian sense of the "happy flaw" (*felix culpa*) has scarcely ever satisfied the majority thought of the church, however. For one thing, it is very complex; for another, even when its complexity is soundly grasped it leaves one with the question whether human freedom is therefore simply an illusion. Such a thought may be attractive to the deterministic temper that can also, here and there, be found among the religious; but it is generally unacceptable as a way of accounting for the fall, even though it may (doxologically) allow a certain breadth of grace and gratitude after the fact.

The only way in which the church at large permitted itself to entertain the reality of radical evil in a world created by the good God was to point to an agency for the evil impulse beyond the Creator's intention—though it could not be beyond the Creator's *awareness* so long as Christians desired to sustain the thought of divine omniscience. In popular Christianity of the early and medieval periods, as well as in some simplistic modern and contemporary forms of belief, the external agency could be identified with supranatural powers antithetical to the Creator God. Indeed, Christianity, following Judaism, has often allowed for a certain provisional dualism with respect to supranatural power. This is because it has never been found wholly satisfactory to explain the radicality of evil on the grounds of human perversity alone. While the modern and contemporary tendency has been to attribute the power of evil to the accumulation and magnification of collective human wrong, with individuals and whole populaces jeopardized by centuries of injustice and revenge (for example, the idea of "systemic evil"), classical accounts have usually resorted to supranatural explanations: there are forces of wickedness afoot in the world over which no one has control. No doubt God *could* overpower these forces, but for God to do so in a direct manner would mean the destruction, not only of the evil forces in question but of that which has been taken over by them—namely, the beloved creature, the conscious center of creation, and through that creature the whole creation. We shall see in the third part of this work that this is in fact the reading of the creaturely condition lying behind one of the most prominent theories of Christ's saving work, the so-called classical or ransom theory.

The problem with the supranatural explanation of existing evil and wrong, however, is that it always courts an ultimate dualism; and the early church had enough of a struggle with various forms of such dualism to realize that it could not embrace that explanation without calling into question both the ultimacy of the one Absolute and the responsibility of humanity for its own condition.

The concept of the fall became a highly important aspect of the story that Christians told, then, because it preserved, at least in theory, the reality and goodness of creation as God's own work and intention (over against gnostic, Neoplatonic, and other accounts); it provided an explanation for the origin of evil in the world without making the Creator directly responsible for it; and it retained in the process an anthropology that maintained at the same time the sense of human responsibility and of human victimization. Through humanity, whose freedom of choice is requisite to its vocation in the midst of creation, evil has entered into the good creation; and this evil has affected first and most devastatingly the very one through whose decisions and indecisions it has been introduced.

14.4. Sin as Deprivation and Sin as Disobedience.   Corresponding to the two conceptions of humanity in God's intention, to which we have pointed in the fore-going discussion of the *imago Dei* symbol, we now encounter two quite different streams of the Christian tradition where human fallenness is concerned. As we reflect on these two distinctive conceptions of sin, the reader will appreciate their correspondence with the two ways of conceiving of the "image of God."

a. Sin as Deprivation.   One way of regarding sin has been to think of it as falling short of potential, or the diminution of some quality that could enable one to achieve one's potential. This indeed is the principal notion informing the word that technically signifies the doctrine of sin, hamartiology. The Greek verb, *hamartano,* from which the noun *hamartia* derives, seems to have originated with the common experience of the archer, an arrow falling short of the target at which it is aimed. Repeatedly therefore the texts of Christian educators inform us that sin means missing the mark.

Since *hamartia,* with its derivatives, is the major term used for sin in the newer Testamental writings, we naturally wonder whether that was the idea the writers wished to convey. By sin did they mean just that—falling short of the desired goal? It seems to me that they did not, on the whole. I do not think that this idea was prominent in the minds of the biblical authors. It is neces-sary here, as elsewhere, to remember that when it came to putting Hebraic categories into the lingua franca of the Mediterranean world of that period, certain compromises had to be made, as in all work of translation. Many of the words that the newer Testament's authors used were, from the point of view of Hebraic linguistics, not entirely satisfactory. The word *hamartia* is surely one of them.

This is shown by the fact that sometimes, where the newer Testament em-ploys the word *hamartia,* the meaning that the text obviously wants to convey is not well served by this language. For example, in the parable of the two sons, where the younger, returning to his parental home, says, "Father, I have sinned against heaven and before you" (Luke 15:11ff.), the thing that is obviously uppermost in the minds both of the prodigal and the recounter of his tale is the son's deep shame vis-à-vis his father. This shame has to do with the fact that he has not measured up to what he might, as the son of such a household, have become. The sin here, however, is not the fact of his failure; it is rather his rank abrogation of this primary relationship, the relationship with his father. It was the memory of the father's love, patience, and generosity that brought the prodigal to the despair that incited him, finally, to return and seek parental forgiveness. It was the accepting, anticipatory pardon of the father that led the son to display his shame openly in his father's presence. Consequently we are not surprised when the resolution of the parable is concerned, not with overcoming the wrong done by the prodigal but with restoring his relationship with both his father and his elder brother.

The reason for such a discrepancy between the textual intention and the vocabulary employed is that the Greek word, apparently the only one available, will not convey the meaning of at least one of the Hebraic words that might have been used to describe adequately the emotions involved in this scene. While there is some parallel between *hamartano* and some of the Hebrew words used in the older Testament for sin, at least one important Hebrew word for sin, *pesha* ("inadequately translated 'trespass,' 'transgress'"[47]) seems to defy translation into the Greek language. It means literally "rebellion," with the cognate idea of rejection, turning away, disobedience. So, for example, what the returning prodigal is saying is not that he has fallen short of his potential for full and authentic humanity but that he has willfully separated himself from his father and rejected his vocation as the son of that household.

Such a linguistic gap between the Hebraic and Hellenic worlds is not accidental. Classical culture, whether Greek or Roman, could readily comprehend the notion of deprivation or diminishment. For Platonic, Aristotelian, and Stoic thought, the concept of failing to achieve the ideal is a familiar one. As for Roman culture, with its morality of moderation, tolerance, and temperance in all things, it is doubtful if any other conception of sin than this would have been understood. It is perhaps no wonder (and this may be our particular inheritance from Rome) that early in the history of the church, sin became associated with immorality, immoderation, intemperance, excess, and similar concepts, all of which could denote deviation from the desired norm. This tendency could only be strengthened with the establishment of Christianity in imperial Rome; for then the church had to uphold the moral code of the dominant classes, and sin naturally came to be associated with the breaking of that code.

---

47. Kenneth Graystone, "Sin," in *A Theological Word Book of the Bible,* ed. Alan Richardson (London: S.C.M. Press, 1950), 227.

Sexual ethics being the most common and conspicuous aspect of most forms of morality, it is not surprising that an indelible connection between sin and sexual deviation from socially recognized norms came to dominate so many centuries of Christian civilization, down to our own period.[48]

This is not to say that the concept of sin as falling short inevitably leads to moralism. Many whose basic understanding of sin runs along these lines are critical of the practice of making sin virtually synonymous with immorality, or of linking it with breaches of the dominant moral code. To understand at depth why the thought of sin as deprivation always had a certain appeal, one has only to remember what has been said already about the substantialistic conception of essential humanity, as encapsulated in the *imago Dei* symbol. Sin as deprivation, a concept closely related to the belief that evil of every sort is "privation of the good" (*privatio boni*), is the negative side of the *imago* conceived as endowment. The two ideas belong to the same thought-world—are in fact two sides of the same coin. Sin here means the negation of that quality that is presumed to be signified by the image of God—for instance, being deprived of, or not fully manifesting, the quality of reasonableness, or freedom, or spirituality, and so on. If our being in God's image is understood to mean that we are rational, then sin, within this same mode of thought, must imply the diminution of our rationality; it is that which detracts from our full potentiality for reasonable thought and behavior.

In short, this way of conceptualizing sin considers it a matter of privation—a lack, a handicap, a deficiency. *Anthropos* the sinner is *anthropos* the perpetual underachiever.

b. Sin as Disobedience. The second way of thinking about sin is so different from the first that one can only conclude that the two conceptions emerge out of two quite distinctive thought-worlds. It is possible that they also overlap, or are mutually informative, in this or that account of the doctrine. Sometimes this overlap occurs intentionally; at other times it is the consequence of a careless eclecticism that does not ask about consistency. The latter, I suspect, is more often the case in our own historical context, where the old authority patterns of classical orthodoxy, especially in the once-mainstream Protestant denominations, have given way to a fantastic admixture of thoughts and half-thoughts whose chief virtue is not that they have either depth or consistency but that they lend themselves to quick communication. In certain ways the relational conception of sin, which I want now to investigate, can incorporate some aspects of the idea of sin as deprivation; yet the foundations of the two conceptions are different, and they lead to different consequences both theologically and ethically.

---

48. The "simple story" of Genesis 2 and 3 "has been made to bear the sins of the whole world." (Phyllis Trible, *God and the Rhetoric of Sexuality,* 72.)

As was the case with the *imago Dei* symbol, it is necessary to employ the word "relational," for what informs this second conception of sin is not the idea of falling short of personal potentiality but that of a breach of relationship. As I have just indicated, the relational understanding of sin can incorporate aspects of the idea of sin as deprivation; for if the human creature is intended for relationship and then breaks it, it has indeed fallen short of what was intended—it has been deprived of something. Yet the original, informing idea behind this second way of considering sin within the tradition is not the idea of deprivation, which is only a consequence of sin, but rather the breaking off of the relation. Sin is what one does, not with respect to one's own human potential, but with respect to another.

This "other" is in the first place God. "Against you, you alone, have I sinned, and done what is evil in your sight," cries the Psalmist (51:4). But (and here again we sense the whole iceberg of which this is merely the tip) sin in this tradition is never just a private affair between the individual and God. God is always more than merely the deity in this drama. God, the Other, is inseparable from the others who are our own kind, and those who are "otherkind." That is why the original disobedience depicted so ingeniously in the third chapter of Genesis is understood to provoke alienation at every level of human relatedness. Accused of disobedience, the man—apparently the passive partner in the act of disobedience—now becomes the active partner when it comes to excusing himself: "the woman," more precisely "the woman whom you [God] gave to be with me," is to blame (Gen. 3:12). Thus, alienation from God issues at once in an alienation between human beings. And it does not end there: The human pair immediately transfer their guilt to the serpent, who at least at this point in the saga must be seen as representative of the nonhuman creation, nature.[49] In other words, nature is brought into the circle of estrangement. The natural order becomes humanity's enemy, the scene of its imprisonment. A struggle is set in motion, one that we should do well to take with great seriousness in our own time. We shall return to this theme in chapter 6.

The idea of sin as broken relationship is not present in the Greek term, *hamartia.* According to Kittel, this is because "the Christian concept of sin does not exist in classical Greek literature. That literature knows nothing of human sin as enmity against God—an enmity in which it is implied that 'humanity does not *want* either to understand or to do what is right.'"[50] This

---

49. See ibid., 125.
50. *Theologisches Wörterbuch zum Neuen Testamentum,* Band 1, ed. Gerhard Kittel (Stuttgart: Verlag von W. Kohlhammer, 1933), 299. The phrase in quotations is from Kierkegaard's *Sickness unto Death,* in the chapter contrasting Socratic and Christian positions. Kierkegaard writes: "Hence Christianity begins . . . by declaring that there must be a revelation from God in order to instruct man as to what sin is, that sin does not consist in the fact that man has not understood what is right, but in the fact that he will not understand it, and in the fact that he will not do it"

judgment would have to be qualified in the case of Greek drama, which certainly depicts human estrangement in all of its forms; but despite its often close parallels with biblical themes, the drama of the classical world seems not to have influenced evolving Christian thought in the manner of its philosophy.

A noteworthy nuance of the relational conception of sin is the presupposition that the relationship can be broken. The human being can turn its back on its Creator, its fellow creatures, and creation itself. This must be considered remarkable, because the scriptural and other sources of the faith assume, as we have seen, that it is the very essence of humanity to live in harmonious relationship with these three inseparable counterparts of our being: to be is to be *with.* Particularly with respect to what we may call the foundational relationship, the relationship with God, biblical faith regards this as the sine qua non of life itself. It was an extension of this presupposition when evolving doctrine conceived of sin as separation from God, and of hell as eternal separation. A humanity that abrogates this foundational relationship thus courts virtual extinction, or (what is worse) damnation—which is certainly the intention of the threat uttered in Genesis 3, that death will follow disobedience. The reference is not to physical death, which (despite ecclesiastical traditions) is taken for granted by the biblical author, but "existential death" (Trible)—which must be understood to include a neurotic preoccupation with nonbeing preventing one from entering fully into life.

In short, everything appears to be dependent upon the maintenance of the relationship between creature and Creator; and yet this relationship can be broken—and by the human partner. What this signifies for Christian anthropology can hardly be overstressed. While mutuality (covenant partnership) is obviously the being for which humanity is intended, according to this tradition, it is not and must not be imposed upon the creature. The relation in question is not to be thought a necessary but rather a voluntary one. It is our destiny; existence is a kind of hell apart from it; yet it is not heteronomously imposed. The imposition of such a relationship would immediately nullify its primary character and the ethical consequences thereof. For love, which *is* its primary character, cannot be forced.

This is evidently why the analogies to which biblical literature turns again and again in its effort to describe the human relationship with God are taken from the realm of human relationships that involve a prominent element of decision: marriage, friendship, adoption. The analogy of blood relatedness is also present: the parent/child metaphor is a dominant one in Scripture, and in this sense the dimension of necessity also pertains to the relationship of creature

---

(Søren Kierkegaard, *Sickness unto Death,* trans. Walter Lowrie [Princeton: Princeton Univ. Press, 1951], 153).

and Creator. As I shall never not be the son of my father, so we shall never wholly escape the divine presence.

Yet even with blood relationships the Bible accentuates the dimension of human decision. The younger son, though clearly deluded from the start, may really leave home. The bid for autonomy is taken seriously, because the obvious alternative to this—that is, the heteronomous superimposition of the divine presence and grace—is entirely unacceptable to this tradition.[51] What counters this strong biblical insistence upon the creature's radical freedom is the even stronger insistence that the Creator, who is certainly free not to do so, nevertheless continues to will the life, healing, and friendship of the creature; therefore, like Hosea in relation to his estranged wife, God pursues humanity relentlessly—and, as the newer Testament especially demonstrates, at great cost.

It is sometimes suggested that these two conceptions of the nature of human sin are nothing more than two versions of a single concept, one of them metaphorical or narrative in nature, the other philosophic.[52] Biblical religion, it is argued, operates within personal, narrative, and historical categories, while philosophic theology seeks always the universal principles that inform these particularities. Such an explanation can seem more reasonable than it really is, however. Its superficiality becomes particularly evident in connection with the doctrine of sin. For it makes a good deal of difference whether that over against which sin is perpetrated is, on the one hand, an abstract ideal of authenticity or righteousness or, on the other hand, "another": another center of consciousness and will, another person, another "thou." The other cannot be easily absorbed into a generalized conception of deprivation or lack of the fullness of being. Where sin means being-against, or being-alone, in defiance of the actual presence of the other, it must be recognized that we have entered an ontological sphere that is recognizably different from that presupposed by the concept of sin as nonbeing. Kierkegaard encapsulates this distinction when he writes, "Sin is not a negation but a position."[53]

14.5. Sin as Act and as Condition.   In discussing the fall, we observed that one of the reasons why this concept came to occupy such an important place in the evolving doctrine of the church was that it made possible an anthropology

---

51. It is true that Reformed teaching accentuates "irresistible grace" *(gratia irresistibilis),* which comes very close to "superimposition," while both Arminians and Lutherans rejected this teaching. For the former, human cooperation is assumed; with Lutheranism, resistance to grace is the characteristically human posture and an aspect of that sinfulness which is present also in the "justified" sinner.

52. In his *Biblical Religion and the Search for Ultimate Reality,* which he intended as a response to the criticism that his "system" was philosophically ("ontologically") rather than biblically oriented, Paul Tillich suggests such an interpretation (Chicago: Univ. of Chicago Press, 1955).

53. *Sickness unto Death,* 155.

that could accentuate human responsibility and at the same time acknowledge human victimization. The combination of these two characterizations of the human situation is not, however, readily comprehended. It must now become the background consideration of our further reflection on the nature of sin as professed in the greater tradition.

That tradition presents us with two unavoidable connotations where sin is concerned. One is that sin is *act*. It refers to a human decision, taken in freedom, to turn from God, to disobey, to rebel. Using the language that has already been employed in connection with the doctrine of God, we may say that sin is the determination of the human creature to secure its being independently of its being-with. It is the act of a creature tempted by its unique potentiality to reach even higher, to become autonomous, indeed to achieve virtual deity through independence from the Creator and at the same time to acquire mastery over the rest of creation.

The second fact with which the tradition leaves us is that sin is a state or condition. In the broadest terms, it is the state of living with the consequences of the act—not only of one's own personal sin, but of the sin of the whole species.

In saying so we have already implied something of the complexity of this juxtaposition of ideas. For if to be human means to live in a state of sin, then how shall the active nature of sin be maintained? The act, after all, presupposes freedom to act otherwise; yet in the state of sin this freedom would appear to be lacking.

The insistence that sin is a human act and not merely a state or condition is necessary to the belief that human beings are responsible for the distortedness of their lives—that it is not something imposed upon us from beyond our own determination; it is not a necessary consequence of our creaturehood. The act-quality of sin is also important because apart from that it would be impossible to retain the relational sense of sin, as something directed against another.

Yet the tradition professes at the same time that sin is a state. For it realizes that human beings are affected by the sin of others: by the generations that preceded them (the parents who "have eaten sour grapes"—Jer. 31:29); by the thoughts, words, and deeds of millions of their contemporaries whose faces they shall never see; by oppressive systems and pursuits of whole collectivities—races, genders, nations, and empires.[54]

---

54. Another way of stating this is to name the heretical positions that result when one or the other of these affirmations is eliminated. Thus those systems that regard sin and evil as inherent in material creation cannot do justice to sin as act; and those systems that neglect the tragic dimension in favor of the human freedom to act necessarily eliminate the reality of sin as state. Berkhof's generalization is an instructive one, therefore, when he writes: "The Western church has always tried to guard against two deviations, against manichaeism which regarded sin as inherent in the creation and against Pelagianism which regarded it as an incidental act of man's free will." (*Christian Faith,* 189.)

Dorothee Sölle illustrates the latter from the experience of her own generation of Germans:

> As a very young woman I went to the Netherlands for the first time and observed that some people did not want to talk to me because I was a German and their relatives had been killed by the Nazis. There it became very clear to me that while I had not "done" anything—I was too young—nevertheless these others had a right to turn their backs on me and not speak to me because by language, culture and heritage I belonged to a human society which lived in a complex of guilt. I cannot get myself out of this; it just is the case.[55]

Every thoughtful person is able to recount a similar experience, even though for many the sense of being conditioned by a sinful environment would be less dramatic than the situation Sölle describes. Yet if sin were only a condition, it would be impossible to maintain the strong sense of human freedom and (especially) responsibility that permeates the tradition. Hence Sölle rightly follows these reflections with a statement that encapsulates both sides of this dialectic: "Sin is certainly also my decision, my free will, my 'no' to God, but it is also the destiny into which I was born."[56]

Both aspects must be maintained: If only the condition side is stressed, then no one in particular could be thought responsible. If only the act side is present, then not only is an entire historical and social dimension of everyone's experience left out of account, but one would have to ask why it was necessary for God to counter the effects of sin through a redemptive event that evidently presupposes sin's universal, unavoidable, ubiquitous, and even transcendent reality. Could not the being who is free to disobey also be thought free to obey, still? Could not this being be persuaded, under adequate tutelage, to turn from disobedient to obedient behavior, from evil to righteousness? Is so costly a redemption required if there is still in the human soul the same freedom to act?

And yet, if both sin as act and sin as condition pertain; if we are accountable because we act sinfully and at the same time victimized in that we are conditioned by a sinfulness far exceeding our personal volition; then how can such apparently contrary assessments of our situation be maintained simultaneously?

There is perhaps no greater point of divergence in historic theology than the one to which we are now addressing ourselves. Clearly, the object of all mature and serious theological work has been to maintain these two aspects of sin in a way that would at least minimize their seeming contradiction. In the systems of theology conceived prior to the modern period, with its recognition of the

---

55. *Thinking About God: An Introduction to Theology,* trans. John Bowden (London: S.C.M. Press; Philadelphia: Trinity Press International, 1990), 55.

56. Ibid.

mythic rather than strictly historic character of the opening chapters of Genesis, this harmonization of sin as act and as state was attempted through a historical interpretation according to which humankind, collectively and individually, was fitted into the cosmic drama whose chief human actors were the "first" and the "second" Adams.

The first Adam—that is to say, the first human pair—is free to act. No external necessity determines the disobedience of Adam and Eve, even though their situation already contains a strong element of external persuasion in the person of the Tempter. It is possible for them not to sin (*posse non peccare*). In their freedom they do, however, capitulate to the temptation; and this, for classical expressions of the doctrine, means not only that they themselves but all those who are born of their union (the entire species) must now live under the condition or state of sin. Their original sin has for its consequence, not only a world in which life is greatly hardened and imperiled in every respect, but an internal condition affecting every subsequent human being, predisposing each toward sin. In the postlapsarian situation, then, the human condition is no longer one accurately described by the phrase *posse non peccare* but rather one in which it is impossible not to sin (*non posse non peccare*). What was *act* for the first humans has become an ineluctable and irreversible *state* for all who follow.

While the modern mind easily manages to dismiss this explanation (and at many points) theology which acknowledges the kind of responsibility to the tradition that we have recommended throughout this work is not at liberty to do so. We are at least obliged to ask what was intended here, what profundity may be hidden by the literary and symbolic forms that were quite naturally taken up by our predecessors.

It is unfortunate that the concept of original sin became bound up with the notion of its transmission to the descendants of Adam and Eve through "concupiscence" (Augustine), or through the very act of generation/procreation even apart from *concupiscentia* (Aquinas).[57] This largely Western explanation, to which the ecclesiastical and public fixation on the combination of sin and sex must be traced, was not part of the earliest theology of the human fall. Basing themselves scripturally on the Pauline statement that sin "came into the world through one man," as a result of which "the many died" (Rom. 5:12-21), the Greek Fathers assumed a collective view of the species: the humanity of which Adam/Eve is the first embodiment was regarded as an organic whole. What happened to the progenitors of the race happened, then, not just to individuals named Adam and Eve, but to the universal named Humankind. And for the Fathers, for the most part, it is the woman who is marked by this distortion, the

---

57. See Eleanor Commo McLaughlin, "Equality of Souls, Inequality of Sexes: Woman in Medieval Theology," in Ruether, ed., *Religion and Sexism,* 213–66.

"original disobedience" having entered through her collective representative, Eve.[58]

In other words, we are in the presence here of a type of realism that regards the individual as a particular instance of the universal. As products of the individualism that commenced with the nominalism[59] that entered Western thinking at the close of the Middle Ages, it is hard for us to grasp this premodern assumption. A contemporary concept like that of human solidarity may, however, help somewhat to overcome the distance. The first human pair are to be regarded, not as unique and unrepeatable individuals but rather as types or prototypes of the whole species. We exist in solidarity with them. Their only distinction is that, being first, their decisions and acts are decisive for all that follow. What happens through them and to them affects the totality.

The next step in this thinking directs us to the "second Adam." The predisposition to sin that followed upon the sinful act of the first humans is opposed now by a grace-given possibility of transcending the sinful condition through adherence to and participation in the life of the Christ. While some theologians insisted that it was not possible for this "true human" to sin (*non posse peccare*), others, rightly wishing to sustain the reality of his human identity, affirmed that it was indeed possible for him to sin; that his situation in this respect, unlike that of all the other progeny of Adam and Eve, was similar to that of the initial pair prior to their disobedience—that is, *posse non peccare*. In contrast to the first Adam, the second Adam did not choose sin but was obedient—as the author of Philippians insists, "obedient to the point of death, even death on a cross" (2:8). This steadfast obedience of Jesus, despite even more persuasive efforts of the ancient Tempter, makes possible a new and victorious humanity for all who, through baptismal incorporation into identification with him, are being lifted up out of the sinful condition and caused to "walk in newness of life" (Rom. 6:4).

What are we to say to this? While the sense of human solidarity, which to some extent we are regaining today, lessens the remoteness of this theo-anthropology, the ancient explanation does not, I think, translate itself easily into the contemporary idiom. Indeed, one wonders whether it was ever a satisfactory response to the question, How can we be thought both active sinners and victims of sin?

Thus, while it seems the intention of most historic theologians to sustain both human responsibility for sin and human victimization by sin, thinkers regularly (and perhaps inevitably) move or are driven to one side or the other of

---

58. See Rosemary Radford Ruether, "Misogyny and Virginal Feminism in the Fathers of the Church," in *Religion and Sexism,* 150ff.

59. Nominalism denies reality to universal concepts, which it regards as merely "names" *(nomina),* and concentrates on particularities.

this difficult combination. Often, it would seem, the positions they adopt are the consequences not so much of their own meditative preference as of excited disputations marked by a strong element of reaction and polarization.

The most famous instance of the latter in the early church was the debate between Augustine of Hippo and the British monk Pelagius, who prefigures a kind of characteristic Anglo-Saxon preference for the side of the discussion that accentuates free will and human responsibility. To Augustine, Pelagius so simplified the human condition by adhering stubbornly to the doctrine of free will that he not only failed to understand the tragic depths of sin but was, consequently, incapable of producing any theology of grace and redemption worthy of the gospel. So one-sidedly did Pelagius accentuate the active nature of sin that he seemed to Augustine blind to the fact that much human evil and suffering is not traceable directly to those who are in fact most affected by it (see Exod. 34:7). For his part, Pelagius could only think Augustine steeped in a doctrine of original sin so fatalistic that it was for all intents and purposes indistinguishable from pagan determinism.

The same struggle occurred in Calvinist and, later, in Methodist circles. Following that epistle (Romans) which has led many to stress the impossibility of avoiding sin "after the fall," Jacobus Arminius (1560–1609), a Dutch Reformed theologian, was inspired to take issue with Calvin's doctrine of predestination. Calvin himself had been moved to adopt what must be regarded as one of the most inflexible of all possible positions on the topic under consideration: He combined an untiring emphasis upon the sovereignty of God with an anthropology accentuating humanity's total depravity, and was induced by his own rigorously logical mind to adopt the position he himself called a "terrifying decree" (*decretum horribile*): that both salvation and damnation are decreed by God. He reasoned that if postlapsarian humanity is incapable of anything but sin, then God alone determines who are to be saved; and if some are quite evidently not saved, this too must be attributed to the divine will. Arminius, on the contrary, insisted that it is possible to sustain an uncompromising emphasis upon God's sovereignty while at the same time assuming a sufficient freedom of the human will to make human beings responsible for their own guilt and capable of repentance when moved by the divine Spirit.

Methodism split over the same question. John Wesley and his supporters, constituting the majority of the Wesleyan movement, strongly urged an emphasis upon sin as act. It was natural for them to do so, for it was the counterpart of a whole theology of evangelization without which the movement would hardly have been what it was. If human beings are free, under the promptings of the Spirit, to repent; if the evangelist indeed bases his whole message on the prospect of this freedom, then to affirm that humanity is caught in an escapable slavery to sin would seem to contradict such an emphasis and thus undermine the entire evangelical thrust. Nevertheless, a part of the movement, led by the great Methodist orator, George Whitefield, supported by Selina, the Countess of Huntingdon, and identified particularly with Welsh Methodism, took up a position that seemed to the leaders of the movement "Calvinistic." Over against this, what was dubbed an Arminian reaction developed, reaffirming the act-character of sin and the freedom of the will.

We have noted earlier that the Calvinist tradition has been particularly influential in North America. Yet the predilection to theological determinism characterizing the Augustinian-Calvinist conception of sin has not been amenable to that New World fantasy that conceives of success on the basis of strong, individual conviction and hard work. In many ways, Pelagius and not Augustine, Arminius and not Calvin, has proven the more natural ally of the American Dream. While there has also been an abiding sense of destiny in the North American (and particularly the U.S. American) public mentality, it has been a highly positive sense—as we argued in the first volume. The idea of bondage to sin is not compatible with a national philosophy of optimism. To speak of "the tragic dimension of the transition from essence to existence," as Paul Tillich did,[60] is to introduce a theme that is almost entirely foreign to the modern American religious mentality. It belongs to the official optimism that we are trying (perhaps desperately) to maintain that "tragedy is . . . an unpleasantness which might have been avoided by better social arrangements and an improved technology."[61]

We are led therefore to conclude this discussion with the following question, to be pursued in the subsequent chapters: How shall we do justice to that aspect of the tradition which acknowledges the fact that sin transcends individual acts and forms a larger framework of reality by which all are affected? To this we may add the following reflection upon our own context: Is there perhaps a greater openness in North America today to the "tragic" dimension expressed here as "sin as state"?

15. Human Vocation

15.1. The Role of Humankind within Creation. We have discussed what the tradition bequeaths to us concerning the knowledge of the human being, and we have reflected upon the nature of humanity under the rubrics of the conventional categories, creation and fall. But in all of this we have left unexplored the question, What, according to this tradition, is the *purpose* of this creature? This is a particularly important question for the church's profession of faith today.

---

60. *Systematic Theology,* vol. 1, 29ff.
61. Robert Langbaum, *The Gaiety of Vision: A Study of Isak Dinesen's Art* (New York: Random House, 1964), 125.

Perhaps no question plagues the contemporary spirit so much as the question of the human *telos*—the "chief end of Man," as the catechists of the past phrased it. "What the hell are people *for?*" asks the American novelist Kurt Vonnegut, with characteristic bluntness—and he speaks for the whole epoch.[62]

It will be understood at once that we are not concerned here only about the practical matter of human activity—What are people supposed to *do?* When we ask about the vocation of the human creature, we are asking about human purpose or meaning. Humanity's end is bound up with the thought of its being intended for some meaningful role in the scheme of things. Clearly, a tradition which assumes as its first principle of anthropology that this being is a *creature* and not a random phenomenon must also assume that the Creator of this creature has some intention for it, and that the creature is at some level capable both of understanding and of undertaking its calling. The idea of a purposeless creation of this particular Creator is inconceivable, even if the ultimate meaning of all creaturely existence remains hidden in the mind of the Creator. Obviously people, according to the Christian profession of faith, are "for" something. Humankind, it must be assumed, has a special part to play in creation's drama. But how does the tradition regard this human role?

From the Bible itself, as I shall try to demonstrate in chapter 6, one is able to derive a rather provocative response to this question, particularly if the Scriptures are approached with explicitly contextual issues in mind. But it appears that when we take the question of human vocation to the postbiblical tradition, we encounter a discussion that touches many of our own most pressing contextual concerns only tangentially.

15.2. Vocation in the Tradition.   To be sure, the tradition is not silent on the question of vocation. When it considers the subject, however, it addresses itself to a question that, while significant in itself, may in some ways obscure or circumvent the problem implied in the phrase, "humanity's role within creation." The question that exercises the Western theological tradition could be phrased in this way: Is the divine calling of human beings a strictly religious or sacred one, or does God call people also to worldly work?

Until the Reformation of the sixteenth century, Christian teaching assumes that *vocatio* is a category applying explicitly to the sacred realm. The necessity of human work and the variety of occupations are taken for granted, but "calling" refers only to the life of discipleship; we are called by God into membership in the holy church. To Christian thinkers in the early and medieval periods, this seemed implicit in the nomenclature of the newer Testament; for the

---

62. Kurt Vonnegut, *God Bless You, Mr. Rosewater: Or Pearls before Swine* (New York: Dell Pub. Co., Delta Books, 1965), 29–30. See also the splendid recent essay by Wendell Berry, "What Are People For?" in *What Are People For?* (San Francisco: North Point Press, 1990), 123–25.

chief term employed there for "church" is *ekklesia,* which contains the Greek equivalent of the Latin *vocatio, klesis:* the church consists of those who are "called out" or "called away from" (*ek*) the world.[63]

Since all members of the church are thus "called," it would seem to follow that the term "vocation" has application to every Christian. This was indeed an idea upon which the reformers relied, but throughout the Middle Ages the matter was not understood in that way. In fact the term "vocation" was normally reserved for those called to holy orders, and more particularly to monastic life. To "have a vocation" meant to be "called away from" the world explicitly and to specify one's calling through the kind of strict separation from normal worldly activities implicit in the vows of poverty, chastity, and obedience (and, in the case of the Benedictines, stability of place). This definition undoubtedly appears restrictive in present-day North America, where vocation is a wholly secularized consideration; but far from being arbitrary or groundless, the concept of vocation understood as separation from the secular world evolved naturally from the original—and indeed the biblical—belief that the disciple community is a community "called apart." In the heyday of Christendom, when virtually everyone was a Christian by birth, it was understandable that those who intended to take faith seriously should have found their Christian calling in communities that at least gave promise of being different from the status quo.

The objection of the reformers to this double standard is also understandable. While monasticism at its best exemplified the seriousness of the Christian calling, it also had the effect (though not always the intention) of locating the arena of Christian obedience outside the ordinary, worldly life of work and play, love and hate, life and death. Great monastics always understood that their vocation consisted in a summons to "come away and be separate" in order that they might the more wisely and single-mindedly enter *into* the world's life. Whatever one may think of his specific deeds, Bernard of Clairvaux exemplifies this motivation eloquently. All the same, the restriction of vocation to the sacred thus understood left the secular Christian in the position of pursuing his or her work without any concrete sense of its connection with divine grace and obedient discipleship. At best, ordinary persons could think of their labors as stations or offices that were necessary to the good order of society and in that sense divinely approved.

It was this lack—one could almost say this vacuum—that was addressed by Luther's "new" understanding of *vocatio.* Employing the German term *Beruf,*

---

63. According to Alan Richardson, the newer Testament itself makes this assumption: "In the NT 'vocation' . . . always refers to God's call to men through Christ to the life of faith within the body of the 'called.'" . . . The word never refers to a Christian's worldly trade, profession, etc. Paul was called to be an apostle, not a tent-maker (Acts 18:3)." *A Dictionary of Christian Theology,* ed. Alan Richardson (London: S.C.M. Press, 1969), 358–59; cf. Alan Richardson, *The Biblical Doctrine of Work* (London: S.C.M. Press, 1963).

a term that in contemporary parlance covers such English words as "calling," "vocation," "profession," "office," "occupation," and so on, Luther insisted that all of the stations to which people are beckoned, whether by choice or necessity, are to be considered sites of Christian obedience to the God who calls us. These *Berufe* include not only "high" callings such as medicine, law, and theology, but every sort of worldly occupation, no matter how lowly; moreover, they encompass those occupations that one acquires simply by virtue of one's relationships—being a parent, a neighbor, a co-worker, and so on.

> Everyone should live his or her life knowing that it is pleasing to God even if it is scorned and insignificant in the eyes of the world. To be a servant, a maid, a father, a mother—these are forms of life instituted and sanctified by the divine Word and well pleasing to God.[64]

Among all the possible callings of God, Christian ministry is one—and as such holy, but not more holy than the others. The sacredness of all work, whether ecclesiastical or worldly, lies not in itself but in its use by God. God's providential governance of the world occurs, in part, through the working and (always mysterious) interworking of these varied human *Berufe*. We for our part cannot discern precisely how our work contributes to the whole divine enterprise, nor should we grasp after such knowledge of God's plan; it is enough for us to endeavor to be obedient to the internal demands and opportunities of our own calling. Yet through faith and prayer, and knowing something of God's overall purposes, we are to watch for the right time (*Stündelein*—literally, the "little hour"), when God requires of us the special contribution for which divine grace has equipped us. Any moment, every moment could be such a time. No one can force it, yet everyone can prepare himself or herself, through discipline and prayer, for the occasion when it arises.[65]

Clearly, Luther's intention in his whole discussion of vocation is to exposit the role of the human creature as participant in God's gracious and providential work; and he does this skillfully, sustaining throughout his central concept of justification by grace, while at the same time lending to all forms of "lawful" human work a dimension of high significance. No matter how menial our task, how unnoticed by others, how apparently incomplete, how mixed

---

64. Kurt Aland, *Lutherlexikon* (Göttingen: Vandenhoeck & Ruprecht, 1983), 39.

65. Luther was deeply impressed by Eccles. 3:1ff.: "For everything there is a season, and a time for every matter under heaven . . . ." "All human labors and efforts have their fixed time to be started, to be effected, and to be concluded. That time cannot be known in advance by man. The moment of all happenings is in God's power. Therefore all anticipatory anxieties and all precise planning for the future are fruitless and meaningless. Man cannot escape that which is to be. But there is no power on earth which can prevent us in the hour when we carry out a work which God wants done." (Gustaf Wingren, *The Christian's Calling: Luther on Vocation*, trans. Carl C. Rasmussen (Edinburgh: Oliver and Boyd, 1957), 214.

with failure, it is lifted out of obscurity by a grace that is able to incorporate it into a meaningful whole.

While this conception of vocation raises certain ethical questions, particularly within the context of a society like our own, where so many are either unemployed, underemployed, or employed in questionable and trivial forms of work,[66] its informing theology seems to me permanently valid. If the purpose of human life is to be understood within the parameters of biblical faith, then the work to which people actually devote their lives must be seen to have some positive connection with God's work. Moreover, Luther's manner of establishing that connection—namely, as participation in God's providential care of the world—avoids the danger into which later Calvinism fell.

Calvin's own interpretation of vocation was similar to Luther's. Rupert Davies helpfully summarizes it as follows:

> God [according to Calvin] has appointed duties and a way of living for everyone, and these ways of living are "vocations," to be compared with the sentry posts which mark the boundaries of a soldier's activities. This is God's provision for the stability of the common life and to counter rebellion. A man of humble station, as well as a magistrate, will discharge his functions the more willingly because he knows that they have been given to him by God, aware that "no task will be so sordid or base, provided you obey your calling in it, that it will not shine and be reckoned very precious in God's sight." (*Institutes* 10.6).[67]

Associated with this teaching in Calvinist circles, however, was the suggestion of prosperity as divine reward for faithful execution of one's calling. While selective quotations from Calvin himself could justify such a concept, his fuller teaching contains many checks and balances against it; yet he seems not to have developed the participatory presupposition sufficiently, and when the ethical aspects of his total theological conceptualization were extracted from the larger discussion by subsequent generations (as frequently happens), the result was a separation of the vocation from relationship with and service of the One who calls.

It is this aspect of Calvinism upon which Max Weber fastens in his famous hypothesis about the relation between Christianity and capitalism. "It is hardly necessary to point out," writes Weber, "that Luther cannot be claimed for the

---

66. Speaking of America as it was coming to be in the mid-1970s, Christopher Lasch writes: "At every level of American society, it was becoming harder and harder for people to find work that self-respecting men and women could throw themselves into with enthusiasm. The degradation of work represented the most fundamental sense in which institutions no longer commanded public confidence." (*The True and Only Heaven: Progress and Its Critics* [New York and London: W.W. Norton and Co., 1991], 33.)

67. In *A New Dictionary of Christian Theology,* ed. Alan Richardson and John Bowden (London: S.C.M. Press, 1983), 602.

spirit of capitalism"; indeed, "from a capitalistic view-point [Luther is] definitely backward." But "Although the Reformation is unthinkable without Luther's own personal religious development, . . . without Calvinism his work could not have had permanent concrete success." Puritanism, Weber asserts, bred an attitude toward human calling that "could not possibly have come from the pen of a medieval writer [and] . . . is just as uncongenial to Lutheranism." This attitude consists in a "serious attention to this world" and the "acceptance of . . . life in the world as a task." It was not this attitude as such that gave rise to capitalism, in Weber's view; rather, as R. H. Tawney later explained, Weber's "main thesis [was] that Calvinism, and in particular English Puritanism, . . . played a part of preponderant importance in creating moral and political conditions favourable to the growth of capitalist enterprise."[68]

The Weber thesis is especially important for North American theological reflection on account of the influence of Calvinism on this continent. Reinhold Niebuhr accentuates the point that we have noticed already in discussing the tendency in Calvinist-Puritan adaptations of the general Reformation conception of vocation to fail to sustain the Lutheran sense of calling as participation in God's providential work. According to Niebuhr, this tendency is emphatic in the American experience, where "the descent from Puritanism to Yankeeism . . . was a fairly rapid one. Prosperity which had been sought in the service of God was now sought for its own sake."[69] With human vocation assuming a status increasingly independent of divine calling, and today almost wholly secularized, we have reached the antithesis of the medieval usage.

15.3. The Missing Dimension. It will be necessary to return to this subject in the subsequent chapters, but it will be well for us to recognize at this juncture what the tradition seems—from the perspective of our present context—to have left out: It has given us little help on the subject of our human calling in relation to our fellow creatures and the order of nature.

This is not surprising, given the assumption of a hierarchic conception of creatureliness, which assumes (1) that the dialogue of faith only concerns God and the human being, and (2) that the nonhuman creatures exist for the enhancement and use of the human. Thus the question of human vocation alternates, as we have seen, between humanity's orientation to God and its potentiality for self-development. One pole in this alternation is the concept of vocation as a sacred calling best undertaken by monastics, the predominant definition of the first fifteen centuries of Christianity, and the other is the

---

68. *Religion and the Rise of Capitalism* (West Drayton, Middlesex: Penguin Books, 1926), 312. All of the Weber quotations are from the English translation by Talcott Parsons of *The Protestant Ethic and the Spirit of Capitalism* (New York: Charles Scribner's Sons, 1958), chap. 3, 79ff.

69. *The Irony of American History* (New York: Charles Scribner's Sons, 1952), 52.

tendency of modern Christianity and post-Christianity to opt for an increasingly anthropocentric and secularized notion of self-fulfillment.

In this polarization, Luther's position is again an interesting one. In keeping with his general understanding of the relation of grace and nature (and his sacramental theology), Luther obviously intends to hold together the two orientations that so easily fly apart: that is, he sees the human *Beruf* as expression of and participation in divine providence.

What is still missing here, however, is some clearer understanding of the end governing the divine work itself. Is God's work, in which our vocations are mysteriously caught up, a work of worldly redemption? Is the *eschatos* toward which holy history moves a consummation also of the whole creation? Does God intend to mend the world? If so, then it will make sense to reflect upon human vocation as a calling which, in its overall intent, is directed toward the stewarding of extrahuman creation. But whether such an assumption can be entertained prior to our own epoch, in which we are seeing clearly what happens when the rest of creation is left out of the discussion of humanity's calling, is a moot point. At any rate, it suggests the question with which we must end this subsection: Is it possible within the parameters of the Christian tradition to fashion a theology of human vocation that does justice to all three orientations of our being-with—God, our own kind, and otherkind—while sustaining a unitary understanding of our creaturely *telos?*

16. Creaturely Destiny and Historical Fulfillment

16.1. Methodological Clarifications. To embark on a statement about creaturely destiny according to the Christian profession of faith is to anticipate the whole subject of Christology, to which the third part of this study is devoted. Christology being the heart of the Christian faith, no aspect of the profession of the faith is independent of it. It has been present in everything that we have attempted to articulate prior to this point—quite openly so in Theology, where the doctrine of the Trinity sustains precisely this dependency of Christian Theology upon the picture of the Christ; perhaps less explicitly but nonetheless as a key presupposition in what we have been saying about creation and humanity. The Christian's paradigm of authentic humanity is Jesus, the "first Adam" (as Paul insists) being for Christians only "a type of the one who was to come" (Rom. 5:14). To reflect on human nature and vocation is to consider the humanity exemplified in Jesus, to see it in contrast to our own, and to know ourselves to be beckoned into this new humanity. Thus in all aspects of Christian thought the doctrine of the Christ is decisively present even where it is not made the explicit subject of discussion.

But with the introduction of the question, What is the destiny of the human creature according to this tradition? we enter a phase of doctrine that is explicitly and profoundly christological from start to finish. This means two things for our approach to the subject: first, that what we shall have to say here anticipates what must be said more expansively in Part III; second, that the discussion here will be incomplete, because its completion requires the more detailed considerations of the christological section.

As a final preparatory note for what follows, let us recollect at this point the introductory statements concerning the threefold focus of the Christian perspective on the world and humanity. Up to now, our concentration has been upon two of the prongs of this focus—namely, those designated by creation and fall. We have seen that this tradition professes a creational intention for the world and human beings, and claims that there is also an existential distortion of this intended or essential being. The world is not what it ought to be; we are not the beings that we are called to be.

Such a statement would be meaningless were it not for the preliminary belief, which is the hidden but decisive assumption of all Christian anthropology, that neither the world nor we ourselves have to be as we are. The "ought" of the sentence, "The world is not what it ought to be"—this ubiquitous Kantian "ought," which continues to punctuate the conversation even of the most secular humans—for Christians presupposes a possibility that, while not automatically present in our actual situation, is continuously being offered.

This possibility, according to Christian profession, is perceived only by faith, and it is associated with two of the constituent foci of what I have called the threefold focus of the Christian profession concerning the world and humanity, namely, creation and redemption. In important respects, these two provide the same fundamental witness to the reality in question; in other respects, they provide quite different dimensions of the total witness of the tradition to this "new" reality.

The two are the same or similar in the sense that they reinforce each other on the chief emphases of Christian doctrine concerning the world and humanity—the very emphases that we have attempted to rehearse in the foregoing. For example, the point of focus called redemption (salvation, consummation, hope, and so on) confirms the creational insistence upon the essential goodness of creation (why else would God bother to redeem it?) *and* of the fallenness of the creation (why else would God *need* to redeem it?). Again, the redemptive perspective assumes the creational affirmation of the human vocation to covenant partnership with God: Jesus Christ is pictured as the one in whom this partnership is at last fulfilled, and the one through whom a new covenantal status is offered to all. The redemptive work in and through the Christ by no means contradicts the theology of creation, but on the contrary confirms it at every point. The Creator and the Redeemer are one and the same. The creation is the object of redemption; the redemption is intended precisely for this creation—not for some other actual or possible world, but for this one.[70]

At the same time, as the adjective "new" in a phrase like "new covenantal possibility" implies, the perspective on the world and humankind provided by the redemptional focus is not simply the same as that given by the creational focus. This has to be noted, because a certain pattern of thought in this regard has implanted itself in the mind of the church here and there. I refer to the idea, partly inspired by a misconstruction of John Milton's intention in his epic poems, *Paradise Lost* and *Paradise Regained,* that redemption in the Christian profession of faith consists primarily in a restoration of the "lost" state of prefallen bliss. This goes back to the concept of recapitulation that is found, for example, in Irenaeus and to some extent in the epistles of St. Paul. The element of truth in this pattern of thought is the one to which we have already referred, namely, the insistence that redemption means the redemption *of creation;* not the creation of a new world but the transformation of the old world by the cleansing and renewal of that which has caused its distortion—primarily the human spirit.

But redemption for this tradition is not merely restoration. The point of the whole gospel is lost if we reduce the movement of the three phases of this doctrinal perspective in some such way as the following: (1) Creation: an ideal condition; (2) Fall: loss of the ideal condition; (3) Redemption: the ideal condition reconstituted. Not even good human stories follow such a pattern—or, if they do, their quality is certainly diminished. Why? Because the primary uniqueness of the third phase is that *it presupposes the second.* Creation only presupposes "the void"; redemption presupposes a whole history—a history which, if it too contains a great deal of "nothingness," if it too gives much evidence of a *habitudo ad nihil* (tendency toward nothingness), is yet a *filled* void. It is filled with possibilities and pains, anticipated joys and terrible disappointments. It is filled with death and new life, new beginnings, new hopes, new anxieties. It is filled with names and events, achievements and wars, sorrows remembered and forgotten. Creation is creation "out of nothing"; but redemption is the creation out of a *nihil* redolent of latent meaning and failed hopes, of heroics and of vanity.

This is why, for the bulk of our tradition, while creation may be called good, redemption must be called better—and its (awaited) consummation best. Paul, in the historically influential fifth chapter of Romans, expresses this progression by the repeated use of the phrase "much more" (*multo magis*):

---

70. This is the foundational insight informing the dogma of perichoresis or coinherence.

For if while we were enemies we were reconciled to God through the death of his Son, much more surely, having been reconciled, will we be saved by his life. (v. 10)

For if the many died through the one man's trespass, much more surely have the grace of God and the free gift in the grace of the one man, Jesus Christ, abounded for the many. (v. 15)

If, because of the one man's trespass, death exercised dominion through that one, much more surely will those who receive the abundance of grace and the free gift of righteousness exercise dominion in life through the one man, Jesus Christ. (v. 17)

. . . where sin increased, grace abounded all the more. . . . (v. 20)

While the thought by which the apostle is grasped here is an explicitly theological and christological one, it is not without human parallels. As I have noted in passing, every really moving human story contains some element of precisely this thought—that the state that *may* (not necessarily does) pertain on the far side of suffering, temptation, or peril could be better than the state that preceded the negating experience. The original state ("original righteousness") is not diminished by this thought: the innocent love of the pair in the garden, like so many (relatively) innocent loves afterwards, is no doubt beautiful to contemplate. But much more beautiful is the reconciliation of lovers who have known estrangement, the hope of those who have known despair, the faith of those well acquainted with the paths of disbelief and doubt.

We are once more, in other words, considering the strange role of the negative—the positive role of the negative, one may almost say—in faith and life. We can only affirm this with a certain caution. The negative—alienation, death, sin, despair, the whole gamut of that which detracts from life—ought never to be celebrated or courted. But as it is in fact present in all life, an aspect of every human story, the existential question confronting every system of meaning is: What shall we make of it? Countless systems, especially those devised by modernity, dismiss, minimize, or repress the negative altogether. The tradition of Jerusalem does not do so. Job, at the end of his great trial, may not have received back all of his goods "a hundredfold," as the legend (but not the poem) of Job would have it; but what Job did receive as a consequence of his humiliation—what he could not have received *apart from* his humiliation—is wisdom (Job 28), and the "peace which passes understanding."

Despite that, the tradition does not make a law of the experience: suffer and you will be rewarded. There is no necessary consequence of that sort; and besides, suffering if it is real is never ordered up at will, as the would-be martyrs of the early Christian movement (as of today) often discovered. Yet suffering belongs inevitably to the human condition, and if meaning is to be found in historical existence at all, then it must be found in the midst of human pain, incompleteness, and ambiguity. Biblical faith does not avoid this requirement. On the contrary, it places it at the center of its concern, causing God—even

241

God, God in particular—to enter fully into the negations of existence, to the point of dereliction. Only from that position, declares the tradition, can our testimony to deity be trusted.

As we turn to the vast question of creaturely destiny, then, we commence already the exploration of that core of the faith to which St. Paul gave the nomenclature, "Jesus Christ and him crucified." The promised end of creation's story is not an eternal tussle between the good that might have been and the evil that is (Romans 7), but the resolution of that struggle toward which (so faith professes) all life now moves.

16.2. New Creaturehood. There can be no doubt in the mind of anyone even cursorily acquainted with the Scriptures and traditions of the Christian movement that humanity is for this faith both the focal point of creation's promise and the agent of creation's greatest peril. This we have argued in the foregoing. Whoever takes up this faith in seriousness must assume the privilege and the burden of living with such an emphasis. It means, to be concrete, living between a very positive and a very negative estimate of the human being. It does not accord with this dialectic when someone stresses the human capacity for good to the neglect of human proneness to evil. The reverse is also true. From the vantage point of this faith tradition, the human creature is both creation's crown jewel and creation's great troublemaker; and both of these claims have their source in the common assumption that this creature's peculiar relationship to its Creator gives it a scope for thought, word, and deed that is unique among the creatures.

This two-pronged assessment of human creaturehood renders the familiar terminology of optimism and pessimism unhelpful and misleading where Christian anthropology is concerned. Over against optimistic evaluations of humanity, biblical faith sets the bleak acknowledgment of human fallenness and an unflinching realism with respect to our actual and potential evil. "People are somehow wrong right through."[71] Even our so-called good deeds are never unqualifiedly praised in this literature, because the tradition is well aware of the unwarranted *superbia* (pride) that we attach to the accomplishments for which society and conscience laud us; and *superbia,* while not the only manifestation of sin, is certainly one of the chiefest. On the other hand, over against every type of pessimism the tradition of Jerusalem holds up the creational vision of this being as the one who images the Creator in the midst of creation—the steward of God's mysteries, the priest, the shepherd and singer of psalms. To shirk from this vocation is to fall into the obverse side of *superbia, acedia* or sloth.

---

71. Sölle, *Thinking about God,* 56.

The World and Humanity as Professed by Faith

While professing and confessing Christian faith involves a life of continuous movement between these two polar conceptions of the human species, it does not result in a prospect of everlasting and unresolved tension. A resolution is proffered. One could in fact say that the whole *problematique* to which the substance of this faith is addressed is the resolution of precisely this tension. But that resolution, to which Paul refers cryptically in the passage from Romans to which I have just alluded for a characterization of the tension (7:25), is not one that grows naturally out of the historical struggle of humankind itself. On the contrary, it must be introduced into that creaturely admixture of good and evil, wheat and tares, from beyond it. The "war" (Rom. 7:23) between good and evil that is taking place in the human spirit, individually and corporately, is subdued by a peace that both transcends and transforms it. The distraught human spirit, caught between "the good that I would" and "the evil that I would not" (KJV), is grasped by the possibility of deliverance from the seemingly endless cycle of mixed motives, duplicitous deeds, and unsettling memories that constitute what we call life but is really, in the apostle's language, a kind of death (Rom. 7:24).

This possibility, according to the Christian profession of faith, is not a natural one—it is not, for example, the consequence of evolutionary development. Yet neither should it be thought purely supernatural, for it is given through the medium and under the quite ordinary conditions of historical existence, without an arbitrary or miraculous disregard for the qualities of creatureliness. It does not reside in nature or history; it must be brought to the process from beyond its own resources. It is, in short, a matter of grace. But grace does not set nature and history aside; it enters subtly into the midst of them. It goes to the very core of their reality, their possibilities and impossibilities. It evokes from them what in themselves and by themselves they could not produce: the truly new.

This sense of the new is what lies behind Paul's doxological ending to his classical characterization of the human condition in Romans 7. He ends, not in a paean of praise to humanity (as Alexander Pope did), nor yet in a lament in the face of human wickedness, vanity, and pathos (with Schopenhauer or Spengler). With the recognition of a new possibility that is neither natural nor yet miraculously supernatural but the consequence of an eternity that works mysteriously upon temporality, Christian faith parts company from both the optimists and the pessimists.

Yet this "final" word to the riddle of human destiny, while retaining its ultimacy, does not and must not lead to complacency. The resolution of the dilemma—the cessation of the spiritual "war"—is *proffered;* it is not imposed. If it is also in a certain sense "finished" (John 19:30), it is not finished in such a way that what we have claimed previously under the juxtaposition of creation and fall no longer pertains. It is not "finished" if that finish is taken to mean that now, in the post-Easter situation, faith no

243

longer feels the necessity of professing that the human creature is highly problematic, a being whose behavior must still be carefully observed, whose motives are still mixed even at the best of times, whose destiny is by no means the rote acting out of a victory already in principle achieved.

The resolution is proffered. This means that it is already present and real; it is not just a wishful thought, a longed-for ideal, a utopian vision. It has been, is being, shall be infused into the process of time, incarnated in history. It is a factor even now in the working out of the conflicts and tensions that humanity experiences daily—for faith, it is the decisive factor.

But it remains grace. It cannot, therefore, be possessed, presumed upon, or taken for granted. There is no automatic transformation, no Aladdin's new lamps for old. The new is *proffered*. This means, too, that some response from our side is expected—is necessary. Our decision, our acceptance, our appropriation of the proffered "new being" is not the decisive thing. The reformers and others have rightly insisted that even the human response to grace—even faith—is a matter of sheer grace. Yet neither is our destiny and that of the "groaning" creation independent of our human decision and appropriation of the gracious resolution of our internal warfare. To have it so (and there can be no denying that some exponents of Christian faith have wished to have it so) is to introduce a wholly different conception of humanity and the world. For, as we have seen, the tradition at its core insists upon a creation whose welfare is bound up with the behavior of that creature that is its articulate center, its steward, priest, and poet. Therefore to introduce, through a theology of redemption, a salvific resolution that in effect bypasses the will of that creature and simply thrusts salvation upon the created order or some members of it would be a flagrant violation of the whole theology of creation and fall.

The point of the resolution that is proffered ("through Jesus Christ, our Lord") is, first, that it is a resolution of a creational dilemma consisting chiefly of *human* distortedness; and, secondly, that it therefore addresses itself precisely to the judging and righting of that same distorted spirit. The *metanoia* of that spirit, understood both individually and collectively, is the heart of the resolving gospel; and therefore, however strongly the profession of faith must emphasize the priority of divine initiative and sheer grace, unless this initiative and grace are understood to work upon, to move, and to alter the wayward spirit of humanity, it will turn out to be a superimposed solution—indeed, a solution to some other problem and not the one that we have been describing in these pages.

We recognize, however, that in making such a claim we are already taking sides in a historical/theological struggle that is far from being so readily resolved itself. We shall therefore attempt now to characterize that struggle, and then we shall turn to the doctrinal area that is presupposed in this whole debate: the doctrine of the Holy Spirit.

16.3. Repentance and the Bondage of the Will. The theological struggle in question stems from two equally emphatic anthropological claims of the tradition, both of them highly visible in the Scriptures. The first is the claim, so significant as to be considered a basic assumption of the tradition, that it is the *will* of the human creature that must be changed. Unlike the high philosophic traditions of ancient Greece, Hebraic thought does not address itself first to the mind. It does not doubt the potentiality of the human intellect for intelligence and even for wisdom, and it does not find the problematic aspect of the human creature in its ignorance. For this reason, neither does it regard redemption primarily as enlightenment or illumination. The trouble with humanity is that it *wills* the wrong thing, not that it is deficient in comprehension.

Of course, will and intellect are not easily segregated. The will that is turned toward evil and not good affects the mind, uses the intellect, in fact applies the most subtle kinds of spiritual pressure upon the mind to produce persuasive reasons why evil and not good should be pursued. Psychology has taught us to call this process rationalization. The term is modern, but the habit is as ancient as the saga of the Garden: "So when the woman saw that the tree was good for food, and that it was a delight to the eyes, and that the tree was to be desired to make one wise, she took of its fruit and ate; and she also gave some to her husband . . . and he ate" (Gen. 3:6). Tempted, the creature finds all kinds of reasons why it should do what it is already inclined to do. It is at least to the credit of the woman in this saga that she found it necessary to search for such reasons. The man, intellectually passive to the point of stupefaction, was not so hesitant to obey the instincts of will and appetite.[72]

The same assumption informs the other great story of temptation in the Bible, that of the "second Adam," first in the wilderness (Matt. 26:36) and then—the continuation and intensification of the wilderness episode—in the Garden of Gethsemane, the "other garden." Here too the Tempter addresses himself to that aspect of human consciousness which the whole tradition regards as decisive: the will. Here too the insinuation of the Tempter is that the human being has the potentiality, if one determines to use it, to achieve a status above creaturehood, above mere stewardship of the other creatures, above dependency upon "daily bread." Jesus is tempted to use his powers to achieve a *status* of power.

Clearly this is not an easy temptation for our representative to resist. It is said that Satan left Jesus "for a season" after the wilderness experience, but one is made to realize, reading these accounts, that temptation is the psychic background of Jesus' whole subsequent life and ministry. Thus his miracles, which in other respects convey a quite different message, may also be seen as

---

72. For a fascinating exposition of the passage, see Phyllis Trible, *God and the Rhetoric of Sexuality*, 106–10.

containing the hint of capitulation to this temptation. Certainly his simple followers understood them in precisely that way, and wished him always to make greater use of these impressive displays of extraordinary power—and, of course, to bestow similar powers upon themselves.

The struggle with temptation on the part of the "second Adam" is infinitely more prolonged than with the first. It comes to a head in that other garden, the dark Eden of the newer Testamental recapitulation. There, temptation sears the very soul of "the true human" (*vere homo*). It has been suggested that Gethsemane should be considered "the crucifixion before the crucifixion." Who knows how decisive was this attack upon the spirit of Jesus, or how much it contributed to the relative swiftness of his physical death a little later?[73]

In Gethsemane, Jesus again turned from the temptation—and precisely, linguistically, as a temptation of the will: "Not my will but yours be done" (Luke 22:42). Even so, the temptation continues to the very end. It is voiced by Pilate, by the crowd (". . . save yourself! If you are the son of God, come down from the cross" [Matt. 27:40]), and undoubtedly by Jesus' own inner voice. The priest and representative of humanity before God has to endure the test to the bitter end. Only in that way can he make good his vicarious solidarity with us.

Throughout, we are to understand that it is the human will that instigates the whole dilemma of creaturely existence; and that it is the will, therefore, that must be converted, freed from its bondage to self-regard, redirected toward "the other."

Yet—and this is the second great claim of the tradition on the subject of the will—precisely the human will seems incapable of willing its own alteration, or at least of sustaining such an intention. This will is what must be changed, but the change will only be genuine if it is in some real and recognizable way *willed*. How can the corrupted will will its own transformation? Even if, in its

---

73. Given the usual agonies of crucifixion, the death of Jesus, according to the record, was remarkably swift. "Crucifixion is the most barbarous form of punishment ever invented. The exquisite cruelty lay in the long-drawn accumulative agonies. Some victims lasted for as long as three days. The cross was usually T-shaped, and the victim's feet did not touch the ground. It is considered a less cruel method if the victim's hands and feet were pierced with nails as this led to a quicker death. When cords were used the feet were not fastened at all so that the weight of the body was borne by the outstretched arms. This position, which soon produced complete immobility and helplessness, led to gradually increasing constriction and agonising pain. The victim was always naked, and his suffering was increased by the scourging which preceded crucifixion. This was so severe that his flesh would hang in strips.

"Crucifixion was originally not a punishment but a form of human sacrifice used in fertility cults because a slow-dying victim was held to produce more beneficial effects on the crop. It was used particularly in the cult of Tammuz, the dying-and-rising god of the Lebanon and Phoenicia. Later crucifixion was used merely as a form of execution, especially when the criminal was considered deserving of the utmost contempt and humiliation. In Palestine the Romans used crucifixion as a deterrent against rebelliousness. They crucified thousands, perhaps hundreds of thousands, of Jews during the period of their occupation." Hyam Maccoby, *Revolution in Judaea: Jesus and the Jewish Resistance* (Great Britain: Darton, Longman and Todd, 1976), 35–36.

corrupt state, it is still able to recognize its corruption and to some extent to abhor it, how far is it capable of sustaining the will to change?

This is the dilemma around which the theological debate of the ages circles, the point at which sides are taken and battles fought. All of those who accentuate the bondage of the will—Augustine, Calvin, Luther, Barth, to name only a few—have on their side, besides much Scripture and a good deal of human experience, the theological point that if in its historical condition the human will were capable of changing, then all that is testified to by the passion narratives would seem superfluous. For law, understood not merely as command but as profound spiritual guidance and the grace of moral illumination, ought to be a sufficient "schoolmaster" (Gal. 3:24-25, KJV).[74] On the other hand, however, the emphasis on the tragic or pathetic bondage of the will leaves all those who follow that path with the question, Is the only salvation, then, one that simply confers forgiveness and new life, setting aside the corrupt will altogether?

Those in the opposite camp—Pelagius, Arminius, Wesley, and others— who, over against the strong doctrine of irresistible grace, wish to hold out for the prospect that the human creature, though spiritually "sick unto death," may in some measure help to effect its own transformation, have on their side the theological point that if the condition of the human will is one that is wholly and irrevocably oriented toward disobedience, then not only law but gospel too would prove ineffectual; for gospel must be heard, received, believed, and lived. If that is denied, they insist, then we have no longer "Good News," to be announced and rejoiced over by all who hear, but a new and yet more imperious type of law, which no longer seeks to convert the will but simply takes it by storm. The weakness of this same position, which is frequently rendered even weaker through polarization, is that it minimizes the dimension of the tragic and underestimates the corporate nature of sin. Frequently, in fact, it gives way to personalism and appeals to those classes of society where *choice* seems a more credible presupposition. It is not well equipped to address the state of great oppression, whether this means the bondage of the will in individuals who are caught in compulsive patterns of destructive behavior or of whole social segments whose willpower is subservient to conditions beyond the scope of their capacity for change.

It is the will of humanity that must be transformed. But how can it be transformed without its being transmuted? How can its wrong-directedness be overcome without, in the process, its being effectively destroyed?

16.4. "Renew a Right Spirit within Me." The answer to this question— which, to be sure, itself poses further questions—is presented by the tradition in the form of a theology of the Spirit, or pneumatology. It has, as we have

---

74. See Gerhard O. Forde, *The Law-Gospel Debate* (Minneapolis: Augsburg Pub. House, 1969).

already noted in connection with trinitarian thought, been said that the doctrine of the Spirit is the most neglected aspect of Christian Theology. This judgment is equally true, I think, of the place of the Spirit in Christian anthropology. While certain well-known spiritualistic groups have accentuated the work of the Holy Spirit in the life of faith, often to the exclusion of other aspects of the tradition, the main body of Christendom has manifested little more than a formalistic, doctrinal interest in pneumatology.

There is a good sociohistorical reason for this. In the Constantinian situation of the church, the doctrine of the Spirit is far from vital to the growth and nurture of the disciple community. People can be brought into "the body of Christ" automatically, without anything resembling decision or spiritual regeneration. They are Christians by birth, not by rebirth. The work of the Spirit came to be emphasized, therefore, mainly in those offshoots and sectarian branches of Christianity which for this or that reason had to exist outside of the establishment. In such movements, since civil law and social custom could no longer be relied upon to replenish the community of faith, the converting work of the Spirit was particularly stressed as a regular and vital aspect of the Christian life. Excesses of spiritism notwithstanding, this has ensured a much more vital concern for the significance of the Holy Spirit among these movements than has ever been the case in mainline Christianity.

While established Christianity has hardly needed the Holy Spirit and sectarian Christianity has often used that emphasis in questionable ways, the biblical testimony to the work of the Spirit has surely to do precisely with the dilemma of the will as we have characterized it above. Wherever this biblical testimony has been taken seriously, pneumatology has been a crucial dimension not only of Theology but also of anthropology.

Although the work of the Holy Spirit is an important aspect of both the Johannine and Lukan documents, it is Paul who writes most systematically and enthusiastically about the role of the Spirit in the transformation of the will. In fact, his most important treatment of this question follows immediately upon the description of the spiritual warfare on which we have drawn in the preceding discussion of the bondage of the human will. Paul concluded that description with the doxological affirmation of deliverance "through Jesus Christ our Lord." The Christ, representative of both God and humanity, has entered into the center of the will's struggle, has triumphed over it, and has resolved it *for us*.

But this christological affirmation (Rom. 7:25) leaves both the writer and the reader of the passage with the question, How? How is the triumph of Jesus Christ over the temptations of the will made available to us? How is this objective deliverance from the vicious circle of a will that cannot and/or will not will its own transformation applicable to our subjectivity?

Paul's answer to this implied question is the "indwelling" of the Holy Spirit (Rom. 8:9). The Spirit, whom Paul here names explicitly "the Spirit of

Christ," enters into an intensive and repeated struggle with our spirits. Unfortunately for much of the doctrinal history that followed, Paul articulates this in the language of struggle between body and spirit (*sarx/pneuma*): "But you are not in the flesh; you are in the Spirit, since the Spirit of God dwells in you. Anyone who does not have the Spirit of Christ does not belong to him. But if Christ is in you, though the body is dead because of sin, the Spirit is life because of righteousness" (Rom. 8:9-10).

Under the impact of Hellenistic philosophies and religions, this language can seem to locate the problematic aspect of humanity in the body—in materiality and finitude. But in reality the text precludes such an interpretation; for the redemptive factor here is not the human soul or spirit but rather the *Pneuma* of God/Christ; moreover, in the verse immediately following the above, Paul insists that the body too is being renewed through the indwelling of the Holy Spirit: "If the Spirit of him who raised Jesus from the dead dwells in you, he who raised Christ Jesus from the dead will give life to your mortal bodies [*somata*] also through his Spirit that dwells in you" (v. 11).

What Paul seems clearly to propose in this and the subsequent discussion of Romans 8 is that the Holy Spirit is effecting (present tense) a change in the disciple community through a continuous intervention in the internal life of its members. The object of this intervention is the transformation of the will. This has to be a continuous work of the divine Spirit because the will is neither easily nor permanently susceptible to the persuasions of the Spirit. That is why the apostle has to warn his Roman readers that if they do not allow themselves to be guided by the Spirit, they will soon fall back into the "death" from which the Spirit is seeking to liberate them (vv. 12-13). The assumption is that the human spirit requires the ongoing and ceaseless testimony of the divine Spirit—there is no suggestion here that, gradually, the Spirit of God achieves a certain success, so that an increasingly sanctified humanity eventually may learn, almost, to stand alone. On the contrary, even the most sincere and pious prayer is the consequence of the Spirit's intervention—not to say intrusion.

It is proposed by this most nuanced biblical discussion of the work of the Spirit in the direction of human destiny, in other words, that the conversion and renewal of the human will can only occur through an ongoing struggle at the core of our being. This is so, not only because of the sheer perversity of the will, or its continuing bid for autonomy; it is also because we do not find it easy or natural to believe that we are forgiven, loved, and offered a new beginning—that we are God's children and heirs: "When we cry, 'Abba! Father!' it is that very Spirit bearing witness with our spirit that we are children of God, and if children, then heirs, heirs of God and joint heirs with Christ . . ." (vv. 15-17).

Then comes the proviso: "if, in fact, we suffer with him so that we may also be glorified with him" (v. 17). The suffering of the church should not be equated with its ill treatment at the hands of an unfriendly world; it is equally the suffering that transpires in this ongoing conversion, this "continuing baptism," of our own inhospitable wills by the divine Spirit. We resist incorporation into the body of Christ precisely because it means the harmonization of our will with that of another. As our representative, even Jesus struggled, in Gethsemane, against this submission, as it is always regarded by that in us which demands preeminence. It is not surprising, then, that human beings who do not share the full freedom of will attributed by Paul to Jesus should continue to struggle against the converting Spirit.

This—to anticipate aspects of our critical work on the subject—has seldom been appreciated by the makers of doctrine. Conservative pneumatology tends to give the Spirit complete freedom to invade and captivate the human will; that is in keeping with its Theology of power. Liberal pneumatology, in contrast, tends to present the human will in such amenable terms that the Holy Spirit experiences little real difficulty in its "gentle persuasion." For the apostle to the Gentiles, the conversion of the errant will is not so easily managed. It involves a suffering so intense that he can consider it part of a cosmic travail (vv. 18-25); and it will not cease, he thinks, until the whole creation bodily (v. 23) has been transformed. What faith hopes for (and does not yet see) is a redemption that applies without qualification or hesitation on the part of the human will to the whole of the created order. Now, we continue to doubt our status as God's children and heirs. We feel ourselves still to be alone. But the Spirit "helps us in our weakness" (v. 26), interceding for us, causing our very sighs to express what our words cannot articulate.

What we have here is surely a sophisticated and delicate response to the historical and theological question posed above. It is as if the apostle had anticipated the whole, colossal struggle of theology over the question of prevenient grace and the freedom of the will in the working out of human and creaturely destiny. With great sensitiveness, he honors both sides of the discussion: The will remains free even in its bondage—free at least in respect to its attitude toward the proffered resolution. It is not coerced, overridden, imposed upon; and certainly it is not ignored. Its wiles, its hesitation, its lack of determination, its very doubt: all of its characteristic behavior is thoroughly acknowledged. At the same time, however, the divine agape refuses to be discouraged by the reluctance of the beloved. The child named as heir will not be dismissed because it is too proud, too ungrateful, or too fearful to claim its new, adoptive (v. 23) status. Grace will struggle with nature, human nature, until it alters nature—without destroying it. It will naturalize nature.

Liberalism is right in thinking this a matter of persuasion; but it is wrong in assuming that the persuasion can occur without a life-and-death struggle, a lifelong struggle—meaning the life of creation as a whole. The love that has gone as far as Gethsemane and Golgotha will not be arrested by the recalcitrant heart of humanity. It will persist. Nothing will ever cause it to refrain from wooing the reluctant and unbelieving beloved: "For I am convinced that neither death, nor life, nor angels, nor rulers, nor things present, nor things to come, nor powers, nor height, nor depth, nor anything else in all creation will be able to separate us from the love of God in Christ Jesus our Lord" (vv. 38-39). In a word, the greater tradition of this faith insists that the resolution of the problem of a will that will not will its own radical transformation is a love that will not let it go.

16.5. On Earth—As It Is in Heaven? The question that is not very satisfactorily answered by Paul's discussion of the Spirit (although it is tackled by him more imaginatively than in a good deal of subsequent church doctrine) is that of the destiny of creation as such. In Romans Paul is addressing the church; therefore he concentrates, as does so much of the newer Testament, upon the meaning of the faith for the community of discipleship itself. We may extrapolate from this on the basis of an ecclesiology that understands discipleship to be the calling, not only of the few who actually "name the Name," but of humankind as such. For if Jesus is the *authentic* human being, and those who are "in Christ" are being incorporated precisely into his humanity, then we must assume that this is a humanity intended for all. Anything less inclusive would immediately call in question the interrelatedness of creation and redemption theologies, which we have relied upon throughout this discussion.

Even if we may assume on the basis of such an interpretation that what Paul says in Romans 8, together with what is affirmed in other ways elsewhere in the Scriptures, is applicable to the entire human community, it leaves us with the question of the destiny of creation. It has been our contention in this chapter that the human species is our tradition's point of concentration, not of its exclusive interest. Therefore the destiny of the human creature cannot be conceived of independently of the destiny of that of which this creature is steward, priest, and poet.

Perhaps in Romans 8 the Bible comes closer to answering that question than in most other places; for here, as we noted in passing, the human redemption is definitely bound up with the redemption of creation:

> For the creation waits with eager longing for the revealing of the children of God; for the creation was subjected to futility, not of its own will but by the will of the one who subjected it, in hope that the creation itself will be set free from its bondage to decay and will obtain the freedom of the glory of the children of God. We know that the whole creation has been groaning in labor pains until now; and not only the creation, but we ourselves, who have the first fruits of the Spirit, groan inwardly while we wait for adoption [as children], the redemption of our bodies. For in hope we were saved. (vv. 19-24a)

There are unmistakable and evocative hints here of a theology of redemption that includes the whole created order. In the history of religions few such affirmations of the eternal worth of the temporal are to be found; there are even fewer such affirmations of the goodness and redeemability of matter and the body.

Unfortunately, however, the thought of creation's own redemption is not developed beyond this almost liturgical affirmation; and, still more regrettably, this emphasis was seldom picked up by evolving Christian thought. Indeed, on the whole one would have to conclude that it had been grandly ignored—replaced, in fact, by a nonmaterial spirituality that assumed, sometimes on the basis of apocalyptic thought misread from Revelation and elsewhere, that as for the destiny of the creation it was essentially unimportant. Humankind having been lifted up from its position within creation, Christian doctrine could occupy itself with the ultimate destiny of the human redeemed; and when it did not assume the actual destruction of creation as a prelude to or consequence of the final triumph of God, it simply left the question in abeyance.

It is in fact this reticence about the fate of the earth which, as we have implied in the discussion of human vocation, constitutes the hiatus that makes it difficult to overcome the dichotomy between an exclusively sacred (indeed, sacerdotal) and an almost exclusively secular understanding of human calling. If it were clearer, from the newer Testament onwards, that the tradition presses toward the redemption of creation, it would be more readily understood that the divine calling of the human species is directed toward the welfare and ultimate wholeness of the earth in all of its variety and interdependence. Until this is clarified, the sacred and the secular are bound to seem alternative and, in practice, mutually exclusive objectives of human purpose and calling.

As is well known, Christianity today stands accused of indifference and perhaps antipathy toward the natural order. This, it is argued, comes about through an anthropology that awards the human being sovereignty over all other forms of life on the planet. It could as well be said to emerge from a redemption theology that leaves unanswered the question of the destiny of the natural order. We have seen that the Spirit of God, according to this tradition, wrestles with the human will, to transform it, to bring it to maturity. Does this same creating, re-creating Spirit, whom the author of Genesis has brooding over the face of the deep before the beginnings of all things, still hover over the whole creation?

With this final question we leave these reflections upon what our tradition has bequeathed us with regard to creaturely being, and we turn to the critical aspect: What is lacking, what inappropriate, what misleading in all of this as we contemplate it under the impact of the present?

CHAPTER ■ FIVE
From Mastery to Passivity

17. The Sisyphus Syndrome

17.1. A Fundamental Weakness. In her moving novel about pioneer days in Nebraska, Willa Cather has her heroine comment, "Isn't it queer; there are only two or three human stories, and they go on repeating themselves as if they had never happened before; like the larks in this country, that have been singing the same five notes over for thousands of years."[1] This sentiment would have to be questioned by Christians were it rendered in absolute terms, for the Judeo-Christian conceptions both of history and of individual life preclude any theory of eternal recurrence. Yet Jerusalem as well as Athens recognizes that there are certain familiar patterns where human stories are concerned; and while each story is unique, it is possible to detect familiar themes, expressed in an indeterminate number of variations, each with its element of novelty and surprise.

One such pattern in particular fascinates the biblical account of the human condition. It is the strange correlation of high and low images of the human: how the one seems to beget, in time, the other; how, like a teeter-totter, human history fluctuates between overly grandiose and overly debased self-perceptions on the part of that creature on whom, as we have maintained, this literature concentrates. Reaching, as it supposes, higher than humanhood, the creature regularly falls—or slinks—into a position far less noble. Seeking knowledge beyond the ken of creaturehood, the pair in the Garden come to know their nakedness. Clamoring for a transcendence above the plains of historical ambiguity and transcience, the builders of Babel are reduced to incoherence and mutual alienation. Lusting after absolute power, Ahab and

---

1. Willa Cather, *O Pioneers!* (Boston: Houghton Mifflin Co., 1913), 119.

Jezebel and many other sovereigns of ancient Israel are cast back upon the essential vanity (Koheleth) of their condition. Saul the conqueror becomes Saul the melancholic, ineffectual old man. In turn, David, the innocent shepherd-king, is corrupted by power and must stand accused: "Thou art the man!" (2 Sam. 12:7 [KJV]). Wanting to have places "at your right hand and your left hand" (Matt. 20:21), the ambitious apostles finally flee in cowardly disgrace from the site of their "King's" unholy anointing, their places assumed by thieves (Mark 15:27). Many other examples could be cited.

Whenever the church has permitted the Bible to be its window on the world, both of these themes, as well as their odd but not illogical interaction, have informed Christian anthropology. Thus the church at its best has remembered that humanity is susceptible both to delusions of grandeur and fits of self-deprecatory torpor, both *superbia* and *acedia*—inordinate pride and abysmal, debilitating sloth. Seldom, therefore, has the human sphere of Christian influence been entirely without testimony to the falseness of both sides of this distortion of human creaturehood. In times of rampant and dangerous national, racial, or cultural pride, at least a few Christians have issued the warning: "Let anyone who thinks that he stands take heed lest he fall!" (1 Cor. 10:12 [ASV]). And in periods of societal lethargy, fearfulness, or desolation there have been prophetic attempts to "strengthen the weak hands, and make firm the feeble knees" (Isa. 35:3).

All the same, it seems evident, as many Christian feminists have insisted, that historic Christianity has been far more adept at recognizing and addressing humanity's exalted self-images than its low self-esteem. Prometheus and not Sisyphus has been the familiar paradigm of the church's anthropology. Despite a considerable lack of imagination in recognizing the subtler forms of human egoism, at least in the presence of unbridled pride what remains of prophetic zeal in the church normally knows what to say and to do. "He hath put down the mighty from their seats" (Luke 1:52). Part of the appeal of liberationism today is associated with this ancient sense of the wrongness of human *superbia*—the pride of oppressors. Hubris in both individuals and collectivities evokes from a vigilant Christian minority the courage to confront overbearing rulers and haughty classes and whole arenas full of jeering mobs. It is perhaps the heroic side of faith that is appealed to in such situations. Flagrant boastfulness on the part of mortals calls forth from the *Defensor fidei* a blast from the trumpet of the Lord. Faced with such pretension, humble faith may rise to heights of righteous indignation, entering the theater of worldly pomp with a fierce dignity, like old Polycarp at his martyrdom.

But it is not heroism that is called for when human civilization falls into decline, its citizens restless victims of self-doubt and moral confusion. David was able through heroic courage to slay Goliath and achieve Israel's deliverance; but he could not in such fashion cure the melancholia of King Saul (1 Sam. 16:14ff.).

Who will speak to Sisyphus, comfort him, help him to hope again? Not conviction but compassion must be the posture of such a one, and not strength but wisdom. And, as Job asks, "where shall wisdom be found?" (Job 28:12). The wisdom even of recognizing, let alone ministering to, human defeatism and despair is never easily acquired. Yet such wisdom is finally more needful than the courage to confront human arrogance. For beneath the facade of our various experiments in mastery, there is an aboriginal, Babel-awareness of human fragility. This awareness is only barely covered by the pomp of empires, the "irony" (Reinhold Niebuhr) of whose histories is invariably the consequence of their vain attempts to conceal their finitude. No ermine, armor, or designer jeans can prevent the worm of self-doubt from entering the soul of the thinking animal. Thought itself will betray the thinker who endeavors to enhance his security by taking thought. "Fool, this night thy soul shall be required of thee" (Luke 12:20, KJV).

The conclusion that we have had to reach in our earlier reflections on the North American context today,[2] to recapitulate them in the metaphoric language of the present discussion, is that the humanity Christians are called to engage in this context resembles Sisyphus more than Prometheus. But to be accurate we should have to devise a more finely nuanced articulation of the ancient myth; for our Sisyphus still parades himself as Prometheus, not knowing any other role. He no longer has the heart to play with conviction the character of Prometheus, stealer of fire from the gods, technocratic hero; for at some unconscious level he is deeply suspicious of his aptitude for that part, having in the meantime discovered how little control he has over the stolen fire. All the same, these are the lines that he has learned, and the character of Sisyphus is wholly foreign to his North American education, which leaves no place for failure. So he continues, year after year, mouthing the old Promethean speeches while silently accumulating the thoughts that have gone into the making of every historical Sisyphus—"thoughts that wound from behind" (Kierkegaard). In the eyes of some observers, he has become an almost comic figure: a fat, drugged, pleasure-seeking, failed, often suicidal Prometheus, chained still to the rock of his well-rehearsed mythology, but no longer believing it. He is Sisyphus playing the part of Prometheus.

As we have received it, the Christian doctrinal heritage concerning creaturely being seems to me ill equipped to engage such a figure. The present unimpressive performance of Christianity in the two northern nations of this continent, which is in part the consequence of ecclesiastical degeneration and mediocrity, is also partly to be explained by the inadequacy of our received theo-anthropological conventions to comprehend the type of humanity rampant in our social milieu. These conventions have conditioned us to think about

---

2. *Thinking the Faith,* chaps. 2 and 3.

the human creature in an exalted fashion; and, intermingled as they are in North America with even less qualified theoretic exaltations of the human coming from the side of the Enlightenment, they prove almost useless in the face of a humanity that is in fact deeply humiliated—but humiliated at a sub- or even unconscious level for lack of any operative paradigms for openly acknowledging its humiliation.

This generalization applies to both conservative and liberal expressions of Christian doctrine in North America. There are, to be sure, exceptions, but the rule, I believe, holds: conservative Christianity, including neoorthodoxy, knows a good deal about the sin of pride but it is hardly acquainted with sloth.[3] Neoorthodoxy has been more faithful to the best of the tradition than has theological liberalism, because it remembers enough of the profound traditions of the faith to know that humanity is fundamentally flawed and in need of radical redemption; but it almost invariably defines this distortion in terms of our inordinate quest for superhuman power and significance. Having received the stamp of strong male personalities ancient and modern— Augustine, Calvin, Edwards, and others—who were themselves rather Promethean; and having honed its sermon against pride in a life-and-death struggle with the Renaissance, modern orthodoxy in the West understands very little the "absurd" human of the existentialists or the "mass" human of the consumer society.

At the same time, theological liberalism has known better than the orthodox that humanity requires compassion and encouragement, not only chastisement; thus liberalism has gone a little way toward addressing human pathos—but only a little way. Having discarded any hint of "total depravity" in favor of sins more amenable to salvation by enlightenment and forgiveness, liberalism has been incapable of realizing the depths of contemporary alienation.

Directly or indirectly, then, both expressions of Christian theo-anthropology at work in our context have promulgated such high images of the human that it is difficult for people who are suffering under the impact of a barrage of evidence of their lowness to find in the church's testimony any sense of their being addressed. A hundred years of science, including the theory of evolution, having successfully persuaded the majority of their ordinariness; daily contact with people of all races and creeds having all but dispelled the myths of specialness; terrible wars, ecological catastrophes, "symbolic" diseases like AIDS, the failure of institutions and consequent public cynicism having robbed most North Americans of their unsullied pursuit of happiness; a gospel that assumes (even if

---

3. I say this in the full knowledge that Karl Barth devoted a large section of his *Church Dogmatics* to sloth, the Sisyphean side of sin. See esp. vol. IV/1, pp. 143ff. and vol. IV/2, pp. 403ff., 483ff., trans. G. W. Bromiley (Edinburgh: T. & T. Clark, 1956, 1958). But precisely this is the aspect of Barth's anthropology that has not been taken up and developed, with appropriate contextual sensitivity, by Barth's North American disciples.

it does not say so) the superiority of the human species, or understands so little the human suspicion of our inferiority, will hardly engage anyone. Or rather, it will function to prevent such engagement. In addressing itself to a species of humanity accustomed to religious and cultural assumptions of humanity's centrality in the scheme of things, it will confirm those managerial segments of society that will do anything to avoid the existential questioning of their mastery, while failing altogether to speak to the actual passivity of the majority. (If we wonder why Christianity of all varieties in North America is an overwhelmingly middle-class affair, we should pause to ponder that statement.)

17.2. Formulating Our Hypothesis. In introducing this chapter of critical theology on the subject of creaturely being, it may seem that I have too narrowly circumscribed the tradition. Let me admit at once, therefore, that Christian traditions respecting creaturehood—notably the creature *anthropos*—are widely diverse. Like Theology, Christian anthropology covers an almost incredible array of opinion. To read side by side Augustine and Pelagius, St. Thomas and Luther, Calvin and Wesley, Richard Hooker and John Knox, Albrecht Ritschl and Karl Barth, Carl MacIntyre and Norman Vincent Peale, Rosemary Radford Ruether and Wolfhart Pannenberg, would be to come away from the exercise thinking that one had been in the presence, if not of another Babel, at least of representatives of many different cults. And it would probably only exacerbate the confusion were one assured that all these commentators on the human condition are professing Christians. It is perhaps presumptuous, therefore, to claim—as I have done in the foregoing—that the Christian tradition concerning human being leaves us more adequately equipped to engage Prometheus than Sisyphus.

It would be presumptuous indeed to register such a hypothesis as though it could account for every exposition of the subject. What I have stressed, however, is that my generalization refers to the tradition *as we have received it.* Here we need to remind ourselves of what has been advanced in the first volume concerning the role of tradition in theological work.[4]

Tradition is not a static thing, a great deposit of inert material, like the archives of some city or university, which remains the same decade after decade, century after century. Tradition as that which the Christian past hands over to us involves not only what is handed over but also those to whom it is handed. Tradition is a living thing because its being received, if it is truly received and not just formally acknowledged, always entails discovery, surprise, nuance, insight, judgment, confirmation, interrogation, and (above all) struggle. We do not hear precisely what our grandparents heard from Tertullian or Thomas Müntzer or Teresa of Avila. Our minds are attuned to other themes,

---

4. *Thinking the Faith,* chap. 4, 263ff.

other questions and alternatives. Today's students of theology reading Karl Barth or Paul Tillich are not arrested by the same things that commanded the attention of the generations actually taught by those theologians. The single fact that many of today's theological students are women makes this inevitable.[5] We do not need from the past precisely what our predecessors needed, nor will our successors need precisely what we need as we search for a usable past.

This methodological observation is particularly important when it comes to the anthropological dimensions of Christian thought. The ever-changing face of humanity requires that what the past enjoins of us must be held in tension with new problems and possibilities that were not present, or not decisive, for our predecessors.[6]

An example is the impact of advanced technology in all areas of life. One looks in vain for any sustained critique of technology in Reinhold Niebuhr's magnum opus of fifty years ago, *The Nature and Destiny of Man*. Although the work must be regarded still as a veritable classic of Christian anthropology, and although it provides innumerable insights needed as background for Christian reflection upon high technology, Niebuhr's Gifford Lectures assume a significantly different human context. More than anyone of his generation of theologians, he anticipated so much about what was coming to be on the face of the earth that we may consider him still immediately pertinent—almost a contemporary.[7] But he does not address the problems of ecological catastrophe, Third World indebtedness, North/South disparities, abortion, gender exclusivism, violence against women, and a whole host of other problems with which faith today must wrestle. Nor does he speak to a world, such as ours has recently become, where the long-standing division between First and Second Worlds has broken down; where communism is more severely criticized inside the countries of the former Warsaw Pact than outside of them; where capitalism indulges in empty boasts about its victory and inherent superiority; where many Americans are confused because the old *Feindbilder* (enemy images) that have been used to bolster our own questionable ideology can no longer serve that purpose.

The situation is even more complicated than these specific ethical issues suggest. What one realizes the more one studies Reinhold Niebuhr's earlier works is that this greatest of all North American contextual theologians is

---

5. See Rosemary Radford Ruether's illuminating discussion of this process in *Sexism and God-Talk: Toward a Feminist Theology* (Boston: Beacon Press, 1983), 12–18.

6. Theology "continues its vital development only to the extent that such thinking remains in touch with depth experience" (ibid., 15).

7. See in this connection Robert McAfee Brown's introduction to his collection, *The Essential Reinhold Niebuhr: Selected Essays and Addresses* (New Haven: Yale Univ. Press, 1986), xx: "To make honest use of Niebuhr in our own time, we must remember what he never forgot, that the gospel speaks different words to different times, and even different words to different participants in the same times."

addressing himself to a human mentality—an *imago hominis*—that is significantly different from the image of the human that has come to be in more recent decades and looms on the horizon altogether too large for comfort. For Niebuhr, who regularly admitted that he "cut his theological eyeteeth" battling the self-possessed automobile magnate Henry Ford, the *problematique* to which the Christian message must address itself is the sin of pride, or rather sin *as* pride. Henry Ford was, so to speak, his paradigmatic Prometheus. So it is not accidental that of the ten chapters of the first volume of the Gifford Lectures, no fewer than three are devoted to the analysis of sin, and precisely sin as inordinate pride, hubris:

> The truth is that man is tempted by the basic insecurity of human existence to make himself doubly secure and by the insignificance of his place in the total scheme of life to prove his significance. The will-to-power is in short both a direct form and an indirect instrument of the pride which Christianity regards as sin in its quintessential form.[8]

That Niebuhr concentrated, in the first place, on the doctrine of sin and, in the second, understood sin's quintessence to be pride ought not to be construed as a fault or limitation in him.[9] On the contrary, it demonstrates his uncanny sensitivity to what Luther called "the little point where the battle rages." For in the context in which Reinhold Niebuhr was reared and "cut his theological eyeteeth," radical sin was not prominent in either Christian or secular consciousness, and

---

8. *The Nature and Destiny of Man,* vol. 1 (New York: Charles Scribner's Sons, 1953), 192.

9. As is well known, an important aspect of present-day Niebuhr scholarship is the feminist critique of his conception of sin, which in its concentration on pride seems to many to reflect a highly masculine bias. See in this connection Valerie Saiving, "The Human Situation: A Feminine View," in *The Journal of Religion* (April 1960); Daphne Hanson, "Reinhold Niebuhr on Sin: A Critique," in *Reinhold Niebuhr and the Issues of Our Time,* ed. Richard Harries (London and Oxford: Mowbray, 1986), 46ff.; Judith Plaskow, *Sex, Sin, and Grace: Women's Experience and the Theologies of Reinhold Niebuhr and Paul Tillich* (Lanham, Md.: University Press of America, 1980); and Judith Vaughan, *Sociality, Ethics, and Social Change: A Critical Appraisal of Reinhold Niebuhr's Ethics in the Light of Rosemary Radford Reuther's Works* (Lanham, Md.: University Press of America, 1983).

In a paper given at the Reinhold Niebuhr Symposium of McGill University, Montreal, in September 1993, Aurelia Takacs Fule reinforces the point I have made here concerning the necessity of reading Niebuhr's works *contextually.* While entirely sympathetic with contemporary feminist reinterpretations of the doctrine of sin, Fule nevertheless cautions that pride should not be regarded as an exclusively male phenomenon: "The work so far is done on a very limited basis: class and race distinctions, so formative of experience, are disregarded; and a great deal of white, middle class, Western women's experience is disregarded also. Surely we are not saying that women who debate planetary communications, or gene therapy, who direct major companies, run for Congress, or dissect Niebuhr's doctrine of sin are strangers to pride. The value, authority, and compensation given to women is universally lower than that granted to men. But the underdevelopment of the 'self' in women is not, and I believe cannot, be documented as nearly universal." ("Being Human before God: Reinhold Niebuhr in Feminist Mirrors," unpublished paper, p. 18; plans are being made for the publication of this and the other papers from the centenary symposium.)

as for pride, it was the very mood of America's dominant classes, the setbacks of depression, racial tension, and wars notwithstanding. The novels of Sinclair Lewis, Theodore Dreiser, John Steinbeck, and many others identify the same *problematique* as does Niebuhr. What remained of the idea that humanity was irrevocably fallen was reduced to trivial, private, and moralistic proportions. In a figure like Ford (and in many more subtle than he) Niebuhr could with perfect right recognize a type of Homo sapiens in the grip of Prometheanism, however unsophisticated and naive.

Moreover, because mainstream Christianity in North America, as in Europe, had allowed itself to be carried along by the bravado of modernity, it had practically lost touch with any of the profound teachings of the tradition on whose basis the tragic, pathetic, and downright evil aspects of the human condition could be recognized, named, and challenged. Conservative Christianity, which remembered the dogmas, was too unimaginative and too implicated with power to apply them. Thus it became the vocation of Reinhold and H. Richard Niebuhr in North America, as of Barth, Brunner, Bonhoeffer, Suzanne de Dietrich, and others in Europe, to recover and enliven ancient wisdom like the dogma of original sin, through which they could derive an alternative perspective on the human situation in the first half of the present century, and fashion their gospel accordingly. In short, their (with hindsight, amazingly correct) perception of their own context evoked and was evoked by their struggle with the tradition.

If we imitate them methodologically, however, I think that we shall not be able to imitate the specific content of their witness, especially where the predominant mood of our society is concerned. For we find ourselves today, I believe, in a significantly different social milieu. Later history may record that the last decades of the twentieth century in North America were in fact very different from the first five or six decades as far as the spirit of the times (*Zeitgeist*) is concerned.

This is not to imply that there are no threads of continuity between the two periods. When Reinhold Niebuhr's portrait appeared on the cover of *Time* Magazine's twenty-fifth anniversary issue in March of 1948, the caption beneath it read: "Man's Story Is Not a Success Story." Niebuhr knew the Bible, and he understood that the inordinate self-regard he felt compelled to denounce was only a slight historical turning removed from debilitating insecurity. Conversely, neither have we seen the end of that mentality to which Henry Ford gave undiluted expression when he quipped that "History is mostly bunk"—the rhetoric of progress. Positive thinkers are still able to achieve a following for their contemporary versions of the early twentieth-century motto invented by Dr. Emile Coué: "Day by day, in every way, I am getting better and better."

Yet today this kind of optimism is forced and often patently hollow. It is the only role that we know well. It is, besides, the part that we feel obligated to play. The very continuation of our society seems dependent upon our playing it. Prometheus American-style is so familiar a model of the human that we are never surprised by it, whether we encounter it in television commercials or in church; and we only find it slightly ridiculous when we see it exhibited in the films of the '40s and '50s. By comparison with present-day cinematography and other art, however, these productions of the middle of the century and earlier seem innocent in the extreme. Nothing indicates so precisely the attitudinal gulf separating the first from the second half of this century as do the films of the two periods; and it is hardly even necessary to specify which films.

To those who have some historical awareness, this observation inevitably invites a comparison with Europe. We have already anticipated that comparison in our use of the Sisyphus/Prometheus typology. These mythological figures have been drawn upon often in twentieth-century European literature. Sisyphus was the very model of contemporary humanity for the existentialists, especially Camus (who may or may not have been an existentialist). Jürgen Moltmann made good use of the two mythic figures in his first influential work, *A Theology of Hope.* That work was in fact written over against two attitudes prevalent in postwar Europe, Germany in particular: Marxian *superbia* and existentialist *acedia*—the Sisyphus syndrome.[10]

It is nevertheless impossible to transfer these insights of European philosophic and theological reflection directly into the North American situation, though many attempted to do so in the wake of Moltmann's "theology of hope." The reason for this is simply and profoundly that our context is infinitely more complex than the European, precisely on the question of our public mood respecting the nature and destiny of humanity. As I have characterized it above, we too have become Sisyphus, but a Sisyphus imitating Prometheus. There is no room for losers in this society, despite the notorious fact that, from the standpoint of the pop philosophy of "winning," greater and greater numbers of North Americans *have* lost—economically, in marriage and family life, in health and self-esteem, and so on. Our public policies insist upon an upbeat approach (reduced to almost vaudevillian proportions in every preelection party convention), despite the facts of staggering national debts, lingering recessions, and permanent unemployment. Task forces on self-esteem are created. Politicians and educators launch programs designed to "make people feel good about themselves"—despite their actual performance and notwithstanding the underlying sense of confusion and loss of confidence.[11]

---

10. Trans. James W. Leitch (Minneapolis: Fortress Press, 1993), esp. 24ff.

11. See the essay by Charles Krauthammer, "Education: Doing Bad and Feeling Good," *Time* Magazine (Feb. 5, 1990), 56.

However understandable this may be, given the history of European civilization in North America, it is apologetically complicating. No wonder so many younger theologians in our context look longingly to human situations where oppression is straightforward, or try to import into our situation liberationist themes like conscientization. It is one thing to "conscientize" the oppressed and marginalized who are surrounded by concrete evidence of their depressed condition; it is something else to "conscientize" the middle classes of North America. To a Sisyphus who cannot avoid the knowledge of his degradation, one may perhaps speak directly about the hope that can be experienced on the far side of despair, and only there. But how does anyone address a Sisyphus who thinks that he is Prometheus, or thinks that he ought to think that he is Prometheus: a Sisyphus who is so conditioned by simplistic variations of the onward-and-upward way of the "religion of progress" that to persuade him of his need is already almost impossible and perhaps unwise?

Against the backdrop of these reflections, we may formulate our critical hypothesis as follows: The tradition as it has come to us too readily conveys a high conception of the human, which, under the impact of the contemporary loss of purpose, fails to engage the low self-esteem entertained at varying levels of awareness by increasing numbers of people in our context. While biblical and minority traditions could speak to this condition, they have not been imaginatively explored by Christians. The appropriate corrective is not a further ontic elevation of Homo sapiens but rather the enucleation of a Christian anthropology that accentuates human creaturehood and develops its teleology in conjunction with a "new" understanding of humanity's vocation within the sphere of creation.

18. The Elevation of the Rational Animal

18.1. The Father Almighty and the Almighty Son. A clever aphorism, which one may hear from various quarters in a world grown irreverent toward both God and humanity, assures us that while the Bible declares that God created man in the divine *imago,* the truth of the matter is the reverse: Man created God in *his* image! This is not terribly profound (Feuerbach's version is better), yet it does point up one important truth: If centuries of Christendom have resulted in the construction and maintenance of a view of the divine as "the Father Almighty" despite the serious critique of such a Theology in scriptural and some authoritative traditional sources,[12] the exercise is not without its anthropological rationale. As Jean-Paul Sartre

---

12. See above, chap. 2.

wrote of his grandfather Schweitzer, who unlike Sartre was a somewhat religious man: "Charles Schweitzer was too much of an actor not to need a Great Spectator."[13]

It is doubtful whether any very different conception of the deity could have arisen in a civilization like ours. The West as we know it could not have come to be had its founders conceived of the supreme being along the lines, say, of Buddhism, or Native Amer-Canadian religion, or Hinduism. Both with respect to God the Father, whom we have considered, and God the Son, whom we shall consider in Part III, the whole tenor and direction of Western Theology has been to ignore and controvert the weakness of God (1 Cor. 1:25) as it is testified to in Scripture, and to maximize God's unconditional power.[14] Behind this tampering with the deity (as from the scriptural perspective we must state the matter), there has been one recurrent though hidden anthropological drive, a drive visible especially since the European Renaissance: namely, the demand of an imperial humanity for the highest possible self-image—the need for a "Great Spectator" to applaud history's "great actor."

It would be naive to propose that this has been a work of deliberate theological engineering. As in the modern world of advertising, the anthropological sources and consequences of our Theology are all the more effective because they operate at the subliminal level. Purposely and in full self-awareness to construct a model of deity intended to reinforce a Promethean anthropology would be to jettison the project in the act of executing it. Obviously this is not how images of the human are fashioned. What happens, happens at a level deeper than intentionality. Conceptions of deity and humanity alike are born out of profound human drives. At base, these drives—for security, love, meaning—are universal and, given the uncertainties and anxieties against which they are pitted, both necessary and understandable. Only cynics and nihilists could ridicule them. Yet the more successful societies are in achieving their ends, the more easily they are tempted to exaggerate their powers. Imperial civilizations are the products of legitimate human aspirations which, through partial achievement, have been galvanized into triumphant world views. Their

---

13. Jean-Paul Sartre, *The Words: The Autobiography of Jean-Paul Sartre,* trans. Bernard Fretchman (New York: Random House, Vintage Books, 1981), 99.

14. "In the framework of the two-nature christology, all statements about 'the lowliness' of Jesus, his humanity, his suffering, and his death on the cross, are reduced, in favor of statements about his divinity, his exaltation and his triumph, and are integrated into these. The history of Christ is essentially the vertical history between God and human beings. It is 'the way of the Son of God into the foreign country,' and 'the return home of the Son of man.' If the history of Christ is essentially this vertical history, then it is a fundamentally 'eternal history.' What emerges as a whole is the picture of the triumphant Christ in the glory of God." (Jürgen Moltmann, *The Way of Jesus Christ: Christology in Messianic Dimensions,* trans. Margaret Kohl [Minneapolis: Fortress Press, 1993], 52.

gods are projections of their corporate ambitions. The "Christian" deity of the West has not escaped this destiny.

What biblical faith demands that we ask, however, is whether humanity is ever well served by such images of deity and humanity. For a sense of purpose—indeed, for the very existence of community—human collectivities need to achieve some measure of regulation vis-à-vis their environment; but do we really need to consider ourselves lords and masters of nature? infinitely higher than other forms of life? capable of unlimited achievements of which the advances of the past are only tokens? veritable demigods, in fact? Is our need for security and meaning so insatiable that we can be satisfied with nothing less than absolute control and the elimination of every negating factor? Must chance be done away with entirely? On the contrary, do not such visions usually function destructively in the end?

Of Western Christian civilization in its North American expression, which is perhaps its purest, least diluted form, must it not now be asked: Who can attain unto it? Having fashioned an "Almighty Father" who could both symbolize and hallow our pretensions to almighty sonship, have we not put ourselves in the way of being weighed in balances of our own devising, and found wanting? Who can measure up to this theo-anthropology? What of those who could never even pretend to do so: the sons who were weak, afraid, "feminine"? the mentally and physically handicapped sons? the black, red, and yellow sons on the edges of our proud white societies? Above all, what of the daughters?

Human beings have indeed the power to create images of deity that serve our grandiloquent aims, cloaking our own craving for sovereignty. But these same images regularly turn into idols. Cultures in their upward and high phases fashion for themselves gods that enshrine their collective pride; and history bears witness to the fact that these false gods do indeed inspire a people's heroic ventures, conquests, explorations, inventions, wars, sciences, and technologies. But in their decline, and as perhaps its chief contributing factor, societies are oppressed by no other factor so much as by their own cultus. Their gods cannot tolerate failure. Like almighty fathers everywhere, the father gods whose main attribute is power will settle for nothing less than stalwart, confident sons. A time comes, however, when the sons of such fathers no longer have the will to believe in their reflected omnipotence. Their self-doubt may then first manifest itself in doubt concerning the might of the gods they fashioned. But as those gods are truly projections of their own bid for preeminence, there can be no critique of almighty divinity that does not return, at last, to its source and question the humanity that devised it. The pathos so ingeniously depicted in Tennessee Williams's *Cat on a Hot Tin Roof* has its genesis in the son's failure of nerve and its resolution necessarily involves the father's terminal illness; but finally it is the son himself whose spirit must be transformed.

(Significantly, his transformation is mediated through the persistent love of a woman.)

Our critical assessment of the doctrine of God (chapter 2) must, accordingly, now in like manner be applied to the doctrine of human being. In undertaking this, we join forces with many, including Christian feminists, who for the past twenty years have drawn the attention of the churches to this problem. Our critique will take the form of a deconstruction of the elements that have provided us with a Promethean conception of human being. In the previous chapter we recognized three such elements: creation, fall, and redemption. We shall return to these now, with a view to showing how each has contributed in its way to an exaggeratedly elevated anthropology, which, at least under our present contextual conditions, fails both to engage the human *problematique* and to provide an alternative vision of human being and meaning.

18.2. Creation: "Man above Nature." Many contemporary ecologists and others lay at the doorstep of the Christian religion and its Judaic parent faith the present-day biospheric malaise.[15] The so-called crisis of nature, they insist, is really a crisis of human nature. Western technological civilization, which has come to dominate the globe, is the product of a cult that lifted the human creature high above all other created life, assigning it a status "a little lower than the angels" (Ps. 8:5, KJV). Thus a climate of expectation evolved in the West that, while superficially appearing to contradict the theocentric assumptions of occidental religion and philosophy, in reality gave birth to an anthropocentric conception of the world: Man as *"maitre et possesseur"* (master and possessor) (Descartes) of nature is the mirror image of the Lord God whom he fashioned.

Elsewhere I have argued that this is a simplistic explanation of a long historical development that was far more complex.[16] Christianity did not single-handedly produce the technological society.[17] Modernity, including the very

---

15. See *Thinking the Faith,* chap. 3, 219ff.

16. See my three books on the theology of stewardship: *The Steward: A Biblical Symbol Come of Age,* rev. ed. (Grand Rapids: Wm. B. Eerdmans Pub. Co., and New York: Friendship Press, 1990); *The Stewardship of Life in the Kingdom of Death* (Grand Rapids: Wm. B. Eerdmans Pub. Co., 1985); and *Imaging God: Dominion as Stewardship* (Grand Rapids: Wm. B. Eerdmans Pub. Co., 1986).

17. "The Jewish-Christian tradition is often made responsible for man's usurpation of power over nature and for his unbridled will to power. It was this tradition, we are told, which decreed that human beings should rule the earth. . . . Yet this allegedly 'anthropocentric' view of the world found in the Bible is more than three thousand years old, whereas modern scientific and technological civilization only began to develop in Europe four hundred years ago at the earliest. So there must have been other, more important factors in its development. Whatever the economic, social and political chances that may require mention, another factor was more important still in determining the way people four hundred years ago saw themselves. This was the new picture of God offered by the Renaissance and by nominalism: God is almighty, and *potentia absoluta* is the pre-eminent attribute of divinity. Consequently God's image on earth, the human being (which in

sciences whose contemporary practitioners now sometimes like to indulge in this new attack upon religion, is a product neither of medieval philosophic theology nor of the Reformation. Something new had to come to be before Western civilization could hear in the biblical commands to "subdue the earth" and "have dominion" the message that God had given humanity license to use the earth and all life for whatever purposes it saw fit. What had to transpire to make such license normative was on the one hand the total neglect of the biblical doctrine of sin (in part, through its reduction to personalistic dimensions) and, on the other, an assessment of human possibilities and rights infinitely more extensive than anything present in the tradition of Jerusalem.

This observation does not, however, exonerate historic Christianity from responsibility for the disastrous course that our society is still blithely pursuing in relation to the natural order. At least through neglect, if not through positive reinforcement, the Christian religion aided and abetted Western humanity's steady quest for sovereignty within creation.

It is not easily managed, however, to excuse Christianity on the grounds of neglect alone; for its neglect of potentially corrective doctrinal emphases was almost inevitable, given Christianity's close, legitimizing ties with the dominant imperial cultures of the West. In its positive doctrine, too, the Christian religion prepared the way for technocratic humanity.

This is particularly noticeable in the key conception of Christian anthropology associated with the doctrine of creation, the *imago Dei* dogma. As we have seen, the comparative motif is almost always prominent in the elaboration of this dogma. It is not enough to speak about the human being as possessing the divine image; it seems mandatory within the annals of doctrine to affirm that humankind alone is the recipient of this wondrous endowment. That is to say, the human is elevated through an explicit and implicit denigration of the extrahuman. Repeatedly we are asked to recognize that, unlike the other creatures, humankind possesses unique capacities, qualities that distinguish it from all the rest.[18] Whereas other creatures live by instinct, humanity lives by thought and decision. Humanity is thus "higher" than other species.[19]

---

actual practice meant the man) had to strive for power and domination so that he might acquire his divinity. Power became the foremost predicate of the deity, not goodness and truth. But how can the human being acquire power, so that he may resemble his God? Through science and technology; for 'knowledge is power,' as Francis Bacon exultantly proclaimed." (Jürgen Moltmann, *God in Creation: An Ecological Doctrine of Creation* [The Gifford Lectures of 1984–1985], trans. Margaret Kohl [Minneapolis: Fortress Press, 1993], 26–27.)

18. E.g.: "Man is a creature divinely endowed with gifts which set him above all other creatures: he is made in the image of God." (J. S. Whale, *Christian Doctrine* [Cambridge: At the University Press, 1941], 44.)

19. E.g.: "In spite of all the marvels of nature, we recognize that it is constituted by *lower grades of being,* that is to say, beings that have a narrower range of participation in Being than has man. Even those animals with which we may feel some kinship are not, like ourselves, answerable for their being. . . . [T]he recognition that nature is creation, and indeed a *lower level of*

As we have noticed, moreover, these uniquely human endowments are most consistently identified as reason and freedom of will—the very qualities taken up by the architects of the modern vision. No one of lasting influence in the tradition speaks about such qualities as gentleness, sacrificial love, compassion, humility, modesty, awe, responsibility for others, meekness, or gratitude as being the qualities intended by the phrase, "image of God." It would appear that Christianity has been almost wholly taken over by Athens at this point—or rather by a particular strain of the tradition of Athens, one that was refined especially by Aristotle.

Beyond that, apart from a critical minority, some of whom have been mentioned previously, few attempts have been made in the past to move the church away from its almost exclusive propensity to think substantialistically about the *imago Dei*. For the majority tradition, the image of God is a possession, almost measurable. This reinforces a thoroughly hierarchic evaluation of all the species. For if only the human species possesses this most precious divine endowment, then all the other species are automatically ranked beneath it, their theoretical value being determined by their degree of intelligence, and their practical value by their usefulness to humans.

Once indulged, this preconception of the ordering of creation bequeaths to all subsequent Christian anthropology a view of the human as being incapable of solidarity with other creatures and, in fact, hardly a creature at all. It could not be denied, of course, that humanity does participate in creaturehood; but this was all too frequently associated with the body—which is to say, the unessential and (usually) detrimental component of human being, that component deemed to be dominant especially in woman.[20] On the contrary the soul, including quite naturally its rational and volitional properties, could be thought immortal in most expositions of the faith. And, since the soul is the essence, according to this thoroughly Hellenized line of thought, one is left wondering whether the profession of human creaturehood has not always been more rhetorical than real within the church. At very least, it has been sharply distinguished from the general creaturely condition. But beyond that even the concept of "creature" as such has been used so infrequently, where humankind is concerned, that it has seemed to many an inappropriate designation. Even in the post-Christian world it is rare to find this nomenclature applied to human beings, though it is

---

creation than man,* destroys animism and the worship of the creation in the so-called 'gods' of nature, thus opening the way to the scientific exploration of nature." (John Macquarrie, *Principles of Christian Theology* [London: S.C.M. Press, 1966], 197 [emphasis added].)

20. "Matter is . . . seen as the source of the moral devolution of mind. Mind entrapped in matter loses its 'wings' and becomes subjected to moral chaos, that is, the passions. Thus the struggle to subdue and order matter ends finally not in the triumph of cosmos as final blessedness but in a flight of the mind from nature and body to a spiritual (disembodied) realm." (Ruether, *Sexism and God-Talk,* 78–79.) See also Moltmann, *God in Creation,* 244–75.

still generously applied to all other species.[21] It is perhaps more difficult for Homo sapiens to profess its creaturehood than to confess its sin! It is even probable that for most Christians and post-Christians, sin and creaturehood are inextricably linked.

In view of this, it is not surprising that one of the most common literary expressions in English rhetoric prior to the emergence of contemporary feminist and ecological awareness was some variant on the theme, "Man above Nature." The irony of this conception of the human, however, lies in the very correlation to which, as we noted earlier, biblical literature consistently testifies: namely, that high images of the human regularly beget low images of the human. So today, when humanity's supremacy over nature is no longer self-evident, we have witnessed the appearance, not only of world views that denigrate the human but also of more subtle public tokens of human self-abasement. The exalted image of the human now begins to give place to a correspondingly reduced self-understanding on the part of beings who, regardless of their indoctrination, do not *feel* exalted. "Man above Nature" threatens to become "Man below Nature"—the *unnatural* animal; the mortal who not only fails to make good its former pretensions to immortality but is questionable even within the sphere of the mortals. It is therefore not uncommon nowadays to hear the dogma of the *imago Dei* openly mocked.

18.3. Even Fallenness Confirms Our Superiority.   It could be thought that the exaggeratedly "high" anthropology that, under present conditions, easily gives way to disillusionment and self-loathing might have been qualified by the theological perspective on humankind coming from the side of the fall. After all, we have noticed how Western Christendom especially became preoccupied with the fall. To be sure, in some classical expressions of Christian anthropology in the West, the consciousness of an innate human distortedness engendered in believers a sense of deep unworthiness and, upon the experience of saving grace, sheer gratitude. This sense is often accompanied by a humility that recognizes human solidarity with all other forms of creaturehood. Thus in African-American spirituality, which was shaped both by a more consistently biblical testimony to the general human condition and by the historical experience of sustained suffering, one finds an unusually gentle attitude toward the creation as a whole. It is as if those who were compelled by "masters" to accept their own status as "critters" were also able to recognize their common bond with the other creatures in a way forever barred to people laboring under the delusion of mastery.

---

21. It is instructive to consult popular dictionaries on this topic. While "creature" is occasionally stretched to include the human being, what dominates is a ubiquitous preference for the pejorative employment of the term: animal, beast, thing, mortal, servant, slave (as in "critter"), etc.

It would be a serious misjudgment, however, to think that the sense of human fallenness has served as a permanent counterbalance to the elevation of the human. As we have interpreted it in the previous chapter, the dominant understanding of the nature of human fallenness has concentrated on the thought of deprivation: in our actual existing we are deprived of qualities that belong to our essential nature. That is to say, *essentially* we are far greater than our actual history demonstrates.

Such a thought can be humbling under certain circumstances, but it can also be exhilarating and salutory. It can function in much the same way as does the family mythology of a glorious past. The middle-class family that can trace its ancestry to some aristocratic European or wealthy American connection is not so much dismayed by its "fallen" circumstances as intrigued by the myth of its high-class origins. If we are encouraged by our religious doctrine to consider our real nature as human beings one that is not only not identical with what we have made of ourselves but infinitely superior to anything that we have yet achieved, such a vision can serve to bolster our self-estimate. Despite its judgment of our actual performance, it confirms our presentiment of a sublime potentiality.

It also has the convenient effect of providing a satisfactory explanation of our obvious continuity with other forms of animal existence. Since the qualities that have been diminished or disordered by our lapse, according to the dominant doctrines of the past, are all of them spiritual and intellectual endowments, we are enabled to feel that our disturbingly excessive animality is consequential upon the diminution of these superior, controlling attributes. We behave too consistently according to our lower nature because our higher nature has been weakened. Thus, by a kind of reverse logic, the notion of the fall can confirm what, in positive terms, the doctrines of creation and redemption are frequently caused to establish: that we are in essence very unlike all other creatures; that our apparent similarity with them is a result of an unfortunate flaw in our historic unfolding.

When this idea is combined with a historical conceptualization of the fall (as has been the case throughout most of Christian history and is still so, probably, among the majority of avowed Christians in North America today), it can add to the attitude we are describing here a dimension of resignation and even complacency. For the flaw by which the race has been affected is then seen to be one for which none of us has direct responsibility; it is simply a condition imposed upon the race by decisions made at the very outset of our appearance. We must live with these conditions, as the middle-class family of my earlier allusion must live with its relative poverty, but we do so knowing that we are really lords and ladies in reduced circumstances. Our place is not in these hovels; our comrades are not these "critters"; our calling is not this ludicrous, repetitive work. In short, the doctrine of the fall can alienate us all the more effectively from our creaturely status, conditioning us to consider ourselves heirs to a destiny far more commensurate with our high aspirations than what has actually befallen us. Even the language of "total depravity" has its highly salutory side effects, and those who have employed it most consistently (for example, the Puritans) have seldom seemed daunted by it.

The total loss of "original righteousness" has, however, seldom been advanced without doctrinal qualifiers. In most medieval and post-Reformation theologies, the spiritual qualities identified with the *imago Dei* are diminished, not wholly lost, by the fall. Not only by means of the reverse logic described above, therefore, but also positively—that is, by accentuating what remains of the endowments of whose fullness the fall has deprived humanity—the doctrine of the fall and its attendant concepts have been far from an operative corrective to the human tendency to "think more highly of ourselves than we ought." Only in those traditions that conceived of sin in relational terms, as a radical abrogation of the interdependent relationships that constitute the integrity of creaturehood, does the doctrine of the fall serve consistently to counteract the pretensions to grandeur readily derived from creation and redemption theologies. For in those traditions, sin is seen from the start exactly as the human attempt to extricate itself from its condition of interdependence, to achieve autonomy, to avoid accountability to its Creator and responsibility for its fellow creatures. Had the doctrine of the fall been informed throughout by "the ontology of communion" rather than a hierarchic ontology of being and valuation, it could not have lent itself so readily to co-optation by the lofty anthropology of Western Christendom. We shall return to this point later.

Such an indirect but ultimately positive functioning of the apparently negative statement about humanity that is contained in the doctrine of human fallenness has seldom been appreciated for what it is. We are easily persuaded by the exaggeratedly uncomplimentary language of Augustinian, Calvinistic, and other descriptions of human wretchedness that such assessments of the human condition must perform in the world as horridly oppressive fantasies, depriving people of the very will to test their human powers. That, of course, can also occur, as the novels of Hawthorne, Flannery O'Connor, Robertson Davies, and many others attest. Yet it must seriously be questioned, when this is put forward as if it were an inevitable consequence of strong statements of human sinfulness, whether such a consequence has in fact usually followed.

No one articulated the depths of sin more tellingly than Calvin; but it may be asked whether, in the history of the world, there has ever existed a race of people more persuaded of their superior powers than are Swiss, Dutch, South African white, or North American Calvinists. The history of the United States of America, whose most significant religious component, historically speaking, has been Calvinism, is hardly the history of a people weighed down with a sense of degeneracy, shame, and guilt. We may conclude that this has something to do with the doctrines of redemption and (especially) election, which also entered this history through the medium of Calvinism and was curiously blended with Jeffersonian idealism. All the same, if the doctrine of the fall so bleakly and even, sometimes, morbidly pursued by this theological tradition really acts to check human pride and assertiveness, one must ask why it has not played a more effective part in our history. Where individual life is concerned, it has sometimes been profound and, often enough, terrifying in its effects. But it appears to have done little to curb corporate or national ambition. Has the American Dream suffered at all, in fact, from Calvin's somber assessment of human prospects?

18.4. Mastery Regained. If the doctrine of the fall has functioned indirectly to exalt the human, redemption theology has done so rather directly. This is not to ignore the fact that, in its most profound articulations, Christian soteriology assumes a critical assessment of humanity—namely, that humankind is so deeply implicated in evil that it needs radical salvation. Nor is it to overlook the eschatological character of redemption, with its implicit warning against presumption (see, for example, 1 Corinthians 9–10). Our concern here, however, is not to critique the theology of redemption as such but to notice how, as one of the three foci of Christian reflection on the human situation (creation, fall, redemption), it has contributed to what, under the present historical conditions, has become a problematic anthropology.

This interpretation may be considered from several points of view, in accordance with differing emphases in redemption theology itself. One influential strand of this theology conceives of redemption almost straightforwardly as redemption *from* the creaturely status. This does not represent a minority position; in fact, it comes close to being the orthodox heart of the tradition. It is certainly suggested, for example, by the famous dictum of Athanasius: "He [the Christ] became human in order that we might become divine." Here the salvific work of Jesus Christ is directed not only toward the overcoming of sin but—with it, as part of it—the overcoming of finitude. The human dilemma is our humanity as such. Jesus must undergo the humiliation of humanity so that he may gain for us the exaltation of divinity. Divinity—that is, participation in God's being—is the true destiny of our creaturehood; and to reach this destiny our creaturehood itself must be overcome.

Such a view of redemption has never been far from the mind of Christendom. It is still powerfully at work in North American Christianity. Combined with the idea of the immortality of the soul, it has the effect not only of denigrating the body but of calling in question the whole historical enterprise, which, from the perspective of its *telos,* must be regarded as being at best a stage—possibly not even quite real. In relation to the redeemed estate, the raw stuff of creatureliness is by definition problematic. In fact, when pressed to its

271

logical presupposition, this view of redemption can only be consistently maintained in implicit antithesis to the doctrine of creation. For what it wants to surpass is the creaturely condition as such. If the object of salvation is that we might become divine, then our humanness must be understood to be the problem. (Otherwise, why should not the formula read, "He became human in order that we might become *human*"?)

While, as I have indicated, the negative side of such a soteriology is its implicit rejection of our present creaturely status, this is more than offset by the presupposition that human destiny is infinitely superior to the creaturely condition. It may not be—in all probability it *shall* not be—that all human beings actually achieve the divine goal; but as a statement about humanity as such, there could be nothing in the realm of anthropology more exalted than the proposal that a redeemed humanity is a humanity partaking of divinity itself.

At the other end of the spectrum of redemption as it applies to our present concern we find variations on the theme of restoration. Here salvation, while not necessarily excluding an afterlife in which the true goal of our being is finally attained, concentrates on this-worldly existence. To experience redemption is to be restored to a more truly human condition. Those flaws that result from sin are subdued, or (depending upon the attendant eschatology) are being subdued, and those qualities of which our fallenness robs us are being restored to us. We are recovering "our rightful mind"; we are being "set free."

The great advantage of this perspective on redemption is that it complements and fulfills the doctrine of creation rather than (as with the previously considered approach) setting itself in something like opposition to creation. It could be said, I think, that most recent theology, whether liberal, neoorthodox, or liberationist in its sympathies, tends toward this understanding of the meaning of redemption. Certainly it is the preference of the present study. For I do not see how a soteriology that is not intentionally oriented toward the healing and fulfillment of our humanity can avoid implying that human creaturehood is itself and as such the problem; and that, I believe, is to part company from the tradition of Jerusalem altogether.

Yet the soteriology of restoration does not necessarily anticipate or correct the problem to which our attention is directed here, that is, the presentation of a too exalted anthropology. It will depend upon how restoration is conceived. Precisely what is restored? If we are thinking of restored relationships, and of a "new" sense of human solidarity with and responsibility for the rest of creation, it is one thing; but if we are thinking rather of the restoration of lost endowments, whose recovery enables humanity to assume once more its high status and office in creation, it is something else. With the latter alternative, we are back in a hierarchic ordering of the world, with all that this means for the inaccessibility and inappropriateness of such an anthropology in an age like our own.

Unfortunately, while various efforts are being made toward the understanding of redemption as the recovery of right-relatedness, it is difficult to establish the meaning of such a view on account of the entrenched character of soteriologies that—whether from the traditional otherworldly or the more contemporary this-worldly perspective—still assume that salvation means being lifted up. (Why not "settled down"?) It is almost impossible to overcome the assumption, centuries in the making, that redemption by definition implies elevation: that to the descent into sin there now corresponds an ascent into salvation. The crown prince of creation, fallen from grace, is now restored to his rightful place—to mastery.

In summary, then, we may say that from the perspective of all three dimensions of the Christian focus on human being—creation, fall, and redemption—doctrine has evoked from Western spirituality a strong tendency to exalt the human. The consequences of this exaltation become clearer as we return once again to the question of the purpose ("end") of human life.

19. Purpose Located in Superior Being

19.1. Being and Meaning. In considering the question of human purpose in the previous chapter, we were made conscious of the fact that the greater tradition appears to devote relatively little attention to the subject. While there is no lack of general affirmations of a doxological nature (for example, that the chief end of humankind is the glorification and enjoyment of God), and while these affirmations are occasionally elaborated in such a way as to suggest more concrete meanings, the whole area of God's intention for the human creature within the sphere of creation seems conspicuously absent from the discussion. This is bound to appear strange to persons familiar with the Scriptures, particularly the older Testament, because a good deal of concern about human purpose is expressed in the Bible. Biblical interest in this area seems both explicit and central—for instance in the concept of the covenant, as well as in the elaboration of the Torah, with its great variety of earthward directives and responsibilities.

Perhaps the clue to this deficiency is suggested in this allusion to the older Testament. We must at least ask whether the attention paid by the Hebrew Bible to Yahweh's intention for humankind has been carried forward into the Christian Scriptures. Is it possible that the latter, written under the impact of an imminent parousia and consummation of all things, are content to interpret the purpose of human being in chiefly spiritual and otherworldly categories—sanctification, regeneration, resurrection, glorification, adoption as sons, and so on? After all, if these documents emanate from communities of faith that expect the old order to end soon, we should not be surprised that they fail to develop the worldly implications of some of the categories that they have taken over from the parental faith—for example, stewardship, priesthood, justice, and even covenant-partnership.

On the other hand, we know that one of the chief reasons for the existence of these documents is the diminishment of eschatological expectation of an imminent nature. Moreover, even if the newer Testamental writings themselves have neglected the elaboration of answers to the question, What are people *for*?—specifically, What are redeemed people for?—they provide a sufficient vocabulary, surely, so that subsequent generations of Christians, who no longer expected an immediate end, might have developed these incipient ideas more fully. Yet, apart from its preoccupation with the Christian mission itself, the evolving church appears to have attached little importance to that question. And while to speak of "the mission" is to speak of the purpose of the church, it does not of itself say much about human purpose or even the purpose of a redeemed humanity—which would be an indirect way of speaking about human purpose in general.

To say that human beings are redeemed in order to facilitate the redemption of other human beings may seem an acceptable sentiment in some pious circles, but in reality it begs the question: redeemed *to what end*? The Christian mission is never self-explanatory, though it is often presented as if it were. Until one understands something of what missionaries wish to bring about through their evangelization, it is impossible to test their authenticity against the authoritative sources of Bible and tradition. Conversion, renewal, and rebirth are certainly biblical concepts, but they always provoke other questions: conversion to what? renewal of what, and why? rebirth into what kind of new life? Here as elsewhere the saying of Jesus applies: "By their fruits you shall know them."

The relative silence of the tradition on the worldly intention of God for "true humanity" therefore presents a kind of historical conundrum, and one that is particularly conspicuous in an age when this question confronts us in existentially gripping ways. As Berkhof writes: "It is remarkable how rarely the question concerning God's *purpose* in the renewal of man has been explicitly discussed in the study of the faith. Its attention was focused on the renewal itself; its results were preferably called 'fruits,' and so the goal-problematics was by-passed."[22]

In the light of the preceding discussion of the tradition's explicit and implicit elevation of human being, I would suggest the following explanation of this conundrum: The reason there is so little explicit treatment of humanity's purpose in the classical doctrinal traditions is that they assume that the meaning or intention

---

22. Hendrikus Berkhof, *Christian Faith: An Introduction to the Study of the Faith,* trans. Sierd Woudstra (Grand Rapids: Wm. B. Eerdmans Pub. Co., 1979), 426.

of God for us is a given of our being as such. That is to say, as superior beings our purpose is nothing more and nothing less than to *be*—that is, to actualize the potentiality of our being; to be or become existentially who we are *essentially;* to overcome the barriers to our fulfillment and make good the promise of our being—or rather, since (certainly) the whole tradition assumes the need for redemption from beyond our own possibilities, to be subject to the grace that renews us. If therefore the tradition focuses "on the renewal itself" (Berkhof) and does not expatiate on the goal thereof, it is because the bulk of the tradition assumes that the renewal or rebirth "in Christ" in itself means the effective achievement of God's purpose for us, which is that we should be the exalted beings we were created to be. In short, being (*ontos*) and meaning (*telos*) are not separate or separable considerations but part and parcel of the same givenness. For such beings, to *be* is already to have meaning. Nothing more needs to be added if this is understood.

Indeed, it may be considered profoundly true that if this is understood, nothing more would have to be said. The trouble is that, under the conditions of existence, being as such seems seldom to bear within itself its own raison d'être. Or let us say, in keeping with our earlier observations, that while there may be occasions when simply "to be" implies "to have significance," there are other occasions when being itself contains no messages whatsoever about its own purpose and may, on the contrary, impart strong intimations of randomness or lack of meaning (Hamlet's problem). Societies with high expectations and manifesting a general sense of well-being, such as the nineteenth century of Western Europe and North America seems to have been for significant numbers of people, may find exhilaration enough in the unfolding of each new day.[23] Promethean Man is seldom found agonizing about the purpose of life! But we have judged that we do not live now in such a society. Being as such, for at least vast (and perhaps increasing) numbers of us in North America, does not automatically confer meaning; on the contrary, for many, being is burdensome. How shall we, who have grown more skeptical about our species' alleged high purpose, appropriate a tradition in which being and meaning are almost equated?

This is our critical question. Before considering it further, however, we shall attempt to demonstrate more concretely the juxtaposition of being and meaning as it applies to different expressions of the received tradition. To

---

23. June Bingham in her biography of Reinhold Niebuhr reminds us that in 1928, the year Niebuhr left his Detroit parish to become a professor at Union Theological Seminary, fashionable businessmen were wearing a small, round gold ornament on their watch chains bearing the motto of America in its latest translation: "Day by day, in every way, I am way getting better and better"—the aforementioned maxim of Emile Coué (1857–1926), the Norman Vincent Peale of his day. (June Bingham, *Courage to Change: An Introduction to the Life and Thought of Reinhold Niebuhr* [New York: Charles Scribner's Sons, 1961], 154.)

that end, we shall first consider the more classical or orthodox theo-anthropology that associates human purpose with the sanctification of the soul, and secondly the more modern doctrine that associates human ends with the restoration and renewal of superior endowments diminished by sin.

19.2. Training for Eternity. Our thesis (that human purpose is not greatly considered by the Christian tradition because meaning is understood to be a predicate of being) seems confirmed by the observations of the preceding chapter concerning the subject of vocation. That Christian vocation could for approximately fifteen hundred years be applied almost exclusively to *religious* vocations, specifically monasticism, is not surprising, given this basic assumption. Or rather, it is only surprising to us today because we do tend to separate being and meaning. Classical expressions of the faith are prone to take for granted that human purpose is given in and with being itself. This applies to the doctrine of creation; it applies even more expressly to redemption. Thus the "new being" *en Christo,* which must be understood as the renewal in us of the being God intended for us from the outset, implies within itself its rationale. Christians who give themselves as unreservedly as possible to the cultivation of that new being are those in whom the meaning of human life is most perfectly expressed. They are "the called," and their calling exemplifies for all others the highest articulation of human significance.

It is thus by no means accidental that, until the Reformation period, the concept of having a vocation referred almost exclusively to the monastic life. The monastic life was based upon the ideal of an untrammeled pursuit of the meaning vouchsafed through the grace of new being. If the essence of that new being is understood as the purification and ultimate salvation of the soul, then a life that is ordered toward the liberation of the soul from bodily passions, temptations, and diversions and its orientation to the eternal most perfectly exemplifies the whole purpose of human existence. The monastic vocation is the model of the soul in training for eternity—that is, for that participation in the divine for which the Christ endured human incarnation.

Against the dangers of Protestant and other bias, let us recognize that this never implied that only those who took the vows of monasticism would be saved. The monk or nun was looked upon rather as a model of the soul's quest for perfection. Nor does such a view necessarily imply strictly cloistered forms of Christian monasticism, as in the purely contemplative orders. The disciplining of the body and the sanctification of the soul might be undertaken as well through works of charity toward others, involving much self-denial and sacrifice. There is no question but that great good has accrued from the institution of monasticism. We are not asking here about its ethical consequences, however, but about its foundational anthropology, specifically the teleological dimension of its anthropology.[24]

What the long association of vocation with monasticism illustrates graphically is a Christian anthropology which takes as its rudimentary assumption the belief that our human *telos* is eternal life, understood as a postcreaturely, otherworldly state. Not all persons are able to devote themselves to the preparation that this goal requires; but through the exemplary discipline of the few, the many may realize more concretely what they, according to their capacities and stations, ought also to strive for.

Together with many other aspects of conventional Christianity, the permanent effect upon Christian piety of this conception of vocation has been to orient the mind of the church toward a goal that can only be attained beyond death. While such a conception of human purpose has the dubious advantage of lending to death itself a positive meaning as the entree to eternal life, the price that is paid for this advantage is a high one. For if the purpose of this life is to pass through it to the next life, it is implied not only that this life in itself and as such cannot be said to have a purpose but that it presents a certain barrier to the attainment of our ultimate goal. And is that not precisely the message that has been conveyed, both explicitly and implicitly, by hundreds of years of Christian spirituality, by no means all of it monastic? How many of the great Protestant hymns are so arranged that by the final stanza the congregation has passed beyond "the Jordan" and has reached its ultimate destiny—"heaven," "the arms of Jesus," and so on? The point is not that such sentiments are always questionable, but that as a recurrent and powerfully entrenched statement of life's whole orientation they convey at best a highly ambiguous message about *this* life. (Let anyone who does not think so sing such hymns attentively alongside his or her teenage children!)

19.3. Human Fulfillment. The reformers' rejection of vocation as defined by monastic exercises in sanctification of the soul in favor of a broader and more this-worldly understanding of the matter introduced a critical principle that exceeds the discussion of vocation and has implications for the whole question of human purpose. If secular occupation, even to the meanest kind of job, can be conceived of as a divine calling, then the purpose of one's existing is not premised upon one's ceasing to exist—that is, one's death—but already

---

24. On monasticism, see Rosemary Radford Ruether, *Liberation Theology* (New York: Paulist Press, 1972), 69, particularly her observation that "originally Christianity, like the Jewish synagogue, modeled its religious community after the family. . . . But, by the fourth century, ascetic spirituality was removing the Christian ministry from normal contact with family life."

manifests itself in everyday life. From the standpoint of an incarnational faith, this must surely be seen as an immense leap forward. At least the locus of meaning is here understood to include the creaturely condition. Even though, in the thought of the reformers, creaturehood as such is neither the source of meaning nor its consummation, the human being is invited and enabled to discover intimations of its ultimate significance in the midst of these transient activities.

And yet, I would submit, the implications of this Reformation teaching about human vocation have by no means been explored and exploited in subsequent forms of Protestantism. Two factors have impeded their development: from the side of Protestant pietism and orthodoxy, a continuing fascination with the otherworldly destination of the soul (as suggested in the above reference to Protestant hymnology); and from the side of Protestant liberalism and secularism, the reduction of human purpose to self-fulfillment and the eventual divorce of vocational theory from theology.

With respect to the first deterrent, while Protestantism may have opened the teleological dimension of human existence to "all sorts and conditions" of human beings who could not or would not pursue a cenobitic path, in its more conservative expressions Protestantism has never seriously challenged the spiritualistic interpretation of human purpose. Despite the fact (in itself laudable enough) that Protestant interpretations of the faith have enabled "ordinary people" to consider their worldly occupations matters of obedience and participation in God's providential work, the notion has persisted in conventional Protestantism as in conventional Catholicism that the goal of the creature is reached, potentially, only in its postphysical or resurrection state. In this case, the same questions pertain as in the discussion of the monastic conception of human vocation.

The situation is rather more complex with regard to the second deterrent in the development of Protestant theologies of human purpose. From the Reformation, Protestant liberalism gladly endorsed the belief that human purpose encompasses the great variety of callings into which, as disciples of the Christ and according to our native gifts, we may be beckoned. Along the way, this endorsement of Reformation teaching produced some admirable, if never wholly unproblematic, practical results: it enabled many lay Christians to consider their vocations, offices, and activities veritable forms of ministry; it lent to the daily round, which otherwise was frequently tedious and trivial, a dimension of eternal significance; it produced in persons of means the awareness of their obligations to others less fortunate than themselves. For example, the practices of stewardship and philanthropy (the voluntary support of Christian and other institutions), which have been mainstays of North American church life, were born largely out of this vocational theology.

278

At the same time, this undoubtedly more incarnational conception of human purpose failed to address the problem at the heart of the teleological question as it applies to *anthropos*. That problem is never stated easily, for it is subtle and complex; but that it has to do with the self's preoccupation with itself seems confirmed not only by biblical thought but also by much modern psychology and psychiatry. The "cure of souls" biblically understood involves liberation from the bondage of the self and orientation toward "the other." As Jesus' summary of the law illustrates graphically, our purpose is to be found in love of God and the neighbor. But with its penchant for individualism, the mainstream of liberal Christianity encouraged instead the notion of *self*-fulfillment. It assumed that our human purpose is to actualize the potentiality of our being—to become the free beings that we have been created and redeemed to be, to attain intellectual and spiritual maturity, to acquire moral authenticity, and so on.

This approach to the meaning of life differs from the more classical approach, finally, only by transferring to the present life what in the latter is reserved for the afterlife. Whether through the soul's purification or through human self-fulfillment, the discussion of the *telos* of human life is still centered upon the self—and to the point that in both conservative and liberal versions of faith, it has always been difficult for Christians, especially Protestants, to avoid the taint of religious egoism and to espouse communality.[25] The appeal to self-interest is present, whether (with old orthodoxy) one posits that the goal of life is to get to heaven, or (with liberal humanism) one thinks it Christian to create for oneself a heaven on earth. Undoubtedly that danger is more conspicuous in liberalism, however; with its high interest in the individual, its loss of contact with older conceptions of radical sin and grace, and its general capitulation to the spirit of modernity, Christian liberalism tended to accentuate the this-worldly fulfillment of the self while classical anthropologies were obliged by their trans-worldly goal to curb the self's worldly ambitions.

Beyond that, liberalism eventually gave way to the secular spirit with which it (quite rightly) attempted to have discourse. Perhaps by the very nature of its enterprise, Christian liberalism was not able to inculcate a spirituality psychically

---

25. See Moltmann's helpful discussion of individuality and community in *The Way of Jesus Christ,* 269. Responding to a poll on the state of Christianity in Canada, Mark Parent writes: "Your poll results mask an important change that has been affecting Christianity ever since the French philosopher René Descartes uttered his momentous phrase—I think, therefore I am. 'God is alive' according to the poll because, in spite of media indifference, the vast majority of Canadians believe in God. This believing subject is what determines the existence of God, while the non-believing subject determines God's nonexistence. In the end, the various differences between 'believers' and 'nonbelievers' are not nearly as important as the similarity, which is that the domination of the self is *the* determiner of all reality, including the reality of God" (*Maclean's*, vol. 106, no. 17 [April 26, 1993], 4).

deep and intellectually profound enough to withstand the inroads of secularity, which increasingly insisted that it was possible to have all the human benefits of religious belief without the inconvenience of antiquated doctrine. Thus the belief that one's lifework is a divine calling gave way more and more to a purely intramundane understanding of vocation; and, while a vaguely religious aura still attends discussion of vocation within the churches, the whole area has virtually been taken over by society at large, mainly through the agency of the educational system, to the point that even the vocation to ordered ministry can be entertained without much theological reflection being attached to it.

In the next chapter, we shall return to the discussion of human vocation. For the present, what we have intended to establish in a critical way may be summarized as follows: (1) The tradition in both its classical and post-Reformation expressions has on the whole assumed that human purpose is a predicate of human being, and that our calling, therefore, is to actualize the superior being that has been vouchsafed to us; (2) in the process of inculcating this conception of human purpose and vocation, however, it has been overlooked by both conservative and liberal versions of such theo-anthropology that *self*-fulfillment may contradict in fundamental ways the biblical ethic of love; besides (3), it fails to speak to a humanity that—as we shall go on to elucidate—may be more skeptical about the validity of schemes for the enhancement of the self than about any other single aspect of human experience.

20. The Humiliation of "The New Adam"

20.1. The Situation: A Basic Confusion. To summarize the argument of this chapter to the present: I have advanced the hypothesis that the general impact of Christian testimony to the human condition has been to inculcate a high conception of the human. By "high" I mean an image of humanity accentuating those qualities or virtues that are generally regarded as desirable; if they are not universally so regarded, they have certainly dominated the anthropological assumptions of the Western world. To speak concretely, a high *imago hominis* upholds such endowments as a superior intelligence, freedom of will, power to facilitate and achieve the goals determined by intelligence and will, domination of "lower" forms of life, leadership in the human community, control of bodily passions and instincts, the maintenance of good order in human affairs, the cultivation of calm in the face of the unforeseen and undesirable, and the effective transmission of all such virtues, through education, to the young.

It is not my intention here to deprecate these and similar attributes. On the whole they may be considered admirable, even noble. I want rather to draw attention to the underlying assumption upon which this entire approach to the question, What is truly human? depends. It is that the essence of human being is to be located in qualities of being for which we have special aptitude, if they are not inherent in our very makeup. It is also presupposed that these qualities may be diminished by other, negating qualities or propensities. Authentic humanity, it is assumed, is achieved through the displacement of negative qualities by the cultivation and enhancement of positive qualities of being.

As we have seen, this procedure almost invariably entails a comparative approach: the human is defined over against the "less than human," the "lower" forms of life, which do not and cannot possess these exalted characteristics. In pursuing this line of thought, we might also have explored (as did most premodern theologies) alleged forms of life "higher" than the human: celestial beings. Such an investigation would undoubtedly have shown that the reason why medieval and other theological conventions could regard angelic creatures as being more exalted than humans is that the former are incorporeal. While there has existed a long tradition, popularized in the Anglo-Saxon world by Milton, concerning fallen angels, the hidden assumption in angelology having particular significance for Christian anthropology is that the (relative) sinlessness of angels is due to their purely spiritual character. Because they are not terrestrial creatures, weighed down as it were by their physicality, angels are more fully in possession of the intellectual and spiritual virtues that, according to the dominant tradition, constitute the human soul and essence.

What this type of thought assumes at its most foundational, in other words, is that the purpose of human life is to maximize the intellectual-spiritual dispositions that constitute its essence and, concomitantly, to minimize the vices or denigrating qualities with which humanity is associated on account of its bodily nature. The goal of terrestrial life is thus to pass through the stage of existence in such a way as to actualize and preserve, so far as possible, one's spiritual essence and so to enhance the prospect of membership in the communion of saints.

Protestantism, it is true, called in question the principle of salvation by works, with which this ideal too readily became associated, as well as many of the rituals and myths by which it was supported and implemented. Significantly, also, Protestantism shrunk from defining angelic beings in the highly speculative manner proposed by Dionysius the Areopagite and others, and maintained, in relation to angelology, a rather consistent agnosticism. Yet Protestantism did not succeed, it seems to me, in challenging deeply the fundamental ontological assumption that the truly human is to be defined in spiritualistic terms. While the externalities of Protestant and Catholic forms of piety can make the two seem very different from each other, internally they are far less distinguishable. Between (say) the Methodist doctrine of sanctification and Roman Catholic rites for the purification of the soul there is little substantive difference.

This is not to say that the Protestant movement presented no alternatives to existing conceptions of human nature and purpose. Luther's doctrine of justification by grace through faith, Calvin's theology of the covenant, and Wycliffe's critique of *dominium,* to name only three aspects of the movement, imply anthropologies quite different from the one that I am characterizing here. Yet Protestantism as represented in these and related teachings seems not to have been strong enough to displace the hierarchic ontology that found the purpose of human life in the successful actualization of "high" spiritual-intellectual-volitional qualities over against temptations accruing from our "lower," "animal" nature. In all of Christian history, it is extremely rare to find unqualified and joyous affirmations of creaturely life in its inextricable admixture of spiritual and bodily realities.

The consequence of this predilection to hierarchic ontologies that place spirit at the top and matter at the bottom of the ladder of being—at least, the particular consequence that concerns us here—is that the whole undertaking ends in a basic confusion: it confuses the meaning (*telos*) of human life with its alleged value on the scale of being. If, as we have argued, there is little discussion within the dominant traditions of Christian belief concerning the calling or vocation of human existence within the creaturely sphere, it is at bottom because the shapers of the tradition could on the whole simply assume that it was sufficient as a vocation for human beings to *be*—that is, to make good their essential identity as spiritual beings; to maintain, or regain—against every temptation toward the "lower" impulses—their high position within the ranks of the creatures of God. The fate of women in both Catholic and Protestant ecclesiastical settings (though in differing ways) is the most concrete and notorious evidence of this assumption; for women, it was almost universally believed, could only with the greatest difficulty overcome their physicality sufficiently to attain full spirituality of being.

In claiming that such an anthropology represents the general impact of Christianity upon church and society, I am not affirming that this is the Christian anthropological tradition. On the contrary, as I shall seek to demonstrate in the constructive chapter that follows this, I believe that it must be adjudged a fundamental distortion of at least the most weighty and contextually relevant elements of biblical testimony to the nature and destiny of humanity, as well as to those minority traditions that throughout Christian history have attempted to be faithful to the tradition of Jerusalem. As with the doctrine of God, so with anthropological theology: radical alternatives are present in minority and submerged professions of faith, and these, if pursued with imagination, can become our best sources of both critical and constructive theological reflection today. The "Father Almighty" is not the only deity familiar to this tradition, however dominant "He" may have been throughout the history of Christendom. Nor is the "almighty son" the only alternative that we have to work with when it comes to professing our belief about the human enterprise, as Christians.

We shall only be inspired to search these alternative traditions, however, if we realize at some rudimentary level of imagination the limited, dangerous, and finally irrelevant nature of so much that has dominated the mind of historic Christendom and is still today put forward and received by millions as if it were indisputable Christian orthodoxy. We shall have to be brought to the awareness that we are living in a society, many of whose gravest problems have been exacerbated if not actually created by supposedly Christian attitudes toward life, before we shall want and need to ask whether there are other attitudes that might more legitimately claim the distinction of being Christian. We shall have to suspect that such phenomena as white racism, male chauvinism, patriarchy, intolerance of sexual difference, class consciousness and upward mobility, the justification of capitalistic enterprise, the segregation of the aged and infirm, and numerous other aspects of everyday life in North America have their roots in that same "high" anthropology that we have been exploring here. Beyond that, we shall have to ask ourselves whether the quest for technological mastery of the natural order, the engineering of all forms of bodily existence including reproduction, and the continued naive idealism and boastfulness at work in our societies are not also directly or indirectly fired by this same allegedly high anthropology.

But above all we shall have to become more conscious than most of us seem to be of the fact that this anthropological doctrine no longer truly engages us. Or, to be more exact, that its impact upon us is the impact of an oppressive past, whose oppressiveness lies, not in its intrinsic persuasiveness, but in the fact that it still functions as the undergirding anthropic philosophy of our society and is still upheld, perhaps with increasing militancy, by elements of our society that are served by it or are fearful of questioning it.

Yet it does not engage us; it does not address us where we are and as we are, because it is the ideology of Prometheus and we have become a type of Sisyphus. This ideology offers us nothing, it only demands something of us; and all that it can demand, whether in sophisticated or crass forms, is that we should again become Prometheus: that we should stand up and be "Men"; that we should "make America great again"; that we should get hold of our families, give leadership in our communities, subdue our enemies (now perceived, not as the Russians but, perhaps, as Japanese and German entrepreneurs), rein in our passions, tighten our belts, jog with our presidents, excel in mathematics and science, clear our heads of drink and drugs, put some iron into our wills, and so on. In short, it can address us only as law and not as gospel. It has no gospel for a failed Prometheus.

20.2. Capable of Failure.[26]   The human being, wrote Paul Ricoeur, is "capable of failing."[27] Tillich put it more strongly still: "there is only one alternative to life with failure, and that is lifelessness without failure."[28] It is just this capability that the Christian conception of humanity as we have inherited and appropriated it has been unable to communicate to us. Or rather, to state the matter more precisely, what our Christian anthropology has not been able to do for us is to incorporate the experience of radical failure into itself in such a way that we might find in it a framework of meaning for our actual failures.

What I intend here by "failure," however, needs to be clarified. It could be heard to connote moral failure, and that would be wrong. Christianity as we have practiced it on this continent is filled to the brim with the recognition of all sorts of moral failures and—it goes without saying—prescriptions for their overcoming. The preaching and worship of the churches are almost universally premised upon the propensity of human beings to moral imperfection and decline, with variations according to the brand of ecclesiastical and societal identity. This in no way fills the vacuum to which I am referring here, however, because the sense of not measuring up to a moral ideal reinforces precisely the ideal. Without the ideal, there would be no failure; and every actual failure, when it is recognized as such, confirms the rectitude of the ideal.

Again, failure could mean the failure to attain a more inclusive goal—not only living up to a moral code but embodying some model of human perfection such as one based upon reasonable rather than emotional behavior, or exemplifying altruistic rather than selfish concern, or manifesting spiritual rather than materialistic impulses. This too evades my meaning. With this type of failure too North American Christianity is familiar, and its ministrations are often intended precisely to reinforce such a sense of failure and to assuage it. "Jesus," in fact, regularly stands for the superior type of humanity intended by such patterns. In the light of ecclesiastical testimony to his perfect humanity, we are to understand that we have failed; but by the same token we become candidates for the grace that the church offers through the mediation of his divinity.

When I refer to the failure that Christendom has not equipped us either to acknowledge or to cope with, I mean something quite different from the sense

---

26. The concerns expressed in this section began to occupy my thought from the early 1970s, and in particular when I noticed the superficial manner in which a serious theological work like Moltmann's *A Theology of Hope* was received on this continent—namely, as reconfirmation of our official optimism. The cultural analysis that I began to develop in *Lighten Our Darkness* (Philadelphia: Westminster Press, 1976), the appropriateness of which has continued to impress itself upon me in the nearly two decades since that work was published, drew heavily on "a theology of failure"—my initial choice for the title of that book (see particularly pp. 15, 111, 170, 211f., 227–29).

27. *Fallible Man,* trans. C. Kelbley (Chicago: Regnery, 1965), 223.

28. *Perspectives on 19th and 20th Century Protestant Theology* (New York: Harper & Row, 1967), 92.

of falling short of a goal, whether a moral ideal or a model of human being more broadly conceived. Although the term is overworked, the failure in question could be called existential failure; what I have in mind is the failure to regard ourselves as being in the first place significant enough to entertain seriously the high ideals and goals that Christian civilization has sculpted for us. I mean the failure even to manifest the residue of idealism that would be necessary in order to regard ourselves as failures. Conventional Christianity on this continent has fostered an exalted image of the human being and, as we have seen, it reinforces this high image *via negativa* even in its doctrine of sin. What most Christianity has not anticipated and does not know how to confront is a mentality that doubts not only our essential exaltedness but also our existential distortion of the exalted essence. This mentality does not find credible, to begin with, such a high conception of the human.

To formulate the same thought in other words: Christianity—especially Christianity in its New World forms—located human purpose in the alleged superior status of the human creature vis-à-vis all other terrestrial forms of created life. But much of contemporary humanity does not perceive itself so. If anything, it is prone to regard itself as inferior to many forms of life, and even to its own invention—the complex machine, in all of its evolving manifestations; or, if not inferior, then certainly on a par with all the rest. What purpose remains for a creature that was taught to value its being and to find its meaning within that being, when it can no longer take the first step and value its own being?

Thus in its most abbreviated form the failure in question is a failure to perceive human life as being purposeful; but it must be understood that the loss of purpose is bound up with the loss of value—that is, with the existential devaluation introduced by the effective reduction of the human to the status of other terrestrial forms of life. And this is a new kind of failure, at least in the sense that it is widely felt—so new in the North American experience, in fact, that it is far more widely *felt* than either articulated or acted upon.

To be sure, the suspicion of our essential purposelessness has never been wholly absent from human consciousness. Fortunately for faith, its reality as part of human consciousness is forthrightly acknowledged in Scripture—particularly in the so-called pessimistic wisdom literature (which is precisely the reason why it has been dubbed pessimistic):

I said in my heart with regard to human beings that God is testing them to show that they are but animals. For the fate of humans and the fate of animals is the same; as one dies, so dies the other. They all have the same breath, and humans have no advantage over the animals; for all is vanity. All go to one place; all are from the dust, and all turn to dust again. Who knows whether the human spirit goes upward and the spirit of animals goes downward to the earth? (Eccles. 3:18-21)

285

Such a frank and open questioning of human purpose is rare, however, even in the Bible; and it is far rarer in the long history of Christendom—excepting, of course, when it is accompanied by an otherworldliness that immediately cancels the shock of it by offering the afterlife as goal and compensation. Yet this deep sense of existential failure is entertained far and wide in our context. It is perhaps the characteristic feature of our *Zeitgeist,* the color of our despair. European Christianity at its best has come to terms with it, at least in the sense of having recognized its reality. The majority forms of North American Christianity have failed even to suspect, let alone recognize and name this failure. Worse still, most of our middle-class Christianity is devoted to the repression of any such thought before it even becomes thought.

20.3. The *Skandalon* of Faith Today: Our High Anthropology. What we are claiming, to employ yet another concept, is that the cutting edge of the *skandalon* of the gospel in our present context is associated with the profound questioning of the meaningfulness of the human project that—silently but effectively—informs our society. That the Christian gospel should evoke any kind of scandal is itself an idea that, in our context, seems incongruous. From its origin in Catholic and Protestant settlements and well into the twentieth century, North American society has looked upon the Christian faith as an almost natural phenomenon, and the gospel as a positive and desirable message: "good news," after all. Little discussion of the biblical concept of faith's "scandal" has taken place even within the circles of academic theology, and it is a theme almost wholly foreign to popular forms of the Christian religion on this continent. Yet the Bible, supposedly the charter of our Christian civilization, is full of testimony to human offense at the presence of God and the consequent and perennial human rejection of the divine.

Skandalon is thus by no means an incidental theme of the Scriptures, and especially in the newer Testament it is at the very heart of the story that is told. It colors the central event of the Gospel narrative: the incarnation, passion, death, and resurrection of the Christ. "Scandal" refers to the human response to God's initiative in the work of redemption—a response of universal resistance and rejection. The scandal is enacted in the rejection of Jesus by his friends and followers, not only by his enemies. It refers not only to Roman, and certainly not only to Jewish, rejection, but to rejection as a *human*—no, as *the* human—response to divine grace, command, and invitation. Scripture assumes that the initial, spontaneous, and honest response of human beings to the approach of God will be one of rejection and deep offense.

For St. Paul, who introduced the word *skandalon* to biblical faith[29] (although he did not invent the idea), the scandal of the gospel—that is, the point

---

29. Especially 1 Cor. 1:23; Gal. 5:11.

at which the world's incredulity and even its wrath are aroused, no doubt because it hits home—is the cross of Jesus. Paul understood that what was for him the very core of the kerygma, "Jesus Christ and him crucified" (1 Cor. 2:2), constitutes a terrible affront to the human soul, more particularly to the religious mentality. For that mentality conceives of deity in the highest possible terms and here, at Golgotha, God defines God's very being in a way that human religious aspiration finds wholly inglorious. In a Christ whose way is the way of the cross, God identifies God's person with the human condition at its lowest, weakest, and most vulnerable. There is in short a complete reversal of expectations, and this reversal challenges not only human preconceptions of the divine but also and simultaneously human presuppositions about authentic humanity. For here God does not choose to enter into fellowship with the successful but with failed and broken human beings—the Messiah of God crucified between thieves! The *skandalon* is the offensive idea that the high and holy God of the most profound of religious traditions (the Judaic), the transcendent one of the most penetrating of philosophic traditions (the Hellenic), should submit to everything that is the antithesis of glory, honor, and power in order to be God-with-us.

This is for Paul the central kerygmatic fact of the evangel, and no apologia can ever overcome it. That is to say, no rational explanation can circumvent this fundamental offense to the human spirit; and whenever in Christian history such an apologetic has seemed to present itself, those who have paid attention to the unfolding drama of the Bible have had to become suspicious of that apologetic. This is what was at the heart of Luther's protest against medieval scholasticism; it was at the heart of Barth's and Niebuhr's protest against the spirit of neo-Protestantism; and it is at the heart of the protest today of radical liberationist theologies against entrenched forms of Christian triumphalism. *Skandalon* is a quality that lies deep within the Christian theological enterprise as a whole, but it manifests itself in different ways in different contexts.

Let us be concrete: In the nineteenth century, what many people experienced as the scandal of the Christian message was the discrepancy between the lofty expectations of the leading classes of Europeans and North Americans in that era and what, from the standpoint of those same expectations, people could only consider a far too negative assessment of human nature and destiny coloring traditional Christianity. Although they had inherited their peculiarly Western Prometheanism in part from the very religious tradition that they now criticized, they wished to eliminate from that relatively positive assessment of human potential the reservations by which, in their view, it was qualified. For the dominant spirit of that age, "Man" was a worthy being indeed, almost a god. "He" was this, moreover, in "his" own right: the seeds of humanity's evolving perfection were as it were contained within the species. Christians, on the other hand, were perceived as guardians of a tradition that not only located the secret of human grandeur in a source external to the creature, but also contained dark symbols like the demonic, spiritual death, the tragic, sin, and wrath. This was an embarrassment to many Christians themselves; and so a Christian avant garde set to work to expunge from the profession of faith everything that made it offensive to that optimistic age. As we have recognized in the earlier discussion of Reinhold Niebuhr, a special target of this renovation of the faith was the elimination of the doctrine of original sin.

This is one way of dealing with the *skandalon* of the gospel: to attempt to eliminate the most offensive elements, so as to make the faith more appealing to the anthropological and other preconceptions of the "high culture" of the age. This attempt frequently fails, however, because the most perceptive people will be well aware of what is being done. Nietzsche, that most far-seeing of nineteenth-century "misevangelists" (Rosenstock-Huessy), was not at all fooled by the attempts of Christian liberals to hide the scandal of the cross. He knew that the Christ is a figure of little glory, and that efforts to render him in heroic proportions go against the grain of biblical evidence. Between the newer Testament's Jesus Christ and Nietzsche's *Uebermensch* (Superman) there is no resemblance, and Nietzsche, the child of the *Pfarrhaus* (rectory), knew it. He despised Christianity precisely because it had to place at the center of its profession what he regarded as a despicable symbol of human weakness and failure. Nietzsche's alternative was a secular messiah who could only appear after the "death of God," when human beings had become bold enough to take charge of their own destiny.

But historical contexts are never static, they are always in flux. Moreover, as we recognized at the beginning of this chapter, high images of the human seem regularly to beget low images. Today the image of the human with which those who profess the faith of the Christ have to dialogue is by no means one of a godlike superhumanity. It is more like the antithesis of all that. For our period the discrepancy is not between the culture's great expectations and Christian knowledge of human contingency, mortality, and sinfulness; rather, it is between the high conception of human nature and destiny that we inherit as Christians and the overt erosion of human expectation. The optimistic secular society of the nineteenth and early twentieth centuries heard the Christians saying that the human situation was finally so impossible that only God incarnate could redeem it. The discouraged and sometimes jaded late-twentieth-century societies of the West hear Christians professing that human life is so significant that God would die to redeem it.

This, I believe, is how we must view the character of the *skandalon* of the gospel today. Its cutting edge is located in Christian anthropology. It is precisely our high anthropological doctrine that seems so incredible to our contemporaries—and even to ourselves. The form of our "unbelief"—the place where the scandal of the cross grasps us—is that we can hardly bring ourselves to believe that the human creature is so significant as to warrant such an assessment as that implied both in creation and redemption theologies and (*via negativa*) in our hamartiology.

This applies, moreover, to all types of Christian anthropology—liberal, conservative, and every shade between. While we have acknowledged the great variety of views that have been put forward as Christian assessments of the human condition, they all in one way or another contain the distinction between essence and existence, authentic and inauthentic, potentiality and actuality. One could generalize about them all in the following way: The human creature is intended for a life to which, in its actual existing, it has not attained. This is a modest and even rather innocuous generalization, but if we tried to introduce the more interesting nuances that would have to be present if we intended to speak for this or that specific tradition, the contrast between essence and existence would be even more pronounced. The point is, even without such nuances, the generalization runs headlong into the doubting spirit of the age.

The scandal begins at the mention of intention. It is terribly hard for people in our time to hold onto any declaration which affirms that human beings are heirs to an essence that transcends their existence. In the age of Auschwitz and Hiroshima and all the subsequent horrors that, like those two names, stand for the apparent cheapness of human life; in the age of massive famines, impossible national debts, and death squads, when lives are determined by apparently capricious yet invincible forces over which individuals have no power whatever; in an age of ecological catastrophes and the prospect of an uninhabitable planet, when every child must reckon with the thought of human regress and possible extinction: who can grasp and sustain, day after day, faith in the human project? Death is all around us. It has become so familiar that it hardly shocks anyone that our news broadcasts are forever full of it. One suspects that the average evening television news today would have left our great-grandparents speechless. Death is so normative for us that violence vies with sex as the main metaphor of our entertainment. And now we know that this means not only the death of individuals; it means the present and prospective death of species—of the nonhuman species, which already succumb (we are told) at a rate of a species per day, but also of our own species's possible extinction, an eventuality which is taken for granted by many and has already perhaps replaced survival as the primary symbol of our thought about the future.

To reiterate: All of this is complicated in North America by our prior commitment to and captivation by the rhetoric of progress. Here, where we have little or nothing to fall back on, people continue to mouth the optimistic credo of modernity, though few are able to do this persuasively. Public figures continue to act out the parts that our modern past has written for them. Leaders of state in both of the northern countries of this continent appear, predictably, with smiles and exaggeratedly positive messages—and the more problematic the actual state of these nations becomes, the more exaggerated are their smiles and their messages. The United States is gravely threatened economically and morally; Canada is at this moment contemplating the prospect of national disintegration. Yet ironically the public of both countries insists upon leaders who will present only slightly altered versions of the theme of unending progress—most recently under the rubric of globalization in trade and commerce. The same leaders who are elected to office because of their apparently positive personal images are within a short time despised for their naiveté or downright falseness of character. We do not believe in ourselves, so we cannot believe in our leaders either, or in the ever-changing platforms (not, please, *philosophies*) of the political parties they represent.

20.4. Covert Nihilism in the North American Psyche Today. To *profess* Christian faith today is to *confess* the meaningfulness of existence. For this reason Christians who have more than a superficial awareness of and concern for the contemporary North American context inevitably find themselves in a strange, unfamiliar position. In the face of the growing cynicism about the human project characterizing our society, we discover, often to our own surprise, that it is necessary for us to defend the human enterprise—and with greater regularity, perhaps, than we are called upon in direct ways to defend any other aspect of our profession of belief. We must be advocates of humanity in order to be advocates of the Deity in whom we trust. We must contend for the creation if we are to be faithful to the creator. There can be no authentic Christian profession of trust in God today that is not simultaneously a profession of trust in life itself. For in a society where the life of creation is threatened, physically and spiritually, to bear witness to "the Lord and Giver of Life" is to bear witness to the essential goodness and purposefulness of the life that has been and is being given: "All things came into being through him. . . . in him was life, and the life was the light of all people" (John 1:3-4a).

This, I say, constitutes a new experience for Christians everywhere, but more conspicuously so in North America. Heretofore the champions of the human project, of history, of the future, of life itself have been humanists, idealists, and rationalists, many of them children of the Enlightenment who looked askance upon religion. "The religious" among us have felt it our responsibility to retain a place for God in the midst of a culture so full of praise for humanity that, despite its exceptional religiosity, it was constantly tempted to dispense with God in all but name. For the majority of North Americans today, God is perhaps still more rhetorical than real; but the object of our deepest skepticism now, I think, is humanity. Suddenly those who believe in God know that they must also learn how to believe in humanity, and help humanity to believe in itself—not, hopefully, in the old way of Promethean bravado, but in a chastened, modest way to cherish life itself, the life of creatures.

Never before has the Christian mission been so directly related to the stewardship of life; for never before has the disciple community had to confront so directly the reign of death: death, not only and not even chiefly in the form of physical demise, but death as a pervasive force and spiritual influence; death as the loss of a positive and exuberant will to be; death as human cynicism and passivity—as a sometimes almost palpable corporate *Todestrieb* (death wish). It is the corporate character of this death wish that renders the situation different from the past. Individual cynics and detractors of life have always been present; but the capitulation to sheer existence that now moves our civilization, the out-of-hand dismissal of essence or intentionality by vast numbers of people, the loss of a capacity to dream: this constitutes a new apologetic phenomenon. It is all the more insidious in our context because it is concealed, for the most part, beneath its oratorical opposite—our official optimism.

The discerning among our immediate Christian predecessors knew that they had to profess their faith in the face of widespread secularity and one-dimensionality. Some of them realized that secularism itself was already a stage on the way to ultimate skepticism. Tillich, for example, contrasted his concept of "theomony" with the "self-complacent autonomy [of secularity that] cuts the ties of a civilization with its ground and aim, whereby, in the measure in which it succeeds, a civilization becomes exhausted and empty."[30] Yet for Tillich, as even more unambiguously for some theologians who later actually celebrated "the secular city," secularity could be appreciated as the vehicle of the holy:

> Everything secular is implicitly related to the holy. It can become the bearer of the holy. The divine can become manifest in it. Nothing is essentially and inescapably secular. Everything has the dimension of depth, and in the moment in which the third dimension is actualized, holiness appears. Everything secular is potentially sacred, open to consecration.[31]

The situation today seems to me conspicuously changed. It is perhaps a dimension of the difference between the two halves of the present century, to which reference was made earlier. While certainly minorities embrace or exemplify the affirmation that "everything secular is potentially sacred"—while indeed the pervasiveness of secular hedonism and cynicism may have provoked

---

30. Paul Tillich, *The Protestant Era,* trans. James Luther Adams (Chicago: Univ. of Chicago Press, 1948), xvi; see also 281.

31. Ibid., vol. 1, 218. In an earlier work, Tillich could even speak about "Protestant secularism" (*The Protestant Era,* 219f.).

new attempts to revive the sacred—the one-dimensionality that was courted by secularism from the middle of the nineteenth century onwards has become more visible, less hospitable to the dimension of the holy. Tillich's sentence, "Nothing is essentially and inescapably secular," simply does not ring true now. Whether it did so in 1951 is already a question; Sartre and Samuel Beckett would have rejected it even then. But half a century later the process of "becoming more and more empty or materialistic without any ultimate concern" has advanced well beyond the immediate postwar situation. This is particularly noticeable in North America, which in spite of its materialism was able to retain at least the external marks of Christian spirituality long after Europe had succumbed to open secularity.

For our current apologetic situation, especially as it relates to humanity, history, and hope, the term *secularism* seems too bland. I suspect that *nihilism* would be more accurate.[32]

But we must exercise caution here. Very few North Americans would be blatant enough to espouse such a position. Nihilism is not only a foreign concept, a term with which, in the first place, only intellectuals are familiar; it describes a phenomenon that is foreign to our whole way of life. If it is to be useful at all in analyzing contemporary North American culture, subtle distinctions will have to be drawn.

Such distinctions were in fact offered in a little-known postwar work of the German theologian Helmuth Thielicke. It is my opinion that Thielicke's analysis can help us to understand North America today—though it was hardly applicable to our society at the time of the book's publication.[33]

Thielicke distinguished between two types of nihilism: overt and covert. Overt nihilism was the nihilism of nineteenth-century anarchists who, to use Nietzsche's characterization of them, announced: "What is falling should be pushed over."[34] As in the work that first used the term nihilism (*Fathers and Sons,* by the great Russian novelist Ivan Turgenev [1818–83]),[35] the overt

---

32. Moltmann speaks about "the nihilistic feeling about life which dominates [in particular] so many people in our mass cities." (*God in Creation,* 23.)

As early as 1969, the late George P. Grant, in his profound analysis of Nietzsche, could write: ". . . if we look at the crisis of the modern world through Nietzsche's eyes, and see them above all as the end of two millenia of rational man, we can see that those crises have come to North America later than to Europe. But now that they have come, they are here with intensity. . . . At the height of our present imperial destiny, the crisis of the end of modern rationalism falls upon us ineluctably. In Nietzsche's words: 'the wasteland grows.' The last men and the nihilists are everywhere in North America" (*Time as History* [Toronto: Canadian Broadcasting Corporation, 1969], 34–35).

33. Helmuth Thielicke, *Nihilism: Its Origin and Nature, With a Christian Answer,* trans. John W. Doberstein (New York: Harper & Row, 1961), see esp. chap. 3, pp. 30ff.

34. Friedrich Nietzsche, *Thus Spake Zarathustra,* in *The Portable Nietzsche,* ed. Walter Kaufmann (New York: Viking Press, 1954), 129.

35. Ivan Sergeyevich Turgenev, *Fathers and Sons,* trans. and ed. Ralph E. Matlaw (New York: W.W. Norton, 1989).

nihilist of Thielicke's description is one who not only believes that the present order is worth nothing but acts upon this belief, obliterating whatever remains of the facade of civilization.

Such nihilism is easily recognized. It has no desire to camouflage itself; it wants to be recognized. But, said Thielicke, it is therefore not nearly so insidious as another type of nihilism that is, in reality, far more prevalent in our time: covert nihilism. This is the nihilism of those who would never admit to being nihilistic. It is a nihilism that is afraid of itself. Indeed it often masquerades beneath its rhetorical opposite. It does not "push things over"; it may even seem to build up, to edify. But its characteristic internal posture is indifference. Like the mysterious figure in Elie Wiesel's *The Town beyond the Wall*,[36] covert nihilism stands at the window and watches the activity of the destroyers. It practices detachment, noninvolvement, "value-free" investigation. In universities and think-tanks, it cultivates the stance of objective Research; that is, it shuns commitment. In the public sphere, it translates into apathy and "psychic numbing" (Robert Lifton) and the loss of "expectancy" (Christopher Lasch). It does not show up in the world as the annihilator; it may even seem to conserve.

Many comfortable middle-class people who inhabit "nice" suburban areas or gentrified inner-city quarters today do not look like nihilists, but many of them are described accurately by Thielicke's category of covert nihilism. While surrounding themselves with good things and pursuing "happiness," they have ceased to expect any good thing for the public realm. Many do not even bother to vote. Their private projects are personal survival tactics undertaken in the company of an encompassing disbelief in the future of society; or perhaps they are just diversions. For in the last analysis, Thielicke's covert nihilists are pretty well identical with Nietzsche's "last men," who say, as "they blink," "We have invented happiness."[37]

The difference between the covert and the overt nihilists is in part a difference of self-knowledge. Covert nihilists are "covert" because they hide from themselves the knowledge of their own nihilism. They are masters and mistresses of repression. They cannot bear to think that they are devoid of operative ethical norms, and so they speak frequently about their "values." They dare not admit their own spiritual emptiness, and therefore they are even found in churches and contemporary substitutes for churches. Above all they repress all awareness of their own proneness to violence, and therefore they bemoan the overt violence of their towns and cities. Since our cities really are increasingly characterized by every type of violence, these secret nihilists are easily

---

36. Elie Wiesel, *Town beyond the Wall* (New York: Holt, Rinehart and Winston, 1967).
37. *Thus Spake Zarathustra,* 129.

distracted from reflection upon their own repressed violence. But as they do nothing to alter the conditions that make for overt violence in their cities, but turn their heads the other way when it comes near, one may well ask who is destroying our cities after all: the few who "push over what is falling" or the many who "invent" private happiness?

But it is easy to accuse, and Christians cannot be satisfied with accusation. Change can only be fostered by understanding, not accusation. If nihilism is at work in North American society today, we must pay more attention to the reason for it than to the phenomenon itself. Nihilism is a response to something else. What I have been proposing in this chapter is that it is a response to a massive loss of meaning. Covert nihilism is the form of this response taken by those who do not have the courage or the wisdom openly to acknowledge that they have ceased to hope. They need to continue to indulge the habit of hope long after its reality has flown from them; otherwise they would not be able to function at all. Yet the field of vision even for this habitudinal hope narrows itself in proportion to the failure of public goals and institutions. It becomes increasingly private. People do not feel that as human beings they are heirs to a civilizational vision and project that transcends their personal histories. They do not hear themselves called to anything purposeful. Often enough, even their own personal existence fails to elicit from them a sense of the mystery and meaningfulness of life; and that is hardly surprising, for it is difficult—perhaps impossible—to sustain private hopes without the corroboration of more expansive social visions.

There is no way of proving such an analysis. For every statistical survey of opinion, a conflicting survey may be found. For every sociological account of our spiritual emptiness, a defense of our high civilizational "gains" may be produced. As we have recognized from the outset, to try to understand the present—one's context—is to find oneself at every turn in the valley of decision. On the basis of the criteria for comprehending contexts established in the first volume, however, it seems to me that Christians in North America today must at least reckon with the probability that, despite the prolongation of the rote optimism of our past, the spirit of our present society verges increasingly on covert nihilism.

Even if this is an overstatement, it must be contemplated seriously by anyone who wishes to profess the faith in this context. For the Christian community that refuses a priori to entertain such a social analysis will almost certainly end by contributing to the perpetuation of the problem. Covert nihilism thrives on nothing so much as sentimental, positive religion. Christianity that rehearses all the predictable values of middle-class existence, examines only a few private sins, and offers the comforts of religion for every hurt is perhaps the most effective agency of repression at work in North America today. It enables millions to conceal from themselves and one another the foundationless character of their daily lives. A church that only knows how to reiterate liberal or conservative versions of the high anthropology of the Christian past and does not allow itself to explore with its people the abyss of meaninglessness over which their lives are being lived serves neither God nor humanity.

21. The Corrective

21.1. On Telling the Truth.[38] The characteristic response of those who sense—a little—the extent of the malaise of our American and Canadian societies is to call for action. From every quarter, especially from our politicians, we hear a familiar refrain, endlessly repeated: We must learn to believe in America again! The cry is taken up by educators, business leaders, and many ecclesiastics. As we expressed it earlier, this approach, whatever its specifics, almost always translates metaphorically into the exhortation, "Let Sisyphus become again Prometheus!"

Christians who have any genuine awareness of the biblical and Reformation distinction between law and gospel will know that such an exhortation is finally absurd and useless. If it is cleverly done—as it often is in an age of subtle and effective technological manipulation of public opinion—it may for a time sway some of the people; and thus it will postpone for a little while longer the meeting with truth that this kind of moral suasion always attempts to avoid.

But authentic morality only comes to existence on the other side of the meeting with truth. No matter how painful truth may be (and truth is always, in some measure, painful), it must be faced. Apart from that encounter, exhortations to change and action can only reflect the general confusion and, so far as the most sensitive or victimized members of a society are concerned, can only beg the question, Why? Prescriptions for cure depend upon honest descriptions of the sickness that needs curing. Christopher Lasch has expressed this straightforwardly and well in a 1989 article for the *New York Times*:

> There is only one cure for the malady that afflicts our culture, and that is *to speak the truth about it*. Once we can bring ourselves to do that, it will be time to worry about "constructive solutions," "practical proposals," and "social alternatives" for our young—discussion of which, so long as it is so absurdly premature, serves only to distract our attention from the truth about ourselves.[39]

21.2. Truth-Telling and the Churches. Lasch's insightful and timely statement, which informs his own attempts at truth-telling in his larger written

---

38. See Dietrich Bonhoeffer, *Ethics*, trans. Neville Herman Smith (London: S.C.M. Press, 1955), Part 5: "What Is Meant by 'Telling the Truth?'"

39. Carried by the *International Herald Tribune* under the caption, "Give Youth Cause to Believe in Tomorrow" (Dec. 29, 1989), 7 (emphasis added).

works, prompts two observations from the side of Christian theology. The first is one of gratitude, because he reminds us here of the prophetic office of faith according to the Judeo-Christian tradition, and this is a reminder that cannot too often find expression in a North American context. For here, not only among Christians and Jews but throughout the society conditioned, in part, by cultural Christianity and Judaism, the prophetic office of truth-telling has been (to say the least) muted. As we have maintained at various points throughout this study, North Americans, whether religious, nonreligious, or postreligious, understand the function of religion to be primarily that of providing solace, on the one hand, and confirmation of the fundamental values of the dominant culture on the other. According to this understanding, comfort and not truth should govern the life of the churches—private comfort for private ills, and public comfort for public ills. The great offense of the churches and synagogues—an offense that they commit, to be sure, all too rarely—is when they place truth before comfort, particularly public comfort.

Examples of what I mean by this are the various recent pronouncements of Episcopal and other councils on unemployment, poverty, sexual harassment, warfare, and the environment. Invariably such statements are met with scorn from the public sector. How could bishops understand the intricacies of economics or international relations? What do church councils know about the job market? What these scornful declamations really mean is that the religious community has, in the view of its critics, stepped out of line. It is not abiding by the long-standing rules of the cultural establishment. The church's task is not to criticize the other institutions of the established order, but to provide them with whatever transcendental sanctioning is still viable.

But the office of truth-telling is not only looked upon with disfavor by the other members of the establishment, it is also hardly understood—let alone consistently practiced—within the churches themselves. The majority of Christians in North America are in fact just as incensed by critical ecclesiastical pronouncements about the economy, war, or women's rights as are those who do not belong to the churches. Clergy and laity alike, on the whole, would be far more comfortable if their leadership were to refrain entirely from discussing "touchy" issues, even when these issues have grown to such proportions that they affect everyone. That the churches should even dare to address the reality of homosexuality, let alone inquire in their courts whether gay men and women should be allowed to exercise ordered ministry: this seems to many—I suspect to the majority—wholly uncalled for. For in this way the church draws attention to what are generally considered negative aspects of our society, when its function is to smooth away such wrinkles in the body politic by accentuating positive values. Certainly the church may comfort the individuals who are afflicted by AIDS—that falls within the pastoral office. But to enter the public arena telling the truth about governments and pharmaceutical concerns and organized crime and public passivity and all the other factors that actually contribute to the spread of that disease—for instance, to call for public education in the whole area of sexual practice: this is to go beyond the bounds of ecclesiastical propriety.

The record of the church as truth-teller is even more questionable, however, than these illustrations would indicate. At least one should be grateful that the once-mainline churches—or rather, minorities within them—are still capable of exploring and articulating dimensions of truth where important ethical issues of our historical moment are concerned, and of making common cause with others who pursue these same problematic areas of life. But this kind of truth-telling is after all only one kind, and while it may be of greater immediate concern than more sustained and profound efforts to comprehend reality, in the last analysis it is impoverished apart from the latter. The prophets of Israel, Jesus among them, did not content themselves with pointing up explicit issues of private and public morality; they attempted to understand the truth about their society at its most fundamental, particularly in terms of what was wrong with it. They risked judging its most deep-seated pursuits, anxieties, and moods; they tried to discern the signs of the times. It was only in the light of the larger analysis—an analysis reaching far back into the past and far ahead into the future—that they dared also to speak about the contributing crises, the specific ethical and other issues of the moment.

To tell the truth as churches and Christians today must mean to risk this larger, deeper analysis. Without this, the few truths that we manage to unearth about the explicit problems of our world will lack both depth and integrity, for they will be fragmented, and they will always beg the question of the total perspective from which they are viewed. In some contemporary ecclesiastical circles where an (admirable) vigilance for social justice issues is maintained, one can hear it said that the church is "at least on the right side of the issues." The question is: How did it get there, and how will it sustain that posture? For the most part, Christian activists have fallen into their (often quite "right") activity by sheer accident or gut feeling. That may serve as a way into the sphere of truth, but it will by no means serve to keep one there. Even to know what "the right issues" are in the first place, and beyond that to know what it would mean to be on "the right side" of them, the disciple community must be actively engaged in an ongoing work of disciplined theo-anthropological reflection.

Truth-telling, Christianly understood, does not mean being *au courant*— "with it," to use an expression of the 1960s; that is, it does not mean keeping abreast of the latest problems and then, predictably enough, siding with that social segment whose approval one seeks (the right, the left, the center). To tell the truth in the manner of prophetic faith means to attempt to see in and under the issues the great currents of history and spirituality by which a society is moved. Issues (for example, economic and racial justice, the deterioration of the environment, waste, violence, sexism) are themselves consequences of these more subterranean currents. Why these particular issues? Why not others? Why did the past see the emergence of quite different issues? Why will the future perhaps present us with new problems undreamt of just now? To entertain such questions is to know that one has to look more deeply into the human spirit than its actions and inactions would by themselves suggest.

Truth-telling in this deeper sense is extremely rare in the churches of this continent today. Novelists, playwrights, artists, musicians, some historians, and social scientists are much more adept at it than are the churches. As it emerges from its Constantinian cocoon, the church in North America seems so fragile a thing that it is hardly able to understand its own identity and mission, to say nothing of discovering truth about its context. I frankly suspect that, so far as any deep probing of the soul of contemporary humanity in its North American form is concerned, churchfolk on this continent, like everyone else, are more dependent upon films than upon any institutional religion. Cinema in its present variety constitutes a very unstable medium for the communication of truth. Yet there are some films—for example, *The Color Purple, Fried Green Tomatoes, Dead Poets' Society, Jesus of Montreal, Grand Canyon, The Prince of Tides*—that delve more deeply into the spirit of contemporary society than almost anything one can hear from the churches.

In short, the corrective to a social malaise whose neglect is threatening to transform it into virulent and perhaps violent forms of nihilism is—for the churches, too—that we must learn how to speak the truth about it in this more rudimentary sense.

21.3. Conditions for Telling the Truth.
The second observation following upon Christopher Lasch's statement about speaking the truth is more complicated; and it concerns a matter with which we shall not have done until we have turned to Christology in Part III of this volume. Here we may only introduce it briefly.

Telling the truth is no easy matter. To begin with, it is not easy because one knows, if one is a Christian at any rate, that one does not *have* the truth to tell. The truth that is the object of this profession of faith cannot be had. It can only be lived with—stood under, not understood—because this truth is not an object but a living Subject. It is not an it, but a Thou. It is not words but a Word. It cannot be translated into words, only into flesh. We have said this. We shall have to say it again, *a fortiori,* in Part III.

Realizing, however, that we may nevertheless be oriented toward the truth (*Wahrheitsorientierung*) even though we cannot possess it, we make bold to become its witnesses in the world. But then we encounter the second part of the problem: To whom may we try to tell the truth? What conditions must we observe as its witnesses? Is it our Christian mandate to speak the truth no matter what the consequences? The truth may destroy people! In the former German Democratic Republic today, thousands of people are being destroyed—just as effectively destroyed as were thousands of others for whom the system produced earlier and more tangible forms of death—by truth contained in dossiers about their pasts and the activities of those who informed on them, often their closest friends and relatives. Many persons—perhaps whole classes of persons—are simply not able to receive the truth. They have developed subtle psychological mechanisms for protecting themselves from the truth that they know, deeply, would destroy them or render them less functional than they are. In our discussion of repression in the first volume,[40] we recognized that whole societies, not just individuals, may be dependent upon the concealment of truth. What we have just identified, with Thielicke, as "covert nihilism" is in fact a way of speaking about this need to conceal. People hide from themselves their deepest subconscious or semiconscious suspicions about their own state because they do not have the courage or the wisdom to absorb this truth consciously.

This is where Christians must go beyond the insight of Christopher Lasch that "There is only one cure for the malady that afflicts our culture, and that is to speak the truth about it." There are many different levels and methods of truth-telling, as there are many differing levels of potentiality for hearing and receiving the truth. It is one thing to write books intended for intellectuals who, at least in a minimal way, will have acquired sufficient objectivity—or perhaps hardness of heart—to open themselves to damning things. It is something else to stand, Sunday after Sunday, before a congregation of "ordinary people" for whom one cares, or even before a classroom of students in training for ministry, and say what one feels must be said about our context.

It is the latter situation that must be the model for the Christian, including the Christian writer of theology. And what one understands, after one has perhaps tried to have it otherwise, is that there is no absolute right to tell the truth. If the language of rights applies here at all (and I doubt that it does), truth-telling is a right that one has to earn. One earns it in two ways, each part of the other: by becoming responsible for those to whom one tries to tell the truth, and by providing them—so far as one can—with a framework of meaning and hope that will enable them, permit them, to receive the truth, especially the uncomforting truth, that one believes they should hear. Apart from these conditions, those to whom one tries to speak truth will be perfectly justified in refusing to hear it.

In this chapter I have testified to truth about the human condition in my sociohistorical context as I understand it. I do not claim that it *is* truth; I can only hope that it is oriented toward the truth. Even so, I know that it is painful. Some, perhaps many, will not be able to bear hearing it said that in this most optimistic of societies our optimism is hollow, rote, insincere; that we are

---

40. *Thinking the Faith,* chap. 2, sec. 9 and 10, 169–96.

Sisyphus pretending to be Prometheus; that we are in decline and courting an even greater decline because of our refusal to think ourselves in decline. I have said these things because I believe them to be true, so far as words can point to truth. But I know that they can only be received—and received so as to be acted upon—where there is a greater truth still.

That is the truth to which—even more haltingly—Part III will attempt to point: the truth that is able to take into itself even the most terrible truth about the human situation, even death itself in all of its guises, and make it serve life; the truth that is not given us, but to which—to Whom—we are given.

CHAPTER ▪ SIX
The Integrity of Creation

22. Perspective and Priorities

22.1. The Task before Us. The most difficult part of any theological work is the part that now confronts us, once more, in this third chapter of Part II: construction. It is easier in theology, as in nearly every other human undertaking, to speak about what has been and what is wrong with what has been than it is to speak convincingly of what might, should, and could be. Perhaps we are always more persuasive in our negative than in our positive analyses.

It will obviate this difficulty somewhat, however, if we first attempt to review in a summary way some of the major problem areas to which, following the discussion of the previous two chapters on creaturely being, this chapter ought to address itself.

22.2. The Quest for an Adequate Ontology. Perhaps the most fundamental question emerging from the previous discussion is the question of being. In this part of our study we are asking about creaturely being, and therefore we must recognize that the concept of being as such is in need of clarification. Many of the difficulties we have encountered in the area of Christian anthropology, especially the exaltation of *anthropos* above other forms of creaturehood, can only be resolved by coming to a better understanding of being itself.

That this question has a certain priority is not surprising. The tradition of Athens understood metaphysics (a term that has since been regarded by some as misleading)[1] as being the first science. This is partly due to the fact that

---

1. From the seventeenth century onwards, "metaphysics" was increasingly replaced by the word "ontology." So Richard A. Norris in *The Encyclopedia of Religion,* vol. 11, ed. Mircea Eliade (New York: Macmillan Pub. Co., 1987), 80–81.

Aristotle's Greek editors applied that term to his First Philosophy. Underlying this historical explanation, however, is the more significant fact that for Aristotle as for many other Hellenic thinkers the "science of being" (*ontos + logos*] is first in the sense of being prior or assumptive: that is, as one thinks about being as such, so one will think about all else. One's (perhaps hidden or unarticulated) conception of "what really *is*" or "what is really *real*" will necessarily inform all aspects of one's thought.

This genuine and important insight of the tradition of Athens ought not to be spurned by those of us who live and work intentionally within the tradition of Jerusalem. Because ontology has been particularly associated with philosophic and apologetic theology, it is sometimes assumed that Christians who wish to be true to the biblical tradition ought to avoid it. It seems to me true that biblically oriented theology must be critical of much of the content associated with Hellenic and other ontologies, but to say that such theology should avoid ontology as such is like saying that it must avoid aesthetics, or ethics, or axiology, or anthropology, or even theology. The question is not whether biblical theology will or will not discuss ontology but *what* ontology it assumes. There is, I believe, a biblical ontology—or, better stated, an ontology that is native to the tradition of Jerusalem. And part of the problem that we encounter in Christian theology, more particularly in its view of creaturely being, has come about because Christian thinkers throughout the ages have been extremely negligent in delineating the conception of being or ontology that belongs to the tradition of Jerusalem.

This negligence would itself require a major study, but one of its causes is plain enough: Christianity entered a world in which a sophisticated metaphysical tradition, that of Athens, had already established itself firmly. There were many variations on themes within that tradition—it was by no means monolithic; yet the themes were well-rehearsed, and most of the questions were in place even if different answers were given them.

As a missionary faith, Christianity almost from its inception had to enter into dialogue with this profound metaphysical tradition in one or another of its several expressions. It even had to use the majority language of that tradition, Greek. It did so, moreover, as the offspring of another and even more ancient tradition, that of Jerusalem. That tradition, however, did not approach the question of being or reality explicitly—that is, as a direct subject of detached or specific inquiry. Jerusalem (as contemporary Jewish theologian-philosophers like Martin Buber and Abraham Heschel have shown) did and does have a theory of reality, but it is implicit and indirect—and above all it is not abstract, which is the reason why it could not be treated in an isolated way.

The ontology implicit in the tradition of Jerusalem, as the most ancient and important writings of the older Testament ought to have made plain from the outset, assumes that "what is really real" is only perceivable in actual

302

occurrences—in historical events, in lives as they are lived, in what transpires between people and God and creatures. Jerusalem, one could say, is suspicious of universals, or at best considers them subservient to particulars:[2] to do justice to the universal called the unity or oneness of God is to describe God's faithfulness vis-à-vis God's people. Abstraction from life, lived and remembered, already distorts the meaning of "divine" attributes like unity and holiness.

What seems to me to have occurred in the meeting of these two very different ways of considering being—the one implicit and unspecified, the other explicit and highly refined; the one native to a religious and cultural minority, the other spread throughout the "inhabited earth" (*oikumene*); the one bound up with a long and detailed historical experience, the other philosophically detached and portable, so that (for example) the whole Roman Empire could appropriate it, simplified but more or less intact—was that the Hebraic was easily and inconspicuously absorbed into the Hellenic. In a short time, in fact already with the Pauline mission to the gentile world, the prospect that Jerusalem had something quite different to offer by way of a "first science" was altogether lost sight of.

Paul himself obviously understood something of this distinction, and some of his most problematic discussions (for example, on the resurrection of the body, 1 Corinthians 15) reflect nothing so much as the conflict created by the meeting, in his own person, of two incompatible ontologies. As long as a relatively articulate Jewish component was part of the evolving church, the stories of Israel could suggest, at least, another way of thinking about reality. But, as is well known, the Jewish component soon was practically lost, and the Scriptures of Israel, which were themselves almost dispensed with through the gnostic temptation of the early church, by the second century had already been assimilated by the spirit of Athens, which knew well how to interpret particular events and personages as allegories and figures and metaphors for universal truths.

Throughout Christian history, the Scriptures of the Jews have been dealt with in various adaptations of that approach, some more and some less sophisticated; and it is only with the emergence of a newly self-conscious form of Judaism and a newly self-critical form of Christianity in our own period that

---

2. In an illuminating letter to one of his critics, Reinhold Niebuhr concluded that "the net effect of this [personal and professional] pilgrimage has been to make me a rather extreme nominalist, too afraid of general concepts, to do creative thinking." (Ursula M. Niebuhr, *Remembering Reinhold Niebuhr* [San Francisco: Harper, 1991], 380.) Whether Niebuhr was really a nominalist may be debatable; what is not debatable is that he represented a biblical faith with a decidedly Hebraic orientation—and therefore he mistrusted abstract universals and what he called "the menace of finality" (ibid.). In short, his ontology (a word that he did not like) grew out of the "tradition of Jerusalem" (George Grant).

attempts have been made to recover what was hidden in those Jewish Scriptures and commentaries by way of a first science.

In the first volume we introduced this subject briefly under the nomenclature, borrowed from Joseph Sittler and Joseph Haroutunian, "the ontology of communion." We have already considered the importance of this understanding of being for the doctrine of God. We shall return to that discussion again in the subsequent section, in order to explore its importance for the subject of creaturely being.

22.3. Affirming and Denying the World. A second problematic area emerging from our reflections in the two previous chapters concerns the Christian attitude toward this world. We have recognized that an abiding ambiguity hangs over this subject in Christian history and still today. Christians have not been able to reject this world outright—at least, if certain sectarian groups have always done so, that tendency is what has kept them sectarian. At the same time, neither have Christians been known for their unconditional affirmation of this world. Their concentration on the fallenness of existence has tempted them to embrace redemption theologies that in effect redeem people *from* creation. Yet because they must believe it to be God's creation, they are not wholly at ease, either, with such a soteriology.

The ambiguity that results from this two-sided tendency is far from neutral. It always serves the vested interests of those who have their own designs on the world. Whether by direct world-rejection or (which is more characteristic) through an otherworldly piety that hesitates in the face of worldly responsibility, the most committed forms of Christianity have frequently left this world to the devices of "principalities and powers" that did not love it but only wanted to control it for their own purposes. Less committed forms of the Christian religion have themselves often been numbered among the latter.

The questions that this history of Christendom vis-à-vis the world raises for all contemporary theology as the church moves into a post-Christendom phase are many: What sort of attitude toward this world ought responsible Christians to assume? Is creaturely being as such the object of divine redemption? Is the profession of faith in Jesus as the Christ also a profession of unswerving world-commitment? Is Christian theology by definition political?

These and related questions will inform the subsequent discussion of the chapter, particularly in the section immediately following this; but the magnitude of this concern must obviously extend itself into the christological part of this volume (Part III) and into the whole structure of the third volume.

22.4. The Place of Humankind in the Theology of Creaturely Being.
We have recognized that humankind is for our tradition its point of worldly concentration. We have also noted, however, that this concentration, under

the impact of hierarchic ontological thought about creation, has regularly been transmuted into the kind of anthropocentrism that relegates nonhuman forms of creaturely life to the sidelines. In considering the criticism of the Judeo-Christian religious heritage that comes from the arena of those who are rightly anxious about the fate of the whole created order, we have had to admit that, as it has been practiced, the Christian religion has seemed to encourage a segregation of humanity from the rest of nature. Other creatures and processes of the natural order seem to be there for human use, convenience, or amusement; therefore human societies under the influence of this religious tradition appear to have felt no consistent sense of wonder at nature, no compulsion to honor its cycles and rhythms, and little desire to preserve it for its own sake.

Today it is largely the Christian West, with its vast technological prowess and its technocratic-managerial attitude spreading to every part of the globe, that is responsible for the prospect of an endangered biosphere. Is there a Christian profession of faith that can counter this avowedly Christian anthropology?

Responding to this question is perhaps the single most important task of Christian theo-anthropology today. It comes close to "the little point where the battle is raging" (Luther). Yet it cannot be answered simply, by taking up this or that aspect of Christian anthropology; and it certainly cannot be answered only at the ethical level, as an issue of contemporary social ethics. The whole of the faith is involved here, including the two problem areas to which we have already drawn attention above. The call for a different anthropology requires a prior search for a different ontology, one that will offer a viable alternative to the hierarchic conceptualization of being that has allowed and encouraged Christians to position humanity so centrally and powerfully among (that is, above) the creatures. Also, unless the faith of Christians expresses itself unambiguously in responsible love *for this world* to begin with, we shall not even feel deeply constrained as churches to correct the anthropocentric misconception under discussion.

Among the many dimensions of thought that must be considered by those who take this task seriously, two aspects of the doctrine of human being dominate. To put them in the form of questions, for the present: (1) How shall we learn to affirm our creaturehood? and (2) How shall we now come to consider our vocation within creation?

In regard to the first question, from the previous considerations of the subject, we recall that conventional Christianity seems to have done little to help human beings joyfully to affirm their creaturehood. It may (we suggested) be easier for people today to confess their sin than to confess their creatureliness. Creatureliness, even in a post-Christian world, seems to suggest an inferior status. The term is most often used pejoratively. A great deal of Christian celebration centers in the thought of redemption, but little of it comes from the thought of creation. Indeed much of what passes for exceptionally pious Christian joy is really joy over the surpassing of creaturehood.

With such a preconception of creatureliness, how could we not end in the denigration of *non*human creation? What would be necessary in order to reinstate the conception of a joyful creaturehood into the Christian profession of faith?

In regard to the second question, the matter of human purpose or calling is, as we have seen, perhaps the most glaring omission of Christian anthropology. On the whole, it has seemed sufficient teleologically, where humanity is concerned, to regard our purpose as being a predicate of our superior being. Since the superiority of human being has been identified chiefly with intellectual, spiritual, and volitional endowments—and so with the soul—the ultimate goal of human existence has been understood as the perfecting of these essential attributes, and thus the transcendence of terrestrial creaturehood. This again leads to an implicit denigration of the stage of creaturehood, and of creation as such.

We approach this chapter therefore conscious of the need to rethink, in the light both of the tradition and the pressing questions of our present context, both the creatureliness of the human being and the vocation of our species within the larger sphere of creation. These aspects of the discussion will be treated particularly in sections 24 and 25.

22.5. Creation's Destiny.   Finally, we have noted that Christian doctrine has been preoccupied with the destiny of the human creature, more particularly humanity redeemed, but that by the same token it has left in abeyance the question, What is the destiny of creation itself? Where that question has not been neglected altogether or suspended in thin air, it has all too frequently been answered in a questionable and even dangerous manner—questionable because of its disregard of consummatory in favor of destructive eschatological testimony in Scripture and elsewhere; dangerous because it has fostered attitudes of disregard and passivity in our present dealings with the natural order. I am referring to "answers" to the question about creation's destiny that posit the annihilation of the world as a necessary prelude to or accompaniment of the fulfillment of the divine will and promise.

It is understandable that traditional dogma has been hesitant to respond to this question. A healthy agnosticism about "the end of the world" is more faithful to the authoritative sources of the faith than are the astonishingly detailed accounts of dispensationalists and others. Beyond that, the advent of modern science and especially the recognition that the physical sources of life will naturally at some future point cease to function make it difficult for theology to speak to this matter without seeming to introduce a false *skandalon*—an unscientific statement about the end, so to speak, to match the tradition's unscientific statement about the beginning.

Yet silence on this subject not only tends to confirm the negative answers provided by both sectarian religion and (in another version) popular science (both of which are extraordinarily potent in North America), but it has a deleterious consequence for many other aspects of Christian doctrine, including anthropology. If creation itself can be thought to have no end (*telos*) other than ultimate destruction and discard, this prospect transfers itself immediately to all creatures, including the human. A purposeless world can hardly be the context of a purposeful worldly being. Or, to state the matter otherwise: If a human purpose is to be found within creation, then the creation itself will have to be seen as having an inherent purpose or end that is more than mere termination.

Specifically, the question that is put to us and to all responsible Christian thought today is whether we have the necessary scriptural backing and the necessary theological imagination to exposit for our time and place an eschatology of consummation that can at least counter the dangerous eschatologies of apocalyptic destruction and secular apocalypse by which our North American religious and secular mentality seems enthralled. The fuller development of this question by the nature of the case awaits the third volume; but it must already be broached here, because apart from establishing something of what we consider the *terminus ad quem* of creation to be we shall have left unanswered many questions about the present and impending future of creaturely being. In doing this, of course, as at so many other points in this volume, we shall be anticipating the subject matter of Part III.

23. Affirming the World/Resisting Evil

23.1. A Remarkable Symbol: Touching the World at Seoul.   The question with which we concluded the discussion of "The Perspective" in the first section (12) of the historical chapter on creaturely being and to which, in this first section of the constructive statement, we now return ran as follows: How is it possible unambiguously to affirm the world as a Christian without courting the sort of acceptance of the world that minimizes the doctrine of the fall and in the end denies the church the possibility of a prophetic and constructive ethic? As the major heading of this section implies, our answer will be that the right and responsible affirmation of the world does not preclude but on the contrary assumes the prophetic renunciation and resistance of evil dimensions of the status quo. Such an answer, however, requires elaboration and substantiation if it is to be anything other than a pious declaration. Our expansion of this thesis will involve two stages (undertaken in the two subsections): a general definition of world-affirmation (23.1), and an explanation of the insistence that such affirmation implies resistance of evil (23.2).

In March of 1990, Christians of all three "worlds" (as they still existed at that time), and all three major branches of Christendom (Protestant, Orthodox, and Roman Catholic) came together in the teeming city of Seoul, South Korea, for a World Convocation on the theme that had been chosen at the Sixth General Assembly of the World Council of Churches meeting in Vancouver seven years earlier: "Justice, Peace and the Integrity of Creation." The theme itself was remarkable, for it implied that for the first time in its history, the World Council of Churches had chosen a focus for its whole work that was not exclusively Christian or even explicitly religious. It was a theme that, without preamble and in the most direct manner, turned the mind of the church toward this world, with its staggering contemporary problems and its possibilities of renewal and life. As such, the theme implied both that Christians would naturally—not even as a second step, but as a dimension of their faith itself—manifest ultimate concern for the fate of the earth, and that in doing so they would be able to join hands with all others, regardless of their creeds, for whom the life of the world mattered greatly.

It must be admitted that the convocation itself, which was to mark the culmination of ecumenical work toward the unfolding of this theme and, in particular, the covenanting together of the churches to continue to strive for "Justice, Peace and the Integrity of Creation" in concrete ways, was less than convincing. The efforts of seven years to bring together representatives of all Christian communions under the umbrella of this worldly theme were hampered by ecclesiastical division and mutual mistrust; and, more particularly, the attempts of many persons and preliminary councils to demonstrate the interrelatedness of all three prongs of the theme were seriously jeopardized by those who, often from ideological commitments that might be questioned theologically, insisted upon the priority of one aspect of the theme over all others (normally this meant the singling out of "Justice," some of whose advocates were bold enough to propose that the other two prongs of the theme had been inserted by the powerful to attract attention away from this one area).[3]

What could not be achieved theologically and intellectually, however, was in some perhaps more impressive way achieved symbolically and liturgically. At the final session of the eight-day convocation, in the context of worship, the assembly of six or seven hundred persons was invited to come forward and lay hands upon a large inflated representation of the planet, which had been borne to the center of worship by children of different races and nations.

Whether this kind of liturgical symbol can ever find adequate expression in theology and Christian ethics is of course a matter for debate—and, in all

---

3. See in this connection, D. Premen Niles, ed., *Between the Flood and the Rainbow: Interpreting the Conciliar Process of Mutual Commitment (Covenant) to Justice, Peace and the Integrity of Creation* (Geneva: W.C.C. Publications, 1992).

likelihood, lasting doubt. Whether most of those who participated in this act themselves realized its full meaning is itself a question. Most Christians today are so ill-versed in the history and theology of Christendom that they are unlikely candidates for recognizing the significance of the very liturgies in which they participate. Even in relatively literate societies like our own (perhaps especially there), so little informed awareness exists of what it means to profess the faith, to say nothing of what it has meant in the formative periods of the past, that few seem capable of grasping even the questions with which that past has left us, let alone the resources that would be necessary for answering them.

To be specific, one would have had to know a good deal about what we named the ambiguity of the Christian past with respect to this world to realize something of the profundity of the symbol of "touching the world" at Seoul—and of doing so as the central liturgical act of worshiping God. To know a little about the history of Christian world-rejection and hesitation was to realize that this event, despite all the frustrations by which it was surrounded, should be considered a point of major transition in Christian consciousness. While it was certainly not the first time that Christians have affirmed this world (we have already noticed that such affirmation is characteristic of much contemporary theology, and indeed one of its most conspicuous distinguishing marks over against the dominant doctrinal and political past), it was, I think, the first time that such an act had been engaged in by so representative a body of Christians, accompanied also by representatives of other religious traditions. Since literally all of the historic churches were represented in this World Convocation, it is appropriate to consider this a symbolically significant moment, marking a major transition in ecumenical Christian consciousness. If that is so, then it compensates somewhat for all the apparent incapacity of Christians to think and act in concert. Perhaps the thought and the action will have to follow the symbol. Perhaps it is only symbolically that we may grasp the inseparability of God and the world, as they are both understood in the tradition of Jerusalem: that to turn toward God (*theo*centrism) must mean simultaneously to turn toward God's beloved world (*geo*centrism).

This is the connection that must be appropriated by Christians everywhere today if we are to overcome once and for all the kind of spirituality that orients itself toward God by psychic and physical acts of dissociation from the world. This is where every constructive theology of creaturely being must begin—with the knowledge that the worship and service of God, as God is conceived of in this tradition, is a travesty and blasphemy if it is in any way a vehicle for the all-too-human impulse to despise and reject this world and to seek to flee from it. That impulse may belong to religion; it is perhaps the essence of religion. But it is the antithesis of a faith which assumes as its most basic tenet that *God's* movement is not away from the world but toward it—the pain notwithstanding.

To touch God is to touch the world—lovingly. Creaturely being in all of its aspects is being beloved by God.[4]

This is the first and indispensable principle of any authentically constructive statement about creaturely being. While it has begun to be understood by minorities in the churches of this continent, it is still mightily countered by self-proclaimed forms of Christian theocentrism and Christocentrism that set love for God over against love of the world and are ready to accuse all who love this world of sheer "humanism," pantheism, and still greater heresies. These God-centered representations of Christianity are not easily dismissed because they can, unfortunately, call up a great deal out of the Christian past—including selected passages of Scripture—to support their cause. Liberal sentimentality and the newfound nature-romanticism of various Christian and semi-Christian movements cannot meet this kind of traditionalism, nor can they provide a viable alternative theology of creaturely being that is sufficiently grounded in Scripture and tradition to provide the necessary ontological foundation for a responsible ethic of creation. Such a foundation can only be established by a sustained exposure of Christian clergy and laity to disciplined study of the sources and history of the faith in the light of the great questions and instabilities of our own context. It is not enough to declare that, in genuinely Christian terms, theocentrism would have to imply at once geocentrism and (in another manner from the earlier use of the term) also anthropocentrism. The church must discover *why* this is so, and that discovery, if it is profound, will carry all who are impelled to embark on it into the heart of the Christian profession of faith: the contemplation of the cross of Jesus Christ.

23.2. Affirmation Implies Resistance. There is no nonproblematic theology. Even the long-awaited affirmation of the world symbolically and liturgically expressed at the 1990 World Convocation of Christians betokens a

---

4. In this connection, Sallie McFague's reflections on the metaphor of the world as "God's body" are evocative and helpful. As she herself recognizes, it is, like all metaphors, open to abuse: specifically, it may become the doorway to yet another pantheistic interpretation of the faith—an ancient temptation, which has been revived in our time partly because of the threat to earth that has been aided and abetted precisely by a "Christian" theism that effectively removes both God and humanity from the mundane sphere. As a metaphor designed (as it is, for McFague) to redress just that separation of the divine and the essentially human from the world, the concept of the world as God's body is particularly useful. It can be related in positive ways both to some developments in scientific thought (e.g., James Lovelock's Gaia Theory) and to theological reflection on the import of God's *suffering*. "The world as God's body . . . , may be seen as a way to re-mythologize the inclusive, suffering love of the cross of Jesus of Nazareth . . . just as once upon a time, in a bygone mythology, human beings killed their God in the body of a man, so now we once again have that power, but, in a mythology more appropriate to our time, we would kill our God in the body of the world. Could we actually do this? To believe in the resurrection means we could not. God is not in our power to destroy, but the incarnate God is the God at risk: we have been given central responsibility to care for God's body, our world." (*Models of God: Theology for an Ecological, Nuclear Age* [Philadelphia: Fortress Press, 1987], 72–73.)

danger present in contemporary theology as it seeks to overcome centuries of Christian world-ambiguity. The danger, to which our opening question points, is that affirmation of this world will come to mean acceptance of the status quo. This is a danger that is present in all religions and philosophies of acceptance, such as Buddhism and Stoicism.[5]

It could be argued that affirming the world must mean affirming whatever actually is, or happens, since "the world" must surely refer to experienced reality—that is, the world as we actually experience it. But to no moral sensitivity, and certainly not to biblical faith, are such realities as genocide, child abuse, violence against the defenseless, deliberate poisoning of the environment, and many other things that occur daily in our world acceptable. What, then, is affirmed, precisely, when faith affirms this world?

Without presuming to answer for every religion of world-acceptance but speaking only as a Christian, I think that it would be necessary here to reintroduce the category of intentionality. When Christians affirm the world they affirm the creation that, in faith, they understand God intends: what God has brought into being, is sustaining, and shall bring to completion. Concretely, therefore, they affirm a material and finite creation, with all the vulnerability that that entails. They affirm the always delicate cohabitation of matter and spirit and the unity of body and soul. They affirm the variety of creatures, with the potentiality for tension as well as for beauty and harmony residing in this variety. They affirm time, and therefore the passage of time—and therefore the potentiality for melancholy, in humans; for, as Dürer illustrates so wisely in his drawing "Melancholia," the passage of time is the very stuff of melancholy. Yet, affirming time, the Christians affirm also growth and maturation, decline and death. They affirm instinct in all creatures and the more complex reflection that is called thought in human creatures. With this they affirm also, necessarily, the possibility of sorrow as well as joy, regret as well as anticipation, fear as well as contentment; for thought is free-ranging, boundless—it must consider nonbeing if it is deeply to consider being.

In other words, to affirm the world that God intends, as God is presented in the continuity of the testaments, does not mean to affirm only what is superficially regarded as positive in the life of the world. For one thing, the so-called positive experiences would be meaningless—the adjective itself would be

---

5. In a conversation with the well-known Japanese Buddhist philosopher, Masao Abe, I called to mind that our common teacher, John Coleman Bennett, suggested to his students a useful hermeneutical procedure: To discern the essence of any system of thought, ask two questions: What does this system hope to preserve? and What does this system wish to guard against?

I asked Professor Abe how he would respond to these two questions if they were asked of his own interpretation of Buddhism. He answered: "I wish to preserve most the sense of the interrelatedness of all that is [a view that is very close to 'the ontology of communion'], and I would like to guard against the danger that Buddhists will too easily simply *accept* whatever is."

without content—were it not for their opposites; for another, it would be impossible even for God to create freely thinking creatures and then to curb their minds and wills so drastically as to prevent them from any sorrowful or anxious thoughts. In short, affirming this world, Christianly conceived, must imply affirming at least some dimensions of what human beings experience as suffering. Finite creatures conscious of their finitude (Tillich) could not help knowing loneliness and impermanency and even anxiety.[6]

Christian affirmation of the world must go even farther, however: it must include the possibility that—from the start—such a world might well be subject to evil and sin, and to the suffering resultant upon these. Christians could not affirm evil and sin as such, but they must affirm the conditions under which evil and sin are possible—perhaps even "inevitable" (Reinhold Niebuhr); because to exclude from the parameters of the affirmation such conditions would be tantamount to affirming some other world, not this one. We must be clear about this: The essential goodness of this world—the world pronounced good by its creator—includes its potentiality for evil and the tragic, and so for a suffering that is not part of the life process but leads to spiritual death.

It will be seen at once, therefore, that world-affirmation is not an affirmation lightly undertaken and sustained; and, seeing this, we may the better realize why historic Christianity, along with so many other religions and quasi-religions of the world, has hesitated and vacillated in this matter. Affirmation of an ideal world, a utopia where all is goodness and happiness, is one thing; affirmation of a world in which positive and negative elements are mixed, where wheat and tares grow up together, where light and darkness struggle together, is something else again. In the end it is possible only as an act of faith. For faith trusts that the intended "good" will ultimately not only use the evil but overcome it—is already doing so.

This trust in the divine intention for the world is engendered by the grace that does not wait to be discovered but openly and willingly manifests this intention—for Christians, manifests it supremely in "Jesus Christ and him crucified." Manifests it, and accomplishes what it manifests. This grace manifests and accomplishes an intention that is consistent and unambiguous, even though it is also full of mystery. In the cross of the Christ, the redeeming God does not reverse the creational conditions that make evil and sin and their dread consequences possible; for that would be to annihilate the world as it is in favor of something very different from "the work of six days." In the cross of the Christ, rather, God takes into God's own person the negating consequences of the conditions of a fallen creation and transforms them so that they serve the good of the world of the Creator's original benediction.

---

6. In this connection see my *God and Human Suffering: An Exercise in the Theology of the Cross* (Minneapolis: Augsburg Pub. House, 1986), especially chap. 2, "Creation: Suffering as Becoming."

To speak concretely, employing the categories of the World Council of Churches, God in Christ absorbs the negating consequences of injustice, unpeace, and the disintegration of the creation. God does not cancel out these realities, but creates new conditions under which they may come to serve God's creational intentions. These conditions are surrounded by a depth of mystery far exceeding our limited comprehension; but they are also in part comprehensible to faith, for faith itself is one of their consequences. Faith, as it is formed within us by the divine Spirit that "proceedeth from the Father and the Son," learns how to affirm the world in spite of everything in us that fears and is prone to reject the world. This is itself an integral part of God's transformation of evil and sin to make it serve the intended good; it is the dimension of that more mysterious transformation most accessible to our understanding. But faith issues not only in understanding; it issues in "works"—that is, in participation in God's own transforming work.

Here we may glimpse something of the distinction between world-affirmation as it belongs legitimately to Christian profession of faith and the kind of acceptance that lacks the capacity for resisting evil in the world. The world that those who trust in God are permitted and commanded to affirm is not to be equated with the world as it appears to ordinary observation—to "sight"—but rather the world that through grace is opened to the "eyes of faith," the world that is being changed through the larger workings of that same grace that calls faith itself into being out of nothing. Faith "sees" this world as it is being altered by grace, and faith affirms it—not only verbally and theologically, but practically, ethically, in solidarity with all others who for whatever tangible reasons are beckoned into this transforming work. Faith resists the actual in the name of the possible. To put it awkwardly but more accurately, faith's affirmation of the possible, of the real-that-is-coming-to-be, entails a simultaneous resistance of the actual, of the real-that-is-being-transformed.

But it will be better to be concrete. Taking up again the theme of the World Convocation, we may distinguish Christian affirmation of the world from the posture of acceptance in this way: The latter posture would have to mean resignation to the conditions of injustice, unpeace, and creation's disintegration; for these are "the three great instabilities" (Charles Birch) by which our planet is presently, visibly threatened. But to affirm the world *in faith* is to be thrust willy-nilly into a posture of resistance in the face of these threatening realities, because the reality that faith entertains is not only the actual existence of injustice, unpeace, and the degradation of creation, but the possible existence of their antitheses. The latter are possible, not merely as ideals to be striven for, but as realities being brought into being by the God who makes even human wrath serve redemptive purposes.

Because the reality that God intends—has from the beginning intended; has in Christ realized; shall through the creative Spirit achieve—absorbs and transforms the realities that threaten the life of creation, faith perceives and sets itself to participate in possibilities that counter the actualities of these three "great instabilities" of our global context. Thus, justice, even in a world where injustice is both present and, apparently, permitted, is nevertheless through the transformative grace of God possible, and therefore injustice is rejected; it need no longer be regarded, in its manifold manifestations, as simply inevitable. Peace, even in a world where unpeace, violence, and warfare are both present and, apparently, permitted, is now possible, and therefore violence and war are to be resisted; there are other ways of achieving just ends than what was supposed to be "just war." The integration of creation, even in a world where disintegration of the created order is both present and, apparently, permitted, is possible; therefore in the name of the creative source of this process the forces and processes of disintegration both may and must be resisted.

To conclude: What we have hoped to show in this discussion is that the affirmation of the world, which we have insisted is the first requirement of a theology of creaturely being, not only need not court the kind of passive acceptance of "what is" that precludes prophetic critique and action, but, understood within the context of the creational and redemptive focus of Christian belief, actually establishes an ontological basis for an ethic of radical transformation. The danger that world-affirmation will end in a premature identification of the status quo with the divine will—a danger that conservative Christianity has always (and often with reason) feared in Christian liberalism—should not be countered by a theology of salvation that ends by so distinguishing God's will from God's own creation that it can only be transferred to an afterlife. Creation itself, creaturely being as such, is the object of divine redemption. If this is not recognized as the preliminary assumption of a theology of the incarnation and humiliation of the divine Word, then the whole discussion to follow will take another turn. What we have wanted to demonstrate here is that this assumption can be made without forfeiting—and in fact giving greater concreteness to—the critical and transformative thrust of the gospel of the cross.

24. Being and Human Being

24.1. "The Integrity of Creation." Of the three prongs of the World Council of Churches' "Justice, Peace and the Integrity of Creation" process, the most nuanced as well as the least understood is the third.[7] What this

---

7. Partly because it was both nuanced and new; partly because it seemed, to some, to compete with the more familiar concerns of justice and peace; partly because in other influential languages (notably German and French) the theme adopted at Vancouver in 1983 was translated in such a

reflects, beyond practical matters of translation, is the general incapacity of contemporary religion and culture to comprehend ontological categories. For the technocratic society, even to think cosmologically (for example, to ask the kinds of questions that Thomas Aquinas asked) is difficult. We have been captivated by an instrumentalist conception of reasoning and scientific-technical variations on the theme, How to? We have all but lost even the language necessary to discourse on the question, What? unless this is confined to externalities, primarily to measurable substances and quantities. What? is that rudimentary question to which ontology addresses itself, and "the integrity of creation" represents an attempt (a rather fine attempt) to return the discourse of Christians to that kind of foundational concern. That it failed to do so on anything beyond a minor scale should be considered by serious Christians as an indication of the need for remedial theological work at every level of ecclesiastical life. Such work is required particularly in the North American context, for here the technological mentality has had its greatest victory.

Children, as Paul Tillich never tired of insisting, instinctively ask ontological questions. It is instinctual with them because, in their earliest stages of self-awareness, their very survival and growth depend upon their coming to terms with the consciousness of their own being—and with the prospect of *not* being. What Tillich called "the shock of non-being"[8] is perhaps a greater shock to the five-year-old than to the thirty-year-old, who has already learned subtle psychic techniques for repressing it. Very young children have been known to be so obsessed with death, despite the relative absence of actual death from their experience, that they could overcome it only with the help of skillful and sensitive adults.

Understandably, therefore, human beings have always had to protect themselves from the ontological question; for consciousness of being can so preoccupy the self that it is prevented from simply *being*. But what has occurred in the technological society that is our present context goes well beyond such necessary protection. We have created in these modern settings an atmosphere that not only diverts the mind from its natural proclivity to ask What?

---

way as to miss the most evocative connotations of the English/Latin word *integrity* (in German it became *Bewahrung des Schöpfungs;* in French, *Sauvegarde de la Creation*), this splendid concept has not yet been appropriated by contemporary ecumenical Christianity in a way commensurate with its potentiality for comprehensiveness and ontological insight. One of the things that became evident at Seoul in 1990 was the incapacity of modern Christianity to absorb the impact of its own symbolic language. In this connection, see Michael Strauss, *Oekumene auf dem Weg: Der konziliare Process zwischen Vancouver und Canberra* (Bielefeld: Luther-Verlag, 1991).

8. See, for example, *The Courage to Be* (New Haven: Yale Univ. Press, 1952), especially chap. 2; *Systematic Theology,* trans. G. T. Thomson (Chicago: Univ. of Chicago Press, 1951–1963), vols. 1, 2, 3, passim.

questions[9] but robs civilization of the language and thought-forms that were built up over centuries to address and cope with that primordial question.

Because in this social context people have lost the sensitivity to recognize the sometimes subtle ways in which children and adolescents (as well as the aged and the dying) raise ontological questions, such questions are regularly transmuted by parents and teachers (and by physicians and others who serve humanity at the other end of the life-span) into technical questions. For example, the child asks, "How did I get here, Daddy?" and the modern father, elated at the precocity of his offspring, proceeds with his son's first sex lesson. But the child is not asking for technical information about the intricacies and delights of reproduction, most of which he could not possibly grasp anyway; he is asking about "being-here." He wants someone to explain, or at least to listen to, his new and unsettling sense of existing, of being different from other existing things, of being, however, like the dead bird he discovered among the flowers, impermanent, subject to overwhelming change, the plaything of time.[10]

Within the ontological question (What?) is an even more insistent teleological question (Why?). In the earlier discussion of being and meaning, we recognized that meaning cannot be simply predicated upon being; being as such seems not to disclose its own raison d'être. Yet the questions of being and meaning are inseparable; and if modern parents or teachers do not answer or even hear the child's What? it is not only because they have been deprived of the language for dealing with the ontological question, it is also because they are positively unnerved by the teleological question.

As we have seen, however, the teleological question—and in its most demanding existential form ("What the hell are people *for?*") is *the* question confronting our entire civilization. The presence of it—the fear of it—lurks behind every honest work of contemporary art. Unlike the ontological question, which can be reduced to abstraction and forgetfulness, the teleological question will not so easily submit to public and private techniques of repression. As the high incidence of adolescent suicide in our context ought to make

---

9. An indispensable aspect of this technological diversion is quite literally the entertainment industry, in particular the ubiquitous television, which both occupies the "spare time" (not leisure) of the vast majority of our citizens and, by the very nature of the medium, "educates" the mind away from all the questions regarded by classical culture as rudimentary: being, meaning, the good, beauty, truth. In this connection see Neil Postman, *Amusing Ourselves to Death: Public Discourse in the Age of Show Business* (New York: Penguin Books, 1985).

10. The best documentation of this phenomenon that I know of is not from the pens of child psychologists but from the pens (and pictures) of children themselves—and adult authors whose imagination has not been dulled by what passes for maturity in our society so that they are able still to speak for the child. In this latter category I recommend highly a work of the French-Canadian writer Roch Carrier, *Prayers of a Very Wise Child,* trans. Sheila Fischman (Toronto: Viking/Penguin Group, 1991).

very plain,[11] the successful dismissal of the child's ontological questions does not end the child's implicit Why? And without some attention to the Why?—even if it is only a matter of hearing the question—it will almost certainly lead to self-destructive behavior—most of it not overt, like suicide, but nonetheless destructive.

It may be that the time has come when the unanswered question of meaning burns so furiously in the heart of allegedly postreligious Homo sapiens that it will necessitate the reintroduction of the question of *being* into our thought and discourse as well. A society in the grips of "future shock," a society reminded of the prospect of nonbeing on a massive, global scale, cannot forever brush aside metaphysics.

For Christians, this deep if still submerged reality of our social context raises the question: What can Christian faith contribute to the contemplation of the ontological/teleological question as it manifests itself in our historical moment? How does this faith-tradition itself understand the meaning of being?

Intuitively, I suspect, rather than by design, the phrase "the Integrity of Creation" was and is an incipient response to that question on the part of the ecumenical church. In a deceptively wise figure of speech, this phrase presents a capsule definition of being, and it implies at the same time a response to the question of the Why? of human being. It declares that in the Christian understanding the most significant thing to be said about being is that it is integrated—whole, interconnected, not fragmented but delicately interrelated, ecological, relational. And with respect to the Why? it implies (given the total context of the World Council's discussion of this) that human being and purpose have something to do with the discovery, nurture, and celebration of this creational integrity, especially in view of the disintegrative tendencies that have been imposed upon the creation by human attitudes, acts, and agencies.

The remainder of this section will be an attempt to expand upon this observation. As such it addresses the question posed in our historical chapter on creaturely being, in section 13.1: How can Christian doctrine simultaneously do justice to the tradition's concentration upon the human species and overcome the danger inherent in this concentration of relegating the larger creation to a position of secondary or peripheral interest?

24.2. Once Again: "The Ontology of Communion." There are good historical reasons why evolving Christianity did not feel called upon to explicate a distinctive theory of being, one that might do justice to the tradition of

---

11. In Canada, where there is a very high suicide incidence among teenagers, a disproportionate number of suicides is found in Native Canadian communities, indicating that the "dismissal" in question can apply also to whole races.

Jerusalem. Among these, the most significant in my view is the one to which we have already drawn attention in the introductory section of this chapter, namely, that as Christianity moved out into the gentile world of the Mediterranean, it encountered and had to accommodate itself to a highly articulate ontology, with variations, stemming from the tradition of Athens. Not only did it begin from the start—already with some of the newer Testamental documents—to frame its message in the categories of that preexisting metaphysic, but its sudden separation from the parental faith of Judaism almost guaranteed that it would not experience the need, in the encounter with the Greco-Roman world, to explore ontological assumptions implicit in Judaism that might well have exercised a critical function in the evolution of Christian doctrine. (Perhaps the frustrations of Tertullian should be considered in that light.)

The ontologies of the Greco-Roman world are not reducible to a single description of reality, but they do share certain tendencies: (1) In their highest expressions, as in Stoicism, Platonism, and Aristotelianism, they press toward systematization and theoretical abstraction. (2) They search for universals, whether as "real" (Plato) or "conceptual" (Aristotle), that explain and transcend all particulars. (3) They tend to identify "the really real" with intangible, spiritual being, which is either limited or positively distorted by material embodiment. (4) They tend accordingly to classify existing entities in a hierarchic manner, with those possessing the greatest potentiality for spirit/reason having precedence over those more subject to their physicality. (5) They tend therefore to consider being substantially, that is, as comprised of qualities or attributes (such as spirit, mind, body) whose presence or absence in existing entities determines their nature and worth.

In the light of our discussion in the preceding chapters of Part II, as well as the discussion of deity in Part I, it can readily be seen how thoroughly the metaphysical assumptions of the tradition of Athens have influenced every aspect of evolving Christian doctrine. Athens was at least more perceptive (I refuse to say, with some philosophic theologians, more advanced) than Jerusalem in this: that it understood early and well how powerfully fundamental consideration of the character of being itself determines all other considerations. To combat the influences of this highly sophisticated and ubiquitous metaphysical tradition, the representatives of the tradition of Jerusalem, whether Jewish or Christian, would have had very early in the dispersion of that community into the *oikumene* to bring into the open and make explicit what in the literature of ancient Israel is concealed—not intentionally, but wisely—in history, story, proverb, lament, and praise. This was most unlikely to happen with Christians drawn from the ranks, mainly, of the uneducated. It does not seem to have happened amongst the Jews of the Diaspora, either.

In consequence, as soon as the Christian message progressed from the stage of plain witnessing to the event—that is, telling the story of Jesus and his teachings and the occurrences of his life; as soon, in other words, as it became necessary to express the import and implications of this primitive witness in the language and thought-forms of a larger and more cosmopolitan public—in short, almost from the start, Christians had no other choice than to express their gospel in categories and in response to questions drawn from the tradition of Athens.

There is no question about the profundity of that tradition. Today we must be grateful that it was *that* tradition that became the vehicle of the evolving doctrine of Christendom, though we may certainly ask why some expressions of that tradition—particularly the pre-Socratic and those preserved in the ancient dramatic productions of Greece—were not taken more seriously.[12] Profundity aside, however, what must be reckoned with now is that the "first science" of Athens was markedly different from that of Jerusalem. Therefore we may legitimately and critically ask why, as Christianity moved from the early into the medieval and then Reformation stages, more Christian intellectuals did not sense the difference. Particularly with the opening up of the Scriptures in the pre-Reformation and Reformation periods, Christianity was given a new opportunity to feel the difference between these two traditions, and at the level of their ontic as well as their noetic foundations.

There can be no doubt that Protestantism in its classical expressions introduced significant noetic changes in theology. With the *sola scriptura* principle there was no escaping the fact that the central claims of Christianity were not accessible to rational investigation, whether rationality were understood in the Platonic-Augustinian or the Aristotelian-Thomistic sense. In its epistemology, the Reformation distinguished itself from the tradition of Athens, therefore, by insisting upon the revelational basis of the faith. On the whole, however, the reformers did not carry this severence from Athens into the sphere of ontology. While many of their principal ideas may be understood to assume a different ontology, there is nothing comparable to the noetic revolution in their ontological thought. Grace, understood as the gracious movement of God toward the creature; faith, understood as trust; sin, understood as rebellion; justification, understood as being considered righteous by God—in all of these teachings the Reformation reaches out for a whole different conception of reality. In the *imago Dei* dogma, as we have seen, the reformers were also searching for another ontology, and so, in principle, in their whole understanding of authentic humanity. Moreover, all of these doctrines may be traced to their exposition of Scripture, with which they were constantly occupied; so that, clearly, it was

---

12. It should also be pondered at length why—under what auspices and influences—the Christians so adamantly rejected the philosophy of Epicurus, a point of view that, while it could certainly not provide an acceptable ontological background for biblical faith, at least shares with the tradition of Jerusalem an acceptance of the materiality of creaturely life.

their exposure to the Bible that brought them to the brink of the discovery of this distinctive "first science" of Jerusalem.

But for the most part, it seems to me, they did not advance far enough toward that alternative to affect deeply enough subsequent Protestant conceptions of God, Jesus Christ, and (in the fuller sense) creaturely being. Insofar as this is true, it is entirely understandable, because no doctrinal areas were more permanently imprinted by the ontology of Athens than were these—especially on account of the trinitarian and christological orthodoxies, which were established entirely within the context of the parameters of Greco-Roman thought, with biblical categories assimilated into the latter, not vice versa. To apply to the ontological assumptions of Nicaea and Chalcedon the kind of critical judgment applied by the reformers to the epistemological assumptions of medieval Christianity would have been to call in question dogmas so indelibly fixed in the mind of Christendom as to open oneself immediately to the charge of rank heresy.[13]

Yet the *sola scriptura* once embraced could not but lead Protestantism toward an ontology which, had it been consistently explored, would certainly have necessitated altering also these central doctrines, and perhaps radically so. Many of the less consciously doctrinal statements of the main reformers— particularly their scriptural commentaries, letters, and sermons—belie the fact that they had already at some profound level of belief adopted an ontological preunderstanding that only ecclesiastical convention, personal habit, and fear of going too far prevented them from making more explicit and consistent. In this connection, Luther's whole *theologia crucis* in fact marks an entree into Theology, Christology, and anthropology far more radical than, perhaps, Luther himself realized; for this, as we have shown in the first volume, was his distillation not only of the christological thought of St. Paul but of the prophetic tradition of the Theology of divine pathos.[14] When various theological movements today urge upon the church other perspectives on the nature of reality itself, many if not all of them are insisting that the *sola scriptura* principle be extended beyond epistemology and beyond the periphery of theological content to the ontic core.

At that core what is discovered, however it may be named, is an understanding of the nature of things that is different from the substantialistic, hierarchic ontology that has governed so much of Christian doctrinal tradition. And it is not accidental that no single word is so frequently used to indicate this core principle than is the word "relation" and its derivatives. For the truth is that *all*

13. Luther's rejection of the pneumatology of the radical reformers, Zwingli's rejection of Anabaptist Christology, and Calvin's fear of the unitarian Theology of Servetus all illustrate how unprepared were the chief reformers to entertain radical questions concerning the conciliar decisions about the identity of the godhead.

14. *Thinking the Faith,* 22ff.

of the key concepts of biblical faith describe relations; they do not describe substances, qualities, or endowments. Moreover, when they are deployed to describe the latter, they are torn from their biblical context and badly distorted.

This applies in an obvious way to such positive concepts as grace, faith, hope, (holy) awe, repentance, gratitude, praise, and so on. These words do not connote substances or qualities that may be acquired; to "have faith" as though it were a possession is a misconception. Faith is trust, we have said, and like all of these and similar terms of biblical religion, faith presupposes another in whom faith is placed.

The same presupposition informs the negative categories of biblical religion such as sin, evil, guilt, the demonic, despair, disobedience, doubt, and disbelief. As we have seen in connection with sin, for example, when it is objectified and quantified—even if quantification means a lack—it acquires a connotation entirely different from the biblical sense of "over againstness" or rejection.

But ontological consistency with the Scriptures must mean that this relational presupposition is carried into our thinking also about the primary actors of the story: God, the Christ, the Spirit, humankind, the elect, the Tempter, other creatures. *Theos, Christos, Pneuma,* and *anthropos* do not name beings who possess being to a greater or lesser extent and can be arranged on a scale of being accordingly. Salvation does not refer to the triumph of a "higher" substance, soul, or a "lower," body. Christology does not consist in the harmonious admixture of seemingly antithetical substances, humanity and divinity. The Trinity does not describe a deity capable of containing transcendent and immanent qualities.

In all of these central categories of the faith professed by Christians there is an assumption of the most elemental nature concerning being itself: namely, that being in all of its aspects and manifestations is relational. It means therefore that the entire system of meaning belonging to this tradition is premised on the ontological assumption of the interrelatedness—the integrity—of all that is. It means, further, that the ethic which emanates from this system of meaning is directed toward the restoration of broken relationship. To state it once more in a single theorem: For the tradition of Jerusalem, *being means being-with*. [15]

When it is understood that the foundational ontology of the tradition of Jerusalem, however unspecified, is one in which being itself is conceived relationally (as with-being or "communion"—Sittler/Haroutunian), all of the major and minor categories of biblical faith fall into place: the ontological house becomes a home. Grace is then not a substance to be meted out like bread and wine, "the medicine of immortality"; it is the active searching and finding of the gracious God. Sin is not the negation or diminution of some endowment but

---

15. See above, chap. 3, sec. 10.4.

the abrogation of relationship, the attempt to undo the relational foundations of our life, born of the desire to have our being independently of our being-with. Salvation is not a status of the entity, soul, liberated from the physical and emotional encumberment, body, but the gift of new relationship—the conquest of alienation by a reconciling love.

God, even God, in this tradition is not "all alone," an entity, a being "greater than whom none can be conceived," and so on; God is rather the center and source of all relatedness, the ground of our human capacity for being-with, the counterpart from whose presence creatures can never wholly escape. And the creatures, all of them, from the smallest and invisible to the planets and interstellar spaces, are living things whose life is dependent upon their interaction. They combine, in ways that defy the human imagination, the principles of identity and distinction; so that their distinctive identity is sustained only so long as it is held in creative tension with their dependence upon the others. Perhaps, as James Lovelock has proposed, the planet itself is a living reality whose being is throughout relational.[16]

Only the human creature seeks to defy this law of intercommunion, to flee dependency, to acquire autonomy, to go it alone. "We alone can 'sin.'"[17] The disordering of relationships that is introduced by this creature's determination—its having to cope with freedom—is what the tradition has meant by creation's fall. All relationships are affected by the self-abrogation of this creature's relationships. Hence redemption, in this tradition, has in particular to do with the judgment, purification, and healing of the human spirit. The Bible's concentration upon this creature, which is not to be confused with anthropocentrism, is in part explained by that recognition. The whole will have achieved the consummation that is intended from the outset only when this errant, pathetic, tragic, and much loved creature finds again its rightful place among the creatures.

It was this "ontology of communion" that, intuitively, the ecumenical movement was reaching out to retrieve when it adopted the nomenclature, "Integrity of Creation." On the surface, it appears a merely ethical concept: the response of conscientious Christians to the manifold problems of the environment. Over against the disintegrative influences that have been introduced into the natural order through unlimited and rampant greed and carelessness on the part of the human population, especially its most "developed" societies, the Vancouver assembly intended to say that as faith calls for justice and peace it also calls for honoring the innate integrity of the natural order.

---

16. J. E. Lovelock, *Gaia: A New Look at Life on Earth* (New York: Oxford Univ. Press, 1987).

17. Rosemary Radford Ruether, *Sexism and God-Talk* (Boston: Beacon Press, 1983), 88. See also Wendy Farley, *Tragic Vision and Divine Compassion: A Contemporary Theodicy* (Louisville: Westminster/John Knox Press, 1990), 61.

But what the churches did not recognize fully, since they are still ideologically so captivated by substantialistic and hierarchic ontologies, is that this turn of phrase hovers on the brink of an entire ontology that, if it were sufficiently exploited and applied to all of the primary categories of the faith, would demand of Christians not only a new environmental ethic but a theo-anthropology at many points new and no doubt unsettling to many Christians. For if human beings begin thinking of everything, their own lives included, in terms of the interrelatedness of all that is, then much in Western Christian culture and cult would have to be challenged and changed. An ontology, the philosophic detachment suggested by the history of the term notwithstanding, is never an innocent, theoretical affair. It has to do with what is "first"—that is, with the most fundamental and foundational realities, with thought that precedes thought. A disciple community that had begun to think along the lines of an "ontology of communion" would be at least as embarrassing in the context of our acquisitive, technically manipulative, anthropocentric, and individualistic society as a scientist who thinks the world itself a living thing or a child who *will* ask ontological questions that her parents have spent their adult lives avoiding.

24.3. Human Being-With. To speak about human being under the aegis of "the ontology of communion" is to speak about human being-*with*. When in the most ancient biblical saga of creation the Lord God realizes that "It is not good for *ha adam* to be alone, I will make for it a companion corresponding to it" (Gen. 2:18),"[18] we find ourselves at once in the presence of an understanding of humanity that is of an order entirely unlike Aristotle's definitive pronouncement, "Man is a rational animal." What humanity "is" is cohumanity—is inconceivable apart from the companionship, both human and extrahuman, that constitutes its original condition.[19] Being truly human in God's intention is being in relationship with the counterparts of our being. Human existence is coexistence.

The most immediate way in which the Scriptures articulate this ontology is, as we have already insisted, in the language of love. It is not accidental that this language, which unfortunately Christians have come to take for granted, is at the center of the entire biblical narrative. Every aspect of Christian theology is in the last analysis a midrash on the theme of love: God "is love." Jesus Christ is the "beloved Son," whom God sent into the world because "God so loved the world." Love is the "fruit of the Spirit." The whole of Christian ethics—"the

---

18. Phyllis Trible, *God and the Rhetoric of Sexuality* (Philadelphia: Fortress Press, 1978), 88.

19. Or should one say its almost-original condition? For the saga of Genesis 2 suggests that Yahweh began with a single being, an "earth creature," and had to "operate on it" after discovering, from its own behavior, that its isolation was "not good." (Ibid., especially 98–99.)

Interesting

law and the prophets"—is summed up in the command to love God and one's neighbor. Love is not only a way of articulating the foundational ontology of this tradition, it is *the* way. No philosophic language—certainly not the language of being—can improve upon the language of love. Contrary to the tendency of most philosophic theology to relegate love, often along with other directly relational and personal biblical language, to the status of the primitive, a theology that honors the tradition of Jerusalem must with St. Paul regard this discourse as greater than any other (1 Corinthians 13). By comparison, ontological discourse is once removed from reality. It is second-order language, whose only justifiable function is to support the primary language of the tradition, which is direct and concrete.

Nevertheless that primary language in almost every instance needs such support, and nowhere is this more evident than in the case of the language of love, the absolutely indispensable discourse of the whole tradition. Particularly in the North American context, the language of love is profoundly spoiled and debased. It is distorted by religious overuse and sentimentalization. It is distorted by crass and manipulative association with sex, to the point of rendering its theological and ethical use difficult even in circles of supposed sophistication.

Beyond this cultural debasement, the deeper and perhaps perennial problem of the language of love inheres in the human experience of love itself, under the conditions of the fall. It is the most difficult thing in the world for beings who love themselves inordinately, or perhaps do *not* love themselves, to love and to accept love when it is offered them. Love in human experience seems continuously prey to two dialectically related distortions: on the one hand an excess of involvement, on the other a fear of involvement. It will prepare the way for the subsequent definition of human being if we consider these two dangers briefly.

The first is the danger of absorption and the loss of identity. In its insecurity and lack of self-acceptance, the self seeks to lose itself in the other. It craves total incorporation into the life of the beloved. It fosters dependency in itself and encourages domination in the other. The end of this impulse is an unwholesome relationship that is achieved only through the almost complete loss of the self and its domination by the other. It has been one of the many contributions of Christian feminist thought to draw attention to the fact that this has been a characteristic fate of women in our Christian society. Women have been conditioned to believe that love must mean the sacrifice of the self for the enhancement of the other. The religious models from which this has been derived can readily be recognized: Christ as the sacrificial lover, calling others to "take up your cross and follow"; the Virgin Mary, submissive and compliant; St. Paul's "wives" who are "obedient to your husbands"; a whole catalog of saintly women, whose sanctity is attributed to their resignation, humility, and self-sacrifice.

324

But, secondly, if mutuality is prevented by excessive self-emptying it is also prevented by the fear of involvement and the loss of autonomy. Desiring to preserve its freedom, the self is tempted to confuse love with the domination of the other. The very pliability of the other, her or his willingness to give, confirms this confusion. Maintaining what is in fact a condescension toward the other, the self esteems itself all the more for its capacity to love; for it knows, secretly, that it loves what is beneath it. It flees from genuine intimacy even while pursuing physical and particularly sexual intimacy with ardor. It guards itself with painstaking care, preserving its distinctiveness even while appearing magnanimous and self-giving. The end of this process is a distorted relationship in which the self goes essentially unchallenged in its bid for mastery, being accommodated by the other. While this is by no means an exclusively masculine scenario, it has been one to which the behavioral patterns and customs of our society have admitted men more freely than women. But the point is that both of these scenarios describe undesirable, pathetic, and occasionally tragic misappropriations of the instinct to love and be loved. The dominating male or female is no less pitiable than the long-suffering wife or the "henpecked" husband. Both constitute distortions of love.

What these reflections illustrate is that love itself, while it is the primary language of the ontology appropriate to this tradition, needs to be interpreted and critically supplemented by other modes of discourse for describing the essence and mystery of human being, the being that acquires its being only in not being "alone." I have used the artificial construct, "being-with," as one way of meeting this need.

Although this is (in English[20]) an awkward form of speech, it can convey precisely the nature of the relatedness that is at the core of the "righteousness" (authenticity) that biblical faith covets for humankind. What it declares is that human being as intended by God is reciprocal being. It is characterized by mutuality, interdependence, communion, dialogue, cooperation, sympathy, sharing, concord. The essence of our humanity is not located in the idealization of some quality, such as purity of will, keenness of intellect, moral propriety, spiritual sanctity, physical beauty, dexterity, or strength. Authentic humanity is humanity in relationship with "the other."

Of course the human creature possesses or is capable of embracing unique qualities, including rationality, volition, spirituality, moral sensibility, and

---

20. It is not so awkward or artificial in German. The term *Mitsein* (literally, "with-being"), which Heidegger employed on occasion, could at least be heard by Germans, whose language has not been so altered by Latin as is English, as a more or less normal form of speech. The German language is full of *mit-* words: neighbors are *Mitmenschen* (literally, with-people); colleagues are *Mitarbeiter* (with-workers) with whom one engages in *Mitwirkung* (cooperative endeavor). When one's friend is ill one feels *Mitleid* (with-suffering), a term we render in English with the Latinized "compassion"; one expresses one's sympathy in *Mitleidenschaft* (with-emotion), and so on.

speech; but these so-called endowments are means, not ends. The end to which they are directed when they are just is the possibility of communion with the other. If this communion is not realized, then the endowments themselves are unfulfilled—like musical or artistic talents that are never developed. For when the receptivity, responsiveness, accessibility, sensitivity, comprehension, empathy, responsibility—in short, the love—for which they equip us is missing, these same endowments are apt to serve other ends that biblical faith does not admire or countenance. It was this recognition that prompted Paul to pronounce such harsh judgment upon even the highest human achievements— wisdom, insight, speech, and even ultimate self-sacrifice: that without love they are "nothing" (1 Corinthians 13). It is to facilitate our orientation toward the other that such astonishing gifts as these are given us. The chief end of human being cannot and must not be regarded, then, as the perfecting of these endowments as isolated capacities, but their faithful deployment in realizing the communion for which we were and are called into being.

"To be" is "to be *with*." The preposition "with," which is (not accidentally) prominent in the Scriptures of Israel and the church, contains a finely nuanced connotation that, if we pursue it with imagination, can help us to grasp the nature of the truly human as it is conceived in this literature. To draw out this connotation, we may again compare and contrast this preposition with the two others that, as we saw in connection with the doctrine of God, have special places in the vocabulary of Jerusalem: "above" and "in." We apply the distinctions now to Christian anthropology, remembering that "above" gives expression to that type of ontological thinking out of which hierarchic theories of reality are fashioned, while "in" is the natural language of all mystical ontologies.

The heavens, declares the Psalmist, the dwelling-place of the "most High," are "high above the earth" (Ps. 103:11). In relation to the God who is above, the human is of "low estate" (for example, Ps. 136:23; Luke 1:52; Rom. 12:16), though perhaps only "a little lower than the angels" (Ps. 8:5, KJV; Heb. 2:7, KJV). Humans can also be considered to be "above" the beasts of the field and the birds of the air and "are of more value than many sparrows" (Matt. 10:31; Luke 12:7), and so on.

Yet the Bible also engages in what should be perceived as an internal and implicit critique of this same above/below conceptualization of reality; and if hierarchic ontologies have evolved within Christendom, it only indicates how little attention has been paid to this internal critique. The aim of the God who is (certainly) "above" is not to remain above but—as we have seen—to be Emmanuel. Truly, God's being "with us" bears the import that it does because God is not necessarily or naturally with us. There is no law demanding of the Creator proximity to the creature. God's being with us is a matter of sheer grace: the condescension of one who is "above."

Is this same as being with each other or is it natural

326

Thus God's transcendence (another "above" word) is not incidental to God's proximity, immanence, or presence. The above-ness of God, God's distinct otherness, ought not to be sacrificed to an undialectical immanence, as happens in sentimental liberalism. When this occurs, grace becomes "cheap" (Bonhoeffer) and the divine agape is reduced to a "monism of love" (Kitamori) that produces neither wonder nor the sense of undeservedness. But the object of the biblical God (and not only with the newer Testamental witness to the incarnation) is proximity and not distance; and therefore while the divine transcendence qualifies the divine immanence by deepening it, it should not become the primary message of faith, as the earlier works of Karl Barth tended to make it. That the essence of God is love—that God *is* love—does not translate into distance but nearness, nor does it court first the sense of undeservedness but rather gratitude. If also distance and the realization of undeservedness are necessary to genuine love, they are necessary as qualifiers of the reality and not as the reality itself.

The same biblical critique of exaltedness applies to human being. It applies in obvious ways to human-to-human relations. The human being who places himself or herself above another human being is consistently denounced in Scripture. No human office, not even that of kingship, gives a human being the right to "lord it over" his or her fellows. This is only what the Gentiles do (Matt. 20:25). Prophetic religion even questions the propriety of the monarchy for this reason. The acceptable monarch for which the prophetic tradition rather reluctantly makes place and by which model it judges existing rulers is one who serves. The kingship as well as the priesthood of Jesus must be viewed as an extension of this paradigm, which is the reason for his association with David, the shepherd king, one of the people. Indeed, throughout biblical literature but notably in the newer Testament the human being who really is "above" all others (in terms of origin, calling, faithfulness, truth of witness, or purity of heart) manifests superiority, not in acting out his or her supremacy but by assuming a position of servanthood.

Does the Bible's internal critique of hierarchy apply also to the relation between human and nonhuman creatures? We must answer that it does not do so, at least not in pronounced and explicit ways. Yet in discussing this internal critique we are not discussing only its biblical application. When the "ontology of communion" has been undertaken, it has in fact unlimited application, for it is an ontology: that is, it does not confine itself to specific aspects of reality but aims to describe "what is" in the most inclusive and rudimentary sense. If the internal critique of hierarchy is applied biblically to the human-divine relation and the human-human relation, it must therefore—especially under contextual circumstances that warrant it, as ours do—be applied also to human-extrahuman relations. We shall return to this observation later.

As we have seen in Part I, the preposition "in" is also prominent in biblical literature. Its use in the newer Testament, especially the Pauline corpus, must be considered in this connection. "In" is the special language of Paul's Christ-mysticism. The *soma Christou* (body of Christ) comprises those who are *en Christo* (in Christ). Through the internal testimony of the divine Spirit, through the preaching of the Word, through baptism, through participation in the Eucharist and prayer, through obedience and sacrifice, the "members" have been, are being, and shall be incorporated into "union" with their "Head." Paul is able to write of this union of Christ and the believing community in realized terms, as though it were a fait accompli:

> . . . if anyone is in Christ, there is a new creation; everything old has passed away; see, everything has become new! All this is from God, who reconciled us to himself through Christ, and has given us the ministry of reconciliation. (2 Cor. 5:17-18)

Or again:

> Do you not know that all of us who have been baptized into Christ Jesus were baptized into his death? Therefore we have been buried with him by baptism into death, so that, just as Christ was raised from the dead by the glory of the Father, so we too might walk in newness of life. (Rom. 6:3-4)

"In" and "into" here denote the greatest measure of identity. This incorporation describes not only the church and the Christian life but the eschatological fulfillment, when God will be "in" all (1 Cor. 15:20ff.)—that is, when all alienation and separation shall have been overcome and perfect harmony and at-oneness shall prevail.

Yet the language of being-in is also subject to an internal biblical critique—to begin with, precisely because of the eschatological dimension. While being-in may envision the deepest goal of the love that seeks us and "will not let us go," it does not accurately describe our present condition; that is, it does not conform to the realism that, for all its visionary impact, biblical thought will not relinquish. The truth is that in our here-and-now reality we are *not* fully *en Christo* and God is *not* "all in all." The new has *not* perfectly overcome the old. The "old Adam" still struggles with the new (Romans 5). The church is *not* the divine realm and reign (Kingdom), and much remains to be accomplished—including the victory over the "last enemy," death.

Beyond the eschatological consideration, the internal biblical critique of the mystical language of being-in stems as well from ecclesiastical and ethical reflection. Mysticism is not unconditionally embraced, even by the most mystical passages of the newer Testament. Paul was not unaware of the mystery cults, with their strange attraction to the human impulse of incorporation—their appeal to the paradox of aggrandizement and abnegation that lurks in the human psyche. Therefore while his concept of the church as the body of Christ contains the dimension of identification, it also maintains a strict differentiation: Christ remains "the Head" of the body, and the body is entirely dependent upon this one Head.[21] Here, as we might put it, the being-*above* of the Head qualifies the being-*in* of the members. This, in addition to the eschatological fact that "the body" is a dynamic and not a static reality, always under way and never having arrived, never "finished," greatly qualifies the mysticism of the apostle.

So does the ethic of love itself. The object of the being into which the Spirit, baptism, and preaching are bringing the community of discipleship is not an undifferentiated oneness but the union and reunion of persons; that is, reconciliation, communion, love. This oneness presupposes distinction and not only identification. Thus, when it is well understood, Christian love does not encourage the kind of merger or conjugation of one with another that is always courted by mysticism and that results in the disappearance of particularity and individuality. As Buber insisted, the mysticism appropriate to biblical ontology preserves and does not absorb the "thou." The "and" in his famous "I and Thou" is not incidental.

If this point is not understood (and frequently it is not) it has dire ethical implications for every manner of relationship, from faith in God to human marriage to the human relation to the extrahuman. Love certainly understands the language of "being-in"—as the romantic idea of "being in love" in its way illustrates. But the internal biblical critique of the mystical language of identification is forfeited at great risk. In practice, when this critique is unheeded the result is capitulation to that dimension of the human quest for love that is seeking the loss of the burden of self through incorporation into another. This impulse has so often been associated with religion, including Christianity, that it is frequently celebrated as true piety. But it must be guarded against by responsible Christian spirituality. It is one thing to lose the self in order to find the self (Matt. 10:39); it is something else to lose oneself in order to avoid the perilous journey of becoming fully human.

By expositing the biblical and theological meaning of being-above and being-in, we have moved toward a fuller comprehension of what is intended by the awkward term "being-with," as this applies to human being. Being-with both preserves what from the perspective of biblical faith are the useful qualities of the hierarchic (being-above) and mystical (being-in) ontological types,

---

21. This is a particularly important Protestant teaching, in contrast to the tendency of Roman and Anglo-Catholic ecclesiologies to overemphasize the "mystical union" of Christ and the church. See in this connection the encyclical of Pope Pius XII, *Mystici corporis Christi.*

and at the same time avoids what from that same perspective must be regarded as questionable in these types. Concretely, it preserves both the principle of identification or union and the principle of distinction or differentiation, and in their lived tension. Both are requisite to love, understood in Christian terms.

On the one hand, to be "with" the other implies a high degree of proximity. The contemporary language of "solidarity," borrowed from Marxism, is useful here. Even in ordinary parlance, to declare "I'm with you" conveys the most unconditional assurance of solidarity and support—not only coexistence but *pro*existence. On the other hand, being-with also implies the maintenance of distinction. While I am "with you," I am also a separate person. Indeed, my being with and for you is dependent upon my remaining other than you. I can only act responsibly *for* you if I also sustain a distinctive identity that is able to think, speak, and act in your behalf.

Being-with, as distinct from the mystical being-in, therefore requires the building up of the other, not the other's incorporation or assimilation. I am not you. You are not me. We are two even in the oneness of our love. More than that: you enable me to be who I am—to say, "I"; and I hope to serve you in the same way. I *and* you, you *and* I. Love does not reduce us to an undifferentiated "we."[22] Our closest communion does not diminish but upholds and enhances our individuality (not to be confused with individualism). Our communion is enriched by the variety that is brought to it by our differences, our different gifts, our different pasts. This common experience was surely in the mind of Paul when he wrote of the "body" with its many "members" and their differing functions.

24.4. Human Being-With "Otherkind."   Our exposition perhaps draws too heavily on the human-to-human relation, though it shares that propensity with the *analogia relationis* of Scripture. The interhuman expressions of the "ontology of communion" are for us the most immediate (after all, we are humans). It is necessary to grasp, however, that what we are seeking to explicate in this way is not confined to human-to-human being but, *mutatis mutandis,* includes all being.

Its appropriateness to the human-divine relation has already been explored a little in the foregoing. According to the dialectic of differentiation and identification that belongs to the language of this ontology, God remains Other, even wholly other, while being God "with us" (Emmanuel). God enters into the closest communion with us, yet God never becomes an extension of our

---

22. See in this connection the first and in many ways the most insightful antiutopian novel of our time, *We,* by the ex-Bolshevik, Evgenii Ivanovich Zamiatin (New York: Viking Press, 1972).

being or a dimension of our subjectivity, nor do we lose our identity in the contemplation and praise of God. The biblical witness to the Holy Spirit is perhaps the strongest possible statement of divine immanence (God *within*); yet in no way does this testimony permit the supposition of a merging of Spirit with spirit. God's Spirit, though penetrating to the depths of our personhood, remains always distinguishable from the human spirit, because apart from this otherness the divine Spirit cannot "help us in our weakness" (Rom. 8:26). Again, both grace and faith confirm this dialectic. Grace as the free movement of the cleansing, forgiving, and accepting God toward us never connotes the absorption of our personhood; on the contrary, grace establishes in us the courage to be and to become truly ourselves. Faith as our response to this movement, as trust, is at the same time the mode of our presence to and with God and the recognition of our distance from God; it is not yet "sight." We might apply the same dialectic to all other aspects of the "divine-human encounter" (Brunner)—to prayer, worship, the sacraments, and so on.

The particular dimension of this ontology to which the *problematique* of our times drives us, however, is the question of its appropriateness to the human-extrahuman relation. Christian anthropology has almost always assumed a close connection between the human-divine and the human-human relation; but the relation of humanity to non- or extrahuman being is an aspect of the subject fraught with difficulties stemming, as we have already seen, from postbiblical neglect, a neglect that is partly explicable on account of the relative silence of the Bible itself in this area. For example, when Jesus summarized the ethical thrust of the whole tradition in which he stood, he made no mention of nonhuman creatures or the creation as such but only of God and neighbor.

Christian thinkers who have become aware of this relative silence of our primary authoritative sources on account of the multifold crises of the biosphere have attempted to find in the Scriptures new evidence of concern for the extrahuman; such evidence, we have noted, may indeed be found. But what is required of theology today (and particularly of systematic theology), I think, is not only that we should discover in the Bible traces of a theology of nature and an ethic of creational care, but rather that we must ask whether there is anything like a foundational basis for such a theology and ethic. Does the extrahuman creation in Judeo-Christian understanding have a central place, or is it only consequential or peripheral? To state the question concretely: If Jesus were summarizing "the law and the prophets" today, would he add a third commandment "like unto the first two," or perhaps extend the second one to include love of creation in all of its variety and integrity?

To answer this question, we must consider the manner in which not only law but also gospel comes to be. This is perhaps more easily demonstrated in connection with the former. The many laws that emerge in the life of Israel and, later, in the newer Testamental *koinonia* emerge in relation to specific historic realities. The dietary laws of ancient Israel are not issued in a vacuum, but in the context of Israel's encounter with other cultures and cults whose religious and social customs are understood to be dangerous to the life (and health) of Israel. The occupation of the land by Rome and the presence of many foreigners, some of them traditional enemies of the Jews, evoked a whole new dimension of the Torah when Jesus considered such questions as the relation of the community of faith to political power ("Render unto Caesar . . . ") or to the people outside the law (the Gentiles), or to "the enemy." The new circumstances introduced by the mission to the Gentiles by Paul and his associates required the revision of many seemingly settled subjects, such as circumcision.

In every case of this sort, there is a necessary return to basics, to the *fundamentum* (foundation), to what is "first"—that is, to the (implied) ontology of the tradition. Thus the foundational assumption of the ethic upon which Jesus draws for his commandment concerning the treatment of the enemy is quite naturally the law of love. As it has been observed often, his precepts are not, therefore, radically new—not independent of the tradition, not arbitrary, for they emerge from the same ontic foundation that produced the old. At the same time, they are bound to be heard as challenges to the old ("You have heard that it was said to those of ancient times . . ." (Matt. 5:21), because the old precepts are deeply entrenched. Yet many of them are no longer capable of engaging the present contextual realities. The "new" ("but I say to you") is occasioned by new or newly realized exigencies of the context. For example, the presence of Samaritans and other traditional enemies of the Jews occasions the commandment, "love your enemies"—a commandment that, however, was certainly at least implicit in the foundations of Israel's faith before it was made explicit by Jesus.

The same observation, with necessary alterations, should be made with respect to gospel. Habitually, Christians speak about *the* gospel, and this creates the false impression that the Christian message is something fixed and unchanging, which the church inherits, must keep intact, and passes along unchanged to the next cohort of believers. But as our whole exercise in contextuality insists, gospel is a witness to truth that is always being discovered as the church lives in the tension between text and context. When Paul moved out into the gentile world, he had not only to reconsider circumcision and other practices of the established tradition, he had to rethink very basic questions, such as: What knowledge of God can non-Jews be expected to have? (Romans 1–3). His whole kerygma as evangelist to the Gentiles was dependent upon the answer to this question. The new reality of Gentiles in the community of the elect occasioned a new expression of the doctrine of the knowledge of God. But Paul certainly assumed, as the whole discussion of the opening chapters of Romans makes clear, that what he answered was not an innovation but the explication of a doctrine of knowledge already implicit in the faith of Israel and the teachings of Jesus.

Today the church is confronted with many problems wholly or largely unanticipated by the tradition, including the biblical tradition. Some of these problems have to do with human attitudes toward and behavior in relation to ever-expanding and complex questions and insights concerning earth's natural processes and other, nonhuman inhabitants. As such they constitute the occasion for a return to and rethinking of the *fundamentum* (foundation) of the faith. In this exposition of human being within the framework of "the ontology of communion," I have intended to describe that *fundamentum* in such a way as to make the inclusion of extrahuman creation in the theology and ethic of love a necessary extension of what is already implicit in it. The agape-ethic has been so thoroughly circumscribed by the habit of associating it exclusively with God and humanity, and in a simplistic and sentimentalized way, that its ontic foundations need to be made clear. Love—agape—is not a purely ethical concept, and even less is it a purely emotional one. Agape describes a profound understanding of the whole of reality, and not only a way in which humans relate to one another and to God. When the real as it is expressed in the concept of "suffering love" is grasped at depth, it affects not only the way in which we understand ourselves in relation to God and our own kind but also our relation to otherkind. The term "ontology of communion" helps us to begin to acquire that greater grasp.

What we may conclude, then, with respect to our relation to the extrahuman creation is of a piece with the Godward and humanward dimensions of our relatedness. To *be together with (Zusammensein)* nature implies once more the dialectic of identification and differentiation. On the one hand, it is to know our essential unity with all creation. Being *with* the other creatures implies, negatively, ceasing to think and behave as if we were above them. The internal critique of hierarchic ontology applies here as much as in the human-to-human relationship. It is more important for us to grasp the reality of our solidarity with earth and its myriad creatures today than to engage in discussions of the rights of other creatures. The language of "rights," which has become ubiquitous in North America, is not compatible with the language of love; love "does not insist on its own way" (1 Cor. 13:5). Not only is the concept of rights a legalistic approach to ethics; not only (in practice) is it almost inevitably adversarial; beyond that, it fails to ask of human beings what, given the initiative of God's love, they are capable of.

If people are interested only in a minimal, survivalist approach to planetary existence, they may be satisfied with the pursuit of rights. No doubt Christians will often have to side with those who advocate the rights of nonhuman creatures. But Christians cannot satisfy the inherent demands and possibilities of their faith in this way; for faith makes possible, not only the acknowledgment of the right to life of other human and extrahuman beings, but *love* of the others—even sacrificial love. In solidarity with all creatures, the humanity that

333

God intends and into which, in Christ, God beckons us, is a humanity that is ready not only to coexist but to proexist vis-à-vis the extrahuman. It is already necessary for the human species in contexts like ours to sacrifice its own desires, rights, and life-styles for our own kind in other, "underdeveloped" contexts; what we shall have increasingly to grasp, at least as Christians, is that this sacrificial approach to planetary existence must extend itself also to endangered species and processes. This at very least is what it means to apply to the earthward dimension of our total relatedness the ontology of communion.

At the same time, this ontology recognizes the distinctiveness of creatures, including human creatures. For humans to be *with* their nonhuman counterparts in the created order does not mean that they should seek to lose themselves in a romantic, mystic identification with nature. Being-with, we have seen, honors otherness. It does not desire amalgamation but mutuality, not sameness but interdependence. Today we see a typical polarization of viewpoints in North America. Against the technocratic exploitation of nature, there has come to be an antithetical insistence that human beings must cease all the willful, rational, managerial activity that has brought our society to the point of environmental catastrophe, and must learn how to "blend in." Some go so far as to suggest that humankind ought to withdraw from any kind of interference—perhaps even will its own extinction. This is a characteristic (and in the case of the latter suggestion, an extreme) application of mystical ontology, and in its most consistent forms it is just as admirable and just as absurd as unqualified mysticism always is. It is right in applying the dimension of identification over against a technological society that has almost wholly ignored this dimension; but it is wrong, as well as foolish, in refusing to recognize distinction. Being-with—here as in the Godward and humanward orientations of this ontology—still implies distinction; and in fact it is obvious that humanity can only make good its co- and (especially) *pro*existence vis-à-vis the rest of creation if as a species it sustains and purifies that distinction.

But the question is: How do we understand the distinction? If we understand it in terms of "being-above," then, as Christians, we shall have no prophetic word whatsoever to offer to a technocratic society that already thinks itself well above the condition of nature—and does so, unfortunately, with the sanction of a majority Christian past. If, instead of continuing to distinguish humanity by the process of evaluation based upon a hierarchic ontology, we are able to appropriate the ontology of communion, then we shall have to look for human distinctiveness in an altogether different area. That is what we shall attempt to do in the subsequent discussion of human vocation.

First, however, we must consider the condition necessary to the right appropriation of our coexistence and calling vis-à-vis otherkind, namely the recognition and acceptance of our own creatureliness.

25. Human Creaturehood and Calling

25.1. Knowing and Accepting Our Creatureliness. Everyone who grasps at some depth the biospheric instability that inspired the World Council of Churches to adopt the phrase "the Integrity of Creation" realizes that the greatest cause of nature's *dis*integration is humanity's seeming inability to understand its essential solidarity with all other forms of life, and to act upon that understanding. While this inability applies in some degree to all humankind, ironically it is most pronounced and most threatening to planetary existence among the most "developed" peoples of earth. Wherever scientific knowledge has combined with human enterprise and favorable economic and geographic conditions to produce high technologies, human beings appear to have recognized no limits in their manipulation of nature for what they regard—often despite conspicuously dire consequences—as desirable ends.

There is a growing consensus among all who consider the future of life on earth that unless humankind achieves some profound awareness of its dependence upon nature, the future will be bleak—if it *is* at all. Most of those who have arrived at that conclusion, from whatever process of investigation and reflection, would add that such an awareness entails the clear recognition of our full human participation in nature: that we are not supranatural, after all, but part of the very process that we are gradually destroying; ergo, that our allegedly progressive civilization is involved in strangely self-destructive pursuits.

In the preceding section, we attempted to lay ontological foundations for the kind of changed consciousness that this situation calls for, as such foundations might be articulated in Christian terms. The question to which we turn in the present section is a necessary extension of these ontological reflections into the realm of the theo-anthropological, understood both theoretically and practically: How, according to the Christian profession of belief, does humankind come to acquire a knowledge and acceptance of its solidarity with nature as a whole?

As we ponder that question, we are made conscious of a number of considerations, some of them introduced in previous sections of this work, by which our response to it will have to be conditioned. The first and by no means least complicating of these considerations is the point made in the previous, critical chapter, namely that Christianity itself has contributed to the problem that modern Western history has finally laid bare. The tendency of historical Christianity to elevate humanity above ordinary nature, locating its end in a transcreational state, is perhaps the single most effective cause of the problem that, as Christians, we have now to help to solve. To speak plainly: There can be no Christian contribution to the solution of this complex *problematique* that

335

is not simultaneously a rejection of significant conventions of the Christian doctrinal and ethical past.

Secondly, the recognition of the disestablishment of Christianity to which we drew attention in Volume I necessitates, with respect to the present consideration, coming to terms with the fact that, while Christianity may have contributed substantially to the creation of the problem, it can help to solve it only in concert with many others. In the pluralistic society that has come to be, Christians must cooperate with others with whom they can make common cause, even where the theoretical background of action may be different and even antithetical.

This concrete contextual reality, however, itself introduces certain ancillary concerns. On what grounds can Christians determine with whom they ought to cooperate, what they ought to support or avoid, how they should balance the various and potentially conflicting elements associated with social action in our present context? In many instances the protection of the environment conflicts with issues of justice: for example, the dependence of thousands of people upon the fishing, sealing, and other industries. From one end of the spectrum, Christians are asked to side with those who counsel an end to human interference with natural processes, while from the other end they are reminded of their commitment to humanitarian concerns that must entail the management of nature. Obviously these types of decisions call for the analyses of actual situations, and therefore they belong more properly to the subject matter of the third volume, *Confessing the Faith;* yet, they also point up more foundational questions of Christian ethics: How do Christians conceive the basic relations with the creaturely sphere? What is to be regarded as good or authentic or righteous in the juxtaposition of these distinctive but always interrelated spheres of relationship? What perspective do Christians bring to bear upon specific ethical issues of this kind?

Thirdly, we have noted Christian culpability in the matter of elevating the human above nature (the first point, above); but in the North American context, according to our critical analysis in this part of the study, this inherited doctrinal convention is complicated by the fact that human beings today do not feel they are in charge of anything, especially not vast natural processes (the depletion of the ozone layer, for instance). The Promethean rhetoric of our Western Christian world view, we have said, is belied by our increasingly passive and fatalistic behavior. How does this affect the way in which we articulate the relation between humanity and extrahuman creation as, in our view, the Creator intends it?

In what follows in this section, I shall not attempt to address all aspects of these problematic areas fully or directly; but they should be understood to be present as background concerns that will inform the discussion both here and in later phases of this study. What all three observations point to is the need for

Christians to formulate as clearly as possible their own rudimentary (professional) presuppositions about the character and calling of human creaturehood.

And in that connection there can be no doubt about what must have priority. It is that the knowledge and acceptance of our own creaturehood, which in a real sense is the very essence of gospel for today, is dependent upon our encounter with and sense of the presence of the Creator.

This rather elementary statement contains more claims to reckon with than meet the eye. For convenience, I will reduce them to four observations: (1) that we do not have what Christians could legitimately call a proper knowledge of our creaturehood until we are able gratefully to acknowledge and accept this as our real, intended, and "good" estate; (2) that such knowledge and acceptance can come to be only *coram Deo*—before God; (3) that this is gospel and not merely law; and (4) that our being-with each other and with the other creatures is profoundly altered by this revelatory experience.

a. Knowing, Acknowledging, and Being Grateful for Our Creaturehood.

Creaturehood is the core of Christian anthropology. It does not describe a penultimate state, a stage on the way to something, a training ground for "real" life. To be a creature, to know oneself to be a creature, and to be glad in one's creaturehood: this comes at least close to the heart of the matter, for Christians. That we should enter into the life of the creature; that with our eyes wide open to the limits as well as the possibilities of being creatures we should embrace our creaturely destiny; that we should not hold back on account of fear—the fear of the unknown future; the fear of the known future (that we must certainly die); the fear of being dependent; that we should nevertheless in all consciousness and decisively affirm and rejoice in our creaturehood: this is what it means concretely, if it means anything at all, "to glorify God and enjoy God forever." *Gloria Dei vivens homo* ("The glory of God is humankind fully alive"—Irenaeus).

To embrace this in its true radicality, one must contemplate it against the background of that world-ambiguity of which we spoke previously. Not the surpassing of creaturehood but its joyful acceptance is what biblical faith professes with respect to true humanity. If we are to take seriously the creation sagas of Genesis; if the doctrine of creation is really an integral aspect of this faith's threefold focus on creaturely being, then we must rid ourselves once and for all of this pious hesitancy about creaturehood. God intends it, and intends it for us as blessing, *shalom*. More than that, if we are really to take seriously the redemption story of the newer Testament; if the becoming-fully-human of the divine Word has any real anthropological significance for us, then we must cease once and for all treating the incarnation as deus ex machina, the "Way Out," and on the paradigm of Jesus believe that our own becoming human is the object of the divine suffering-love. We shall have to exchange Athanasius's "He became human in order that we might become divine" for the yet more incarnationally oriented summarization of soteriology: "He became human in order that we might become truly human." which is what?

Moreover, this emphasis in both the creational and redemptive foci of Christian anthropology is fully upheld and strengthened by the third dimension of this threefold focus: the fall, upon which Western Christianity fixed its gaze in questionable ways. What is the human lapse except the attempt of the creature to escape its creaturehood?—to become God, suprahuman (pride); or, conversely, to become subhuman (sloth). Falling from creaturehood, refusing the creaturely status, wanting to be more, better, higher, lower, or at any rate different: that is what sin surely means in this tradition. It means rejecting the state of creaturehood and the relationships belonging to this state and the vocations implied in this state.

It belongs to the human form of creatureliness to know this about oneself; and knowing it, not only to accept it, fatalistically, stoically, but gladly. "This is the day that the Lord hath made, let us rejoice and be glad in it!" This is the life that God has given us, let us accept this gift with gratitude. We do not have to be disappointed by it, like children expecting something more impressive for their birthdays. This knowing and this accepting may not be asked of any other terrestrial creature, we do not know; but we do know that it is asked of us, it is part of our being. And that has nothing at all to do with our alleged superiority; it has to do with the particular character of our being-with; concretely, it has to do with our vocation among the creatures—to which we shall speak in a moment. To realize the full blessedness of our creaturehood; to take up the calling of our peculiar creaturehood, the knowledge of it and the glad acceptance of it are prerequisites. Mere knowledge is not enough. Knowledge is easily enough come by. Beyond knowing—as the most significant dimension of our knowing—is the question of acknowledgment, free and unconditional and glad acknowledgment. Will we say "Yes!" to being creatures? That is the question. Until we are ready to repeat our own "Amen!" to the Creator's gift of life, we have not made good our own peculiar creaturehood.

And that is why the leading statement above insists that the knowledge and acceptance of our creaturehood is dependent upon our experience of the presence of the Creator.

b. **Coram Deo.** The truth of the matter is that it is the very knowledge of our creaturehood that militates so powerfully against our full acceptance of this state. Many of the other creatures, who seem not to have our kind of consciousness of their creaturely condition, are obviously subject to fears—for example, the fear of predators. But so far as we can discern, they do not have the fear that is most typical of humankind—that unspecified fear that is simply there in us, that transcends all descriptions, the fear that Kierkegaard named

Angst, the fear that is not exhausted when we have enumerated all the things that we are anxious about.

Angst is, apparently, for us already present in and with the thought: "I am a creature." It means: I am mortal, finite, subject to processes over which I have little or no control. I shall become old, ill, a corpse, dust, nothing. I do not have within me the wherewithal to comprehend all the processes and influences that surround and enfold me. I cannot even answer my own deepest questions. I cannot even ask them! With diligence, I may touch the surface of the questions that I am: What? How? And—the most abysmal of the questions—*Why?* I have been aware of this question, at some level of apprehension, since my earliest days, my first conscious thoughts. Why have I been born? Why do I live? Why do I suffer? Why can I not simply be? Why must I keep asking Why? I devise ways of subverting the question. I arrange a certain modus vivendi with my consciousness. I must—how else could I function reasonably, responsibly?

Fortunately I am required to be a good citizen, a provident spouse and parent, a reliable co-worker, a serene grandparent. Without these daily requirements I could not abide the attacks of teleology. All the same, my life is lived over an abyss of that forever unanswered question. It inserts itself into my subconscious despite all my precautions. My dreams are full of the confusion and chaos that flow from that source. Sometimes I long for oblivion because of it. As one of those fortunates of the First World, I am spared the immediate and vulgar threats to which so many of my kind are subjected every day. Yet sometimes I even envy the ones who suffer physically. I should not mind suffering in the flesh myself, if it would rid me of this disease of thinking.

I am of course characterizing what so many of the great novels and plays of our epoch express: the burden of creaturehood. Heretofore, religion has served as the chief reliever of this burden. Religion understands very well the demands that are evoked by the human consciousness of creaturehood. It is the primary supplier of the needs that issue from these demands. The human need to surpass creaturehood is great, perhaps the greatest instinct of all. It is innocuous to call it "the survival instinct." It wants more than mere survival. And religion speaks directly to this instinct, it offers an "out": this is only a stage, a testing ground, a preliminary exercise, at best the dress rehearsal—this creaturehood. Like the chrysalis you will slough off this flesh. And so on.

But religion as such should not be blamed, as Lenin blamed it. For the most part, it is not superimposed from above; it originates from below, in the human consciousness of creaturehood. However overlaid with great and petty forms of corruption (the power-seeking of a priestly elite, for example), at its most basic religion is a strictly human instinct, a crying out for relief from the millstone of creaturehood. And if today there is, as some insist, a return to religion, we may be sure that it has not been engineered by bungling electronic evangelists and ambitious prelates, however useful it may be to them; it too is bound up with the ancient cry of humankind: O gods, save us! Deliver us from creature-hood!

The biblical God does not respond to this cry, because the God of Abraham and Sarah, of Mary Magdalene and John the beloved disciple and Judas Iscariot, does not want to save us *from* creaturehood but *for* it. Redemption is redemption from our fear, distaste, and rejection of creaturehood, our fall. Sanctification is the sanctifying of creaturely life. Prayer in the name of Jesus Christ is a way into the world, not out of it. The baptism of water quenches the false spirituality of the ecstatic, fiery baptism that is our soul's vain attempt at flight from earth, from the body. The flesh and blood that is "remembered," taken and eaten at the Supper, is given in the form of nourishment for our bodies; it is not "medicine of immortality," it is to restore our mortality, to make us whole, to make us truly human (*vere homo*). And consider: "the resurrection *of the body.*" Creaturehood is so very good that the biblical God intends not only to save it, provide for it, clothe it—but to repeat it. *Da capo:* Go back to the beginning! This music should not be played only once; it is too beautiful. This picture should not be passed by quickly; you have to live with it. There is more in it than meets the eye. Quite naturally, then, the biblical God opts for "the resurrection of the body and the life of the world to come." Anything else would be a non sequitur.

But let us not mistake it: Only in the presence of God can the grace of accepting our creaturehood be undertaken with jubilation. This has nothing to do with bourgeois mysticism or the celebrationism of suburban Christianity. It is not a conclusion reached by the blithe spirit of healthy, well-fed, insulated bodies, contemplating in their user-friendly universe how splendid life really is. It is only genuine when it is professed and confessed from the vantage point of a full and unprotected immersion in the often turbulent waters of life. It presupposes the darkness, the impossibility, the *Anfechtung* (sense of abandonment) that real knowledge of creaturehood entails. Even in Eden, according to the saga, Eve could intuit from afar the perils of the creaturely condition. East of Eden, none who live wholly escape the knowledge of those perils. Therefore it is only grace and not nature that permits us to know and to rejoice. And this is in fact the essence of the grace that we profess. It is gospel.

c. Creaturehood as Gospel. Today, the most appropriate articulation of the meaning of gospel (*euangellion* = good news) might be: You are free to be a creature. You are liberated for creaturehood. You do not have to be a god or a demigod or a superman/woman, a Prometheus. Nor do you have to be subhuman, a robot, programmed by your television set, reading the lines and going through the motions, a Sisyphus. You may be a human being, nothing more and nothing less. Bonhoeffer said it half a century ago. So did Barth. So did many others. But we have still not heard this gospel, because we are still conditioned by religion to hear the gospel of deliverance from creaturehood.

Now, however, there is a new reason why we must hear this as gospel, and perhaps if that "must" is grasped the "may" will also be understood, finally. The new reason is the one to which we have drawn attention already: that until human beings become deeply aware of their own creaturehood, there will be no noticeable change in their comportment vis-à-vis the earth itself and its "others." The humans will continue to think themselves masters of nature (Prometheus), or victims of nature (Sisyphus), or confused combinations of the two. The only really significant "paradigm shift" will occur if and when human beings attain, not only knowledge of their creaturely solidarity with all the birds of the air and beasts of the field, but some measure of positive acceptance of this status. That acceptance, we are affirming, is always a matter of grace. It is gospel.

That does not mean that it is only Christians who can or do experience such a possibility. The divine Spirit is not confined to whatever calls itself "church," though by the same token wherever Christ's church is found it knows itself to be the creation of the Lord and Giver of life. Specifically, if the preceding assumptions have any truth in them, "church" in the North American context today will at some level of faith and understanding recognize that the knowledge and acceptance of our creaturehood is gospel.

This will be experienced as a matter of both continuity and discontinuity in the cooperative endeavor of Christians with others who know this same truth: that the point of departure for all serious concern for the biosphere today is human recognition of our participation in the general conditions of planetary existence. It will be experienced as continuity in that Christians will be able to recognize in all these others some common basis of thought and action. Those with whom knowledgeable Christians will not be able to work today are those who do not admit the need for such a radical conversion to creaturehood but think that we may continue being masters or that we must continue being mastered. The great bulk of persons and movements in whom the recognition of creation's disintegrity has taken shape have already been, as it were, converted to that need.

But (and this is the point of discontinuity with others) for the most part this conversion to the need has not been accompanied by any persuasive conversion to the possibility of meeting such a need. Thus, for the most part it is only the need that we hear about from these others. Their exhortations and the manner in which they "practice what they preach" are often truly remarkable. They shame us. They have been powerfully altered by what they have seen—in the ruination of ecosystems, the disappearance of species, the destruction of processes vital to planetary life, the waste and pillage of vital resources, the unconcern about practices that will impair or perhaps prevent altogether life and civilization in the future. They have become in our time the great moralists; and their morality is not a rhetorical affair, any more than was the morality of the temperance advocates of the nineteenth century or the morality of the social reformers against slavery, against the oppression of children and women. This morality can be effective; it can challenge the best motives, the idealism of the young, the compassion of the old. It is never to be despised by sincere Christians, who should see in it the best efforts of those who have in some way remembered the law of God.

With most it is, however, law and not gospel; imperative and not indicative. It understands what has to be done—at least, it often does. But it does not know how such a thing can be done; it does not have a foundation for its ethic, and whatever substitutes for a foundation are put forward are patently substitutes. Moralists have always pointed to the consequences of our failing to do what they direct must be done; but while that may frighten some people into action, fear will not serve as a sound foundation. Nor will the opposite approach of rewards for well-doing. Hell and heaven are just as effective and just as ineffective in their secular as in their religious deployment. This is just as true with respect to the environmental apocalypse, if we may call it that, as with respect to war, economic, racial, sexual, and other forms of injustice, and a host of other issues. In some ways, it is even truer of the whole set of problems associated with environmental deterioration; because what is being demanded here clearly is nothing short of a human *metanoia,* a fundamental change in human perception and conduct. And exhortation, even when it is astute and persuasive, cannot achieve or sustain such a fundamental change.

To speak plainly: "I do not see how man can get along without God" (Margaret Drabble). That is to say, I do not think it probable that, apart from some profound experience of a grace that at the same time convicts us of our creaturehood and reconciles us to it, we shall ever find the wisdom and (especially) the courage that are needed if we are to learn to become creatures among creatures. The whole superstructure of religion and most of what we call civilization is built on the hypothesis that we do not have to be creatures among (with) creatures, that we are above the creatures, or soon shall be. This, I think, cannot be altered by exhortation.

And therefore Christians, who consider themselves professors of a gospel distinguishable from law and the basis of authentic law (the "new law in Christ"), have a particular apologetic responsibility in this situation. They may not assume that theirs is the only rendition of the truth of God; but unless they come to believe and to understand that their gospel is intended for humanity, and that it may indeed address humanity within this particular context, they shall be salt that has lost its savor. Law that is active and alive is always better than a gospel hidden underneath the bushel of received doctrine. The question is: Can we as Christians in this historical context translate our doctrinal-theological heritage into gospel? Can we proclaim the gospel of human liberation for creaturehood?

d. Being-With All Creatures.

The test of Christian liberation, accordingly, is the manner in which it qualifies and translates into our being with all other creatures, humankind and otherkind. In the past, when it has been obedient, the disciple community has understood well enough that the fruits by which its faith and obedience were to be known were its thoughts, words, and deeds vis-à-vis other human beings. There must be no diminishment of this test because of any new awareness of the wider field of our coexistence. There need not and must not be any principle of conflict between justice and the integrity of creation. Practical difficulties will always exist, and some of these will be conflictual, because it is impossible to sort out in advance the many realities that have to be taken into account when explicit questions of human and extra-human welfare have to be answered and decisions made. There is therefore a necessity for vigilance from all sides. But that the church should divide into parties of justice and parties of ecological concern only indicates our captivation by sub-Christian ideologies. Ideologies always know in advance what is to be done, because they are abstractions from reality. Theology is not abstraction but ongoing commentary on reality from the perspective of faith—a commentary which, of course, always runs the danger of devolving into abstraction.

The revelatory experience of creaturehood places its recipients in solidarity with all other creatures, processes of creation, and the whole creaturely sphere. The ark of Noah could be our scriptural paradigm, although it would be limited as such because it is not possible to get whole ecological systems and climatic conditions and the like inside even such a parabolic ship. Despite these limitations, however, there are certain lessons to be drawn from that biblical saga.

The first is so obvious that it is regularly overlooked: What the Creator wills to preserve and cause to prosper is the very same creation that was begun before. Through moralistic and other interpretations of the mythology of Noah, the primary salvific intention of the Creator has been obscured. The flood is not the consequence of divine wrath against human evil-doing, it is a strategy of Yahweh for saving the world from the creature's *self*-destructiveness. God does not obliterate the first creation and begin anew, creating other kinds of creatures—creatures, perhaps, without even the possibility of sinning. Rather, God assembles representatives of all the species just as they are, the humans included. They are not particularly fine specimens, either, as the events immediately after the successful landing of the ark graphically illustrate. The creation *as it is* will work. It is still approved in principle and in practice by its Creator.

The second lesson that comes to us from this ancient source is simply and profoundly the lesson of solidarity. They were all "in the same boat"! There could be no hard and fast distinctions between species, humans included. No lifeboat allegory is set up here: Who will be sacrificed first? No list of hierarchic prioritization is established—we do not hear about the way in which "the law of the jungle" prevailed, so that one species consumed another, the last remaining members of that species. There is no word about separate living quarters for the humans, with or without bath!

The third lesson is that we find, however, a particular concentration upon the human species—as we would expect in this literature. To begin with, more human beings than representatives of the other species (whether two or seven) enter the ark. The Creator is obviously especially concerned for the preservation of human life. But this should not lead us back immediately into prioritization and hierarchic thinking about creaturely being. The concentration upon the human must rather be understood in relation to two considerations, one negative and one positive, that are symbolically present in this myth only because they are present everywhere in this tradition. Negatively, God's concern for the human is warranted by the divine recognition that humankind is the problematic species, the weak link in the chain of creation. Positively—and this will become our point of transition to the subsequent subsection—it has to do with humanity's function within the whole. It was not the elephants or the apes who were called to build the ark in the first place, but a human being. And not, *nota bene,* for the purpose of human self-preservation alone.

25.2. Creation as the Context of Human Vocation.   Throughout recorded history, human beings have marveled at one phenomenon more consistently than any other: their own existence. Seldom is this beguilement a matter of unalloyed adulation: the grandeur and the misery are both present in humanity's soliloquies. Yet both evoke wonder—and the more so because they are finally inseparable.

> What a piece of work is a man! how noble in reason! how infinite in faculty! in form and moving how express and admirable! in action how like an angel! in apprehension how like a god! the beauty of the world! the paragon of animals! And yet, to me, what is this quintessence of dust? man delights not me: no, nor woman neither. . . .[23]

The tradition of Jerusalem shares this awe. It is an integral part of what we have termed that tradition's anthropological concentration. The very impermanence and fragility of "this quintessence of dust," when compared with the immensity of the cosmos, only enhances the biblical sense of wonder over human being:

---

23. William Shakespeare, *Hamlet,* act 2, sc. 2, lines 317–22.

When I look at thy heavens, the work of
    thy fingers,
  the moon and the stars which thou hast
    established;
what is man that thou art mindful of him,
  and the son of man that thou dost
    care for him?
Yet thou hast made him little less than God,
  and dost crown him with glory and honor.
Thou hast given him dominion over the works
    of thy hands;
  thou hast put all things under his feet,
all sheep and oxen,
  and also the beasts of the field,
the birds of the air, and the fish of the sea,
  whatever passes along the path of the sea.
(Ps. 8 8, RSV)

What this historically important Psalm of Israel once more demonstrates, however, is that the Bible's concentration upon humankind presupposes a much broader context. Unlike Hamlet's soliloquy, the Psalmist's awe is not the consequence of reflection upon the perfections of the isolated human subject. Such reflection, as nearly all Shakespeare's plays so eloquently illustrate, easily leads to disillusionment and despair; for this so excellent creature regularly applies its faculties to dastardly and ignoble ends. The author of Psalm 8 is not indulging in anthropocentrism when he marvels at his own kind. In marked contrast to the humanistically inclined moderns who have loved to cite this passage of Scripture, the Psalmist does not begin with "Man" at all; he begins with God—and this is no mere formality.

O Lord, our Lord,
how majestic is thy name in all the earth!

Thou whose glory above the heavens is chanted
    by the mouth of babes and infants,
  thou hast founded a bulwark because of thy foes,
    to still the enemy and the avenger. (vv. 1-2)

The Psalmist's soliloquy on humanity is set within this thoroughly doxological context. Human "glory and honor" (v. 5) do not accrue to humanity *in se* but to the one who created this creature and called it to a particular vocation within the sphere of creation.

Are we then to consider the tradition theocentric and, with a growing segment of the church and the theological guild, to counsel a return from liberal Christian anthropocentrism to theo- and Christocentrism? Certainly God—

345

and for newer Testamental faith God-in-Christ—is central to this story: God initiates, God creates, God calls, God judges, God redeems, God is "all and in all." And as for *anthropos,* clearly the tradition envisions essential humanity as humanity *centered in* God. At its most basic, the biblical concept of repentance (*metanoia*) means turning away from "idols" (Ezek. 14:6), stubbornness (Deut. 9:13ff.), "evil ways" (Jonah 3:8), and turning toward God (Zech. 1:3, and elsewhere). The whole thrust of the theology of redemption is, in short, humanity's reorientation toward God.

Yet to conclude that the tradition therefore is theocentric is not wholly adequate or accurate. Particularly in a religious context like our own, where theocentrism is all too explicitly understood to mean a God-centeredness that excludes or marginalizes every other interest, a faith professed in these terms will hardly speak to the crisis of a world that is perhaps being rendered uninhabitable on account of human rapacity and neglect. Besides, even apart from this contextual concern, theocentrism does not do justice to the tradition as it stands. For as we have already seen, the God who is certainly central to this story and in whom humanity is called to center itself *is not God-centered.* The fundamental Theology of this tradition will have us contemplate a deity whose own orientation is toward the world, and who looks to the articulate component of that world—the "speaking animal," humankind—for response, discourse, conscious participation. Oddly enough, given the usual megalomania of humanity's gods, the God of Abraham, Isaac, and Jacob, the Father of Jesus Christ, is not turned in upon Self but outward toward the other—is geocentric and anthropocentric. To the God-orientation of repentant humanity there corresponds a human-orientation of the gracious God: "Turn ye unto me, saith the Lord of hosts, and I will turn unto you" (Zech. 1:3, KJV). A religious tradition whose very *Theos* is other-centered cannot be described adequately as a theocentric tradition.

If anything is central to the narrative core of this tradition, it is the story itself—the whole, unfolding drama of God's venture, the creation, with its historical and natural dimensions, its diverse inhabitants, and the always surprising interactions of all of its personages and components. It is of course God's undertaking, and therefore God is always prominent in the story. But as in a drama the action constantly shifts from one center of concern to another, so biblical faith does not lend itself to permanent concentration upon any one center, not even God. As for theological midrash on this story, concentration will fall upon that aspect of the whole to which attention is evoked by contextual realities. Thus, over against modern liberal concentration upon humanity, it was necessary for neoorthodox and other critics of liberalism to stress the theocentrism of the biblical story; just as, over against the single-minded and oppressive theocentrism of Protestant orthodoxy, it had been necessary earlier for liberalism to accentuate the humanism of the tradition. The whole drama is distorted if one facet of it is abstracted and made permanently decisive. A strategic, contextual theology concentrates upon the dimension of the whole which, in that particular here-and-now, requires faith's attention.

It is both faithful to the tradition and contextually sound, I believe, to insist that what should occupy the mind of the disciple community in North America today is creation in its totality. Neither deity nor humanity nor nature alone should be thought central, but what must command our attention is the whole enterprise in which, according to the narrative basis of this tradition, both *Theos* and *anthropos* are engaged—God's creation project. Creation, including its mending, is the perspective from which we may most faithfully discuss the question of human vocation in our time and place. The appropriate form of this question is the one that we have used in the historical and critical chapters already: What is the role of the human creature within the creation? *employees of God?*

The Psalm quoted above immediately answers this question with the word "dominion" (*radah*). It is impossible to read Psalm 8 today, as it is impossible to read the Priestly account of creation in Genesis (1:26), without hearing that word as the point of stumbling for many. Is it not precisely this biblical assumption of and exhortation to "dominion" that has introduced into the Western Christian world an image of the human that is not only anthropocentric but dangerously, uncritically managerial? Are not the exaltation of the human and the concomitant objectification of nature the consequences of such a conception of humanity's calling?

What I would like to propose is that, on the contrary, the dilemmas of the technological society have been brought about by a complete failure on the part of Christendom to comprehend human "dominion" as it is conceived in this literature. Furthermore, so far as the Christian contribution to the correction of this life-threatening situation is concerned, nothing could be more significant than our coming to understand human vocation in terms of "dominion" comprehended within the total context of biblical faith.

25.3. Vocation as Representation of God's Dominion.   Assuming, then, that what is central to the narrative foundations of the faith that Christians profess is the creation project of God, how does this enable us to regard the concept of human "dominion" in a contextually appropriate way?

First, it effectively refutes the notion that is the silent presupposition of "dominion" understood in hierarchic terms, namely that the human creature is the pinnacle of the Creator's work, and as such transcendent of ("above") all the rest. So far as its biblical basis is concerned, that long-standing assumption stems from a misappropriation of the story of creation in Genesis 1: As the work of the sixth day, it was assumed, the human creature is the goal of the entire enterprise, creation's crown jewel. Jürgen Moltmann has insightfully reminded us,[24] however, that the Priestly account of creation does not move inevitably toward, or come to its climax with, the work of the sixth day; the goal is attained rather on the seventh. "And on the seventh day God finished his work that he had done, and he rested on the seventh day from all the work that he had done. So God blessed the seventh day and hallowed it, because on it God rested from all the work that he had done in creation" (Gen. 2:2-3).

Like every artist and artisan, God does not reach the envisioned goal of God's project until it has been completed and the Creator may gaze upon, contemplate, and take pleasure in the finished work. The *telos* toward which Wisdom directs the mind of the Creator is not attained until the seventh day, when God is at last able to see what was only envisioned before, and so to confirm the rightness of the vision: "God saw everything that he had made, and indeed, it was very good" (Gen. 1:31). The sabbath is hallowed, not by a divine rest (Gen. 2:2, 3) understood in passive terms, but by a rest that incorporates the delight of divine Wisdom in what it has fashioned:

> The Lord created me [Wisdom] at the beginning of his
> work,
>   the first of his acts of long ago. . . .
>   then I was beside him, like a master worker;
> and I was daily his delight,
>   rejoicing before him always,
>   rejoicing in his inhabited world
>   and delighting in the human race. (Prov. 8:22, 30-31)

Humankind has thus its place within that divine delight, but as part of the whole, contemplated in its wholeness—its integrity—by its Maker.

Second, when the creation as an integrated work is understood as the Creator's goal, it follows that humanity must be viewed in relation to the totality and not the other way around, as if the rest of creation had been brought into being as a stage on which the human actor might strut. Instead of picturing the Creator as fashioning a world fit for humanity, we must think of God devising humanity in such a way as to suit the requirements of an earth whose rudiments, laws, and potentialities precede the *adam* in the plan of God. The Creator's question, so to speak, is not, What sort of world shall I make for this splendid creature, this centerpiece of the project? but rather, What sort

---

24. *God in Creation: An Ecological Doctrine of Creation* (The Gifford Lectures of 1984–1985), trans. Margaret Kohl (Minneapolis: Fortress Press, 1993), "The Sabbath: The Feast of Creation," 276–96.

of creature shall I need to do justice to this kind of world? In other words, the character of the human creature is determined by the inherent needs of the creation as it is envisioned by its Creator. Humanity is fashioned as to its peculiar capacities and endowments by the worldly office for which the Creator intends it. Its raison d'être is to be found outside itself, in the mind of the Creator and in the structure of what the Creator calls into being.

Now we may return to the knotty term, "dominion." The office for which the human creature is fashioned is "dominion." What does this mean? The term is by no means self-explanatory. In fact, as soon as it is separated from the scriptural and theological context in which it is used in both Psalm 8 and Genesis 1, it lends itself to flagrant misinterpretation. We do not have to speculate about that; it is a matter of historical observation. As with nearly every other key word of the Bible, "dominion" has been fantastically misshapen through wrong association. Under the impact of almost every historical model one can name, from Caesar to General Electric, the biblical "dominion" becomes *domination.*

The misinterpretation of this term is more complicated still, because, as we have seen in Part I, even if "dominion" as it is used in these biblical references is (rightly) perceived to be associated with the character and rule of God and not of human paradigms of power and authority, the fact remains that Christendom has been at work for centuries depicting God in the most unambiguously *dominant* terms. So that, far from introducing a prophetic critique of fallen humanity's own habitual experiments in domination, the Christian religion has on the whole legitimized human domination by presenting the divine model of "dominion" as "the Father Almighty."

The restoration of Christian anthropology in general, and of the Christian understanding of human vocation in particular, thus entails the restoration of biblical Theology. For the human vocation biblically understood is in the first instance the representation of God within the sphere of creation.[25] And if our preconception of deity is nothing more than an abstract apotheosis of the power principle according to (for example) white, Western, masculine forms of ambition, then of course we shall end with nothing short of human domination

---

25. "The command to have dominion *(radah)* actualizes the divine intention already stated in Gen. 1:26, where the link between creation in the image of God and the charge to have dominion is even clearer. It is as representative (image) of God that we are given capacity for power in the world. This is not the granting of an absolute human prerogative to do with the earth what we will. If the term 'dominion' has royal connotations of rule, it is as representatives of divine rule that we exercise authority. We are not absolute monarchs in the world but trustees or stewards acting in behalf of God's sovereignty as Creator. Thus, the implied moral norm is a measuring of human actions by reference to their faithfulness in reflecting God's will and ultimate rule." (Bruce C. Birch, *Let Justice Roll Down: The Old Testament, Ethics, and Christian Life* (Louisville: Westminster/John Knox Press, 1991), 89.

of everything that can possibly be dominated But what we have claimed about the nature and purposes of God as they should now be professed in our context—that God is "a suffering God"—must of necessity radically alter our understanding of "dominion" to which such a God calls human beings.

It belongs to that divine suffering—that voluntary relinquishment of absolute power, that kenosis—that God will exercise God's own dominion indirectly, through a creature, one who shares with all creatures their ephemeral and vulnerable nature and destiny. God limits Godself in creation. The creation is "other" in relation to God, and its otherness must be respected. That God's rule is mediated through a creature that is itself part of creation, subject to all of creation's laws, rather than imposed directly, heteronomously, upon the creation is an integral aspect of the divine respect for creation's otherness.

By the same token, in its internal dominion the human creature is required to emulate God's own character and manner of rule; it is to image God within the creational realm. God wills to be represented concretely within the creation by one whose orientation toward God may make it possible for that one to mirror God's own way with creation as a whole. And if we take our cue from what is actually claimed about this God in the continuity of the testaments, this can by no stretch of the imagination lead to human domination, whether the domination of our own kind or of otherkind. On the contrary, representing God's dominion would have to mean almost the antithesis of what this concept regularly means in human experience. It would have to mean resisting the temptation to "lord it over" the others; it would have to mean long-suffering, compassion, solidarity, mercy, grace, edification; it would have to mean servanthood, selfless stewardship[26] of creation; it would have to mean love—sacrificial love, agape.

---

26. Because I have already expressed my thoughts on the theology of stewardship extensively, I shall not develop this subject here beyond the present reference, which sets stewardship in its proper theological context. Because of a certain simplistic representation of this theology current in the present theo-ecological debate, however, at least a footnote is mandatory. It is given out in certain circles of "environmental concern" that stewardship is a too "managerial" notion. For example: "Even such theological concepts as stewardship have to be viewed with a degree of healthy scepticism. Though it emphasizes a more responsible and caring relationship to Creation, stewardship still places humans in the position of power. It is *a management model.* It assumes that we know what is best for the Earth, although the tree has done a pretty good job of growing on its own, and the loon has known how to survive for 50 million years. Now human societies are threatening the loon's very existence. . . ." (David G. Hallman, *A Place in Creation: Ecological Visions in Science, Religion and Economics* [Toronto: United Church Publishing House, 1992], 101 [emphasis added].)

Not only does this kind of analysis betoken a conception of stewardship fundamentally uninformed by biblical and theological research and imagination, but it capitulates to the bourgeois mysticism that is stealing over the spirit of affluent Western societies, capturing in particular the allegiances of certain classes of intellectuals and "religious" persons. Its appeal cannot be divorced from the affluence of these same classes, who in their newly acquired concern for nature

The Integrity of Creation

The full impact of what we hear in Psalm 8 and Genesis 1:26 cannot be grasped by Christians until it has been submitted to the christological basis of the faith. The only paradigm worthy of the biblical assumptions concerning the term "dominion" is the one whom the Latin church called *Dominus*. If the following two verses of Scripture are read and contemplated side by side, they will suggest something of what is intended by this statement:

> You have given them dominion over . . . all sheep and oxen. . . . (Ps. 8:6-7)
>
> "I am the good shepherd. The good shepherd lays down his life for the sheep." (John 10:11)

Nothing is more needful in our present context than a new appreciation for the human "dominion" that God our Creator exemplifies in the authentic human being, Jesus, the shepherd who lays down his life for the sheep. Over against a domineering, manipulative, smug technological humanity that tries to control the whole world; but also over against a frightened, bored, or pleasure-seeking humanity that lets the world go its own way so long as it is not too directly affected by the degradation that inevitably results, it is precisely human "dominion" that is called for. Neither domination of the world nor withdrawal from the world meets the requirements of this tradition under the impact of the contemporary situation. More than ever, the human being is called by God today to assume "dominion"—only this refers, not to the dominion exemplified by Caesar but to that exemplified by Jesus Christ.

---

are able to assuage their incipient guilt about nature's deterioration by discovering how truly they have always loved the wilderness.

I too stand in awe of loons. But I do not expect them to do much about the starving thousands in Somalia!

Larry Rasmussen's account of the discussion of this topic at Canberra (the Seventh General Assembly of the World Council of Churches) should be taken seriously. He notes that "many Europeans and North Americans were fearful that 'steward' too easily backslides into the familiar domination model." On the other hand, "Both the Jews and early Christians understood 'image of God' and 'dominion' as a message of cosmic dignity that affirmed human agency and responsibility. *From the perspective of the less powerful at Canberra, to be named by God the custodians of creation is an empowering word. The steward model empowers such people to recognize themselves as created in the image of God—the subjects, not the objects, of history.*" "The Assembly, the majority of whose delegates represented the majority of the world, namely the poor, quite naturally affirmed the dignity of the human person and gave central place to the suffering of millions, even billions, of people. These delegates had nothing in common with those environmentalists (mostly romantic, mostly white, mostly rich) for whom the most pristine picture of the world is one in which homo sapiens are nowhere to be seen—only sunny, harmonious 'nature.' . . . Such views were voted down, however, on the grounds that they offended the biblical dignity of human beings and their high stewardly calling." ("Toward an Earth Charter," in *The Christian Century* [Oct. 23, 1991], 964ff. [emphasis added].)

There is something ironic about intellectuals who, from their comfortable, air-conditioned studies, write books about a world in which homo sapiens "is nowhere to be seen—only sunny, harmonious 'nature.'"

25.4. Vocation as the Representation of Creation.   The vocation of the human being is representational also in a second sense. Not only is this being called to represent to all creatures the God who "is love," but it is called as well to represent all creatures before God. If the first aspect of the representational vocation can be expressed in the language of dominion understood as sacrificial servanthood, the second should be expressed chiefly in the language of gratitude, thanksgiving, and praise.

Psalm 8, whose use of the concept of "dominion" has suggested the first aspect of our exposition of human vocation, can provide us with an illustration also of this second aspect—though it shares this with all the Psalms, and with much else belonging to the Scriptures of this tradition. For the presupposition of the whole statement of this Psalm—so thoroughly presupposed, indeed, that it can escape our attention altogether—is its form as an address to God. Here the human being, the speaking animal, comes before its Creator with words. It is not there for its own sake alone; it is there in behalf of all the others. It is the priest who represents them all before God. It is the poet (Brueggemann) who articulates what the other creatures express in their very being.

Therefore this creature expresses, first and last, praise: "O Lord, our Sovereign, how majestic is your name in all the earth!" (Ps. 8:1, 9). Praise, thanksgiving, and gratitude flood the psalms of Israel and are recapitulated in the prayers of Jesus, the "high priest." But the response of the human representative of creation to its Creator cannot, under the conditions of existence, be praise, thanksgiving, and gratitude only. Even in this brief Psalm, with its exceptionally doxological spirit, the shadow side of creaturely existence also makes its appearance in the form of "the enemy and the avenger" (v. 2). In so many of the other Psalms, the tone is far darker—is one of lament, or fear, or even anger. And Jesus too, in the Garden of sorrows, recapitulates this side of the human representation of creation. For creation "groans" (Rom. 8:22), and our human representation of creation is not true if it does not reflect, as well, this travail.

Today especially, it belongs to the Christian understanding of humanity's calling to bring before God the groaning of a creation that can scarcely bear the burden of existence. Those who believe that the prayers of the church and of the pious should contain only gratitude "for the beauty of the earth" need to reconsider the psalms and laments of Israel, summed up in the cry of dereliction from the cross. Humanity repents of the evil that it has visited upon the inarticulate creation only as it articulates the groaning of the creation. For that is the only legitimate sign of its solidarity with the other creatures in the reality of their existing in a still-unredeemed world.

Both from the perspective of humankind's representation of God within the sphere of creation, then, and from that of its representation of the creation before God, what is presupposed is precisely the community of humankind with

352

otherkind. Far from removing the human creature from the rest of creation, the stewardly, priestly, and poetic vocation of humankind as it is understood within this tradition presses toward an even greater sense of being-with in relation to the others. This sense is not one of merger, nor of undifferentiated union—difference is honored here—but of the highest form of communion.

26. The Destiny of Creation

26.1 The End as Catastrophe. We concluded our historical reflections on creaturely being with the observation that Christian doctrine on the whole leaves the question of the destiny of creation unanswered. While there are biblical themes that are suggestive of a positive statement concerning "the fate of the earth," historic Christianity has seldom pursued these. Instead, the tradition's concentration upon the human creature has encouraged the dominant theological conventions of Christendom to regard the earth as the stage setting for the human drama; so that, having in sundry ways settled the question of human destiny, the destiny of the creation as a whole could be more or less ignored—as the props of great plays and operas, no matter how impressive they may have been throughout the drama, fade from memory with the resolution, in the final act, of the human dilemma.

The notable exception to this generalization is apocalypticism. Apocalyptic expressions of the Christian religion almost invariably entail the destruction of the "stage setting" along with the evil-doers who are judged and condemned. There is in this more than a hint of Manichaeanism. That is to say, the entertainment of the end as catastrophe seems to have its genesis in a deep suspicion concerning the redeemability of anything so prone to decay as the material universe. Whether this suspicion is the consequence of an innate sense of the vulnerability of finitude or experienced disillusionment in the face of specific private anxieties and public fears, it is after all a rather common one, one to which most human beings are at least intermittently drawn. Who has not been assailed by the thought that life in this world is so problematic that the only resolution honest reflection could entertain would necessitate an alteration so radical as to entail the dissolution of life as we know it? This apocalyptic sense, which is naturally heightened in periods of historical instability, is perhaps, as has been proposed, "the mother of religion." The religious impulse, which seems indigenous to the human spirit, is at least strongly activated by the sense of an ending.

Here we encounter what within the spirit of our own age demands of us as Christians of the nonapocalyptic mainstream in North America a more explicit response to the question of the destiny of creation than we have ever before given or even considered. For the sense of an ending that conditions all sentient life has, in our present context, been greatly aggravated by a whole spectrum of public realities that raise the private anxieties of human beings to new planes of concern and preoccupation.

The realities to which I refer are not all of them dramatic or conspicuous. Though it is customary to think in this connection of the great physical threats to life that have accentuated our "future shock," any discussion of the factors contributing to the public mood described by that term must take account of realities far less tangible than warfare, economic upheaval, and environmental deterioration. It would have to extend into that mysterious realm of spiritual transition that witnessed the birth of the so-called scientific outlook.

Sometime between the High Middle Ages and the Enlightenment, the spirit of Western humanity began to turn away from belief in the worldly governance of an exacting yet ultimately benevolent deity toward the cosmos itself, with its apparently unchanging laws and processes—processes that were subject to human investigation and could, if understood, serve human ends; yet processes, too, that were fundamentally indifferent to the ambitions of human individuals and societies. And among these processes the wary side of the collective human psyche became conscious also of the process of decline and inevitable decay: entropy. The diminishment of energy in a closed system like the universe could be retained as objective information, without adverse emotional effect, in a society persuaded of historical progress. But the knowledge that mortality applies to the earth itself; that the universe will itself grow old, sicken, and die: such knowledge has become existentially significant in our own time, as we consider many of the immediate natural threats that can seem to us, now, like so many symptoms of the winding down of the system.

Together with the effective disappearance of the highly positive conception of history and human agency that is the birthright of European civilization on this continent, this newly gripping awareness of the expendability of the natural life-forces of the universe has created in our midst an apocalyptic consciousness so powerful that it conditions our whole behavior as a people. The fact that it is not, for the most part, acknowledged is not only not surprising in view of what has been argued earlier concerning our need to continue seeming optimistic; it is also the dimension of this sociopsychic posture that makes it particularly virulent. Precisely because we do not possess a language for articulating this secular apocalypse; precisely because modernity robbed us of any frame of reference for permitting such prospects of a catastrophic ending to come into consciousness, let alone be vocalized by more than a small minority—in short, just because they are and must be repressed, these feelings of termination are all the more effective among us. This of course belongs to the characterization of the dominant culture of North America that we created earlier: Sisyphus playing the role of Prometheus.

The situation begets two different but closely connected responses: On the one hand, that segment within our majority culture which still nurtures and is nurtured by the mythos of mastery and progress, and is sufficiently insulated against the coarser assaults of the times by stabilizing economic and psychic conditions, continues to demand a return to the posture of control. The political right in both Canada and the United States becomes increasingly adamant on this point. In an almost total psychic denial of all aspects of the secular apocalypse, this segment insists that the good destiny of our society is assured, if only government and the other institutions of society will encourage self-reliance and a return to belief in ourselves. It is not accidental that this approach necessitates isolationist national policies always verging on racism; for when the global character of contemporary life is taken into account, the prospect of a return to mastery and progress is less readily envisioned.

On the other hand, those more vulnerable to the realities of the ending that is sensed, including many whose material circumstances are affected by economic recessions as well as persons who are not psychically capable of sustained repressive behavior, with ever greater frequency capitulate to the apocalyptic atmosphere. A significant proportion of these resolve the inevitable anxieties of such a capitulation through the adoption of an apocalyptic religious faith, whether Christian or otherwise. Apocalyptic religion is powerful in our context because, whatever one may think about its specific dogmas, it offers people a framework of meaning that is needed if they are to cope in such an age. In a real sense, from the standpoint at least of personal health, apocalyptic religious faith acts as a safety net for many who, in our time, would (and do) otherwise become mentally ill; and therefore in an odd way it performs a public service.

That does not, however, alter the fact that it does this by supporting the much more extensive (if devastating) public conclusion that the fate of the earth has already been sealed. Those who cling to the religious belief that the destruction of earth is a necessary accompaniment to or consequence of the salvation ("rapturing") of the elect confront earth's doom with equanimity or even rejoicing, while those who enjoy no such faith can do so only through the development of a programmed indifference or sheer fatalism. One way or another, however, the mind-set that results from this capitulation profoundly affects our whole social enterprise. We appear to have determined—and at the subconscious level where it is most devastating—that there is no future for earth, really; that we may pursue our own little ambitions and programs as long as this is possible, but that we must know we are doing this "on our own," with no external backing. The stage setting itself may go up in smoke before our drama is done!

The power of this public mood demands of Christians of the classical traditions that they break their silence on the question of the destiny of creation. More than that, it challenges us to make, if we can, a positive statement about the fate of the earth; for apart from this all talk of Christian hope is finally otherworldly and little more, in the end, than a variation on the theme of human redemption that has been our soteriology all along.

26.2. The End as Consummation.   To think of the end of creation as consummation is to engage in two bold acts of Christian profession that have rarely achieved in the church the fullness to which divine grace invites the disciple community: First, it is to engage in an act of faith which defies much that is unavoidable to "sight"; second, it is to engage in an act of truth that is quite probably inconceivable apart from faith.

To profess the end as consummation is an act of truth because such a thought can only emerge from the reflections of a community that contemplates in all honesty the real prospect of "the end," with all the uncertainty, apprehension, and fear that such thought engenders. The conventional forms of mainstream Christianity have seldom demonstrated their capacity for this kind of reflection. Indeed, the formerly established churches in North America automatically assume—with the whole social stratum of which they are part—that any talk of "the end" belongs to the crassest sort of sectarianism. Within the safe environs of middle-class churches, the only persons who would resort to such ideas, it is assumed, are individuals who have become unhinged mentally. Contemplating death, whether in its microcosmic or macrocosmic forms, the churches have habitually stopped short of facing the stark reality of such a terminus. Whether through an exposition of resurrection transformed by Hellenistic ideas of the immortality of the soul, or through a liberal-romantic camouflaging of the fact of death itself, North American Christianity has characteristically refused to face death as the end of human possibilities. It has accepted neither biblical nor modern scientific realism about death, but has clung to dogmas and sentiments that insulate it from the awesome reality. This has been enacted perennially in the Holy Week liturgical sequence, which in both conservative and liberal Protestant expressions presents the "crucified, dead, and buried" Christ as if he were not really crucified, dead, and buried, but only temporarily detained, and the risen, glorified Christ as a phenomenon almost natural.

This paradigm, so practiced in our treatment of personal death, is the one that is drawn upon also in contemplation of the death of the macrocosm—insofar as we consider it at all. This enables us to think of the end of the world without pain, because it is not really an ending. In this way, all that is accomplished, beyond the peace of mind of a few middle-class people, is that the churches cut themselves off all the more from those who cannot avoid the pain of the contemplation of earth's ending, or civilization's ending—which in particular means the young. Our doctrinal triumphalism, sentimental and inarticulate as it is, keeps us from experiencing the truly traumatic feelings that are inspired in every young person as he or she is assailed by the data—the increasingly explicit data—of earth's decline. To profess the end—that is, to incorporate an omega as well as an alpha, an ending as well as a beginning into our profession of the faith—is in our particular context to engage in an act of unusual truth-telling, and as such it is never pain-free. Until we can do this, however, we shall not only be denying and subverting a great deal of scientific evidence about the nature of the universe and taking less seriously than we should the data of decline that pour in from every source today, but we shall also be proving once more that we are not quite capable of exposing ourselves to the realities that must be confronted by others who do not possess our psychically insulating system of belief.

The second boldness implied in the profession of the end as consummation is in reality the presupposition of the first; for without faith the contemplation of the realities of the end is neither probable nor, on the whole, advisable. Trust in God, which is what faith has been interpreted to mean throughout this exposition of Christian belief, enables us to consider the terrors of death and life, and of death that is always in the midst of life, without being entirely debilitated by such reflection. In fact, such trust thrusts us into the zone of truth, because unless we are truthful about death we cannot be truthful either about that which "gives life to the dead and calls into existence the things that do not exist" (Rom. 4:17).

Trusting in the God of life, the faithful regard with eyes wide open the destructive capabilities of the powers of death and profess, despite them, that the end toward which creation moves is not ultimate catastrophe but consummation.

At the risk of repetition, we must underscore the insistence that this profession is a matter of faith; and here we should hearken to the reformers and understand this to mean "sheer faith" (*sola fide*)—that is, faith understood not only as ordinary trust but as response to unusual and unheard-of grace (*sola gratia*). It is by no means necessary for such faith to overlook or underestimate the power of life to heal and renew itself. There is, as the reformers knew, a common grace upon which every breath we draw depends and without which every new day would be unthinkable; and this grace is so common that to distinguish it from nature itself is only given to those who believe that nature as such is gift—is creation. But the open contemplation of the end and the trust which sees through that end a beginning: this requires more than common grace, and as for nature, it is of little or no support in the construction of such a conclusion.

Faith as response to exceptional grace is the acceptance of an invitation to see the cosmos as God sees it—though, certainly, "through a glass, darkly." In reality, nothing more than an occasional glimpse is given. But it is enough. It enables the disciple community to contemplate the fate of the earth from a perspective external to the earth itself, the perspective of earth's Maker, Judge, and Redeemer. From that point of vantage, the earth is not "the late, great planet" but a creation greatly loved, whose Maker has declared it "very good," whose Judge has foresworn its annihilation, whose Redeemer came "not to destroy but to give life." Here the very world that so easily seems to us who are within it the most fragile thing, whose long-term survival in any form is highly unlikely, is "seen together with . . . what is already evident to God's foresight." And faith is given to trust that God "sees better";[27] for God sees not only what is and what is coming to be but the glory (*doxa*) by which the entire process is surrounded. The "very good" of the Creator is, for faith, not merely the pronouncement of a worker about the product prior to its actual use; it is a statement about the whole concept and vision that the creation embodies, and of which it can never be robbed. Human sight—even human insight—sees only the externalities of the thing; thus, says Luther, "the fools of philosophers look at God's creature" and are appalled. They do not understand that "it is constantly being prepared for the glory that is to come, but they see only what it is in itself and how it is equipped but [they] have no thought whatsoever for the end for which it was created."[28]

To profess that the end is to be understood as consummation and not catastrophe is to profess that God is committed to God's creational project and will bring it to its proper fulfillment, in spite of and even through "the wrath of men." It is to profess that redemption, as it is glimpsed in Jesus Christ, has a cosmic and not only a human dimension. It is to insist that resurrection—not immortality, but resurrection—applies to the whole created order, and not only to the chosen among the human species. Accordingly, in all of this we are presupposing what must now, in Part III of this study, become our point of concentration: the doctrine of Jesus as the Christ.

To conclude this discussion: If it is asked how such a thing could be, how a finite universe moving inevitably toward its termination could be thought by anyone to have an inner aim (*telos*) sufficiently substantial to be the subject of human hope, then of course the disciple community is thrown back upon its unadorned noetic assumption: *Credo*—I believe, I trust. With the macrocosm it is the same as with the microcosm, our own selves: the possibility does not lie in the creature but in the Creator. With the one who brought the cosmos into being, *ex nihilo,* there is also the possibility—for there is the will—to bring it to its intended perfection.

While faith therefore leaves to God the "how" of such a consummation, it is never silent about the "what" and the "why" of it. For while biblical religion consistently and necessarily avoids explaining how God could be God, it does not withhold but on the contrary is at pains to divulge what God is doing in the

---

27. Eberhard Jüngel, *The Freedom of a Christian: Luther's Significance for Contemporary Theology* (Minneapolis: Augsburg Pub. House, 1988), 35.

28. *Lectures on Romans* (Philadelphia: Westminster Press, 1961), 237.

world, and why. God in this tradition manifests an abiding commitment to this world (our nonreligious definition of the theology of the cross), and this commitment would be questionable from the start if it were not understood as the determination to see the cosmos through to the "very good" omega that is already implicit in the "very good" alpha.

It is time, therefore, for the remnants of classical Christianity on this continent to counter all the rumors of a catastrophic ending that emanate from either religious or secular sources by professing their faith in a God who wills to complete and fulfill the promises of a creation that has been visited and redeemed by the love that made it.

PART III
JESUS THE CHRIST, SAVIOR

CHAPTER ■ SEVEN

Jesus: His Person and His Work

27. The Foundation and Core of Christian Profession

27.1 "Jesus Christ, and Him Crucified." In this volume we are seeking to answer the question, What is it that constitutes a Christian profession of faith? What makes it Christian? The answer in the briefest possible terms is that Christians profess Jesus as the Christ. They are called Christians, properly speaking, only for this reason.

That is not to say that the Christian profession of faith is exclusively a statement of belief in or concerning Jesus as the Christ. When St. Paul wrote to the Corinthian Christians that he had "decided to know nothing among you except Jesus Christ, and him crucified" (1 Cor. 2:2), he did not mean that he intended to confine his witness to statements directly related to Jesus. Glancing at the headings provided by most editions of Paul's letters, one notes that the apostle covers a great variety of subjects. Even in the two relatively lengthy letters to the Corinthians, there are excursuses on stewardship, the keeping of festivals, the body, marriage, idolatry, the glory of God, the Eucharist, love, speaking in tongues, the Spirit, contributions of money for Christian work, the new covenant, the suffering of the disciple community, the marks of apostleship, and other topics. With all that Paul has to say here and in the other epistles about human behavior, the law, Judaism, Christian freedom, and many other subjects both theoretical and concrete, one could hardly accuse the apostle to the Gentiles of Christomonism.

What Paul means when he asserts that he is determined to know and to preach only the one thing, "Jesus Christ, and him crucified," is that for him this represents the foundation and core of the whole Christian profession of belief. That is to say, he intends to consider every subject from the perspective that one acquires upon it when it is considered from the vantage point of the cross.

That someone should contemplate existence from a particular point of view is not unusual. It is what we all do, whether or not we acknowledge the fact. If we are to achieve any sort of coherence at all, if we are to avoid the intellectual and psychic confusion of being recipients of impressions, random thoughts, and emotions that we cannot hold together in any meaningful way, then we must attain some perspective on the world, some window through which to observe and relate the great variety of things that we see, hear, feel, sense, experience, or know. Without such a perspective, we are at the mercy of the world's apparent randomness. For the sake of truth and in all humility we must periodically be cast back upon the chaos of raw experience. Perhaps we learn all too soon how to "order" everything, subjecting all the astonishing diversity and unpredictability of existence to little systems that reflect no more than the narrowness and provinciality of our own exposure to reality. Who is not familiar with the vociferous bigot for whom every actual and possible event is fitted without surprise or effort into a well-rehearsed "philosophy" or "faith"? This, however, is an exaggeration and distortion of a process entirely needful to life: the building of a perceptual foundation through which to gain sufficient insight and foresight so as to make sense of existence.

For the former Saul, persecutor of Christians, the very thing that he had struggled against and sought to eradicate—the message concerning the crucified one—had become that perceptual foundation. He found in the gospel of Jesus as the Christ a core of meaning through which he might open himself to all else, whether unseen or seen, whether thoughts of the mind or impulses and instincts of the flesh, whether private anxieties or public events and the great movements of history. "Everything," in the sense in which we have established that term, could be submitted to the *Sophia* (wisdom) God had put forward in this person and event regarded by worldly wisdom as "foolishness" (1 Cor. 1:18ff.).

Not every Christian has agreed with Paul's particular appropriation of "the wisdom of the cross" or his application of it to every subject upon which he expressed himself. Not every Christian has endorsed even the manner in which Paul speaks of the core event itself, the foundational theology of the crucified Christ. Yet it would be difficult to justify the use of the adjective Christian to describe any posture that did not adhere to the principle that Paul establishes here. Positions that do not take "the Christ event" as their perceptual founda-tion; positions that, while they make space for aspects of this event, subsume even those aspects under some religious or philosophic point of view that functions more significantly for them: such positions could hardly qualify as Christian. A theology is Christian if and when it finds in Jesus as the Christ the meditative core in and around which it intends to weave its reflections about "everything."

Expressed in such a way, this affirmation will not satisfy those who want to reserve the appellation Christian for persons who endorse explicit christological doctrines and dogmas. The point which, in one way and another, I shall reiterate throughout the three chapters of this final part is that what makes anyone a Christian is not adherence to specific doctrines about Jesus Christ but adherence to Jesus Christ. As far as doctrine is concerned, serious Christian faith will sustain, I believe, an attitude that is both respectful and critical. It will be respectful because it will assume that doctrine, at least in its intention, is nothing more nor less than the halting attempt of the formulators of our tradition to express in words the mystery of this person and the meaning of this person's work. But genuine faith will also be critical of doctrine, and more explicitly of the way in which doctrine functions in communities of belief, because it knows, insofar as it knows the person, that no doctrine whatsoever can adequately express this mystery.

This does not mean that the Christian community is called to capitulate to undifferentiated mystery. St. Paul, along with most of those whose names have to appear in any discussion of what Christians profess, tried hard to express and communicate the sense made by the "foolish wisdom" of God: ". . . among the mature we do speak wisdom, though it is not a wisdom of this age or of the rulers of this age, who are doomed to perish. But we speak God's wisdom, secret and hidden, which God decreed before the ages for our glory" (1 Cor. 2:6-7). As we insisted in the Introduction to this volume, there is good reason to think that a serious and disciplined attempt to articulate Christian doctrine, and to do so in terms that can engage our own context, is one of the most important callings of the disciple community in North America today. All the same, it is not doctrine that constitutes the foundation and core of the Christian profession; it is Jesus. He himself, and not our so-called Christology, is our wisdom. Being Christian means allowing this "secret and hidden" wisdom of God that Jesus "is" (Paul did not say that Jesus "imparts") to inform and direct, question, stimulate, and criticize all that comes to us from the world of our internal and external experience.

It is highly significant that Paul, for all his alleged intellectualism and theological abstraction (terms that are once more beginning to be used about this first great theologian) does not begin his first letter to Corinth by listing a series of doctrinal fundamentals; in fact he nowhere indulges in that kind of doctrinalism. Rather, he alludes in a manner that is both explicit and full of mystery to the person and the event at the center of this profession of faith: "I decided to know nothing among you except Jesus Christ, and him crucified." Although Paul himself was not present at the crucifixion and did not meet Jesus in person at any point in Jesus' brief life; although he himself, therefore, would seem a prime candidate for the reception and promulgation of second-hand information about all this, he goes instead directly to the heart of the matter, anticipating in his own way the (later) Gospels, which also do not tell us what we should think about Jesus and all that he began to say and do but witness directly to his life, death, and resurrection. Paul is frequently accused of having rationalized the primitive faith of the earliest Christian community, the simple faith of Jesus and the disciples; but in fact his avowed point of departure is not at all such an intellectualized discussion of the meaning of all that occurred but a direct witness to the occurrence: "Jesus Christ, and him crucified."

In what follows in these chapters on Christology and soteriology, we shall have to engage in much doctrinal and theological discussion; it cannot, nor should it be, avoided. There is no person, living or dead, about whom much can be understood without a great deal of reflection, speculation, discussion, research, testing, and reformulating. Whole libraries are devoted to the investigation of persons and events associated with such names as George Washington, Mahatma Gandhi, Rosa Luxemburg, and Helen Keller. Without such second-level discourse, the reality even of these recent lives would soon be lost in a shower of legend and speculation. Even as it is, they and countless others readily become mere receptacles for the ideals and prejudices of others.

Early in its history—already with the newer Testamental writings, in fact—the church discovered that the real human being named Jesus of Nazareth would have to be protected against the propensity of his followers and his detractors to make of him what they would. Obviously enough, neither the earlier efforts (the Gospels and epistles) nor those that have been undertaken since can prevent the co-optation of "Jesus" by anyone. Yet the Christian profession of faith depends upon this work of sober, restrained, and scholarly exegesis and theological reflection. Without it, we would have in North America today not four thousand or so denominations but four hundred thousand! There is a need for sobriety here, and that need will never lessen until the Parousia itself.

Yet we must keep ever before us the fact that what is foundational in this theology is neither our exegesis nor our Christology but Jesus Christ himself. This means that from the start we must reckon, not only with the possibility of error in our attempts to describe this one, but with the inevitability of error. That does not give us license to err boldly, but it does give us a certain freedom with respect to our subject. Jesus Christ will be who he will be, whether through our witness or despite it. What is required of us, then, is not that we should set out to "tell the whole truth" about Jesus but that we should try in our own way and in our own context to point to the truth that Jesus "is."

27.2 Dividing the Indivisible. From the outset it is necessary to introduce a theoretical distinction that, if it is not straightforwardly acknowledged as such, easily threatens the integrity of the one who is the subject of this thought. I am referring to the fact that this doctrinal area, historically considered, falls under two subcategories: Christology, used in the more restrictive sense, that is, as a way of speaking about the person of the Christ; and soteriology, meaning the church's contemplation of the nature of that salvation accomplished by the one whom it acknowledges as *Soter* (Savior).

This is an artificial separation, and one that probably has had serious negative consequences in Christian history.[1] By way of explaining, without attempting to justify, the distinction, we may draw attention to two factors that have been at work in Christian theology.

The first is that the two dimensions of christological doctrine correspond to two questions that, while they are not separable, are nonetheless different. Christology proper asks the question of the identity of Jesus: Who is this? Soteriology asks about the work of the Christ: What has he done for us? Obviously the separation of any person from the work of that person is an artificial one. Biographies that attempt to treat the life and the thought of their subjects in two parts often fail. In the case of the person Jesus, called by faith the Christ, there is however a certain reason for the separation, if one considers (1) that the question of Jesus' identity was from the outset a highly disputed one, and (2) that the question of the salvation that he brings is not just a question about him but also about us—human beings, whose condition is the effective cause of this work of redemption. These considerations explain in part why what can be thought almost independent doctrinal discussions arose around each of the two dimensions of Christology.

The second reason for the separation of Christology and soteriology is more complex, for it relates to the whole task of a theology that, while governed by the overriding thought of the unity of truth, has yet to communicate this truth effectively. Systematic theology is systematic precisely because it is bound to the assumption that truth is one: everything is related to everything else. Systematic theology is also in the service of a community commissioned to bear witness to the one truth, and it is not possible to say everything at once; it is not even good to do so, because saying everything too often amounts to saying nothing—a fact of which contextual theology is especially conscious. Theology has to break up the one truth in order to communicate it—even to comprehend it. Theology has this in common with every other type of intellectual endeavor that is imbued with a strong sense of the integrity of "what is." Faithful theologians have always known that the identity and work of Jesus are indivisible. But it is one thing to know this and another to articulate it in such a way that the divisions that are made necessary by the process of understanding and communication do not end by inculcating in the hearing community the impression of divisions within the reality being testified to.

---

1. See Jürgen Moltmann, *The Way of Jesus Christ: Christology in Messianic Dimensions*, trans. Margaret Kohl (Minneapolis: Fortress Press, 1993), 44–46, 107f.

Perhaps only art can come close to presenting life whole. This is undoubtedly why "the story" is a special category in Jewish and Christian theology and why narrative theology has become a particular interest of many in our time.[2] Jesus himself used the form of the story in his parables; and when the first Christians tried to communicate the significance of the events of which Jesus was the center, they told the story of his life, death, and resurrection. "And the gospel," wrote Luther, "is nothing more than the story of God's little son, and of his humbling."[3] By comparison with the gospel story, systematic theology is a secondary and dependent discipline. It functions as it should only when it is understood to be an ongoing commentary on the fundamental story that Christians tell, the narrative around which their movement has grown. As we have put it earlier, theology is comparable to literary criticism or musicology: it analyzes the story in order that the church may hear the story more intelligently, with greater understanding of and appreciation for its many nuances and turnings, and so also with deeper comprehension of its meaning. It would be as unthinkable for theology to replace the gospel story as for literary criticism to replace literature or musicology to replace music.

Yet even stories divide the indivisible. Even the gospel story, as we have it in the Synoptics particularly, presents the one life in episodes and sequences, with attention to this aspect here, that aspect there. It is possible to lift out whole portions of the Gospels (for instance, the little apocalypses) and turn them into authoritative texts that are no longer counterbalanced by other texts. Even art divides.

Fortunately, the writers of the newer Testament seem to have been aware of this, and therefore they point us to the person and to the moment, knowing that they cannot capture either adequately. The most poignant expression of this is in the Gospel of John, with its final apologia: "But there are also many other things that Jesus did; if every one of them were written down, I suppose that the world itself could not contain the books that would be written" (21:25). Narrative theology may have certain advantages over conventional systematics so far as its capacity for preserving something of the livingness and unity of truth is concerned; but it would be less than perceptive to imagine that it had overcome or ever could overcome the difficulty to which we are drawing attention here. Finally only the moment of "insight" (Lonergan), only the "being grasped" (Tillich) can gather all the parts into an integrated and compelling

---

2. The tradition of Jerusalem is throughout a tradition of narration, of the impartation of knowledge through story. "The form which this knowledge takes, and the way in which the history of God's promise is communicated, can only be narrative, not a systematic and generalizing concept." (Jürgen Moltmann, *God in Creation: An Ecological Doctrine of Creation* [The Gifford Lectures of 1984–1985], trans. Margaret Kohl [Minneapolis: Fortress Press, 1993], 120.)

3. *Church Postil Sermons,* vol. 1, trans. John Nicholas Lenker (Minneapolis: Lutherans in All Lands Co., 1905), 11.

whole—which is to say, only the Spirit of God can cause the witness of the disciple community to its foundational story to be heard in the way that it is intended to be heard, as "good news." Perhaps this Spirit can even employ the halting and disparate attempts at ordering truth called systematic theology to bring to pass this moment of encounter with truth.

If, then, we understand that the division of this doctrinal area into two parts arises from the limitation of the discipline itself, which in turn reflects the limitation of the human mind when it comes to grasping wholeness, we may avoid making the doctrinal division of the study of Christ into an existential division. From the Christian past we are—or should be—aware of the danger of doing this, for whole branches of Christendom have been affected by it. Some Christians pursue with special interest the christological side of the question. Those, for instance, who in our own context forever ask, "Do you believe in the divinity of Christ?" as though salvation depended upon giving a positive answer to the question, have given too little attention to soteriology. Other branches of Christendom attach themselves with special fervor to the soteriological side of the doctrine of the Christ. In a real sense, the whole of Western Christendom has been characterized by a soteriological attachment that is impoverished because of its separation from the person of Christ. In the Eastern churches the opposite tendency has perhaps prevailed.

Over against this historical tendency, it is important to realize that when we discuss this person we are discussing the one who performs such and such a redemptive work *pro nobis* (for us), and that therefore an abstract Christology is out of the question; conversely, when we discuss the work we are not discussing a disembodied process but the work of a historical person. For the sake of speaking in an orderly way, theology habitually divides the indivisible; but the order exists only for the sake of the living truth that defies ordering—the truth that we must always stand under because we cannot understand it.

One more word by way of introduction to this doctrinal area: In only one of the two dimensions of christological thought has the church ever made an official pronouncement. By official pronouncement I mean an ecumenical, conciliar statement representative of the church at large, and therefore given early enough in its history to be regarded subsequently as normative. This is the area of Christology, in the restrictive sense. At Chalcedon in 451 C.E., the church made a decisive statement concerning the identity of Jesus: the Formula of Chalcedon. While this pronouncement has never been felt to be wholly satisfactory (could a wholly satisfactory definition of Jesus Christ even be conceived of?), it has all the same functioned in a regulative manner, more or less as the measure of orthodoxy. Later we shall consider why this could have been the case.

No such statement has ever been made in the realm of soteriology, and this must be regarded as very significant, even indicative of a kind of intuitive wisdom. It is wise because the soteriological question, as I have suggested earlier, contains in itself a vital anthropological component—indeed, a contextual component. To say what Jesus Christ has done *pro nobis* is at once to say, or to assume, what needs to be done for us. But "we" do not stand still. Our condition is different from age to age, place to place. Imagine the confusion if sixteenth- and twentieth-century Christians were expected to accept at face value soteriology created in (say) the fourth century C.E.

Unfortunately, there is no need to imagine this; in fact soteriological theories (as we shall soon see) did become so entrenched that they functioned as though they were official, as *theologia eterna.* They still do. But there is nevertheless some consolation for those of us who try to think the faith contextually in the fact that while the church is in some way beholden to an official Christology, it has witnessed the clear evolution or development of soteriological doctrine. If one studies that evolution imaginatively, as we shall try to do in what follows, one finds that it confirms obviously and instructively the most salient point of theological contextuality: namely, it responds to the human *problematique,* to what is there in the context, and therefore it must constantly readjust and reform itself.

With this introduction to the doctrine of the Christ, we move now to a consideration of the two components. It is assumed that the reader will supplement the generalizations that will be drawn in this discussion through a more detailed reading of the historical and intellectual developments upon which they are a commentary, including the original documents.

28. Christology: The Identity of Jesus

28.1. Biblical Background: The Significance of the Question.   However exasperating the contemporary Christian mind may find the christological debates of the early centuries to be, it should be understood from the start that the question of Jesus' identity is not one that subsequent theology simply imposed upon the gospel. It is present, and prominently so, in the original testimony of the early disciple community concerning the events out of which the Christian message emerged. It is present there, moreover, as a fundamental question—perhaps even as *the* fundamental question of the whole record. People who make their appearance in this scriptural narrative are forever asking, "Who is this?" The birth narratives, with their testimony to the mother's own astonishment as well as that of those who appeared at Bethlehem and at the dedication in the temple; the calling of the Twelve, who follow almost without hesitation; the deep concern and suspicion of the priestly element, which fears to strike without a carefully conceived rationale; the fearsome recognition of

Jesus on the part of the "demons" who possessed the beings of the mentally ill—in all of these we sense, and often hear, the question: "Who is this?"

The question comes to its most fevered expression (no doubt intentionally, on the part of the authors) with the so-called triumphal entry into Jerusalem: "When he entered Jerusalem, the whole city was in turmoil, asking, 'Who is this?'" (Matt. 21:10). Not only is the question of Jesus' identity one that is put into the spirits and mouths of those who come into contact with him; it is also recorded as having been Jesus' own question:

> Now when Jesus came into the district of Caesarea Philippi, he asked his disciples, "Who do people say that the Son of Man is?" And they said, "Some say John the Baptist, but others Elijah, and still others Jeremiah or one of the prophets." He said to them, "But who do you say that I am?" (Matt. 16:13-15)

There are of course also answers to this question all along the way. Nevertheless, the picture that we derive from our exposure to the newer Testament's story of Jesus among his contemporaries is one in which the question is more prominent than any of the answers. To be sure, the answers have seemed to subsequent Christianity very important. No doubt they are important—especially the answer of Peter that immediately follows the sequence cited above, the famous confession at Caesarea Philippi: "You are the Christ, the Son of the living God." Yet we should realize that these answers (and especially that one) have played a particularly important role in the history of the church. Because of their ecclesiastical significance, they may seem more prominent than they really are in the story itself.

Certainly in the case of Peter's confession, even if it is a historically accurate account, the answer seems not to put an end to the question. In fact, the answer is forgotten—even contradicted—at once. At the end of the story there is still an overwhelming sense of interrogation, both in the minds of the disciples and in the narrations of their amanuenses. The famous remark of that centurion who exclaimed (according to the record), "Truly this man was a son of God!" (Matt. 27:54), has been interpreted by a triumphant church as a decisive end to all questions. But is it not in fact another statement of the question? It does not stem from true belief (the speaker does not say this was *the* Son of God) but from astonishment at the whole manner in which this "criminal," one among thousands who suffered this form of Roman execution, endured his suffering. Who among the race of Adam and Eve could do this? *Who is this?*

We enter this commentary here because, later, we shall need to draw upon it significantly. The history of Christology has been a history of answers to the christological question. But it may be that the biblical answer to this question is its accentuation of the question. It may be that answering such a question is the beginning of a process of reductionism that the biblical record itself fears, and that Jesus also feared, according to the record.

What I am suggesting is that the question about the identity of Jesus may constitute the heart of the newer Testamental fascination with and testimony to him. Could it not be that what we must take with the greatest seriousness in the biblical record is the fact that the question of Jesus' true identity cannot be satisfactorily answered? Is this after all what lies behind the messianic secret? Must Jesus remain in some basic way the unknown one, the stranger, the outsider, the one whose story remains unfinished? Were not the first disciples and their amanuenses sophisticated enough to know that as soon as we think we know anyone, we have begun to dispense with that one? How soon the historical Jesus disappeared beneath a mountain of exegesis and church doctrine!

To propose such a hypothesis is not arbitrary. The biblical tradition of divine encounter, with special reference to the theology of the name, is part of the background of the drama of the Gospels. The God who becomes present to the leaders and prophets of Israel will not allow God's Self to be named either, even though the human recipients of God's Self-manifestation always demand to know God's name. The name that God reserves for those who come closest to God is one that at the same time conveys and withholds the essence of the divine: YHWH—"I am who I am," "I will be who I will be," "I cause to be what I cause to be" (the translation itself is uncertain).

Much has been made in theology and newer Testamental studies of the various names and titles that the biblical writers assign to Jesus; we shall look at this presently, too. But is it perhaps more important still for us to recognize that what the writers of these early testimonies seem most conscious of is the question? Within the centrality of the christological question for biblical thought, there is perhaps already an incipient recognition that every answer to this question will be both limited and misleading. The "true God"/"true human being" must appear among us—that is to say, among false and fallen creatures—first as a question, not as answer, first as mystery, not as clarification. As a being of mystery, who causes us not only to ask who he is but (as they all do in these accounts) who we are, Jesus moves toward the center of the story and of the life of the church as one who puts to us ultimate questions, not as one who brings answers. We could dispense with him if he were just the bringer of answers. If they were engaging answers we could worship the answers and forget the one who brought them. But they would probably not be good answers because, as the Bible knows throughout, there are no really good, sufficient answers to our deepest questions. There is only an Answerer—who appears more often than not as Questioner (think of Job). The presence of the Questioner is the only finally satisfactory answer.

Let us be clear, however, about the nature of the mystery that Jesus represents in this biblical story. He does not appear on the scene of life in ancient

Judea simply as a human curiosity, a conundrum, such as that found in the myths and legends of many peoples when gods or demonic beings take on human form. He appears rather as the sort of mystery who, in raising the question about his own identity, simultaneously causes those around him to wonder, "And who am I?" If the Christ of the Gospels is a question, or a questioner, it is also true that he encounters other human beings who through their encounter with him become conscious of themselves in a new way: conscious of their tentativeness, their uncertainty, their vulnerability and sin; conscious that their very being participates in questionableness, falseness. "Go away from me," begs the same Peter who was ready with an answer to the christological question; "I am a sinful man!" (Luke 5:8).

What we are touching upon here is what may be called the encounter quality of the first christological reflections. The question of Jesus' identity originates, not with a theoretical problem (How can a historical person be said to combine the essences of humanity and divinity?) but with the meeting of a specific person, Jesus, with other persons. We cannot very well perpetuate this situation. Despite accounts of miraculous appearances, no one has met Jesus in the way that he was met by his contemporaries. Yet, must not this encounter quality of the first christological reflections be, in some form, a permanent feature of any Christology? If it is not, then will not our attempts to answer the question of Jesus' identity end by destroying the very thing that, in the first place, drew people to him? To have answered the question; to have developed, perhaps, a highly sophisticated and technically satisfying Christology—this may in the last analysis have been to dispel the very mystery that engenders faith.

Must we not apply to the christological question what we apply (when we have understanding and respect) to every question of personal identity, namely the modesty and honesty of recognizing that the other is and must remain other? At the point where I can believe it possible to define another person, I have turned the other into a thing, an object. There is no longer any question of relationship with this other, because the center of mystery that was the other has become for me an extension of my own mind and will; "thou" has become "it," an image—a graven image, dependent upon my determination with regard to it. It is no longer free in relation to me, no longer capable of challenging me, no longer capable of loving me, either.

This is the warning that biblical Christology writes over the subsequent christological attempts of the church—all of them. Unfortunately, it is a warning that few have heeded. As Karl Barth wrote,

When has theology not attempted to entrap the divine logos in its analogies, setting these analogies, in fact, on the throne of God, worshipping and proclaiming them or recommending and acclaiming them for worship and proclamation? What else could the theology of these theologians be—when they contend for

themselves and against one another (regardless of how good they might otherwise be)—than theology that is placed in temptation by its own object.[4]

28.2 Biblical Background: "The Historical Jesus." It was partly on account of the temptation and idolatry to which Barth alludes in this warning
that, beginning in the nineteenth century, Christians were inspired by certain
biblical scholars and theologians to engage in a search for the "real" Jesus, the
historical Jesus. With the breakdown of classical christological orthodoxies, a
breakdown that can be traced back to the Reformation and is naturally associated with the Protestant emphasis upon the priority of Scripture over tradition,
it became important for all who were exposed to these influences to ask: How
does the newer Testament itself present Jesus? What do the writers of the
Gospels and epistles have to say about his identity? Can we read these earliest
documents without bringing to them the assumptions of a later age?

This attention to the biblical background led gradually to the recognition
that the Bible itself showed a tendency to branch out beyond the apostolic testimony to the historical figure at the center of this literature and to interpret him
on the basis of personal and communal faith—a faith informed both by categories drawn from the sacred texts of Israel and from Greek and Hellenistic
philosophic and religious traditions. Thus the attempt to discover the genuine
historical personage and to distinguish him from the faith of the early church
became a problem of biblical interpretation, and not just one of the evolution of
doctrine.

Under the impact of scholars from Ritschl to von Harnack, the mind of liberal Christianity was trained to regard the three Synoptic Gospels (Matthew,
Mark, and Luke) as the most trustworthy records of the life of Jesus, and in one
degree or another to mistrust Johannine and (in particular) Pauline christological thought. This could be substantiated moreover by the dating of the Gospels,
John being considerably later than the others, and by the biographical data sup-
plied by the biblical literature itself concerning Paul, whose rabbinic training
had conditioned him to consider the core events of the faith from the perspective of a Hellenized Judaism that had already discarded the more earthy historical realism of classical Hebraic thought.

With such provocative thinking in the air, the nineteenth and early twentieth centuries saw the production of many "lives of Jesus," some of them highly
sophisticated works of critical scholarship, others popularly and imaginatively
conceived. This was by no means the merely fanciful and naive enterprise that
subsequent religious and theological scholarship sometimes made it seem. Behind it was the intuitive wisdom of a Christian faith which realized that Christology had replaced and displaced Jesus the Christ, and that if faith were not to

---

4. *Evangelical Theology,* trans. Grover Foley (New York: Holt, Rinehart and Winston, 1963), 138.

be robbed of its encounter basis, Jesus would have to become again for the church a living, credible, and charismatic *person.*

It is true nevertheless that most of these lives of Jesus indicate more about the virtues and values of their writers and of the contexts to which they belonged than about anything else. They characteristically depict a gentle, pious, modest, truth-telling, underdog-loving person, almost always utterly transcendent of his Jewishness, or perhaps a social reformer—a slightly Jewish Wilberforce, full of the best Victorian and Wilhelmian moral virtues. Most of the lives are the literary equivalents of the paintings of Jesus that belong to the same era, such as Sallman's *Head of Christ* or Hoffmann's *Christ in the Garden.*

For the world of Christian scholarship, the process of writing biographies of Jesus was thrown into confusion by the explosive 1906 study by Albert Schweitzer, *The Quest for the Historical Jesus.*[5] The impact of this work was to question the whole endeavor of contemporary consciousness, which, Schweitzer believed, could not begin to comprehend the strange, apocalyptic figure at the heart of the Christian story.

While Schweitzer's and subsequent exegetical and theological scholarship (notably that of the Bultmann school) has influenced all later christological discussion at the level of academic theology, its influence upon the churches is not, I think, conspicuous. It belongs to a contextual theology undertaken in the service of the church to recognize that here, as at many other points, popular Christianity is not immediately susceptible to the often swift and passing transitions that sweep the world of Christian scholarship. It may also be, let us add, that in some things at least, it would be well for Christian scholarship to pay more attention to this discrepancy and to inquire more seriously about why the laity holds to positions long banished by scholarly opinion. If the public libraries of small towns all over North America still contain more lives of Jesus than books by experts who have long ago discarded that approach; if Sunday-school rooms in many of our churches still display Sallman's *Head* and similar portrayals of Jesus, this may tell us more than that the Christian laity is always reactionary and simplistic. It should inform us that faith requires a living being, and not only ideas, however sophisticated, at its center.

Can we find any reliable knowledge of the living human being called Jesus of Nazareth? Are we confined to a literary testimony in which, not only in the epistles and the Gospel of John but in the Synoptic Gospels as well, what dominates is the faith of the early church, the belief that this was indeed the Messiah of God, the divine Word and Wisdom made flesh? In the foregoing subsection, we proposed that the christological question of the newer Testamental writings may be the most important aspect of this biblical testimony. But even this kind of fascination with Jesus' person, based as it is upon the sort of wonder that

---

5. First published in English in 1910 (trans. W. Montgomery [London: A. & C. Black Ltd.]).

suspects the extraordinary beneath the ordinary, presupposes the faith of those who were able finally to affirm his extraordinariness.

Certainly there is no going back behind the scriptural record, and this is the only historical testimony to Jesus that we have. Whenever people seek to distinguish the historical Jesus from the Christ of faith on the basis of what is actually presented to us in the Scriptures, they are bound to apply criteria of judgment derived from subjective sources, even if these sources are allegedly gleaned, in turn, from the Scriptures themselves. The reaction of twentieth-century theologians of many schools to "the quest for the historical Jesus" confirms, on the whole, the impossibility of reconstructing a picture of Jesus that is independent of the disciple community's pentecostal faith.

Besides the practical barriers to any such undertaking, many have with Søren Kierkegaard made the theologically significant observation that even if we could reconstruct Jesus' life it would be no guarantee of faith. Jesus' own contemporaries had more than a "life of Jesus"; they had Jesus himself, present in their midst, eating, talking, sleeping, praying, and personally responding to their (usually false) assumptions about him. With all that they failed utterly, according to their own testimony, to understand who he was and what his mission was. They came to faith only afterwards, and through the most radical sort of internal transformation (*metanoia*)—a transformation inspired by the internal testimony of the Holy Spirit.

The alternative to a fully developed and nuanced biography of Jesus is not, however, the simple affirmation that such a person once lived, taught, and died. Obviously we cannot know very much about the Jesus of history. If the three brief writings called the Synoptics are compared with the mountains of data that we possess concerning historical figures like Charlemagne, Elizabeth I of England, or Adolf Hitler, they appear terribly insignificant—almost ludicrous. And even if the whole of the newer Testament can be trusted to provide absolutely reliable information about Jesus, the comparison with most of the other figures who command our historical attention would be discouraging to contemplate. Besides, it must surely be conceded that there is probably nothing that we can know of Jesus that has not been influenced by the church's confession of faith in him.

But does faith necessarily and inevitably distort reality? Evidently it does color everything; but does it entirely change everything?

Christian theology has vested interests in answering that question in the negative. Theology itself brings to the contemplation of reality a perspective (what we called earlier a perceptual foundation) that, it believes, not only does not distort reality but enables one to see more clearly what is already there, which even by ordinary standards of verification is always partly hidden from immediate view. Faith does not aim to acquire extraordinary information that is inaccessible to sight. Contrary to Gnosticism, faith in the biblical sense neither seeks nor possesses data hidden from ordinary view; rather, its object is to open itself to the *meaning* present in occurrences that are common and perceivable by all. That is why, considering especially the character and standards of religious experience and testimony acceptable to the historical period concerned, the canonical writings of the Christian Scriptures are extraordinarily factual and cautious with regard to their presentation of events.

It is necessary to consider in this connection the pressure under which the small Christian communities of the beginnings of this movement must have been to embellish every detail of the life, ministry, death, and resurrection of Jesus with miraculous and otherworldly accompaniments, whose function would be to demonstrate the ultimate authority of their claims. As it is, one finds certain inclinations in that direction, particularly in connection with the birth narratives and the resurrection appearances. But by comparison with what was allowable by the religious and cultural standards of the age, and particularly in view of the fact that the apocryphal "gospels" that did indulge in this kind of embellishment in a major way were not regarded, finally, as acceptable, one must admit that the Gospels, including John, are amazingly restrained.

This is not accidental, nor is the reason for it remote. It is not a matter of intellectual virtue on the part of the biblical writers and their apostolic forebears and informants; it has to do rather with the nature of their fundamental faith commitment. They evidently believed that the truth to which they were obliged to point was entirely bound up with the real, humanly observable events and experiences through which they had passed. They believed that the good news they were commissioned to announce required the closest possible attention to what, so far as they could remember, had actually taken place. They believed, in short, that it was precisely in and through these occurrences—occurrences open to ordinary human perception—that the extraordinary thing had happened. Their object, therefore, was not to change what had happened (for instance, to surround Jesus with all the usual paraphernalia of divinity) but rather to preserve its ordinariness, earthiness, and human credibility. It was the essence of their faith that the absoluteness of the message concerning the Christ lay in the particularity of this man who had called them friends, that the eternality of this kairos was inextricably bound up with its occurrence in time, that the ultimacy of "the Christ event" was inseparable from the contingency of this particular life.

"The Word became flesh and lived among us" (John 1:14). The very transcendence of this claim bound the original Christian witnesses to a sort of historicity that, while it is not governed by the empirically verifiable objectivity to which our contemporary historians (perhaps vainly) aspire, is nevertheless remarkable for its time. But it is remarkable, not as a scholarly virtue anticipating modernity, but purely as the extension of the theological presupposition that informs it. It would hardly serve the purposes of a faith that wanted principally to uphold the incarnation of truth to end by giving the world truths remote from the everyday world of carnality.

What faith added to what was open for all to see was what it believed to be the unseen and unseeable significance of these occurrences. That, too, belongs to the fundamental theological presupposition of the whole newer Testament undertaking. No one, not the disciples themselves, not even the mother of Jesus, could discern that significance, though like Mary many were evidently given to pondering what was happening in their midst. Everyone sees but no one understands. Everyone hears but no one comprehends. Everyone is present at the baptism by John, but no one sees the dove descending. Everyone knows that something unusual may have happened, but most say that "it thundered." Everything takes place publicly. Even on the Mount of Transfiguration there are witnesses. Even in Gethsemane what can be seen is seen. The betrayal, the arrest, the trial, the flogging, the grim procession to the Place of the Skull, the execution: all are credible occurrences, presented with an absolute minimum of religious theatrics.

There is little here comparable to the miraculous appearances and heavenly voices and disturbances of the laws of nature and history that soon became the standard fare in every story of Christian martyrdom. The recorders of these events were being guided by an unspoken but firm rule. It is not a literary or historical rule (these are modern) but a theological one: that the whole presentation must be as ordinary as possible because the extraordinary thing cannot be perceived by human beings who have come so far from God, who are so deeply alienated from their own origins. The significance of these quite normal occurrences can only be understood afterwards—after a radical transformation of spirit, will, and mind has taken place within some of the witnesses. Only then will it be possible for them—the few—to know that the words they heard from this rabbi were "words of eternal life," that the suffering of this rejected one was "for our sake and our salvation," that this cross, so like all the others, was in reality utterly different because of the one whose forsakenness it effected.

What I am arguing here with respect to the question of the historical trustworthiness of the scriptural accounts is that the so-called Christ of faith, profoundly understood, itself drove the writers of these brief testimonies to a greater faithfulness to the Jesus of history than much modern theology and exegesis have suggested. This is not to say that the records as we have them should be construed as biographies in the contemporary sense. I am in agreement with those who say that everything is conditioned by faith. My point, however, is that faith, far from requiring the abandonment of factuality or encouraging the sort of fantasy that sits lightly to data, on the contrary begets the desire to be true to what actually happened—given the fact that it is faith in the incarnation of the Word.

If this is so, then we may at least endorse a claim to the historicity of this testimony that is strong enough to perform the minimal services that an authoritative scripture must perform.[6] What, in relation to the person of Jesus, would these minimal services be? To answer briefly, they would constitute a characterization or picture of Jesus sufficiently integrated and detailed (1) to constitute a positive historical testimony to a believable human being, an external testimony to which the internal testimony of the divine Spirit might correspond; and (2) to provide a basis for a critical Christology, through which the disciple community could assess the validity of spiritual claims to knowledge of the Christ.

Both of these services, which are two sides of the same coin, are required by a community of faith that places at its center a historical person. Without some external testimony to this person on the part of those who can legitimately claim historical proximity, little or nothing remains of his reality beyond the period of his life and the lives of his contemporaries. Worse still, what does remain, if (as is likely) it has come to be surrounded with an aura of sanctity, is subject to indiscriminate and indefinite manipulation by those who have claims upon it. We know that both of these problems were recognized by the first Christians, particularly when it began to dawn upon them that the anticipated Return (Parousia) would not occur before all of the original witnesses had passed on. Subsequent Christian history has only demonstrated all the more clearly how justified were their fears; for even with what they have given us there seems no end to the fantasies and fabrications that are devised by the human—especially the religious—imagination, and then set forth under the name, Jesus Christ.

There is enough in this scriptural testimony, nonetheless, to convey to age after age the memory of one who, though subject to the great and jumbled variety of human preference and prejudice, remains at the same time free to impress upon human beings of diverse contexts an *imago Christi* that is remarkably consistent, all things considered. And, perhaps most importantly, there is enough in this scriptural witness to enable a faithful, studious, and prophetic church to distinguish Jesus from at least the worst of the distortions of his memory.

In short, there are limits—and despite the propensity of religion to transgress them, there has always been and still is a minority among Christian believers who try to honor the scriptural limits. Thus, to the upright citizen who

---

6. The recent study of John Dominic Crossan seems ready to press considerably beyond my claim here. In the Epilogue of his book, *The Historical Jesus: The Life of a Mediterranean Jewish Peasant* (San Francisco, Harper, 1991, p. 424), and with specific reference to Chalcedon, he writes: "I find . . . no contradiction between the historical Jesus and the defined Christ, no betrayal whatsoever in the move from Jesus to Christ." This appears to me rather grandiose. Chalcedon, after all, occurred *after* the establishment of Christianity. Crossan ought perhaps therefore to have reconsidered the above statement in the light of the sentence that follows it: "Whether there were ultimate betrayals in the move from Christ to Constantine is another question" (Ibid.).

calls for law and order and cites Jesus Christ as an authority for his insistence upon the validity of capital punishment, it may safely be said, "No, Mr. Chief of Police, Jesus did not say, 'an eye for an eye and a tooth for a tooth'; he said, 'forgive your enemies, do good to them that hate you.'" And to the moralist who calls upon Jesus to undergird his homophobia, it may be said that Jesus, in distinction (perhaps) from Paul, did not consign homosexuals to hellfire; he sought the internal motivation of our acts and therefore was more inclined to denounce the sin of self-righteousness and spiritual smugness than to belabor the failures and foibles of the flesh. And of the laughing Christ, which in some circles of middle-American "churchianity" threatens to displace even the ubiquitous Sallman *Head,* it may be said that Jesus is not pictured in the texts as one who is forever laughing and enjoying; Jesus is not Dionysius. There are limits.

Therefore, while the quest for the historical Jesus will never be successful—while it is in fact forever barred from success on account of its object, who is no object but a living subject—it must nevertheless in some modest way continue to inform the life of the Christian community. If it does remain at the level of modesty and does not, with so much christological orthodoxy both of the right and the left, presume too much, it will be successful enough to do what must be done in this regard, namely, to help faith to "see Jesus" (John 12:21) and to prevent religion from imagining that it has captured Jesus.

28.3. The Biblical Background: Jesus in the Record. This is not the place to attempt a full-fledged discussion of Jesus as the Gospels and epistles of the newer Testament bear witness to him. What *is* required of systematic theologians is that they provide a sufficient indication of their own interpretation of the biblical text to enable others to assess their reading of this foundational literature. It must at least be shown that a theologian who dares to speak about Jesus intends to do so as one who attempts to be faithful to the Scriptures, seriously considered. No Christian is at liberty simply to speculate where this name is concerned. The most refined and logically satisfying Christology in the world, if it does not consciously seek to ground itself in the newer Testamental witness to the one that faith named *Christos,* is sheer abstraction.

My observations here are intended to fulfill that office at least minimally; they are also governed by what will follow by way of an analysis of the evolution of Christology in the church. I shall reflect briefly, first, on the events themselves, and then on the search for their meaning within the newer Testamental corpus.

It has already been proposed that the most salient feature of the Gospels' presentation of Jesus may be the fact that his presence as such elicits the question of his identity. He raises in the minds of all whom he encounters, especially those closest to him, an attention that is more than curiosity. It is rightly described as existential, for it is always also a matter of personal concern. None of those who appear in this story is neutral, merely an observer. One supposes that there were observers; there always are. But they are not part of this story. Whether enemy or friend, scoffer or disciple, betrayer or family member, they are all intensely involved with this person, and Jesus' own personhood is shaped by this involvement; it is not an abstraction.[7] Even the people who appear in the narrative only momentarily, like Zachaeus or the woman at the well, are deeply affected by the encounter. Even the crowds react passionately, whether out of a celebrative or a violent temperament. An expectancy, perhaps a hope, is felt in his presence—though for some, chiefly those in power, the expectancy has a negative connotation, because hope for the deliverance of some must always mean the accusation and dethronement of others: "He has brought down the powerful from their thrones, and lifted up the lowly; he has filled the hungry with good things, and sent the rich away empty (Luke 1:52-53).

This fascination with the man Jesus, this puzzlement about his identity, and especially this sense of expectancy surrounding all that he does cannot be divorced from the history of the people into whose midst he comes: the Jews.[8] That is where Christology must start, and today we can no longer fail as Christians to recognize that when Christology does not start there, or starting there quickly moves out into the wide world of universals no longer grounded in this particularity, something questionable happens to it—and through it.

Jesus was a Jew. He appeared at a crucial period in the history of the Jews. Given the torturous history of the Jews, it may seem a tautology to call that period crucial; yet both Jewish and Christian historians agree that the era which constitutes the sociopolitical context of Jesus' life was one of particular significance for Judaism. The word kairos would not be out of place here. As one studies the period, one gains new appreciation for Paul's statement in Galatians 4:4-5: "But when the fullness of time had come, God sent his Son, born of a woman, born under the law, in order to redeem those who were under the law, so that we might receive adoption as children."

At this time, the life and faith of the Jewish people was threatened by two powerful forces, the Roman imperium and Hellenistic culture. Both of these influences found their natural ally in the house of the Herods. Herod the Great was appointed king of the Jews by the Romans in 40 B.C.E. and ruled from 37 until 4 C.E. It was consistent with Roman policy to use members of the royal families of the lands they conquered; "Herod was merely one of the most

---

7. "Jesus' personhood does not exist in isolation. . . nor is it determined and fixed from eternity. It acquires its form in living relationships and reciprocities. . . ." (Moltmann, *The Way of Jesus Christ*, 136.)

8. See *Thinking the Faith*, 212.

prominent among these rulers."[9] The monarch under whom Jesus was born went out of his way to court Rome's favor. He was also drawn to Greek culture.

> By sympathy and character he was more Greek than Jew and it was his dearest wish to gain the reputation of being a great Hellenistic monarch. His Gentile subjects soon understood his love of power, and he, in turn, appreciated the simplicity of their religion, the beauty of Greek art, and the charm of Greek modes of thought. He filled his court with Greek hangers-on, mostly parasites who lived by their flattery. . . . Herod's ideas about government were the same as those which at that time were common throughout the Roman empire. It was government not for the sake of the people, but for, of and by men of wealth and aristocracy. The common people had only one duty—to obey their masters.[10]

The policies of Herod the Great were carried on, though with less ability, by his heirs, notably his son Antipas, who ruled the region of Galilee—the home of both John the Baptist and Jesus. The pattern is not an unfamiliar one; parallels can be found in Latin America and elsewhere today: A powerful empire finds within the nations it dominates elites through whom it can rule. These privileged minorities have on their side not only the might of the imperium but the glitter of what can seem a superior culture—a cosmopolitan culture, in comparison with which local customs appear rustic and naive. But with the increase of oppression, both economic and cultural, movements of opposition come into being, particularly among the poor.

According to Ben-Sasson, resistance to Rome must be traced especially to the governorship of Pontius Pilate (26–36 C.E.). Until that time, "relations between the Jewish nation and the Roman Empire were not markedly hostile. . . . [but] from the time of Pilate onwards, reports of unrest and riots become more frequent, and a gradual disillusionment from the hopes that had been attached to Roman rule is evident." Heavy taxation, the arrogant disregard of Jewish traditions, and outright acts of violence "contributed to the growth of the Jew's hatred of Roman rule" during this period. Not only did Pilate insult the Jews by taking money from the temple treasury and bringing the banners of the Roman army into Jerusalem, but dramatic acts of tyranny occurred—including the one of which we learn in Luke 13:1, where pilgrims from Galilee, as they were engaged in worship, were slaughtered by Pilate's soldiers.[11]

Such a time naturally evoked in the most subjugated and sensitive Jews the thought of deliverance. Messianic expectation drew upon many sources, positive

---

9. H. H. Ben-Sasson, ed., *A History of the Jewish People,* trans. George Wiedenfeld and Nicolson Ltd. (Cambridge, Mass.: Harvard Univ. Press, 1976), 239.

10. Solomon Grayzel, *A History of the Jews,* rev. ed. (New York: New American Library, Mentor Book, 1968), 103–4.

11. *A History of the Jewish People,* 251.

and negative in their impact, including the earlier Maccabean resistance and the holiness or covenanting communities such as the one described in the Dead Sea Scrolls. But without the sense of an ending, created by the spread of an empire that could easily absorb into its all-embracing yet all-effacing system even such particularized local traditions as that of the Jews, the messianic hope would probably have been confined to the more exotic and radical religio-political movements, such as the Zealots. As it was, the collective memory of a distinctive Judaism was strong enough that a figure like Jesus could spark intimations of a hope that was quickly dissipating through the co-optation of this small people by the crass glories of a great world power.

Jesus, whose early life is certainly obscure, was apparently swept up into this largely amorphous mood of disillusionment and expectancy through the apocalyptic preaching of John the Baptist. In his decision to accept the baptism of John, which was not understood only along the lines of initiation into purity of faith against all hypocrisy and mere formalism but as "the eschatological sign of the conversion of all Israel,"[12] Jesus appears to have come to some firm conclusion about his own vocation. It is a matter of dispute among biblical scholars whether he ever thought of himself as the Messiah;[13] but certainly he believed it his God-appointed mission to engage in a public ministry aimed at transforming the life of his people.

At the heart of this ministry was his message concerning the reign of God. Upon hearing of the arrest of John, he began to announce the inauguration of the divine kingdom—God's reign is "at hand" (Matt. 4:17, par.). This ought not, in my opinion, to be rendered in such a way as to place all the emphasis upon the present, as if Jesus were announcing a program that he intended to put into effect. Such an interpretation not only "reduces the matter to moralistic terms"[14] but it overlooks the "not yet" of the world transformation ("new creation"—

---

12. Moltmann, *The Way of Jesus Christ,* 88. (See also Crossan, *The Historical Jesus,* chap. 11, "John and Jesus," 227ff.)

13. On this much-argued question, Moltmann's proposal seems to me theologically important, regardless of its exegetical correctness: "The Christian community rightly understood the cross and resurrection as the revelation of that which Jesus truly is. In this light of what comes later, what is earlier appears as the way that leads there. The words and ministry of the earthly Jesus, and his fellowship with other people, are therefore presented in wholly messianic terms. But Jesus is as yet only *the messiah on the way* and the *messiah in his becoming,* led by God's Spirit and sustained by what he has experienced with other people through his energies and his words. That is why he responds to the question whether he is the one 'who is to come' by pointing to the 'signs and wonders' which take place in his presence (Matt. 11:5). Jesus does not *possess* the messiahship; he grows into it, as it were, since he is moulded by the events of the messianic time which he experiences. These events find their completion in him through the sufferings of the new Servant of God and the birth pangs of a new creation" (*The Way of Jesus Christ,* 139).

14. I am in full agreement with Moltmann's criticism of "recent Protestant theology" in which "it has unfortunately become customary to interpret *Basileia tou Theou* solely as the present rule of God" and thus "to reduce it to moralistic terms" (ibid., 98).

Moltmann[15]) that God is "already" bringing to pass. That great transformation remains for the present "hidden beneath its opposite," though faith perceives its reality there—among the poor, those who despair, those who possess nothing, those who hunger and thirst for a righteousness they do not have, those who strive for peace in the midst of violence, those who are persecuted (the Beatitudes).

Unlike the militant wing of Judaic feeling, Jesus did not embrace a policy of violent revolution. God's reign *(Basileia)* would be inaugurated, rather, by deeply spiritual means. By this I do not intend to say that Jesus exemplified the sort of religious privatism that conceives of social change as the end-product of personal conversions, but that as a Jew of the prophetic and mystical tradition he understood God to be at work in the great movements of history. God's reign was not to be effected by private conversion and healing, but the latter should be considered points of symbolic importance, tokens of the great change being brought about as history neared the end of an age.

In this connection we should think in particular of the healing ministry of Jesus, which is not adequately understood if it is privatized, and is badly misunderstood if (as happens regularly in our context) it is considered proof of his divinity. No doubt many—perhaps all—accounts of his miraculous healings belong to the dimension of the biblical witness we are calling here its search for meaning. But it is not necessary (as with theological modernism) to legendize the miracles away if one understands them as indicators of the more cosmic transformation ("mending") of the world that Jesus evidently conceived to be the clear determination of divine providence.

> When Jesus expels demons and heals the sick, he is driving out of creation the powers of destruction, and is healing and restoring created beings who are hurt and sick. The lordship of God to which the healings witness, restores sick creation to health. Jesus' healings are not supernatural miracles in a natural world. They are the only truly "natural" thing in a world that is unnatural, demonized and wounded. As parables of the kingdom, Jesus' parables are also parables of the new creation in the midst of the everyday life of this exhausted world. Finally, with the resurrection of Christ, the new creation begins, *pars pro toto,* with the crucified one.[16]

In the course of his ministry of teaching and healing, Jesus created both a following and—not unpredictably—the enmity of certain powerful elements, including the Pharisees, with whom in some respects he had much in common. The more enthusiastic and influential his followers became, the more he was opposed by the priestly and Pharisaic groups within Israel. He appears to have been reluctant to accept the adulation of his supporters, particularly their attempts to

---

15. Ibid., 98.
16. Ibid., 98–99.

define his mission in their own terms—invariably power terms. Increasingly, it would seem, he understood that he would nevertheless be cast into the role of political leadership whether or not he approved of it, and that his own closest associates, the disciples, seemed incapable of thinking in any other terms. The confession of Peter at Caesarea Philippi, rather naively though not innocently heard ever afterwards by the church as *the* moment of great recognition ("You are the Christ") is followed immediately in Matthew's account by a scenario in which the enthusiastic *confessor fidei* makes it clear, as he does at many other points as well, that he too is thinking in purely power terms.

Jesus, meanwhile, has learned to contemplate his vocation and his destiny in a different way. He would not have to be clairvoyant, given the circumstances, to understand that with such expectations on the part of his supporters and such fears on the part of his detractors he would end up in trouble.[17] How was he to think, then, about the suffering that would undoubtedly be his lot? Could this suffering and rejection also be encompassed in his calling? Was the reign of God the *telos* to which not only his teaching and healing pointed but also that which gave the rationale to his probable suffering?

While we may debate the question of Jesus' consciousness of his messiahship, I do not think that it is unclear what we must answer to *this* question. The one point that shines through all the historical ambiguity of the record and is confirmed not only by its consistency in all the accounts, including Paul's, but by the prominence that it received in the early church's process of contemplating and determining the meaning of "these things," is that Jesus not only came to understand that he would have to suffer, but that he came to believe that his suffering was the primary focus of his mission. Thus, knowing full well by that time that his presence in Jerusalem would be the occasion of his decisive rejection by the powers that were, he nevertheless "steadfastly set his face to go to Jerusalem" (Luke 9:51, KJV).

Did he himself understand this necessary suffering, rejection, and death as vicarious atonement? as the means of cosmic redemption? as the prelude to resurrection victory? as the birth of a new covenantal community? as the turning

---

17. Crossan writes: "What would happen to Jesus was probably as predictable as what had happened already to John. Some form of religiopolitical execution could surely have been expected. What he was saying and doing was as unacceptable in the first as in the 20th century, there, here, or anywhere." ("The Life of a Mediterranean Jewish Peasant," in *The Christian Century* [Dec. 18–25, 1991], 1199.) While I agree entirely with this statement, I find it lacks the more subtle theological dimension to which I am leading here. If the violent death of Jesus, like that of John, is attributed solely or chiefly to the incendiary character of his message and activity, it is effectively removed from the sphere of soteriological discussion and becomes yet another, if impressive, instance of the martyrdom of the just. There is a dimension of mystery in the crucifixion, as not only Paul but also the Synoptics insist; and this mystery has primarily to do, not with the role of human beings in that event (an entirely predictable role) but with God's relation to it. I wonder if this is not a question that has to be asked of Crossan's whole treatment of "the historical Jesus."

point in history? We do not know precisely how he interpreted the meaning of the end that he obviously contemplated; but we can know, I believe, that he did not think it random or ignominious or simply, predictably, the revenge of the powerful. By all accounts, he did believe it to be a destiny ("cup") full of meaning and therefore one that "must" be. He could hardly have intuited the "must" of the later and no doubt stylized "predictions of the passion" without linking it in some way with the divine intention to alter the destiny of Israel; and he could hardly have considered a divine alteration of Israel's destiny without linking *that* with the larger destiny of the world.

Being a student of the Scriptures, he was certainly not unfamiliar with the suffering servant and other prophetic literature in which suffering was closely and even inevitably associated with the working out of God's purposes. In fact, if Abraham Heschel is right in contending that "divine pathos" is at the heart of all prophetic consciousness,[18] then it would be less than astute of any student of these Scriptures to miss the point of the connection between God's power and the apparent vulnerability of God's messengers. Jesus' principal teaching, after all, was the law of love: self-giving, unmotivated, sacrificial love; the love of the one who "lays down his life for his friends." It does not require very great insight to see indelible links between "divine pathos," sacrificial love, and the sense of vocation entertained by one who believed that he had some vital role to play in effecting a new situation within the world of his experience. If the prophets before him could understand precisely such connections, and if the apostles after him could do so, then we may surely suppose that, even humanly speaking, a man of Jesus' apparent sensitivity and intelligence, faced with such a prospect, would be drawn to interpret it along the lines of that *necessitas* which punctuates the Gospel accounts like a leitmotiv—explicitly in the "predictions of the passion," implicitly throughout. And if he made these connections, is it not also possible that he began to help his closest associates to make them?

What I am proposing is that the quest for the significance—the unseen and unseeable meaning—of the events that constitute the focus of the newer Testamental witness already begins with the one who is the chief protagonist of this story. It seems to me, in fact, naive in the extreme to imagine that Jesus' contribution to this story is limited to that of a teacher of higher righteousness or an idealistic revolutionary. He should be given credit for at least a sufficient degree of human insight to have reflected on his own life and the end to which, given such a life, he would likely come. Even dull and unreflective people are given moments of clarity when they reflect upon the course their lives are taking. A man teaching nothing but the so-called higher righteousness, and accumulating in the process a sufficient following to threaten the institutions of

18. See *Thinking the Faith,* 26f.

religious and political authority, would be dull indeed were he not to ask himself what possible purpose his likely ignoble end could serve. And, given the fact that Jesus' primary frame of reference for such contemplation (as was the case for his disciples after his death) was the sacred Scriptures of Israel, with emphasis upon the prophetic, apocalyptic, and sapiential traditions, is it not in fact highly probable that he would have been given the courage and imagination to think of his end in terms, not of defeat and despair, but of the strange yet not absurd logic of the suffering love—the agape—of God?

When, therefore, we move from this brief meditation on the events to what must be an equally brief meditation on the meaning of these events as undertaken by the biblical writers, we are not entering an entirely new phase, as was often suggested by those who made an absolute distinction between the Jesus of history and the Christ of faith, but we are in fact proceeding along a course of interpretation and contemplation already begun in the midst of the events, as part of them. That this interpretation is now carried far beyond those beginnings may be taken as historical fact, so far as the language of fact has meaning in any connection. But at very least it should not seem that later reflection on the event took on a form of thinking entirely discontinuous with the thinking that had already begun *in medias res*. I am suggesting that the propensity of the later disciple community to perceive deep and inscrutable significance behind all that was visible to "the eye of flesh" is a propensity that that community learned first of all from the one at the center of the events, whom it called "Rabbi."

To state the matter in different terms (which, however, mean the same thing): Christology began with Jesus himself.[19]

28.4. The Biblical Background: Faith Seeking Understanding. The question of Jesus' resurrection is a complex one both biblically and theologically speaking. That something out of the ordinary happened cannot be doubted. That it was expressed by the biblical writers in the language of an empty tomb, angelic presences, miraculous appearances, and the final ascension of the Lord into heaven is not surprising in view not only of the early church's quest for the meaning of its core event but also of the contemporary religious and social mentality, which would not find such testimony incredible in the way that our own

---

19. "[T]he earthly life and ministry of Jesus contains within itself what Conzelmann calls 'an implicit christology,' which after Easter led to the explicit christologies of the Christian congregations. . . . The implicit christology of the gospels is therefore theologically required. Is it also historically probable? If we judge the matter historically, unprejudiced by dogmatic or humanist postulates, we have to assume that there is a correspondence between the community's remembrance of Jesus, and their Easter experience of the One risen. Inconsistencies would have destroyed either the remembrance of Jesus or the experience of the risen One, and would in either case have broken down the identity involved in the acknowledgment 'Jesus—the Christ.'" (Moltmann, *The Way of Jesus Christ,* 140–41.)

scientific age is prone to receive it. But, by the same token, when it is put forward today as an adequate articulation of the resurrection it not only places a false *skandalon* in the way of communication, but it does grievous injustice to the meaning of the resurrection. And where the resurrection of Jesus is concerned, everything depends upon the question of meaning.

Meaning is not located in the fact of the resuscitation of a dead body. Not only is human history full of tales of dead persons coming to life again, but contemporary medical history now documents instances of clinical death having been overcome. Aside from the curiosity (both morbid and existential) aroused by such accounts, however, they communicate little or nothing in the realm of meaning; and the whole intention of the biblical witness is to say that with Jesus' resurrection new *meaning* is given—not only to the import of his life but, more significantly still, to the import and end of *ours*. For with the theology of resurrection we have moved over the invisible line between Christology and soteriology.

Whatever, therefore, may be said about the "event of the third day," what is most important is not that we should have some clear conception of the physical details (in any case if the event is, as it is maintained, unique, a clear conception of the physical details is out of the question), but that we should try to understand the effect of "whatever happened" upon the disciple community. In outline, what we may say on that subject is: (1) that this community found itself becoming for the first time a real community; (2) that it felt this enlivening of its corporateness to be a direct consequence of the presence of the Lord and/or the Spirit; (3) that it found itself spiritually and intellectually stimulated by this presence, not only to remain together (despite its earlier readiness to disband) but to engage in a prayerful and studious quest for the understanding of what lay behind the occurrences in which it had participated; and (4) that as soon as it had begun to be grasped by the meaning of these occurrences, it was seized by the impulse to share its insight with others.

The reader may deduce from the foregoing paragraph that I am ready to leave the question of Jesus' resurrection in abeyance; and that impression would be correct insofar as it refers to the factual question, What happened to the dead body of Jesus? I am not prepared (with liberalism in its more radical expression) to say, "Nothing—except the usual." But neither am I prepared (with fundamentalism) to name the physical resurrection as one of the five fundamentals of faith. As I have said in parentheses above, if the resurrection of Jesus is unique, then to comprehend it is impossible, because comprehension of anything requires previous experience and comparison. As for the sheer acceptance of a bodily resurrection, I cannot think what such a thing could do for faith, other than to constitute yet another of the many historic instances of making faith a matter of consent (*assensus*) to otherwise unbelievable data—

and that is to demean faith.[20] Faith, as we have continuously interpreted it—in keeping with the reformers' understanding—means trust: trust in God, analogous to the trust that I may learn to have for some other human being who has demonstrated particular and sustained concern for me. Unless the resurrection of Jesus has something to do with the engendering of that kind of faith,[21] it is nothing more than an abnormality, which, if it interests anyone more than other abnormalities, does so for reasons extraneous to itself (for instance, for the reason that it has become a touchstone of "true belief" in the religious group whose approval one cherishes). It would be a misreading of the foregoing paragraph, however, if one concluded that its writer intends to keep silent about the resurrection. Both here and in what follows, it will be vital to everything else that is said; for apart from the resurrection faith of the community of the cross, we would not even be discussing these matters.

This resurrection faith, to reiterate the above summary, (1) creates the community, the church; (2) apprehends the continuing presence of the crucified one; (3) drives the disciple community to an ongoing search for understanding; and (4) impels it to engage in mission. The first and fourth of these summarizing statements will receive elaboration in the final volume of this trilogy. The second point, which is partly anticipated in our discussion of the Trinity and of the theology of revelation, will become an integral part of the treatment of the second aspect of the doctrine of the Christ, soteriology. Our present concern is with the third point: the fact that the resurrection implies an intensive and ongoing search for understanding of the events preceding it.

That search centers in the christological question: Who is Jesus? Who, really, was this one who for these few months intimately entered the sphere of our lives? Who is this man whose presence, despite his departure, we continue so strongly to sense that we cannot confine our understanding of his being to *human* being, pure and simple?

We have suggested that Jesus himself, as a vital aspect of his ministry to them, began already to point them in the direction of whatever answers they might need in the face of this question—assuming, however, that the answers would never render the question passe. And, so far as that direction involved an

---

20. Fundamentalism insists that Jesus' resurrection proves his divinity. But what does his "divinity" prove? The argument is circular: one fundamental is demonstrated by another fundamental—but both are in the first place dependent upon *faith*. See Tom Harpur, *For Christ's Sake* (Toronto: Oxford Univ. Press, 1986), 81f. The Jewish theologian Pinchas Lapide writes: "If the defeated and depressed group of disciples overnight could change into a victorious movement of faith, based only on autosuggestion or self-deception—without a fundamental faith experience— then this would be a much greater miracle than the resurrection itself" (*The Resurrection of Jesus: A Jewish Perspective,* Introduction by Carl E. Braaten [Minneapolis: Augsburg, 1983], 126).

21. "The resurrection of Jesus came not by hope but by faith." (Tom F. Driver, *Christ in a Changing World: Toward an Ethical Christology* [New York: Crossroads, 1981], 115.)

objective aspect, we have adduced, it must mean for Jesus, the Jewish teacher, the Scriptures of Israel. These Scriptures themselves and as such could not, Jesus believed, fully enlighten his followers; for true understanding depended upon transformed expectations, perceptions, and attitudes ("the circumcision of the heart") that nothing external, not even his own physical presence in their midst, could effect. But with the experience of the burning, winnowing Spirit (Acts 2), such a transformation began to occur among them; therefore we are not surprised to learn that almost the first thing they were led to do in their search for understanding was to search the Scriptures. The sermons of the Book of Acts are full of references to what we have come to call the Old Testament—a collection that (it cannot too often be said) constituted for the first Christians all there was by way of a Bible.

From this source of reflection and inspiration, the disciple community derived its first christological ideas. This is not to deny that other, extrabiblical influences were brought to bear upon these ideas; obviously they read their Scriptures, as we do, under the impact not only of the events they were attempting to decipher but also of assumptions, longings, and influences present in their milieu, including influences emanating from religious and philosophic sources other than Judaism. These latter became more prominent as the movement spread beyond the Jewish community into the Jewish diaspora and the gentile world. Already with the earliest christological reflections, however, we can sense the direction in which the church's thought was likely to move.

To begin with, it was established, evidently, that what had happened in the constellation of occurrences and relationships of which they were part had not happened accidentally, or incidentally, but was decisively purposed; and now it is established (what may only have been suspected by Jesus himself) that the purpose by which his life and ministry had been guided from the beginning not only included his passion and death but was concentrated on these, with his teaching and prophetic and healing ministry being something like a prelude and preliminary to the chief goal:

> "Men of Israel, hear these words: Jesus of Nazareth, a man attested to you by God with mighty works and wonders and signs which God did through him in your midst, as you yourselves know—this Jesus, delivered up according to the definite plan and foreknowledge of God, you crucified and killed by the hands of lawless men. But God raised him up. . . . For David says concerning him. . . ." (Acts 2:22-25, RSV)

The characteristic appeal to the Scriptures followed. Or again:

> "And now, brethren, I know that you acted in ignorance, as did also your rulers. But what God foretold by the mouth of all the prophets, that his Christ should suffer, he thus fulfilled." (Acts 3:17-18, RSV)

390

The well-crafted sermon of the first martyr, Stephen, in Acts 7[22] goes all the way back to Abraham and the patriarchs and Moses to show the logic of the hidden purposes of God in the "betrayal and murder" of "the Righteous One." This theme of the purposefulness of all that had happened, a purposefulness based not only on God's plan of salvation but on the *necessitas* that evoked this plan in the first place—namely, the human condition—this insistence that what had happened *had to happen,* became now a prominent feature and presupposition of the whole testimony of the newer Testament.

It is not surprising that this should be so, and that it should have been conceived of so early in the history of the Christian movement. For if meaning was to be found here—a meaning profound enough to become the basis both of an entire interpretation of reality and a community of belief and discipleship with a mission to the world—then the foundational events of this teleological source would have to be thought of as partaking of a destiny more mysterious and eternal than the immediate, external circumstances would seem to warrant. Clearly, very soon after their separation from their teacher, these mostly untutored men and women began to believe that they had been unwitting actors in a drama of unthinkable historical and transcendental proportions.

In more ambitious elements of that society (or any society), such a supposition would have to be assessed by the cynical as a delusion of grandeur not untypical of those who think more highly of themselves than they ought. But there is no hint in the record that this first great step toward the promulgation of special significance—of gospel—was part of a bid for glory on the part of the disciples and their first converts. Not only were there no rewards available to the dreamers of such a dream, but on the contrary they faced only demerit and punishment. Besides, in their oral traditions they evidently made themselves out in a bad light: far from offering any positive contribution to the process at the basis of their gospel, they presented themselves as dolts and detractors, capable at best of occasional insight and occasional loyalty. Obviously, they are men and women caught up in something much larger than themselves—and they are astonished. Their sense of their own utter unworthiness must be taken as it stands, as entirely sincere. What inspires them is not that they had merited special attention but that the gift of meaning had been given them despite their reluctance, dullness, and desertion.

Once the community has entertained the thought that these occurrences in time are the working out of purposes that are eternal, however, the direction of

---

22. It must also be realized that this sermon constitutes a highly judgmental account of the apostasy of Israel and has played an unfortunate role in the history of Christian anti-Judaism. (See Rosemary Radford Ruether, *Faith and Fratricide: The Theological Roots of Anti-Semitism* [New York: Seabury Press, 1974], 77f.) The ill effects of this may, however, be somewhat mitigated if it is understood that the author is pressing toward his primary point—that the death of Jesus was part of God's plan for universal healing.

the community's reflections has been set. From that indeterminate moment onwards (the pentecostal moment, as we may call it), there is no extraneous limit to what may be claimed for the identity of the one at the center, the crucified one. Between the postpentecostal recognition that the crucifixion and resurrection of Jesus were central to the "very plan and foreknowledge" of God and (for example) the Pauline theology of the second Adam or the Johannine theology of the divine Logos or the later epistles' conception of the preexistent Son, and so on, there is an unmistakable continuity. In all of the christological or protochristological thought of the newer Testament, including the names and titles assigned to Jesus in the Synoptic Gospels as well as the more complex discursive Christology of the epistles, the church is at work, imaginatively, prayerfully, speculatively, liturgically, poetically, doctrinally, in an attempt to understand what it believes.

The belief (*fides*) is not attached to this or that proposition, including propositions about the resurrection. It is an expression of existential trust in the purposing agency behind all that they had experienced. Once this trust is present, the drive to comprehend it is open to a certain freedom—the freedom of the Christian to use whatever is at hand to enrich understanding and facilitate communication. And, as the newer Testament demonstrates liberally, much was at hand.[23]

But while there are no external limits to what may be used in the service of expressing this faith in the ultimate meaning behind the events, there *is* an internal limit, and it is decisive. The limit is this: Whatever lofty, eternal, transcendent, suprahistorical, and supernatural concepts may be employed in the service of this sense of ultimacy, it must not be overlooked for a moment that the figure around whom all these concepts are woven is *Jesus*. That is to say, he is a human being like themselves "in every respect," a Jewish man living under specific historical circumstances, a person who, though the bearer of a transearthly ultimacy, was himself no less contingent than they.

Do the newer Testamental claims for the ultimacy of what was revealed in Jesus as "the Christ of God" themselves in some cases transgress this internal boundary? When the crucified one is presented as the very mind of the Eternal, God's own *Logos* and *Sophia;* when he is depicted as the preexisting Son, the incarnation of truth, the heavenly Son of Man foretold in the apocalyptic literature of late Judaism, the Lord (*Kurios*), the ultimate Judge of all the living, and so on, has the *koinonia* already begun to lose touch with the carpenter's son, the itinerant teacher, the compassionate healer, the despised and rejected and mocked "King of the Jews"?

---

23. "Belief in resurrection is not summed up by an assent to a dogma and the registering of a historical fact. It means participating in this creative act of God. A faith of this kind is the beginning of freedom. If God reveals himself in the raising of the Christ crucified in helplessness, then God is not the quintessence of power, such as the Roman Caesars represented. . . ." (Moltmann, *The Way of Jesus Christ,* 241.)

It is not easy to answer this question. While the internal evidence of the texts may help us to understand what such names and titles and concepts conveyed to the earliest Christians, we, the inheritors of sixteen-odd centuries of Christendom, cannot readily overcome the attitudes and connotations associated with such claims. It is hard for us to hear even common christological titles like "Lord" and "Savior" without being drawn into the whole vortex of triumphalistic religion that has exploited such nomenclature. Whatever the first Christians felt when they employed the title *Kurios/Dominus* to Jesus, they did not have the dubious benefits of centuries of Christian theological exclusivism and ecclesiastical imperialism as their background. On the contrary, so long as the "eyewitnesses" were still among them, or were remembered for the very human beings that they were, the primitive Christians would not be able wholly to apotheosize or etherealize Jesus. As an often persecuted minority, they needed the interpretive symbols and nomenclature requisite to the courage to believe in their *Christos*. But there is a world of difference between the quiet, often secret and whispered confession of the earliest centuries, *Jesus Christos Kurios* (Jesus Christ is Lord), and the same declaration shouted by crusading European knights in the face of "the infidel" or lustily sung by well-clad North American congregations on Easter Sunday morning.

Contexts alter meanings. The context of most forms of the Christian movement prior to its adoption by empire permitted and even required a high Christology. But when this same high Christology is extended beyond the circumstances of Christian minorities; when it is not only carried over into the post-Constantinian situation but elevated and exaggerated through association with dominant cultures and institutions; when at the same time it is no longer checked by the lively memory of Jesus, the "despised and rejected" one, then the same language acquires a meaning and a function very different from what it could have had for the earliest Christians.[24]

The question therefore is not just what the Bible says about Jesus Christ, but how to distinguish what it says from what it in all likelihood says *to us*. Under the circumstances of Constantinian religion, even though we must now speak in almost post-Constantinian terms, we cannot simply repeat the newer Testamental titles, names, and concepts associated with the Christ and assume that we are being faithful to the biblical witness. We may in fact be giving the lie to the biblical witness by failing to recognize that all of this language (Christ,

---

24. "The process of Christologizing Jesus of Nazareth may indeed 'freeze' or neutralize his message and praxis but lose sight of him and leave us with only a celestial cult mystery: the great Ikon Christ, shunted so far off in a Godward direction (God himself having already been edged out of this world of men) that he too, Jesus Christ, ceases to have any critical impact on the life of the world." (Edward Schillebeeckx, *Jesus: An Experiment in Christology,* trans. Hubert Hoskins [New York: Crossroad, 1981], 670–71.)

Word, Wisdom, Son of God, and so on) now has a long history of its own, quite independent of its first usage.

What then may we conclude about the biblical witness to Jesus, called the Christ? In my view, we may construct some such generalization as the following: Two vital affirmations about this person are present as formative assumptions in the newer Testamental witness as it communicates itself to thoughtful faith today: first, that this person must be regarded as having been a genuinely human being, whose real humanity must not be sacrificed for the sake of accentuating or seeming to accentuate faith's claims to his ultimacy; second, that this person must be regarded as being uniquely related to the being and purposing of God.

I have tried to choose my words carefully in making this summary statement. No words will be faultless in this respect; all will cause some to stumble or turn away. But until we are ready to revert to silence or to doxology, some words must be found. It will perhaps be understood by those who have tried to find the right words for this purpose that the words of the above summary do presuppose both silence and doxology; but theology cannot abide in either. It is driven on by the same drive that fired the prophets and apostles—to understand what has been experienced and is believed.

29. Christ for the Church

29.1. The Formalization of Christology. In Part I of this study we saw that the scriptural testimony to God left the Christian movement with what may be called the trinitarian problem. It will now be our claim that the same thing must be said of the biblical witness to Jesus as the Christ: namely, it leaves the people of "the Way" with the christological problem.

It is not difficult to appreciate how this could be so. Consider the two aspects of the generalization made in the previous subsection: first, the insistence that Jesus was and must be regarded by the disciple community as a fully human person. This affirmation, as we shall see in the critical chapter that is to follow, was and is in constant danger of being lost. Yet there were (and still are) minority traditions that functioned as watchdogs also in relation to this affirmation. For that reason, accounts of Jesus' life and deeds that went too far beyond the internal limit named in the foregoing discussion (that is, the recognition of his true humanity) were rejected.

In other words, Docetism, the concept that Jesus only seemed to be human, was rejected. Jesus had to be understood as a fully and perceptibly human being, and not only for incidental reasons but because, apart from this insistence, the whole central conception of the meaning of the Christ event, namely the becoming flesh of the Word, would be lost. It would not be incorrect to say that this rationale for the maintenance of the full humanity of the Christ functioned more formally than materially, in the end; but that it was retained at all, even formally, may be considered a kind of miracle, for it is evident that the early church was under enormous internal and external pressure to succumb to the divinity principle. In a context of powerful alternative theologies at the level both of popular religions and philosophical theism, a faith that was ready to keep at its center a "mere man"—indeed, a failed hero in a society that much honored heroes—must have been sorely tempted simply to turn Jesus into a god. The great wonder of early Christology is that this did not happen officially; the great pity is that it did happen too often at the level of Christian piety. To state the point more cautiously, it is unfortunate that the humanity of Jesus, while formally *retained,* was not imaginatively *sustained.*[25]

The second part of our generalization about the newer Testamental teaching concerning Jesus affirms that these canonical writings leave us with the insistence that, although Jesus was fully human, his life was bound up with the being and purposing of God in a way both unique and decisive. It seems to me that we must put the matter in such terms even to be fair to what is there in the scriptural texts; for to say in the more conventional way that Jesus was "divine" has always been to run the risk of what later was rejected as the Sabellian heresy; and in the North American context, where "the divinity of Christ" functions as an authenticating test of orthodoxy for whole segments of the Christian population, it is almost certain to provoke misunderstanding. The Gospels and epistles associate the life and death of Jesus with God's being and purposing in the closest possible way, but without ever making (what would have been the simplest formula, after all) the straightforward claim: "Jesus was God."[26] Not only do these texts manifest an inherent awareness of the internal limit placed upon their association of Jesus with divinity (that is, his full humanity), but they also maintain a clear desire to remain within the monotheistic traditions of Israel—even when, as in the case of the Johannine material for example, there is a certain pull toward the Hellenistic world.

In short, the biblical material requires of us both affirmations: Jesus is human—"tempted in every respect as we are"; yet God is present to, with, and in Jesus in a way that could not be claimed for any other human being.

This dual claim is what constitutes the christological problem. We do not find any "theology of the two natures" in the biblical texts; and yet we can

---

25. "The proclamation and ministry of Jesus between his birth and his death are never mentioned in the christological dogmas." (Moltmann, *The Way of Jesus Christ,* 70.)

26. "In applying to [Jesus] such terms as [Messiah, king, savior, Lord] were the Gospel writers stating outright that Jesus was God? The answer assuredly is in the negative. To claim to be, or to be called by others, 'Messiah' is by no means the same thing as claiming to be or being thought of as God-in-the-flesh, on a par in every way with Deity." (Tom Harpur, *For Christ's Sake,* 70. See also pp. 9, 59, 97–98, 103.)

understand why a theology of two natures might have developed out of the con-sciousness of those for whom these texts became vital. What occurred within the next few centuries, and came to a certain point of resolution at Chalcedon in 451 C.E., was the attempt of Christians in the postbiblical period to explain how these two affirmations could be maintained simultaneously. How could a mere human being bear such a unique relationship to the one, transcendent God?

This attempt presupposes one other factor of which we must be conscious as we move into these early christological discussions: The theater of reflection and discussion has now shifted, perhaps gradually but decisively, from the He-braic to the Hellenic and Hellenistic world. The great historian of Christian dogma, Adolf von Harnack, believed that this shift from Jerusalem to Athens ended in a complete transformation of the faith, especially at the level of its Christology. On the other hand, Paul Tillich believed that this transition was not so conspicuous, and that it should certainly not be regarded (as Harnack regards it) as a total distortion of the original.[27] I shall reserve my comments on this matter for the conclusion.

In considering the doctrine of the Trinity, we found it a useful device to think of the long debate about the godhead as involving the elimination of what came to be regarded as false alternatives. In clarifying its belief concerning God, the church was adopting a working (not necessarily a conscious) *via neg-ativa.* With the negation of various possible or actual interpretations, a space was left in which the contemplation of deity might safely be undertaken; and this "clearing in the middle," as I designated it, was given the symbolic nomen-clature, *mia ousia kata treis hypostaseis/una substantia et tres personae* (one essence or substance in three distinctions or persons).

We may approach the early church's handling of the christological problem bequeathed to it by the newer Testamental witness by adopting a similar her-meneutic. In the process of decision-making, what is happening is that certain heretical positions are being identified gradually and rejected. This process eventually creates its own boundaries, within which, in the minds of the major-ity of those involved, it is permissible to contemplate and describe the identity of the Christ. The Formula of Chalcedon is the documentary consequence of this lengthy process.

It is not difficult to anticipate, on the basis of the generalizations we have drawn from the newer Testament, what opinions had to be questioned and eliminated—at least formally—in and through this elaborate and often chaotic process. As there are two rudimentary affirmations deriving from the biblical witness to Jesus Christ, so there are two christological positions that will have

---

27. See Adolf von Harnack, *Outlines of the History of Dogma,* trans. Edwin Knox Mitchell (Boston: Beacon Hill Press, 1957), esp. chap. 7, pp. 242ff.; and Paul Tillich, *Systematic Theology,* vol. 2 (Chicago: Univ. of Chicago Press, 1957), 140.

to be subjected to strong criticism. The first is the tendency to undermine the newer Testament's affirmation of the full humanity of Jesus; the second is the tendency to make too little of Jesus' unique relation to God, the Father.

Among those who denied the full humanity were the Docetists and Gnostics. For these positions, which were more like pervasive attitudes than specific schools of thought, the full humanity of the Christ had to be questioned because, out of a Hellenistic orientation toward the inferiority of matter, they conceived of ultimacy in purely spiritual terms. To be embodied was to be distorted. Salvation meant salvation from the creaturely state.[28]

This tendency came to be associated in particular with Apollinaris, Bishop of Laodicaea (310–390 C.E.), who believed that while Jesus had a human body and a human soul, his spirit (in effect, his quintessential self) was not human but divine. In the unique case of Jesus, he declared, the human spirit had been replaced by the divine Logos. The position was condemned by the Council of Constantinople in 381, after Apollinaris had already seceded from the church. The reason for the rejection of his position was that the humanity had to be maintained in order for the full humanity of human beings, and not just their spirits, to be redeemed. In other words, the principle of Jesus' humanity was upheld.

The second type of answer to the question of the Christ's identity that was eliminated in these discussions of the early centuries was one that minimized, or seemed to endanger, the centrality of the biblical claim concerning the uniqueness of Jesus' relation to God. This thinking was present in the positions of various parties, including those stemming from the views of Arius. The Arians wanted to uphold the transcendent otherness of God, as we have seen, and therefore they refused to affirm the Athanasian insistence that the Son was *homoousios* with the Father. Semi-Arianism could admit of the Son's similarity *(homoisios)* vis-à-vis the Father; but even this was too bold for the strict Arian. The adoptionists, on the other hand, wanted to uphold the humanity of Jesus, but they could see no way of making his humanity contiguous with his divinity; therefore they solved the problem by claiming that at some point in his life the man Jesus was taken up into or adopted by Deity.

It was the wisdom of the church that if this minimization of the Son's oneness with the Father prevailed, Christianity would present itself to the world as another of the many accounts of apotheosized beings, and therefore a faith whose central figure is one in and through whom we encounter, not ultimate truth and salvation, but an intermediate revelation on the way, perhaps, to something more complete.[29]

---

28. See Rosemary Radford Ruether, *Sexism and God Talk* (Boston: Beacon Press, 1983), 78–79.

29. In this connection see D. M. Baillie, "Christology and the Nature of God" in *God Was in Christ* (London: Faber and Faber, Ltd., 1948), 63ff.; Williston Walker, *A History of the Christian Church,* rev. ed. (New York: Charles Scribner's Sons, 1959), chap. 9, pp. 131ff.; and Jürgen

The elimination of these two positions meant that the evolving church had upheld, technically, what it had gleaned from the biblical witness concerning the human and divine natures of the Christ. But there was yet another dimension of the problem: How are the two natures to be combined in one person? How, without presenting to the world a freak of duality, is Jesus to be seen as incorporating in his one life two apparently vastly distinct if not utterly incompatible natures?

Again we may make use of the language of elimination. Two positions are negated in the painful process that resulted, finally, in Chalcedon: one, which is associated in particular with the name of Nestorius of Antioch, seemed to the majority questionable because it did not overcome sufficiently the danger of duality. Nestorius and his followers maintained that there were two natures, distinct from one another organically; in Jesus they were joined, not in a physical or ontic sense but in a moral union. That is, Jesus the man unites with Jesus the divine Son at the point of the will. The two essences, divine and human, remain separate in him, but they are united through a continuing determination of the will of each to be one. Although many interpreters have concluded that this in fact anticipates Chalcedon itself and that Nestorius's position was rejected more out of political than theological causation, on the face of it the question of the integrity of Jesus' person does not seem to be sufficiently maintained by this school.

The opposite solution, however, was also rejected. This was associated with the school of Alexandria, and it came to be linked in particular with the name of Eutyches (378–454), though its first and more subtle exponent was Cyril of Alexandria. The basic insistence of this school is upon the unity of Christ's nature, hence it is designated the monophysite controversy (*mono* [= one] + *physis* [= nature]). It was rejected because, in its eagerness to combine the two natures and at the same time to stress the ultimacy of the Christ, it effectively eliminated the principle of Jesus' full humanity. While in Cyril this elimination is implicit and cloaked in complexity, in the simpler, almost naive Eutyches it becomes plain that for this whole school what matters is the retention of the divinity principle.

With the elimination of all four of these positions, the formulators of Chalcedon had their work cut out for them. They had to summarize in a convincing, formulary way the conclusions already implicit, if not quite explicit, in the decisions leading to the denunciation of the positions outlined above. That is precisely what they did. The decisive part of the formulation reads:

> Therefore, following the Holy Fathers, we all with one accord teach men to acknowledge one and the same Son, our Lord Jesus Christ, at once complete in

---

Moltmann, *The Crucified God: The Cross of Christ as the Foundation and Criticism of Christian Theology,* trans. R. A. Wilson and John Bowden (Minneapolis: Fortress, 1993), 87ff.

Godhead and complete in manhood, truly God and truly man, consisting also of a reasonable soul and body; of one substance [*homoousios*] with the Father as regards his Godhead, and at the same time of one substance [*homoousios*] with us as regards his manhood; like us in all respects, apart from sin; as regards his Godhead, begotten of the Father before all ages, but yet as regards his manhood begotten, for us men and for our salvation, of Mary the Virgin, the God-bearer [*theotokos*]; one and the same Christ, Son, Lord, Only-begotten, recognized in two natures, without confusion, without change, without division, without separation; the distinction of natures being in no way annulled by the union, but rather the characteristics of each nature being preserved and coming together to form one person and subsistence [*hypostasis*], not as parted or separated into two persons, but one and the same Son and Only-begotten God the Word, Lord Jesus Christ; even as the prophets from earliest times spoke of him, and our Lord Jesus Christ himself taught us, and the creed of the Fathers has handed down to us.[30]

We shall make four brief observations about the process of formalization, and then in a concluding subsection on this aspect of christological doctrine we shall enter certain more substantive questions that will be taken up later in the critical chapter.

1. Throughout the process leading to Chalcedon, and in the Formula itself, we note the admixture of biblical and philosophic-religious language. The biblical titles (Christ, Son, Lord, Word) are combined with language entirely foreign to biblical thought: *physis, hypostasis, homoousios, theotokos*. Given the background of the document, there was probably no way in which Chalcedon could avoid this combination; but does the Formula not indicate that the philosophic-religious language is by now the real point of comprehension, discussion, and contention? Has the relational language of biblical faith not given way entirely to the substantialistic language of the Greco-Roman world?

Related to this is the charge of feminist christological thought, which rightly notes the patriarchalization of the whole tone of the discussion, including the loss of earlier female representations of the divine, especially the *Sophia* of Proverbs and the Wisdom of Solomon.[31]

2. The full humanity of Jesus is affirmed—and in a way that Nicaea had not been able to manage. Not only is Jesus "of one substance" with God, but he is also *homoousios* with us and indeed "like us in all respects, apart from sin." This is undoubtedly the most remarkable aspect of the Formula, and its presence must be attributed to the insistence chiefly of the school of Antioch.

---

30. Formula of Chalcedon in *Documents of the Christian Church,* ed. Henry Bettenson (London: Oxford Univ. Press, 1943), 73.

31. See Ruether, *Sexism and God Talk,* chap. 5, 116ff.

Without this school, which Father George Florovsky characterized insightfully with the expression "anthropological maximalism,"[32] the church "would probably have lost entirely the human picture."[33] The question to which we shall have to return is whether this albeit bold affirmation of the "very humanity" of the Christ is sufficient to deliver Christianity from a theoretical incarnationalism lacking in existential depth and human credibility.

3. The strength of the Formula lies in its skillful summation of the negated positions. As an instance of theology performed *via negativa* it is almost exemplary. This is not to be taken lightly, for perhaps the only trustworthy Christology is a negative Christology. It is already presumptuous of anyone to say of anyone what he or she is not; but to say who a person—any person—*is,* is to go well beyond presumption toward audacity. In the case of this person, given what is being claimed about and for him, positive definition always verges on blasphemy. The very modesty of Chalcedon, considered in the light of so many of the immodest statements that preceded and have succeeded it, is not only morally commendable; it is theologically perceptive.

4. As a positive statement about the identity of the Christ, Chalcedon is unsatisfactory—fortunately. It settles for the affirmation of both the full divinity and full humanity of the Christ as well as both the unity and distinctiveness of the natures combined in him—and without saying how this could be. Surely that is commendable, apart from whatever problems it points up; for there is no way in which a unique and unrepeatable occurrence of sheer grace can be explained. *Deus non est genera* (God is not one of a species). "*Incarnation* has no presuppositions."[34] The sin of nearly all Christology is that it seeks to define a person, Jesus, by having reference to categories ("divinity" and "humanity"), neither of which it can adequately comprehend. Yet faith cannot remain silent. It must try to understand, and to communicate its understanding in comprehensible terms. There is, however, a fine distinction between seeking comprehension and assuming that comprehension is perfectly possible. Chalcedon may be regarded as a model of theological sobriety because it knows how to navigate between the Scylla of presumption and the Charybdis of mystical silence.

To state the matter in the most positive and appreciative terms available to me, I would summarize the formalization of Christology briefly as follows: Through trial and error and in the confusion of motives that always accompanies intense religious struggles, the church at last came to certain definitive conclusions as to what should *not* be said concerning the one whose life constitutes its raison d'être. In doing so, it also risked positive affirmations concerning this one, but with these it was content to state the matter without explaining

---

32. John Meyendorff, *Christianity in Eastern Thought* (Washington: Corpus Books, 1969), 6.
33. Paul Tillich, *A History of Christian Thought* (New York: Simon and Schuster, 1967), 81.
34. Moltmann, *The Way of Jesus Christ,* 84.

its possibility. Since, if God and humanity met uniquely in this one life, the possibility of such a thing must remain for us a profound mystery, Chalcedon has chosen the better path. The task of theology is here, as perhaps always, more negative than positive. Christology exists to identify the false shepherds, so that the true shepherd may the better identify himself.

29.2. The Question Implicit in the Process. Our recognition of the appropriateness and even brilliance of the Chalcedonian resolution of the christological problem bequeathed to evolving Christianity by the earliest witnesses ought not, however, to be construed as a blanket endorsement of Chalcedonian Christology. Given the circumstances—the changed context; the language available; the strife between contending factions; the need to strengthen the unity of the church; the new, political functioning of the Christian religion—Chalcedon may be regarded very highly. But if one asks whether Chalcedon and the whole process leading up to it constitute a solid basis for the ongoing christological reflection of the Christian movement, then one must register serious reservations.

The fact is that Chalcedon has functioned as though it were such a basis. It has been regarded as the measuring-stick of orthodoxy by a remarkably diverse Christian majority. That Christians as different from one another as ancient orthodoxy and present-day U.S. and Canadian Protestants could find in the Formula of Chalcedon an acceptable doctrine of Christ's person is attributable, chiefly, to the factor mentioned above: the Chalcedonian emphasis upon the *via negativa*. Without overlooking the positive aspect of such an appeal, we must at the same time recognize the danger implicit in it: the substitution of a highly theoretical approach to faith for one that retains something of the encounter quality of which we spoke earlier.

What I mean is that the historic church's adherence to Chalcedon, while it has made possible a modicum of consensus with respect to the central figure of Christian belief, has also encouraged a faith that is more nearly assent to doctrine (*assensus*) than trust in the one to whom doctrine tries feebly to testify (*fiducia*). The internal question implicit in the process leading to and following Chalcedon is whether it does not signify a quite different kind of interest in the Christ—different, that is to say, from what is present in the witness of the newer Testament itself.

One way of designating that different interest is to employ (as I have done above) the term "theoretical." Another is to distinguish between what we may call the existential-soteriological interest of the biblical writings and the abstract-metaphysical preoccupation of the christological debate. With the newer Testamental writings, we know that we are hearing the testimony of people for whom the question of the Christ's identity was also and simultaneously a question of their own; and therefore we are never able to separate the question of who Jesus is from the question of what he has to do with and for us. It is possible to hear behind the christological debates of the early centuries a soteriological concern (especially in Athanasius, and in the school of Antioch); but that concern is not prominent, and its background importance is often so obscure that the impression is created that salvation depends upon a nuanced, rational explication of the identity of the Christ as a matter of definition.

The continuing influence of such a christological posture cannot escape anyone who is even peripherally aware of religion in North America today. For whole segments of what passes for the most earnest and committed type of Christianity in this context, the cornerstone of true belief is "the divinity of Christ." It seems not to matter so much what this means or where it leads ethically; it is sufficient for eternal salvation to believe that Jesus "was divine." We may regard this as a gauche and simplistic reduction of Chalcedonian orthodoxy, or even as a perversion of the same; but the power of the theory is such that we must ask whether, behind it, there lies a whole history of reductionism in Christology, and whether in fact this history is not the dominant type of christological reflection over the Christian centuries.

The other side of this same coin is a humanistic reduction of the Christ, the power of which, in the North American context, is in considerable measure due to the liberal reaction to conservative and fundamentalist representations of Christ's divinity. Jürgen Moltmann asserts that this "anthropological christology," "Jesuology," or "christology from below" represents the great shift in christological thought in the modern era: "The christological disputes and discussions of the last two hundred years reflect a radical change in European theology as a whole."[35] I would add to this that in North America the move to anthropological Christology in mainstream liberal Protestant churches is even more marked than in Europe—partly, again, because of the more pronounced and unnuanced opposition to this "Christology from below" represented by those who, with a single-mindedness hardly known in European Protestantism, insist upon "Christology from above."

Both of these positions, which have their historic roots in the "two natures" conceptualization of Chalcedon, and which mutually antagonize and perpetuate one another, must be questioned; for both reduce the mystery of the person of Christ to typologies, and sometimes caricatures, drawn from preconceptions of divinity and humanity. It will be evident from the foregoing discussion that, for contextual as well as biblical and historical reasons, I am anxious to retain in particular the profession of the real humanity of Jesus. But this should not be interpreted to mean that humanity as it is experienced, understood, or idealized by this or that stratum of society (for example, middle-class Christian) becomes the entree to our understanding of Jesus Christ, any more

---

35. Ibid., 55.

than a preconceived "divinity" ought to do so. Jesus Christ confronts and challenges our preconceptions of both God and ourselves. For faith, his humanity defines authentic humanity and not the other way around.

Further elaboration of this concern must await the critical chapter to follow.

30. The Work of Jesus Christ

30.1. Historical Fluidity and Dogmatic Tenacity in Relation to This Subject. While Christology received a great deal of attention in the early centuries and was resolved in at least a quasi-official manner at Chalcedon, soteriology evolved gradually and in response to specific, changing contexts. Especially with respect to what from the outset was understood to be the principal aspect of Christ's saving work, the so-called priestly aspect, it is possible to show an almost exact correlation between the human predicament, as it was perceived in the varying historical situations concerned, and the manner in which the church articulated the meaning of the atonement.

This applies particularly within the Christian West. We shall argue (with many others)[36] that all of the prominent theories of the atonement can be classified according to three basic types: one whose fundamental theme is the idea of deliverance or (to use a contemporary term) liberation; another that is woven around the commanding thought of sacrifice in behalf of others; and a third that concentrates on the motif of demonstration or revelation. The rudiments of each of these may be said to be present in the scriptural testimony to the cross and resurrection of Jesus, and each type has advocates throughout the whole history of Christendom; yet in a given context, one of the three tends to dominate. The dominant type corresponds to the perceived condition of humankind during that particular period. Part of our task in this subsection, therefore, will be to show in some detail the correlation between the historical context and the soteriology that achieved classical expression within it.

Indeed, the doctrine of the work of the Christ demonstrates more graphically than any other aspect of Christian theology the inherently contextual character of this faith. Wherever the disciple community has tried in an earnest and original way to answer the question, What has Jesus Christ done for us? it has been obliged to answer in such a manner that the human *problematique* as it is experienced and articulated in that context is existentially engaged. Without such engagement, the redemptive answer appears as an answer to a question nobody asked. It would not be an answer *pro nobis* (for *us*). The great theories of Christ's atoning work, in their most persuasive

---

36. Most recently, Daniel L. Migliore, *Faith Seeking Understanding: An Introduction to Christian Theology* (Grand Rapids: Wm. B. Eerdmans Pub. Co., 1991), 152ff.

expressions, have all of them emerged from a profound, original exposure to historical human suffering.

This does not mean that in every case the formulators of the atonement traditions were aware that they were doing their work contextually. As we have argued in the first volume, the awareness of contexts is a modern phenomenon, a consequence of historical consciousness in general. When the theologians who gave classical expression to all three types of atonement theology developed their theories (for they all worked in premodern settings), they simply thought of themselves as exploring the meaning of the gospel. They did not ask whether their work had particular import for the age or locus in which they lived, nor did they suppose that it might not be relevant under other historical or sociological conditions. Yet because they were persons who were in fact deeply immersed in the *problematique* of their own contexts, what they said about the atoning work of the Christ really did correspond with the problems and possibilities of life as they were experienced in that particular situation. It was for them, in other words, a matter of intuitive inspiration and participation.

Our situation is different. We have become conscious of the fact that people always think and write, pray, speak, and work as persons who reflect their particular contexts. We are prevented by this awareness, where it is refined, from assuming that what we shall say with respect to the work of the Christ has universal and eternal applicability. We know that it grows out of an explicit kind of human experience, and that the circumstances of life to which we believe the gospel of the cross speaks will be different—are already different—in other times and places. If, for instance, we live in First World contexts, we know that we cannot and must not presuppose that our particular answers to the question, What has the Christ done *pro nobis?* are immediately applicable to Third World contexts. This consciousness of the context poses for us problems of which the classical formulators of the dominant atonement theologies were not aware. They, or their disciples and hearers, could think their answers absolute, or at least permanently valid. We know that ours—and indeed all possible answers to this question—are relative.

While this knowledge may diminish some of the boldness of our soteriology, it has at least the advantage of making us more vigilant with respect to both the temporality and the tenacity of dogma. And this is salutary; for not only does the history of atonement theology demonstrate the inherently contextual character of the Christian message, but it also demonstrates an antithetical proposition, namely, the propensity of powerful theological dogmas to persist well beyond the point of their timeliness.

To be concrete, so overwhelming has been the influence of those atonement traditions centered in the idea of sacrifice that, in the West, they have continued to this day to dominate the field. And this is no minor problem; for these atonement traditions were addressed to apologetic contexts characterized by readings of the human predicament quite different from the analyses of that predicament by which the most sensitive minds of our own context have been grasped.

We see here, in short, contradictory tendencies at work in the life of the community of faith. On the one hand, the work of the Christ is articulated responsively in relation to the perceived predicament of humanity. On the other hand, entrenched theories of Christ's work so predispose the believing community to certain assumptions about what is wrong with the world that the community fails to remain sensitive to changes in the human predicament. Thus, soteriology leads away from pure theory to participation and reformulation (*praxis*) of theological understanding; at the same time, it can prevent precisely that participation and reformulation, by stubbornly adhering to atonement theories which assume that the human condition has been understood once and for all.

We shall need to be aware of this dual tendency as we turn to the discussion of the historical evolution of the priestly work of Jesus Christ in particular. But it permeates the whole discussion, and therefore we introduce it at the beginning of our soteriological reflections as a methodological reminder.

30.2. The Threefold Office of Christ. In much Protestant theology, and especially (following Calvin[37]) in the Reformed tradition, it has been conventional to consider the work of the Christ under the nomenclature of the "threefold office" (*officium triplex* or *munus triplex*). This refers to the three essential *officia* within the community of Israel as Christians read the Scriptures of the older Testament, namely, the offices of prophet, priest, and monarch (king). The underlying assumption of this Christology is that Jesus both took up and fulfilled each of these offices: He is not only the one to whom the prophets pointed; he is himself the supreme prophet. He is not only the one who stands in the succession of Israel's priests; he is both the final priest and the one who, as priest, assumes the place of the sacrificial victim. And he is not only the legitimate successor in the line of Israel's monarchs, especially David the shepherd king; he is the last king, the one who rides in eschatological simplicity into Jerusalem, the king whose coming kingdom, though not "of this world," has already broken into history, calling in question the kingdoms of this world, and soon to be established in reality as it is already established in principle.

This is not the only schema under which it is possible to discuss the work of the Christ, or soteriology. Obviously there is something arbitrary about it, despite its familiarity in certain circles. Not only does it lead to "artificial divisions,"[38] but it easily succumbs to the theoretical approach to the faith that perpetuates the notion that the life of Jesus is an almost mathematical

---

37. *Institutes*, 2.11.

38. Hendrikus Berkhof, *Christian Faith: An Introduction to the Study of the Faith*, trans. Sierd Woudstra (Grand Rapids: Wm. B. Eerdmans Pub. Co., 1979), 295.

abstraction: one component in a triune being, with two natures, fulfilling three offices. Besides, it may be questioned whether Israel's faith and life are adequately summarized through the allusion to the three offices. The Hebrew Scriptures also speak of the judges, the authors of wisdom, the lawgivers, and others. There is evidently here, as elsewhere in Christian doctrinal history, a certain fascination with the number three. In view of all this, one can only agree with Tillich when he asserts that if the threefold office is considered an indelible way of discussing soteriology, then it must be questioned.

At the same time, the tradition must be said to have some merit. Three advantages may be named: First, it offers a convenient way of discussing what is otherwise a difficult subject. As we have remarked earlier, theology must divide the indivisible; and the most acceptable divisions are those, surely, that facilitate communication while at the same time not doing grave injustice to the subject. Prophecy, priesthood, and sovereignty may not encompass all that must be covered in any discussion of the work of the Christ, but these categories are nonetheless substantial ones and a reasonable way of arranging the material that must be considered.

Second, and more important, so long as the profession of faith remembers the three aspects of Christ's work, it is prevented from capitulating altogether to the tendency to concentrate exclusively on one of them. That tendency is a real danger, as the Western concentration on the priestly work amply demonstrates. There is in fact a certain potentiality in the device of the *munus triplex* to offer a more rounded and holistic portrayal of the whole work of the Christ than has regularly occurred within Christendom. The Gospel records themselves concentrate on the passion and death of Jesus, the nucleus of the priestly work; the two historic creeds allude only to Christ's "suffering" when they wish to say something about the life of Jesus as distinct from his birth, death, and resurrection; and throughout the history of doctrine there has been a preoccupation with the priestly work, as though it were all that faith had to profess in this regard.

While it is natural and right that the priestly work should dominate the discussion, in my opinion, the biblical testimony is falsified or reduced when this work becomes an almost exclusive interest of soteriology. Even the priestly work itself suffers, in the explication of it, when it is not understood to be the work of one who conducted an influential if brief ministry of teaching and prophecy, and who is acknowledged by the church as the one who "reigns at the right hand of God." Too often the cross and resurrection are lifted clear out of the whole biblical account and treated, almost, as a problem to be solved by soteriological theory. The recall of the other offices, imaginatively pursued, could prevent this.

The third and most important aspect of this dogmatic device is that it helps the disciple community to maintain its necessary continuity with the community of Israel—a continuity that is constantly being lost sight of. Wherever the threefold office has been taken seriously, there has been not only a vigilance against the Marcionitic heresy but also an exceptional consciousness of the importance of the older Testament for the faith and life of the church. Jesus has been seen in this tradition, not as an independent figure or innovator, but as being himself the inheritor of a rich and wise tradition. His work is not a work upon which he arbitrarily, or in communion with God alone, decides; it is a work whose outlines are already determined prior to his appearance. It is a work therefore whose necessity is already known to the prophets and lawgivers and wisdom-writers of Israel. Part of the destiny ("cup") of which Jesus in the newer Testamental record is clearly conscious is his calling to accept and fulfill this preconceived work.

The importance of this continuity with Israel can hardly be overestimated. If Christianity from the outset and in all of its major expressions had in fact perceived its *Christos* as one whose whole ministry is already anticipated by the fundamental faith of the Jews, it would not have been possible for the Christian faith to become, as it did become, the spiritual climate favorable to the development of anti-Semitism. As a vital ideational and symbolic dimension of the mentality that produced the Holocaust,[39] we must recognize today a Christ-figure who, both in his person and his work, suggested no essential continuity with Israel. In view of the fact that Christology (in the restrictive sense of the term) constantly succumbed to the divinity principle and therefore constantly minimized the personal, historical, and genetic connection with Israel, a soteriology which took seriously the fact that Christ's work was an extension of the work of Israel's prophets, priests, and monarchs could have offset considerably the propensity of Christianity to adopt a working Marcionism and thus an anti-Judaic spirit.

In relation to one aspect of the threefold office device, however, great care must be taken precisely in this connection. I refer to the notion, which I have faithfully represented in the introductory paragraphs of this subsection, that in Jesus the three offices of Israel's faith and life are "fulfilled." This fulfillment can be understood in two ways, and from the standpoint of the present work only one of them is acceptable. First, it can mean that Jesus Christ finished once and for all a work that the prophets, priests, and kings of Israel could not complete, and that this fulfillment constitutes a finality with respect both to these Hebrew callings and the legitimacy of the mission of Israel itself. Obviously when it is understood in this way, the fulfillment of the offices by Jesus not only constitutes a judgment of Israel (that is, the Jews were not able to do it) but also points, along with the other aspects of the avowedly Christian witness, to the redundancy and superfluity of any continuing community of Israel, the work of the Jews having been finished. In short, it is inherently supersessionistic.

---

39. See *Thinking the Faith,* chap. 3, sec. 13; 210ff.

The fulfillment of the offices can also be understood, however, in a second way; and it is this that I shall intend in what follows. It can mean that the work in which Israel had long before Jesus been engaged is the very work that Jesus now takes up, and that the fullness of Jesus' assumption of this work is a mission in which, not only his "body," the church, now by grace participates, but one in which also the continuing community of Israel has its share.

The latter point, I am persuaded, is exactly what Paul contends in Romans 9–11. Jesus' fulfillment is not final in the sense that nothing more needs to be done. Obviously that would leave no room for the followers—for the church. According to the Pauline tradition, it is the essence of the disciple community that it is being incorporated into the work that Jesus fulfilled (Col. 1:24). But the eschatological fulfillment that in Christ already impinges upon history is one which involves not only the people of the newer covenant but also those of the older. This fulfillment is nothing more nor less than the realization of a covenant that is as old as Abraham, or Noah—or Adam and Eve. Jesus, for Christians, represents the decisive moment in the realization of this covenant; but as such this does not exclude but on the contrary includes both the people of the old and the people of the new.

With this qualification, and understanding the threefold office as a dogmatic convenience and not as the entire substance of what faith professes concerning the saviorhood of Jesus, we shall consider the work of the Christ under this nomenclature.

30.3. Jesus as Prophetic Figure and Teacher. As we begin to reflect on the work of Jesus, it is well to remind ourselves of what is stated implicitly in the immediately foregoing paragraphs: namely, that this is a work into which we ourselves, as members of the covenant people, are called. If we discuss any aspect of the work of the "head" of the "body" as though it were exclusively Christ's work, we shall miss the point. In every aspect of it, it is a work that describes also the vocation of those who are being incorporated into the Christ.

Nowhere is this more provocative than in connection with the prophetic work. Only the church that is prepared to take such a work upon itself has the right to discuss Christ's prophetic work. Perhaps one reason why so little attention has been paid to this office is that historic Christianity has been so ill prepared to be a prophetic community—"salt," "yeast," "light." Christendom excelled in modeling itself upon a distorted conception of Christ's monarchic office, and it has honored those in its midst who assumed the priestly office; but Christendom has neglected with great skill all but the most innocuous aspects of the prophetic role. To speak of the work of the Christ in this period of transition from establishment to diaspora[40] is to ask concretely whether the

---

40. See *Thinking the Faith,* chap. 3, sec. 11; 200ff.

Christian movement is at last willing to participate also in this office. If it is not, then it will be unable also to comprehend the other two offices in anything but a rote manner.

As we have already noted, the priestly office, to which historic Christian doctrine in the West has been most attached, is really incomprehensible apart from the prophetic work of Jesus. Jesus as the priest who becomes the victim is brought to the point of physical martyrdom (*martyreo* = to witness) because of his spoken witness—his continuity with the prophets of Israel. He would not have become the slain "lamb of God" had he not first been the roaring "lion of Judah." He is no silent victim. To be sure, he is silent before Pilate at the last; but by that time he does not have to speak. He has spoken already. He has already played the prophet's role: every pretentious authority has been called in question, every hypocrisy denounced, every hidden motive brought to light.

As prophet, Jesus not only challenges the authority of the secular authorities but he defies the religious authorities as well. Indeed, he appears as one who is ready to question all authority—not because he is against authority *in se* but because he is conscious of the propensity of authority to wield power for the sake of self-aggrandizement. Most scholars agree that Jesus was not a member of the revolutionary Zealot movement, though he may have been sympathetic to its cause in part; yet neither was he apolitical in the way that respectable Christianity always wants to have him. Clearly his bias (and this is in strict continuity with the whole prophetic tradition) is in favor of the powerless, the oppressed, and the poor; he is especially—and for his age unusually—sensitive to the oppression of children and women: those, in short, who do not have power but are the victims of power.

This does not mean that Jesus simply despises the rich and powerful, as social revolutionaries would like him to have done. It does mean, however, that he is not prepared to be all things to all people. It is not only banal but also biblically questionable to turn the prophet Jesus into the sort of preacher who is equally critical of all and equally open to all. As John Coleman Bennett pointed out in his book *The Radical Imperative,*[41] it must not be thought accidental that the Magnificat of the Virgin heralds the advent of the Christ with the statement, "He hath put down the mighty from their seats." The same note is struck in Jesus' opening sermon in his native town of Nazareth, when he audaciously announces his mission in the words of the prophet Isaiah:

> The spirit of the Lord is upon me because he has anointed me; he has sent me to announce good news to the poor, to proclaim release for prisoners and recovery of sight to the blind; to let the broken victims go free, to proclaim the year of the Lord's favour. (New English Bible, Luke 4:18ff.)

---

41. (Philadelphia: Westminster Press, 1975), 39.

The permanent truth that has been discovered again in our time by various liberation movements—for example, Minjung theology in Korea[42]—is that the work of Jesus is directed in a primary way toward the afflicted, the tyrannized, and the impoverished. Liberation theology has helped us to rediscover this and, along with Marxism, with which this theology is sometimes linked in Third World contexts, it has helped us to recognize also the class interests in states and churches that have perpetuated the picture of a Jesus who brings comfort to the poor without disturbing the political and economic circumstances that keep them poor.

Moreover, this bias of the Christ in favor of the downtrodden is combined with an equally prophetic attempt on his part to break down the false security of the strong, the self-satisfied, the righteous, the powerful, the rich. Nietzsche, with the keen eyes of the enemy, saw this clearly, and he rejected Jesus precisely because of Jesus' critique of power. Nietzsche wanted the human being to become more Promethean, more aggressive, to lay claim to the natural human will to power. Jesus the prophet struggles against all that, and not even because of the hubris of which it gives evidence so much as the fact that it is such a pathetic way, finally, for human creatures to behave. What a pathetic person is the fool in Jesus' parable who wants to build larger barns in order to amass a bulwark against the future (Luke 12:18f.). He has only been able to do this by repressing the knowledge of his own tentativeness. And how pathetic is the one who hides his treasure in the ground so that no one will take it from him (Matt. 25:15f.). And how pathetic is the Pharisee who thinks that he is secure because of his superior righteousness (Luke 18:10f.). It is the whole aim of the prophetic rabbi, Jesus, to break down all of this pretense, whether it is based on possessions of a physical nature or the more subtle possessions of a false and proud spirituality.

Is this not in fact the central thrust of Jesus' ethical teaching? As it has been said often enough, there is little that is new in Jesus' ethic. Yet a characteristic note sounds throughout the newer Testament's summation of his teaching: his concern for internal goodness or "purity of heart," to use Kierkegaard's term. Jesus does not minimize the stringency of the law of Moses; on the contrary, he increases its demand: "Do not think that I have come to abolish the law or the prophets; I have come not to abolish but to fulfill. For truly I tell you, until heaven and earth pass away, not one iota, not one stroke of a letter, will pass from the law until all is accomplished." (Matt. 5:17-18).

Jesus' manner of accentuating the cutting edge of the Torah is to draw attention to its hidden implications. Concretely this means that he shows the necessity not only of external but of internal obedience. One is not only to refrain

---

42. See, for example, David Suh Kwang-sun, *The Korean Minjung in Christ* (Hong Kong: C.C.A. Commission on Theological Concerns, 1991).

from adultery but from lust. Lust is already the adultery of the spirit (Matt. 5:27f.). One is not only commanded to refrain from murder but from thinking murderous thoughts (Matt. 5:21f.), and so on. The question that Jesus searches out always has to do with the motives for the deeds. He is if anything more critical of the "good" people who perform their goodness out of duty than of those who simply follow their own selfish instincts. Those who "do the right thing for the wrong reason" (T. S. Eliot) are just as guilty as those who simply do the wrong thing.

By the time Jesus finishes his discourse on obedience, anyone who has been listening carefully will likely respond in the way that, on at least one occasion, the disciples themselves responded: "But surely this is not possible!" (Matt. 19:25, par.). Is this not, however, precisely the response for which the prophetic teacher of the law is waiting? If the first effect of his teaching is to demonstrate that the law requires purity of motivation and not only external compliance, the second is to show his hearers that all claims to purity are without foundation. Who can avoid the conclusion, reading the Gospels of the newer Testament, that for Jesus of Nazareth the greatest unrighteousness would be to imagine oneself righteous?

Saint Paul more than any other author of the Christian Scriptures (and certainly more than any of the theologians of the second century C.E., who for the most part adopted a highly legalistic version of the faith), understood the whole thrust of prophetic religion along these lines. For that reason he wrote his famous "schoolmaster" statement about the law in Galatians: "the law was our schoolmaster to bring us unto Christ, that we might be justified by faith" (Gal. 3:24, KJV). That is to say, whoever hears the law in depth, with its demand not only for outward observation but for inward purity, with its insistence not only upon morality but upon love, knows that its deepest effect is to discourage human beings from any attempts at self-justification. It is only in this mood of *krisis* and new self-knowledge that a person can be open to free grace. So long as we believe that we are fully in charge of our lives; so long as we think ourselves rich, we shall not be ready to receive what God intends to give us. The task of the prophet, with Jesus as with John the Baptist and Amos and all the prophets, is to open the eyes of the blind, arrogant, and unknowing who "think more highly of themselves than they ought"; to unveil their pretensions and their pomp, their naive self-indulgence, their myopic innocence; to prepare them, through an unwelcome exposure to their real unacceptability, for the unwarranted acceptance called grace.

This ought not to be interpreted to mean, however, that Jesus is antinomian. His primary intention as prophetic teacher of the law is to demonstrate that before God "all have sinned and fall short of the glory of God"—Paul's conclusion about the human condition (Rom. 3:23), which Jesus as he is presented in the Gospels would certainly have endorsed. The law of God cannot be fulfilled as law, because the essence of God's law, as Jesus summarizes it, is love: love toward God, toward the neighbor (Matt. 22:37-40), toward the enemy (Matt. 19:19). Love cannot be achieved in response to a command. Before the command to love, and to love without condition, without thought of rewards, without even the prospect of being loved in return, we are all weighed in the balance and found wanting. But this recognition of our want is the *conditio sine qua non* of our preparation for the grace of justification (being made right, authentic).[43]

The moment of justification, however, is also the moment of a new openness to the law. The Torah of God is not false or merely instructive because we cannot fulfill it. It is . . . true. Only through its fulfillment can our humanity be righted. By true I mean that it describes reality. It is not in the first place *prescriptive,* it is *descriptive.* We have been created for love—for being-with: this is simply the case. So long as we do not love we are living contradictions of our own being. Thus Jesus the teacher of the law has not only to show us the implications of God's command; he has also to bring us toward its fulfillment, to help us become who we are.

This is where the office of prophecy is inseparable from that of the priest. The prophetic teacher cannot lead his disciples into true obedience. Instead, he has himself to experience, representatively, the judgment that comes of human lovelessness. He himself fulfills the law of love—and is broken in doing so. But precisely as such a one he becomes the savior who brings others into the sphere of his fulfillment. Those who with him are caused to experience the impossibility of their condition, who are "buried with him by baptism into death," are given a new way into the future; they "might walk in newness of life" (Rom. 6:3-4). Humbled in their relation to their own false love of self, they are being turned toward "the other" in love.

While therefore Jesus quarrels with the guardians of the law because he does not regard the law itself as redemptive, he by no means embraces an antilaw position. Not only does the law function to bring us to greater self-knowledge and thus to repentance, but, in the new situation of justification, the law functions as guide and possibility—"a lamp to my feet" (Ps. 119:105). Calvin spoke of this as the third use of the law.

It would be incorrect, however, to leave the discussion of the prophetic work of the Christ at the point of his ministry as a teacher of the law. Even here we have had to touch upon matters that far exceed the usual discussion of such an office. The teacher who points up the internal requirements of the divine command must, we have said, himself submit to these requirements—in the summary statement of Philippians 2:8, he must "become obedient"; and this obedience, given the conditions of history, means obedience "to the point of death—even death on a cross." If one asks what informs such a conception of the prophetic teacher, one

---

43. The doctrine of justification will be treated at length in volume 3.

is led once more to the heart of Israel's understanding of the nature of the prophetic office. "To the prophet," as we recall from an earlier discussion, "God does not reveal himself in an abstract absoluteness, but in a personal and intimate relation to the world. He does not simply command and expect obedience; He is also moved and affected by what happens in the world, and reacts accordingly."[44]

There could be no more fitting way of summarizing the prophetic work of Jesus than through Heschel's "divine pathos." Not in his teaching alone, his parables, his acts of healing, his denunciations and blessings, but *in his person* Jesus must be seen as the inheritor of this prophetic tradition. As we have finally had to say in the foregoing discussion about the teaching ministry of Jesus, the prophetic teacher must himself submit to the highest requirements of what he teaches. In his life, and above all in his suffering and death, Jesus fulfills the prophetic office. He reveals—what has been implicit and explicit in all the prophets before him—the profound involvement of God in the life of the creation. He exemplifies unconditionally what Heschel describes as being the very substance of "divine pathos"—that "God is concerned about the world and *shares its fate*. Indeed this is the essence of God's moral nature: His willingness to be intimately involved in the history of man."[45]

In this we see that the separation of the so-called offices is artificial; for to come to the heart of the prophetic office, the enactment of the "divine pathos," is to be led without a break into reflections upon the *passio Christi*—the passion of the Christ, which is the heart of the priestly work.

30.4. The Priestly Work. Already with the earliest testimonies to the work of Jesus Christ we are introduced to the thought that the core of this work is to be located in Jesus' passion and death. As we have seen, Paul summarizes his message in the phrase, "Jesus Christ, and him crucified." Obviously, he intends by this more than a narrow concentration on the crucifixion as such. Presumably the historic creeds also wished to symbolize more than that when, in speaking of the life of Jesus as distinct from his birth, death, and resurrection, they employed the one word, "suffered." Yet it is clear from the start that the passion of the Christ occupies the mind of the movement in a dramatic way, and that when the first Christians applied the term *Soter* (Savior) to Jesus of Nazareth, they were conscious of this in particular. Soteriology thus from the outset has been especially concerned to understand the meaning of the cross.

Whether the category of priestly work is adequate to describe what Jesus does as *Soter* is a question. The Epistle to the Hebrews and also the Gospel of John use the category of "priest" in central ways. There are other categories.

---

44. Abraham Heschel, *The Prophets* (New York: Jewish Publication Society of America, 1962), 223f.

45. Ibid., 224 (emphasis added).

Nevertheless the link with Hebraic faith is important here, as elsewhere, and if it is borne in mind that the priest is first and foremost a representative figure, then, in my view, we can still find in this category a provocative and helpful theological and apologetic term. In the critical chapter that follows, I shall have occasion to return to this observation when I contrast representation and substitution; and in the final (constructive) chapter I shall use the concept of representation as the central, informing category of both Christology and soteriology.

While soteriology has concentrated on the meaning of the cross, it has understood what occurred at Golgotha as the culmination of a way that can be traced back far beyond Gethsemane and even beyond the life of Jesus. When medieval painters showed the infant Jesus in his mother's arms with a little cross in his hand where otherwise a toy might have been, they were representing this profound theme of the newer Testament's proto-Christology. Already with the annunciation there is a strong hint that the child to be born will be born to a life of suffering and rejection. Thus another motif familiar to the art of the Middle Ages (for example, the fifteenth-century Merode Altarpiece) depicts a divine sprite, bearing a cross, descending to the womb of the Virgin as the great angel announces God's choice of her as the bearer of the divine life.

The suffering of the Christ is present, in other words, as a destiny, and one that awaits him, perhaps, from the beginning of time—though we must at once qualify this by recognizing that it is a destiny that is held in strict tension with Jesus' freedom to embrace or refuse it. If we ask for the rationale of this destiny (and that is precisely what soteriology asks for), then we must press back beyond the cross itself to the *necessitas* that informs it. *Why* must Jesus suffer?

The answer that only a few historical theologians have dared to give, though it has become something approaching a primary motif of contemporary theology, is that God suffers. And if we ask why God suffers, then we are cast back upon the whole theo-anthropology of biblical faith: God suffers because God's creation suffers and "God is love." The one therefore who is to represent both "true deity" and "true humanity" (Chalcedon) necessarily inherits the destiny of carrying to its apex this double suffering of the Creator and the creature. Given this God and this creature, the cross is necessary.

We have seen that the theme of necessity permeates the entire newer Testamental witness. Not only is it made explicit in the predictions of the passion, it is implicit throughout. It was therefore no innovation but a logical progression of thought that in the postpentecostal situation the preaching apostles not only made the cross of Jesus their central theme but insisted that, far from being accidental, this apparently tragic end of their leader had been the point of fulfillment of the divine plan (*boule*). Similarly, the epistles of Paul, the Johannine Gospel and letters, and indeed most of the components of the newer Testament are concerned primarily with the provision of a rationale for the suffering and rejection of the one who is the source of their hope. How could life and hope be discovered in the midst of death, tragedy, and despair? This is their confronting question.

It was out of this initial reflection of the first generations of Christians that the atonement theology of the church evolved. If Jesus did not suffer arbitrarily; if his suffering and rejection were purposeful and indeed the key to the whole purposing of God for the life of creation, then it was and is imperative that the disciple community should try to understand the meaning of this apparent paradox. It is not a mystery to be accepted blindly. Or rather, if it is in the most profound sense a mystery, it is not the kind of mystery that simply muffles thought but one that begets rapt reflection and sets the mind racing.

In its search for understanding of the meaning of the suffering of the Christ, culminating in the cross, the Christian movement advanced many different explanations. While these cannot be classified in a precise way, and while some scholars have found as many as five or six different types,[46] it is common to identify three basic approaches and variations on these three themes. There are many ways of naming these types, and in what follows I shall refer to some of the alternative nomenclature in each category. What is most important, however, is to grasp the fundamental ideas that inform them. For that reason, I classify the three according to the following schema: (1) those answers to the *ev* question about the meaning of Christ's suffering that are characterized by the idea of rescue or deliverance; (2) those characterized by the idea of sacrifice; *sub* and (3) those characterized by the idea of demonstration or revelation. *moral*

Each of these types of atonement theology presupposes a different reading of the human predicament. It is not accidental, therefore, that each type of theory has grown out of a different phase of cultural history, particularly that of Europe. In discussing the three types, we shall have to refer frequently to that history. Paul Tillich's analysis of anxiety in *The Courage to Be*[47] is particularly useful in this connection. Tillich names three types of anxiety: the anxiety of fate and death, the anxiety of guilt and condemnation, and the anxiety of meaninglessness and despair. These anxieties, he claims, belong to the human condition as such and are therefore always present in one form or another, to one degree or another. Yet it must also be said, he believes, that one or another of the three dominates any particular period.

My intention in what follows will be to show that: (1) the atonement theologies characterized by the idea of rescue and deliverance should be correlated with the anxiety of fate and death—the typical anxiety of the ancient Mediterranean world into which postbiblical Christianity first came; (2) the atonement

---

46. Emil Brunner enumerates five types (*The Christian Doctrine of Creation and Redemption, Dogmatics,* vol. 2, trans. Olive Wyon [Philadelphia: Westminster Press, 1952], 283ff.); Berkhof identifies six types (*Christian Faith,* 305–6).

47. New Haven: Yale Univ. Press, 1952.

415

theologies characterized by the idea of sacrifice should be correlated with the anxiety of guilt and condemnation—the typical anxiety of the medieval and early Reformation period; and (3) the atonement theologies characterized by the idea of demonstration or revelation should be correlated with the anxiety of meaninglessness and despair, though in this case the correlation is inadequate and unfinished, for reasons that will be considered in the two subsequent chapters especially.

Because in my view the correlational dimension is vital in the discussion of the priestly work of the Christ, I shall begin each commentary on the types of atonement theology by indicating the nature of the anthropology it assumes. Only then shall I seek to describe how the work of Christ is understood to address and answer the predicament so described. In this as in all discussions within the three chapters of historical theology, I wish to present the tradition in as sympathetic and appreciative light as possible. None of these theories of Christ's atoning work is eternally true or fully adequate even to its own dominant period; yet all of them have grown out of the church's exposure to human suffering, and all have given comfort to millions of human beings. It behooves us, then, before we ask for their weaknesses and failings, to listen attentively with open minds both to the analysis of the human condition that they presuppose and to their way of applying to it the gospel of the cross.

30.5. The Soteriology of Rescue. This version of Christ's priestly work, which is considered by some historians and theologians to be the oldest type of atonement theology, is usually designated the ransom theory. Gustav Aúlen, in his influential book, *Christus Victor,* [48] dubbed it "the classical theory" because he insisted that this theory not only dominates the early church and all of Eastern Orthodoxy, but is also the chief biblical teaching concerning the cross as well as the major emphasis of Martin Luther. In claiming this, Aúlen was going against the grain of most Western theology since Anselm of Canterbury, and there can be no doubt that the success of his small book was due to its provocative thesis. Many others have denied such generalization as being altogether too doctrinaire. The ransom theory, they have insisted, is certainly not the only one for which biblical grounds can be discovered. As for Luther, he is capable of drawing on all three types of atonement theology—and in the same paragraph! [49]

---

48. Gustaf Aúlen, *Christus Victor: An Historical Study of the Three Main Types of the Idea of Atonement,* trans. A. G. Herbert (London: S.P.C.K., 1953).

49. I am strongly inclined to agree with Aúlen's critics, particularly when it comes to Luther interpretation and for a number of specific as well as more general reasons. A careful study of Luther's works does indicate, I think, that he is eclectic in his way of articulating the meaning of the atonement. He does not dismiss the (Anselmic or Latin) theology of sacrifice in the way that Aúlen claims. More importantly, I do not find it either helpful or accurate to single out one theory

The anthropological presupposition of the soteriology of rescue is that the human condition is one of oppression. Humanity is enslaved, in bondage, caught, trapped in a tragic predicament.

Enslaved to whom or to what? The earliest articulations of this type of atonement theology would have answered straightaway: to Satan, to the demonic, to supernatural forces of evil—what St. Paul named "principalities" and "powers" (Rom. 8:38, Eph. 6:12, RSV).[50] We must remember that for people of the first Christian centuries, and indeed (for many) well into the modern epoch, the world was full of demonic and supranatural influences. Such things as mental illness, various crimes and passions, and even the less heinous sins of the flesh could be attributed to demonic persuasion. One has only to remember the terrible witch trials of New England to realize that, throughout most of its history, the human race has looked for the causes of what it has felt to be evil in dark, unearthly sources. Few people in Puritan New England would have thought of seeking the causes of witchcraft in the social environment, with its oppression of women. Few would have thought to find the causes of this type of behavior in the neuroses of the women and men who believed themselves to be in communication with dark powers. The natural thing, so far as the bulk of humankind until today is concerned, has been to suppose that persons who behaved in eccentric ways were "possessed."

When early Christians described the human situation as one of enslavement to supranatural forces of evil, then, they were not, as Christians, inventing their own anthropology. They were using the common assumptions of the day, embroidering them with their own religious nomenclature, and attempting to put the Christian message into correlation with them. In their view, not only conspicuously disturbed persons but in one degree or another all human persons are dominated by extrahuman forces over which they have no or little control. Christians could readily explain why this was so: in the fall, humankind through its representatives, Adam and Eve, had committed itself to the service of Satan. In permitting themselves to be enticed by the subtle temptations of the serpent, the first humans had in effect inclined the collective human soul toward evil. There was then no turning back. As we have already observed, the dogma of original sin came to mean a quality of (fallen) being itself, transferred from one generation to the next in the act of propagation. What the first pair did had a tragic effect upon the whole succeeding race. By their original

---

as if it were unconditionally true. Aúlen is so thorough an advocate of the so-called *Christus Victor* theme that he does not tell us about the problems associated with this theory. Each of these theories has its attendant problems; and if we are going to be responsible in our discussion of them we shall have to notice not only their strengths but also their weaknesses. From the perspective of the *theologia crucis,* one of the serious weaknesses of the ransom theory is its tendency to supersede the cross. What comes to occupy the central place is the resurrection victory *over the cross.*

50. Aúlen, *Christus Victor,* 63ff.

disobedience, the entire species was committed into the hands of the Prince of Darkness. Some might resist the evil inclinations of the collective human spirit more successfully than others, but all were in some degree of bondage to evil.

Behind this theological-metaphysical statement about the human condition as one of tragic enslavement to the demonic, there stands the sociological reality of a world in which the anxiety of fate and death is prominent. World views are never only metaphysical or religious; they are also political and economic, cultural and environmental. The background of a world peopled with supranatural influences is the real experience of fate and death—from our twentieth-century perspective, a fixed fate and an early death. To be born into the lower strata of society in the Greco-Roman world was to have one's destiny assigned, almost, from the point of conception. Slaves did not know "upward mobility."

It is extremely difficult for us, members of dominant classes living in the post-Enlightenment societies of the West, to put ourselves emotionally into the shoes of the vast majority of persons throughout history, for whom our most ordinary assumptions about our work, our relation to nature, and our feelings about those in authority would be absolutely foreign. Emotionally we are so conditioned by the ideas of freedom, mastery, progress, and the capacity of technologies to overcome human problems that we are cut off at a rudimentary level of comprehension from the vast majority of those who preceded us—and, of course, from many of our contemporaries in less "developed" societies as well as the poor within our own society. It is not accidental that the soteriology of rescue emerged out of an earlier form of the church, many of whose adherents were slaves and citizens of the lower classes. Nor is it accidental that liberation theology, which in some respects incorporates an adaptation of the soteriology of rescue, has evolved largely in Third World settings and among oppressed groups in rich societies. For those whose primary condition is one of oppression, however that may be understood, the only news that could be truly good would have to be a message of liberation.

That is precisely how the work of the Christ was understood in the ransom or classical theory of atonement. Jesus appears here as the deliverer, the liberator. He is Christ the Victor, whose victory frees those with whom he has identified himself. As the human condition is one of bondage, so the savior can only be savior if he appears as the one who frees people from their bondage. For biblical background, one could think of Moses, or the judges of Israel, or David the slayer of Goliath. Mythically, one could consider St. George, whose story was told throughout the ancient world: George, the slayer of the dragon, is a Christ-figure understood according to the ransom theory of atonement. Like St. George, the Christ is a miraculous rescuer of the community from the tyranny and gluttony of the demonic.

The manner of Christ's liberation was conveyed in the early church through metaphor and legend—which will not surprise anyone who has come to appreciate the value of narrative in theology. One of the most popular legends, often verging on allegory, involved allusion to Leviathan and the story of Jonah. In it, the human race is depicted as being trapped in the belly of the great sea monster, a symbol of the demonic. God wills to rescue the race, but this cannot be achieved straightforwardly simply by slaying the monster, for then the humans who are held captive would perish too. How to destroy the sin without destroying the sinner? The divine decision involves the putting forward of another human, a new human being who is not mortally infected by sin, a second Adam. This pure human being will be, as it were, bait. The primeval monster sees in him only what it has seen in all the others—a vulnerable, easily tempted mortal. The monster grasps at the innocent one, swallows him—and is himself caught! For the Leviathan has not reckoned with the steely hook of this one's divinity. Not only is *this* Adam not tragically involved in the universal sin of the race, but he is the one "begotten of his Father before all worlds," the second person of the holy Trinity, the Word incarnate. The monster of evil may capture him (the crucifixion), but it cannot hold him. On the contrary, the monster itself has now been captured, and the creatures held in its sway are set free. The resurrection is the victory point of this divine defeat of the demonic.[51]

While fifteen or more centuries later, we may find such a tale ludicrous or even embarrassing, we must ask what our forebears were thereby attempting to say, and not be preoccupied with the way in which they said it. Obviously we cannot repeat such legends as this as if they were capable of conveying to our own contemporaries what they conveyed to earlier generations. Yet we cannot dispense with the theme that, in their own manner, they are exploring. For one thing, it is a theme that is very much part of the biblical witness: Christ as liberator from evil.

At least one barrier to a sympathetic hearing of this classical soteriology is giving way in our time, and this is one salient reason why the soteriology of rescue has achieved once again a certain appeal—and not only among liberationists,

---

51. The idea of the deception of the devil lends itself to imagery. Aúlen claims that Gregory of Nyssa first developed "in greater detail than any before him" the imagery of the fish (ibid., 68); but the popularity of the image was widespread. A good example is found in the writings of Rufinus of Aquileia (ca. 400 C.E.): "The purpose of the Incarnation . . . was that the divine virtue of the Son of God might be as it were a hook hidden beneath the form of human flesh . . . to lure on the prince of this age to a contest; that the Son might offer him his flesh as a bait and that then the divinity which lay beneath might catch him and hold him fast with its hook. . . . Then, as a fish when it seizes a baited hook not only fails to drag off the bait but is itself dragged out of the water to serve as food for others; so he that had the power of death seized the body of Jesus in death, unaware of the hook of divinity concealed therein. Having swallowed it, he was caught straightway; the bars of hell were burst, and he was, as it were, drawn up from the pit, to become food for others. . . ." (Bettenson, *Documents of the Christian Church*, 49). See also Emil Brunner, Appendix to chapter 2, *The Christian Doctrine of Creation and Redemption*, vol. 2 of *Dogmatics,* trans. Olive Wyon (Philadelphia: Westminster Press, 1952), 308f.

but in more existential circles as well.[52] I am referring to the fact that in the postmodern world a reconsideration of the nature of evil has arisen that is more compatible with the fundamental assumptions of this theory than was the modern world view. Few of our contemporaries, even among those who are still open to great mystery, would be ready to accept the idea that human bondage means a direct enslavement to Satan or demonic forces (though there is also a revived interest in the demonic today). More significantly, however, there is a growing sensitivity toward the concept of corporate or systemic evil.

The modern, liberal reduction of existence to a one-dimensional secularity manifesting clear cause-and-effect relations, and the concomitant reduction of evil to an ignorance soon to be overcome by scientific enlightenment, is less credible to the majority of thinking people today. There is a new readiness to consider evil a transcendent phenomenon—not transcending human genesis and maintenance, necessarily, but in the process of history becoming far greater than the individuals and collectivities that perpetuate it. Auschwitz was not just Auschwitz; it is a symbol infinitely transcending the statistics of the death camps. The Bomb means more than our stockpiled weapons; it is the symbol of an evil reality hanging over the heads of nations like the sword of Damocles. Technology as a whole, indeed, constitutes for many a vast evil mystery, a process evading human efforts to direct and control it. For us the great Leviathan could well be a technocratic system and mentality become "leaderless" (Buber), subject to no command, moving inevitably forward, poisoning the earth, alienating workers from their work and farmers from their land, threatening to master whatever remains of the vaunted autonomy proclaimed by the Age of Progress that spawned it.

The openness to a transcendent dimension of evil applies at the personal level as well as the societal. The idea of an enslaving sin, or of sin as enslavement, is no doubt more accessible to some than to others. The alcoholic who has come to the point of admitting her alcoholism; the neurotic who feels as though his body had been taken over by a stranger; the drug addict who is not capable of "just saying no"; the man or woman "addicted" to sex:[53] such persons are able to recognize in their compulsions a kind of bondage not wholly discontinuous with the demonic as it was experienced in other periods of human history. And such human beings are no longer rare among us. Not only do they frequent our daily lives but they are present in our imaginations through literature, cinema, and all forms of pop culture. This presence is a vital part of

---

52. E.g., John Macquarrie writes of Aúlen's restatement of this soteriology: "It seems to me to offer the most promising basis for a contemporary statement of the work of Christ" (*Principles of Christian Theology* [London: S.C.M. Press, 1966], 286ff.).

53. According to some psychologists and others, sex addiction is not only a genuine addiction but one of the most prevalent addictions of North American society today. See "Do People Get Hooked on Sex?" *Time* Magazine (June 4, 1990), 48.

the Sisyphus phenomenon, for it reinforces a fatalism that is also present through other agencies and militates against the notion that human beings are themselves "masters of their fate and captains of their souls."

Wherever people are open to such a recognition, they are also open potentially to the presentation of the Christ as liberator from the state of bondage. This has been an aspect of the Christian gospel from the beginning. It may have dominated the early church, and it will always have currency wherever the human condition is experienced as one of oppression—being "overwhelmed," as it is frequently put today. The anxiety of fate and death is a permanent human anxiety according to Tillich; and therefore the Christ as one who frees the human spirit from this anxiety will have lasting importance in the life of the Christian movement.

In keeping with the earlier observation about the tendency of powerful doctrinal conventions to manifest a tenaciousness of their own even when they no longer speak to the human situation, however, we must caution against the propensity in certain Christian circles to apply contemporary versions of the rescue soteriology to every situation. The theme of liberation can apply to every life, every context; for none is truly free. But when liberation is pursued by Christian communities that are part of an oppressing society, it is necessary to ask whether this theme does not function more to conceal than to reveal the truth. We shall return to this concern later.

Apart from possible and actual misuse of the soteriology of rescue, it must also be acknowledged to contain certain inherent difficulties, as all of these models of atonement do. Three must be named here for purposes of clarity in connection with the chapter to follow.

First, they usually court triumphalism. It is always difficult for Christians to employ such terms as "victory" and "triumph" without soliciting the triumphalism that is so much a part of the story of Christendom. It has been observed by many that the theory says much more about the resurrection than about the cross. The cross is present, not as the focus of the story, but as a preliminary occurrence, almost a foil to the reality that precedes and succeeds it. Such a triumphal rendition of the meaning of Christ's saving work may be appropriate under certain conditions, particularly when the community that believes and announces this victory is itself far from being triumphant. It is therefore conceivable that in its minority status, whether prior to the Constantinian-Theodosian establishment or in diaspora contexts today, the *Christus Victor* concept is contextually appropriate. But for most of its history the church has itself been such a power in the world that when its imperial status combined with an unconditionally victorious message, the result has been an oppressive church. One would have to have been a Jew to have understood how the Christ who rises triumphant over death and the demonic so consistently becomes the oppressor of all who fail to acknowledge his victory.

Second, this theory of atonement entails an almost exclusive emphasis upon the divinity of the Christ. In fact, it has frequently if not always fostered and been fostered by a docetic Christology. What Jesus Christ does, he does as the triumphant Son of God. His humanity, as in the analogy of the sea monster, is chiefly for the sake of appearance; it is meant as a deception. Given what we have already noticed about the tendency of the divinity principle to overwhelm Jesus' real humanity in the christological discussions, a soteriology that makes so little of Jesus' humanity only contributes further to this same tendency.

The third danger inherent in this soteriology is what is usually identified as its objectivity. By this is meant its lack of existential involvement on the part of those for whom salvation is intended, human beings. What is described here is a transaction occurring, almost, on a plane outside history, and involving suprahistorical beings (the divine Father and Son, and the devil or transcendent Evil). Humanity is offered the benefits of the outcome of this transaction—as happens also in the second type of atonement theology to which we shall turn. But if we are considering Jesus Christ as our priest, his priesthood in this case is wholly imposed from above and entails little that is representative or participatory.

This latter difficulty has been noted by many modern theologians, even those who (like Macquarrie) have a high regard for it. But it is by no means only a contemporary criticism. Already Peter Abelard, who gave classical expression to the third type of atonement theology that we shall consider, was conscious of the externalism of the ransom theory. While it may express important aspects of the work of the Christ, it may also, when pursued as an exclusive expression of Christian soteriology, do so at the expense of essential dimensions of the biblical narrative, particularly the incarnational dimension.

30.6. The Soteriology of Sacrifice.   The second type of atonement theology, the one that most capitalizes on the concept of atonement, is discussed under such nomenclature as the Latin theory, the satisfaction *(satisfactio)* theory, and substitutionary Christology. While Calvin's so-called penal theory is thought by some to be a sufficiently independent explication to warrant separate consideration, I would agree with those who see it as belonging to this model.[54] The central informing idea of the type is the Christ as sacrificial victim.

Again it will aid our comprehension of this theory if we ask first about the character of the human *problematique* that it presupposes or elucidates. We have seen that the rescue type conceives of the sinful condition in terms of bondage to forces stronger than the human. For the sacrificial type, humanity's predicament is quite different. Here, the human problem is not enslavement to evil powers but guilt before the author and source of all goodness.

---

54. *Institutes,* 2.16.

It will be instructive for us to recall at this point that this type of soteriology, in one or another of its various forms, came to dominate the Middle Ages of the West, replacing for the most part the earlier theory Aúlen designated "classical." What this means is that in the changed context between the early and medieval periods, assessment of the human dilemma was altered dramatically. To use again Tillich's categories, the anxiety of fate and death as the dominant anxiety gave way to the anxiety of guilt and condemnation.

There can be no doubt that the influence of the Christian faith was one of the reasons this change occurred. In a real measure, Christianity challenged the classical age's anxiety of fate and death. It provided for those burdened by this anxiety a gospel of freedom: even earthly destiny (that of persons born into slavery, for example) might be changed, and death could be regarded, not as oblivion, but as the way into eternal life. This indicates something of the effectiveness of a soteriology that is capable of contextual engagement.

The other side of this same coin, however, does not flatter the Christian religion. For while this faith had the effect of dispelling some of the old pagan sense of fate and mortality, it also had the effect of reinforcing the human consciousness of guilt and condemnation. Christianity gave people a certain freedom for the pursuit of life here and now, but it also gave them cause to worry about their destiny in the future life. Under the conditions of Christian establishment, this factor became a significant one in European life; for a vital aspect of the power of the church was its custodianship of the afterlife. The system of indulgences, which provided the immediate catalyst for the Reformation, was only the logical consequence of a religious system that, whether intentionally or not, capitalized on human guilt and the gnawing fear of eternal damnation.

Yet it would be foolish to insinuate that the anxiety of guilt and condemnation was created by the church in its post-Constantinian role as priest to the official culture. Given the customary abuse of power, the exploitation of the human sense of guilt and unacceptability may account for a good deal of the popularity and tenacity of the sacrificial theories of atonement. But this abuse should not blind us to the fact that guilt does seem endemic to human beings, and that it is particularly conspicuous in the medieval and early Reformation period. Luther, with his quest for a merciful God, exemplifies the late medieval preoccupation with guilt and punishment in the afterlife.[55]

The soteriology of sacrifice conjures up one name in particular: Anselm of Canterbury. This eleventh-century monk provided Western Christendom with what must be regarded as its most succinct and authoritative theology of atonement. So influential has Anselm's substitutionary Christology been in

---

55. For an informative and detailed discussion of the type of anxiety prevailing in the late Middle Ages, see Bernd Moeller, "Religious Life in Germany on the Eve of the Reformation," in Gerald Strauss, ed., *Pre-Reformation Germany* (New York: Harper & Row, 1972), 12–42.

all forms of Western Christianity, whether Catholic or Protestant, that it would be difficult to conceive of the history of Western civilization without it. We have already alluded to its tenacity (it is still by far the most common atonement theology of the West); we must now consider what internal logic lends it this power of endurance.

Anselm developed his theory of the atonement in a short work entitled *Cur Deus Homo?*—literally "Why God-Man?" meaning "Why did God have to become human?" This theologian, who more than any other historically important figure taught Christians to realize that true faith "seeks understanding,"[56] in *Cur Deus Homo?* applied this theological principle to the central symbol of the faith, the cross of Christ. Why was the incarnation—why was the cross necessary? The suffering of the Christ is not just part of the story, to be accepted and transmitted by the church. It contains high meaning, and this meaning can at least in some measure be comprehended by faith.

The work takes the form of a dialogue between Anselm and an imaginary companion, Boso. In the typical fashion of a teaching dialogue, Boso raises questions to which Anselm provides learned answers. The foundational question is the one indicated in the title of the work.

It does not take long to establish that God became incarnate in the Son in order to alleviate the condition of the sinner. Boso, however, wants to know why, it being in any case the will of the Deity to redeem sinful humanity, God could not have done so more straightforwardly—*sola volante,* simply by willing it. To this Anselm responds with one of the most important sentences in theological history: *Nondum considerasti quanti ponderis sit peccatum* ("You have not yet considered the great weight of sin"). In other words, sin and its consequence, guilt, are matters too profound (ponderous) to be solved simply by pronouncement of forgiveness. The world can be created by fiat, but not even God's creative command can redeem the world.

Why? For two reasons, chiefly: First, because God is God; that is, the Deity is holy and righteous and as such cannot simply overlook human unholiness and evil. We are not dealing with a relationship between two equals, both of them guilty, neither of them able without hypocrisy to judge the other—as would be the case between humans. We are treating of the relation between God and human beings, the Creator and creatures who have fallen from their Maker's high intention for them. God is the author of justice, and cannot tolerate the sheer injustice, the distortedness, the generations of revenge upon revenge, the incalculable debt of guilt that has been incurred by humanity over the centuries.

This conception of God has been found questionable by many. Is Anselm's God so intensely righteous as to be incapable of compassion? Many have felt

---

56. *Fides quaerens intellectum (Faith Seeking Understanding)* was the subtitle of his book, *Proslogion.*

this to be the case.[57] In the light of that criticism, I suggest that we should be willing to interpret the eleventh-century thinker in a way more consistent with later thought on the subject of sin and guilt; otherwise we may not achieve an understanding sufficiently sympathetic to enable us to appreciate either the strengths or the weaknesses of the interpretation.

To that end, we may propose a second reason why God could not forgive *sola volante:* Would the declaration of sin's forgiveness really solve the problem of sin? Sin is not only God's problem, it is ours too. The "great weight" of sin and guilt of which Anselm reminds Boso is perhaps chiefly, in fact, its weight upon human shoulders—like the millstone about which Jesus spoke (Matt. 18:6). Possibly Anselm himself intended this; for in the last analysis his God is able to bear the weight of sin, though at great cost. Had Anselm been writing in the nineteenth or twentieth century, he might well have drawn upon depth psychology. Freud and others could certainly have helped him to demonstrate that guilt is indeed a weight, a preoccupation, a burden preventing people from entering into life, a reality whose repression consumes much private and public energy. Insofar as sin and guilt permeate the whole life of humanity, this condition is not relievable through a mere assurance of forgiveness.

While such a rationale may help us to gain more sympathy for the position, it is not, however, the one that Anselm actually employs. The weight of sin is for him its affront to God. We are guilty before God and our guilt is infinite. How could it be borne by anyone? Satisfaction must be made for it, but no human being can make satisfaction, for each of us is thoroughly implicated in the guilt of the species. Yet, since it is human guilt, only a human being *could* atone for it. But what human being could be found who is "good enough to pay the price of sin"?

The argument is circular and already anticipates the answer that is given: Infinite human guilt can only be atoned for by perfect human innocence. No human being qualifies, all being guilty; therefore God must assume human form and become, as human, the substitute for all other, guilty men and women. As the sacrificial victim, Jesus thus receives in his own person the righteous judgment of God against human unrighteousness.

---

57. E.g., feminist Theology according to Elisabeth Moltmann-Wendell finds that the atonement theory based on such an interpretation of the Deity is steeped in sadomasochism. God appears as *"ein grausame Vater"* (a cruel father). (*God—His and Hers,* trans. John Bowden [New York: Crossroads, 1991], 81.) A more pointed criticism is offered by the English lay theologian and writer, Dorothy L. Sayers, in her provocative and often humorous work, *Christian Letters to a Post Christian World* (Grand Rapids: Wm. B. Eerdmans Pub. Co., 1969). "What is meant by the Atonement?" she asks; and with tongue in cheek and drawing upon popular interpretations of Anselmian/Calvinist soteriology she responds: "God wanted to damn everybody, but his vindictive sadism was sated by the crucifixion of his own Son, who was quite innocent, and, therefore, a particularly attractive victim. He now only damns people who don't follow Christ or who have never heard of him."

If certain scriptural passages are read in the light of this deeply entrenched soteriology of sacrifice, they can seem to confirm it almost to the letter; and of course that is precisely what has happened through the centuries. The suffering-servant poems of Second Isaiah are especially susceptible to this hermeneutic:

> Surely he hath borne our griefs, and carried our sorrows; yet we did esteem him stricken, smitten of God, and afflicted. But he was wounded for our transgressions, he was bruised for our iniquities; the chastisement of our peace was upon him; and with his stripes we are healed.
> All we like sheep have gone astray; we have turned every one to his own way; and the Lord hath laid on him the iniquity of us all. (Isa. 53:4-6, KJV)

It is almost impossible for those influenced by Anselmic and Calvinistic traditions to hear such Scripture without assuming that it is a clear statement about the cross of the Christ. The power of this soteriological tradition in Western Christianity is enormous, and not only among the more conservative and evangelical sectors. For a theologian of Karl Barth's sophistication, this was still the basis on which the meaning of the passion and death of the Christ must be understood and communicated.

> Through the total suffering of Jesus the total sin which is its cause breaks out. . . . Thus Jesus alone knows the totality of suffering. Man, thrown into the conflict of his existence, into the impossibility of living, into the abyss of solitude, of war, and finally of death and hell, is disclosed through the person of him who was God and man in his own person. But not every man suffers such total suffering: Jesus Christ alone does. We believe we know suffering, conflict, sorrow, death. The truth is we know only vague glimpses of them. To suffer what man *should* suffer because he is God's enemy would mean our annihilation. Precisely here, God's mercy bursts out: it is God himself, who in the person of his son suffered that very total suffering. God himself, in Jesus Christ, offers himself to man in order to bear, as representative of mankind, the suffering that man had to suffer.[58]

Despite its wide influence in the West, this soteriology contains inherent problems, which have not gone unnoticed. Besides its questionable picture of God, to which Christian feminists and others have drawn attention, three other problematic aspects should be noted here; some of them will be recalled for further discussion in the succeeding chapter.

---

58. Karl Barth, *The Faith of the Church: A Commentary on the Apostles' Creed according to Calvin's Catechism,* trans. Gabriel Vahanian (New York: Meridian Books, Living Age Books, 1958), 89.

First, many from Abelard onwards have complained, not only that the concept of God is distorted in this theory but that, like the older classical theory, this one too is lacking in any participatory (subjective) dimension. The classical theory describes a transaction between God, Christ, and Satan; the sacrificial theory depicts a transaction between God the Father and God the Son (Anselm disapproved of the older theory because it gave Satan too much power). Human beings appear in the Latin theory as guilty ones for whom a substitute appears; but how does the substitutionary act of the Christ become transferred to the guilty in such a way as to assuage the burden and weight of their sin? Anselm's answer seems artificial: God, he affirms, rewarded his beloved Son by passing on "the benefits of his passion" to the guilty sinners with whom the Son had voluntarily associated himself.

In other words, human beings appear in this soteriology as recipients, or potential recipients, of a transaction in which they have had no involvement.

Second, and along similar lines, the theory lends itself to a highly theoretical treatment. It easily devolves into doctrine of a highly doctrinaire sort. Its deepest appeal comes from its basis in the reality of human guilt. But while this accounts for its significance at a profound level, it is doubtful if the theory could have achieved the breadth of its influence in Western Christendom had it not also been reducible to portable, almost mathematical theory: (1) We are guilty debtors; (2) Jesus redeems our debt; (3) We are forgiven if we believe this. An existential dimension is present in the theory because of the first point, and wherever there is a genuine consciousness of guilt this dimension does qualify the present criticism. But on the whole (and, as I shall argue presently, in our own historical epoch especially) genuine consciousness of guilt is rare. Moreover, little has accompanied the promulgation of this theory in the written or spoken word to give it the depth of religious and psychological meaning that it could have had. It has been advanced chiefly as theory, and that is at least partly because in both its Anselmic and Calvinistic forms it lends itself to rationalistic and abstract explication.

Third, a particularly superficial aspect of the soteriology of sacrifice is bound up with the concept of substitution. Not only is this informing motif of the theory questionable because of its connection with the two critical points registered above; it is also objectionable on more subtle grounds, which we shall pursue further in our discussion of the distinction between substitution and representation. Here we may state the criticism briefly in this way: In the historic versions of this theory, the Christ as substitute for guilty humanity stands before the holy God and offers his life as a propitiation for human guilt. Jesus' suffering, in other words, is bound up with the human need to make amends in relation to God. But is that all that can be said about the cross? Is it only the point of human suffering before God—and even at the hands of God?

Is nothing said here about God's suffering before and with humanity? Does Jesus only receive in his person the consequences of God's rejection of unacceptable humanity? Does he not also suffer because of human enmity toward and rejection of God?

Anselm, along with the great bulk of Christendom, could not indulge such a thought, for his God was above suffering. But as we have seen in the first part of this study, precisely that is what has to be questioned about the whole history of the doctrine of God.

Fourth, at least in our own historical moment we Western Christians, who have been so deeply affected by this soteriological type, must seriously raise the question whether, even when it is sensitively presented, this is the appropriate soteriology for our context. It is addressed to a world that felt overwhelmed with guilt before God and the prospect of eternal punishment. In the feudal situation in which it was first conceived, this theological posture of fearful awe before the divine Judge was reflected in and undergirded by a sociopolitical system based upon the maintenance of a code of honor that, for those among the lower levels of the social order, translated at once into plain fear.

Both the religious aspect, which the young Luther still felt keenly, and the political aspect of this system have been greatly altered in nearly all parts of our world. The anxiety of guilt is a continuing reality; and wherever this anxiety is strongly present, an atonement theology that can seem to address it will find hearers. But in a society like that of North America today, the guilt that becomes the prelude to the acceptance of this form of gospel is almost always artificially stimulated by evangelical preaching aimed precisely at such an effect, and the identification of sin with largely personal guilt deflects the religious community from the awareness of societal guilt and hides the fact that there are other anxieties at work among us that are not addressed by this particular soteriological tradition. To proclaim forgiveness for guilt to a people whose condition is "the anxiety of meaninglessness and despair" all too easily serves repressive ends. So long as we can believe that our real problem is personal guilt, we do not have to confront either the great social evils perpetuated, in part, by our own corporate life-style or the underlying apathy of spirit that feeds the life-style. It is altogether possible that the soteriology of sacrifice, more than any other single aspect of Christian doctrine, prevents large numbers of churchfolk in North America from coming to the point of a more genuine self-knowledge. It is therefore no innocent matter of doctrine to which we are turning our attention here.

30.7. The Soteriology of Demonstration. The third type of atonement theology is particularly associated with the name of Peter Abelard (1079–1142), but it came into its own when versions of it were adopted by Protestant liberalism. As the "moral influence theory," it became the most popular expression of the atonement in nineteenth- and early twentieth-century liberal Protestant thought in North America.

The core concept of this theory is the idea of demonstration or revelation. In distinction from the two types that we have already considered, what God intends to accomplish through the cross, according to Abelard and his more modern counterparts, is neither a rescue mission nor an expiation of guilt but a lasting demonstration of the depth of the divine love.

We may glimpse, once again, the inner logic as well as the appeal of this theory if we inquire about the character of the human predicament that it presupposes. Soteriologies of rescue presuppose oppression or bondage; soteriologies of sacrifice presuppose guilt; and soteriologies of demonstration presuppose ignorance.

This can be misleading if it is understood to mean a mere lack of knowledge. The ignorance of being loved is never merely an intellectual failing. The ignorance of being loved by the Eternal, of being a beloved creature, is—as the best advocates of this theory would insist—a truly pathetic condition. It is in the most profound sense existential ignorance. The incapacity to realize that one's very life is enfolded in transcendent love may be the most devastating thing that could be said about human existence.

It must be admitted that, at least in its typical modern expression, the moral influence theory seldom achieved that kind of depth. It was bound up with an overall assessment of human life and history that, from the perspective of all classical and Reformation forms of the faith, would have to be regarded as optimistic (some would say shallow). This assessment derived from the Enlightenment's faith in rationality, qualified by nineteenth-century romanticism. For the Enlightenment, salvation comes through knowledge. The romantics did not trust reason so unconditionally, but the more optimistic among them transferred to "feeling" and "the heart" the kind of human hopefulness located by the Enlightenment in rationality. What deters humanity, according to this mentality, is not simple ignorance but *moral* ignorance. The impartation of information alone will not save, nor will the liberation of the intellect from inauthentic forms of authority. What is required is a new sense of self-worth that will inspire the human spirit to venture forth into the future with something like heroic courage.

Under the impact of such a reading of the human condition, modern theologians from Schleiermacher and Ritschl to Walter M. Horton, Vincent Taylor, and others[59] were able to find in the work of Abelard a "usable past." Abelard did not have the Augustinian sense of "total depravity" that inspired the soteriological reflections of his older contemporary, Anselm. His loathing for both of the previous types of atonement theology was in large measure a protest against the dark assessments of humanity they assumed. With respect

---

59. See, e.g., L. Harold DeWolf, *A Theology of the Living Church,* rev. ed. (New York: Harper & Brothers, 1960), 264ff.

to the ransom theory he felt (as did Anselm) that it was far too respectful of the demonic. Was the devil so powerful? Did this not betoken a lingering dualism? As for Anselm's own theory, Abelard found it even more objectionable. What sort of God is it who requires the death of the "only-begotten Son"? Besides, is the sin of humanity so desperate? And how, in any case, could the death of the innocent Jesus alter the condition of the guilty?

The work of the Christ for Abelard, therefore, is not sacrificial in the sense of being a substitutionary recompense for an impossible debt. Abelard's explanation of the cross does involve sacrifice, and even prominently so; but the intention of the sacrifice is not the making of amends (and in that sense atonement) but the setting forth of ultimate truth, which, if it is received, will alter the whole perspective of the recipient. To quote the most important passage from Abelard himself:

> Now it seems to us that we have been justified by the blood of Christ and reconciled to God in this way: through this unique act of grace manifested to us—in that his son has taken upon himself our nature and persevered therein in *teaching us by word and example even unto death—he has the more fully bound us to himself by love; with the result that our hearts should be kindled by such a gift of divine grace, and true charity should not now shrink from enduring anything for him. . . .* everyone becomes more righteous—by which we mean a greater lover of the Lord—after the Passion of Christ than before, since a realized gift inspires greater love than one which is only hoped for. Wherefore, our redemption through Christ's suffering is that deeper affection in us which not only frees us from slavery to sin, but also wins for us the true liberty of the sons of God, so that we do all things out of love rather than fear—love to him who has shown us such grace that no greater can be found, as he himself asserts, saying, "Greater love than this no man hath, that a man lay down his life for his friends."[60]

The effect of the passion and death of Jesus, in other words, is that, looking upon it, pondering it, contemplating its nuances and turnings and strange reversals, hearing it described and proclaimed in preaching and teaching, seeing it depicted in Christian art and iconography, we are moved to a new consciousness of God's love for us. The cross is God's supreme revelation of mercy and grace. The divine love and forgiveness are communicated to us as we become hearers of the gospel through the testimony of the church, brought home to us through the internal witness of the divine Spirit. Being thus moved by love, we are (to use the language of the modern version of the theory)

---

60. Abelard, "Exposition of the Epistle to the Romans (An Excerpt from the Second Book)," in *A Scholastic Miscellany,* The Library of Christian Classics, vol. 10, ed. Eugene R. Fairweather (London: S.C.M. Press, 1956), 283–84.

"morally influenced" in our whole attitude, not only toward God but toward our own kind as well: being loved, we learn to love.

The American theologian L. Harold DeWolf, a revered mentor of Martin Luther King, Jr., rightly observed that this approach to the meaning of the work of Christ has influenced many modern Christian thinkers who would avoid an "explicit avowal" of the theory. This is "not to be wondered at," he writes, in view of the inaccessibility of the older theories to "the modern mind."[61] DeWolf's judgment seems to me especially true of the North American context. All of the once-mainline denominations of the church in this context have felt the persuasive power of this more "psychological" interpretation of the cross. Even among the more conservative theological communions, where substitutionary soteriology prevails at the level of official doctrine, it is probable that the majority at least of the laity will express their personal belief in terms more nearly Abelardian than Anselmic or Calvinistic.

This too is "not to be wondered at"; for the anthropological assumptions of the Abelardian type are far more compatible with the New World outlook than are those of the two older theories. Both of the latter draw heavily upon the tragic dimension of the human condition, and modernity has been nothing if not an insistent protest against the idea of the tragic. Despite so much of our contemporary experience, so far as Middle America is concerned, "tragedy is . . . an unpleasantness which might have been avoided by better social arrangements and an improved technology."[62] A view of the cross as the positive demonstration of universal love appeals both to our kindlier conception of humanity and our friendlier conception of deity.

It is therefore all the more necessary for us to consider the criticisms that are made of this type of atonement theology. I shall identify three. First, it seems to many to lack any objective basis. While the theory overcomes one of the perennial problems of both of the older types—their lack of a participatory dimension—it courts the opposite danger: apart from our human reception of the demonstration of divine love in the suffering of the Christ, the cross would seem to be of no avail. For the older theories, "something happened" in the death and resurrection of Jesus Christ, and its occurrence does not depend upon its reception by faith. In the ransom theory, evil is overcome; in the sacrificial theory, guilt is atoned for. In the moral influence theory, on the contrary, the effect of the cross depends wholly upon our subjective response (hence it is sometimes called the subjective theory). Does this not give too much credit to the human potentiality for faith and too little recognition to the reality of prevenient grace?

---

61. *A Theology of the Living Church,* 264.

62. Robert Langbaum, *The Gaiety of Vision: A Study of Isak Dinesen's Art* (New York: Random House, 1964), 125.

Second, and pursuing this same line of reasoning, it is asked whether this type of atonement theology can really provide the basis for gospel. Both of the older types insist that a new situation pertains in consequence of Christ's work *pro nobis:* evil and death have been robbed of their power (the *Christus Victor* theory); the debt owing to God on account of human guilt has been paid (substitutionary soteriology). This new situation precedes any human awareness of it, and its truth is not dependent upon our acceptance or denial of it. It is therefore good news and can be proclaimed as such. In the light of this tradition, the Abelardian type of soteriology seems to offer only a conditional gospel: it is good news if we consider it so. But is that gospel or law?

Third, one asks whether this theory has done justice to the radicality of the biblical conception of evil and suffering. We have already acknowledged that the lack of love in human life is by no means a minor problem of existence. Yet there appear to be levels of wickedness and suffering that are not explicable on the basis of lovelessness and cannot be touched significantly by the manifestation of "greater love." Certainly they are not to be accounted for on the grounds of moral or existential ignorance. Europe's death camps were constructed by members of intelligent and morally sophisticated societies, and the greatest wars of the world have been made possible by weaponry invented in nations scientifically more developed than any others. The very points on which the earlier theories of atonement seem strongest—their insistence upon the transcendent power of evil and the depths of human guilt—have commended them in new ways to late twentieth-century experience, which, in distinction from earlier expectations, seems not to warrant such unquestioning faith in human goodness and historical progress. Besides, if redemption can be achieved through the revelation of transcendent love, why was it not achieved before the Christ appeared? Israel's God never withheld love from the creature.

Fourth, it must be asked whether the soteriology of demonstration adequately addresses the anxiety of our own age—the anxiety of meaninglessness and despair, according to Tillich's analysis—the dull, nameless despair of Sisyphus. In its best representations, it may have been precisely this anxiety that this explication of the meaning of the cross has dimly sensed. It meets— even if it does not satisfy—the experience of purposelessness with the declaration, "You are significant, you matter, you are loved." In this respect at least, this type of soteriology seeks to address a society that is no longer sufficiently convinced of eternal goodness to believe in radical evil, and no longer sufficiently idealistic to feel guilt at having fallen short of any great expectations.

Perhaps any contextually pertinent discussion of the meaning of the cross in North America today must be in some way an extension of this soteriological strand. At least it must recognize, with this approach, that the predicament that has to be engaged is an internal one, a loss of purpose and of confidence. Only love can penetrate the depths of abandonment and alienation that accompany this loss and this crisis. What must be questioned about the theory as such, however, is whether it could be extended to incorporate the dimension of the tragic thus understood.

30.8. Concluding Observations on Soteriology.

Before we turn to the final aspect of the work of Christ—his sovereignty—it will be well to register certain observations that have been gleaned in the process of considering the tradition concerning the atonement. These will be recalled in the subsequent chapters.

First, in view of the fact that the atoning work of the Christ can be considered so only to the extent that it meets and in some way resolves a human dilemma or predicament, the soteriological aspect of Christology always involves anthropological analysis, and in particular analysis of what is problematic in the human situation. While this analysis has often been implicit rather than explicit, it is clearly present in all three types of theory as the necessary background of the question, What has God in Christ done *for us*?

In the contemporary situation, the profession of Christian belief in this connection necessarily implies explicit attention to this background question. This is not only because of modern historical consciousness; it is also because of the insights of present-day theological praxis: when soteriology is engaged in without conscious attention to the existing human *problematique*, it almost always ends in theoretical abstraction and the superimposition of doctrinal conventions that have acquired their own momentum through familiarity and the exclusion of lively criticism.

Second, insofar as Tillich's analysis of anxiety is genuine, it will be mandatory for a faithful disciple community always to be conscious of the three anxiety types and to recall, in its reflection on the tradition, the wisdom that the tradition preserves in relation to each of these types. A rigid adherence to one or another atonement theology means that the church is capable of addressing only the anxiety that corresponds with that particular type. In every human context, all three types of anxiety will be present; therefore it is part of the task of faith's profession to remain in dialogue with the whole tradition even when, confessionally speaking, one type of atonement theology needs to be pursued more imaginatively and vigorously than the others.

Third, while faith's profession requires ongoing reflection on all three models of atonement theology, and while elements of all will be found in the gospel proclaimed by the witnessing community in every context, it must also be recognized that there are incompatible components among the three. An eclectic atonement theology is therefore not the answer to the narrow adherence to one theory. One cannot have a theology of salvation that assumes simultaneously the anthropology and Theology of both Anselm and Abelard.

Fourth, the most significant thing to be learned from the history of this doctrine is that the great expressions of the atonement all grew out of an original exposure to the human condition as it was lived in various ages and places. As was noted at the outset of the discussion, this doctrinal area is clearly the most contextually conditioned of all. What this means, however, for any present or future soteriology worthy of the tradition is that it must be ready to expose itself afresh to the sin that the grace of the cross is intended to address. The mere repetition of theories devised by the past can never suffice for Christian profession of the faith in the present; indeed, it is likely that such repetition will constitute a handicap to the profession of faith. Imagining itself to possess permanently valid truth about the meaning of Christ's suffering and death, the church only insulates itself from the raw stuff of existence—and, concomitantly, ensures that the world will find its message largely irrelevant. The one thing that is needful for authentic soteriology is continuous and unprotected experience of that in relation to which salvation is needed. And that, as we have seen from this review of the tradition, is never quite the same from one context to the next.

31. *Christus Rex*

31.1. "He Sitteth at the Right Hand of God." From the beginning, the movement that formed itself around the memory of Jesus did so under the impact of experiences that rendered this memory more than, and different from, the usual acts of collective human recall. Indeed it was conscious of itself as having come into being as a fellowship (*koinonia*) and evangelical movement only because of these extraordinary experiences. These experiences constituted for it the condition without which it would neither have comprehended the meaning of Jesus' priestly and prophetic work nor itself have achieved sufficient unity and direction to become, in the first place, such a community of remembrance and hope.

The experiences to which I am referring are detailed in the narrative of the newer Testament's message in ways familiar to most of those who will read these words: the empty tomb, the postresurrection appearances to Mary Magdalene and other members of the first disciple community, the Emmaus road, the incident of the doubting Thomas, the farewell discourses, Jesus' disappearance in a cloud, and (perhaps above all) the Pentecost experience. Theologically, these experiences are gathered into the doctrinal conventions of resurrection, ascension, glorification, and the advent of the Holy Spirit. Each of these biblical and doctrinal motifs contributes its own particular nuance to the profession of faith, but in all of them one fundamental point is being made: namely, that the work of the Christ is first of all a work of enlightenment and spiritual-intellectual transformation, that is to say a *present* work.

The kingly or (as I shall now consistently designate it) monarchic office of the Christ refers precisely to this fundamental point of Christian experience. As such, it even has a certain priority. I do not mean that it precedes chronologically what has been summarized in the prophetic and priestly categories. On the contrary, the tradition assumes that the monarchic office can only be attained after the prophetic and priestly work have been completed. That they are necessarily prior, chronologically, is an aspect of the dialectic of humiliation and glorification that informs the whole Christ event. Nevertheless the monarchic office is noetically prior; that is, it is the condition necessary to the reception and comprehension of the other two offices. It is only as the community is grasped by the spiritual power of the glorified Christ that it is made capable of perceiving and exploring the meaning of the Christ's earthly pilgrimage and ministry. The past work of prophecy and priesthood is dependent for its reception and dissemination upon the present work of the one who "sitteth at the right hand of God" (the only phrase in the second article of the Apostles' Creed that is expressed in the present tense) Apart from the church's faith in and relationship with this living, reigning, and returning one, its recall of the one who "taught with authority" and "laid down his life for his friends" must tend to devolve into nostalgia and melancholy.

31.2. The Lord and the Spirit. The monarchic work of the glorified Christ presents several complicated problems for theological reflection, and it is perhaps for this reason that this third dimension of the work of the Christ has been, on the whole, neglected by Christian faith and doctrine.[63] The first problem concerns a certain confusion that arises at this juncture over the trinitarian distinction between the Son and the Spirit. It may be asked (the question can hardly be avoided) whether what the church attributes to the risen, glorified Christ cannot as well be attributed to the Holy Spirit. Is the present work of Christ really distinguishable from what faith has experienced as the internal testimony of the Spirit? On the basis of the dogma of perichoresis (coinherence), one does not look for an absolute separation of the offices of the second and third persons of the Trinity; but is there a sufficient distinction between them to think still in trinitarian terms at all?

The church historian, the late Cyril C. Richardson, in his study of the Trinity, proposed that there may not be. He cited St. Paul's statement in 2 Corinthians 3:17-18 as evidence of a proneness in early Christianity to make little of the distinction between the risen, reigning Son and the divine Spirit: "Now the Lord is the Spirit, and where the Spirit of the Lord is, there is freedom. And

---

63. See Emil Brunner's discussion of W. A. Visser't Hooft's *The Kingship of Christ* in *The Christian Doctrine of Creation and Redemption,* 315–21.

we all, with unveiled face, beholding the glory of the Lord, are being changed into his likeness from one degree of glory to another; for this comes from the Lord who is the Spirit" (RSV).[64]

The history of dogma is not clear on this point. The one distinction that seems generally present in all major traditions of doctrine is that between the internal and external manifestations of divine sovereignty. The glorified Christ, presently in closest proximity to the Father and therefore still discontinuous with or external to us, rules as "head" of the "body" from a position of exaltation or transcendence. But the internalization of Christ's rule, its intimate communication to believers, belongs to the realm of the Spirit.

This, however, appears an arbitrary and perhaps even a superimposed distinction. It not only seems to originate in a trinitarian theory that for theoretical purity must keep the lines of distinction clear, but in doing so it fails to negotiate reasonably around the concept of the mystical union between Christ and the church, with its Pauline background not only in the language of the body imagery but also the *en Christo* concept. The question cannot be avoided whether the whole monarchic aspect of the work of the Christ could not be as well attributed to the divine Spirit; or, on the other hand, whether what is attributed to the Holy Spirit ought not to be attributed simply to the continuing presence of the risen Christ.

One argument against the identification of the reigning Christ and the Holy Spirit is that unless faith retains a strong sense of the sovereignty of "this Jesus" (Acts 1:11b)—this very one who was in our midst, who was one of us, who was tempted as we are, who suffered and was rejected, who died and was buried—it will easily revert to a general theism or an indeterminate spirituality. To state the matter concretely: In answer to the questions of ultimacy—"Who is Lord? Before whom are we accountable? Who is the final arbiter of our life?"—the disciple community must be able to believe: "None other than the God whose will and whose way has been shown us in Jesus, the crucified one."

Along these lines, Paul's seeming equation of the Lord and the Spirit may, on the contrary, be thought a definition of the nature of spiritual authority: "The Spirit is certainly divine and therefore, to mortal beings like ourselves, a source of unknowable mystery; yet we are bold to believe that this divine influence is none other than the spirit of that same one who lived and walked, taught and suffered in our midst." In other words, Paul is perhaps anticipating the problem as well as the decision of the third Council of Toledo (589 C.E.), which resolved the issue of an insufficiently defined Spirit by inserting the *filioque* clause into the Nicene creed ("who proceedeth from the Father *and the Son*"). Without something like this, the rule of the Holy Spirit easily becomes divorced from the work of the Christ. Ecclesiastical history from Montanism until the

---

64. Cyril Richardson, *The Doctrine of the Trinity* (New York: Abingdon Press, 1958).

various Charismatic movements of our own period testifies powerfully to this danger. Wherever Christians have become especially conscious of the commanding presence of the divine, there has existed a strong tendency to substitute for Jesus' sovereignty, which necessarily involves the discipline of recall and study of the past, a more immediate and less explicit devotion to the Spirit.

This question is by no means a merely theoretical one in North American Christianity today; for in this context not only are many of the liveliest forms of the Christian religion oriented toward the Spirit but an inchoate spiritualism informs most denominations of the church. The sovereignty of the Spirit frequently expresses itself in a lack of interest in Scripture and doctrine and the disciplines requisite to their contemplation. Spirituality under these conditions comes to mean an immediacy of relationship with the divine that finds tedious and unnecessary the mediation imposed by historical considerations. But a faith that is centered in a historical person cannot avoid the discipline of historical reflection and study without endangering its own identity. The doctrine of Christ's sovereignty is thus a critical one in this context. If Christian obedience loses touch with the christological tradition in favor of a pneumatic, mystical authority that may seem more immediate and more open, there can be no end to the fragmentation of the church. Perhaps no aspect of Christology is more in need of clarification in our context than the office of Christ's monarchy.

31.3. The Linguistic Problem—and More. A second difficulty with the discussion of the monarchic work of the Christ is linguistic—but finally it is more than merely linguistic. Linguistically, it is hard to avoid masculine imagery in this connection: *Christus Rex*—Christ the King. Superficially, this dimension of the problem may be solved by substituting gender-neutral language, as I have done here. As with the terms Kingdom of God or Kingdom of Christ, one may (and should) speak of the Christ's "sovereignty" or "monarchy."

While such substitution may satisfy superficial criticism, it does not go to the heart of the problem of which the linguistic problem is only a token: the problem of christological triumphalism. The profession of Christ's sovereignty, whether it is called kingship or monarchy or sovereignty or lordship or whatever else, invites the religious tendency to turn the whole character of Jesus Christ's person and work into one of blatant triumph. At this point more than any other, whatever vestiges of a theology of the cross survived the Constantinian adoption of the Christian faith have been swept up into an overwhelming *theologia gloriae*. There is no more imperialistic image of the Christ at work in Christian history than the *Christus Rex;* and it does not matter that this image is often portrayed against the background of the cross. The message of the image is all too plain: the vilified, rejected Jesus has become in the end the glorious victor. The crucified "King of the Jews," a figure almost laughable, has become the Ruler of the Universe. The simple rabbi who could not find a place to lay his head is now understood to be royally ensconced at the right hand of the Absolute. Symbols abound in Christendom, West and East, that reaffirm this message. In short, the whole work of humiliation is shown to be nothing but a brief prelude to glory, making the glorification seem all the more impressive because of its temporary (and illusory?) mortification.

Here we encounter the perennial danger of this third office: that through it the church rationalizes the cross as a necessary but preliminary stage. When this identification of Christ's "kingship" with resurrection triumphalism is combined with an equally undialectical stress upon his divinity, as it usually is, the whole intent of the humiliation and crucifixion of the Word is undone. Nothing then is to prevent the Christian church from conceiving of itself in terms of power and glory. This theoretical possibility, which certainly predated the Constantinian-Theodosian establishment and is already occasionally envisaged in the newer Testamental writings themselves, will not disappear with the disestablishment of the Christian religion in the West.

The only way in which this corruption of the third office can be prevented is by submitting it to a radical transformation under the aegis of the theology of the cross. Concretely this means that the church must be vigilant against its own temptation to enthrone the Christ on the model of earthly power and majesty. If the sovereignty of the Christ is to be retained at all, it must be retained as the sovereignty of the crucified one. The life of Jesus as it is testified to in the Scriptures must be the stuff out of which the church understands what is ultimate. Christ's "kingship" is a meaningful and even a highly evocative concept if the metaphor of monarchy is radicalized by the story of the "royal" person who rides into Jerusalem on a humble donkey, is adorned with the purple office while being whipped and spit upon, is crowned with a wreath of thorns, is presented to the public by his executioner, and is established in office by being nailed to a cross. A total "transvaluation of values" (Nietzsche), constantly and critically reconsidered against every triumphalistic temptation, is all that will save this office from co-optation by power, whether that means the real power of passing Christendom or the longed-for power of a post-Constantinian church that will still be tempted to "conquer the world for Christ."

As such a radicalized conception of ultimate authority, this office can be highly suggestive and meaningful in a world that still today, as always, honors power and ostentation. When the early Christians affirmed (their first creed) *Jesus Christos Kurios,* they were engaging in a highly dialectical (and not only a courageous) profession of faith. Their avowal of the lordship of Jesus Christ was made—secretly and silently most of the time—as a direct response to the Roman cry, *Kaiser Kurios* (Caesar is Lord). In other words, they were saying that, appearances to the contrary, the one who is really in charge of the course of this world is not the fantastically bedecked and exalted emperor, surrounded by all the symbols and weapons of power that the world can devise, but one whose sovereignty expresses itself in readiness to serve, to the point of laying down his life for his friends. Victory is not dismissed from this office and metaphor, but it is a victory very different from the kind honored by the world at large. It is the victory of meekness, voluntary powerlessness, truth, and love. And that kind of victory is accessible only to faith, for it is necessarily "hidden beneath its opposite" (Luther).

CHAPTER ▪ EIGHT

Incarnation or Apotheosis?

32. Christology—and Jesus, the Christ

32.1. Christology as Temptation. While the Christian churches still produce and hold fast to a remarkable variety of Christologies, it is possible to glimpse a certain consensus today among critical theologians with respect to the functioning of Christology in general and classical Christology in particular. This consensus holds that the traditions we have inherited have not only failed to convey adequately the person who stands at the center of the Christian profession of faith, but have actually prevented this from happening. The end governing the "science" of Christology is that it should facilitate the perception and reception of Jesus the Christ within the disciple community. Christology cannot give us Jesus Christ any more than Theology can give us God. Only the divine Spirit can communicate Christ to the church. As it was in the beginning (Acts 2), it is now and evermore shall be.

But Christology can disencumber this act of communication—if in no other way, then, as we have already proposed in connection with Chalcedon, by identifying some of the false "Christs" so that the one who *is* the Christ will not be confused with the "saviors" that religion, including the religions of the ideologues, always tries to have.

Christology can perform this service, but it does not do so as a matter of course. What Christology seems to have done on an all too regular basis throughout the history of the Christian church, in fact, is to constitute an end in itself. Instead of being an aid to the Self-communication of the one who cannot be communicated, christological doctrine has too often been substituted for that one. Just as human beings are constantly at work creating images of one another, on whose basis they may then avoid the difficult and always unpredictable

440

business of relating to one another as living persons, so it is habitual in the Christian community to fashion images of the one called Jesus Christ and to treat these images, works of our own minds, as though they were God's own representative among us. Christology thus becomes the particular form of idolatry having to do with the second person of the Trinity. Christology becomes Christolatry. Tom F. Driver points to this danger as a salient one in North America today:

> Much of the churches' teaching about Christ has turned into something that is dictatorial in its heart and is preparing society for an American fascism. Most people do not notice, because they think it is enough to call upon the name of Jesus. It is not enough, as Jesus himself said; it never has been, and it has always been dangerous.[1]

That such a transmutation should occur is not surprising. As Dostoyevsky illustrated so persuasively in his tale of *The Grand Inquisitor,* it is perhaps unthinkable that the historic church could have permitted itself to be governed by the living Christ. Especially after it exchanged the form of movement for that of institution—indeed, a vast and worldwide institution serving and being served by whole nations and empires—the church required a dependable, objective, and easily accessible conception of its "head." If we are not overcome by the sheer details of history and doctrine, we can perceive this need to be a primary force driving the church of the first five or six centuries toward doctrinal uniformity.

To be sure, the church had to guard its own unity and ward off internal heresies and conflicts, most of which represented parallel competing power interests; but from the perspective of almost twenty centuries, the most recent of which have witnessed the emergence of a great variety of Christologies, one may be allowed to wonder whether, on internal ecclesiastical grounds alone, such a doctrinal consensus was necessary. The church depicted in the newer Testament is already lacking in strict christological consistency, yet it seems to manifest a working unity. The truth surely is that when the theological-ecclesiastical need for unity combined, after the fourth century, with a political need for order, the result was a new demand for uniformity—also at the level of doctrine. Under these circumstances, the doctrine of Christ assumed a new importance.

It would have been as impossible for the Constantinian church to live with newer Testamental christological variety as for a totalitarian state to live with alternative political visions. At any time, the most difficult aspect of the life of the community of faith is the existential character of its relation to the living God. The whole Bible is a documentation of that difficulty. But whenever

---

1. *Christ in a Changing World: Toward an Ethical Christology* (New York: Crossroad, 1981), 3.

the community of faith attempts cultural or political establishment, the normal difficulty of living in obedience to "the Lord [who] is the Spirit" is intensified, often to the point of conflict. And what is usually sacrificed under the pressure of the contradictions between divine sovereignty and the sovereignty of nations and empires is the former. The livingness of the divine Spirit is always a threat to established order.

In our own historical moment, serious Christians in many different contexts have become conscious of the tendency of christological doctrine to function immodestly. Instead of helping people to "see Jesus," Christology has too often erected intellectual barriers between the life experience of people and the one who came to share our life experience—to be "with us." Doctrines of the Christ, remnants of which are to be found in most churches, not only fail to facilitate the awareness of Christ's presence but come to people as something esoteric and remote from daily life. Doctrinal formulations of the person and work of Jesus Christ may have served the purposes of an established religion, but they do not meet the needs of the present. As Christianity is forced out of its monopolistic position; as being a Christian becomes, once more, a matter to be decided upon, and not only once; as the movement quality of the "people of the Way" is again somewhat recovered; and as, consequently, those who remain within the movement seek again to *know* this one in whom they desire to put their trust, there is a growing dissatisfaction with Christology and a corresponding need for greater familiarity with Jesus, the Christ.

32.2. Catholic and Protestant Distinctions in Christology.   This dissatisfaction and need are perhaps most conspicuous where classical christological doctrine has been most prominent—in Roman Catholicism. There is therefore no more determined search for the Jesus who has been hidden by Christology than among leading lights of Catholic liberation theology in Latin America. In the preface to the English translation of his *Christology at the Crossroads: A Latin American Approach,* the Jesuit theologian Jon Sobrino writes:

> Here in Latin America we can read many of the old, classical treatments of Christology as well as more current ones. When we do, and when we notice their practical repercussions on the life and praxis of Christians, we cannot help but formulate certain suspicions. Basically those suspicions come down to this: For some reason it has been possible for Christians, in the name of Christ, to ignore or even contradict fundamental principles and values that were preached and acted upon by Jesus of Nazareth.
>
> Thus we are led to analyze how it has been possible for christological reflection itself to obscure the figure of Jesus and to examine the dire consequences of such christological reflection. . . . Christ has been reduced to a sublime abstraction.[2]

---

2. Trans. John Drury (Maryknoll, N.Y.: Orbis, 1978), xv.

Because of the christological obscuring of the Christ, Sobrino in his book makes "the historical Jesus" his point of departure:

> We choose to adopt the historical Jesus as our starting point. . . . Our Christology will thereby avoid abstractionism, and the attendant danger of manipulating the Christ event. The history of the church shows, from its very beginning . . . that any focusing on the Christ of faith will jeopardize the very essence of the Christian faith if it neglects the historical Jesus. Finally, we feel that the historical Jesus is the hermeneutic principle that enables us to draw closer to the totality of Christ both in terms of knowledge and in terms of real-life praxis. It is there that we will find the unity of Christology and soteriology.[3]

To Protestant ears, this is an intriguing statement, both because of its forthright criticism of official christological dogma and its rather innocent assumption concerning the way in which "the historical Jesus" delivers faith from the coils of dogma. It could not, I think, have been made by a knowledgeable Protestant scholar, given our quite different backgrounds in relation to this subject.

The Protestant background involves two factors that have not affected Roman Catholicism materially. The first belongs to the beginnings and the core of the Protestant protest, namely, the primacy of Scripture: *sola scriptura*. While Protestantism has by no means escaped the cloying dogmatism that Sobrino associates with classical Christologies, it has always had to contend with the Bible and has, in addition, been subject to biblical criticism coming from the side of its own traditions of belief and scholarship. Even seventeenth-century Protestant orthodoxy's attempts to concoct new forms of doctrinal certitude could not ward off the antidogmatic watchfulness (on the part of pietism, for example) which insisted that dogma might never replace the biblical testimony to Jesus. According to Protestant tradition, extrabiblical tradition is secondary to Scripture, and scriptural interpretation is not the sole prerogative of ecclesiastical or even scholarly authority. Traditional dogma is not insignificant in classical Protestantism, as we have seen, but it is decidedly conditioned by the ongoing exposure of faith to the Scriptures.

Nor is this primacy of Scripture a mere formality. *The* authority among all of the provisional authorities[4] is the Bible, so far as Protestantism in all of its many expressions is concerned. While a cursory study of Chalcedon and other formal Christologies has remained, in most cases, part of the theological training of Protestant clergy; while phrases like "the divinity of Christ" and "the two natures" are certainly known to many Protestant laypersons (largely, one must add, on account of conservative influences), the picture that dominates

---

3. Ibid., 9.
4. See *Thinking the Faith,* chap. 6, sec. 32: "Authority in Faith and Theology," 427f.

Protestant consciousness of Jesus Christ is a biblical picture, or at least one that has been derived from aspects of the Bible's presentation of Jesus. Few among even the clergy of the Protestant denominations would be able to recite the main clauses of the Formula of Chalcedon or trace the logic of Anselm's *Cur Deus Homo?* but every Protestant, lay or clerical, is able to articulate some notion of the Jesus of history. This is not reported as a boast, for it is no virtue to be ignorant of doctrine and, besides, much of what Protestants have retained as "Jesus" would not stand the test of scriptural exegesis. The point is only that, in some real if limited sense, the *sola scriptura* principle has made a difference in Protestantism.

The second factor governing Protestant as distinct from Roman Catholic Christologies is the influence of theological liberalism. It was precisely the liberal intention, as we have seen, to rediscover the living Jesus behind the Christ of dogma. At the level of theological scholarship, this attempt failed—or seemed to fail. At the level of Christian piety, on the other hand, it has been permanently influential. What I purposely styled the Protestant "picture" of Jesus is one whose character has been determined, not only by the biblical testimony to Jesus (with little input from classical Christologies) but also from the "lives of Jesus" produced by liberal scholarship and piety. It would not be an exaggeration to say that, in mainstream Protestantism in North America, the Sermon on the Mount and Sallman's *Head of Christ* have exerted an infinitely greater christological influence than has the Formula of Chalcedon or even the distinctively Protestant Christologies of the reformers and their theological heirs.

This does not necessarily imply that Protestant theology in North America has an advantage over Catholic theology in Latin America. If there is any advantage, it is limited to an awareness that North Americans ought to have, but have not necessarily appropriated—namely, that the disciple community is not delivered from obscuring images of Christ just because it is influenced by the Bible and by a search for the Jesus of history. In other words, we ought to recognize that Sobrino's assumption that the historical Jesus will avoid abstraction and allow us "to draw closer to the totality of Christ" is rather innocent of experience in these matters.

While the two influences cited above have certainly kept the mainstream Protestant churches in North America from christological dogmatism of the classical variety, they have by no means prevented the development of working Christologies that may function in essentially the same way as do the more formulary Christologies of orthodoxy. Precisely on the basis of the Bible, received (for example) through the lens of liberal Christian values, the typical pictures of Jesus that dominate in mainstream Protestantism in North America are often formidable barriers to the development of responsible christological thought. Jesus, in these "pictures," is not, to be sure, the same kind of abstraction as one has in the stilted language of formal christological or soteriological doctrine; but he is still very much an abstraction, and one that easily translates itself into ironclad (if velvet-wrapped) ideology.

This is not to suggest that the attempts of Sobrino and others to avoid abstractionism through a new submission to Scripture are wrong. Such attempts must always be undertaken, and we shall do so here too. But it is naive to assume that the human, religious temptation to make christological reflection a means of controlling or perhaps even avoiding Jesus Christ will be overcome if only one turns again to the Bible and to historical reflection upon Jesus. The fact that liberationists conduct their search for the historical Jesus in the context of oppressed and economically poor communities will certainly help to ensure that the bourgeois, Victorian, personalistic, and other elements in the picture of Jesus produced by nineteenth- and early twentieth-century liberalism will not be present or dominant. But will it prevent other, perhaps equally constricting cultural assumptions and values from coloring the picture? A Christology emerging from the context of poverty or marginalization, whether in Latin America or in North America, may attain greater faithfulness to important dimensions of Jesus as he is attested in Scripture. But will it really "avoid abstractionism, and the attendant danger of manipulating the Christ event"?[5]

We must, it seems to me, begin all critical theological reflection upon Christology by recognizing that there can be no Christology that avoids temptation and the prospect of misleading the church. Jesus Christ does not give himself to any of our Christologies. The most that we can do in our reflections on this existential core of faith is to try to avoid the worst temptations and, in the process, communicate to the disciple community whatever positive hints and clues we may discover to help the church and the world hear for themselves "the voice of the good Shepherd."

The worst temptations, in my view, are those that I shall now seek to characterize in the three major sections of this chapter: (1) divinization and the forfeiture of Jesus' real humanity; (2) the failure of soteriology to engage that

---

5. The Chinese theologian Bishop K. H. Ting warns against the "idealization of the poor" in some forms of liberationism. After acknowledging an affinity between liberation theology and the emerging theology of Chinese Protestant Christianity, he takes exception to the former's tendency to "absolutize liberation and make it the theme or content of Christian theology." Ting grants that the poor may have an "epistemological advantage" in being able to perceive issues of injustice and domination, but he does not believe that all truth is necessarily in their hands. In fact, he argues that the Cultural Revolution was precisely a consequence of this idealized view of the poor. It pitted them against not only the rich but also against intellectuals, veteran revolutionaries, and all aspects of enlightened culture. Writes Ting in his *Theological Review* essay: "The poor deserve justice. But poverty is not virtue, unless voluntary, and it does not always bring with it wisdom." Don Browning, "The Protestant Church in the People's Republic of China," *The Christian Century* (March 4, 1987), 221.

in relation to which salvation is actually needed in a given time and place; and (3) the reduction of the living Savior and Lord to dogma—in Sobrino's language, "abstractionism." In all of these temptations, as I shall explain in a concluding section, what seems to me to have been transpiring throughout Christian history (and what still exists as temptation for the church today) is the submission of Christology to the preconceived and largely unrecognized assumptions of the theology of glory. The *Christologia gloriae* with which, all too consistently, we have ended in the church has been gained at the expense of "Jesus Christ, and him crucified"; and that Christology is finally a glorious one only for those who are able in one way or another to avoid the existential inglory of the human condition.

33. The Divinization of Jesus of Nazareth

33.1. Classical Christology and the "Cloud of Divinity." It cannot, I think, be said that in the historical summary of the preceding chapter we have been unsympathetic in our treatment of Chalcedonian Christology. Chalcedon managed, despite popular as well as political pressures, to avoid the most simplistic and undialectical affirmation of the divinity principle. But it did so, finally, in a manner more formal than real. It retained the humanity of Jesus only by the skin of its teeth.

That retention belongs specifically to one party in the debate, the school of Antioch. "Without Antioch," writes Paul Tillich, "the church would probably have lost entirely the human picture."[6] The Antiochene theologians do not appear to have been very adept at defending the humanity of Jesus against the rival Alexandrian school. Nestorius, though the ablest of the Antiochian theologians, ended with a Christ-figure who could be thought schizophrenic, a marvel of humanity and divinity united morally but ontically strictly separable. Yet despite the discrediting of the whole Antiochian school after the Council of Ephesus (431 C.E.) and the outright denunciation of Nestorius himself, Chalcedon sustained the humanity of the Christ in a way not dissimilar to Antioch. Without this critique, it is likely that the voice of Alexandria, with its strong preference for divinity, would have prevailed formally as well as in the general imagination and piety of the church.

What must be asked, however, is whether this explicit affirmation of the *vere homo*, "*homoousios* with us as regards his manhood," represents anything more than a formality. Does Chalcedon intend us to think of Jesus in fully human terms? Does it intend us to picture Jesus as one who shares our flesh

---

6. *A History of Christian Thought* (New York: Simon and Schuster, 1967), 81.

truly, not only formally?[7] Does it direct us to consider him as one who, like us, is not only born but also dies—and knows daily that he must die? who, like us, is limited in knowledge, capable of hunger, loneliness, uncertainty, disappointment, anger; who, like us, passes through a stage of puberty to one of sexual adulthood . . . and so on? The "yet without sin" of the famous declaration of Hebrews 4:15, which the Formula also cites, has always provided an interesting out for those who fear that the first part of the phrase ("in every respect . . . tempted as we are") will lead to an all-too-unconditional homoousial identity with ordinary mortals "like us." One must certainly ask the writers of Chalcedon, all of them men, whether Jesus' temptations included the typical masculine temptation of considering women less than persons, objects of sexual pleasure. And by Jesus' own allusions to the nature of sexual temptation (Matt. 5:27ff.), where is the line to be drawn between the temptation and the yielding? If "looking at a woman with lust" is already "adultery of the heart," such a line of distinction is indeed a fine one; and the same thing would have to be said about the line between anger and hate, passion for justice and the desire for revenge, and every other mixed emotion and motivation of the human spirit.

Clearly there has been and continues to be an immense fearfulness on the part of the church that the profession of Jesus' full humanity may ruin everything. It almost seems the natural heresy where Christology is concerned. For this reason, D. M. Baillie in his classical study, *God Was in Christ,*[8] cautions against "high Christologies" because they seem inevitably to lead to the denigration of Christ's humanity, and he pleads: "no more docetism!"

Carl E. Braaten, reviewing classical Christology, agrees that Docetism is the perennial heresy of the church; but he balances this (too dexterously, in my opinion) with the observation that while Docetism is the heresy of "the right wing of christology," through whose influence "the human life of Jesus evaporated in a cloud of divinity," the opposite heresy is also present, namely, treating Jesus as a "mere man." The latter danger he associates (rightly enough) with the Ebionites. But because the Ebionitic influence has always been minimal, it seems to me misleading to present these two faults as if they were equally dangerous.[9] Historically speaking, the two temptations may hardly be thought to have had equal weight. The liberal attempt to reemphasize the

---

7. Jürgen Moltmann rightly suggests that "If we wished to bring out [the incarnational] intention of the nativity story today, we should have to stress the *non-*virginal character of Christ's birth, so as to 'draw Christ as deep as possible into the flesh,' as Luther said." (*The Way of Jesus Christ: Christology in Messianic Dimensions,* trans. Margaret Kohl [Minneapolis: Fortress Press, 1993], 84–85.

8. (New York: Charles Scribner's Sons, 1948), 20, 60–62.

9. Carl E. Braaten, *Christian Dogmatics,* vol. 1 (Philadelphia: Fortress, 1984), 499–500.

humanity of Jesus, which we shall discuss presently, is only superficially a resurgence of Ebionitic Christology. Moreover, far from being a "mere man," Jesus for liberal piety was such a (capital M) Man that his humanity removes him from the sphere of our "mere humanity" just as effectively as does his divinity in conservative Christologies.

Certainly it must be admitted that during the period that is decisive for classical christological formulation there was no danger whatsoever that the church would fall into humanism. I consider Harnack to have registered a permanently valid insight when he claimed that the formal upholding of the humanity of the Christ by Chalcedon represents a doctrinal necessity rather than a commitment of faith to the flesh-and-blood reality of the man, Jesus. It is not, I think, in the profoundest sense incarnation that the fourth- and fifth-century theologians upheld but (to use Harnack's term) *ensarkosis*. They needed to sustain the principle of Jesus' humanity since otherwise they would have had difficulty justifying the entry of the eternal Logos into history. But that formal requirement of doctrine is a far cry from affirming that this was, after all, a real human being. "[During this period] no single outstanding thinker really accepted the humanity [of the Christ] in an unqualified way [and although] most theologians contented themselves with the *ensarkosis*, they nevertheless clung to the most naive docetism as regards details."[10]

It was noted earlier that between the biblical attempts to respond to the christological question and those of the fifth-century church, a conspicuous shift of language occurred. What we must now propose is that the linguistic shift represents a deeper, theological shift, the essence of which is this same process of divinization; and that what is entailed here is not only the overwhelming influence of Hellenistic thought upon the mind of the church but the virtual loss of the Hebraic background.

It is necessary, I think, to stress the deprivation of the Hebraic matrix in the evolution of Christology. The recognition of Greco-Roman influence in this development, while usual, is not by itself sufficient to grasp the nature of the transition involved. The Judaic commitment, which is still present in the thought and language of the Antiochian school, brings to bear upon the christological question a distinctive perspective, one that affects every aspect of the subject; but in two ways particularly the difference between Athens and Jerusalem becomes visible at the point of the doctrine of Christ's person.

The first has to do with divine revelation. In the typical religion and mythology of Hellenistic culture, the manner of the deity's self-manifestation is extraordinary. The divine bursts in upon history, setting aside the laws of nature, cause and effect, and astonishing the recipients of this communication. Mystery here is associated with the unusual. It would be difficult in contexts

---

10. *History of Dogma*, trans. E. B. Speirs (London: Williams and Northgate, 1898), vol. 4, 169.

preconditioned by such expectations to sustain any conception of divine revelation that was not associated with such exceptional experiences. The consequent pressure upon the Christian movement to present the Christ as one surrounded from the start by extraordinary signs and wonders must have been great. In such a setting, to expect that people would be impressed by tales of a simple teacher of the law and the prophets and of his humiliation is perhaps comparable, in our contemporary milieu, to assuming that people would be ready to believe in the earthly advent of extraterrestrial beings without any rumors of spaceships and other "unidentified flying objects."

This "epiphanic"[11] conception of deity, which is the cultural background of Chalcedon, must be contrasted with the Hebraic conception of divine revelation. It is true that in biblical religion too there are moments of the extraordinary; and in connection with the life, death, and resurrection of Jesus such a signs-and-wonders approach is part of the record. It must be remembered, however, that the record appears after the fact, is heavily informed by theological interest and the conclusions of faith, and is already in some measure also influenced by Hellenistic presuppositions. It must also be borne in mind, as we have insisted earlier, that the record retained as Holy Scripture in the churches of the early period is not only remarkably restrained where the out-of-the-ordinary is concerned, but does not include those accounts of Jesus' life that indulged themselves freely in the epiphanic approach. The reason is obvious to anyone who remembers the Judaic background. God's mode of relating to the creature in the literature of the older Testament is not normally through ostentatious display of power; rather, the biblical God works within the historical process, honoring the laws of nature as well as human freedom, and altering the course of events through subtle and quiet intervention, usually involving the calling and activity of some human being. In fact, the calling of and covenant with Israel as a whole, with its connotation of worldly servanthood, is the foundational assumption of the Hebrew Bible.

Despite and even through the newer Testamental willingness to resort, on occasion, to the epiphanic, the fundamental note that is sounded by this postpentecostal record is one of great historical sobriety and realism. To be sure, there is (in Luke) a virgin birth. But this is what faith says about the birth—and for subtle theological reasons. It is not a public affair, this nativity, open for all to behold. It occurs in the obscurity of Bethlehem, in a stable, in the midst of beasts of burden, and witnessed by the simplest of folk. Epiphany is, to be sure, involved: the birth is manifested also to important personages—but they are foreigners, who depart from the land immediately and without fanfare. Their adoration has theological significance for the later, gentile church; but at the time, even if it is considered in the usual sense historical, the appearance of the

---

11. Sobrino, *Christology at the Crossroads,* 4.

wise kings prevents nothing and achieves nothing of immediate worldly significance. The nativity is an entirely inconspicuous and ordinary affair, seen from the perspective of the world.

> How silently, how silently
> The wondrous gift is given.[12]

What about the resurrection? This too is faith's confession. "Faith in the resurrection . . . sees the raising of the tortured and crucified Son of Man as God's *great protest* against death and everyone who plays into death's hands and threatens life."[13] It involves no public spectacle, no undoing of all the obscurity of the past, no overcoming of the humiliation that has preceded it. It too prevents nothing that worldly powers determine to undertake. It gives the believing community no power of its own beyond the power of memory, love, and courage. It can hardly be received even by faith, because this is the faith of a Jewish people (the first Christians) and therefore not one that is evoked by the extraordinary. The revealing God is the hidden God, whose glory is hidden beneath its opposite, whose truth is concealed from "the wise and prudent" (Luke 10:21, KJV), whose presence is recognized, usually, only after the fact. ("Surely the Lord is in this place—and I did not know it!"—Gen. 28:16.) The divinization of Jesus can only occur when this indirectness of divine revelation has been replaced by an immediacy foreign to Hebraic sensibilities.

The second factor in the Judaic background of Christianity that, had it not been lost, would certainly have militated against the process of divinization is an entirely different evaluation of the human. The Hellenistic world, particularly as it shows through in Alexandrian religion, thoroughly distrusts the human as a medium of ultimacy. Popular thought since the Renaissance imagines that Greece is the great source of humanism, while Jerusalem is too pessimistic about humanity. This is true only in one respect—and that one respect gives the lie to the assumption as a whole. Athens, unlike Jerusalem, thinks highly of rationality. But the rationality honored by Athens can only be attained by humans who overcome what, for biblical faith, is inextricably part of their essential humanity—their physicality, their capacity for emotion, their will to love what is other (the man the woman, and vice versa), their urge to

---

12. Moltmann's discussion of the virgin birth appears to me one of the most helpful statements on the subject to date. He insists that it is the Holy Spirit, not the Virgin, who is central to this aspect of the narrative: "If we take the birth of Christ from the Spirit seriously, then much that the church has ascribed to 'the Virgin Mary' is transposed to God the Holy Spirit himself, and Mary can once again be that which she was and is: the Jewish mother of Jesus. . . . The so-called 'feminine' side of God, and the 'motherly mystery' of the Trinity, is to be sought for, not in Mary but in the Spirit." (*The Way of Jesus Christ,* 86.)

13. Jürgen Moltmann, *Experiences of God* (Philadelphia: Fortress Press, 1980), 31. See also Moltmann's *The Way of Jesus Christ,* 214.

beget progeny, their joy in food, dance, laughter—life. From the vantage point of Jerusalem, Athens only affirms humanity at the expense of human creature-hood.[14]

It must therefore be considered a foregone conclusion that in the world of Hellenistic discourse the humanity of Jesus could not be greatly emphasized; or, to state it otherwise, one is not surprised that Jesus' humanity was acknowledged only in a formulary way. In a Hebraic context, on the other hand, it is by no means unusual that the human could be the bearer of transcendent purpose. In fact it is assumed that the normal medium of the divine would be the human; and while such human media would have to be in some way exceptional—as Abraham, David, Miriam, Jeremiah, and the Mary of the Magnificat are exceptional—it would by no means be expected of them that they should no longer manifest the admixture of positive and negative attributes that constitutes, for Jerusalem, actual human life. The Hebrew Bible is almost at pains to demystify every human bearer of divine purposing—from Noah, who gets drunk; to Sarah, who laughs at angelic promises; to David, who lusts after another man's wife. It seems mandatory, with this tradition, that the human emissaries of the divine should not only be human but very human. Only such credibly human beings could be received by the community of Israel as bearers of transcendent purpose.

This was lost to Christianity as it moved away from its homeland into the gentile world. Under these new auspices, the christological reflections of the church were no longer constrained to accentuate the credible humanity of Jesus; on the contrary, his obvious marks of solidarity with us, some of which are still discernible in the Synoptic Gospels, fade into the background in the evolving church. The formal profession of his humanity is required, but it is devoid of recognizably human content. The Jesus of the Synoptic Gospels is not simply human—nobody ever is. Jesus was a particular human being, a Jewish man living and dying under specific, unrepeatable historical conditions. It seems to me that we must at last be prepared to acknowledge, as Christians, that this Jewish human being called Jesus was almost wholly superseded, in evolving Christendom, by the theoretically human but really divine Christ. We would do well to add to this acknowledgment that it is therefore not surprising that those who were defeated in the process of the formalization of Christology were those who remembered what historic Christianity has always forgotten—that Jesus Christ was a Jew.

33.2. "Jesus Is God": Contra Fundamentalism. The critique of Christology as tending toward apotheosis is one that applies to nearly all Christians, for

---

14. See Rosemary Radford Ruether, *Liberation Theology* (New York: Paulist Press, 1972), chap. 5.

we tend to perpetuate this long-standing convention even when we do not do so intentionally. It is ubiquitous in the collective consciousness of the church; it is recited in hymns and liturgies composed in the past; it is carried in symbols and pictures, phrases and slogans; it silently informs our missiology. Looking at the stained-glass representations of Jesus in most Protestant, Catholic, Anglican, and Orthodox churches of the West, one would not suppose that this most important figure of the Christian religion was, in his lifetime, a wandering Jewish rabbi, "watched by the cold, hard eyes of peasants."[15]

In the present study, however, we are concerned about the profession of the Christian faith in a specific context: the two northern nations of North America; therefore in the critical chapters of each of the three parts we intend to draw attention especially to problems indigenous to that context. With respect to Christology, there are two apparently contradictory but really polar interpretations of the person of Christ in our midst that function in an anti-incarnational manner. The two are accurately described as polar because, while they have evolved in direct opposition to one another, they perform similar services within the quite different ecclesiastical communities with which they are associated.

The first is the Christology of fundamentalism. In its most influential form, this is a simplistic and dogged appropriation of the orthodox doctrine of Christ, goaded into single-mindedness by the presence and opposition of its liberal antithesis. While there are degrees of sophistication among those who claim this posture, the characteristic mark of the Christology that emerges from this branch of Christianity is an almost exclusive stress upon the principle of divinity. In its most vociferous expressions, fundamentalism in North America could be considered the reductio ad absurdum of the tendency toward apotheosis or divinization about which we have been thinking here. While a strict Chalcedonian orthodoxy insists upon Christ's two natures, fundamentalism affirms the divinity of Christ in such a way as to make his humanity little more than a cipher. The message that "Jesus is God" is perhaps the most frequently repeated formula of American media-conscious evangelicalism; and there are seldom any indications of the fact that the promulgation of such a message conjures up the most ancient christological heresies in the world (Sabellianism, Monophysitism, Docetism). As James Barr writes, "The basic answer furnished within fundamentalism [to the question, 'Who is Jesus?'] is: Jesus is God. He is the Son of God, supernatural in essence, miraculously manifested within the world in human form."[16]

While there are conservative scholars of biblicistic persuasion who are critical of such one-sidedness, the fundamentalist position is significant for theological

---

15. John Dominic Crossan, *The Historical Jesus: The Life of a Mediterranean Jewish Peasant* (San Francisco: Harper, 1991), xi.

16. James Barr, *Escaping from Fundamentalism* (London: S.C.M. Press, 1984), 56.

awareness within the churches partly because of its one-sidedness. For one thing, its appeal lies largely in its lack of nuance, and for another that appeal by no means confines itself to churches designating themselves as fundamentalist. The fundamentalist impulse, as one might designate it, is also to be found in most of the once-mainline Protestant churches of this continent.

Where Christology is concerned, what is attractive to this impulse is particularly the assurance that no human weakness or fault mars the figure at the center of the Christian gospel. This mentality would rather submit to the most blatant Docetism than to leave its Christ vulnerable to any human failing. The insistence upon Jesus' full divinity has frequently led, therefore, to claims more extravagant than any to be found in the annals of Christendom. Thus, for the Canadian-American evangelist of the earlier part of this century, T. T. Shields, the Christ could be described as basically unkillable: "You must not say that the death of Christ was caused by the cross of wood, by those who drove the nails and platted the thorns and pierced Him with a spear. These instruments could never terminate the life of the Son of God, an indissoluble life."[17] Not only was Shields's Jesus immortal, but as God he himself effects his own resurrection from the dead: "Jesus, and He is God, most emphatically, He is God—God never said, He never did a mightier thing than this, 'I lay down my life, that I may take it up again.'"[18]

Fundamentalist Christology is significant in North American Christianity and society, not only because it can claim the allegiance of a significant portion of the population, but—more to the point—it can seem to the general public as well as to many Christians in nonfundamentalistic denominations the purer form of Christology. Fundamentalists themselves have not been slow to convey to the populace that it is they who have preserved the authoritative Christian sources—the Bible primarily, but also classical doctrine and the theology of the Reformation. A public that is biblically illiterate and wholly innocent of any knowledge of the history of doctrine is prone to regard the fundamentalist witness to the Christ as normative Christology, even when it finds this witness unacceptable or repulsive.

In fact, secularism in North America is conspicuously colored by the assumption of the general public that "real" Christianity is the Christianity of the most biblicistic and doctrinally simplistic elements of the church. A major factor in the decline of Christianity in this context may thus be the association of the Christian religion with its crassest and least sophisticated expressions. If all that the Christians can say about Jesus is that "he is God," then a public

---

17. "The Power of an Indissoluble Life," a sermon in *The Gospel Witness* (Jan. 2, 1930), 9. I am indebted to Mark Parent for the references to Shields. See his unpublished doctoral dissertation for McGill University, "The Christology of T. T. Shields: The Irony of Fundamentalism," 1991.

18. From an unpublished sermon entitled, "He Shall Not Strive," based on Matt. 12:19-20, preached on April 26, 1903.

that has become conscious of religious pluralism and skeptical of every kind of exclusivism will not likely wait to hear more.

33.3. "Jesus the Perfect Man": Contra Liberalism.

It was the strength of religious liberalism that it understood the importance of keeping Jesus human. Unless we are able to discern in the church's testimony to Jesus a human being like ourselves (Heb. 4:15), there can be no inherent reason for anyone to think that this human being in particular is the mediator of good news to other human beings. The Bible's own witness ought—here above all—to be regarded as normative for all testimony to Jesus Christ. The first disciple community was not confronted by christological claims but by a human being, Jesus of Nazareth. These men and women are described as having lived in close proximity to the man Jesus for a short but significant period of time. They wandered about the countryside with him, ate with him, shared his waking and sleeping hours. They heard him speak, observed his ways with children, women, sick persons, men of authority; they witnessed his conflicts with those in religious and political leadership. They were impelled by some inner need to follow him, though they hardly knew why. They were never absolutely certain that they wanted to go all the way with him, but where else, to whom else would they go (John 6:68)? Gradually they found themselves swept into the orbit of his destiny—and it was not the destiny they expected, for it seemed incongruous with his talk about God's kingdom. Finally they had to see him taken from their midst, arrested, tried, condemned, and executed. And while none of this was in itself sufficient to elicit faith in him, the faith that *was* elicited, later, was absolutely dependent upon all this. Because they had had to do with the man Jesus, they were able, under the influence of what he had named "the Paraclete," to confess that, despite the discrepancy between popular expectations and the actual life of Jesus, he was indeed the Christ, the anointed one, the hoped-for savior of his people.

Liberalism understood much better than had most previous formulators of christological dogma that something like this is the pattern that must always apply to the church's reflections on and testimony to its "head." Faith is not a direct consequence of encounter with Jesus; but apart from that encounter it is impossible to elicit the faith-response for which the newer Testamental witness is asking. Without some lively memory of this human being, faith turns into assent to propositions about the nature and work of a doctrinal construct, a mythic or symbolic figure who never quite achieves flesh-and-blood reality.

Prompted by this right epistemological insight and by the immense dissatisfaction with christological conventions that had proven inept in the face of the growing skepticism and secularity of the West, liberal Christianity set out to help us actually to "see Jesus." It attempted this, not only through the aforementioned "lives," but in countless practical ways: in materials created for

Sunday schools and religious education; in a whole genre of hymnody and sacred song; in Christian art, drama, and story; above all, in the sermons and meditations that dominated Protestant pulpits throughout the late nineteenth and early twentieth centuries.

It is misleading to think that liberalism concentrated chiefly on revamping the faith intellectually and morally; or, rather, if it did this, it did so less directly than is sometimes asserted by those who have no personal memory of the movement in its heyday. The dominant feature of this whole episode in modern North American theology was its characterization of Jesus. Through its portrayal of Jesus, liberal Christianity effected changes in the church's theological and moral understanding. Its Jesus was more than a teacher of religion and morality. He was a paradigm, model, and pattern of genuine humanity. He was the Great Example. He met us—in Bible stories, in songs, in sermons and lessons, in dramas and paintings, and above all in persons who themselves had been deeply affected by their own encounter with his example; and in meeting us he challenged *our* humanity. We too could become lovers of neighbors and helpers of the sick and lonely and outcast; we too could be lifted out of self to give our time, talents, and treasures for the coming kingdom. We did not have to follow the crowd; we could be different. We could be "like Jesus."

It will be evident to the informed reader that I am not speaking here out of the high intellectual traditions of liberal theology—of Schleiermacher, Ritschl, Harnack, and others. I am referring rather to the impact of the liberal presentation of Jesus upon the North American church at large—an impact that was possible, in part, because of the work of the great scholars. It will also be obvious that the type of liberalism to which I am referring here is that liberal spirit which aligned itself with Christian pietism rather than the more critical, academic variety, which functioned more as an attack upon old orthodoxy and, later, upon the fundamentalism to which, in the North American situation, much old orthodoxy was reduced in the face of the liberal critique. I concentrate here on popular, believing liberalism for the simple reason that this is the type that most profoundly affected the churches of Canada and the United States. In the main, its approach was personalistic and not directly political. It aimed for changed lives—lives altered by their contact with *that* life.

There was always, however, an indirect political thrust within the liberal message, for the changes that it wished to effect were radically altruistic and never, therefore, quite compatible with the spirit of capitalism. A moral concept like that of Christian philanthropy, deriving from the brotherly love manifested in the life of Jesus, could be (and frequently was) manipulated into compatibility with capitalism: the "stewardship" of money and skills could be conceived in such a way, even, as to demonstrate the rectitude of the capitalist quest; for the more one had, the more one could give. And if, to this, were added the deuteronomic concept of earthly reward for righteous living, so that giving almost automatically promised benefits both spiritual and material, the philanthropic way could seem Christian indeed.

Yet, as is demonstrated not only by the rise of the social gospel within the liberal camp but also by the direct and indirect influence of liberal piety on political socialism (particularly in Canada), the picture of Jesus promulgated by liberalism was never quite innocent of its critical potential in a society where people were conditioned to behave in a manner very different from the self-sacrificial way of the Nazarene. Thus even those who, eventually, had to become highly critical of liberalism[19] still had to acknowledge their indebtedness to the ideal for which it stood. And that ideal was always one most perfectly embodied in "the Man of Nazareth."

It is my conviction that any viable Christology, in whatever historical setting, must imitate this liberal quest to "keep Jesus human" and to present him to the church and the world as a believable human being. It should not be thought that this attempt is simply equatable with "the quest for the historical Jesus." Some liberal scholars were intent upon discovering the Jesus of history behind the Christ of dogma, that is true. But it is misleading to think that the main thrust of liberalism was the intellectual's search for authentic historical data. It was rather the chief aim of this movement to present faith (and unfaith) with a human model of goodness and truth, a paradigm of belief in "the Fatherhood of God and the Brotherhood of Man"; and the failure of the "quest for the historical Jesus" is only tangentially consequential for that aim. What the failure to "get behind the record" means for the liberal attempt to depict Jesus is that all future attempts are bound to recognize that the Jesus whom they present to the world and the church is never strictly identifiable with the Jesus who actually lived, and probably manifests more of the biases of the presenters than they care to admit. But the analytical problem of recovering the historical Jesus is not the same as the theological and missiological problem of conveying to church and world an *imago Christi* that is believably human and existentially gripping.

No amount of scholarly difficulty in connection with the historical-analytical problem can discourage the Christian movement from attempting to overcome the theological and evangelical problem; and when, today, liberation theologians in Latin America affirm, over against an entrenched christological "abstractionism," that they intend to turn to the historical Jesus, what we should hear is not that they intend innocently to begin yet another impossible search for the Jesus behind the record but rather that they want to find a Jesus who *speaks*— prophesies, judges, consoles—and through the engagement of the present brings

---

19. Like Reinhold Niebuhr; see *An Interpretation of Christian Ethics* (New York: Meridian Books, Living Age Books, 1956 [Orig. New York: Harper and Brothers, 1935]), esp. chap. 4, "The Relevance of an Impossible Ethical Ideal."

about changed lives and changed societies. They want a living, humanly concrete Jesus, not an empty vessel meant for containing all the stale dogmas of Christendom. And that is precisely what the liberals wanted. It is what an obedient church must always want.

What, then, was the problem with the liberal Jesus? If it was not simply that such a picture of Jesus could not be authenticated, finally, by the actual record, what was it?

The problem was, I think, that Jesus for liberalism became a model of humanity so perfect, so absolute in every virtue, so blameless in respect to every sin recognized by his Victorian and other champions, that in the long run the very humanity of the liberal Jesus functioned in much the same way as did the divinity of the conservative Jesus—that is, to distinguish him conspicuously from the rest of us.

There are shades of meaning here that do not impress themselves upon the mind at once; therefore we must pause to reflect on this last generalization. First we should contemplate the nature of an ideal. Jesus for liberal theology and piety was a paradigm of ideal humanhood. His main work as person was to show us the way, to provide a model. It is commonplace to recognize that human beings must have such models. Without patterns of behavior individuals end in confusion. "Where there is no vision, the people perish" (Prov. 29:18, KJV). Children require of their parents and teachers that they exemplify humanity, not only that they describe and command it. Congregations demand of their clergy and lay leaders that they exemplify Christian behavior, not only preach it. All through our lives, from childhood to old age, we are dependent upon the exemplification of knowledge, wisdom, and (above all) courage that we can derive only from those who have "been there before," or can in some manner enlighten us. Ideals and idealism are not the foolish and dispensable attitudes that self-styled realists have always made them out to be. Without the guidance of a credible and in some measure realizable ideal, we are at the mercy of a realism so bleak that, where it is embraced without illusion, it destroys—often literally.[20]

Jesus has always been for faith, where it has been genuine, an ideal. His "true humanity," affirmed at least formally by Chalcedon, means the humanity for which we were all intended and to which, through grace, we might yet attain. This is part of the meaning and task of Christology: to show the way, to demonstrate authentic humanity.

But the ideal always walks a narrow path between showing us the way that we, too, might go, and showing us how impossibly far from that way we have come. The ideal may encourage us to dare great things, but it may also discourage us

---

20. In this connection, see the discussion of the work of Ernest Becker in *Thinking the Faith,* 179–89.

from imagining such possibilities for ourselves. Ideal beauty inspires some to emulate it and persuades others that it can never be theirs. The Miss Americas and the "Marlboro Men" of the entrepreneurial world still function with sufficient power to persuade millions that they could obtain physical attractiveness if only they would make use of certain products; but the seductive beauties of the commercials and the slick magazines only persuade countless others of their lifelong imprisonment in bodies that repel (consider the high incidence of anorexia nervosa in North American society today). Ideal teachers, clergy, parents, wives, husbands, and families may keep before us virtues that would otherwise seem merely rhetorical and remote; but they may also, under certain circumstances, simply judge our humanity and exist for us as constant reminders of our inferiority and failure.

What, we may ask, makes the difference? Why do ideals function sometimes to reaffirm, encourage, and inspire, and sometimes to condemn, discourage, and fatalize?

To respond wisely to such a question would require greater space—and greater understanding—than can be managed here. Two observations may, however, be offered. First, to function positively an ideal must combine two qualities that are never easily combined: participation and distance, identification and differentiation. An ideal, to inspire, must at the same time touch my life and transcend my life. If it only touches my life, manifesting only what is already there, it will not inspire change in me. On the other hand, unless it is appreciably grounded in the same reality in which I am grounded, its superiority will appear to me unattainable and, in the end, it will serve only to remind me of the impossibility of my condition. Thus the older brother whose intelligence is comparable to my own but who makes better use of his mind than I do may inspire me, finally, to work harder at my lessons; but an older brother whose IQ greatly exceeds my own and who therefore invariably performs "miraculously" in every mathematics examination will be for me a living reminder of my incapacity for demanding intellectual work. This admixture of participation and transcendence is rare, but it is the very stuff out of which viable ideals and visions are made.

The second remark that must be made about ideals and idealism is that they are strongly conditioned by historical contexts. There are idealistic periods in history and there are periods that manifest a dearth of idealism. In an idealistic period, individual idealism, including religious idealism, is made to seem good and right because idealism of one kind or another characterizes the whole epoch and culture. Conversely, in a period of low expectation the ideals of a former age will seem naive and woolly-headed, lacking in realism, childish.

Both of these observations apply to our consideration of the North American form of Christian liberalism and the Christology at the core of it. To take the second observation first, liberalism emerged in the nineteenth century—by comparison with the twentieth, a highly idealistic period in Western history. That it could therefore develop a picture of Jesus informed by the highest virtues, devoid of ambiguity, pure of deed and intent; and that this picture could be received and honored by so many was in considerable measure because of the spirit of the age, which not only entertained the heroic in every sphere of life and society but positively demanded of religion in particular that it should foster the highest ideals and thus undergird the positive outlook that reigned everywhere in the dominant culture of the land.

This idealism held sway in the North American context especially, for it incorporated and was continuous with the world view at the heart of our continental experiment. In Europe and in older cultures that were also grasped by the idealistic spirit of modernity, earlier elements of philosophy, religion, and culture could act as countervailing agents against a too one-sided optimism; but in North America (especially the United States), the religious idealism that centered in "Jesus" knew almost no bounds. We are speaking, after all, of the age that saw the emergence of one-world visions of every sort, including the ecumenical movement and the League of Nations; therefore the ideal associated with Jesus' kingdom of God did not seem, in such a context, a terribly impracticable vision.

This cultural mood, however, is not the outlook of our present society. We live in a time of "diminishing expectations" (Christopher Lasch). The ideal humanity for which the liberal Jesus stood in the nineteenth and early twentieth centuries, therefore, is no longer undergirded by a societal readiness to dream. Liberalism failed among us, not because it could not discover an authentically historical Jesus, but because its Jesus was the representation of a heroic humanity in which the majority can no longer spontaneously believe.

The earlier observation about the character of idealism also applies to the liberal treatment of Jesus. Liberalism lost whatever it may once have had of the magic combination of participation and transcendence in its picture of Jesus. The two observations come together at this point, because this loss was partly attributable to the changed sociohistorical circumstances. The idealistic age could absorb a great deal of transcendence in the presentation of Jesus, because it was open to great expectations of every variety. But the changed contextual circumstances do not wholly explain this loss.

The truth is, I think, that liberalism was always tempted to accentuate the humanly exalted qualities of Jesus. This was perhaps its heritage from two thousand years of orthodoxy. It lost interest in orthodoxy's divinity principle because the divinity seemed formulary and outdated; but it carried over from orthodoxy the habit of treating the Christ-figure grandly. Not grandly *divine* but grandly *human* virtues were now grandly explored. Jesus became the name for a humanity so blameless, a clarity of purpose so lacking in doubt, a vicarious suffering so selfless, a life-style so courageous, a morality so unambiguous, a

459

social zeal so vigorous, and above all a love so pure that in the end the effect produced in those with a modicum of self-knowledge was: "Such a life is completely beyond me." It was (as one of the great homileticians of the century, Paul Scherer, used to tell his students) as though someone had held up an ostrich egg to a Bantam hen and said, "Do your best!"

In short, the participatory side of the dialectic necessary to a viable ideal was lost. Jesus—*vere Homo*—became so unearthly perfect as to be of little earthly use. Not his divinity, but his divine humanity became the device separating him effectively from the actual human condition for whose redemption he came among us. It is an exaggeration (but an instructive one) that in some of the more unsophisticated circles which had fallen under the impact of a liberalism that built upon centuries of orthodox apotheosis, Jesus was reputed to be perfect not only in his spiritual and moral aspect but even physically. As I child, I was given to understand that Jesus was exactly six feet tall, not an eighth of an inch more or less. Since it was by then becoming apparent to me on the basis of my own growth rate and my parentage that I would never attain such a splendid stature, the message was clear: My humanity had nothing in common with that of Jesus, and I was fated forever to stand outside the circle of his stalwart company.

It was only under the impact of the modern failures that began to appear in the second decade of this century, and of the theology that noticed these failures and attempted to rethink the faith in the light of them (so-called neoorthodoxy) that this liberal habit of idealizing Jesus' humanity in a way strikingly similar to orthodoxy's idealization of him through the accentuation of the divinity principle was called into question. "At least [says Zooey Glass to his sister Franny in J. D. Salinger's *Franny and Zooey*] I've never tried, consciously or otherwise, to turn Jesus into St. Francis of Assisi to make him more 'lovable'—which is exactly what ninety-eight percent of the Christian world has always insisted on doing. Not that it's to my credit."[21]

33.4. Why Christian Theology Must Sustain the Real Humanity of Jesus, the Christ. If there is anything distinctive about Christianity, it is that this faith is focused, not on a general theism, not on religious principles, not on ethical teachings, not on ritual observance, not on heavenly appearances or worldly observations, but on *a life:* a life lived under the same basic conditions that affect all life. Through this life, faith perceives what, to be sure, transcends that particular life. For faith, that life is transparent of an eternal love in which all life is wrapped. And because that which faith sees in and through that life is eternal, it is not surprised, and it is certainly not threatened, if it

---

21. J. D. Salinger, *Franny and Zooey* (Boston and Toronto: Little, Brown and Co., 1955, 1957, 1961), 164–65.

now and then sees this same eternal love manifested in other places as well. Yet it clings to that particular life. It does not find it dispensable or merely a temporary vehicle for its journey toward understanding. It could no more dispense with that life than could a lover dispense with the life of the one who introduced him to the vast, unending universe of love. Faith is all the more bound to that life because of its particularity; for the only way to the universal (here too) is through the particular.

We have learned in twentieth-century theology to speak about the scandal of particularity, and this is both a biblically sound and (in a pluralistic age) a contextually responsible form of speech. Yet particularity is not really very scandalous. It is scandalous only to those who imagine, in their vanity, that they have immediate access to universals. Such vain imaginings are unfortunately the common failing of intellectuals, who are prone to forget that their discoveries are inseparable from the intensely particular beings whose small and great sacrifices have enabled them to arrive at their laws and theories. Theology, too, readily falls into such vanity.

But the religious experience upon which theology comments is always particularized. Without some solid grounding in what is concrete and accessible, the human quest for the ultimate devolves into endless speculation and abstraction. The speculation may prove interesting, of course. Games of every kind can be interesting, and the more complex the game the more interesting to the clever mind. But religion is not for minds only; and even those with agile minds are eventually introduced to needs that cannot be met by the mind. Fortunately, the Christian religion has never been wholly abandoned by those whose minds were keen and who demanded excellence of thought. But the great thought of the tradition has been inspired by the experience of the incapacity of our minds for greatness of thought in relation to the Author of thought. Before the mystery of that unknown God, great thought is silenced; only mediocrity imagines itself capable of cleverness and insight there. Blinded, repulsed, humiliated, like Saul on the Damascus road, the ambitious spirit may learn how to know God through the very particular that it had rejected and persecuted.

The judgment against intellectual pride that is an unmistakable theme of all the Scriptures is not to be construed as a concession to anti-intellectualism or the elevation of the soul over the mind. It is rather an application of the general biblical theme of *metanoia* to the realm of thought. With thought as with every other work of the fallen creature, rejection and humiliation must precede and condition depth and authenticity. The mind too must be born a second time, baptized into death, so that it may learn to live more abundantly, more freely. And the mode of this rebirth of the mind is its being turned away from the garden of universals, which is guarded by angels with flaming swords. Its humiliation—and its salvation—is to be reduced to the condition of the child, dependent upon what is immediately present to it. The repentant mind must begin all over again with what is there, accessible, available:

> "I thank thee, Father, Lord of heaven and earth, that thou hast hidden these things from the wise and understanding and revealed them to babes; yea, Father, for such was thy gracious will. All things have been delivered to me by my Father; and no one knows the Son except the Father, and no one knows the Father except the Son and any one to whom the Son chooses to reveal him. Come to me, all who labor and are heavy laden, and I will give you rest." (Matt. 11:25-29, RSV)

Jesus is the response of the gracious God to fallen creatures who long ago and perhaps always forfeited their capacity for immediate discourse with the Absolute. Through this particular—the Son—faith is delivered of the heavy burden of living with an ungraspable Absolute, a hidden Judge, an ultimate as inaccessible as the inhabitants of Kafka's castle. And something within the human spirit longs precisely for this response, and finds in it precisely the "rest" for which it has waited.

Why then has the whole course of historic Christianity's life with this mediator been one of undoing the very concreteness of such a revealing presence? Why, from the outset and still today, has so much of the intellectual inventiveness of the church been devoted to the reduction of this person to theory, this particular to yet another statement of the universal, this concrete to an absolute? If Jesus is the answer of God to the human quest for God, then why has Christianity itself expended so much energy substituting for this answer abstractions, Christologies, which have the effect precisely of turning the whole quest back into a speculative and futile search for absolutes?

In defense of the christological history of Christendom, one may say that every particular needs to be protected from the human habit of misidentification and misappropriation. That which drives us to make graven images of one another also drives us to create graven images of Jesus; and therefore a corrective "science" of Christology has always been required. It is, as we have seen, already begun in the newer Testament itself—and by Jesus.

But this alone does not explain the phenomenon of Christologies, for they go far beyond the requirement of correction and become themselves the objects of belief, displacing the person who, according to faith's own profession, still "lives and reigns" and ought, therefore, to continue to be the "Thou" to whom faith is oriented.

It is exactly because this person is no object but a living subject, surely, that "he" is constantly transmuted into an "it." For while the particular is the only path to the universal, the cost of that assumption is a willingness to submit to the particular. And, like most particulars, like all living particulars, the particular person called Jesus can only be lived with. He cannot be appropriated, manipulated, arranged and rearranged, managed, mastered, speculated about, possessed. With him it is a matter of discipleship. Only as he is "followed" (Bonhoeffer) will he lead to the throne of the ultimate; only as the disciple community "takes his yoke upon it" will it find rest.

This is what Bonhoeffer rightly called the real "cost of discipleship," and it is always too great a price for "the wise and understanding." Hence the temptation of the theological community of the Christian movement particularly has always been to exchange the reality of this human being for theories about this human being. Some of these theories have been formulated through submission to the principle of divinity, and some through speculative and idealistic thought about true humanity; but the effect is the same in both cases: namely, the loss of the "Thou" at the center.

And this constitutes, in reality, the loss of whatever genius informs this faith. The humanity of Jesus must not be retained for theoretical purposes only—including the purpose of affirming a theory called the incarnation. It must be retained because apart from it the very particularity that our humanity requires and which the biblical God knows that we require is lost; and we are thrown back once again upon religious and theological universals that must remain as remote from our lived lives as every other abstraction.

34. The Missing Ingredient: *Pro Nobis!*

34.1. The Existential Remoteness of the Traditions of Salvation. In our historical reflections of the previous chapter, we noted that while the church produced a doctrinal definition of the person of the Christ that has been regarded as official—if not always satisfactory—by all the major branches of Christendom, no such pronouncement has ever been made concerning the work of the Christ. On the contrary, the soteriological dimension of Christology evolved gradually, and in response to the changing perceptions of the human predicament in the history of the West. The traditions of salvation associated with the Christian profession of faith are enshrined in three types (with variations) of atonement theology, each of which correlates with an assumed reading of that in relation to which human beings require redemption. The work of the Christ is not encompassed wholly in any or all of these theories, for, as we have affirmed through the adoption of the "old Protestant"[22] concept of the three offices, Jesus Christ exists for faith not only as savior but also as prophetic teacher and as Lord. In a subsequent discussion we shall return to the consideration of those two offices; but since, traditionally, the work of the Christ is particularly bound up with the question of the

---

22. *The Way of Jesus Christ*, 286.

atonement, it is the priestly office that must occupy the bulk of our critical assessment.

To come directly to the point, which I shall elaborate in several cognate observations, it is my opinion that none of the three types of atonement theology that we have considered as having dominated the Christian past is capable of engaging the human *problematique* as it is experienced within our contemporary North American context.

This undoubtedly bold and sweeping generalization will be challenged by individuals and groups whose religious experiences corroborate one or another of the atonement theologies in question. I hasten therefore to say that I have no wish to discount anyone's personal religious experience. My attempt here is based on a different kind of concern. I am trying to understand who "we" are—not just as individuals or various collectivities within the greater society, but as a people, a culture, part of a civilization. Within any larger social unit, whether it be ancient Rome or the present-day "developing" world, it is possible to recognize a great variety of human experiences. Just as our physical and material needs differ, so our spiritual conditions manifest many differing tendencies. This is why a contextual theology that is more than merely ideological in its concern for concreteness always presses toward a personal as well as a social ethic, and expresses itself in pastoral as well as prophetic ministry.

But societies, as we have argued in the first volume, are also characterized by common motifs, goals, values, fears, and so on; and Christian theology that wishes to be faithful to the greater evangelical thrust of the gospel (by which I do not mean proselytization) must always endeavor to discern these. If the disciple community cannot or will not do this, its message will be frozen in the past. It will then continue to speak to those who for one reason or another are also conditioned by problems and possibilities carried over from that past, but it will not engage the cutting edge of the future-oriented sections of the culture. And because it does not engage the culture where it is most responsive to the "now and here," it will also fail to engage most of those individuals and groups which determine the course of that future. The mainline churches of North America should be concerned about the loss of youth, the poor, and the intelligentsia, not because of the prestige or numerical strength that these segments might bring to it, but because their sparsity or absence may well mean that the church's message has ceased to be meaningful to those most affected by the winds of change.

The brief survey of atonement theology that we undertook in the previous chapter illustrates graphically the capacity of theological imagination, which has never been wholly absent from Christendom, to grasp at the key points of cultural transition the nature of humanity's new perceptions of itself, and to reformulate the meaning of the cross accordingly. Three preconditions for this work of "sanctified imagination" seem to be mandatory: (1) unprotected exposure of the theological community to the human situation in its altering or altered form; (2) the willingness of that community to relinquish older soteriological doctrine, or even to reject it outright (as both Anselm and Abelard did); (3) the capacity of faith to present the Christ as one who understood and was able to participate in the human predicament as it is now perceived, and to engage it from within. Unless the theological community itself experiences in its own being something of the "sickness unto death" that is gripping the spirit of the times, soteriology will lack depth. And unless the theological community is willing, in the light of new faces of human sin, to distance itself from the hold of the old versions of salvation, there will be no movement of the community into the altered situation; it will remain the purveyor of old remedies for old diseases, and will serve those who still suffer from the old diseases and those who do not wish to know the extent of their suffering from the new ones.

Luther's theological biography illustrates the three preconditions poignantly: (1) His great spiritual struggle—the quest for "a gracious God"—was not only a personal struggle, though he certainly experienced it as such; it was a representative struggle. Luther's life absorbed, like a magnet, the spiritual crisis of his age. (2) While Luther did not permit himself Abelard's type of strong rejection of the Latin theory of atonement, neither, evidently, could he find the theory of sacrificial substitution adequate as a salvific answer to the human dilemma as he lived it. The truth of Aúlen's excessively one-sided theory[23] lies in Luther's sympathies with the ransom theory as a "usable past" on which he could build in his attempt to present Christ's work as the conquest of radical evil ("the devil"). (3) Luther and his colleagues had not only to decipher their own situation in new ways, but they had to present Jesus Christ himself in a way different from the bulk of the tradition—not as a St. George who triumphs visibly over evil, but as one whose victory is "hidden beneath its opposite" and so looks for all the world—*to* all the world—like defeat.

My contention in this segment of the critical analysis is that in the North American situation today we seem to be wanting where all three of these preconditions are concerned (and here I refer, not to individuals or avant garde groupings within and around the churches, some of whom constitute exceptions to this generalization, but rather to what seems to be meant by "mainstream" Christianity). The typical salvation theology of the more established forms of Protestantism in North America is still, in my judgment, captivated by one or other of the three types; and nothing significant will occur in any of our churches until there is a greater readiness to entertain the preconditions described above.

In what follows, I shall deal first with the inadequacy of the demonstration type of atonement theology, since it is the one that tends to dominate in the

---

23. *Christus Victor.*

vaguely liberal denominations. Then I shall move to the sacrificial type, which has preeminence both in the more conservative traditions and, at a theoretical level, among historically knowledgeable persons in denominations that have in other respects become liberal. Finally, I shall ask about the adequacy of the rescue type, which is attractive to some who follow the lines of liberation theology. In the concluding section of the chapter, I shall return to the prophetic and "kingly" offices.

34.2. Love *Is* the Answer—But . . . The permanently valid insight of Abelard's teaching concerning the meaning of the atonement is that it does not stray, as do both of the older, "objective" theories, from the rudimentary point that what informs the cross from the side of biblical Theology is from start to finish *love*. Both of the older theories lose this rudimentary basis, however much they have wished to sustain it, because of their fascination with (one could almost say their fixation upon) that which the divine love intends to *overcome*—in the sacrificial type, guilt; in the rescue type, transcendent evil. Unerringly and with something like what Kierkegaard meant by "purity of heart," Abelard insisted that the love of God, and neither God's righteous holiness nor God's omnipotence, was the point of the whole event; and that when the older ("classical") theory concerned itself so emphatically with the power of evil it was not only giving the devil more prominence than he deserved but, to overcome demonic power, it had to present a still more powerful Deity, thus both courting dualism and accentuating power instead of love. Likewise, Abelard sensed that the so-called Latin theory was so preoccupied with guilt and the offense of sin to God that it both exaggerated human guilt at the expense of other dimensions of the human being and robbed God of God's chief attribute, agape, in order to accentuate that which, in the best traditions, can only serve love—namely justice and holiness.

While this single-minded devotion to God's love on the part of the passionate medieval scholar must continue to commend him to all who take the biblical story for their point of departure, the weakness of Abelard's teaching should no longer be missed by the remnants of liberal Christianity in North America today. The truth is that love, from our human side at least, is never so easily received and appropriated as either Abelard or his later admirers appear to have thought. It is necessary for serious readers of the Bible to affirm that the God who "is love" is, in and through the Son and the Spirit, preoccupied with the manifestation and transmission of that love to unloved and often unlovely creatures. But part of the cost to God, incurred through this attempt at "reconciling the world to himself," is that the creatures are seemingly incapable of accepting love when it is given spontaneously and without ulterior motivation (Aúlen). It may be debated whether this is because their own loves are so calculating and unsteady, or because of their incipient and dark

466

awareness of their own unworthiness, or because of their abiding cynicism about the very possibility of love in such a world. But whoever thinks that love is received as unreservedly as it is (according to Abelard) given by the one who "lays down his life for his friends" will have missed not only the lessons of the great psychologists of the modern epoch but much, as well, in the ancient wisdom of the tradition.

Jesus once depicted God as a mother hen who wishes to enfold Jerusalem like chicks beneath her wings—"and you were not willing" (Matt. 23:37). It is human to want to be loved; but it is also human to fear love and to accept it only on one's own terms, for love contains within itself an invasion of the self and a terrible judgment of the self's bid for autonomy. At the same time, paradoxically, the self desires and repulses love. It also no doubt fears, at the deepest level of unconscious awareness, that it is neither good enough to be loved nor capable of loving in return. Perhaps the two older theories of the atonement understood this better than either Abelard or his later admirers. In Anselm, particularly, with his expansive guilt consciousness, there is a strong hint of what Tillich termed the lack of courage to "accept our acceptance."

The idealistic age during which, in North America, liberal Christianity betook itself enthusiastically to the soteriology of "love demonstrated"—the age that is still present in the Hollywood films of the 1940s and '50s—could imagine that love solves everything. If only one is loved, all things will turn out for the good. But as we now view those same films, however nostalgic they may cause us to become, they seem almost absurdly naive about the realities of existence; similarly, we are prone to regard the religion of love as a superficial if well-meant sentimentality that is almost wholly out of touch with life today.[24]

Like the model of wholesome, small-town simplicity and goodness that the suburban bourgeoisie still attempts to re-create, the Christian faith is enacted every seventh day throughout our continent as a litany of love: God's love, Jesus' love, our love for each other, family love, marital love, the love of teachers for their pupils and presidents for their fellow citizens and patriots for their country. But even most of those who participate in this litany must, in order to go through with it, close their eyes to the world they experience every day. With their minds full of the violence, loveless sex, rapacious consumerism, and "future shock" that characterize their workaday worlds as well as their "entertainment"; with their children in schools where drugs are readily available and truth and wisdom are in short supply; and, perhaps most important, with a whole cultural apparatus that, from Freud to Tennessee Williams and Andy Warhol, has taught them to look for the seamy side of all apparent virtue, they are hardly candidates for an atonement theology that enthrones love without knowing much about the interstellar spaces of insecurity, pride, revenge,

---

24. Barbra Streisand's recent film *Nuts* is perhaps the best illustration of this point.

and cynicism that have to be traversed if the message of divine, healing love is ever to reach us.

It must, I think, be regarded as one of the reasons for the absence from the churches of large numbers of people in our society that, given the sophistication of our psychological indoctrination and the hardness of the world we experience daily, Christianity as it is practiced in most once-mainline liberal congregations must seem a terribly naive, insipid thing. How could it understand the bleak impulses that drive the young to "crack" and rock and suicide? How could it deal with the appalling noise and almost tangible hatred of the great emporia of electronic games? Before the disillusionment and pathos of one violated woman or one unloved old "bag man," the Christianity that ritualizes love, whether to the accompaniment of Bach or the modern guitar, shows up as a travesty—and not only to those on the outside of the sanctuary.

None of this renders untrue the belief that love truly is the ground and purpose of all that biblical faith wants to communicate to us in and through the cross of Jesus. What is criticized here is not the insistence of the moral influence theory that "love is the answer"; what is and must be criticized is the assumption that love can be so effortlessly mediated to *us*. For our problem is not ignorance, whether intellectual or moral; our problem is that we have been "enlightened." We have "come of age" (Bonhoeffer). We have seen through the sweet virtues and ideals of our progenitors. The scientists and social scientists, the historians and literati, the politicians and artists, and above all the raw events of our lifetime have impressed upon the great bulk of us how ambiguous, at best, are human motives and how illusory human hopes. The message of love, however well intentioned, is simply not capable of engaging the depths of skepticism and suspicion that we bring to every golden discourse of conquering love. The anthropology in which, by sheer osmosis, we are steeped is one that neither Thomas Jefferson nor George Washington nor Mary Baker Eddy nor Walter Rauschenbusch would have understood very well. Increasingly, this anthropology expresses itself openly, but it is also hidden behind the magazine-correct decor of many middle-class dwellings.

And at the heart of it is this: We do not see ourselves lacking love so much as lacking purpose. Love of one sort or another may help to assuage our lack of purpose, but it will not *speak to* it. A church that announces love and goes through the motions of being "a loving congregation" may help some of us to suppress or repress the dull despair of our waking hours; but it will be a holding operation and not the site of a genuine spiritual struggle for life. Jesus Christ must either be the bringer of life ("New Being"—Tillich) or else he will be a mere vestige of his former saviorhood. Significant numbers among the liberal churches have sensed this, and more than a few have renounced the soteriology of sentimental love for the older, more drastic soteriology of sacrifice (the conservative backlash). But is that soteriology any more engaging?

34.3. Guilty—but Unmoved. What is attractive to many about the Anselmic-Calvinistic soteriology of sacrifice is that it offers a clear-cut definition of the problem and an equally decisive statement of the answer. The problem is that we are all immeasurably guilty; the answer is that through Christ's substitutionary sacrifice the punishment we deserve has been endured already, the debt we owe has been paid.

In addition to the fact that this soteriology can claim a thousand years of almost unrivaled indoctrination in the West, it derives no small portion of its present-day appeal from its simple straightforwardness. In a spiritual context as contourless and complicated as our own age, the clarity of the Latin atonement theology provides, for all who seek relief from this complexity, both a ready-made analysis of what is the matter and an accessible remedy. Combined, as it is in both Catholic and Protestant renditions, with well-rehearsed religious rituals for its appropriation, this substitutionary soteriology is ideally suited to the religious simplism to which we referred in the first volume.[25] Not only is it one of the five basic teachings (fundamentals) of North American fundamentalism, but in less doctrinaire forms it lingers like a familiar specter in all of the churches of our continent. Even where it has been replaced at the conscious level by the more liberal soteriology of "love demonstrated," it continues to assert its seemingly ageless impact through hymns, collects, and pious slogans.

Nevertheless, we should not associate substitutionary soteriology with religious simplism alone. There is within it a more profound appeal, and this can be recognized wherever one encounters within the Christian community persons encumbered by a sense of guilt. In a way not true of the moral influence theory, substitutionary Christology understands the tragic element, particularly as it is expressed in the anxiety of guilt and condemnation. That anxiety appears to be a lasting one. As the stories of Kafka—especially *The Trial*—and of Flannery O'Connor and many other contemporary authors illustrate, even postreligious humanity is subject to an inexplicable and often objectless sense of condemnation. The secular person who suffers from this malaise, unlike those who in the past were conditioned from their youth onwards to locate their accuser in the righteous and holy Deity of Christendom, does not know before whom or what he or she is guilty. Yet far from lessening the burden of the guilt, this can intensify it. What the school of Kierkegaard called "existential guilt"—guilt whose potency lies precisely in its failure to manifest either its cause or its accuser—is evidently still with us today. Without it, the couches of the psychoanalysts would be emptier.

We may go beyond even this personal level where guilt is concerned, for we are part of a world—the so-called First—that today stands accused corporately

---

25. *Thinking the Faith*, chap. 3, sec. 17.

and en masse. Our way of life is eked out at the expense of two-thirds of the global human population, and in this case our accuser is by no means silent. The all-too-familiar symbol of the child with distended stomach (as in Somalia, for example) is for us a constant reminder of our corporate guilt. So is the unborn child, the unwanted, aborted fetus, who for many represents not only a sign of our moral callousness but our unacknowledged rejection of the future generations from whom we are borrowing so recklessly the wherewithal of our life.

Not only are we accused by the poor and by generations yet unborn; our accusers are now made up of myriad creatures, large and small, animal, vegetable, and mineral, whose wholesale sacrifice is necessary for the continuation of what we imagine to be our high quality of life.

Not only privately, then, but also publicly, politically, the concept of guilt as basic to the human condition does seem viable still. Where it is exploited with imagination and fervor, and especially where it is lifted out of the merely personalistic mold, it can and must continue to be a dimension of the analysis of the condition from which human beings and the human species need redemption.

Yet there are limitations to the usefulness of this soteriological tradition even at the level of analysis, not to speak of "the cure." Two such limitations can be named forthwith: First, the concept of guilt in the received tradition is so religiously colored that it is hard to apply it where today it must be applied, namely psychologically and politically. So necessary is the Theology of divine righteousness and holiness to the convention of this atonement theology that it has little possibility of addressing the secular mentality. In fact, of all the atonement traditions, this one is most inextricably bound up with a theology of revelation that verges on positivism of revelation. As can be detected from its twentieth-century renaissance in the school of Barth, its exposition seems to require a strong prior sense of the divine presence and judgment, and it does not welcome but on the contrary suspects any nonrevelational corroboration from the side of human science and wisdom. Part of what lay behind Karl Barth's rejection of what he called "existential screaming"[26] was the fear that an existentialistic sense of guilt or dread might be seen too readily as being continuous with the consciousness of sin felt in the revealing Presence. While therefore the sense of guilt that is still felt by post-Christian humanity could become an entree and apologia for this soteriological type, there is a curious need on the part of its fundamentalist, old and neoorthodox defenders to keep it discontinuous with ordinary experience and rather exclusively related to the kerygma.

---

26. *The Doctrine of the Word of God: Prolegomena to Church Dogmatics,* vol. 1, Part 1, trans. G. T. Thomson (New York: Charles Scribner's Sons, 1936), 22.

The second limitation of this atonement tradition at the level of its anthropological assumptions is more serious. It is that while guilt may still abound, both privately and corporately, it is not at the forefront of the *problematique* to which, at least in the North American context, the Christian gospel must be addressed. Such a thesis cannot, of course, be demonstrated conclusively; one can only "talk around" it.

To begin with, it seems unlikely that guilt is the dominant anxiety in our culture. While specific forms of guilt naturally exist and may even be said to be common, guilt as a form of spiritual anxiety as distinct from regret or shame in relation to explicit causes does not frequently find its way into either art or public discourse in our context. To attempt to teach the *Confessions* of Augustine to a class of contemporary university students is to encounter a wall of noncomprehension: why would anyone feel such abysmal remorse over the remembered stealing of a pear, or even promiscuous sexuality? In the realm of public morality, nothing is more objectionable than the suggestion that someone may be "trying to lay a guilt-trip" on (for example) middle-class people by telling them about poverty in Central America and the Caribbean.

In the lives of generations still present in our midst, though disappearing, such matters as divorce, bankruptcy, abortion, indebtedness, deception uncovered, and the like could be expected to produce feigned if not genuine guilt. The later generations that have been indoctrinated by popular and semiprofessional forms of psychology have been conditioned to regard such guilt as an antiquated and unhelpful response to human behavior. For many, *all* behavior is explicable without any recourse to the subject of guilt. Psychological reasons can be found for every type of conduct, including, of course, belief. Given the relativization of morality and its replacement (if at all) by "values," there is for many of our contemporaries no standard of acceptable or normative behavior over against which one might sometimes experience even the moderate guilt of the transgressor. Without limits, transgression is an empty category. Our pluralism is not only a pluralism of religion, it is also—and more so—a pluralism of ethics. Morality by consensus—values-morality—may result in the alienation of those who stand outside the majority culture, but it can hardly produce genuine guilt.

More significantly, the attempt of Christians to move beyond private to social forms of guilt (an attempt that must be made by any serious Christian faith today) is hampered by a fatalism with respect to change. I refer not to the fatalism of the oppressed but of the oppressors. Many good and sensitive people in our society recognize that there is justice in the claims of the underdeveloped and undeveloped peoples that our "developed" world is preventing them from achieving even a modicum of human dignity and freedom. The liberal mind of our dominant culture is not given over wholly to crass survivalism. It would truly like to see all people prosperous and happy. It turns away from frank revelations of inconceivable degradation, which is the lot of millions of human beings today, and it is capable of expressing indignation over the exploitation of the animal kingdom and the spoliation of nature.

But the incipient guilt that these revelations (now part of the daily media diet of all North Americans) may inspire in some is quickly countered by another, stronger mentality. This latter is what I mean by the fatalism of the oppressor. It is an attitudinal mechanism that immediately squelches our twinges of guilt by assuring us that the inequality of the world and the exploitation of other species and resources are inevitabilities. It is "the way the cookie crumbles." Since "the cookie" has so conveniently crumbled to the advantage of the rich, we are highly unlikely to protest against this fate and even less likely to counter it by allowing the incipient guilt concerning the poor to do its proper work.

Here and there, it is still possible for those who are skillful at constructive accusation to effect changes in some among the rich peoples of the northern hemisphere, and this skill should usually be fostered by those of us who profess the prophetic faith of the Christ. But I think that this cannot be the main route to be taken in our search for a meaningful soteriology. What most people in our context need to be saved from is not guilt but the fatalism, apathy, and "covert nihilism" (Thielicke) that allow us so quickly to repress whatever pale reminiscences of shame we feel.

Guilt when it is religiously significant presupposes purpose. Martin Luther felt terrible guilt because he sensed the presence of One before whom he stood accused. *Coram Deo:* Before God, before One who had a definite plan and purpose for his existence, Luther could not feel just, righteous—authentic. Existential guilt, which is the only legitimate background anxiety for the soteriology of substitutionary sacrifice, is the guilt of those who have some prior intimation of the authenticity that is being thwarted by their behavior, the essence that is being contradicted by their existence.

But what if one cannot feel, even tentatively, the presence of purpose, let alone a Purposer? What if the sense of randomness has swallowed up the remnants of the teleological impulse? If the universe is utterly indifferent to our human pursuits, as Camus claimed, then guilt may be nothing more than a vestige of our teleological past. Those for whom that past still bears some weight may find in the soteriology of Anselm and his school a little respite from that "great weight of sin." But few, I suspect, of our contemporaries are still sufficiently in touch with that past to find even a formal point of contact with this soteriological convention.

If even at the level of anthropological analysis that tradition encounters serious limitations, what must be said of its exposition of the salvific answer to the human predicament? A Christ who substitutes himself or is substituted for the guilty and condemned seems to most of our contemporaries, I suspect, not only a remote and improbable notion, but repulsive as well.[27] The strangeness of this idea is due in considerable measure to the fact that few of us today seem capable of knowing the depths of guilt that cry out for help in the face of an intolerable burden. Even intellectually, however, it is hard for the contemporary mind to grasp the intelligibility of the substitutionary idea: How could the substitution of one man's innocence and righteousness make amends for the guilt of all the others?

Here we come face-to-face with the thoroughly contextual character of this soteriology: The sacrificial theory came to be and was operative within a sociohistorical milieu where substitution and exchange were part of life. In the feudal society that was the context of Anselm of Canterbury, and still in a revised form in Calvin's society as well, substitutionary exchange was practiced at every level: the exchange of military protection for labor and a portion of one's crops; the exchange of goods for serfs, or serfs for other serfs; the exchange of daughters and sons for lordly favors; the exchange of freedom for the remission of crime, and so on. Anselm's soteriology of sacrificial substitution was in short thoroughly conditioned by the specifics of his milieu; and, apart from extraordinary examples, usually drawn from the literature and history of the past, it is no longer supported by the realities of our context. It can only seem to most contemporaries an artificial, forced, and formulary sort of thing—a *religious* idea, having no existential ties with life as we know it.

To most of those who learn the theory, even if they also learn to supplement it through the use of more recent psychological insights (as we did in the historical discussion of the theory), the idea of a God who substitutes his innocent son for an indeterminate number of guilty men and women is literally a fantastic notion. Not only does it present the spectacle of a deity that only sadomasochists could learn to appreciate (as Abelard already felt), but it offers as salvation an act of transfer that is psychically and rationally almost impossible for the modern mind to grasp.

I seriously doubt that our contemporaries can be moved by this soteriology, particularly in its classical expressions. If it still seems exceptionally alive in North American religious conservativism, this must be attributed, I suspect, either to skillful "updating" or (which is more likely) to extraneous causes. By the latter I refer to the religious conditioning that is effectively undertaken in many evangelical circles. In these circles, ideas do not have to sway the mind.

---

27. A popular Canadian Christian journalist speaks for many when he writes: "Perhaps I am lacking in piety or some basic instinct, but I know I am not alone in finding the idea of Jesus' death as atonement for the sins of all humanity on one level bewildering and on the other morally repugnant. Jesus never to my knowledge said anything to indicate that forgiveness from God could only be granted *after* or *because of* the cross. . . . This theory is not only crude but immoral." (Tom Harpur, *For Christ's Sake* [Toronto: Oxford Univ. Press, 1986], 75–76.)

It is not what is professed there but the technology of profession that achieves the aimed-for conversion. Playing upon the high degree of personal guilt that is constantly nurtured in fundamentalist contexts, and relying upon a millennium of formulary soteriology drastically reduced to slogans and incantations, the evangelist easily brings souls to the altar without any help from hard thinking. But the "success" of this religion by no means demonstrates the continuing relevance of the Latin atonement theology; it only illustrates the power of a well-honed religious technique within pockets of our society that are most successful in resisting the real questions that historical providence is putting to us.

Let me be quite clear: I do not think that any responsible theology will be ready to discard the whole Anselmic-Calvinist atonement tradition. But unless we are prepared to wonder whether this same tradition in its reduced forms may not be one of the most potent religious forces preventing Christians on this continent from facing the real questions, we shall not be able to recover from this soteriological tradition the dimensions of it that can and should inform our whole message. A religion offering salvation to the guilty within First World contexts today may be one of the most effective betrayals of Jesus Christ conceivable. The path to our salvation is far narrower than that. It will deny salvation to the globally guilty and cause us to confront the shallowness and pettiness of our guilt feelings; and it will carry us into dark places of the soul and of the body politic that are far more shattering to spiritual smugness than the ritualized recitations of sin that are wrung from overfed and self-indulgent penitents exhibiting their "sincerity" in front of the television cameras. Jesus Christ, the Savior, has a more honest work to do with such human beings as we than to forgive us our peccadillos and set us back onto the road of self-satisfied and frequently bigoted Protestant piety.

34.4. Liberation of Oppressors?   The impact of liberation theologies in Latin American and other contexts, including certain segments of our own society, has revived in the church at large an openness to the soteriology of rescue. While it is not always recognized that liberationism is able to call upon this ancient tradition, the spirituality to which it has provided a new access is close to that which we have seen to have been at work in the formation of the ransom soteriology of old. In fact, wherever human beings are most conscious of their oppression by seen or unseen forces, the most obvious and even necessary manner in which the gospel will be experienced by or communicated to them is through some form of liberation. The surprising thing is not that liberation theology (under various names) has arisen in Third World and other contexts of oppression today, but that it did not arise earlier.

The tardiness of its appearance demonstrates an important aspect of the thesis that I am advancing here, namely the power of established soteriological doctrine to stifle and inhibit the development of indigenous theological reflection. That the traditional Western (Latin) atonement theology and its ritualistic accompaniments were able to dominate the piety of (for example) South and Central American Catholicism, despite the fact that the most conspicuous public anxiety in those contexts was far closer to the anxiety of fate and death than to that of guilt and condemnation, provides a graphic illustration of the entrenchment of Anselmic doctrine. When a whole populace has been conditioned to believe that the sin for which atonement has to be made is personal guilt, it requires a very persuasive countervailing doctrine to effect a theology more in keeping with reality. Perhaps such a change could not have come about without the aid of a powerful secular ideology (Marxism) and an effective pedagogical program of "conscientization" (Paolo Friere). Similar statements would have to be made about the evolution of Afro-American and feminist theologies in North America.

The consequence of this extensive and many-sided recovery of the theme of Christ as Liberator is that the Christian movement throughout the world has been stirred to explore this neglected tradition. The fact that this recovery has been accompanied by a weakening of both of the other types of atonement theology has rendered the rescue type all the more interesting to many. First World—and especially North American—Christians, long since dissatisfied with substitutionary Christology and too hard-headed to be moved by the moral influence theory, have been quick to apply new versions of the *Christus Victor* soteriology to specific contexts of oppression in our own situation.

It is my impression, however, that this approach is not satisfactory in our context, especially if it is understood to be an appropriate soteriological response to the situation of the dominant (largely white, middle-class) culture in North America. I would qualify this judgment in three ways.

First, as with both of the other types, the denial of the contextual appropriateness of a theory does not mean that it is dispensable. The disciple community must continue to reflect upon and struggle with its whole received tradition precisely because it is oriented toward the present and impending future. History moves quickly, and contexts change. No one knows what "usable past" will have to be drawn upon tomorrow. The tradition that I have named here the soteriology of rescue contains permanently true elements. As the anxiety of fate and death is a perennial anxiety of the human condition, so a redemption theology which speaks to that anxiety will always be in some way pertinent. No humanity, under the conditions of existence, is perfectly free, is not oppressed by something greater than the personal or collective will. To be human is to be bound—if not dramatically and obviously, then subtly; if not by an identifiable oppressor, then by elusive structures or systems; if not by clear addictions or neuroses, then by ambiguous motives, selfish concern and ambition, manipulative dealings with others, dark urges of psychic or sexual punishment. There is no end to the "principalities and powers" by which human beings may be enslaved. The variety and subtlety of such forces may be more extensive in our complex global society than they were at the time of the early theologians who first devised this atonement theology. Because of this, the liberating Christ is in some sense always a necessary dimension of gospel.

Second, it must be understood that this soteriological tradition is appropriate, in contemporary modes, for particular segments within our society. We recognized in our discussion of the nature of context in the first volume that there are contexts within contexts. What may be appropriate for the dominant culture of a society may be quite inappropriate for minorities within that society, and vice versa.

It is especially necessary for Christians in the North American context to come to a better understanding of what is involved here. Dominant cultures, which continue to constitute the once-mainline churches of the United States and Canada, spawn and sustain their own minorities—the excluded ones, the "different" ones, whose outsider status is guaranteed by the dominance of the majority culture. There can be no single Christian message in such a situation. What may or should be confessed as gospel in the context of oppressed minorities, when it is appropriated as gospel by the oppressing majority not only fails to engage the real condition of the latter but positively confirms them in their attitudes toward their minorities. A theology of liberation announced as *the* Christian message in white middle-class congregations in North America must be questioned in principle even if it is, in practice, sensitively and imaginatively done. At the same time, there are minorities within our cities and towns, and in some cases within our congregations, for whom some articulation of the liberation theme is mandatory.

It is a rudimentary assumption of this work that minorities not only have the right and duty to pursue their profession and confession of the faith in ways appropriate to their own particularity, but also that the larger Christian community must provide a willing and receptive forum for them to do so. The biblical priority is clear on this point: those who are "last" within the kingdoms of this world will be "first" in the divine kingdom, which is being anticipated within the church. The attitude that struggles against the testimony of Christian minorities—testimony that necessarily calls into question the Christian majority in North America—is not only at fault morally; it is delinquent in its perception of the gospel and of the nature of the community of truth that Jesus Christ creates.

Third, the soteriological tradition appropriate to minorities, which will usually be heavily informed by the theme of liberation precisely because of their minority status, is not usually appropriate to majorities; and the present work is addressed primarily to those churches that, though they are not themselves majorities any longer, still represent the dominant culture of these northern nations. What I find questionable in the present fascination with liberation theology on the part of significant numbers of First World Christians generally is that it deflects attention away from the real *problematique* of our larger cultural context. Of course the need to master, to succeed, to dominate, to win—and in the process to oppress—can itself be regarded as a form of oppression. And so of course one may sometimes speak of a Christ who liberates oppressors from their need to oppress. But such a soteriology is not existentially right for the majority cultures of First World societies, including the Christians among them. It is in fact nothing but a subterfuge when it is pursued consistently and as though it were contextually appropriate.

Liberation is an appropriate metaphor for the work of the Christ where oppression is the real condition of those who are addressed. The condition of First World Christians whose economic, educational, vocational, and value identification is with the dominant middle classes of these societies is simply not one of oppression. When theology in North America takes up the theme of liberation, it is engaging in the old habit of the churches in this context of borrowing their theology ready-made from the struggles of others. The seminary or theological college which insists that its faculty and student body be representative of feminist, black, Hispanic, or other minorities is certainly to be commended. But if it then relies upon these minorities to provide for it, besides their own analysis and critique, a theology pertinent for the whole "mainstream" church, it has not yet begun to understand the meaning of contextuality in theology.

The context that has to be investigated—and investigated by those who are part of it, as well as those who in relation to it are outsiders—is the dominant culture of this continent, which is the cultural background of these mainstream denominations. In relation to this larger context, the minority contexts that are within it without being part of it may and must bring their critical insight to bear upon the analysis of it; and they will be able to do this in a unique and irreplaceable way because they are in various ways victimized by that culture. But when no imaginative analysis of the dominant culture comes from inside its own structures, pursuits, visions, and failures, depth of analysis can never be achieved. Each of the minorities will naturally and necessarily stress the aspects of the dominant culture by which they are themselves oppressed. They are prevented by their external status from entering deeply enough into the ethos and the positive aims that drive the majority culture to experience the failure, disillusionment, and deception that may be known, in a measure, only by those who have been identified with that ethos and those aims.

To exemplify: It is possible to learn from the indigenous peoples of North America that traditional forms of Christian faith are deficient because of their anthropocentrism. Unlike some Native American/Canadian religions, modern Christianity has neglected the extrahuman creation and reduced "nature" to raw material intended for human consumption and aggrandizement. It happens—perhaps with increasing regularity—that Christians of Euro-American descent are moved by this testimony of the indigenous peoples to engage in a critique of their own Christian culture. This sometimes is a useful and important exercise, and the whole Christian community benefits from the minority protest that informs it. But it is not enough to set over against traditional Christian doctrine and practice the thought and life-style emanating from another culture or cultus. If Christian attitudes toward nature are to be altered significantly, the doctrine and history that gave rise to existing attitudes must be entered into at depth, must be owned, must be understood anew from the perspective of the problems to which they have given rise. Only as the church experiences the admixture of good and evil in its own traditions of belief; only as it opens itself to the pain of discovering its own culpability, which is never just the guilt of "the fathers" but is also our own—only then will the work of critical theology be productive of genuine change.

The question arises whether this observation also applies to feminist or women's theology. Women's theology in most of its expressions pursues some variation on the theme of liberation from the oppression of a majority culture. Yet women do not represent a minority in the same manner as do native peoples, ethnic and racial groups, or gay and lesbian coalitions. The oppression of women is at the same time more subtle and more consequential for the whole society. Moreover, women for the most part participate in the majority culture, even though they have not been in a position heretofore to determine the course and character of that culture directly. These exceptional factors have important consequences for the question at hand. They mean, for one thing, that women are in a position both to understand the status of the victim and to explore, from within, the world view of the dominant culture. For this reason, their mission within the mainline Christian community is particularly important, and today it is not an optional matter for all serious forms of the disciple community to include and foster this dimension.

No theology, however, can afford to overlook its own potential misuses. It would be unfortunate if feminist theology allowed itself too uncritically to analyze societal and ecclesiastical structures from the side of the victim—particularly the victimization of women—and made too little use of its participation in the majority culture, which gives it the unique possibility of seeing from the inside how apparently good and positive goals may create terrible problems for others who are outside the limits of the society that dreams those particular dreams. Except in the case of women who are excluded from the dominant culture for reasons other than their gender, a feminist critique of the ruling classes in North America and the West generally must always be in part self-criticism. When it becomes too one-sidedly accusatory—that is, when it exempts itself from all the negativities it ascribes to patriarchy—it loses its potential for prophetic depth. Fortunately, this earlier and perhaps necessary stage in Christian feminism is now challenged within the women's movement itself to avoid typologies that effectively exempt women from the society they critique and in the process diminish the strength and credibility of their criticism.[28]

To conclude: Like the soteriologies of sacrifice and demonstration, that of rescue or liberation must continue to inform the theological reflection of the church, as it speaks in various ways to minorities within the North American context as to other oppressed peoples in the world. But it does not, in my opinion, engage the dominant culture and the churches whose membership still draws largely upon that culture. The faithful community of Christ's disciples in North America today must explore another path if it is to discover in what way Jesus Christ may be known to us as savior.

34.5. Identifying the Question to Which the Cross Responds. Summarizing these reflections on the received traditions of atonement and their pertinence to the dominant culture that is our context, we may say that while each of them still speaks to dimensions of our experience, none goes to the heart of the matter. If we recall the three anxiety types named by Tillich in *The Courage to Be,* we are helped to understand why none of these inherited theories addresses us directly. The anxiety of fate and death, in response to which the ransom or rescue theory of Christ's work evolved, can be found among us still, particularly among segments of our society that have been marginalized by economic, racial, ethnic, gender, and other realities, but it is not our primary anxiety. The anxiety of guilt and condemnation that was the existential (if unconscious) background of the sacrificial theory of Christ's work is likewise a part of our experience, individually and corporately, but it could hardly be counted the dominant anxiety of our context.

We are in agreement with Tillich that the dominant anxiety of our culture is the third, the anxiety of meaninglessness and despair. But, as we have been at some pains to show in the first volume, unlike the European existentialist expressions of this anxiety that constituted the basis of Tillich's cultural analysis, the North American mode of living out of this anxiety is more complex on account of the enormous difficulty that we have in expressing it.

The point is: None of the received traditions of atonement addresses this anxiety satisfactorily. They may do so tangentially, but not in the manner of encounter. That is, they do not engage the *problematique* of our dominant culture but tend, instead, to deflect attention away from its core by identifying our dilemma with some of its consequences. Almost any of us can find evidence within our lives of the three conditions assumed by these soteriological types; and therefore if any of the three is skillfully enough presented, it can impress

---

28. See Wendy Farley, *Tragic Vision and Divine Compassion: A Contemporary Theodicy* (Louisville: Westminster/John Knox Press, 1990), 151–52; also Daphne Hampson, *Theology and Feminism* (Oxford: Basil Blackwell, 1990), 170 and elsewhere.

at least some in our midst. But in the process the real question of our corporate existence will have been transmuted and suppressed. For as a people we are not first and foremost either enslaved, guilty, or unloved; we are lost. We do not believe deeply anymore in the goals that we still announce rhetorically or the "values" that we try to retain and inculcate. We are no longer motivated by the high vision that brought us into being as a people. We have no more great expectations.

Most of the time, most of us are completely silent about this state, but our individual and corporate pursuits betray us constantly. Our religious pursuits betray us perhaps more pathetically than anything else. To deflect attention away from our disillusionment and lostness, we will gladly subscribe to even the most archaic expressions of sacrificial atonement theories. If we can continue to believe that our problem is guilt, we will not have to face up to the more complicated question with which historical providence has confronted us: whether the human enterprise has any purpose.

Is there a soteriology for those who are in this sense lost? Can the gospel of the cross address those who suspect that life is meaningless beyond the goals and values that we arbitrarily impose upon it—who suspect this yet dare not suspect it?

In times past, Christians have professed a faith that could address the enslaved (Christ sets you free), the guilty (You are forgiven), and the unloved (God loves you unconditionally). Each of these summations of the kerygma continues to have its own necessity and its own appeal, for human life is perennially challenged by bondage, guilt, and the feeling of nonacceptance. But beneath all the negations to which, in the interplay of their witness, these atonement traditions speak, there is a great negation which, unless it is itself in some measure negated, has the effect of canceling the positive responses to all the attendant negations. It has surfaced at various points in the history of the race, and it has never been without its individual amanuenses; but in our time and place it has become something very public, despite—or perhaps because of—its nonacknowledgment. Koheleth long ago gave it a name. He called this great negation "vanity." Is it possible to articulate a soteriology that engages and may even negate *that* negation? And which may do so, not only in its overt but in its covert expression?

This must be the attempt of our final chapter.

35. Before Christology—Jesus, the Christ

35.1. The Need for a New *Imago Christi*.   In discussing the tendency of historical Christian thought to permit the divinity principle in Christology to overwhelm the real humanity of Jesus, we advanced the thesis that when this occurs the personhood of the one whom the newer Testament places at the center of its testimony to the love of God tends to be replaced by impersonal theory: instead of Jesus, Christology. It is this hypothesis that we must now expand in our final critical commentary in the chapter.

The point of departure for the faith of the first disciple community is clear: it is the memory of Jesus, enlivened and enlightened by what the community considered the decisive event in its formation as *koinonia,* the advent of the divine Spirit. The Spirit does not bring new information, however. The experience of the upper room enlivens and enlightens precisely the previous experience of this community, its experience of Jesus. After the fact, the disciple community is enabled to "see" Jesus in a way that it could not see him before, while he was still present physically. The faith, discourse, prayer, planning, thinking, and activity of the community created at Pentecost unfold themselves as response to the newly felt spiritual presence of the one who is no longer present bodily.

Before Christology there was Jesus Christ—or, to be more precise, there was Jesus, whom the community learned to profess and confess as the Christ. The Christian movement did not begin with a Christology—*any* Christology; it began with this person, remembered and contemplated on the strength of his continuing presence through the Spirit. That a christological reflection very soon, perhaps almost immediately, came to be is no more surprising than that a family, following the death of one of its members, will rehearse in its thought and conversation aspects of the deceased person's character, statements, and actions.

With this we do not mean to insinuate that Christology is inherently questionable. What is questionable is when this necessary consideration of the dialogue about the person called Jesus becomes detached from any recognition of his real and ineffable personhood. What is questionable is when christological reflection becomes christological speculation and achieves a life of its own. What is questionable is when the encounter quality of the formative experience is lost and belief, instead of being belief *in* or *through* the person who is remembered and spiritually present, becomes belief *concerning* this person. In short, what is questionable is the substitution of dogma for person.

Before Christology there was Jesus, called the Christ. And every reformation of the disciple community involves and must involve the rediscovery of the person, who in the interim has been obscured by theory concerning him. The monastic movement, the Augustinian renewal, the Christian mysticism of the late Middle Ages, the Reformation of the sixteenth century, nineteenth-century liberal Protestantism, neoorthodoxy, liberation theologies of our own time—all these represent rediscoveries of the living Christ behind the Christ of dogmatic convention and popular piety.

As we have already noticed, this same rediscovery was particularly prominent with the liberal movement. It would even be possible to say that the attempt to "see Jesus" was at the heart of this movement, uniting dimensions of the movement as diverse as the more individualistic and the more collectivistic expressions of liberalism. Jesus, characterized not only by liberal theology but in descriptive prose, art, and symbol, was the great inspirer of this colossal attempt of Western Protestantism to move beyond what it regarded as the static and outmoded dogmatism of orthodoxy.

The attempt failed, as we have already noted. It failed because it incorporated into its Jesus too uncritically—almost naively—the assumptions and values of the age, assumptions and values that were soon to be contradicted, and brutally, by a succeeding age. But was the procedure wrong as well as its application by the liberal thinkers and activists?

Before we respond to this question, we must reconsider what came to replace the liberal attempt to depict Jesus alive and compelling. Since the appearance of Albert Schweitzer's *The Quest for the Historical Jesus* (1906) and Karl Barth's *Römerbrief* (1918), the theological discourse of Western Christendom has been inspired, not by "the life of Jesus," but by strong, imaginative, critically intelligent, biblically based, historically knowledgeable and insightful theology.

Only persons who are insufficiently informed or innately prejudiced against neoorthodoxy and the movements that it, in turn, spawned, will want to assess this relatively lengthy period in recent Christianity in a one-sidedly negative manner. It was surely necessary, in the light of the inadequacy even of the best of liberalism, to comprehend and address a world that had taken directions almost entirely discontinuous with the expectations of modernity. Liberalism had failed to apply to the (modern) present the same critical acumen that it had brought to bear upon the past. It had capitulated, often without even recognizing it, to assumptions about human goodness, historical progress, technological genius, and the like that were present in the society at large. Naively, it had presented Jesus as a model of humanity all too acceptable to the optimistic spirit of the age; so that when that spirit was countered by realities that did not corroborate its positive thinking, the liberal Jesus himself was shown up as being naive, lacking in realism, sentimental, and incapable of understanding the dark events that were occurring as Reinhold Niebuhr finished delivering his Gifford Lectures in Scotland (1939). It was entirely necessary for responsible Christian thought to enter a period of critical and corrective doctrinal reconstruction, to distinguish the Christ testified to by Scripture and tradition from the Jesus who had become carrier of the ideals of an epoch.

We ought to pause here to notice something that may be generally instructive in theological work. It is possible that the church's endeavor to "see Jesus"—that is, to fashion and live with images of the Christ—is perennially in danger of adapting itself too uncritically to the present. The need to have "Jesus with a human face" leaves the disciple community vulnerable to those images of the human that are most influential in a given context; a Jesus wholly other than the humanity that has established itself as being desirable or at least viable in that context will, as we have seen, hardly achieve sufficient proximity to people to seem credibly human. Yet precisely in their desire to achieve such proximity, Christians have often sacrificed the otherness of Jesus altogether. Their image of the Christ turns out to be a self-image, or a type of the humanity they hope to project. There is no better modern illustration of this than the laughing Christ who was portrayed on the posters of the youth culture of the 1960s and '70s. This Bacchic representation of Jesus had considerable appeal to the "Age of Aquarius," for it legitimated many of the permissive life-styles of that era. It challenged little or nothing that was au courant ("with it!") in that context—and much about that era, as we now know, *ought* to have been challenged by a responsible and faithful Christianity.

It is altogether likely, therefore, that the corrective "science," the science of dogma, must always be prepared to critique the images of the Christ operative in the Christian and human community: to demonstrate their discrepancy with respect to the authoritative sources of the faith; to reflect critically on the manner in which they function, whatever the intentions of their formulators may be; to be vigilant with regard to the segments of society whom they ignore, or intimidate, or oppress; above all, to remind the church that in spite of its need for such images, the images that it actually creates will always be inadequate and, when they draw too much attention to themselves, dangerous. The living Christ defies every attempt of ours to image him. He remains a mystery; he remains the stranger of Galilee; he remains person; he remains "Thou"— and this is as much part of his humanity as of his divinity, for it belongs to the humanity of all of us. Critical theology with respect to Jesus Christ is as indispensable as critical theology with respect to God and creaturely being.

But if it is true that dogma in this sense is a necessary corrective science, it is by the same token true that it is not sufficient in itself. Correction presupposes that there is something to correct. This something, in the case of Jesus Christ, is the church's image of the Christ; and that image must be portrayed also by theology. Indeed, when the theological servants of the church leave the imaging of the Christ to other elements within the Christian and human community—the arts, liturgists, poets and hymn-writers, story-tellers, and (almost the most powerful) those who testify personally to their encounter with the Christ—they ought not to be surprised if the results are (from the perspective of scholarship) questionable.

It could be said, in my view, that serious theological and biblical work during the past half century, especially in North America, has neglected this whole dimension of its task. It has (perhaps naturally and necessarily) concentrated almost exclusively on the corrective side, often too narrowly conceived, and has limited its constructive work to the production of doctrine. Sometimes the doctrine has been of a recognizable and conventional nature; sometimes it has been self-consciously avant garde and philosophically or ideologically nuanced. But in either case the theological enterprise has in a marked way separated itself from the community of belief. It is in fact a highly academic affair, and touches the life of the church only tangentially. Its ideas are sometimes stimulating, but it has done little or nothing to give Jesus a human face.

Ought we not to wonder, at this juncture, whether the perhaps-better Christologies that may have emerged through this dogmatic-scholarly winnowing process are not profoundly inept as a core of belief? Faith (and not only the faith of "ordinary Christians" but the faith of the theologians and biblical scholars, too) needs to *see* Jesus; and it is not sufficient for it to entertain all kinds of fascinating, dialectically exciting ideas about Jesus Christ. Before Christology there was Jesus, called by faith the Christ *because* faith was grasped by something in and around this person which elicited from it that confession. What we need today, I suggest, is not more Christology but a new *imago Christi*.

35.2. Rediscovering the Jesus of the Scriptures.   Images of the Christ do not—must not be allowed to—emerge out of sheer speculation. There will always be a subjective element in the attempt of the disciple community to "see Jesus" because, as we have maintained throughout these reflections, what faith sees in Jesus is *Soter* (Savior), and this means that in seeing Jesus we also see ourselves in another light. Particularly, we see that within ourselves in relation to which salvation is needed. Our own perceived need, both as individuals and as cultures, will therefore always color our perception of Jesus.

But the formulation of appropriate images of the Christ is not a case of demand and supply. The revelatory basis of Christian faith means that Jesus, as the concrete particularity through whom faith encounters ultimacy, participates in that mystery and Self-determination that belong to the One whose name means, "I am who I am." Not only will Jesus be for us many things that we did not anticipate and (probably) would prefer not to encounter, but in seeing him we, like the original disciples, will also discover needs that we did not know we had, needs that we have perhaps spent a lifetime erasing from our consciousness.

This revelatory basis of the church's *imago Christi* is to be sustained, according to the best of our received traditions, by four referents that condition and limit the subjective factor that is part of the process of "seeing Jesus": (1) the biblical testimony to the historical Jesus; (2) the testimony of the Holy Spirit; (3) the testing of truth that occurs within the dialogue of the community of faith; and (4) the encounter with the incognito Christ who meets us in the world, and especially among those who suffer. Each of these constitutes a source of faith's ongoing perception of the Savior, and each exercises an ongoing critique of the *pictura Jesu* that dominates in settled, institutionalized forms of the church. In concluding this critical chapter of Christology, we shall think briefly of these four constitutive elements of the image of the Christ, and in this way prepare for the constructive statement to be offered in the final chapter.

We begin by turning once again to the scriptural witness to Jesus. This is where all Christology that intends to be faithful to the *sola Scriptura* of the Reformation must begin, and there is perhaps no branch of the ecumenical church that is more in need of such a beginning today than is Protestantism. For the impression is far too easily maintained with this camp, with its deliberate emphasis upon the Bible, that its dearly held preconceptions about the Christ are true because they are (naturally) "biblical." It is too little realized that within the broadly Protestant fold, "biblical" regularly stands for long-established conventions that, while they might have had their origins in Scripture, have become so stylized and sterile that they no longer challenge the church but may be treated as possessions—familiar patterns of belief so predictable as to contain no element either of surprise, offense, or wonder.

Thus Jesus, for perhaps the vast majority of Euro-American Protestants in North America, is a good, mild-mannered, sexless, kindly but serious, nonpolitical male of indeterminate age, who counsels devotion to God, evenness of temper, patient acceptance of difficult experiences, courtesy in one's dealings with others, obedience to those in authority, and resignation with cheerfulness in the face of sickness and death. This Jesus, in short, looks much like a white Anglo-Saxon Protestant, also in his implicit but decisive renunciation of any Jewish traits, and he behaves in a way that is quite unlikely to throw into question any of the mores, taboos, and values governing mainstream culture. And those who carry about such a mental image of the Christ can do so, being Protestants, in the firm belief that it is entirely biblical.

What is at fault here is not only a fundamental ignorance of the newer and older testaments (we have become biblically illiterate) but a total misconception of the nature of scriptural authority. Considering widely held preconceptions of Jesus that are, if not precisely equivalent to the above characterization, certainly similar to it, one is able to recognize elements of conservative and liberal Christologies derived from the biblical and theological reflections of past generations. Powerful images of the Christ gleaned from the religious struggles of the distant and nearer past become entrenched, simplified, sloganized, and rendered basically harmless by pious and secular usage over time. The struggles that gave rise to aspects of these familiar images (for example, the "gentle Jesus, meek and mild," which was originally a polemic against the stern and unbending Jesus of a severe orthodoxy) are lost in the mists of history, and what remains are the positive aspects, made innocuous by their disengagement from the ideas and practices they originally intended to challenge or negate.

The authority of the Scriptures for faith, as we have argued in the first volume, is not to be understood as the scriptural guarantee of established religious conventions. On the contrary, it is part of the struggle of prophetic faith against the habit of all "religious" authority of sanctifying entrenched conventions of belief and practice. The Bible is to be studied and listened to continuously, and never under the assumption that its primary function in the life of the community of faith will be to confirm and strengthen religious beliefs and customs that are already axiomatic. The *sola Scriptura* is for classical Protestantism primarily a critical principle, intended to offset the danger (of which the reformers were well aware) that truths once grasped would be hallowed into lifeless theorems and thus, in effect, reconfirm the validity of ecclesiastical and other authorities. Bonhoeffer's criticism of American Protestant Christianity is as pertinent today as when he wrote it fifty years ago:

> American theology and the American church as a whole have never been able to understand the meaning of "criticism" by the Word of God and all that signifies. Right to the last they do not understand that God's "criticism" touches even religion, the Christianity of the churches and the sanctification of Christians, and that God has founded his church beyond religion and beyond ethics.[29]

The classical (not fundamentalist) Protestant principle of *sola Scriptura,* which assumes that the Bible is the primary witness to God's living, reforming Word, serves the ongoing reformation (*semper reformanda*) of the church by calling in question our genuine apprehension of truth and thus preventing us from imagining that truth is our possession. The Word of Truth lives. It cannot be possessed. It can only be lived with.

And Jesus said, "I *am* . . . the truth."

Not through Bible study alone is the truth that Jesus "is" grasped by the community of discipleship, but so far as the Scriptures are concerned in this process the procedure is rather clear: the disciple community must subject itself always anew, every day, in every new context, to the scriptural testimony to this one who is concretely our entree to universal truth. We must in a real sense be prepared to sacrifice the Jesus of our fondly held conventions and biases to the one who emerges through these words as they are illumined by the Spirit within the context of the Body as it tries to perform its mission in the world.

Today the kind of Protestant Jesus characterized earlier as containing no element of challenge is called into question in ways that are almost too dramatic and unsettling for most First World Protestants, and there is a consequent and understandable tendency to set the biblical Jesus over against all the alternative images of the Christ that emanate from feminist, African American, Hispanic American, Native Amer-Canadian, and other contexts. But in fact we are seeing

---

29. "Protestantism without Reformation," in John de Gruchy, *Dietrich Bonhoeffer: Witness to Jesus Christ* (London: Collins, 1987), 216.

that these alternative images often *can* claim biblical warrant, and we are forced to recognize that the Jesus of our conventions is at least as culturally conditioned as any of the alternatives. This situation is particularly evocative of a new openness to the Jesus to whom Scripture bears witness, and who transcends all of our predispositions. The new *imago Christi* that may eventually emerge and (for a time) serve God's purposes in the world will be a consequence of this unsettling; therefore, however uncomfortable it may be to live without a fixed image of the Christ at present, we may learn to consider our discomfort a necessary stage on the way to a picture of Christ that may be more real, because more alive, than either the christological theory of the dogmaticians or the "Jesuology" of Christian pietism.

35.3. "The Spirit Will Lead You into All Truth Concerning Me." In the discussion of the Trinity we argued that there are good reasons why an "ungrounded" Spirit must be caused again and again to conform its testimony to the One who has "come in the flesh" (1 John 4:1ff.). Spiritualistic religion not only robs the community of faith of its "concrete universal" (Tillich), but it inevitably results in the fragmentation both of truth and the community that is grasped by the quest for truth's unity. A pneumatology that is not christologically shaped and rooted becomes the source of religion that, while it may be enthusiastic enough, can be both humanly divisive and productive of a spiritualism no longer rooted in God's love for this world.

It is equally true, however, that devotion to the second person of the Trinity can breed rank distortions of the faith. And it is in fact of the essence of these distortions that they substitute doctrine for life, dogma for experience, theology for relationship with God. Jesus Christ will only live for us, who are not his historical contemporaries, if he is made lively by the one whom the Nicene Creed wisely described as "the Lord and Giver of Life."

Nothing is more threatening to established religion than the Holy Spirit. Already prior to the political establishment of Christianity, the Spirit presented problems for evolving Christianity (for example, Montanism); but with the establishment spiritualistic faith became perhaps the primary enemy of Christendom. The story of the religion of the Spirit within the church is a story of persecution. Nothing by way of heresy has ever been so mercilessly extinguished as the spiritualistic movements of the twelfth and thirteenth centuries, especially the Cathari and the Waldenses. In Bohemia, loyal Catholics and moderate reforming elements joined forces to extinguish the Taborites, and in northern Germany Catholics and Protestants, themselves at enmity, recognized in the Anabaptists a yet greater enemy and found it possible to cooperate in their destruction, especially at Münster, Westphalia.

In our own context as well, spiritualized Christianity, as found in the Pentecostal movement and its various offshoots, has been the subject of almost

487

irrational suspicion and ridicule. No one in my youth was more vilified than the "Holy Rollers" (Pentecostals), who greatly upset not only the religious respectability of our village but constituted an affront to the rustic decorum honored by that rural society. Anglo-Saxon Christianity has perhaps been particularly unnerved by the lingering tendency of religion to burst the bonds of respectability and become ecstatic.

The consequence of this history is that the Holy Spirit is not only the most neglected doctrine of Christendom but the most neglected person of the Trinity. Religion has been with us a matter of the head and the hands— particularly, among North American liberal Protestants, the latter; the heart has been consistently suspect.

But there can be no renewal of the living Christ in the church without a renewal of faith's recognition of and possession by the Holy Spirit. The real problems attendant upon this exposure to spiritual energy must be risked if "dead Christendom" is to be given some measure of new life.

The *testimonium Spiritus sancti internum* is inseparable from the other three factors, named in this discussion, that contribute to the formation of the image of Christ in the disciple community. Spiritualistic religion as a religious phenomenon usually tries to isolate the Spirit and spiritual experience from ordinary experience, including that of exegetical and theological work. To be grasped by the Holy Spirit in this type of religion means to be lifted out of the world of everyday reality and exposed to something unnameable and fantastic.

But we are not evoking spiritualistic religious practice and method here. The divine Spirit in whose work we are interested is a transcendent dimension and quality of worldly, historical life, distinguishable in terms of its consequences for faith from ordinary experience, yet found within and under the conditions of life as it is lived from day to day. We may think of the Holy Spirit as that extraordinary dimension of the ordinary, which illuminates and integrates the disparate elements of our life and thought and creates within us the strong and grateful impression that our existence is enfolded in a meaning that, for the present, we can only glimpse occasionally. For Christians, this meaning is given expression and concreteness in the sense of the presence of Jesus, whom the Spirit makes contemporary to us as we expose ourselves to the historic testimony to him, to the community that perpetuates his memory and work, and to the world for whose future he gave up his own. The Holy Spirit is thus not, for Christian faith, one formative factor among others but the creative power that makes of the scriptural, ecclesiastical, and world-experiential fragments of our life a whole that is sufficiently integrated to function as our source of purpose and guidance.

Constantinian religion, or the religion of culture, has consistently resisted this creative force, because order and the institutions that retain order in society always fear the chaotic potential that is necessarily present within creative energy. We have spoken, however, in the first volume, about the end of the Constantinian era. While this end is by no means uniformly disclosed among us, its effects are already everywhere present. One of these effects is the new openness to "spirituality." By this term, a great many uncertain and amorphous things seem to be intended; yet the reality to which it points contains at least the prospect of a form of discipleship that is ready to regard the Spirit as more than a silent partner in the Trinity.[30] Constantinian religion is and must be a religion of the letter, for its whole function is the regulation of those aspects of humanity and society that are not directly controllable by secular authority. Post-Constantinian Christianity may become, what in the beginning and at certain times and places throughout its history the Christian movement has been: a religion of the Spirit. The hope for a new and living image of the Christ is largely inspired by this emergent freedom of a faith that is being relieved of its civil office and therefore may become newly conscious of the Lord whose "body" it is. As the Christian movement is distanced from Caesar, the image of Christ becomes, not only more needful for its life, but more viable as well.

35.4. The Body and the Head. The *imago Christi* always in some sense signifies a personal experience of and relation to the one called by the tradition Lord and Savior, for each individual has his or her own imaginative faculties, as well as his or her unique biography. Biblical faith does not despise the concern for the individual in the way that ideological communism has done. Though it greatly distrusts the corruption of individuality that has accompanied capitalism, it honors the uniqueness of persons and therefore recognizes that the personal element will be present in all aspects of faith, including the imaging of the Christ.

It is a matter of unwarranted oppression of the most subtle sort when religious bodies insist upon a single *imago Christi* as if it were accessible to all and pertinent to all. As the various sexual, racial, economic, and other communities of concern within the ecumenical Christian movement have reminded us for decades, it is one of the most effective elements in the repressive mechanism of the dominant structures of the church when Jesus Christ is presented to all the faithful as a strong, young, white male.[31] Such a symbol immediately excludes not only the weak and handicapped, the old and feeble, the members

---

30. "Spirit is the 'more' of any relation. The ethical person will be keenly aware of Spirit and for that very reason will not claim to know it directly. When Christian theology put Christ Jesus at the center of time, regarding his unity with God as forever decisive, it put a frame around the divine/human context, setting limits to the Spirit. Its ethics have been crippled ever since." (Driver, *Christ in a Changing World,* 111–12.)

31. See ibid., 44–45.

of nonwhite races, and women,[32] but it also places upon those who can more or less identify with it in external ways the terrible pressure of an ideal to which none of them can measure up.

What this accentuates for our present discussion is that no image of the Christ is universally valid. There must be room within all viable pictures of Jesus for the particularity of those who would "see" Jesus to discern itself. Otherwise, the declaration of the incarnation of the Word and the "being with us" of God is contradicted by the symbol that is the medium of this act of solidarity. Always, it must be necessary for me to see my own face reflected in the face of Jesus, even though what I shall have to see there is of course more than merely my own reflection.

The other side of this same coin is nevertheless highly important, the more so in a culture like our own that has always courted individualism, and perhaps more blatantly in its religious pursuits than anywhere else. If Jesus is not in some sense personal to one, he cannot be *person*. But the pious individualism that prays to "my Jesus" and "walks in the garden alone" with him ends in a privatistic religion that is not only incapable of the unity and reconciliation which lie at the heart of the biblical message but is also unable to be salt, yeast, and light in the society at large because it has no corporate image of the one whose name it bears.[33] Our search in this work is for a contextual theology, and while that does not mean in a direct and exclusive sense a political theology, it does mean a theology that is capable of public witness and concern and is therefore at least prepolitical. Such a theology requires a conception of the "head" that is sufficiently integrated to encourage "the body" to act in concert.

In practice, of course, there will always be tension in the church's ongoing attempt to envisage its head. This tension is already a conspicuous element with the first disciple community. Evidently Peter and John have different perceptions of Jesus (see John 21), and the tax collector, Matthew, brings to his discipleship very different experiences and needs from those belonging to the

---

32. "Consider . . . the following. A book, edited by Hans-Ruedi Weber, . . . *On a Friday Noon*, shows illustrations of Christ crucified, drawn from all cultures and times in history. The variety is fascinating. There are yellow Christs and brown Christs, Christs who are serene and Christs in agony, Christs who are stylized and Christ in the image of the people who depicted him. But one thing these pictures . . . have in common: they are all images of a man." (Hampson, *Theology and Feminism,* 77.)

33. "A theology which with its christology goes along with the modern experience of subjectivity, and now conveys the content of the Christian doctrine of salvation only in as far as this is related to the individual subject of experience, is no longer willing—and no longer able—to call in question the social conditions and political limitations of this experience of subjectivity. This theology fits without any conflict into the requirements of the 'civil religion' of modern society. As the 'civil religion' of that society, it ministers to its educated and ruling classes, but not to its victims." (Moltmann, *The Way of Jesus Christ,* 63.)

former fishermen. The great example of this internal tension is Judas Iscariot, who earlier and with greater self-knowledge than the others sensed the totality of Jesus' claim upon all their lives and, in advance of his fellows, fled this "hound of heaven." Clearly also, the tension continues to inform the early church, with Paul and the Jerusalem disciples almost capitulating to the distinction between their conceptions of the head; and in the communities to whom the epistles are addressed, this enormous and always potentially destructive variety of imaging the Christ plays a major role in the subject matter of these letters.

We should not be surprised, therefore, when today vastly different and conflicting images of the Christ are at work in the ecumenical church. Our investigation particularly of the atonement theologies that have informed empirical Christianity ought to prepare us for the fact that diverse human experiences and needs will be productive of very different conceptions of the one whom faith trusts to illuminate and alleviate these experiences and needs. We know that in the *oikumene* today there are liberating Christs and Christs who console the rich; Christs who identify with the peacemakers and Christs who understand the need for arms; Christs who accentuate the human and Christs who identify with the creatures maltreated by humans; masculine Christs and feminine Christs; black, white, red, and yellow Christs. The enormously different requirements that Christians from all parts of the world, all races and genders and sexual orientations, all ages and economic states, bring to the imaging of the Christ make it appear, often, that this is finally an impossible undertaking; that we are in fact worshiping different gods under a more or less common nomenclature.

It is too easy in the face of this conflicting image-making to say that it is all wrong and that Jesus Christ will remain who he is and withhold himself from all. I think that we must rather allow this conflict to occur and seek to learn from it. We are undergoing a period of unprecedented transition where this necessary Christian imaging of the head of the body is concerned. We are moving not only from a Christendom toward a diaspora church, and not only from a sort of superimposed universalism to one in which specificity is important, but we are also freeing ourselves from a highly entrenched Christology that has been dominated by the affluent of the West and that is by now not even acceptable to many within the "developed" West.

The dogmatized Christ of Western (largely European) Catholicism and Protestantism is giving way to a great variety of more experientially influenced images of the Christ. This variety is in some sense overwhelming to all who treasure both the tradition and the unity of truth; yet it is essential if Christology is to become an authentic contemplation of the person, Jesus, called the Christ, and not merely the reception of received theories that for the most part not only do not "save" but perpetuate patterns of economic, sexual, and other forms of bondage from which, in fact, salvation is needed. It belongs both to the discovery of Scripture on the part of new Christians and to the freedom of the spirit, that the Christ who is "seen" in so many different contexts today must be experienced by older forms of the church as being antithetical to or discontinuous with the christological conventions of the tradition.[34]

Part of what must be understood by the guardians of the tradition is that it belonged to the triumphalism of Western Christendom (and not in any pure way to its sophistication of theory) to control the imaging of Christ through strong and authoritative dogmatic and hierarchic conventions, including the Formula of Chalcedon and Anselmic-Calvinistic soteriology. If what I have maintained in the foregoing is in any respect justifiable, then the overcoming of the sterility of the Christology of dogma through a reimaging of the person, Jesus Christ, will require the deposition of this controlled doctrine of the Western churches.

Such a deposition cannot be achieved peacefully, in the still atmosphere of academic discussion. Like the deposition of flesh-and-blood monarchs and potentates, the deposition of entrenched christological dogma calls forth visible opposition. A period of wildness, misrule, and chaos may well accompany it. African, Asian, Native American, and other Christians tell us today that they do not need to be burdened with all the contradictions and niceties of European and satellite European Christianity, which after all represents contextually conditioned struggles not germane to their experience. They can go (as they say) directly to Scripture; they can call directly upon the Spirit; they can discern Jesus Christ alive and active in their own contexts. Their point is surely well taken, however much it may hurt the pride of the ancient guardians of truth.

It may well be, in fact, that out of this clash of old and new doctrines and images of the Christ there will come to be an image of the Christ that is appropriate to the contexts of the established yet tired and ineffectual churches of Christendom, as well as those who attack and challenge them. There are already signs to this effect, for the contextually aware thinking about Jesus Christ that is prominent among the newer churches and certain minorities in the older forms of Christendom has begun to make the inheritors of traditional christological dogma conscious of the fact that their own doctrine has been hammered out on the anvil of specific historical experience and may not have the eternal weight that its greater age and influence have caused it to seem to possess.

35.5. Christ in the World. The *imago Christi* is informed by Scriptures, the testimony of the Spirit, and the internal dialogue and struggle of the Christian

---

34. See Driver, *Christ in a Changing World*, 20.

community itself; but in a real sense the most significant ingredient in this picturing of Jesus that is necessary to the faith of the disciple community and its profession in doctrinal form is none of these, but is rather the world. The world, which is the immediate theater of the judging, healing love expressed supremely in the cross, is the place where faith meets Jesus and learns once more how to recognize him, how to distinguish him from "false shepherds," how to see his face and hear his voice and not only second-hand descriptions of him and arid theories about his life and work.

The world, for whose future this one sacrificed his own, is the context whose ongoing life is always in some measure—for faith—the scene of the life of the risen Christ. The resurrection is not a dogma to be believed despite its incredibility; it is a reality to be experienced in the living of life within this world. It means entering into worldly life—really, consciously, intentionally, and with expectancy, for faith expects to meet the redeemer there. Without waxing romantic about worldly wonders and delights; without closing its eyes to all that is ugly, evil, and dangerous; without expecting miraculous occurrences and signs and wonders, faith enters the world with hope, believing that despite, in, and through all the bleak and negating as well as good and delightful things that it finds there, there is a presence that is transforming death into life.

There can and will be no commanding image of the Christ that does not entail, for the community of discipleship, a new and no doubt unsettling exposure to the world that is the context of the risen Christ. Apart from this exposure, the imaging of Christ remains fundamentally a religious work, and the resultant image inevitably lacks the incarnational dimension that is the source of its spiritual meaning. Even the best study of the Scriptures will not lend to the *imago Christi* the life that it needs if it is to inspire and renew the pledge of discipleship. Even the most enthusiastic openness to the Spirit will not produce a human face of Jesus. And even the most dedicated listening and dialogue within the *oikumene* will fail to allow faith to glimpse once more, and with conviction, the person who transcends all the dogma, symbols, and metaphors. Apart from a new and unprotected meeting with the real world, all that will happen in the church's attempt to see Jesus is that one idea will be exchanged for another, one symbol for another, one dogma or popular slogan or "theology of" for another. The Christ himself will remain silent, as in Shusaku Endo's great novel;[35] for the living Christ is always too preoccupied with the actual life of the world to devote his attention exclusively to those who are supposed to be following him into it.

---

35. *Silence,* trans. William Johnston (Tokyo: Sophia University, in cooperation with The Charles E. Tuttle Co., Rutland, Vermont, and Tokyo, 1969).

It is necessary to reiterate that we are not here offering alternatives, as if attention to the world were one method of envisioning Christ, and the study of Scriptures, openness to the divine Spirit, and ecumenical discourse another. There is no reason—especially not in North America—to perpetuate the absurd idea that there are two kinds of Christianity, one that is world-oriented and activistic and one that is church-centered and contemplative. Each of these without the other is impoverished. Activistic faith that has no contemplative side is soon lost in the welter of worldly discourse and deed.

This entire work is premised on the belief that without a clear intention faithfully and wisely to *profess* the faith, the activistic Christianity that is in many ways the best and most authentic form of discipleship in North America will be dissipated, and will soon lose even the foundational rationale necessary to its acting. Without a disciplined contemplation of the Christian Scriptures and traditions; without earnest listening to and openness toward the spiritual presence; without engaged ecumenical dialogue, all the activity of Christians, however inherently good, will contribute little to the envisioning of the Christ that is necessary for the life of the whole church today. For without scriptural, spiritual, and ecclesiastical help it is impossible to recognize the Good Shepherd who is at work in the world and to distinguish that work from other works.

Our concern at the moment, however, is that the opposite is also true: Apart from ever-renewed openness to the world, the consequences of exegetical, spiritual, and ecclesiastical discipline will lack the animation that comes only with exposure to life in all of its particularity. If the Christian witness to Jesus Christ is to rise above the recitation of precept and dogma, it must always rediscover afresh the face of the Christ in the faces of those with whom he identifies himself.

The grounds for such an affirmation are not to be found in the worldliness or penchant for humanism of which certain self-styled conservative elements in the North American churches accuse any Christians who turn to this world for the invigoration of the faith. They are located in Scripture and in the best and most authoritative traditions of our faith. From the outset, and again as part of its heritage from Israel, the primitive church recognized that the Christ to whom it bore witness in its own way was not dependent upon its witness, and was indeed present in the world already, infinitely transcending not only its powers of containment but also its capacity for discernment. The little flock remembered what it had heard from Jesus, the prophetic teacher: how there were "other sheep," and how the work of God is done by many who remain unaware of their obedience, and how the mere reiteration of religious formulae and sentiment has finally little to do with the state of the soul. It remembered his parable of the "blessed" ones who, having acted in compassion toward "the least," had shown compassion upon himself, incognito (Matthew 25).

494

The concept of the hidden Christ, *Christus absconditus,* was particularly important for Luther. His best-known sermon, a Christmas sermon,[36] exemplifies how necessary it was, in his view, to lift the gospel out of its sacrosanct context and establish anew its essential worldliness. Jesus Christ is not to be equated with the stained-glass representations of him or with the formulae and pious phrases that two thousand years have accumulated "round that head sublime." He must ever and again be rediscovered by faith in the midst of the secular and profane.[37]

In particular that means in the midst of those who suffer—"the least of these. . . ." It is regarded as an affront by many respectable churchfolk today when they are confronted by representations of the crucified Christ as black, or a person with AIDS, or a migrant worker, or a child hanged at Auschwitz. It is especially offensive to this mentality when the crucified one is presented as a woman—as in the sculpted *Crucified Woman* now displayed in the garden of Emmanuel College in the University of Toronto, one of several such representations.[38] But why should this offend? The whole point of the cross is God's solidarity with those who in the world are "crucified," in whatever form that may be.[39] Nor is it by any means a new device when this fundamental theological point—the Emmanuel point, we might call it—is applied to unconventional or unrecognized forms of suffering. During the fourteenth century, when much of Europe's population was carried off by the black plague, there were many "black Christs." They were black not because they were African but because they were dying of the plague.

If Jesus is not recognized in the faces and forms of those who suffer, then neither will he be recognized as savior in relation to any of us except in the most theoretical manner. The theology of glory may be upheld by such theory (in fact, the only way it *can* be upheld is theoretically), but in real life, where finitude and failure are inescapable, the only glory that is credible, finally, is the glory of a compassion that identifies itself with "the least."

It has been the folly of most of Christendom that it has imagined that only a conquering Christ could meet the needs of humanity for God and salvation. We are still laboring under this pathetic illusion. In some ways, North America is its last stronghold. We think that Jesus must be strong, a winner. But this Jesus only does for us, individually and collectively, what all highly positive images

---

36. *The Martin Luther Christmas Book,* trans. Roland Bainton (Philadelphia: Fortress Press, 1948), 19–21, 37–40.

37. "As Christians, our first concern should be neither Christ nor the Bible but the world of God, the world in ethically creative relation to God's creating . . . this was Jesus' own concern." (Driver, *Christ in a Changing World,* 83.)

38. See in this connection Doris Jean Dyke, *The Crucified Woman* (Toronto: United Church Pub. House, 1991). See also Elisabeth Moltmann-Wendell, "Is There a Feminist Theology of the Cross?" in *God—His and Hers,* trans. John Bowden (New York: Crossroads, 1991), 88.

39. See C. S. Song, *Jesus, the Crucified People* (New York: Crossroad/Meyer-Stone, 1989).

of the human do: he makes us all the more conscious of our weakness, absurdity, and lostness. He may, for a time, serve empires and the rich and successful. But empires decline, the rich are required to give up their souls, and the successful enjoy their success only briefly, if at all. When will we learn that Jesus, the crucified one, is with us in our decline, our extremity of soul, our failure? When will we discover the one whose power has to be manifested in weakness because it is the power of love?

CHAPTER ▪ NINE

Emmanuel

36. "Who Is Jesus Christ for Us Today?"

36.1. "We" Are Part of the Christological Question. Half a century ago, Dietrich Bonhoeffer, awaiting the final verdict on his life in the Nazi prison of Tegel, raised a question that has stimulated and perplexed thoughtful Christians ever since: "Who is Christ for us today?"[1] Whatever one may think of Bonhoeffer's own necessarily tentative and brief response to this question, it will be evident to those who have followed at least one of the primary motifs of the present work that its author would consider Bonhoeffer's formulation of the question to be the correct one. To ask the christological question in this way is to lift it out of the murky waters of dogma and place it where it belongs—at the heart of a gospel that is intended, always, for "us," whoever we are, at whatever time, in whatever place.

Who is Jesus Christ *pro nobis?* Asking the question in this way does not imply that one has no interest in who Jesus Christ was and is for others—for the original disciple community; for the early church that wrestled with the christological problem bequeathed to it by the evangelists; for the medieval scholastics and the sixteenth-century reformers; for our liberal forebears with their "lives of Jesus"; for our own contemporaries in other parts of the world, other contexts. A contextual theology worthy of the gospel does not sit lightly to Scripture, the history of doctrine, and the global discourse of the contemporary church.

---

1. *Letters and Papers from Prison,* enlarged ed., trans. Reginald Fuller, Frank Clark, et al. (London: S.C.M. Press, 1953), 279.

Nevertheless all genuine theological work must finally come down to . . . us. Until we ourselves, with all the specificity of our historical moment, allow the great questions of the faith we profess to penetrate our spirits and unsettle our minds, we are not engaged in theology but only paratheological work—doctrine, exegesis, historical research, social analysis, and so on. In no part of what we profess as Christians is this more conspicuously the case than in Christology. This is not only because Christology is central to any belief that is professedly Christian, but also because of the internal requirements of this doctrinal area. For the question about Jesus is never just about Jesus. If it is a serious question, a question of faith, it is also a question about those who ask it. It is a question about us.

That is the case even when we reduce the christological question to a matter of Jesus' identity—the christological question in the more restrictive sense. Seriously to ask who Jesus is, is to betray an existential concern that is qualitatively different from what the wording of the question superficially suggests. It is not coincidental that the same Bonhoeffer who asked who Jesus is also asked, "Who Am I?"—the title of his best-known poem. We proposed in the historical chapter that the question about Jesus' identity may be the most significant original (biblical) aspect of christological reflection because, unlike all the answers that have been offered in nearly two thousand years, the question itself contains a dimension of involvement with the person that cannot be dismissed without serious consequences for the whole endeavor.

This involvement is made still more unavoidable when faith moves from interrogation concerning Jesus' identity to ask, as it must, what he has done for us. For *us*! The soteriological side of the christological question, without which the christological side regularly degenerates into metaphysics, makes explicit our participation in this question. We shall never be able to comprehend the doctrine of the Christ apart from a good deal of investigation of our own identity and condition. And that investigation is never wholly painless.

Who is Jesus Christ *for us today?* The last three words of Bonhoeffer's question are in many ways the most complex. For who are "we"? And how shall we understand "today"?

So far as the first question is concerned, the subtitle of these volumes indicates that their author has identified "us" as North Americans, specifically citizens of the two northern nations of this continent, living at the close of the twentieth century C.E. There are of course many different sorts of collectivities within this larger context. I have not understood it to be either my prerogative or my calling to address all of them. I want to speak to and for the remnants of "mainline" Protestantism, chiefly, and as one whose life has been lived within the context of what is still the dominant culture of this society, however questionable its dominance may be. I have neither the right nor the capacity to represent any other segment of our society, though I have been helped to understand my own segment by listening to the others.

Rightly or wrongly, it is my perception that the once-mainline Protestant traditions within our context are confused and demoralized, and that this state also manifests itself in their theology—their Christology, perhaps, in particular. There is a hesitancy to speak out of this identity and these traditions, because they generally bear the brunt of so much criticism. Few Protestants other than the most conservative seem willing to own their past, even for the sake of critiquing it from within. Instead, we wait for the latest attack from "the victims" of our dominance, some of whom truly are victimized by us, or by the shadows we cast.

This waiting may be necessary. It may be an important stage in our conversion. Perhaps we need to be silent, simply to accept the many-sided debunking of our pretensions. On the other hand, our waiting may be nothing more than another facet of our well-practiced pride: Why respond? Why not just wait it out? Or perhaps it is pride's alter ego, sloth. Perhaps the Sisyphus syndrome has taken over our theology, too.

Whatever may be the case, I do not think that silence is a reasonable or helpful alternative. Unless the churches that have been most conspicuously identified with the dominant culture of these nations enter into a theological inquiry that is their own, neither they nor the victims of the dominant culture will be aided. Only we can discover who Jesus Christ is for us today. And only we can discover who he is *not* and must not be any longer—for us.

And then, what shall we understand by "today"? It is always easier to answer the question, Who was Jesus Christ for the church *yesterday?*—or even for *us* yesterday (say, those of us who lived through the 1950s and 1960s). "Today" is an elusive word. Tomorrow people will speak about our "today" with understanding, perhaps even wisdom—or so it will seem. But to comprehend today *today* seems an impossible undertaking, always. Yet a contextual theology must risk it, and particularly in its Christology; for Jesus Christ is either Lord and Savior *today* or he is nothing but a memory and a hope. Faith, it is true, lives on memory and hope, so it does not aspire to the kind of existentialism that knows only the moment. Still, in the last analysis the purpose of our remembering and our hoping is to strengthen our trust in this One *now* (Rom. 3:21). What has made (for example) liberation theology in Latin America and Minjung theology in Korea the lively discourses that they are is that they have been prepared to enter the presence of the Christ with the uncertainties and realities of today at the forefront. By comparison, the settled theologies of the "developed" churches regularly hide those uncertainties and realities beneath calm, scholarly discussions about yesterday's Christologies. It is hard for the rich, or the once-rich, to enter that presence.

36.2. What We Bring to the Christological Question: Difficulties with the Tradition. Before we attempt to speak constructively about Jesus Christ, then, it will be well to reflect briefly on what we bring to this discussion. In this subsection we shall consider certain difficulties that we carry with us to our reflection on the received tradition, and in the next we shall ask about some of the expectations that are part of our quest for a positive Christology. I shall name four barriers to our immediate reception of established christological dogma.

a. The Language of Substances. With a great deal of patient historical, philosophical, and philological work, it is possible for those who study the christological heritage of Christendom to grasp and communicate something of its meaning for past generations. But this is exceptionally demanding work, and even when it can claim a measure of success it is work that remains for the most part at the level of knowledge as distinct from genuine understanding. Chalcedonian Christology may, with diligence, become familiar; but very few of those who adhere to the denominations for whom I am writing may lay claim to grasping or being grasped by the Formula of Chalcedon—to speak only of this one key christological document.

Our difficulty with much of the christological thought of the tradition is that it assumes an ontology that is neither biblical nor contemporary. While a concept like "the two natures of Christ" may be advanced as a theory that people once believed, it does not find in us the sort of spiritual resonance that is required if language is to become the medium of transforming truth. While at the intellectual level we, too, have been taught to divide reality into substances, intuitively we think relationally, especially where human beings are concerned.[2] What is important for us—what is *real*—is not what individual entities are made up of but what transpires *between* entities, *between* persons. Unfortunately, substantialistic thought still conditions too consistently our practices vis-à-vis the extrahuman world, nature. But through the influence of the social sciences, art and story, ecology, and feminist thought, relationality has increasingly colored our perception of life.

This constitutes a barrier to our reception of the christological tradition; but it should also be regarded as an asset for the reformulation of Christology in more biblical terms.

b. The Notion of Sacrificial Substitution. We have noted that by far the most influential atonement theology of Western Christendom hinges upon the concept of sacrificial substitution: Jesus, the pure and innocent Lamb of God,

---

2. See Tom F. Driver, *Christ in a Changing World: Toward an Ethical Christology* (New York: Crossroads, 1981), 101–2, 104.

accepts in his own person the just judgment of God, thus propitiating for "the sins of the whole world"; if we believe this and avail ourselves of the ritual and other means of grace, we may be saved from the divine wrath and become recipients of eternal life.

But "we" do *not* believe this. Some in our midst do believe it, or say they do, and we are not permitted to discredit the sincerity of their claim; but the vast majority of those who will read these words not only do not but probably cannot believe this, or even comprehend profoundly what believing it entails. For the theory is impossibly interwoven with medieval feudal and even superstitious practices and folklore, to say nothing of its unworthy representation of the biblical God to whom sacrifice was made.

In other words, the most powerful and (so far as Western Christendom is concerned) almost exclusive doctrinal tradition concerning Christ's priestly work seems fundamentally inaccessible to us. This by no means disqualifies every facet of the theory or renders it uninteresting. It may even continue to convey important dimensions of the meaning of Christ's work. Seen illustratively, Jesus' innocent suffering for others serves as a metaphor for sacrificial love. That, I suggest, is how it is understood among us today; but that is to understand it in an Abelardian and not an Anselmic way. The emotion that it inspires (if it inspires any emotion) is not one of gratitude at having been substituted for by another, but at most of a quickening of the sense of divine love.

At the same time, the Abelardian atonement theology, revived by liberalism, seems to many so general, if not sentimental, that it has little to say to us—for we have become conscious, in ways that our forebears were not, of the inadequacy of all easy declarations of love, human or divine.

Thus, what we bring to the christological question by way of an appropriation of the received traditions is hardly calculated to contribute much to a constructive Christology. Both the person and the work of the Christ, as they are set forward in the most prominent historical doctrines, seem disturbingly foreign to our preunderstanding, even when we, as believers, wish that it could be otherwise.

c. Particularity and Exclusivity.   Not only does the tradition fail to grasp us existentially, it places upon us a burden of absoluteness that most of us in the once-mainline churches of North America are very reluctant to bear. We feel overwhelmed and chagrined by the claims of utter uniqueness, supremacy, and ultimacy that are made by the tradition in the name of the one who claimed so little for himself.

This is undoubtedly in part because we are no longer living in an exclusively or even predominantly Christian world. North America may be unique in this matter. While other religions now invade the old European flagship of Christendom, they are still perceived as the religions of foreigners. In Canada and the

United States, on the contrary, while there are pockets of Christian monopoly in rural and small-town areas, other religions of the world are present in all their variety and concreteness in all of our cities, and they can no longer be relegated to second-class status. It is impossible to live in proximity to Jews, Muslims, Buddhists, and newly conscious Native Amer-Canadian religions and continue believing that the profession of Jesus as Christ is the exclusive entree to truth and eternal felicity.

This does not translate into eclecticism, necessarily, though it has done so for many; but it does constitute a barrier to the reception of christological traditions that were formulated in the monopolistic situation of Christendom. If we cannot articulate the meaning of Christ for faith in ways that avoid the exclusion of all non-Christians and the humiliation of many even within the churches, then we shall have conceded that the fundamentalists within our midst have correctly assessed the implications of professing the Christian faith.

d. Existential Remoteness. It belongs to the doctrine of the Christ, notably to the profession of his "kingship," to insist upon his contemporaneity with us. Jesus is not only the rabbi of the Gospels who once walked the paths of Galilee; he is the risen one, whose presence the community of faith continuously senses, whose "body" that community is.

We would be less than honest were we not to acknowledge that for most of us who find our ecclesiastical home within the older denominations of this continent, this sense of the real presence and companionship of Jesus Christ is hard to sustain. Pockets of spirituality and piety exist, but the one-dimensionality of modern secularity has infected almost everyone, including theologians.[3] Liberalism tried to address this by presenting a historically credible Jesus, who could provide a moral example for modern people. But while liberalism was in some ways more successful than later doctrinalism in providing the church with a "living" head, it could not displace the secular banishment of transcendence, and in some ways only furthered the latter.

It is doubtful whether we can arrive at a meaningful Christology apart from a greater struggle with secularity than has yet been undertaken in these major denominations. Charismatic Christianity, which is present in a minor way in and around all of the old Protestant denominations, may be symptomatic of this greater need; but as we have seen in earlier trinitarian and christological discussions, the religion of the Spirit can also create its own problems for the doctrine of the Christ. How can an essentially secular people acquire a sufficient sense of

---

3. "What strikes me . . . about much modern theology—and this is not least true of feminist theology—is how profoundly secular it is. It is as though theology has lost its moorings." (Daphne Hampson, *Theology and Feminism* [Oxford: Basil Blackwell, 1990], 170.) See also Van A. Harvey, "On the Intellectual Marginality of American Theology," in *Religion and Twentieth Century American Intellectual Life,* ed. Michael J. Lacey (Cambridge: Cambridge Univ. Press, 1991), 172ff.

transcendence to entertain the presence of the Christ without falling into spiritualistic distortions of the faith?

36.3. Christological Intimations in Our Human Quests. The christological debates of the classical period were necessitated by the incorporation into the Christian movement of large numbers of people who had no background in the Hebraic tradition that was presupposed by the original disciple community. The human quests of these people were shaped by the events and interpretations, aspirations, and anxieties of Hellenistic civilization. In its mission, the Christian movement had to relate itself to these existing human quests. We may judge that what emerged from the resultant refashioning of the movement was a questionable interpretation of the person of Jesus. But this does not alter the truth of the assertion that the Christian apologia had to enter into dialogue with what it found in the gentile world by way of a human search for meaning.

The soteriological history of the tradition is even more illustrative of this truth. As we have seen, the various types of atonement theology were informed by changing human quests for salvation.

In discussing the christological doctrine of the faith historically and critically, we have implied that the human quest for salvation in our own context is significantly different from the answers that are derived from much of the received christological tradition. In this subsection we shall summarize some aspects of that quest in which there are intimations of a Christology appropriate to our situation. I shall identify three of these.

a. Our Quest for Meaning. The overarching search of all societies that have experienced the malaise of modernity is a search for meaning. Modernity insisted that meaning was built into the historical process as such: whether gradually or in a revolutionary manner, there would be progress toward a conspicuously purposeful earthly existence. This progress was independent of human agency, though it would so to speak employ humanity by liberating the species from ignorance and aligning its potentiality for rational behavior with the patterns of historical destiny.

There could be little need for a redeemer, or for the assumption of need for radical redemption, in such a view. The salvific principle was built into the process of history itself. Jesus could be an exemplar of moral and even rational behavior, but he could not be treated as savior.

The failure of modernity is nothing more nor less than its failure as a system of redemptive meaning. Not only has enlightened rationality been unsuccessful in banishing the most bestial aspects of human behavior, but where modern rationality has been most successful in ordering life, it has brought about forms of society unprecedented for their captivation by boredom, apathy, and the sense of purposelessness. It is not in societies that have failed to achieve the "developed" status, but in those of high, technological "development," that we find today the greatest instances of human despair and *acedia*. There is "a growing collective indifference toward life."[4]

Our own society, we have argued, is a special case in point. While older societies possess symbolic and linguistic frames of reference for the experience of negation, ours is so much a product of modernity that we lack any operative intellectual-spiritual referents on the basis of which even to express our negations, let alone do battle with them. Moreover, religion—meaning in particular the Christian religion—functions for many or even most people who maintain some affiliation with it to keep from their conscious thought the frustrations and failings that they actually experience. It is a religion of postponement: it helps to put off until tomorrow any reckoning with the data of despair that we cannot and will not face today.

"Jesus," under these circumstances, almost inevitably becomes a figure of false comfort. It is not the comfort about which the prophet Isaiah spoke (Isa. 40:1). It is comfort for those who are still relatively comfortable but sense, a little, the prospect of discomfort and wish to erase it as effectively as possible. There is no common denominator more conspicuous among all sorts and conditions of Christians on this continent than the idea that "Jesus Loves Everybody."[5]

Such a blatant misuse of "Jesus" and of the whole tradition not only betrays its shallowness even to those who profess it, but it also evokes a protesting minority within the community of faith. It becomes clearer almost daily that we are a people nearly bereft of any credible system of meaning, and the misappropriation of "Jesus" as a psychic stopgap for our incipient despair provokes a thinking minority in the churches to ask with renewed fervor whether the profession of Jesus as Christ can be anything more than a sop to frightened middle-class people.

b. The Quest for Truth.

Churches in which solace in the name of Jesus is offered to people who, because of their relative affluence, could make a difference in the world may be the most questionable expression of Christianity ever

---

4. Jürgen Moltmann, *The Way of Jesus Christ: Christology in Messianic Dimensions,* trans. Margaret Kohl (Minneapolis: Fortress Press, 1993), 192.

5. This is the title of a splendid, timely article by Ronald Goetz (*The Christian Century* [March 11, 1992], 274–77). Commenting on "the recent Interchurch Features Survey . . . sponsored jointly by a Roman Catholic journal and seven mainline Protestant denominational journals," Goetz's article is a cogent update on what we have called earlier (following Kitamori) the "monism of love" in so much contemporary Christianity. Despite the unprecedented poverty, violence, famine, and conflict of the age, Goetz reports, "mainline Christians, . . . far from despairing are nearly unanimous in their buoyant conviction that Jesus loves people of other faiths and even unbelievers as much as he loves Christians. . . . America's characteristically optimistic piety seems to have grown even more optimistic."

to have been practiced. There is an almost palpable demand for the preservation of untruth in much of our mainline Christianity. Clergy who are imbued with a sense of the urgency of the times can hardly sustain long-term ministries in our churches, especially the more prosperous; and laypersons who appear in the midst of "friendly" congregations with burning personal or social questions are regularly edged out onto the periphery. The reason is clear enough: People want the churches to provide comfort *without truth*. Jesus, who called himself "the Truth," is for many respectable citizens of our continent a more effective opiate than can be found among the sad victims of the drug culture.

Again, however, this visible misuse of Christian faith has called forth minorities within and around the churches who insist that the purpose of our trust in Jesus is to open our eyes to reality no matter how discomforting it may be—to give us the courage of truth-orientation. Must the comfort of the Savior be a comfort that represses truth? Can anything comfort truly, when in the very act of receiving it we must agree not to press too insistently toward the truth?

c. The Quest for Reconciliation. Reconciliation is a conspicuous theme of the whole christological tradition, and it is a theme that can be plausibly explored today because the human need for reconciliation is unavoidable in the global society that we have become. Only—as the final phrase of that sentence already anticipates—the focus or theater of this need has shifted.

What I mean is that the quest for reconciliation has acquired for us a distinctly this-worldly connotation. Both of the older atonement theories that have been most influential in the West presuppose that the reconciliation for which human beings are searching is reconciliation with God and, perhaps in consequence, with one another. In the Anselmic type it is God who has to be reconciled to us, and in the Abelardian type the need is more directly ours. Perhaps it has been the success of the latter in modern, liberal churches that has helped to shift the need for reconciliation from heaven to earth. We are, in any case, conscious of an alienation that pertains at the creaturely level, and in almost every realm of our life. We need to be reconciled to other human beings, and not only personally but socially and politically. We need also to be reconciled to nonhuman forms of life and to the earth itself. Part of our quest for meaning stems directly from our sense of alienation from our own kind and otherkind. We anticipate the chaos and impossibility that is coming upon the world, and is already part of its reality, because we have not learned even the rudiments of respect, mutuality, sharing, solidarity. How can reconciliation, as it is effected by Jesus, meet this quest for a new way of living in and with the world?

What is being asked for both in relation to our alienation from other human beings and our alienation from nature is really conciliation *to our own creaturehood*. This complicates the christological task noticeably, because so much of the tradition concerning the Christ has been preoccupied with a reconciliation to or with divinity and the transcendent that the idea of being reconciled to our creaturehood is an almost foreign concept. Frequently it is dismissed as humanistic or even pantheistic. Salvation has been so exclusively directed to the religious longing to transcend our creaturehood; Jesus has been so consistently regarded as the door to heaven, that it seems to many a veritable betrayal of the gospel when the Redeemer is presented as one redeeming us *from* "religion" and "heaven-storming" and *for* the life, work, and joy of creaturely being.

At the same time, it has happened once again that a minority within the contemporary churches has grasped the internal demands of a faith claiming to be incarnational to make heaven serve earth, eternity serve time, and hope serve history. There is no need to question Jesus' promise of an ultimate state of reconciliation, when all the dividing walls of hostility will be broken down; but this future-eschatology of reconciliation also applies here and now, and if approximations of it cannot be sought for and achieved contextually, the question of its ultimacy is also begged.

To summarize: We bring to the reformulation of Christology problems, attitudes, and needs that affect our task both negatively and positively. There can be no christological work within the disciple community that does not also, simultaneously, expose us to these realities of our own situation. We cannot pretend that either the christological or the soteriological traditions are easily accessible to our experience; we shall have to labor hard for the meaning that is in them for us. Nor can we ignore our own quests, which in themselves are never wholly uplifting; for to understand them fully we must come to understand as well the deep and inscrutable unfulfilled needs that they represent. Yet a picture of Jesus Christ that is authentic *for us* may emerge as we permit the divine Spirit to lead us into these mostly unexplored spaces of our personal and public souls. If that occurs, it will not matter that this picture is incomplete or blurred.

37. Representation as a Contemporary Christological Term

37.1. The Hermeneutics of Representation.   Who then *is* Jesus Christ for us today? To respond constructively, however hesitantly, to this question, we need to find a language with metaphors and symbols that can create a bridge of communication between the biblical and traditional witness to the Christ and our own world of experience. Each of the formative christological/soteriological stages of the Christian past has done this, and in doing so each has had to break with the regnant conventions that, in the minds of the reformulators, were no longer capable of communication. We have determined above that the language of substances in christological discussion as well as that of substitution in soteriological discussion constitutes barriers to communication in our time. Is there a language that can *facilitate* communication?

[handwritten marginalia: Are we talking to God? Christ represents us? or us?]

A number of contemporary theologians have answered that such a language may be found in the concept of representation. Dorothee Sölle developed this metaphor suggestively in her 1965 book *Stellvertretung—Ein Kapitel Theologie nach dem "Tode Gottes."*[6] Sölle distinguished representation sharply from substitution, as I shall also do. Hendrikus Berkhof, who also favors this metaphor, thinks that Sölle makes too much of the distinction:

> Dorothee Sölle . . . fears that the substitution which leaves room for the other has in the Christian faith often become the replacement [*Ersatz*] which renders me and my actions superfluous. Without concurring with her conception, one can appreciate her fear. In the NT, however, there is no ground for such fear, because the other side of the substitution is our participation through the Spirit.[7]

Surely it is not necessary, however, to neglect the work of the Spirit if one insists upon the participatory dimension also in Christology. As we have noted in our historical discussion of the soteriological formulations in particular, it is precisely for want of that dimension that the two older types of atonement theology appear (at least for us) objectivistic and remote. It would seem to me possible, through the use of the representational concept, to retain what is important in the older traditions, especially Latin substitutionary Christology, and at the same time avoid the danger that both Sölle and Berkhof acknowledge in the latter.[8]

In view of the claim that we are making for this language, we should begin by noting six of its inherent characteristics. If we remind ourselves in this way of the implications of "representation" in ordinary usage, we shall be in a better position to assess its application to Christology.

a. *Representation is a concept and reality that applies concretely and naturally to daily life in our context.* It is explicitly employed in the realms of politics, law, and business, and it is implicit in almost every area of our life. Government is by representation in democratic states. Given the complications

---

6. Kruez Verlag, 1965. The book appeared in English under the title, *Christ the Representative: An Essay in Theology after the "Death of God,"* trans. David Lewis (London: S.C.M. Press, 1967).

7. *Christian Faith: An Introduction to the Study of the Faith,* trans. Sierd Woudstra (Grand Rapids: Wm. B. Eerdmans Pub. Co., 1979), 305.

8. Many other contemporary Christian writers employ the language of representation. In this connection see (e.g.) Letty M. Russell, *Human Liberation in a Feminist Perspective: A Theology* (Philadelphia: Westminster Press, 1974), 182: "Whatever models may develop as we move toward the future, they will need to follow the life-style of the Representative of new humanity in such a way that openness for service will lead to a continuing process of communion and dialogue as the praxis of freedom"; David Tracy, *The Analogical Imagination: Christian Theology in a Culture of Pluralism* (New York: Crossroad, 1981), 302: "In sum, for myself . . . the symbol 'incarnation' also has a properly christological use. The incarnation is a symbol employed *in relationship to cross and resurrection* to reexpress their meaning: viz., that for Christian faith Jesus Christ is the decisive representation of God; that Christians believe that in this one man Jesus, God's own self is present amongst us."

of civil, criminal, and corporate law, anyone who must conduct transactions having public implications (virtually everyone, at some point in his or her life) must seek representation by lawyers. In large businesses and industries, boards and committees represent the interests of the shareholders. Even in private life—for example, family life—representation is implicit at every turn. Mothers and fathers represent their children to teachers, doctors, and courts. Children carry into the playground the opinions of their parents. Parents and grandparents represent to the younger generations the mores, opportunities, and demands of the larger society (often to the chagrin of the latter). Beyond the family, teachers and professors represent disciplines with long histories; medics represent the traditions, methods, and discoveries of their profession; musicians represent the musical traditions of their society, and so on. The idea of representation, in our social context, is not only an idea but a ubiquitous reality. It is at least as indigenous to our historical context as the concept of substitution was to that of Anselm.

b. One can only represent another if she or he is qualified to do so. I hire a lawyer to represent me in court. I go to a real-estate agent to purchase a house. I seek medical advice from my physician. In all such instances, the presupposition is qualification. I could no doubt represent my own interests in all of these instances, but I am not qualified to do so in the best way even in purchasing a house; and in most instances I am wholly inadequate. The concept of representation includes the nuance not only that the representative is and must be qualified but that the one being represented is not. In seeking the representative, the latter acknowledges, tacitly, his or her own inadequacy.

c. Representation almost always has a dual character. Representatives regularly must face in two directions. This is obvious in the case of government in democratic states: The person whom the people elect to parliament is responsible (1) to represent her constituency in the decisions of government and (2) to represent the decisions of government to her constituency. In other vocations this duality of the representational act may be less obvious, but it is usually present in some way. For example, a teacher has an obvious responsibility to his pupils; and in much modern pedagogical theory this appears to be his only responsibility. But in fact if he is a conscientious teacher he will realize that he has an equally decisive responsibility to the tradition of knowledge and wisdom that he is trying to impart; and indeed unless he feels this latter responsibility, he will not be acting very responsibly as teacher in relation to his pupils either. What is important in the relation between teacher and pupils is not only that it should be a pleasant, supportive relationship, but that it should be the medium through which the young are introduced to the mysteries of (say) mathematics.

Another way of stating this is that representation is usually a mediatorial activity, and mediation involves duality—turning, as it were, from the one to the other, interpreting one to the other. This is very different from the idea of substitution. The substitute represents one party to the other. A substitute ballplayer, teacher, or violinist represents to the team, classroom, or orchestra the person for whom he is substituting; and even that may be questioned, for in practice most substitutes have no intention of representing anyone but themselves. It would be a rare occurrence for a professor, called at the last minute to substitute for a sick colleague, to conduct his class from start to finish with only the reputation of the absent colleague in mind.

   d. Suffering often belongs to the representational act.   Suffering is not an unusual dimension of representation. Not every lawyer suffers deeply as she represents her clients—but Abraham Lincoln did. Not every president of the United States suffers personally when his country is torn by war or economic depression, but some have done so. Most politicians who are in office out of a sense of public service and not mere personal ambition suffer. A caring parent who must appear before the parole officer in behalf of his or her offspring certainly suffers. Suffering in some degree belongs to the representative life and role, and this is not surprising; for the representative must live between two others, in some kind of solidarity with both; and often the two are not only distinctive but in real or potential conflict. One could be crucified, living between others.[9]

   e. Representation is frequently an activity flowing from a lifework or vocation.   We often use the word "office" in connection with representation. Many representational acts are simply isolated deeds, but more often representative work is the consequence of a lifework or vocation, an office. The work proceeds from the life; the life issues in this kind of work. There is a certain element of destiny in the idea. The work is not taken up or laid down at whim. The drunken priest in Graham Greene's novel *The Power and the Glory* is a priest still even in his failure. The physician who cares about his patients takes them home in his mind; perhaps he does not sleep easily; perhaps he is himself sickened by the sickness of others.

   In other words, when one's lifework is inherently representational, representation is no longer just a deed. Fathers and mothers, we noted, are representatives of families. No loving parent thinks that he or she has done all that needs to be done when the child reaches eighteen, or twenty-one, or fifty.

---

9. Even when the "others" in question are not, in both cases, persons, suffering may accompany the representational role. A conscientious grade school teacher who identifies with his pupil and feels at the same time responsible to the traditions of learning that he is employed to communicate suffers when the pupil fails. A minister like the priest in Georges Bernanos' *The Diary of a Country Priest* (trans. Pamela Morris [New York: MacMillan, 1937]) suffers terribly—and why would he not? He has to represent the justice and purity of God to unjust and impure people; yet he also has to represent the poor, failing people before God. It is no wonder that the priest, like so many ministers and priests in our own context, experiences acute pain.

There is literally no end to the representative work once a person has grasped the representational nature of his or her *life*. [10]

f. *Those who are being represented know themselves—or come to know themselves—as being involved in the representational event or act.* The five previous observations about the language of representation focus on the representative; but of course representation also involves those being represented. In some ways, particularly for christological purposes, this observation is the most important of these; for it lifts Christology/soteriology out of its isolationist frame of reference ("Jesus *alone!*") and establishes his connectedness with us—us Christians, us human beings.

We have seen that the idea of substitution is theologically and biblically limited because it lacks what is usually called the subjective (I prefer to say the relational) factor. Substitution grows out of an ontology of hierarchic, substantialistic thought. Representation is essentially and necessarily a relational concept. Everything about it has to do with the relation between the representative and those whom he or she represents. We used the term "solidarity" a moment ago to describe the intensity of this relation, this "being-with." And we said that the suffering that accompanies the representational act is bound up with the fact that solidarity must be achieved, by the representative, with two parties who are not necessarily compatible and may be (often are) in conflict.

In this final observation about the term, we want to note how representation applies relationally to those being represented. The substitute does not really have to achieve proximity vis-à-vis the one for whom he substitutes, and the latter does not have to participate in the substitutionary act at all. The substitute steps in and does the thing instead of me. This certainly conveys *to me* the message that I am myself inadequate (which is just what both Anselm and Calvin intended us to hear). But it does not convey the other part of the story—by which I mean both the story told in the continuity of the biblical testaments and the story that is told in an infinity of variations wherever someone represents another. That other part of the story is about the involvement of the one who is being represented.

This may be discussed discursively, but it can be communicated in a more direct way through illustration—through story.

There is a story about a young Indian brave who has come of age and must now go into the wilderness by himself for a year. If he survives and returns, he has earned the right to be a mature member of the tribe. If he does not, then he has failed the time of testing.

The young man is terribly afraid, but also anxious to prove himself. He knows about the wild beasts who seek their meat from God, and about the

---

10. This should be borne in mind especially as we consider the necessity of keeping the person and work of Jesus Christ together, reflectively, and also the continuity of the "offices"—prophet, priest, and sovereign.

inhospitable weather and terrain through which, all alone, he is to go. He knows too about the demons and spirits that haunt those who are alone—the demons encountered by St. Anthony.

As he is about to leave, he approaches his mother with a strange request: he asks her to make up his sleeping place every morning, just as if he had slept in it.

The mother does this, and when the young brave returns a year later, a wise, strong, and mature adult, he tells his mother: "I succeeded because of your faithfulness."

This story is about the son, chiefly; but it is the mother about whom the present observation is being made. What does her role in the story signify? Only the son goes out. Only he leaves the parental home to face the unknown terrors of the future, the *tentatio* of the outer and inner worlds.

Is the mother merely passive? Do her personal security and the safety of her home ensure that she will have no part in the temptations and dangers that must come to her son? Is the period of her son's absence just another year, like every year? Parents who have watched sons and daughters go into the world to be tested will know the answer to such questions. Of course the mother is not passive. She thinks constantly of her son. She can do nothing for him directly, but she can make his bed. This is her symbolic participation in his ordeal. This is the act of remembrance through which she puts into effect, ritually, her very real involvement with this one who is representing his tribe, including herself, in its quest for courage and a way into the future. She is "with him," though she is also not with him. The outcome of the year of trial matters ultimately to her, too, though she is not personally out there doing what must be done, what can only be done by him.

Here we may introduce certain connections with the story at the heart of the Christian message. In that story, too, a young man has to go out alone into the wilderness to be tempted. His whole story is one of temptation, with one explicit episode (the temptation of the wilderness) at its beginning and another (that of the Garden) at its end.

In the latter, the young man has taken a band of his associates with him. At a certain point in their progress toward the place he intends, he leaves most of them behind and goes ahead with three of them. He tells the three, "Watch and pray." Then he goes forward by himself. Only he can go all the way to the place of meeting; only he is qualified for this act of representation. The others, however, he intends to involve so far as possible. The story illustrates this intention graphically: all twelve are brought toward the place of meeting; three go a little farther—perhaps they have shown that they are ready for this.

But they fall asleep. They are not yet capable of such proximity. They cannot even stand, consciously, in the environs of Gethsemane, let alone of Golgotha.

Yet everything that follows—everything!—is geared toward the equipping of these ordinary human beings, and countless others like them, for just such participation. Only afterwards, when it is all over, do they realize that already at that point, in Gethsemane, their life of participation in the life and work of the Representative had begun. Their discipleship is nothing more nor less than the extension of this realization.

In developing this sixth observation, I have obviously moved from reflection on the metaphor of representation as it affects our life generally to the more specifically christological application of the metaphor. In doing this, I have wanted to show that one of the advantages of this metaphor is that it applies equally to Christology and ecclesiology; so that when we move between these two doctrinal areas, as we must, it is not necessary to engage in awkward shifts of language. The doctrine of the church is a consequence of the doctrine of the Christ, and this should be reflected linguistically—though it has seldom been done. The representative who is Jesus calls into being a representative community—to use the older language, "a priestly people." This theme will be developed in the third volume.

The primary intention of this final observation, however, has been to illustrate that representation, if it is understood profoundly, assumes the formation of a bond between the representative and those being represented. From the standpoint of the latter, the representational act of the former is not merely an external act but one in which there is a high degree of participation. Those being represented, when and as they come to know themselves as such, cannot remain detached from the representative act itself. They are being carried forward in and with the one who goes forward for them. It is they who are being represented; the outcome of the act matters ultimately to them.

We should perceive in this a substitutionary dimension in the act of representation: only the one goes into the wilderness. This is, however, merely one dimension, one that Anselm understood well. But he did not understand the other side. Perhaps that dimension can only be described adequately through story and drama, for it has to do with the difficult role—the agony—of those who cannot go all the way, who are not qualified, but who know that everything depends upon the one who is anointed to that office.

37.2. Representation Applied to Christology and Soteriology. In the concluding observation of the previous subsection, we have already made a transition from the metaphor as such to its christological application; but we have observed only one aspect of the latter. To suggest the more holistic application of the metaphor to christological and soteriological reflection in our context, we shall develop five hypotheses.

a. Continuity with the Tradition. In the foregoing, it has been our intention to show something of the apologetic coinage of the concept of representation. It is our task here to show that it also maintains continuity with the other

512

pole of theology, the tradition. I believe that it is able to do this, moreover, without erecting the kinds of false scandals that are present for contemporary sensibility in the substantialistic language of Chalcedonian Christology and the substitutionary language of Anselmic soteriology.

To take the christological aspect of the tradition first, we argued in the historical chapter of Part III that the christological problem with which the newer Testament's testimony confronted the early church was a two-pronged affirmation that insisted on (1) the full humanity of Jesus and (2) his unique relatedness to the One God of Israel's faith. Chalcedon's resolution of this biblical problem, insightful as it was in some respects, created other, lasting problems for the church whenever it applied to its theology the rule of Scripture; for it substituted for the relational language of the Bible a substantialistic language that, while perhaps comprehensible within the Hellenistic framework, is no longer helpful even if it can be made to overcome the basic ontological leap—which is doubtful. We have seen that the "two natures" Christology never has been an adequate positive statement of the biblical witness to the Christ, and today it is usually falsely scandalous and a barrier to faith.

The metaphor of representation permits us to sustain the fundamental profession of belief that the newer Testament as well as Chalcedon, in its way, wished to affirm, without indulging in the substantialistic-ontological language of the latter. Instead of translating the biblical profession of Christ's unique relation with the Father into his divinity, we may profess Jesus Christ as God's representative;[11] and instead of translating the biblical witness to Jesus' real humanity as his human nature (*ousia*), we may affirm that he is our human representative.[12] In other words, his being is described in terms of his with-being. Thus we do not say he "is" divine (a statement that always courted the Monarchian heresy and is a permanent offense to the religion of the older Testament), but we say that he appears before us as the representative of the divine person, the one whose being-with-God is such that it communicates God's being-with-us. We do not say that he "is" (also) human (a statement that is both self-evident and in itself empty of content), but we say that he is *representatively* human: that is, that his being-with-*us*, in solidarity with our humanity, constitutes a decisive representation of us *coram Deo* (before God).

It is true that this leaves unanswered the question, *How* is this special representational life possible? or What sort of being could be so described? But that question cannot be answered. There is no rational explanation, no satisfactory response to it. It is a matter of experience and of faith; it can only be professed and confessed. I am in complete agreement with Berkhof here: "In these words [representative and representation] we hit upon the final, solid

---

11. See the statement of David Tracy in n. 8 above.
12. See the statement of Letty Russell in n. 8 above.

core of our salvation, and it is very much a question whether this core can be further split or elucidated."[13] Encountered by Jesus Christ through the testimony of the Spirit and the Word, the disciple community professes: "This one represents God to us and us to God. We do not know *how* this can be, only *that it is*. We are content to be represented by this one, and we believe that this one represents to us all that we need to experience of God."

We are left, then, with a "leap of faith"—and also a "scandal of particularity." But it is at least faith and not credulity, and at least it is a real *skandalon* and not a false one—not simply a barrier to comprehension and communication. Faith confesses Jesus' dual representation and its uniqueness. It would not be Christian faith were it otherwise. It remains for us in Volume III to address the question whether this particularity jeopardizes dialogue with other faiths. For the present we only want to profess that faith's affirmation of Jesus as representative of God and humanity avoids the false scandal of positing a historical person who combines in his being two apparently incompatible substances, divinity and humanity. The key christological question is not about Jesus' individual, isolated being but about the mode of his being-*with*— with God and with us. Jesus is with us so unreservedly that he may represent us before God; and Jesus is with God so unreservedly that he may represent God to us. This is quite different from saying that he *is* simultaneously true God and true man. Yet it retains what the profession of the "two natures" might have intended had it been cast in the language of Jerusalem and not of Athens.

Secondly, representation as a symbolic device for the discussion of Christ's person is also and immediately applicable to the discussion of his work—and without a shift of metaphor. In fact, as I shall attempt to say more systematically in the second point, the concept of representation enables us to overcome, in a remarkable measure, a long-standing problem in this doctrinal area, namely the separation of Christology and soteriology. With this metaphor it would be artificial to separate the two. We could not even speak about Jesus as the representative without constantly resorting to reference to his representative office. The concern of the present hypothesis is, however, to demonstrate continuity with the tradition; and here I am thinking in particular about that soteriological tradition which, as we have seen, has been so influential in the West as to be named *the* Latin theory.

As we noted in passing, the idea of Christ as our representative does contain a dimension of substitution. A representative is a substitute insofar as he or she does something for one, in one's behalf. As we put it earlier, the representative who is qualified for this office in a way that the ones represented are not "goes all the way." There is this singling out, this anointing (Messiah, we recall,

---

13. *Christian Faith*, 302.

means the chosen or anointed one). One does what the others cannot do, are not able to do, will not do, are not asked to do.

This is the essential aspect of the substitutionary concept—and by that I mean that it is necessary to the biblical testimony. For the idea of election, as of anointing, as of the sacrifice of one for others, *is* biblical; indeed it is of the essence of the biblical narrative. It is bound up with the whole conception of the covenant. Israel is called out from among all the peoples of the world, and is therefore "judged" (Amos 3). But this does not mean that Israel *alone* is judged, shown mercy, restored; it means that Israel is the medium through whose judgment and mercy God "blesses" the many (Gen. 12:1f.). Israel does not *replace* the others (that is substitution); rather she is there *in behalf of* the others (that is representation). She is singled out, but for a mission infinitely more inclusive than her own welfare. In representation, the substitutionary dimension, in short, is retained so far as the singling out or calling is concerned, but it is strictly inadequate when it comes to explaining the intention of this anointing.

Both with respect to the person and the work of the Christ, then, representation provides a thread of continuity with the essence of the church's doctrinal past for a contemporary mentality that cannot and does not have to accept the *accidens* (inessentials) of that past.

b. A Holistic Approach to Christology.

The preceding point is a reminder of one of the perennial dilemmas of christological thought: the division of person and work. It is hard to overestimate the negative consequences of this division; yet so entrenched is it that it is scarcely possible to discuss the subject historically without falling into the practice. There are some good reasons why the subject must be considered separately: in particular, we have seen that soteriology involves anthropological theory and social analysis in a way that Christology in the restrictive sense may not, or in a way that is at least distinctive. For the Eastern church, Christology as such has seemed more or less sufficient; in the West, on the contrary, christological clarity was sacrificed to an overweening soteriological preoccupation. Both branches of Christendom were impoverished by this division.

Part of the reason the person and work of the Christ have been treated separately (or rather, tended to separate because of the way they were treated) is that no common language was found to serve both at once. Most of the christological language of the early debates was borrowed from the Greco-Roman world of the first four Christian centuries. While the soteriological doctrines and theories that we considered have reflected the changing human needs of nearly two thousand years, the linguistic base of soteriology has been biblical: triumph over evil and death, sacrifice for sin and guilt, love and forgiveness revealed. It is almost impossible to move back and forth between the christological language of essence and substance, unity and distinction (*hypostaseis*), and the soteriological language of conquest, suffering, and love. Two different language-worlds are present in these two sides of Christology, and it was almost inevitable that they would seldom be held together by anything beyond the insistence of faith that they both have to do with one and the same person, Jesus.

Representation does not solve all problems, but it does solve this one, if it is imaginatively deployed. Without any linguistic shift, representation serves both areas equally and helps to prevent the distinctive concerns of each from detracting from their essential unity: Who *is* this? The representative. What does he *do* for us? He represents us to God and God to us. With one and the same language, one speaks of both aspects of the doctrine; in speaking of the person one necessarily refers to his work, and vice versa. This is perhaps an obvious point, but after the linguistic and conceptual confusions of the ages, it is both intellectually and spiritually liberating.

c. Identity-with-Distinction.

The hypothesis I wish to defend here is an extension of what has already been said about the relation between the convention of substitution and the idea of representation, but it also involves us in a closer look at the meaning of representation as such.

Representation connotes a dynamic of relationship comprised of the tension between two opposite or polar qualities of relation, identity and distinction. A representative must have, or achieve, a high degree of identity with the one to be represented (we have already used the word "solidarity" in this connection). I can represent my son because of our blood relationship. My wife can represent me because of our chosen and legal bond. If a lawyer is to represent me in court, however, she has in one way or another to acquire a sufficient knowledge of and sympathy with my case so that she can "be there" in my behalf, and not only to defend her own ideas or professional reputation. Representation is bound up with the proximity to and identification with the one to be represented; for the latter is precisely to be re-presented, to become "present" through the presence of another.

At the same time, there can be no necessary or meaningful act of representation without distinction. The only reason for resorting to the practice of representation in the first place is because the party desiring representation is for one reason or another incapable of "being there" personally: his personal presence or identity is insufficient. The representative therefore must not only have or achieve a high degree of identification with the one to be represented; he or she must also be distinctive: the representative must bring something of her or his own to the representational act. To be present *for* (*pro*) another, the representative cannot be there simply *as* the other one. Without identification with the other, the representative will be unable to "present" the other; but without distinction from the other one, the representation will be ineffective. The mother who appears before the principal of her daughter's high school in order to interpret the latter's unacceptable grades can do so because she has her daughter's good at heart and wishes to help her; but she will not help her very much unless she has acquired, in the process of life and parenthood, a more mature understanding of the world than her young daughter possesses as yet. The diplomat who enters into difficult peace negotiations with the deputation from a potential enemy state is qualified to represent his own country because of his citizenship and his sympathetic identification with the aims of his people; but if he has no more than citizenship and sympathy—if he is not also exceptionally knowledgeable about both his own and the enemy nation—he will prove a poor representative. He will perhaps be a spokesperson or delegate without being a representative.

This dynamic of identity-with-distinction is not only inherent in the concept and office of representation generally, it is also a significant nuance in christological thought. In Christology proper (that is, discussion of Christ's person), it is essential for our understanding of the relation between Jesus and God, Jesus and humankind. Jesus, to be God's representative, must be seen to have a high degree of identification with God. Because of the power of the linguistic traditions of Athens in christological evolution, we should have to say that Jesus must "have" this identification with the Father. But without resorting to adoptionism (which was also a consequence of substantialistic thought), we could just as well say that Jesus "acquired" a high degree of identification with God; that is to say, in his own personal development he became increasingly conscious of God's presence and purposes and felt himself profoundly called by God.

If we are thinking relationally and not substantially, it is wholly unnecessary and even misleading to consider the dimension of identification as a matter of possession (having). Using a previous illustration, we may say that the mother's ability to represent her daughter to the school principal may be partly due to her blood relationship (and to that extent something possessed); but blood relationship as such contributes nothing to this representative act. There are no doubt millions of parents who have neither the ability nor the desire to assume such deputations in behalf of their children. By the same token, we might say that it would be possible for God to have "begotten" many sons, and yet it would not follow that all of these sons automatically, through their "physical" relation with their "Father," would have achieved the high degree of identification necessary to the office of representation. According to the Bible, Jesus did not "have" the qualifications necessary for this office; rather, "Although he was a Son, he learned obedience through what he suffered; and having been made perfect, he became the source of eternal salvation for all who obey him, having been designated by God a high priest according to the order of Melchizedek" (Heb. 5:8-10). What is important here is not the "sonship" as such, but the behavior of the son—the obedience, "to the point of death—even death on a cross" (Phil. 2:8), which must be "learned."

But representation also implies distinction from the one represented. God, as God, cannot perform this office; God cannot represent God's Self. Nor is this a Christian invention. It is a direct heritage from the tradition of Jerusalem, and as such it is shrouded in mystery. At base, it has to do with God's otherness. The transcendent God whose love drives toward communion with that which God infinitely transcends, the creature: this God always calls and sends forth messengers. Rarely are they heavenly messengers. Normally they are earthly—*very* earthly—beings. This God, who "in many and various ways" spoke through the prophets, now "has spoken to us by a son" (Heb. 1:1-2).

The dimension of distinction is already implicit in the affirmation of this identification. The whole notion of a son who is identical with his father is in the first place an impossible one, given the relational ontology of the Bible; but in the case of this particular father it is absurd.[14] God remains God. Even though the categories of Athens would have permitted it to some extent (and to some extent they did), the evolving doctrine of the Christ in the early church rejected the formulation, "Jesus is God." Intuitively, though seldom out of conscious faithfulness to Israel, the Christians recognized in the monophysitic formulation a fundamental break with the Scriptures. Jesus, to represent God—to be Emmanuel—cannot simply *be* God. His necessary identification with the Father implies a necessary distinction from the Father. Is it then a matter of subordination? No, because that concept lands us back in hierarchic, substantialistic thinking. Relationally considered, the representative cannot *be* the one represented. He must be "with" the latter intensively (see the Prologue of John), but as we have noted throughout, "with-being" always implies otherness. In fact, what we are now observing in this whole area is nothing else than elaboration of the basic ontology of biblical thought—the "ontology of communion"—with respect to Christology. This ontology is always a matter of identity-with-distinction—naturally—because its core is love.

This construction also applies to Jesus' representation of humankind. In order to represent us, he must have or must acquire a high degree of identification with us. We have seen how important this is, not only for Christology proper but for soteriology as well. Jesus must not only "be" human—this in itself would mean little; he must participate in our humanity. Scripturally stated, he must "in every respect [be] tempted as we are" (Heb. 4:15). If he is to liberate the oppressed, he must himself know oppression. If he is to be the medium of

---

14. On the question of Jesus' relation to the "Abba God," see Moltmann, *The Way of Jesus Christ,* 142, 165.

divine mercy and forgiveness, he must himself come close to human sin and guilt—be tempted. If he is to demonstrate God's love to the loveless, he must experience alienation, forsakenness. Being born makes him technically human, but only suffering will render him human enough to represent us. We shall have to recall this when we come to speak about Jesus and the quest for meaning in our present-day context.

But identification with us is also not sufficient for the representational act of the one who would represent us *before God*. Jesus must also be different from us if he is to be our "vicar." Scripturally stated, he must be "without sin" (Heb. 4:15). Sin here must be understood biblically, that is, relationally. What this means is not that Jesus must be morally pure, personally blameless; rather, he must be in the kind of relationship with God and the neighbor that leaves him free for them. He must not be bound to himself. He must not have fallen into our kind of self-preoccupation. He could not and would not even desire to represent us if he had. To be our "high priest" (a purely representational concept) he must achieve a high degree of freedom: the freedom that is necessary to accept the destiny ("my cup") of representation. He must be ready (using scriptural language) to "lay down his life for his friends." The one who goes forward in our behalf—who goes all the way—is not allowed to indulge in our kind of reservations about self-giving. In this he is distinct, and only so is he able to represent us.

What we are claiming, to put it into other words, is that the unity of Jesus' life and work is posited on the confluence of the two sides of his representational vocation. It is his identification with God that gives him the possibility of being sufficiently different from us to represent us to God; and it is his identification with us that gives him the possibility of being sufficiently different from God to represent God to us. The Nestorian idea of Jesus' unity as a unity of will or a moral unity is thus in some respects one with which we can find sympathy. But unfortunately it was so befuddled by metaphysical substantialism that it could not free itself from the charge of ontic dualism. We are thinking relationally, and therefore we leave behind the language of substances. It is neither biblically justifiable nor apologetically useful; it is in fact an immense barrier to communication, despite its great age and entrenchment. Jesus' so-called divine nature is far more scripturally conceived as his relational identification with God, which manifests itself, not in the miraculous, ordinarily conceived, but in his exceptional capacity for compassion and for solidarity with humanity ("divine pathos"). And Jesus' so-called human nature is his relational identification of himself with us, manifesting itself in his readiness vicariously to represent us before the eternal. The two sides of the representational life are not only two sides of the same person, they are wholly interdependent, the one expressing itself externally on the internal basis of the other.

d. Representation and Participation.   We have seen that a perennial problem of the Christian soteriological tradition is what is usually called its objectivity: that is, in both of the older types of atonement theology the salvific event is presented in such a way as to eliminate the dimension of subjectivity or (better stated) participation. In the ransom or classical theory, the core event is depicted as an interplay between God and Satan, with the Christ himself as an almost passive partner. In Anselm's theory, Satan is eliminated as having no right to such prominence; but the drama is still one involving chiefly the transcendent personae, Father and Son, with humankind introduced only as recipients of "the benefits of his [Christ's] passion."

Abelard was particularly conscious of this mythic objectivity—and overcorrected it. His theory, sometimes called the subjective theory for this reason, so concentrates upon the human response to the cross that it leaves in doubt the whole matter of the divine initiative and the question of grace.

If the metaphor of representation is imaginatively developed, it is capable of retaining both the necessary accentuation on the divine initiative and grace *and* human participation. We did not and do not choose Jesus to be our priest, our representative; he has chosen us (John 15:16f.). And the representation that he enacts—not only the cross, but his entire life process—is clearly his own. It is certainly not due to our support—a point that the newer Testament almost shouts. Unlike us, unlike even the most loyal of his twelve disciples, he "goes all the way" toward the place of encounter. Through him we may learn how to stand in "the *environs* of Golgotha" (Barth), but we are not the one "crucified, dead and buried." With and in him we may learn how to suffer with and for others, but this is his gift to us and not our achievement. In short, the objective side of the salvific event is maintained.

But we have also shown that representation, even as it is ordinarily conceived and lived, connotes a high degree of participation on the part of those being represented. Only the one who represents me goes forward to the place where I cannot go (whether that refers to the court of law, the office of the school principal, or the negotiating table of diplomats charged with securing world peace); but insofar as I am conscious of the representation being made in my behalf, insofar as I am brought to know how profoundly it affects my own destiny, I am *carried forward* in spirit even though I am not physically there at the place of the encounter.

This is where representation differs most conspicuously from substitution. When substitution is the guiding concept of our atonement theology, the behavior of the disciple community during the arrest, trial, scourging, presentation, crucifixion, and death of their master is almost a matter of indifference. What is vital is being done, all alone, by "the substitute." Where representation becomes the informing metaphor of the story, in contrast, the behavior of the disciple community throughout the entire ministry of Jesus

520

and particularly at its ending is an integral aspect of what is being done. And does not the scriptural story as it is presented in the Synoptic tradition assume precisely that? Why else would the Gospel writers tell us so much about the activities of the twelve and others—the initial attempts of Peter impulsively to resist the arrest; the flight of all from the scene, one even running away naked; the vehement denial of any relationship to "that man" by a Peter more calculating than at first; the tragic recognition and suicide (or accidental death?) of the betrayer; the pathetic figures around the cross; the loyal women; Mary in the Garden. All of this is calculated to tell us that even prior to its spiritual "enlightenment" (Acts 2) the disciple community is deeply involved with what is going on

True, only the one goes forward—all the way. But are the others, who could not bring themselves to leave him earlier ("to whom can we go?"—John 6:68), who have just shared the most intimate participation in his life (the meal in the upper room)—are they indifferent? Incidental to the story? Of course not. They know that they are themselves being brought forward to the place of judgment. They know that this event has to do with their own destiny. In spirit, and with every fiber of their being, they are with him. Their behavior, including their utter dejection during the postcrucifixion period, is otherwise inexplicable. And this involvement is only intensified and given new meaning by what they experienced as Jesus' resurrection, postresurrectional appearances, ascension, and the advent of the Spirit.

In practice, representation as it occurs in our lives daily can fail to incorporate the dimension of participation. Perfunctorily executed, an act of representation may be nothing more than the substitution of another person's time, skills, connections, and so on, for one's own lack. But almost anything can be reduced to the perfunctory—including love. What we have to recognize is that when it is seriously undertaken, representation always implies the participation of the one being represented—*re-presented,* being caused to be present through the being-there of another. Jesus represents us *coram Deo* seriously; and therefore insofar as we acquire any deep consciousness of his "priesthood" we know ourselves to be "present."

Does the latter phrase imply that the objective factor is left out of account? Must consciousness or awareness of the representative life and event be made the decisive aspect? Certainly it is vital to the profession of a Christian faith. I can see no way of avoiding that, biblically. To present the sacrifice of the Christ as a vicarious deed that is wholly independent of any awareness on the part of those for whom it is undertaken seems to me to overstep the bounds of biblical sensibility—including the entire sacrificial system of Judaism, out of which the sacrifice of the cross emerges. To present the cross as an objective satisfaction with no referent in subjective experience is to adopt a legalistic point of view that is antithetical to the biblical concept of grace.

Nevertheless, the prominence of human awareness that is present in the biblical story—and not only in connection with the Christ but even more so in connection with the work of the Spirit—does not mean that awareness is the decisive thing. It is the means to our consciousness of what is decisive. And that consciousness knows that it cannot even begin to grasp the full implications of what is decisive: Who knows how expansive is the suffering love of God? Who knows this even for himself, herself—to say nothing of those who seem not to know? To state the matter in any other way would be to fall into Gnosticism.

e. Representation as a Bridge between Christology and Ecclesiology.

Repeatedly in works of systematic and practical theology it is affirmed that Christology is the basis of ecclesiology. Yet this intimate connection is seldom mirrored in ecclesiological language. With many of the newer Testament's own metaphors, an obvious connection is linguistically present: vine and branches, bride and bridegroom, head and body. Because the latter especially—the Pauline metaphor, which is more than a metaphor—has been so significant in ecclesiological dogma, the continuity between the doctrine of the Christ and the doctrine of the church has at least never quite been lost. But without the help of nonbiblical and nonreligious language, the "body of Christ" imagery devolves into pious jargon and the in-language of the church. It becomes more liturgical than descriptive, so that in the end it communicates little even to those who belong to "the body of Christ."

Beyond that, unless it is carefully interpreted, the *soma Christou* symbol too easily lends itself to that type of ecclesiology which loses sight of the distinctions that must be made between the Christ and the church, on the one hand, and between the church and the divine realm ("kingdom") on the other. The notion of the church as Christ's very body becomes a convenient way of undergirding the ultimacy and supremacy of the church. In both Roman and Anglo-Catholic doctrine, there has been a constant danger of overlooking the fact that Jesus Christ remains the "head" of this "body," and also of the fact that, biblically speaking, there is no easy correlation between the church and the kingdom.[15]

The inner logic of the motif of representation can provide precisely what is required by way of a nonreligious linguistic vehicle for the necessary theological interface of Christology with ecclesiology—and, as in the case of the two aspects of Christology itself, without an artificial shift of metaphor. As with the

---

15. The Pauline metaphor of the body should be juxtaposed with the Johannine metaphor of the bride (Revelation 18, 21–22). As Claude Welch has pointed out, the church as "bride of Christ" is presented in the apocalypse as one tempted to harlotry. In other words, the bride imagery is thoroughly eschatological: The church is not the kingdom. See Claude Welch, *The Reality of the Church* (New York: Charles Scribner's Sons, 1958), 132–33.

biblical symbol of the priest, theologically applied to Jesus as our "High Priest," so representation can be considered a mode of translating into nonreligious language the priestly vocation of the church. Like so much of the church's language that has been hallowed by centuries of pious usage (including "body of Christ"), "priest" and "priesthood" do not constitute a very good vehicle for the discussion of the church's life and mission today. This vehicle is steeped in practice that renders it questionable.[16] This does not mean that it should be abandoned altogether, but it does mean that when it is used theologically and doctrinally, even within the disciple community, it must be *explained.*

And when it is explained it spells out precisely: *representation.* Thus, when it is said that the church can be regarded as a priestly people (1 Pet. 2:9), as was and is Israel (Exod. 19:6), what is meant is that the disciple community is a representative community: it stands before God in behalf of the world God loves, and before the world in behalf of the God who would mend it.

Employing this language, we are able to cement and simultaneously interpret the relation between Jesus Christ and the church. The church is that community of discipleship which is being brought to live the representative life of Jesus Christ in the world. Through hearing, through the sacraments, above all through the enlightening and life-giving work of the divine Spirit, this community is being enabled to participate in his participation in the life of God, and this enables it to represent God's presence in the world. By the same token, it is being enabled to participate in Christ's participation in the world's life, so that it may authentically represent the world before God.[17]

In this representational pilgrimage, the church also knows suffering. This is part of its incorporation into the life of the crucified one. It suffers as it appears before God in behalf of the world, for it must hear God's judgment of the world in order to become the bearer of God's mercy toward the world. And it suffers as it appears before the world representing the divine Word, because

---

16. I am not thinking only of its almost exclusive use in catholic circles in the West, though that too must be taken into account; but beyond that the model left us by the historic priesthood, with its insidious and perhaps unfair but nevertheless unavoidable connotation of authority, hypocrisy, status, and finally archaism, severely limits its usefulness. For most people, it is also inherently sexist.

17. If especially this latter dimension of the church's representative life were a little appreciated, it would transform the worship of congregations—particularly those small and often demoralized congregations that are becoming increasingly the norm in North America today. Ben Smillie relates a moving episode in his own life, illustrating just this point: "While an undergraduate at Westminster College, Cambridge, I had been asked to provide pulpit supply for one Sunday at a small Presbyterian church that stood in the shadow of Canterbury Cathedral. On the Monday following I went to the daily morning prayers in the cathedral. With some awkwardness, I found myself following the congregational responses of the Prayer Book—I was the entire congregation! After the service the rector shook my hand and said, 'Thank you for representing the world before God.' I floated out of that service with a feeling of utter well-being." (*Beyond the Social Gospel: Church Protest on the Prairies* [Toronto: United Church Pub. House and Fifth House Publishers, 1991], 148.

the world does not want to hear this Word. Thus the suffering of the church— certainly the most consistent and well-developed "mark of the church" in the Bible—is a direct consequence of its participation in the (dual) representational life of the Christ.

What is of particular importance in the application of representational language to ecclesiology is that it contains an inherent warning against the ever-present danger of ecclesiastical exclusivism. Here too the distinction from substitutionary language is vital. The church is *not* a substitute community but a representative community. It does not take the place of the world, it exists in behalf of the world. It is not an elite but an elect community: that is, it is chosen for service and as a means, not an end. It is the world that God loves and wills to engage, embrace, and heal. The church as means to that end is brought to appear before God, in and through Jesus Christ, to represent creaturely being. And it is sent out into the midst of the (fallen) creation to represent in thought, word, and deed God's redemptive intention and presence. The church has this two-sided representational life and work as it is caused by the divine Spirit to participate in the life and work of the one who has bidden it, "Follow me."

f. Representation as Link between Christology and the Christian Ethic. Both the previous hypothesis and the present one must await further development in the third volume; but we are seeking to establish the viability of a language that has important possibilities in the realm of Christology, and Christology is the central and foundational doctrine of this profession of faith. It is therefore necessary to show not only the implications of this language for ecclesiology in general but also for the daily life of the disciple community in the world.[18] Presently we shall see that representation has anthropological potential as well, for the "new humanity" that is being given through the redeeming work of God in Christ is to be understood as a representative creaturehood: the "new" man or woman *en Christo* is a creature who is "there" representatively in behalf of the other creatures. This will become part of the final discussion of this chapter. For the present we wish only to observe that, beyond the ecclesiological connections that can be sustained through this language, it is also well-suited to holding together two branches of theology that are constantly coming apart: systematic theology and ethics or ethical theology.

One of the main reasons why Christian ethics has so frequently been allowed to shape itself into a separate discipline is that theology can seem to be sufficient in and of itself. This is particularly so on account of the types of Christology and soteriology that have characterized classical and dominant traditions of the

---

18. See John Howard Yoder, *The Priestly Kingdom: Social Ethics as Gospel* (Notre Dame, Ind.: Univ. of Notre Dame Press, 1984).

faith. In these latter, the life and work of Jesus are in themselves so final and complete that it is almost redundant to speak of the church at all, let alone of a Christian ethic. "*He* paid the price" (a popular slogan for the Latin and penal theories); we live off "the benefits of *his* passion."[19] Particularly in the strong theology of grace expressed in some aspects of the Lutheran Reformation, this all-sufficiency of Christology can end (as Bonhoeffer warned) in a neglect of Christian ethics altogether, or its relegation to the theological sidelines.

It is not very much better, however, where the dogmatic/systematic side of theology is insufficiently developed. In Anglicanism, Methodism, and other ecclesiastical bodies of the Anglo-Saxon world especially, where piety and activism predominate over doctrinal struggle, there is no lack of concern for ethics; but the ethic frequently lacks any clear foundation in theology, and especially in a christologically based theology. Where it is not a poor imitation of the Catholic "natural law" basis, the Christian ethic as practiced in North American Protestantism is often an equally flat duplication of the *imitatio Christi* of medieval or liberal piety. The substitutionary character of the sufficiency-of-grace approach leaves an ethical vacuum; and the detached ethic of Christian morality begs the question of its foundational raison d'être.

Language will not solve the problem, for the problem is not linguistic at base, nor even intellectual. It is a spiritual problem: We fear and resent the ethical demands of the gospel, and therefore we invent theologies and Christologies that are interesting in themselves; or, conversely, we invent moral codes that do not have to come up to the demands of the cross.

Yet language can help; and in the motif of representation we have a common conceptual basis for both sides of the Christian profession of faith. To say (as I have done above) that the Spirit of God incorporates us into the representative life and work of the Christ is to say that we are given a distinctive ethical direction and calling. *With* and *in* the Christ, we are to live out of a redeemed creaturehood, a new humanity, that lives not for itself but for others—lives, that is to say, representatively. Here life and work, being and doing, are clearly part of the same reality and can be described by the same language. Of Jesus himself we put it this way: the Representative represents. Of the disciple community we may say the same thing, with the christological premise intact: taken up into the life of the Representative, the work of this community is—to represent. Grace is presupposed. It is not just our decision to become representatives, it is a gift of new identity, a new creaturehood for which we must be freed. But the moment of this grace is also the moment of our initiation into the

---

19. Some feminist Christians speak of "the lone heroism" of this concept of the Christ and attribute it to the masculine dominance of the christological tradition. See June Christine Goudey, "Theologians Re-Imaging Redemption," in *The Christian Century* (July 11–18, 1990), 675ff.; Rita Nakashima Brock, *Journeys by Heart* (New York: Crossroad, 1991), 58.

discipleship it assumes. To be given the gift of representation—to be there "with" and "for" others—and not to use this gift is the essence of disobedience. The work of the community that is liberated from self-preoccupation is to be occupied with the representation of others.

It remains for us to elaborate this. What the representative life and work of the disciple community means concretely in our context—this is the end for which we are now trying to lay the foundation; and it will occupy our attention also in this volume, but more particularly in the third. Part of what is involved in laying this foundation—the prerequisite for understanding our representative existence as Christ's *body*—is to ask concretely what such representation must mean for the *head*. Hence we turn from our methodological reflections on the hermeneutics of representation to their application, contextually, to the meaning of "Jesus Christ *for us today.*"

38. Christ *Our* Representative

38.1. Jesus Christ: "God with Us." As the positive core of the Christian profession concerning the character of redemption—as gospel—the doctrine of Jesus as the Messiah of God incorporates two interdependent phases or movements. For purposes of discussion they are separable as perspectives on the one life and work; in reality, they are inseparable. We may describe them as the movement of God toward humanity and the movement of humanity toward God. Faith perceives both of these movements in Jesus as the Christ. Representing the God of the Scriptures, Jesus moves toward humanity in unqualified commitment and love. Representing humanity, Jesus moves toward God in trust, obedience, and expectation. The first movement—rather, the first aspect of this indivisible act of representation—is what we shall have to consider here. Subsequently, we shall think about Jesus' human representation.

One of the most significant of all the biblical titles assigned to Jesus Christ, significant not least of all because of its implicit affirmation of continuity with the faith of the older Testamental community, is the term Emmanuel: God-with-us. It is also, interestingly enough, one of the least-mentioned in the history of theology and Christology. By comparison, such titles as Savior, Lord, Son of God, and even Son of Man abound in this doctrinal history. Yet Emmanuel tells us something that none of the more popular titles communicates. Emmanuel is in fact in itself almost a full and sufficient confession of faith: God is with us. In Jesus, God is with us.

Straightforward as this capsule confession of faith seems, however, it is by no means as simple as it appears. (Or perhaps it is the essence of simplicity, and therefore utterly profound.) Much—indeed everything—depends upon the matrix of the religious sensibility in which it is announced. Both from our

526

discussion of God in Part I of this work ("the Father Almighty") and from our historical and critical reflections on Christology in the first two chapters of this third part, it has been maintained that the matrix of religious sensibility pertaining throughout the history of Christendom and still, largely, today is such that a statement of this nature would have to be heard in a certain way. How shall we characterize that way? We may say, I think, that the Emmanuel-confession, so far as it was even employed in Constantinian ecclesiology, would have to be heard in that context as a strong reaffirmation of the power of God and of the divinity of the Christ. The accent has been on the first word: God. *God* is with us. And God, being understood primarily in terms of omnipotence, can only be "with us" powerfully. The accentuation of Christ's divinity, the repeated danger of losing touch with his humanity, is therefore a logical christological consequence of this Theological premise.

But such a God cannot be with us, because such ultimate power can only intimidate the ultimately powerless. Omnipotence will hardly convey divine solidarity with the creature; on the contrary, it will have the opposite effect. Luther understood this very well (few others have) when he wrote, "Let us then meditate upon the Nativity just as we see it happening in our own babies. I would not have you contemplate the deity of Christ, the majesty of Christ, but rather his flesh. Look upon the Baby Jesus. Divinity may terrify a man. Inexpressible majesty will crush him. That is why Christ took on our humanity, save for sin, that he should not terrify us but rather that with love and favor he should console and confirm."[20] God's almightiness and, as its christological corollary, Christ's monarchic "deity," under the conditions of Constantinian religion strictly circumscribe the character of God's being "with us." Sooner or later, any doctrinal genuflection before the idea of divine solidarity with the creature will have to be offset by the renewed recognition that God, after all, is *God*. Thus God the Father is exempted, so to speak, from any direct participation in the human sufferings of God the Son (the Patripassian controversy), and even the Son is relieved of any profound and sustained participation in the human condition—if not through a docetically inclined Christology proper, then through the swift and decisive proclamation of his resurrection as a glorious overcoming of the confinement of mortality.

What we are really speaking about here is the historical hegemony of the theology of glory. It is typical of this theology that the whole incarnational thrust of the newer Testament is held in check by an overarching and a priori theological triumphalism. Incarnation, to use the language introduced above, means the movement of God toward creaturely being. It means that this movement, which is already very pronounced in the life of Israel long before the manger of Bethlehem and the cross of Golgotha, and which is therefore by no

---

20. Hugh T. Kerr, *Readings in Christian Thought* (Nashville: Abingdon Press, 1966), 157.

means an innovation of the newer Testament, now reaches its climax: complete, unreserved, unconditional identification with the creature. Here, as we have put it sermonically, the representative "goes all the way" to the place of encounter. Here the Creator enters into full communion with the creature.

But theological triumphalism has never been prepared to allow God to go all the way. It is the very aim of the *theologia gloriae* to prevent such a thing. For complex reasons—"religious" reasons that embrace everything from grand political to private psychological motivation—the theology of glory from the outset fully intends to keep God from solidarity with the creature; or, if it allows God to seem for a moment (three days?) to have gone all the way, it recovers itself quickly and decisively through recourse to the triumph of the third day. Nothing equals the triumphalism of Christian resurrectionism (I do not say "the resurrection"). Resurrectionism achieves the ultimate coup of triumphalistic religion: It permits deity to seem, for a moment, to have been overcome— and therefore it makes the triumph of power and glory all the more impressive.

The price that resurrectionism pays for this quite predictable and, in practice, highly manipulative tactic (though it is a price that can only be understood as such from another point of view altogether) is the effective nullification of the incarnation. And the reader will understand, on the basis of what has already been said, that I do not mean merely the denial of Jesus' full "humanity," that "substance," but I mean the denial of God's determination, in and through the Representative, to move toward the creation and the creature without reservation. I mean God's achievement in the Christ of the closest possible proximity to humankind, the divine goal that has been visible throughout the life of Israel.

The theology of glory is not able really to profess, "Emmanuel!" This, in the long run, is why that particular christological title has been underdeveloped in the history of Christendom. If Constantinian Christianity sometimes adopts this confession, what it means is that *God* is with us, namely God in "his" power, divinity, ineffability, immutability, total otherness. The theology of glory does not and cannot, without contradicting itself, accentuate the "with us" of the Emmanuel-confession of primitive faith; because to be truly *with* us, God would have to let go of the very exaltedness with which this theological mood and preference always intends to surround deity. It is power and glory— and at that quite obvious glory, the glory that empires understand, the glory of winners—that this broad theological stream of Christendom intends always to stress, even when it bows temporarily to divine humiliation. Its gospel is the good news of glory brought down to the state of inglory; therefore it fears above all taking that latter state into itself and making of it the contributive basis of its understanding of the character of authentic glory. Sheer glory, as glory is commonly conceived, may penetrate and overwhelm inglory. It may even negate human ignominy. But the movement is always from glory to the inglorious, with the object of overcoming the latter. There is no way, on the basis of the rubrics of this great triumph song of Constantinian Christianity, for the inglorious, sinful, fallen, beaten, and broken world to become a positive contributing theme, a theme actually informing the meaning of glory and power itself.

It is otherwise with the thin tradition: the *theologia crucis*. Here the foundation of the Emmanuel-confession is the "with us." This concreteness, this rootedness of the confession in the reality that "we" are, with all the pathos, weakness, yearning, regret, guilt, contrition, pain, and incompleteness of our being, is what sets the tone for the Emmanuel-confession when it is heard within the matrix of a faith informed by the theology of the cross. The confession in this case is not based upon a triumphalistic Theology that makes it impossible for God to be with us; on the contrary, our situation is the given in relation to which the "God [who is] with us" graciously conforms. What sort of God would this have to be to be with us? Clearly, this could not be the God of power and glory as these attributes are usually understood. A powerful, glorious God could only be in our midst as an "over-againstness," an overwhelming Other. To be sure, the theology of the cross also confesses God's otherness, but this otherness lies, not in divine power and glory, but precisely in the voluntary relinquishment of these because of love. God's transcendence here is understood as God's willingness to be found in our company, imminent, under the conditions of our history, our inglory.

Jesus Christ can be called "God with us" only as he enters unreservedly into the condition of our humanity. This is not a theoretical humanity; not a substance that can be added to or taken away from another substance, divinity; not a formula—*vere homo*. Rather, it is an existing, living, breathing, interacting humanity, alive within the web of the universe—in fact, not even "humanity" at all, since no such universal actually exists, but human beings in their private and social reality, generation after generation; male and female human beings; adults and children; healthy, sick, dying, and dead people. In short, the actual condition of humankind describes and determines the conditions under which God may be "with" it. God cannot (the biblical God seems not to wish to) create a different humanity from that which God has already created. If God wills to be "with us," then it is really "us" with whom God must enter into relationship, and to do so there must be a good deal of "emptying" (kenosis), surely, on God's part.

38.2. Jesus Christ and the Crisis of Meaning. If this has been established, let us now consider what God's being with us must mean—not with humanity generally, since a general humanity does not exist, but with human beings in the North American context in and around the final decade of the twentieth century. If Jesus as the Christ is truly with us, as he has been with human beings in other contexts throughout history, then according to our earlier analysis of the human condition as we are experiencing it presently he would have to participate in our anxiety over the loss of meaning, our disillusionment, our repressed despair, our unconvincing, Sisyphean enactment of a Prometheanism in which we no longer believe.

To claim that Jesus' representation must be understood to involve him in our kind of anxiety and quest is not at all innovative. It is nothing more than the strict application of the tradition as we have received it. We have seen in connection particularly with the soteriological dimension of Christology that all three types of atonement theology assume that Jesus must and does participate in the predicament of humanity if he is also to be understood as the one who liberates. The humanity presupposed by the ransom theory is an oppressed humanity; therefore Jesus must himself undergo oppression—indeed ultimate oppression—by the very forces that hold humanity captive. The humanity presupposed by the soteriology of sacrifice is a guilty humanity; therefore Jesus is caused to participate in this guilt—indeed, to become the guilty one—despite his personal innocence. The humanity presupposed by the soteriology of demonstration is a humanity ignorant of the divine love; therefore Jesus must experience lovelessness and rejection—indeed, must be forsaken—if he is to become the revealer of God's suffering love.

Always, the salvific principle is the same, though the character of that in relation to which salvation is needed always differs. And the first principle of salvation is that of participation. In order to alter the human condition, the Savior of that condition must participate in it. Moreover, the participation is not just a token role—the participation of being or becoming human, of "being found in human form." It is the participation, rather, of one who enters still more deeply into the human condition—who "goes all the way," to the point of his abandonment by any factors of differentiation that would prevent or soften or qualify in any way his total immersion in our condition.

The truth of the much-debated kenosis theory lies precisely here: Insofar as the divine representative is allowed to retain special powers or graces attached to his origin and mission, he is prevented from full participation in the condition of those whom he has been anointed to redeem. We may go so far as to say that this is the primary christological assumption of biblical faith. It is on account of his representation of God that the Christ must empty himself of divinity, God's intention being to be with us. And within this we find also the Bible's primary soteriological assumption, namely, that the human condition can be altered only from within. Biblical Christology begins with the insistence upon the Christ's full participation in the human condition because of the soteriological assumption that that condition can only be significantly altered ("saved") through a reformation and redirection of its given reality. Anything else would not constitute salvation *of* the world but salvation *from* it.

Does this not accord with the whole biblical approach to divine-human relations? There are, to be sure, "attempts" on the part of the biblical God (as one might put it) to have it otherwise, but through these very "attempts" God learns the truth of what God has known all along: that the creation can be changed—transformed without destruction—only from within.

The history of God's covenanting with the creature marks the Bible's recognition of this conclusion (one might almost say, this foregone conclusion). The Adamic covenant assumes the viability of a modicum of mutuality even beyond the point of the original abrogation of relations. The Noachic covenant, based on the divine hope that at least a remnant can be trusted to be faithful, is already less optimistic about external change in the human condition. The covenant of Sinai from at least one perspective (that of prophetic religion) recognizes frankly that any agreement between God and fickle humankind must be spelled out clearly with respect to the specific obligations of the latter. But with the development of the traditions of the "higher prophets," especially Jeremiah, the hidden or partially hidden presupposition of all the covenants is brought into the open: the only relationship with humankind acceptable to God is one that, from the human side, issues from the very soul of the creature, not from outward observance of the law. Moreover, this *Innerlichkeit* (inwardness) is not merely a selfish desire on God's part; it is for the sake of the creature, who, apart from communing with God "in spirit and truth" (John 4:24) is a living contradiction of its own essence.

"The days are coming, says the Lord, when I will make a new covenant with the house of Israel. . . . I will put my law within them, and I will write it on their hearts; and I will be their God, and they shall be my people" (Jer. 31:31–33). Too often, the "new covenant" concept of Jeremiah is understood by Christians as a novel approach; this accords with the tendency of liberal Christianity to advance a progressivistic view of revelation, and of most historic Christianity to sustain a decisive discontinuity between the "old" and the "new" covenants—Jeremiah's being an early anticipation of the "new covenant in [Christ's] blood." On the contrary, it seems to me that Jeremiah's message represents the unfolding of an assumption that is present throughout biblical history—as I characterized it above, a kind of foregone conclusion. Jeremiah only articulates openly the preunderstanding of the earlier writers; namely, first, that the only relationship with God that the Creator desires and the human creature needs is one that is joyfully willed by and not imposed upon the latter; and, second, that the present state of creaturely alienation from the Creator can only be altered from within the life of the creature.

The question that this now fully acknowledged presupposition raises, however, is the most difficult one for the entire tradition of Jerusalem: How? How is it possible for God to alter the human condition from within? That it must be altered is the universal assumption of biblical faith. Apart from its alteration, it will simply self-destruct. But how alter it without destroying it? How change the whole orientation of the human will? How achieve this "circumcision of the heart"? It simply cannot be done externally. This is not a newer Testamental conclusion; it is the foregone conclusion of the older covenant; it is already assumed by the writer of Genesis 3.

The newer Testament's answer to this problem is also not really new; it is only the enactment of the prophetic formula for the "circumcision of the heart." It is also, to be sure, an original and apparently complex (or profoundly simple?) enactment of this biblical formula for change—and therefore it is full of wonder and is "good news." The nonrealist, the educator, the utopian in all of us supposes that it could have been much more straightforward: spiritually, hiddenly, deeply within the dark recesses of whatever mysterious channels of communication exist between Creator and creature, God might effect an alteration of the human mind and soul—perhaps as an evolutionary process, a process of spiritual evolution (à la Teilhard). Is this not partly what process theology has in mind?

But then, it is *God* who effects the change. And it is no less a matter of manipulation and heteronomy because it occurs in an unostentatious, evolutionary way rather than in a burst of glory. Such a turn of events—from the standpoint of the tradition of Jerusalem—would in fact represent the undoing of the whole covenantal basis of the divine-human relation as God intends it and as human authenticity requires it. To occur within the parameters of that preconception of authentic relationship, there must be some movement also from the human side: a decision is required, a consent to the meeting, the intimacy—nothing less, finally, than love responding to love given.

Thus the complications of the newer Testamental faith, complications that certainly center in the second person of the Trinity, are by no means arbitrary ones. There is a "*logic* of the cross" (Reinhold Niebuhr). The Christ must appear and must precede the "internal testimony of the Holy Spirit" because, while the human transformation may and must be elicited, it cannot simply be imposed, whether by external or internal power. It is part of the "foregone conclusion" of this tradition that the transformation may only be elicited by humankind's encounter with that which it can in some fundamental way receive, engage, and comprehend—namely, another human life, but a life lived in unreserved identification with others, a life transparent of something, therefore, beyond the possibilities that seem to open up to those who live strictly within the cause-and-effect sequences of historical existence. That part of the transformative event which has to do with humanity's residual capacity for decision is what Christology is all about. Pneumatology, the doctrine of the Spirit, is not thereby excluded, but it is secondary. Without the Spirit, the human will to change could never be sustained; but without the person of Jesus, the Christ, that will would not be awakened to the radical need to change and the possibility of change in the first place.

When we use the expression "from within," therefore, we mean this need for the representative of the God who would be "with us" to be in our midst as one who can be understood as truly participating in our existence—"tempted like us in every respect." The life that he pursues in our midst must give concrete evidence of being lived under the very conditions that affect us; otherwise, the possibility that this life opens to us, awakening in us the will to change, will not be grasped—or it will be grasped only as a possibility for those, whoever they may be, who are not "like us."

The latter phrase describes precisely the way in which Jesus Christ is perceived by many outside the churches in North America today—and by many who are inside, who may silently accept what the church professes yet without believing its applicability to themselves. For while we are still trying—intuitively and by rote, for the most part—to present Jesus Christ as one who is "tempted like us in every respect," the "us" whose condition we professional Christians have in mind is a humanity that is not the humanity of our actual context. It is a humanity, perhaps, that knows guilt and shame (Anselm's or Calvin's paradigm), or lovelessness and discouragement (Abelard's and the liberals' paradigm), or oppression (the classical paradigm, which is still applicable to some segments of our society); but seldom is it a humanity that knows the loss of purpose in the face of an indifferent universe, a humanity that suspects (in a new version of Koheleth) that human existence is precisely what it seems—vain and absurd, and may be in what Moltmann has called its "last era."[21]

To be "with us"—to make good the incarnational quest of the Word to alter "from within"—Jesus will have to be known by us as one capable of entertaining and of living out of such anxiety. So long as we present him as one who knows nothing of this, who never doubts as we doubt, who never knew our kind of disbelief and despair, God's movement toward us in him will remain nothing more than a pious and anachronistic myth.

It is, I suspect, the lingering power of theological triumphalism in our churches and ourselves that keeps us from presenting Jesus Christ as one who knew and knows that anxiety. For the anxiety of meaninglessness and despair (to use Tillich's terminology) is undoubtedly the most debilitating of all the anxieties and, for North Americans especially, the one with which we want to have the least to do. Perhaps our continuing if increasingly pathetic cultural triumphalism expresses itself most characteristically in our confinement of the Christ to the known anxieties of the race, the "tried and true" anxieties of fate and guilt and lovelessness. Perhaps we think that the Christ, and the gospel, and we ourselves could not survive exposure to the absurd.

---

21. *The Way of Jesus Christ,* 159, 191, 194, and elsewhere.

The truth, however, is that Christian faith cannot surv:ve *failure* to engage precisely that anxiety.

That failure, however, is inevitable only for the church that refuses to shed its imperial trappings. If and insofar as we can free ourselves from the cloying presuppositions of christological triumphalism, we may not only risk the possibility that the gospel of the crucified one could be brought into direct contact with the anxiety of meaning; we may even learn to believe that it is precisely for that encounter that this gospel of the crucified one is intended. For is not the frantic quest for meaning the quintessentially human anxiety?—the anxiety that is still present after the anxieties of oppression and guilt have been assuaged?—the anxiety that is found in "the world come of age" (Bonhoeffer)? Is it not possible that in these so-called developed societies of the North Atlantic, which have experienced the amelioration (not, of course, the overcoming) of so many of the ancient and more immediate anxieties of the race, our relative freedom from preoccupation with these has left us the more vulnerable to the anxiety that remains? And is not precisely this, religiously speaking, the great challenge and opportunity with which historical providence has confronted Christians in these societies: to test whether this gospel speaks, not only to those who are in bondage to powers and principalities, and not only to those who fear for their eternal salvation, but also to those who ask whether the whole process, from beginning to end, has any purpose in it?

What seems to me astonishing is that the churches of this continent have learned so little about this challenge, while some outside the churches (ostensibly) seem to have grasped it with great imagination. I shall illustrate what I mean by reference to two popular dramas, in both of which Jesus is the central figure and as such is depicted as one of "us," tempted as we are tempted, asking whether and how, in such a nonteleological universe, there could be any meaning.[22]

The first illustration is *Jesus Christ Superstar*. While this "rock opera" was written by an English author and composer, it was received more keenly in North America, perhaps, than elsewhere in the West. To the conservative Christian mentality it was often thought offensive; and the point of offense, apart from its possible hint of sexual relations between Jesus and Mary Magdalene (and "the beloved disciple"?) was, predictably enough, that it did not offer a clear statement of christological triumph. (In an ecclesiastical production that I attended in the midwestern United States, this omission was "corrected" by the addition of a victorious resurrection scene, replete with new, upbeat (and decidedly inferior)

---

22. I am purposely choosing popular art forms here rather than more sophisticated literary and other examples because my point has to do with the broad appeal of these examples. They are, however, examples of a much wider phenomenon.

musical numbers. This of course cast an entirely different light on the whole piece—and in the process rendered it completely innocuous.)

The lack of an unambiguous, third-day triumph, a grand finale that would set everything to rights again, was only the most conspicuous point of a much more inclusive *skandalon* to the conventional Christianity—whether liberal or conservative—of the officially optimistic society. Throughout the opera, Jesus is a figure of little glory, a kind of first-century James Dean, locked in struggle, not with oil barons but with Herod and Pilate and his own disciples— and with God. This Jesus is possessed of a strong passion for justice, championing the rights of the poor against the rich, of the weak against the strong, of sinners against the righteous, of women against brutal and censorious men. He feels a deep sense of mission, but without knowing quite what his mission is, or whether it has any meaning beyond his own visceral reactions to evil and his captivation by goodness and compassion.

His struggle with God (his passion) reaches its peak in the Garden of Gethsemane where, in a song that could well be compared with Bach's passion music, Jesus "only wants to know" what precisely God has in mind, whether it makes any sense, whether it is worth dying for, whether to begin with it is anything more than a projection of his own mind. This Jesus understands well the plight of so many young men and women of our epoch who must fight in wars they do not believe in and prepare for careers for which they may never find employment. He also understands the poets who write about the age of anxiety, the philosophers who write about the absurd, and the social scientists who write about "radical futurelessness." In short, he embodies the anxiety of meaninglessness and despair.

And precisely such a Jesus spoke to millions of ordinary people who remain untouched by the Jesus of ecclesiastical convention. The reason is obvious: The humanity actually experienced by multitudes in our context was moved by this story of God's deputy.[23] People could see in him a figure who "knows our frame" and "remembers that we are dust" (Ps. 103:14, RSV). Without this initial sense of full and unguarded identification with "us," everything else that belongs to this story is lost. No amount of triumph can overcome the failure of the church to allow this story to achieve (what it still can achieve) the initial and foundational sense of God's being "with us" in and through this one, Jesus. That is how it occurred with the first disciple community, and that is how it must always happen if it is to happen at all. I do not suggest for a moment that *Jesus Christ Superstar* is a full-blown answer to the christological problem of the age. It is nonetheless an astonishing secular exemplification of the principle

---

23. At a more profound and "high" cultural level, Rolf Hochhuth's play *The Deputy (Der Stellvertreter)* accomplished a similar communicational breakthrough with his figure of the priest, Ricardo.

we are discussing here: that Jesus will be perceived as God's movement toward "us" only if Jesus is seen truly to participate in *our* condition.

The second illustration of this principle is the film *Jesus of Montreal.* This 1989 work of Quebec producer Denis Arcand presents what could be thought an updated version of the earlier drama, but it also contains nuances that set it apart. It is also more contextually interesting than the English production, for despite (or perhaps because of) its setting in French-Canadian Catholic particularity, it is representative of much in North America today.

The film depicts the story of a young actor, an appealing but by no means heroic type, who has been employed by the Roman Catholic church in Montreal to play the role of Jesus in an annual passion play held on Mount Royal. In the process, the actor not only unmasks the pathetic emptiness of the conventional ecclesiastical rendering of the story of Holy Week but finds himself more and more drawn into the biblical story as it is opened up for him through some rather bizarre theories of a university theologian concerning crucifixion and (more importantly) through the actual suffering of those around him, including a failed though still active priest of the church. In his subsequent portrayal of his character, Jesus, the actor both demythologizes Jesus and remythologizes his own formerly one-dimensional, secularized life. Jesus of the biblical passion story enters so completely into the young actor's own story that the actor becomes a re-presentation of the Jesus of the stations-of-the-cross—to the point of having to die.

Obviously these secular presentations of the Christ owe part of their appeal to the vestiges of the traditional story that Christendom has kept alive despite its own characteristically religious distortions of the same. There continues to be a background of expectation: Many people still hope that something good could come out of Nazareth. Amazingly enough, the post-Christian society has not entirely forgotten that story.

But it is just as obvious that the communicational success of such presentations is made possible by the sensitive and skillful recognition, on the part of their authors, that the human condition is different now from what most of the doctrine and practice of the church continues to assume about it; and that if there is to be any incarnational identification of the divine representative with lived humanity, it must be achieved in terms of the passions that are indigenous to our own context.

What professional theology needs to acknowledge, however, is that the most authentic sources of the faith can themselves support such a presentation of the Christ. The biblical Jesus, as distinct from the ecclesiastical Christ, is also a figure of little glory: "he had no form or majesty that we should look at him, nothing in his appearance that we should desire him. He was despised and rejected by others; a man of sorrows and acquainted with infirmity . . ." (Isa. 53:2b-3a).

From the heights of its own imperial status, Christendom bequeathed to us a Christ who is in every respect precisely *not* "like unto us"—a victorious Christ, victorious in his humanity as in his divinity. So long as Christianity monopolized the spirit of the West, the flaw in this theology of glory was not conspicuous. Only a few detected it. It was strategically unimportant that the victorious Christ-figure could not really be with *us*—a fact illustrated by the cult of the Virgin and of the many thousands of intermediary saints, all of them filling the vacuum left by the false elevation of Christ beyond participation in the life of earth.

With the breakdown of Christendom, however, this flaw becomes increasingly visible. Christendom could command attention for its *Christus* because it was Christendom. The diaspora church that is on the horizon and, in many places, already here can only invite humanity's attention to its Christ if the latter emits a sufficient degree of divine solidarity with the humanity that we are and makes us curious about the humanity that we might become.

Wherever this historical challenge of the death of Christendom is felt, a resurgence of interest arises in the biblical Jesus and in those ecclesiastical traditions that have retained his memory. It is remarkable in this connection that the "cry of dereliction," which for centuries was treated by the church as a purely formal point of self-giving on the part of the sacrificial lamb, has been taken up both in theology and imaginative literature as the clarifying moment of the whole story.[24] The Jesus who thus protests his abandonment by the God whose purposes he believed he was enacting is a Jesus who knows the loss of purpose and the sense of universal indifference.

Only if this Jesus is presented by the witnessing community—and not in words only, but in acts of solidarity with "the crucified people"[25]—will it be possible for the church to profess him as the source of its life and "the life of the world." Jesus' participation in the human sense of dereliction is not all that the disciple community has to say about him; but if *this* cannot be said, and lived, then the rest will fall on deaf ears. This—for our time and place—is the core of the divine representation to us. This is "God with us."

---

24. "'My God, my God, why hast thou forsaken me?' Why does that cry hold our faith and our lack of it? Was Christ doubting his own reading of God's plan for himself? Did he question God's ultimate power and goodness, or was he feeling just dreadfully alone? Naked I came into the world, and naked I go out, clothed in nothing save myself. Naked and alone, as removed from the fellowship of family and friends as when one is wheeled, doped, antiseptic and anonymous, into an operating room. . . ." (Ursula M. Niebuhr, *Remembering Reinhold Niebuhr* [San Francisco: Harper, 1991], 253.)

25. C. S. Song, *Jesus, the Crucified People* (New York: Crossroad/Meyer-Stone, 1989). See also Song's more recent work on Christology, *Jesus and the Reign of God* (Minneapolis: Fortress Press, 1993).

38.3. Jesus Christ, Our Advocate.   Jesus' representation of humanity before
God is not another aspect of his person and work, it is the same person and work
viewed from another perspective. What from the perspective of his unique participation in the life of God is seen as God's movement toward the alienated
creature is, from the perspective of his participation in creaturely being, seen as
humanity's movement, in him, toward God. The full humanity to which his divine commission as God's anointed one inevitably leads him is now seen as the
necessary prerequisite for his priestly representation of fallen humanity before
God. In him the two movements converge: God's movement toward us and our
movement toward God. Given the biblical presupposition of the brokenness of
the divine-human relationship, this convergence in the one person cannot occur
without pain. But precisely out of the pain of this meeting, a new beginning is
made possible. As Isabel Carter Heyward has insightfully commented, following
Dorothee Sölle's exposition of representation: "in this dialectic of identification
both God and Jesus were changed—as is always the case in mutual relationship—revealing something new about both God and being human. And that
something new—that revelation—is that when God and humanity act together in
the world, human action and divine action are the same action, the same love,
the same justice, the same power, the same peace."[26]

It may seem strange, but I would judge that the human representation of Jesus is undoubtedly the more complex side of Jesus' dual life and work of representation. The reason why Jesus' humanity has been so terribly neglected by
traditional christological and soteriological dogma no doubt has something to
do with its sheer complexity; it requires an almost Kierkegaardian or Dostoy-
evskian "sixth sense" to grasp what is transpiring here. It is one thing to understand Jesus' representation of God (though this, as we have seen, has seldom
led to the realization that, if pursued biblically, it must express itself in the
strongest possible affirmation of Jesus' *humanity*); for to represent God as one
strongly seeking relationship with humanity is, after all, familiar not only to
Christian but also other forms of Theology.

Humanity, on the other hand, does not move toward God with God's kind of
eagerness. On the contrary, the biblical picture of the human creature is of one
seeking wherever possible to avoid and evade such a meeting. Or if—as in some
biblical and traditional anthropology—the human being searches after God, it
is in such ambiguous, roundabout, and distorted ways that it cannot be relied
upon (as, for example, the rich young ruler of the Gospels). Moreover God, in
appearing, is generally unwelcome; humanity prefers divinities of its own devising. Humanity regularly creates gods and worships them; and in this god-
making, as in its frantic love-making, perhaps humanity *is* seeking its ultimate

---

26. *The Redemption of God: A Theology of Mutual Relation* (Lanham, New York, London:
Univ. Press of America, 1982), 199.

Source. Paul in the opening chapters of Romans seems to think so. But in any case, no exact parallel may be drawn between the divine seeking of lost humanity and the human seeking of its Source. Complicating factors—perhaps paradoxical in nature—attend the latter.

If we try, as we must, to comprehend what is entailed in the representation of human creaturehood that Jesus offers to God, we are soon made conscious of the limits of our capacity to understand this "high priestly" act. Who can know with anything approaching depth what is involved in this advocacy? The newer Testament itself, in its most nuanced attempt simply to describe the pivotal moment in this meeting,[27] is reduced to relating externalities: Following his last meal with his disciples, Jesus takes them to Gethsemane. He bids them to wait while he goes, with Peter, James, and John, a little way farther. The three in turn are bidden to "watch" (Mark, KJV, RSV)—or "watch with me" (Matthew, KJV, RSV)—and Jesus, "going a little farther . . . fell on the ground and prayed" (Mark). The prayer, according to the Lukan version, is so intense that "his sweat became like great drops of blood falling down on the ground" (22:44). What is recorded of the content of the prayer in the Synoptic sources is Jesus' repeated plea that the "cup" may be taken from him—which seems clearly to be a reference to the destiny that he has just enacted symbolically in his supper with the disciples and that is soon to be realized at Golgotha. After a prolonged struggle, Jesus finally accedes to God's will: the "cup" must be drunk to the dregs. Immediately there follows the scene of betrayal and arrest.

John's account (chap. 17), insofar as it may be thought to be a commentary on this same pivotal moment, accentuates the representational character of the prayer. While in the immediate sense it is a representation in behalf of the disciples ("I am not praying for the world but for those whom thou hast given me," v. 9, RSV) it is indirectly for the beloved world (3:16) into whom, now, the disciples are to be sent.

Christological interpretation, which is already imaginatively at work in John's rendition of the "high priestly prayer" of Jesus, can only offer commentary on the moment the Synoptics describe. The full significance of this moment of divine-human encounter can never be grasped and communicated by the human mind; it can only be meditated upon by faith, and the only appropriate response to it, finally, is gratitude. It is this gratitude that is most prevalent in the epistolary contemplation of this event:

> If we say that we have not sinned, we make him a liar . . . . But if anyone does sin, we have an advocate with the Father, Jesus Christ the righteous; and he is the atoning sacrifice for our sins, and not for ours only but also for the sins of the whole world. (1 John 1:10, 2:1-2)

---

27. Mark 14:32-42; Matt. 26:36-46; Luke 22:39-46.

Since, then, we have a great high priest who has passed through the heavens, Jesus, the Son of God, let us hold fast to our confession. For we do not have a high priest who is unable to sympathize with our weaknesses, but we have one who in every respect has been tempted as we are, yet without sin. Let us therefore approach the throne of grace with boldness, so that we may receive mercy and find grace to help in time of need.

. . . In the days of his flesh, Jesus offered up prayers and supplications, with loud cries and tears, to the one who was able to save him from death, and he was heard because of his reverent submission. Although he was a Son, he learned obedience through what he suffered. . . . (Heb. 4:14-16, 5:7-8)

What must be noticed by the ongoing community of discipleship as it contemplates this moment and the scriptural commentary upon it is that from its inception the church not only felt gratitude for the advocacy of Jesus, the pioneer of our faith, but attempted to express this gratitude in meaningful language. The advocate or mediator,[28] it is assumed, performs an office that human beings may at some level of comprehension grasp. As we recognize in the two passages cited above, this human possibility lies particularly in the realization that we need such a representative, for we are unworthy or incapable of immediacy before God. It also has to do with the emphasis of our preceding reflections—that the reason why Jesus may be perceived by us as having the capacity for such mediation is that he participates fully in our condition. He is not so far beyond us that his representation would be mere condescension. He understands our weakness, our temptations, our sin. He goes forward to the meeting place as one of us.

It is the responsibility of faith—which necessarily "seeks understanding"[29]—not only to contemplate the scriptural and historical testimonies to this moment but to continue the interpretational work that is already under way in the Gospels and epistles. Two questions are implicit in this work of interpretation: (1) From the christological side we ask: Is our humanity truly represented by this one? (2) From the soteriological side we ask: How are we redeemed through this representation?

In the elaboration of Jesus' representation of God to us we have already had to respond to the first of these questions; for Jesus is able authentically to represent the biblical God to us only as he achieves in God's behalf full solidarity with us in our lived humanity (incarnation). His being "from God" (John 17:8 and elsewhere) manifests itself to his disciple community in the completeness

---

28. Cf. 1 Tim. 2:5; Heb. 8:6; 9:15; 12:24.

29. See Daniel L. Migliore, *Faith Seeking Understanding: An Introduction to Christian Theology* (Grand Rapids: Wm. B. Eerdmans Pub. Co., 1991), 1: ". . . faith and inquiry are inseparable. Theology arises from the freedom and responsibility of the Christian community to inquire about its faith in God."

of his eschewing of every sort of suprahuman power that would constitute a separation of himself from ordinary human creaturehood. The divine love requires of the anointed one that he should enter without reservation into the creaturely condition. Thus, "though he was in the form of God, [he] did not regard equality with God as something to be exploited, but emptied himself, taking the form of a slave, being born in human likeness. And being found in human form, he humbled himself and became obedient to the point of death—even death on a cross" (Phil. 2:6-8). We have attempted to show, moreover, that this self-emptying or humbling may be said to incorporate also the sense of purposelessness—the repressed *acedia*—that has come upon *our* humanity. What is "divine" in Jesus presses toward its fullest expression in its movement toward the human, whatever "the human" means in a given context.

But we may and must consider the question of Jesus' humanity also from the perspective of his representation of our humanity before God. We have said that it is his unique relationship with God that propels him toward solidarity with humanity, and that it is this solidarity with us which must then be understood as the prerequisite of his representation of us before God. How then may we think about Jesus' representation of *our* humanity?—the humanity whose content, positive and negative, is defined or at least highly conditioned by the realities of our context? In what ways can we see the moment of Jesus' appearing before God in Gethsemane, "the crucifixion before the cross," as incorporating also our historical moment? Does he bring us, with all the particularity of our contemporary life, as far as possible toward this encounter?

Like the first disciples, we cannot go all the way with him. Even if we are chosen to go farther than others, as were the three, there is a point beyond which we cannot go; we are not qualified, we could not endure it. Even to have gone that far, Peter, James, and John had to protect themselves through repressive sleep. Undoubtedly they were baffled by the strange behavior of their teacher at the time. Later, however, they understood (a little) what it meant that he took them at least that far. They knew that he was doing it for them, and that by bringing them with him physically that night, he was preparing them for the spiritual participation in his representation which, later, they would begin to comprehend and live. The point is that unless we, too, can know ourselves brought forward at least a little way toward the place of encounter, we shall not be able to consider ourselves among those who, in turn, are being brought to live, with and in Jesus, his mediatorial life in the world.

Throughout this study in various places we have tried to understand who "we" really are. It is neither an easy exercise in theo-anthropology, nor one to which any one response will suffice to include all of "us." But theology, we have said, particularly a theology that hopes to be public or at least to provide some understanding for the church's public witness, must risk making decisions about the existential character of the public that it hopes to engage.

Accordingly, it has been our decision that the dominant spirit of our context is one of a repressed but increasingly conspicuous disillusionment over the loss of the meaning that profoundly shaped our earlier New World history.

If and insofar as this truly does represent our contemporary North American humanity, it is precisely this humanity that, as Christians, we must understand Jesus to represent before God. Undoubtedly we are still also the guilty whose guilt disqualifies us from representing ourselves; undoubtedly we are still also the oppressing oppressed whose bondage to false power renders us incapable of standing in that presence; undoubtedly we are still also the unloved and unloving whose moral ambiguity stands in the way of any direct encounter with pure love. But above all we are the lost—afraid even to admit our lostness. Vision has failed us, personally and corporately. Hope has been reduced to slogans in which we no longer really believe, though we continue to mouth them—for the children's sake. The light that we celebrated, of which we thought our democratic civilization was the highest manifestation, has given way to an incipient darkness that, though we consistently deny it, spreads visibly over our cities and infiltrates all of our institutions.

Is it not precisely as such human beings that we may discern, in Jesus, "an advocate with the Father," who is able to "sympathize with our weakness"? We do not even have to alter the scriptural record or concentrate only on this or that emphasis. Far more faithfully than Chalcedon, which as we have seen only affirmed Jesus' humanity in a formulary way, and which required the translation of the newer Testament's historical-narrative categories into the metaphysical language of the Greco-Roman world, Christians today are free to take seriously the truly human character of Jesus as he is presented in the Gospels. We are no longer constrained by political and cultic considerations to accentuate either his glorious divinity or his victorious, unsullied humanity. We may hear the scriptural record as bearing witness to a credible human being, a Jewish man of a specific time and place: a person who is capable of a great range of emotions, from tenderness toward women and children to anger in the face of self-righteousness; a person who is vulnerable to the insults of his enemies and the false expectations of his followers; a person who is able to weep over the death of a friend and to share meals with strangers and to argue with the learned; a person who knows hunger, thirst, weariness of body and spirit, and who may become impatient, even frustrated, even angry enough to curse nature; a person tempted, and therefore knowing at least the mixed motivation of human goodness and evil; a person crying out, at last, in the face of his terrible abandonment.

In short, Jesus is one of us. This person was lost sight of by evolving Christendom, which, to fill the vacuum left by his apotheosis, had to manufacture a whole spectrum of intermediaries and advocates. Today—and not after the too sentimentalized fashion of the liberals, who made him as remote in his splendid humanity as the orthodoxy made him in his splendid divinity—we may in some sense recover the real Jesus behind the official Christology. That is more important than trying to find the real Jesus behind the newer Testamental Christ-figure; because for all of its faith perspective, the newer Testament never substitutes for the man mere doctrine, as evolving Christology did. Biblical studies (perhaps also "the Jesus Seminar") certainly help us to rediscover the human Jesus. But more important than biblical studies in this endeavor is our new freedom from the need that was imposed by our establishment status to "keep Jesus divine." We shall never penetrate to the heart of his representation of us before God, but as we contemplate his humanity under the conditions of our own new freedom for this contemplation, we may and do discover how inherently capable is the Jesus of the newer Testament of being also *our* advocate. The glorious Christ was perhaps never really capable of this; the crucified Christ has always been.

But how shall we respond to the second question implicit in the Christology of advocacy? How are we redeemed through his representation of us before God?

38.4. Jesus Christ, the Bringer of New Meaning. Paul Tillich sought (as he would say) to remythologize the meaning of the work of the Christ through the use of the language which informed his entire system of theology, that of being: Jesus, he affirmed, should be presented as "the bringer of new being."[30] I shall follow Tillich's method but not his content. Since I have understood the fundamental ontological category of the tradition of Jerusalem to be, not "being" but "being-with"; and since I have understood the fundamental *problematique* of our context to be, not the diminution of being but the loss of meaning, consistency requires that I interpret Christian soteriology within the parameters of these same categories.

What I shall say in answer to the question posed at the end of the preceding subsection may therefore be summarized in the following way: In entering into full solidarity with us as God's anointed one, Jesus carries our humanity with him to the encounter with God, our Creator. Through the suffering that is the inevitable consequence of this encounter, we are enabled at last to accept our creaturehood—to cease both trying to rise above it and trying to avoid its true calling. As we begin to experience the "righted" relationships that are consequent upon this acceptance, we discover new meaning in our creaturehood.

There will be four stages in the elaboration of this statement. 1. To begin with, I am associating the redemptive work in a special way with Jesus' human representation. Since throughout this discussion I have insisted that there are not two works but only one, as there is only one person, I hope it will be understood

---

30. *Systematic Theology,* vol. 2, sec. 2B (Chicago: Univ. of Chicago Press, 1957), 118ff.

that I am by no means confining the soteriological side of Christology to Jesus' humanity. At most we are able, theoretically, to consider this one person with his unified work from two perspectives: the movement from God to humanity and from humanity to God. The metaphor of representation, as we have seen, facilitates this unification in a way that has seldom been possible historically.

This having been said, I should like all the same to consider salvation in a concentrated though not exclusive manner from the perspective of Jesus' representation of humanity before God. I do so, not only because it seems to me more consistent with biblical narrative, and not only because it avoids the Deus ex machina soteriology that has so consistently arisen from redemption theology conceived "from above," but also because it belongs to the theology of the cross to do so. The humanity of Jesus has, as we have seen, been consistently neglected, and not only in christological but also in soteriological theologies. In the two older atonement theories, Jesus' humanity is logically required, but it carries mostly negative connotations. In the classical or ransom theory, the Christ's human nature is a foil—to the point of verging on Docetism. Through it God lures the demonic to destruction. The active, salvific principle is clearly associated, not with Jesus' humanity but with his divinity. In the Anselmic, substitutionary theology, Jesus' humanity is indeed essential to the argument—but for the sake of sacrifice. Its proper end is extinction: vicarious death.

Abelard rightly recognized the negative statement that was being made, not only about deity but also about humanity through this treatment of Jesus' humanity. For his theory therefore the humanity becomes exemplary of a highly positive quality: the faithful love of one who "lays down his life for his friends." This positive consideration of Jesus' humanity points us in the right direction; but as the sentimentalization of Abelardian atonement theology in the hands of the liberals demonstrates all too plainly, it is not an adequate expression of the significance of the cross. What it lacks is the concreteness of participation in the human condition, which belongs to the concept of representation, and which entails a greater appreciation for the "tragic" dimension of sin (Tillich) than Abelard and his later followers seem to have understood. This leads directly to the second consideration.

2. When we affirm that Jesus as the anointed one of God, the Messiah, is propelled toward greater and greater identification with humanity; and when we then affirm that it is precisely this lived humanity which Jesus represents before God, what we are claiming is no empty, theoretical thing. We are professing that Jesus accepts as his destiny the representation of a creature deeply estranged from its Creator, profoundly disoriented in all of its relationships, and, apart from radical grace, destroying itself from within. Such a bleak picture of the human condition offends our modern sensibilities, but it is certainly present in the Bible and in the classical traditions of the faith—particularly, but not exclusively, the Reformation of the sixteenth century. We are perhaps

in a better position today to appreciate just how accurate a description of the human condition this might be; for we have been confronted, in late modernity, by a whole spectrum of truths about ourselves and the world that are even more devastating than anything found in the Augustinian traditions of "total depravity"—for one thing, they contemplate our horrors, including the doom that is now no longer mythic, against the backdrop of a secularity that contains no ameliorating transcendental "nets." Our apocalypse is a secular one.

As the advocate of humanity, Jesus' movement toward the meeting with the Eternal One should therefore not be thought of piously. This is not the picture of a sweet and gentle man—Hoffmann's *Christ in the Garden*—praying earnestly and so very altruistically, after all, on behalf of others. Nor is it the picture of a crucified one who goes "gentle into that dark night" (Dylan Thomas). The almost hysterical Christ of *Jesus Christ Superstar* and the confused Christ of *Jesus of Montreal* are better representations of biblical faith—better at least for our time; perhaps better for every time. They are reminiscent of the "plague Christs" of the fourteenth century, of Grünewald's Christ, of "the crucified woman." For if there is to be contextually viable truth in this representation and not just doctrine and pageantry, Jesus must appear before our Maker and Sovereign God with a great deal to quarrel about. His questions will have to be at least as insistent as Job's. After Auschwitz they could well be far more insistent—for a Jew. To be "the man for others" (Bonhoeffer)—for *us*—Jesus will need to come before the Creator with the great question of the age, vulgarly phrased by Vonnegut as "What the hell are people *for?*" Human life has been rendered so cheap in our time; thousands die daily in senseless accidents, violent explosions, genocides, famine. Thousands more experience the death of the spirit because they can find no good reason to live. Representing all that is not a passion play, nor is it a soteriological formula. Jesus is asked to drink *this* cup. In faith—therefore no doubt also foolishly—we have professed that as we know him, he can do this. He *has* done this.

3. We must at this point, however, confront the most difficult problem, theologically speaking—perhaps existentially speaking as well. Granted that faith may profess that Jesus has done this—that what Jesus has done includes "our" particular quarrel with life—how shall we understand and speak about this representation as involving us? When I am being represented by a lawyer in a court of law, I know perfectly well that I am involved. But we are speaking of an event some two thousand years ago, and one, besides, that lacks the specificity of most of the acts of representation that are part of daily life today. How does anyone come to understand that Jesus carries our humanity forward into the presence of the eternal, pleading our cause, voicing our questions and our forsakenness?

There is no universally applicable answer to this. Moreover, no doctrinal answer can do justice to the mystery of the answers that are given it existentially.

We may only say what it seems to have usually entailed in the experience of the disciple community. To begin with, it certainly entails hearing: that is, the sense of our involvement—that *we* are being represented by this "high priest"—can only occur if we are told of this event. The scriptural testimony to it is indispensable. But by itself this testimony seldom suffices, for its form and language are very different from ours. There must be a bridge between then and now. Jesus must become for us in some sense our contemporary (Kierkegaard). This is why we have elaborated his representation of our humanity, above, in terms of the crisis of meaning. Even in the earliest disciple communities this necessity was understood. That is why Paul wrote about the "foolishness" of preaching (1 Corinthians 1, 2) and asked straightforwardly:

> . . . how are they to call on one in whom they have not believed? And how are they to believe in one of whom they have never heard? And how are they to hear without someone to proclaim him? And how are they to proclaim him unless they are sent? . . . So faith comes from what is heard, and what is heard comes through the word of Christ. (Rom. 10:14-17)

All the same, there is nothing automatic here: The proclamation of the faithful may fall on deaf ears, like the seed that falls on infertile soil (Matt. 13:3ff.). If genuine hearing is to take place, more than our words are required—though the tradition of Jerusalem by no means despises our words. We are driven back therefore to the Theological basis of the theology of redemption: only God can cause the words of Scripture and of the preacher to become *the* Word. Only the Spirit of God can bring us forward, to the point of our knowing ourselves to be the ones re-presented by this one. This is why we cannot separate the two perspectives from which the work of the Christ is viewed—movement of God toward humanity, and the movement of humanity toward God. The trinitarian basis of the faith is here particularly needful. If we in fact come to know ourselves represented by Jesus in his appearing before God in our behalf, it is because the divine Spirit is at work through the words of the witnessing community and through our own internal struggle of soul to carry us, as it were, into the Garden with the praying Christ. As the first disciples only later knew that, while they slept, their cause was being represented by the one who went forward alone, so it may happen that we, in our always-unique ways, come to know this about ourselves.

(4) How then shall we characterize this meeting? We have said that it could not have been a placid encounter. For the two who meet here, in this Garden of Sorrows, the second Garden in which cosmic temptation occurs, are estranged from each other. In this Anselm and Calvin were surely right, biblically speaking: from both sides, if truth is here at stake (and it is), there must be a frank admission of the reality of the brokenness of this relationship, and there can be

no easy reconciliation. The God of justice cannot simply accept and forgive the unjust creature; neither can the creature simply accept and forgive the Creator. That is what Anselm and Calvin failed to understand.

It is what Christian theology has almost never understood. Judaism understands it much better. Christianity, partly in consequence of its political establishment and partly because of its loss of the Jewish foundation, but mostly because it has dealt in the theology of glory, has always been the self-appointed defender of God. It has found it acceptable to argue in God's favor against failed, pathetic, or despicable humanity; but only very rarely has it entertained even the thought that humanity, from its side, might have a legitimate quarrel with God. So while Western Christianity was ready for a thousand years to present Jesus as the human substitute and sacrificial victim who must be damned in place of all of us, only rarely—and at that mostly on the edges of Christendom—have Christians contemplated the prospect that, in this meeting, God too might have to suffer, and as one in some real way recognizing, if not personal fault, at least the awesome plight of the human condition.

For it is a plight, and until the Christian church is able to absorb this reality, it will never attain to the depths of the gospel "treasure" whose "earthen vessel" it is. The Bible—not consistently, perhaps, but in a way that puts to shame the Christian doctrinal traditions—understands that our humanity represents an almost impossible kind of creaturehood. Consider: A creature which not only knows that it is a creature, is not only expected to accept and rejoice *in* its creaturehood, but at the same time is supposed to behave in the world with the kind of responsibility and wisdom and goodness that quite clearly exceeds its creaturely grasp—why would not such a creature try to get hold of something higher, divinity? Or, failing that, why would it not try to slink out from underneath the responsibilities of its peculiar creaturehood?—to become, perhaps, a happy animal, to foreswear thought altogether, to lose itself in pleasure, perhaps, or to seek oblivion in drugs, in practiced indifference, in death?

The tragic dimension of human creaturehood is not due only to the creature's failing; it is a flaw in the very concept of human creaturehood. To be sure, it is present in human creaturehood for a very good reason—and it is not the last word. The reason is that apart from the real possibility of failure, there could be no possibility either of this creature's responsiveness to the Creator. Humanity must bear the consciousness of its precarious creaturehood because without this neither could it bear the joy of communion with God, with its own kind, with otherkind. It is not necessary to say with the supralapsarians that God created fallen creatures; but it is necessary, if one wants to remain within the house of biblical faith, to say that the human creatures God created are, for the sake of their peculiar relation with God and their fellow creatures, almost inevitable candidates for a tragic destiny. Inevitable, though not necessary (Niebuhr).

The meeting to which Jesus' destiny takes him as our deputy—this divine-human encounter that, in the Gospel story, reaches its dialogical climax in Gethsemane and is then enacted at Golgotha—is therefore a meeting that might well produce, in the one whose life is its very locus, a "soul exceedingly sorrowful, even unto death." From both partners in this dialogue a "No!" must be heard. The human rejection of God and the divine judgment of humanity: both must come to clearest expression here. History—universal history and also our own individual history—has been a question begging just this encounter. The resolution of the estrangement that is, if not prehistoric, the most original historical reality, can occur if the truth and depth of its reality is finally faced—faced and *endured*. As with ancient enemies, who have perhaps pretended friendship from time to time, the only authentic reconciliation between the alienated creature and Creator must pass through the narrow door of honest confrontation. The author of the poem of Job understood this; so did the author of Jeremiah 20; so did the writer of the suffering-servant poems. The passion of Jesus, the Christ, is the final scene in this long, long dialogue.

And the enactment of the conclusions of this dialogue a little later, at Golgotha, involves a suffering that must be seen from both perspectives if it is not to be misunderstood completely. This is not only the suffering of the human priest become victim, the one "bruised for our iniquities," hearing God's "No!" against unholy creaturehood; it is also the suffering of God's representative, God's own Son rejected—as were the forerunners—by the tenants of God's vineyard. Behind the cross of Golgotha stands a cosmic rejection coming from both Creator and creature.

But this point of rejection is also the point of resolution: here God assumes the suffering of humanity, and humanity assumes the suffering of God. Here, through the truth of confrontation, the peace that passes understanding is made possible. In the encounter, both God and humanity are changed (Carter Heyward). The peace, the *shalom,* that comes to be is the consequence of the Creator's compassionate identification with our creaturehood and the creature's long-awaited acceptance of its creaturely role. Befriended by the God who not only understands our frame and remembers that we are dust, but assumes our flesh, we are enabled to begin to assume the full burden and glory of our creatureliness.

CONCLUSION AND TRANSITION:

"I Am with You Always. . . ."
(Matt. 28:20)

In the end, we are brought once more to the beginning, the point of departure, the presupposition of all the words that have preceded these and of the centuries of professing and confessing and living this faith that *these* words, in their way, have sought to honor: the resurrection. If from the newer Testamental writings onwards the very best thought that the universal church has managed has been devoted to pondering the meaning of the cross, it has been because the cross of Jesus was and is not the last word that must be said about him. It was and is the *decisive* word, but that is only because it is not the last word.

How difficult—how almost impossible—it is to speak about the resurrection, especially "in a North American context." We have encountered this difficulty throughout; for while literally everything that I have wanted to say in this volume is dependent upon the resurrection faith of the people of the cross, the word "resurrection" can hardly be uttered in this milieu without its conjuring up whole legions of misconceptions and wrong associations.

"Resurrection" must stand on the one hand for an exultant religiosity, a pious conceit enabling its champions to overlook all that the cross of Jesus represents by way of injustice, agony, and incompleteness. It becomes the basis of a smugness never encountered in the Scriptures, "Christian" smugness, the smugness of those who "know" that they are saved and that nothing untoward can happen to them or to the (neatly fenced) world that matters to them. It covers the cross with daffodils. It leaps across eons of human wretchedness, creational "groaning," and cosmic longing, and in precepts and postulates acquired without tears declares that everything has now been cleared up—"the strife is o'er, the battle won," and this is "our triumphant day." Humanly speaking, this is undoubtedly understandable, but it is still a betrayal of the gospel of the crucified and risen one. The community of the newer Testament, whose occasional exultation over the triumph of the third day should be seen within the context of its astonishment and terror (Mark 16:8) and of its decidedly nontriumphal worldly status, does not permit itself such delusions of finality:

> As it is, we do not yet see everything in subjection to him. But we see Jesus, who for a little while was made lower than the angels, crowned with glory and honor because of the suffering of death, so that by the grace of God he might taste death for everyone.
> For it was fitting that he, for whom and by whom all things exist, in bringing many sons to glory, should make the pioneer of their salvation perfect through suffering. (Heb. 2:8b-10, RSV)

In the North American context, besides this cultic resurrectionism, as we have named it earlier, the symbol of the risen Christ must also bear the immense burden of our cultural and political imperialism, an imperialism made still more insistent and virulent today by our self-doubt concerning its veracity. If Easter Sunday still marks the pinnacle of church attendance on this continent (and it does), it is because this cultic symbol of victory quite naturally and without notice functions admirably—for us as for the ancient Romans—as "the sign by which we conquer." In old Europe, it was Good Friday that the Jews feared, for it frequently served as the occasion for pogroms: all the frustrations of an impoverished, illiterate, and oppressed peasantry could then be visited upon the "Christ killers."[1] In North America it is Easter that should make Jews and all other minorities nervous; for while it will seldom incite physical violence, this national feast-day of the New World contributes much to the atmosphere of untruth that permits America to overlook and repress the subtle and not-very-subtle violence that it does to those who are "other" in its midst.

One approaches this subject, the resurrection, with fear and trembling, then, for it is almost bound to darken the very thing that it is meant to illumine: the abiding presence of the crucified one, who is "with us always," from whose love nothing, not death itself, can separate us (Rom. 8:35f.).

Observing this caution, it would, I think, be best to listen to Jewish testimony when it comes to the question, What happened on that first Easter? Those who were involved in it were, after all, every one of them, Jews. As with so many other aspects of Christology, historic Christendom consistently bypassed the Jewish background of Jesus' resurrection in favor of the mystery cults and philosophies of the Hellenic and Hellenistic world and its successors. A usually silent (but sometimes quite vocal) assumption persists, even in the

---

1. See Adele Wiseman, *The Sacrifice* (Toronto: Macmillan of Canada, 1956).

scholarly world of Christians, that from the Jews nothing significant could be learned about all that; that Jewish rejection of our Messiah is at least in part due to a Jewish incapacity to believe in resurrection or even life after death. Thus we turn to the tradition of Athens and its heirs, and almost invariably end by substituting for the biblical thought of resurrection a very unbiblical notion: the immortality of the soul.

But in fact Jewish thought is not silent on this subject, and it provides the best possible antidote to a Christian resurrectionism that, in the North American setting at least, is a combination of cultic doctrines of the soul's imperishability and cultural optimism over our imperishability as "the new Eden for the new Adam" (Mead/Ahlstrom).

In his evocative study, *The Resurrection of Jesus: A Jewish Perspective,*[2] the German Jewish scholar Pinchas Lapide locates the Jewish belief in resurrection in Judaism's insistence upon the commitment of God to this world (the very point I have identified in this work as the essence of the theology of the cross):

> The historical fact that the resurrection of the dead was solidified into a doctrine of Judaism not until a relatively late time explains also its rationality. Unlike the mystery cults of Egypt, Greece, and Asia Minor, which also believed in the resurrection, it is free from magic, mysticism, miraculousness, and lengthy burial rites, which often degenerated into worship of the dead.
> *If God is all-just and all-merciful, then death in this world cannot be the final end.*[3]

Lapide, like most contemporary Christian scholars, acknowledges the fact that in the early church—already beginning with the newer Testament—Jesus' resurrection was adorned with anecdotes, legends, and utterances sometimes verging on the "magic, mysticism, and miraculousness" of the mystery cults. But as a Jew he can believe, without overstepping the bounds of his Jewish faith, that "something" happened; that this something was comprehensible, without being predictable, within the Judaic categories of the first disciple community; and that it was *decisive:*

> . . . as a faithful Jew, I cannot explain a historical development which, despite many errors and much confusion, has carried the central message of Israel from Jerusalem into the world of the nations, as a result of blind happenstance, or human error, or a materialistic determinism—although all these factors possibly may have helped advance the divine plan of salvation. The experience of the

---

2. Trans. Wilhelm C. Linns with Introduction by Carl E. Braaten (Minneapolis: Augsburg Pub. House, 1983).

3. Ibid., 54 (emphasis added).

resurrection as the foundation act of the church which has carried the faith in the God of Israel into the whole Western world must belong to God's plan of salvation. . . .

Indeed this world remains unsaved, and we all are still suffering in it just as we also are still responsible for it. But that experience of a handful of Bible-believing Jews who were able to carry their faith in God into the Gentile world must surely be interpreted as a God-willed encouragement in a world that so often seems hopeless.[4]

Let us accept this testimony and be grateful; and let us explore further this so-neglected source of understanding our originating event, the tradition of Jerusalem. If as Christians we ask (and against Christian liberalism I agree with conservative Christians that we must ask) what actually happened "back there," let us cease running all over the world to find out about immortality and the afterlife and let us listen, for a change, to the Jews.

If we listen to them, if we hear them out on the subject of resurrection and its application to their Brother,[5] we shall be carried by their concern well beyond the question, What happened? For the Jewish explorations of resurrection (why have we not noticed it in the excruciating meditations of the former Saul of Tarsus—for instance in 1 Corinthians 15?) are all premised on the belief, the summation of belief, that God is the God of *life,* and that this means the life of creation.

On that premise (which I suggest is also the foundational premise of the newer Testament, overlaid as it may be by other *Weltanschauungen*), Jesus *had* to be brought from the dead; it is a "must"—not in order to get us into heaven (though one has no quarrel against that prospect, either) but *to get us into earth!* To bring us fully to *life,* creaturely life, the life that we spend our days and nights trying to escape from, avoid, reconstruct along ideal lines, control, transcend, manipulate, resign ourselves to.

Jesus *saves.* He saves us for life, for giving ourselves over to its joys and sorrows, its predictable and unpredictable occurrences, its routines and its surprises. He saves us from the awful habit we have of saving ourselves, of sparing our energies, of protecting our minds and souls and bodies from the life struggles they are in fact well equipped to undertake. He saves us for the spendthriftness of love, of work, of play. He saves us from Promethean but also from Sisyphean fatalism and for "the freedom of the Christian person." He points us back into the *civitas terrena* (the earthly city), its disappointments and its tragedies notwithstanding—back into burning Rome, whose tribulations are (apart from grace, recognized or unrecognized) impossible to bear, yet the

---

4. Ibid., 142–46.
5. See Hans Küng and Pinchas Lapide, *Brother or Lord?* (Glasgow: Collins, Fount Paperbacks, 1977).

scene of the unfolding of the city of God, the *civitas Dei.* Jesus the Christ, Savior, trains our souls for creaturehood, weaning us from our need to be gods and to be less-than-human too. (*"Wir sollen Menschen und nicht Gott sein. Das ist die summa; Es wird doch nicht anders. . . ."*[6])

Jesus *saves.* His person and his work, his representative life, belong to that drama of God's long "labor": the bringing forth of creatures who, in the midst of this "good" world are ready to say Yes to their creaturehood, to take up their vocation within creation, and to find precisely there—*here*—all the meaning that they need.

And it continues!

---

6. "We should be human and not God. That is the summation [of Christian belief]. It will never change." Luther, *Letters,* 1530, Selections, *LW.* 49.337. See Eberhard Jüngel, *The Freedom of a Christian: Luther's Significance for Contemporary Theology,* trans. Roy A. Harrisville (Minneapolis: Augsburg Pub. House, 1988).

INDEX OF SUBJECTS

Index of Subjects

INDEX OF NAMES

INDEX OF NAMES